Over tł

US Army Amphibious Operations in the Korean War

Colonel (Retired) Donald W. Boose Jr.

Combat Studies Institute Press
US Army Combined Arms Center
Fort Leavenworth, Kansas

Library of Congress Cataloging-in-Publication Data

Boose, Donald W.
  Over the beach : US Army amphibious operations in the Korean War / Donald W. Boose Jr.
      p. cm.
  1. Korean War, 1950-1953--Amphibious operations. 2. Korean War, 1950-1953--Participation, American. 3. United States. Army--History--Korean War, 1950-1953. 4. Amphibious warfare--History--20th century. I. Title.
  DS919.B66 2008
  951.904'242--dc22

                                            2008038959

First printing, December 2008.

CSI Press publications cover a variety of military history topics. The views expressed in this CSI Press publication are those of the author and not necessarily those of the Department of the Army or the Department of Defense. A full list of CSI Press publications, many of them available for downloading, can be found at http://usacac.army.mil/CAC2/CSI/RandPTeam.asp

The seal of the Combat Studies Institute authenticates this document as an official publication of the CSI. It is prohibited to use CSI's official seal on any republication of this material without the written permission of the Director of CSI.

Foreword

The Combat Studies Institute is pleased to present the latest publication in our Special Study Series, *Over the Beach: US Army Amphibious Operations in the Korean War,* by historian and retired Army Colonel Donald W. Boose Jr. Colonel Boose has exhaustively studied and skillfully written the little known history of the Army's amphibious operations during the Korean War. This book is part of our tradition of publishing high-quality historical studies from outside authors that have continuing relevance to the US Army today.

Building on its extensive experiences in World War II, General MacArthur and the US Army conducted three major amphibious landings during the war, including the brilliant counterstroke in September 1950, an assault at the port of Incheon behind North Korean lines. After the massive Chinese attacks of November and December 1950, the Army conducted a number of amphibious withdrawals as it fell back southward on the Korean peninsula to more defensible positions. Throughout the war, the Army also conducted a number of non-assault amphibious operations and over-the-shore logistical operations.

Since the Korean War, the Army's amphibious role has greatly decreased in importance. The Army, however, conducted extensive riverine operations in Vietnam and continues to employ them in Iraq. Additionally, over-the-shore logistics remains an important part of Army doctrine and logistical capability today. This historical study chronicles an aspect of the US Army's history that may seem remote from the challenges facing the Army in 2008. If history "proves" anything, however, it is that the hard-won lessons from the past tend to be relearned in the future. If this study makes that relearning process faster and more effective, it will have fulfilled its purpose. CSI—*The Past Is Prologue!*

Timothy R. Reese
Colonel, Armor
Director, Combat Studies Institute
US Army Combined Arms Center

Acknowledgments

This study was begun at the direction of General Richard Cody, the Vice Chief of Staff of the Army, at a time when he was the Army Deputy Chief of Staff, G3, and General Leon J. Laporte, US Army (Retired), who was then the Commander, Republic of Korea–US Combined Forces Command; Commander, United Nations Command; and Commander, US Forces, Korea. The initial G3 Project Officer was Lieutenant Colonel Robert R. Mackey. For most of the years of research and writing, the project officer was Mr. James C. Boyt. Both Colonel Mackey and Mr. Boyt have been exceptionally helpful throughout the process, as has Mr. John Auger, the Booz-Allan-Hamilton project officer.

The former Chief of Military History, Brigadier General John S. Brown, US Army (Retired), was supportive when I began this study and Dr. Jeffrey J. Clarke, the current Chief of Military History, continued that essential support throughout the period of my research. Dr. William M. Donnelly; Colonel Jon T. Hoffman, United States Marine Corps Reserve (USMCR); and Mr. Frank R. Shirer of the Center of Military History at Fort McNair, DC, provided valuable advice and recommendations based on their extensive knowledge of the Korean War and amphibious operations. Professor Allan R. Millett, a retired Marine Corps Reserve colonel as well as one of the preeminent historians of the Korean War, graciously offered encouragement, support, and advice.

Much of the research for this book was conducted at the US Army Military History Institute (MHI) at Carlisle Barracks, Pennsylvania. The entire staff of MHI has my gratitude, in particular, the Director, Dr. Conrad Crane, who was instrumental in my being selected to do this study; Dr. Richard Sommers; Dr. Arthur Bergeron; Ms. Louise Arnold-Friend; Mr. Richard Baker; Mr. Clif Hyatt; and the Circulation Desk Staff, Mr. Tom Buffenbarger, Ms. Isabel Manske, Ms. Amy Pealer, Mr. Shaun Kirkpatrick, Mr. Gary Johnson, Ms. Jessica Sheets, Mr. Steve Bye, Mr. Billy McElrath, and Ms. Youngae Raymond.

My principal guide, mentor, colleague, and friend at MHI, Mr. David Keough, provided indispensible advice, suggested avenues for research, and tracked down obscure sources. He and Colonel Walter Wood, USMC (Retired), have been my close companions throughout this project, serving as sounding boards and counselors, and reading the entire manuscript. Dr. David Jablonsky also read the manuscript, sharing with me his deep and broad knowledge of modern military history. Captain Albert Lord, United States Navy (USN), the Senior Navy Representative at the Army War College, reviewed the manuscript and made helpful suggestions.

Colonel Clark Summers shared his experience with Transportation Corps watercraft and over-the-shore logistics with me while he was a student at the Army War College. Colonel (Retired) George Rasula read portions of the manuscript and provided unique insights based on his own participation as an officer in the 31st Infantry Regiment in the Incheon and Iwon landings, the battle east of the Jangjin (Changjin/Chosin) Reservoir, and the Heungnam evacuation.

Dr. Lewis Bernstein, the United Nations Command/Combined Forces Command/US Forces Korea Command Historian has been exceptionally helpful, and I also wish to acknowledge Mr. Karl Swanson and Mr. Bruce Conard, United States Forces Korea historians; and Major Patrick J. Berry, of the Eighth Army G5. I have fond memories of retracing the Incheon Landing with these four men. Dr. Choi Yong Ho, Dr. Nam Jeong-ok, and Dr. Kang Ch'ang-guk of the Korean Institute for Military History Compilation made great efforts to help me acquire material from Korean archives and were unsparing of their time. Mr. John A. Burzynski of the United Nations Command Component of the Military Armistice Commission (UNCMAC) provided advice and assistance, including communication with sources and contacts in Korea, and UNCMAC interpreter/translators, Mr. Ham, Chi Min; Ms. Kim, Hyun-young; Ms. Kim, Mi-na; and Mr. Yim, Chae-sul, provided advice on current geographical nomenclature and translated some of the Korean sources.

At the National Archives at College Park, I was greatly assisted by Mr. Richard Boylan. Dr. Paul K. Walker, the Chief Historian of the Corps of Engineers, provided useful leads for research and Dr. Michael J. Brodhead spent many hours helping me find my way through the Engineer historical archives. At Fort Eustis, Virginia, the Transportation Corps Command Historian, Mr. Richard E. Killblain, was also unstinting of his time and effort. Dr. Jim Ginther, Ms. Patricia A. Mullen, and Mr. Michael Miller at the Marine Corps University Archives were unfailingly helpful. Captain Patrick Roth, USN (Retired), of the Center for Naval Analyses, Dr. Edward Marolda, the Senior Historian at the Naval Historical Center, and Ms. Kathleen M. Lloyd, the head of the Operational Archives Branch of the NHC, provided helpful information on naval matters.

I have received much encouragement and support from the US Army War College Department of Distance Education, in particular from the Department Chairman, Dr. C. Clayton Chun; the Directors of Second Year Studies, Dr. Stephen Lemons and Colonel Dwight Raymond; and the Second Year Administrative Staff, Ms. Kathy Ramsey and Ms. Sylvia Hollenbaugh. My friends at the US Army War College Library could always be counted on for cheerful and professional assistance and support. I wish to thank in particular the Director, Mr. Bohdan Kohutiak, Ms. Jacqueline Bey, Ms. Virginia Shope, Ms. Margaret D. Baumgardner, and Ms. Kathy Hindman. In Carlisle, I was provided with books, friendship, and a pleasant working environment through the courtesy of Elizabeth and Jeffrey Wood; Robert and Naomi Pham; Amy, Doug, and Andrew Fulton; and Linda McBeth.

The following members of the Combat Studies Institute, US Army Combined Arms Center, Fort Leavenworth, Kansas, exhibited great professional skill as well as patience and understanding in shepherding this manuscript through the editing and publication process: Mr. Kendall D. Gott, Chief, Research and Publications Team; Ms. Elizabeth Weigand, editor; and Ms. Robin Kern, illustrator.

My wife, Lil, assisted in the research, tracked down the history of every LST that ever landed on a Korean beach, proofread the pages, and provided the love and encouragement that have sustained me through the years of research and writing.

Any errors or omissions in this book are, however, entirely my own.

Contents

Maps

Chapter 1

Introduction

In the summer of 1950, when the North Korean Army attacked South Korea, a US Army infantry battalion landing team was conducting an amphibious landing exercise in Japan. Over the previous 5 years, the Army and the Marine Corps had struggled bitterly over which Service should have the responsibility for amphibious warfare. During the 1920s and 1930s, both Services had grappled with the problem of transporting and landing ground forces from the sea, but the Marine Corps systematically developed doctrine, tactics, techniques, procedures, and equipment for assault landings against defended shores. During World War II, both Services made use of those techniques and developed improved methods for conducting amphibious operations. In Admiral Chester W. Nimitz's Pacific Ocean Areas (POA), both Marine and Army forces carried out landings against Japanese-held islands in the South and Central Pacific, culminating in the seizure of Okinawa and the Ryukyu Islands by forces of Tenth US Army under Lieutenant General Simon Bolivar Buckner Jr. In the Mediterranean Theater of Operations (MTO) and European Theater of Operations (ETO), the Army, working with the British who had pioneered their own approach to amphibious operations, had developed doctrine and capabilities for continental assault landings and had carried out some of the largest amphibious operations in history in North Africa, Sicily, Italy, Normandy, and Southern France. In the Southwest Pacific Area (SWPA), General Douglas MacArthur used predominantly Army and some Marine forces to carry out a series of landings along the coast of New Guinea and the nearby islands before conducting the amphibious invasion of the Philippines, which included several landings of various sizes. MacArthur's ground forces were transported in these operations by Rear Admiral Daniel E. Barbey's Seventh Amphibious Force and other Navy amphibious elements and by the very versatile engineer special brigades that, unique to SWPA, included engineer boat units operating landing craft. By the end of the war, more amphibious operations had been conducted in MacArthur's theater than in any other theater of war.

When World War II ended, the Army leadership believed their Service should assume the amphibious warfare mission, but it was the Marine Corps that emerged from the defense unification and roles and missions struggles of the late 1940s with their amphibious warfare mission validated by Congress, the Secretary of Defense, and the Joint Chiefs of Staff. Despite this validation for the Marines, the Army was also charged with providing forces for joint amphibious operations. Thus, the Army maintained an amphibious capability in the form of one understrength engineer special brigade and one amphibious tank and tractor battalion, developed amphibious doctrine, and conducted several large-scale amphibious exercises with the Navy.

Fortuitously, in the months prior to the Korean War MacArthur's Japan-based General Headquarters (GHQ), Far East Command (FEC) had initiated an amphibious training program that introduced key members of the staff to the concepts of amphibious warfare and predisposed them to consider amphibious operations when war came. The landing exercise phase of the training had just begun when the North Koreans attacked and so there were in Japan a Marine training team and a Navy amphibious group able to provide amphibious expertise and the nucleus of an amphibious task force. General MacArthur, as the Supreme Commander of the Allied Powers (SCAP) in charge of the occupation, also had available under his control the Shipping Control Administration, Japan (SCAJAP)— a fleet of Japanese-manned landing ships, tank (LSTs) and cargo ships. The recently formed Western Pacific (WestPac) office of the Military Sea Transportation Service (MSTS) provided an organization with cargo and transport ships and the ability to lease additional civilian shipping to supplement the amphibious force.[1]

Thus, within weeks of the North Korean attack, Navy Amphibious Group One and the Army's 1st Cavalry Division were able to mount an unopposed amphibious landing with a hastily-trained landing force and a mixed assortment of US Navy, MSTS, SCAJAP, and Japanese civilian shipping. The 1st Cavalry Division's landing at Pohang in July 1950 was unopposed, but in September the US Army X Corps carried out the only seaborne amphibious assault landing of the war at Incheon (Inch'on)[2] with the 1st Marine Division accompanied by an element of the US Army's 2d Engineer Special Brigade (ESB) and a company of the 56th Amphibious Tank and Tractor Battalion (ATTB) making the initial assault, the 2d ESB in charge of the shore party and logistical operations, and the Korean Marine Corps (KMC) regiment and the Army's 7th Infantry Division as the follow-on forces.[3] In October the 7th Infantry Division made an unopposed landing at Iwon in northeast Korea as the Marines went ashore, also unopposed, at Wonsan. Following a massive Chinese assault in late November and December 1950, Army units then took part in the amphibious withdrawals from Jinnampo (Chinnamp'o) in the west and from Wonsan, Seongjin (Songjin), and Heungnam (Hungnam) in the east.

While no further amphibious assaults were carried out after Incheon, Army Engineer and Transportation Corps units conducted over-the-shore logistic operations throughout the war. Most of the wartime amphibious raids and reconnaissance missions were conducted by the United States, Republic of Korea (ROK), and British Navy and Marine forces, but US and ROK Army special operations forces conducted some such missions and supported Korean partisan forces operating from off-shore islands. In April 1951 US Army Rangers and soldiers of the 7th Cavalry Regiment attempted a waterborne attack against the Hwacheon (Hwach'on) Dam in central Korea. Army units in Japan planned and trained for major amphibious operations that never took place, and the last amphibious operation of the war, a demonstration off Gojeo (Kojo) on the east coast in October 1952 by a regimental combat team of the 1st Cavalry Division, was an Army–Navy operation.

In the years after the Korean War, the Army further refined its amphibious doctrine, carried out amphibious exercises, and, during the Vietnam War, conducted large-scale over-the-shore logistics and riverine operations. Beginning in the 1970s, the Army gradually lost interest in amphibious operations, but retained an over-the-shore logistic capability. Today, the Army's role in forcible entry[4] is seen primarily as the conduct of airborne operations, but Army interest in strategic and operational maneuver by and from the sea and other water areas continues.

This study examines Army participation in amphibious and over-the-shore operations in the Korean War, beginning with a backward glance at the Army's amphibious heritage; its participation in the development of amphibious doctrine prior to World War II; the World War II experience that shaped the Army's Korean War era amphibious doctrine, techniques, and attitude; the 1945–50 inter-Service unification and roles and missions struggles; and the pre-Korean War training and exercises. The study also briefly reviews Army amphibious doctrine, units, planning, and training following the Korean War and the current state of Army waterborne strategic and operational maneuver capabilities.

The study concludes that, while the Marine Corps will continue to be the nation's amphibious warfare specialists, and future assault landings on hostile shores are likely to be conducted by Marines, the Korean War experience indicates that Army forces should be prepared to conduct or participate in amphibious operations in the absence of or in conjunction with Marines. It would be prudent for the Army to maintain a small amphibious support element that can develop and test Army-specific doctrine, tactics, techniques, procedures, and equipment and serve as the basis for an Army amphibious-capable force for situations in which Marine Corps and/or Navy amphibious forces are insufficient or not available.

A Note on Definitions[5]

Most amphibious operations are joint, which "connotes activities, operations, organizations, etc., in which elements of two or more Military Departments participate," while combined activities are those involving "two or more forces or agencies of two or more allies."[6] The current joint doctrinal definition of an amphibious operation is a "military operation launched from the sea by an amphibious force, embarked in ships or craft with the primary purpose of introducing a landing force ashore to accomplish the assigned mission."[7] The definition has varied over the years, with the Army sometimes using or arguing for a broader definition that includes other waterborne operations, including those on inland waters. The types of amphibious operations currently include the amphibious assault (the principal type of amphibious operation that involves establishing a force on a hostile or potentially hostile shore); amphibious demonstration (a type of amphibious operation conducted for the purpose of deceiving the enemy by a show of force with the expectation of deluding the enemy into a course of action unfavorable to him); amphibious raid (a type of amphibious operation involving swift incursion into or temporary occupation of an objective followed by a planned withdrawal); amphibious reconnaissance (an amphibious landing conducted by minor elements, normally involving stealth rather than force of arms, for the purpose of securing information, and usually followed by a planned withdrawal); and amphibious withdrawal (a type of amphibious operation involving the extraction of forces by sea in ships or craft from a hostile or potentially hostile shore). Other amphibious operations include noncombatant evacuation operations (NEO) and foreign humanitarian assistance (FHA).[8] Amphibious landings may be conducted against undefended or lightly defended areas to bypass or envelop enemy forces, or they may be conducted against defended areas in operations known at the time of the Korean War as "landings on hostile shores" and currently called amphibious operations against coastal defenses.

During World War II and at the time of the Korean War, the Army made a distinction between "ship-to-shore" and "shore-to-shore" operations. Ship-to-shore movement was conducted by transferring troops, equipment, and supplies from transports to the beach in landing craft or landing vehicles. Shore-to-shore movement was the movement of troops, equipment, and supplies directly from the embarkation area to the beach without transfer at sea, except for that portion of the landing force that landed directly on the beach from landing ships. These short distance operations were normally made mostly by landing craft and only a very few landing ships.[9] Most amphibious operations were a combination of both types because of the mix of ships, including attack transports (APA) and attack cargo ships (AKA) that required ship-to-shore movement and ramped landing ships that could land troops and equipment directly onto the beach.[10] Some of General MacArthur's operations along the New Guinea coast and in the Philippines were purely shore-to-shore operations using predominantly Army landing craft, but most of the SWPA and European and Mediterranean operations used a combination of ship-to-shore and shore-to-shore techniques. The long-range operations in the Central Pacific were by necessity largely ship-to-shore operations, although shore-to-shore operations were often conducted among closely neighboring islands.

Related but different from amphibious operations are those activities to sustain combat operations on shore by means of landing supplies, personnel, and equipment over beaches rather than through port facilities. Currently called logistics-over-the-shore (LOTS) operations, they are defined as "the loading and unloading of ships without the benefit of deep-draft-capable, fixed-port facilities; or as a means of moving forces closer to tactical assembly areas dependent on threat force capabilities."[11] During the Korean War, the lack of adequate dock facilities and problems caused by extreme west coast tides also required the frequent use of lightering in which troops, cargo, and equipment were transferred between ships anchored in the harbor (in the stream) and the shore using landing ships, landing craft, powered barges (lighters), or other vessels collectively called lighterage.[12]

Amphibious and LOTS operations may be conducted as part of an expedition (defined by both the Department of Defense and the Army as "a military operation conducted by an armed force to accomplish a specific objective in a foreign country").[13] Naval expeditionary warfare is currently defined as "military operations mounted from the sea, usually on short notice, consisting of forward deployed, or rapidly deployable, self-sustaining naval forces tailored to achieve a clearly stated objective."[14] The US Navy defines "expeditionary maneuver warfare" as "the ability to mass overwhelming naval, joint, and allied military power, and deliver it ashore to influence, deter, contain, or defeat an aggressor. Naval expeditionary forces provide the Joint Task Force Commander with the ability to conduct military operations in an area of control, extending from the open ocean to the littorals, and to accessible inland areas that can be attacked, supported, and defended directly from the sea."[15] The Marine Corps has tended to conflate the terms "expeditionary" and "amphibious," exemplified by its renaming the newest amphibious assault vehicle as the "Expeditionary Fighting Vehicle."[16] In 2005 the Marine Corps introduced the Expeditionary Warfare Family of Concepts that includes Operational

Maneuver from the Sea, Ship-to-Objective Maneuver (landing operations), Sustained Operations Ashore, and Other Expeditionary Operations.[17] A related concept is sea basing, in which ships and other platforms would be combined to form a base at sea from which Marine or Army forces could conduct and sustain amphibious operations.[18]

Some of the same techniques and equipment used in amphibious operations may be used in river crossing operations or on inland bodies of water. From time to time, the Army, as well as the Navy and Marine Corps, has also conducted military operations along rivers and inland waterways. These riverine operations make use of amphibious techniques and materiel as well as specially adapted tactics, weapons, and equipment, but while water is an obstacle to be overcome in amphibious and river crossing operations, in riverine warfare the fluid concourses of rivers, lakes, bays, and estuaries are avenues of approach providing access to the enemy and routes of transportation and sustainment for friendly forces.[19]

See appendix C for definitions of terms applicable to amphibious operations as they appeared in doctrine during the Korean War period.

Notes

1. The landing ship, tank (LST) was a 328-foot long ship with a bow ramp that was capable of running up onto a beach (beaching) to discharge tanks, vehicles, personnel, or other cargo and then pulling back off the beach (retracting). Gordon L. Rottman, *Landing Ship, Tank (LST) 1942–2002*, New Vanguard 115 (Oxford, UK: Osprey Publications, 2005); Norman Friedman and A.D. Baker, *U.S. Amphibious Ships and Craft; An Illustrated Design History* (Annapolis, MD: Naval Institute Press, 2002), 117–124. A descriptive list of amphibious ships and craft in use at the time of the Korean War is at Appendix B, "Landing Ships, Craft, and Vehicles in Use during the Korean War." SCAJAP in June 1950 consisted of 12 ex-US Navy freighters and 39 LSTs manned by Japanese but controlled by SCAP. These ships had been used to repatriate Japanese from the continent following the war and continued to be used for Far East Command (FEC) logistic support and as interim transport in the Japanese islands until the war-destroyed Japanese Merchant Marine could be reconstituted. James A. Field Jr., *History of United States Naval Operations, Korea* (Washington, DC: GPO, 1962), 46, 54, 71–74.

2. Korean place names are presented in this study using the National Academy of the Korean Language style. On first use, the Modified McCune-Reischauer (*Times-Herald*) style generally in use at the time of the Korean War is provided in parentheses. See Appendix A, "Korean Geographical Names," for the place names used in this study in both the new and old styles.

3. In Korean War era Army doctrine, a shore party was an organization formed to provide logistical support within the beach area to landing force units during the early phases of an amphibious operation. Its basic mission was to unload supplies and equipment; to receive, segregate, and safeguard this materiel; provide services and facilities ashore; maintain security of the beach area; and evacuate casualties and prisoners of war. The Navy equivalent was the beach party: the element of a shore party that controls the landing of craft and larger landing ships and regulates water traffic near the beach. The beach party was controlled by the Navy beach master. Roughly speaking, the beach party was responsible for activity below the high tide line and the shore party for activity above the high tide line. However, under Army doctrine, the shore party commander had overall control of the beachhead, including the beach party, except for purely Navy matters. See Appendix C, "Amphibious Terms, Abbreviations, and Acronyms: Army Doctrine in Effect 1950–53."

4. Forcible entry is the seizing and holding of a military lodgment (a designated area in a hostile or potentially hostile territory that, when seized and held, makes the continuous landing of troops and materiel possible, and provides maneuver space for subsequent operations) in the face of armed opposition. *Department of Defense Dictionary of Military and Associated Terms,* dtic.mil/doctrine/jel/doddict/index.html (accessed 7 May 2007), hereafter, *DOD Dictionary.*

5. The material in this section was current as of June 2008.

6.   Unless otherwise indicated, these definitions are all from the *DOD Dictionary*. During World War II, the British used the term "combined" in the way "joint" is used today and generally used the term "combined operations" to describe amphibious operations.

7.   An amphibious force is an amphibious task force (a Navy task organization formed to conduct amphibious operations) and a landing force (a Marine Corps or Army task organization formed to conduct amphibious operations) together with other forces that are trained, organized, and equipped for amphibious operations.

8.   US Joint Chiefs of Staff, Joint Publication 3-02, *Joint Doctrine for Amphibious Operations* (Washington, DC: GPO, 2001), I-2–I-3; Joint Publication 3-18, *Joint Doctrine for Forcible Entry Operations*, Appendix A, "Amphibious Operations" (Washington, DC: GPO, 2001).

9.   Headquarters, Department of the Army, Field Manual (FM) 60-10, *Amphibious Operations: Regiment in Assault Landings* (Washington, DC: GPO, 1952), 2–3.

10.   Attack transports (Navy designation APA) and attack cargo ships (AKA), originally called combat loaders, were transports (troop carriers) and cargo ships modified to carry landing craft suitable for amphibious assaults. An APA could carry a battalion of troops. Three APAs and an AKA could carry a regiment. Tanks and other heavy equipment were normally carried in LSTs. The other major Korean War era amphibious ship was the landing ship, dock (LSD), a 475-foot ship that could carry landing craft, amphibious tractors, or amphibious trucks in a well deck that could be flooded to allow the craft to be launched under their own power through stern gates. Smaller landing ships were 203-foot long landing ships, medium (LSMs) and 120-foot landing ships, utility (LSU), which had been known as landing craft, tank (LCT) during World War II and were redesignated landing craft, utility (LCU) after the Korean War. Landing craft were ramped vessels small enough to be carried aboard APAs, AKAs, or LSTs and included several types of 36-foot vessels designed to put troops and light vehicles on the beach and 56-foot landing craft, mechanized (LCM), originally intended to carry tanks. Some rubber boats were also designated as landing craft. Amphibious vehicles included landing vehicles, tracked (LVT), which were amphibious tractors; armored LVTs mounting howitzers; and amphibious trucks, of which the most important and numerous was the DUKW, or "Duck," an amphibious 2½-ton truck; Friedman and Baker, *U.S. Amphibious Ships and Craft,* 117–124. The development of these ships, craft, and vehicles is discussed in chapter 2. A descriptive list of amphibious ships and craft in use at the time of the Korean War is at appendix B.

11.   *DOD Dictionary.*

12.   René de Kerchove, *International Maritime Dictionary*, 2d ed. (Princeton, NJ: D. Van Nostrand Company, Inc., October 1961).

13.   de Kerchove, *International Maritime Dictionary*; Headquarters, Department of the Army, FM 1-02, *Operational Terms and Graphics* (Washington, DC: GPO, 2004).

14. *DOD Dictionary.*

15. US Navy, *Seapower for a New Era: A Program Guide to the New Navy* (Washington, DC: Department of the Navy, 2007), 22, www.navy.mil/navydata/policy/seapower/spne07/top-spne07.html (accessed 20 June 2008).

16. Headquarters, United States Marine Corps, Direct Reporting Program Manager, Advanced Amphibious Assault, "Expeditionary Fighting Vehicle," efv. usmc.mil/ (accessed 7 May 2007).

17. Headquarters, United States Marine Corps, "Expeditionary Maneuver Family of Concepts," *Marine Corps Concepts and Programs,* 2005, hqinet001. hqmc.usmc.mil/p&r/concepts/2005/PDF/Ch2PDFs/CP05%20Chapter% 202%20 Warfighting%20Concepts%20pg%20025_Expeditionary%20Maneuver%20Warf are%20Family%20of%20Concepts.pdf (accessed 13 May 2007).

18. Henry B. Cook, "Sea Basing and Maritime Pre-positioning," *Army Logistician*, Vol. 35, Issue 3 (May–June 2004): 36–39. The latest statement of Marine Corps doctrinal concepts as of the time of this writing (June 2008) is, US Marine Corps, *Concepts and Program 2008* (Washington, DC: Headquarters, US Marine Corps, 2008), www.usmc.mil/units/hqmc/pandr/Documents/Concepts/2008/toc.htm (accessed 20 June 2008).

19. George E. Buker makes this point and uses the term "fluid concourses" in *Swamp Sailors: Riverine Warfare in the Everglades, 1835–1842* (Gainesville FL: University Presses of Florida, 1975), 4–5. The *DOD Dictionary* defines riverine operations as "operations conducted by forces organized to cope with and exploit the unique characteristics of a riverine area, to locate and destroy hostile forces, and/or to achieve or maintain control of the riverine area. Joint riverine operations combine land, naval, and air operations, as appropriate, and are suited to the nature of the specific riverine area in which operations are to be conducted." Scott C. Truver, "The Sea Base: Cornerstone of the U.S. Tri-Service Maritime Strategy," *Naval Forces*, Vol. XXIX, No. II (2008): 9–19; *US Navy Seapower for a New Era*, 24–25, 114–130.

Chapter 2

Amphibious Heritage

American Amphibious Warfare to 1919

With its long indented coastline, bays, lakes, and rivers, the North American continent has always lent itself to waterborne operations, which were an essential part of military campaigns from the beginning of European colonization. Colonial and United States military and naval forces conducted many river crossings, operations on inland lakes, riverine operations, and small-scale amphibious raids in their long history. A series of expeditions beginning in 1645 by British and colonial troops against the French settlement of Port Royal in what would later become Nova Scotia is among the earliest recorded amphibious operations by Europeans in North America. In 1690 Sir William Phips led some 450 colonial militiamen in the seizure of Port Royal during King William's War (the War of the League of Augsburg). Later that same year he failed to capture Quebec with a much larger expedition. Colonial troops also participated in Admiral Edward Vernon's generally unsuccessful amphibious operations in the Caribbean during the War of Jenkins' Ear (1738–48).[1]

In 1745, 4,200 Maine volunteers, led by William Pepperrell, sailed in 90 ships to capture the French fortress of Louisburg on Cape Breton Island. Louisburg was returned to France under the provisions of the Treaty of Aix-la-Chapelle, but in 1758, during the French and Indian War (Seven Years War), General Jeffrey Amherst and Admiral Edward Boscowen recaptured the fortress with some 14,000 British regulars and American Rangers carried in 150 transports escorted by 40 fighting ships. The following year, General James Wolfe carried out a brilliant amphibious landing to seize Quebec, an operation that General Douglas MacArthur would use as an example in his arguments for the amphibious landing at Incheon (Inch'on) 191 years later. Some 4,000 Americans of Amherst's New York forces also participated in Admiral Sir George Pocock's amphibious assault on Havana in 1762.[2]

The first eight American combatant ships of the Revolutionary War were ordered into service by General George Washington as commerce raiders and manned by Army troops, many of them soldiers of General John Glover's 14th Massachusetts Continental Regiment (The Marblehead Mariners).[3] Under Commodore Esek Hopkins, 250 sailors and marines who raided the British port of New Providence in the Bahamas in March 1776 carried out the first American amphibious operation. The only other amphibious operation of any size during the Revolutionary War took place in 1779 when an expedition of 40 ships and 21,000 soldiers, sailors, and marines, under the joint command of General Solomon Lovell and Commodore Dudley Saltonstall, made an unsuccessful attempt to recapture the Castine Peninsula on Penobscot Bay, Maine. However, Continental Navy ships and craft and Continental Army forces carried out frequent coastal defense operations and used lakes and rivers for transportation. Indeed, an iconic image of the Revolutionary War is that of Washington being rowed across the Delaware River by soldiers of Glover's regiment.[4]

Following the Revolution, river transportation sustained Anthony Wayne's 1792–93 Ohio campaign and the Lewis and Clark exploratory expedition to the Pacific coast.[5] Throughout the War of 1812, American forces carried out coastal, lake, and river operations. These actions saw some of the best and the worst examples of the then-standard American approach to command and control in joint operations: the principle of voluntary "mutual cooperation," with the land and naval commanders of equal status, neither subordinate to the other, and the effectiveness of the operation depending on the willing cooperation of each with the other.[6] The height of effective cooperation was reached in October 1813 during the Battle of the Thames, when Commodore Oliver Hazard Perry, having swept the British from Lake Erie, supported Major General William Henry Harrison's forces with naval gunfire and over-the-shore logistics. Perry then turned command of his squadron over to Captain Jesse Elliott and went ashore to serve at Harrison's side during the ensuing campaign.[7] The actions of Commodore Isaac Chauncey the following year were in stark contrast. Following effective but troubled Army–Navy cooperation in the attack on Sackett's Harbor, Major General Jacob Brown called on Chauncey to support the Niagara campaign in July and August 1814. The commodore replied that, while

> You might find the fleet somewhat of a convenience in the transportation of Provisions and Stores for the use of an Army and an agreeable appendage to attend its marches and counter marches . . . the Secretary of the Navy has honored us with a higher destiny—we are intended to Seek and fight the Enemy's fleet . . . and I shall not be diverted in my efforts to effectuate it by any Sinister attempt to render us subordinate to or an appendage of the Army.[8]

Keel boats and other river boats supported the postwar Western expansion, and the Army's overland expedition during the First Seminole Wars of 1816–23 made some use of water transportation. During the Second Seminole War of 1836–42, Army units, watercraft of the US Revenue Marine (predecessor of the US Coast Guard), and a fleet of Navy ships and craft that came to be known as the Mosquito Fleet conducted amphibious landings and riverine warfare, carrying out waterborne raids and counter-guerrilla operations along the coast and rivers and through the swamps of Florida, with waterborne logistical support provided in part by Army-owned or chartered ships and craft.[9]

During the Mexican War of 1846–47, Commodore Robert Field Stockton and US Army Major John C. Fremont conducted a small landing at San Diego in July 1846 and Navy forces of the Home Squadron under Commodore David Conner carried out landings along the Rio Grande and Tabasco Rivers and at Tampico on the gulf coast. A superb example of cooperation and the largest seaborne US amphibious operation to date took place on 9 March 1847 at Vera Cruz under the command of Major General Winfield Scott and Commodore Conner. This operation had many of the hallmarks of modern landings on hostile shores. Scott, the senior officer of the US Army, planned the operation carefully and arranged for the procurement of 141 40-man surf or flat boats for his assault troops, the first landing craft specifically designed for amphibious landings in US history. Scott's relations with Conner were exemplary. Prior to the landing, Scott organized his 8,000-man force into boat teams. He and Conner conducted a joint beach reconnaissance, and then Scott placed his Army forces under Conner's control for the landing. On the morning of 9 March, steamers towed the surfboats to the troop-carrying transports. At 1530 Conner signaled and the soldiers clambered down into the boats, and at 1730, after a brief naval gunfire bombardment that scattered the Mexican troops on the beach, Conner signaled to land the landing force. Rowed by Navy crews and guided by control vessels on the flanks, the boats sped toward shore in 10-boat waves with signal flags and regimental colors fluttering in the breeze and fixed bayonets glittering in the afternoon sun. Just before 1800 the first wave splashed ashore to find that the Mexican defenders had fled behind the sand dunes. Bands aboard the ships began playing the "Star Spangled Banner," and within 5 hours 8,600 troops had been landed without loss of a single life. After capturing the city of Vera Cruz, Scott's forces began a march to Mexico City, which they occupied on 14 September 1847. The expedition was logistically supported during the 15-month campaign through the ports and beaches of the Mexican gulf coast.[10]

Although there was no strong defense of the beach and the landing was essentially unopposed, the Vera Cruz operation nonetheless demonstrated appropriate organization of a landing force, smooth ship-to-shore troop movement, and effective coordination of naval gunfire support. While there is little evidence these lessons entered the doctrine of the Army and

13

Navy, the Army engineers responsible for the planning and execution of the Army part of the landing came away with experience that would be reflected in Army waterborne operations during the Civil War.[11]

Although frequently marred by erratic strategic direction, divided counsels, and poor inter-Service cooperation, major joint amphibious and riverine operations were carried out during the Civil War. The initial Union strategy was one of coastal blockade combined with a large expedition down the Mississippi River. The latter operation never took place as originally conceived, but the coastal blockade, including the seizure of lodgments at key points along the Confederate coast, was carried out much in the way it was planned by the 1861 Blockade Board, which was chaired by Navy Captain Samuel F. DuPont and included Army Engineer representation.[12] Early amphibious operations included the capture of forts at the entrance to the Hatteras inlet in North Carolina by Navy Flag Officer Silas Stringham and Major General Benjamin F. Butler in August 1861 and the seizure of Port Royal off Hilton Head, South Carolina, by Captain DuPont and Brigadier General Thomas W. Sherman in November of that year.[13]

Early in the war, Major General George B. McClellan proposed a plan to use joint operations to penetrate the Confederacy by way of the great river systems and the coast to seize key railway junctions and thus paralyze the Southern transportation and communications systems. The strategy was never fully implemented, although McClellan did arrange for the activation of a special amphibious division comprised largely of New England seamen and commanded by Major General Ambrose E. Burnside. Initially operating with Army-owned and chartered ships and then in conjunction with naval forces under Flag Officer Louis M. Goldsborough, Burnside's Coast Division captured Roanoke Island and New Berne on the Carolina coast in February 1862 before being diverted for operations against Richmond.[14]

The capture of New Orleans by forces of Butler and Navy Flag Officer David G. Farragut in April 1862 and joint Army and Navy operations on the Western rivers in 1862 and 1863 were vital contributions to Union victory.[15] The Army operated transports on the Western rivers throughout the war and, until they were turned over to the Navy in October 1862, maintained a small force of gunboats. The Western theater also saw the operation of a unique Army amphibious force—the brainchild of Lieutenant Colonel Alfred W. Ellet, a self-taught engineer, who had long argued for swift, unarmored vessels with reinforced rams that could destroy enemy ships. In March 1862 Ellet persuaded Secretary of War Edwin M. Stanton to allow him to outfit a flotilla of seven paddle steamers with armored prows, wooden bulwarks to protect the machinery and boilers, and hoses that could spray scalding steam on the enemy in battle. Beginning in April 1862, Ellet's Army Ram Fleet operated on the Mississippi directly under Secretary Stanton's control and independent of Army and Navy commanders.

In August 1862 Ellet proposed the formation of an amphibious riverine force to deal with Confederate guerrilla bands that were harassing and interdicting Federal lines of communication. The newly arrived Navy commander, Acting Rear Admiral David Dixon Porter, saw merit in the idea. Ellet was promoted to brigadier general and in October 1862 was given command of the Mississippi Marine Brigade, consisting of one infantry battalion, one cavalry battalion, and an artillery battery. Although officially designated a "Marine Brigade," the roughly 1,500 troops were all Army volunteers, some of them recruited from among the convalescents at hospitals in Saint Louis. The brigade's transports were converted river packets fitted with ramps so troops and horses could debark quickly. Operating in conjunction with the Army Ram Fleet, initially under Porter's control and later under General Ulysses S. Grant, the brigade conducted operations with mixed results until 1864 and was disbanded in January 1865.[16]

In the east, the movement of McClellan's Army of the Potomac by water to the Virginia peninsula (and its later withdrawal) was a major operation that involved Navy cooperation and the use of Army watercraft. Particularly notable was the training and equipping of Brigadier General William B. Franklin's division as an amphibious assault force that included an engineer brigade equipped to support river crossings and amphibious landings. Lieutenant Colonel Barton S. Alexander, who had developed methods of landing heavy equipment over beaches while supervising the construction of fortifications and lighthouses during prewar service, trained these engineers. In April 1862 in preparation for a proposed landing below Gloucester, opposite Yorktown on the York River in Virginia, Alexander directed the construction of amphibious assault vessels, including landing barges each capable of carrying and landing a battery of artillery. Pontoon boats originally intended for the construction of floating bridges served as 40-man infantry landing craft. The infantry practiced boarding the pontoon boats from transport ships (Alexander designed special ramps to speed the process) and landing in battle order while the artillery rehearsed loading and debarking its guns and horses. The Confederates abandoned Yorktown before the landing could take place, but the division used its special equipment and techniques to make an unopposed landing at West Point, some

25 miles upriver from Gloucester on 6 May 1862. At 1600 the first wave of 2,000 men went ashore and formed a line of battle. Within 3 hours 10,000 men were ashore, and by dawn the next day all of the artillery and supporting equipment had been landed and the division had gone into action. Franklin's division was the most well-trained amphibious force in the Union Army at that time, but like Burnside's Coast Division, it was thereafter used in conventional military operations. Nonetheless, the West Point landing is an indication of what might have been had the Union leadership elected to put more emphasis on Army amphibious operations.[17]

In January 1865, after a failed attempt in December 1864 that reflected the worst of the American cooperation approach to joint warfare, Army and Navy forces successfully captured Fort Fisher at the mouth of the Cape Fear River. In spite of previous friction between the two officers, Major General Alfred H. Terry and Admiral Porter cooperated closely. The operation was well planned, the preliminary naval bombardment was accurate and intense, the unopposed landing north of the fortress was well organized, and Porter's ships provided close support fires during the final assault, which included a 2,000-man naval brigade of sailors and marines as well as Terry's army forces. The seizure of Fort Fisher opened the way to the capture of Wilmington, North Carolina, thus establishing a secure line of communication for Major General William T. Sherman's army advancing northward from Georgia.[18]

The Army's extensive amphibious and riverine experience in the Civil War was not codified into formal doctrine, although some institutional memory of these operations is likely to have survived.[19] During the last decades of the 19th century, the few amphibious operations carried out by US forces were generally conducted by Navy landing teams of sailors and marines, exemplified by the seizure of forts along the Han River in Korea in June 1871 by a naval landing force.[20] In the words of historian Brian McAllister Linn, these "punitive strikes, naval landings, amphibious raids, and other landing operations . . . were ad hoc incidents of military forces assisting the commerce-protecting gunboat diplomacy of the era."[21] However, in the 1890s the Navy began to consider the possibility of large-scale overseas expeditions, and the first of such operations came in the Spanish–American War. While Army–Navy cooperation was often good at the tactical level, those landings revealed problems in inter-Service cooperation and coordination and Army preparedness.

In a preliminary operation on 10 June 1898, Lieutenant Colonel Robert T. Huntington's 650-man Marine battalion temporarily based at Key West, Florida, was landed at Guantánamo, Cuba. The landing went smoothly and, reinforced by some 60 Cuban insurgents, the Marines held off a Spanish attack with light casualties. The US expedition was thereby provided with a useful anchorage, coaling station, and base of operations, and the Marine Corps increased its focus on the seizure and defense of advanced bases as their special role.[22]

General William R. Shafter's US Army V Corps then made unopposed landings at Daiquirí and Siboney in Cuba between 22 and 26 June 1898. The landings were impeded by heavy surf and a lack of docking facilities and lighterage, but after a preliminary bombardment of suspected Spanish positions by Navy ships, the 16,000-man V Corps was put ashore with the loss of only two troopers of the 10th Cavalry who drowned. However, there were no special craft to land horses and mules, some 30 of which perished after the animals were pushed into the sea to swim ashore.[23] In July, 27,000 troops under Major General Nelson A. Miles landed unopposed at Guánica, Ponce, and Arroyo, Puerto Rico. With the help of an engineer unit with small craft and pier-building materials and a fleet of captured lighters, these landings went smoothly, reflecting "the Army's growing skill at amphibious campaigning."[24] Following Commodore George Dewey's destruction of the Spanish fleet at Manila Bay in May 1898 and subsequent occupation of Manila by a naval landing force, the Army dispatched an 11,000-man expeditionary force under Major General Wesley Merritt. Cooperation between Dewey and Merritt was close and the landings of this force also went smoothly, using Navy launches, ships' boats, and improvised landing craft.[25] During the long war against the Philippine insurgents that followed, there were many instances of Army–Navy cooperation in operational and tactical movement by water.[26] The shipment and landing of troops in the Caribbean and the Philippines, while generally successful, demonstrated the need for transports and lighterage. In November 1898 the Army Quartermaster Corps established an Army Transport Service (ATS) that, except for a brief period during and after World War I, operated a fleet of large ocean-going transports until it was absorbed by the Military Sea Transportation Service (MSTS) on the eve of the Korean War.[27]

The Spanish–American War provided rich lessons for joint operations in general and landing operations in particular. It also set the stage for a continuing US military and naval presence in the Western Pacific. After the Japanese military and naval success in the 1904–05 Russo–Japanese War, this presence provided the focus for Pacific strategy over the next four decades. The problems of conducting joint operations during the war led to reforms by both Services that included establishment of an Army General

Staff, the Navy General Board, the Army War College as both an educational institution and as an extension of the Army Staff for planning and strategic thought, and, in 1903, the Joint Board of the Army and Navy.

The Joint Board was intended to provide a forum for the discussion of matters that required the cooperation of the two Services. The Board engaged in some war planning in the years prior to World War I, including joint studies for a possible war with Japan, and considered command and control of joint operations.[28] In 1908 Dewey, the senior member of the Board, recommended that when Army, Navy, and Marine forces were engaged in joint operations on shore, the senior line Army officer should command the joint force and have authority to issue orders to the officers in command of the forces of the other two Services. At the time, both Service Secretaries agreed, but such action required legislation and by 1913 the Navy had reversed its position and the project ceased.[29]

During this same period, the Marine Corps underwent changes that would ultimately result in the adoption of landing force operations as its primary mission. The Marine success at Guantánamo coincided with a growing sense within the Navy that a force devoted to the landing mission should replace the traditional ad hoc landing forces.[30] In 1900 the Navy General Board gave the mission of seizing and defending advance bases to the Marine Corps after considering, and dismissing, Army forces for this role, because an appropriate Army force might not always be available. In 1901 the Marine Corps designated a battalion for the advance base mission, carried out landing exercises in the Caribbean, and in 1910 established an Advance Base School at New London, Connecticut.[31] While far less focused on the issue than the Marines, the Army produced a rudimentary manual on landing doctrine in 1908 and conducted a landing exercise on the coast of Massachusetts in August 1909.[32]

The most significant landing operation before World War I took place in April 1914, when a US Naval Division composed of marines and sailors from ships of the Atlantic Fleet, augmented by a Marine battalion from the Advance Base Force, seized the Mexican port city of Vera Cruz. On 24 April Brigadier General Frederick Funston arrived with a reinforced Army regiment to replace the naval division, take operational control of the marines, and begin an occupation that lasted until 23 November.[33]

World War I provided no opportunities for US amphibious operations, but other belligerent powers carried out several landings. In September 1914 the Japanese landed on the coast of China to seize the German colony at Qingdao (Tsingtao). They also occupied German possessions in the Marianas, Caroline, Palau, and Marshall Island groups in the Central

Pacific; while Australian forces seized the German holdings in New Guinea, the Bismarck Archipelago, and the Solomon Islands; and New Zealand occupied German Samoa.[34]

All these were traditional landing operations against undefended or lightly defended beaches followed by movement to the objective. However, in April 1915 British troops conducted an assault landing against defended beaches at the southern tip of the Gallipoli Peninsula in an attempt to force passage through the Dardanelles, capture Constantinople, put Turkey out of the war, and reopen the southern route to Russia. In spite of the use of innovative landing craft by the British, the Turkish defenders immediately pinned down the landing force. Turkish forces also contained a second landing at Suvla Bay on the west coast of the peninsula by an Australian and New Zealand Corps (ANZAC).[35]

Although they had no tradition of amphibious warfare, in October 1917 the German Army and Navy conducted a well-planned landing to seize islands at the mouth of the Gulf of Riga and trap Russian warships. The amphibious phase of the operation went smoothly and the Germans gained access to the Riga Harbor facilities; however, several German ships were lost and most of the Russian warships escaped.[36] The last major amphibious operation of the war took place in April 1918, when the British tried to block the German submarine bases at Ostend and Zeebrugge, Belgium, by sinking concrete-laden ships in the entrance channel and detonating explosive-filled submarines. A commando force of some 200 Royal Marines sent in to disable the coast defense guns took very heavy casualties and the channel was only partially blocked. The US Army and Marine Corps would study all of these operations in the years after the war.[37]

Amphibious Doctrine and Planning, 1919–38[38]

After World War I the United States turned inward, but could not completely disengage from a world in which it had economic interests in Europe and Asia, overseas possessions (most notably Hawaii, the Philippines, and the Panama Canal Zone), and cultural links. There was no realistic threat from Europe for the near future, but Japan's acquisition of the German Pacific island possessions, Japanese expansion into Manchuria, and the growth of Japanese naval and commercial maritime power raised the possibility of war between the United States and Japan. The Philippines and Guam would be at immediate risk, because they were at the end of a long sea line of communication and vulnerable to interdiction from the Japanese-held islands. Under the provisions of the 1922 Washington treaties, the United States and Japan agreed not to fortify their island possessions in the Western Pacific and the United States agreed not to improve its existing fortifications at the mouth of Manila Bay.

The Navy saw Japan as the only likely enemy and did its war planning based on the assumption that war would begin with a Japanese attack on the Philippines and end, after a climactic naval battle in the Western Pacific, with a blockade of the Japanese home islands. By the 1930s the general outline of Navy planning was for a counteroffensive across the Pacific that would require long-range ships and aircraft and the ability to replenish ships at sea, and also the seizure of Japanese-held islands for use as intermediate bases.[39]

The Army's challenge was to balance requirements for the continental defense of the United States with the defense of the Panama Canal, Hawaii, and the Philippines as budgets and the size of the Army shrank. Any adequate defense of the Philippines would require the use of Philippine troops, but in the aftermath of the Philippine War and subsequent operations against the Moros in the south, the Army was reluctant to arm large numbers of Filipinos. By the late 1930s a force of some 11,000 US and Filipino troops guarded the Philippines and the issue of whether and how they would be reinforced in the event of war with Japan was still being debated.[40] The Army also considered, more as a theoretical exercise than a likely scenario, the possibility of the United States going to war with a European power or Mexico. In either case, or in the event of an intervention in Latin America or China, the Army would have to transport troops overseas and might have to land on a hostile shore. By 1938 events in Europe made this possibility far less theoretical.[41]

The Joint Board

While both Services grappled with the problems of how to defend US overseas territory and interests as the military budget shrank, joint consideration of these issues was carried out by the Army and Navy Joint Board, reorganized in 1919 after languishing during World War I. The members of the Board were the Army Chief of Staff, the Chief of Naval Operations (CNO), their deputies, and the chief planners. For the study of joint issues, the Board created a Joint Planning Committee (JPC) consisting of officers from the Army War Plans Division (WPD) and the Navy Plans Division and generally referred to as the Joint Planners.[42] Over the next two decades, the Joint Board would establish doctrine for joint expeditionary operations, develop a range of war plans, and examine command and control in joint operations. The Board also provided a structure and procedures for joint deliberations that would smoothly transition to the Joint Chiefs of

Staff organization in February 1942. The war plans developed by the Joint Board and the study of joint overseas expeditions pursued at the Army and Navy War Colleges in the 1920s and 1930s provided the strategic context within which the Marine Corps and Navy, with some contribution by the Army, developed the tactics and techniques for landing operations on hostile shores.

With regard to command relations, the joint planners initially considered whether there should be a single commander (unified command) for joint operations. They concluded in 1919 that the "paramount" interest of one or the other Services would be evident in such operations and that "intelligent and hearty cooperation" would be just as effective as unity of command under a single commander of either Service, which "might cause jealousy and dissatisfaction."[43] This principle of "paramount interest" was incorporated into the first document designed to address joint operations, *Joint Action of the Army and Navy in Coast Defense*, published in 1920, and replaced in 1927 by *Joint Action of the Army and Navy (JAAN)*, which provided for coordination of joint operations either by paramount interest or unity of command, with the method of coordination specified in the war plan for each phase of a campaign. A 1935 revision stated that unity of command could only occur by specific order of the President; otherwise, the commander having "paramount interest" would exercise "limited unity of command." He could designate Army and Navy missions, but could not control forces from other Services.[44] During the 1930s the trend was toward unified command in joint operations, but in 1938 the Service chiefs agreed that, except for specific, specified operations, coordination of joint operations should be by mutual cooperation, with unity of command only when ordered by the President, by agreement between the two Service Secretaries, or when "commanders of Army and Navy forces agree that the situation requires the exercise of unity of command and further agree as to the Service that shall exercise such command."[45]

In 1904 the Joint Board had begun assigning colors to identify major potential adversaries and allies in war plans. The revived Joint Board continued this practice. The major war plan in the 1920s was a Red–Orange Plan based on the scenario of a war with an Anglo–Japanese alliance. Such a war was not deemed likely, but it provided a useful exercise to consider strategy and the size of forces required in a two-front war. One lasting legacy of these plans was the inculcation of an assumption that if the United States was faced with a simultaneous war with a European power and Japan, US interests would best be served by initially concentrating on the defeat of the European power while pursuing defensive operations in the Pacific.[46] Beginning in the early 1920s, the Joint Board also developed a plan for operations against Japan fighting alone (Joint Basic War Plan Orange). This plan originally envisioned operations across the Pacific to transport an Army expeditionary force to rescue the Philippines. While all the variations of the Orange Plan called for the Navy to fight its way across the Pacific, capturing Japanese-held island bases en route, the Army's role in the Philippines varied from reinforcement, to holding out with the forces available, to abandonment. The last version of the plan before World War II began was approved in 1938. Under this plan, the Army would reinforce Alaska with 7,000 troops, Hawaii with 25,000 troops, and the Panama Canal Zone with 15,000 troops. Neither the Philippines nor Guam would receive reinforcements. Guam was undefended in accordance with the Washington Treaties and was expected to fall quickly. The Army would hold out in the Philippines with the forces available as long as possible.[47]

The third area of Joint Board deliberations relevant to amphibious operations was the publication of guidance for expeditionary warfare. The Army and Navy had conducted joint maneuvers in Hawaii in 1925 that included a landing by two battalions of marines.[48] In 1929 the Joint Board published *Joint Overseas Expeditions—Tentative*. Revised and reissued in 1933 as *Joint Overseas Expeditions*, this document addressed cooperation between the Services and the functions of each during joint landing operations. It provided broad guidance on the organization of landing forces into battalion combat teams, the functions of Navy beach masters and Army shore parties, commercial versus combat loading of transports, the necessity of Army and Navy commanders to be aboard the same ship, and the selection of beaches. It also addressed the advantages and disadvantages of day and night landings: better control of landing craft and troops, better air and naval fire support coordination, and better defense against hostile air and naval units in the case of the former; increased chance of tactical surprise and reduced efficacy of the defenders' fires in the case of the latter. However, it did not provide specific guidance on the tactics and techniques of landing on a defended beach—a subject the Marines would take as their special mission.[49]

Marine Corps Developments

Major General John A. Lejeune, who became commandant of the Marine Corps in 1920, put particular emphasis on the advance base force mission. Under his direction, a group of staff officers headed by Major Earl H. Ellis produced a detailed study of the requirements for "Advanced Base Operations in Micronesia." Approved in July 1921, it served as the basis for Marine Corps planning, mobilization, and training.[50] In 1922

Lejeune defined the primary mission of the Marine Corps as "to supply a mobile force to accompany the Fleet for operations on shore in support of the Fleet [and to be used] in conjunction with Army operations on shore, when the active naval operations reach such a stage as to permit its temporary detachment from the Navy."[51] Although the *JAAN* and *Joint Overseas Expeditions* presumed that the Army would provide large-scale expeditionary forces, and the language of the documents was in terms of Army–Navy coordination, the document recognized the role of the Marines in the seizure of advanced bases for the Navy. The 1927 version of *JAAN* assigned the Marine Corps the responsibility to "provide and maintain forces . . . for land operations in support of the fleet for the initial seizure of advanced bases and for such limited auxiliary land operations as are essential to the prosecution of the naval campaign." Because the Marines were in "constant association" with naval units, they were to be given "special training in the conduct of landing operations."[52]

In 1933 the Marine Corps schools at Quantico discontinued classes to devote the full efforts of the students and staff (including at least one unidentified Army officer) to the development of a landing operations manual.[53] Until then Navy doctrine for landing operations was contained in the *Landing Force Manual, United States Navy,* which, in various editions since 1905, had remained basically unchanged in its guidance for getting troops ashore. Lines of whaleboats towed by motor launches would carry the troops ashore while other launches on the flanks provided fire support with machineguns.[54] The new manual dealt with naval gunfire and air support, ship-to-shore movement, security of the beachhead, and logistics. Because the Marines at that time were an integral part of the Navy, the issue of command relations was not developed. A naval officer would have command of the attack force, consisting of the landing force and the supporting naval forces (consisting of a transport group, fire support group, air group, mine group, screening group, and salvage group). The Navy published this manual in June 1934 as the *Tentative Landing Operations Manual.* This document would provide the template for all later Service doctrinal literature on amphibious warfare.[55]

While the intellectual work of developing the manual was underway in 1933, two brigades of marines were established, one on each coast, as the Fleet Marine Force (FMF). This force could put into practice the doctrine prescribed in the new manual through a series of fleet landing exercises (FLEXs). In the words of one Marine historian, establishment of the FMF "would dedicate a body of Marines to the full-time study, development, and practice of amphibious war."[56]

Army Activities

Although not becoming as deeply involved as an institution in the study of landing operations as the Marine Corps, the Army did not ignore these operations. Army members of the Joint Board were actively involved in the examination of and promulgation of joint doctrine on expeditionary warfare. The War Plans Division of the War Department General Staff studied landing operations as part of its war planning duties and some Army officers attended the Naval War College, where they studied expeditionary and landing operations. Students at the Army War College studied the preparation of joint Army and Navy war plans, many of which included landing operations. Naval officers gave lectures at the Army War College on expeditionary operations and joint landings.[57] Faculty and students at the Infantry School and the Army War College studied the Japanese landings of the Russo–Japanese War and the World War I amphibious operations.[58]

In 1923 the Army General Service Schools (later the Command and General Staff School) collaborated with the Naval War College in producing an exercise based on a joint expeditionary force landing in the Lingayen Gulf to recover the Philippines, and in 1926 and 1927 the two institutions conducted joint Army and Navy exercises involving expeditionary operations.[59] In 1928 the General Service Schools studied the requirements for ship-to-shore movement of divisional and corps artillery in an opposed landing on a hostile shore.[60] The following year the Army War College studied the problems involved in training, planning, deployment, execution, and sustainment of a joint Army–Navy expeditionary force using Gallipoli as a historical case study and a landing to recapture Luzon in the Philippines as a theoretical study. The study included examination of the nature of beaches, naval gunfire support, deception operations, beach master and shore party operations, and the types of ships and craft available.[61]

Throughout the 1930s, students and faculty at the Command and General Staff School and the Army War College continued to examine landing operations in the context of planning for future coalition warfare. Student committees in the Conduct of War and Analytical Studies courses repeatedly examined the Fort Fisher landing operations in the American Civil War; the Japanese Port Arthur Campaign in the Russo–Japanese War; and the World War I Tsingtao, Gallipoli, and Baltic Islands campaigns.[62] By 1940 they were also studying Japanese landing operations in the Sino–Japanese War that had begun in 1937.[63]

Army observers participated in the first two FLEXs in 1935 and 1936.[64] In 1937 the Army formed the First Expeditionary Brigade, consisting of the 30th Infantry Regiment and attached artillery and engineer elements to participate in FLEX 3. Three regiments (one Regular and two National Guard) and supporting troops participated in FLEX 4 in 1938.[65] Following the exercise, the Chief of Staff of the Army expressed a desire for greater Army participation in amphibious training, but was rebuffed by Admiral William D. Leahy, then Chief of Naval Operations, who argued that amphibious operations were essentially naval in character and so the Navy and Marines were best suited to conduct amphibious doctrine and tactics development.[66]

In late 1939 the Army began its own independent efforts at amphibious training. The Corps of Engineers conducted an Engineer School problem in 1939–40 to assess the engineers' role in an opposed landing and in late 1939 the 3d Infantry Division at Fort Lewis, Washington, began preparations to begin amphibious training.[67]

Amphibious Developments on the Eve of World War II

This increased emphasis on amphibious training took place in the context of dangerous world events. In 1937 increasing Japanese aggression in China prompted the Joint Board to direct a review of War Plan Orange. The war in Spain, the German expansionism and alliance with Italy, and the 1938 crisis over Czechoslovakia that resulted in the ill-fated Munich accords all provided further evidence that the United States faced the very real possibility of war. Accordingly, in November 1938 the Joint Board ordered a study of joint action to be taken in the event of interference in the Western Hemisphere by Germany or Italy and in July 1939 directed the development of a new family of plans known as the Rainbow plans because they envisioned war with more than one country. All plans focused on the protection of the Western Hemisphere, but Rainbow 5 involved the dispatch of forces to Europe or Africa to assist Britain and France. This was the first time since post-World War I joint planning had begun that a joint expeditionary operation to Europe or Africa was seriously contemplated.[68]

Amphibious training continued at a stepped-up pace. From January to March 1940, the Navy carried out FLEX 6 without Army participation. The landing force was provided by Brigadier General H.M. Smith's 1st Marine Brigade. The exercise tested various experimental landing craft and demonstrated the need for specialized transports, rather than warships, to carry the troops.[69] In lieu of participation in FLEX 6, the Army requested Navy support for a joint landing exercise on the West Coast in January 1940. The 9,000 troops and 1,100 vehicles of the 3d Infantry Division were to be lifted by Army transports and chartered vessels from Puget Sound and then landed in Navy landing craft in the Monterey area. The Navy refused to risk its landing craft in the beach assault and insisted on landing most of the troops at a pier, so the division conducted its landing exercise in an open field (the alfalfa assault) with trucks playing the role of landing craft.[70] At about that same time, the 1st Infantry Division's 18th Infantry Regiment began studying amphibious operations with on-shore training at Fort Devens, Massachusetts, and boat exercises at the Edgewood Arsenal in Maryland.[71]

As part of the hemispheric defense mission, various studies were conducted for assembling troops and shipping for expeditions to the Caribbean and Latin America. When Germany invaded France in June 1940, preparations were made to land the 1st Marine Brigade and 1st Infantry Division on the French islands of Martinique and Guadeloupe in the Caribbean to prevent German acquisition of French fleet units stationed there. This plan was forestalled when the French admiral neutralized the ships, but it was the beginning of serious US consideration of joint amphibious operations. German success in Europe put amphibious operations in a new light. Previously, US planners had assumed that forces sent to Europe would land through existing French seaports. Now that Germany was in control of the ports, the only way to return to the continent of Europe was through a large-scale amphibious invasion. On 26 June 1940 the War Department established an Army General Headquarters (GHQ) with responsibility for supervision and direction of the training of Army tactical forces and officially directed the 1st and 3d Infantry Divisions to conduct amphibious training.[72]

In September 1940 the Chief of Naval Operations directed the establishment of a large-scale program to train landing craft crews for assignment to transports and cargo ships. The training began in November of that year, with the assignment of US Coast Guard warrant officers and enlisted personnel to Navy transports to provide their special expertise in small boat operations in heavy seas and surf. Preparations were already underway for the potential transfer of the Coast Guard from the Treasury Department to the Navy.[73]

Throughout 1940 and 1941, coordination between the still-neutral United States and the beleaguered British grew. Rear Admiral Robert Ghormley became a permanent observer in London in the summer of

1940 to discuss US–British naval cooperation if the United States entered the war. In January 1941 an American, British, and Canadian Conference (ABC-1) was held in Washington. In the spring of that year, a 17-man team of special observers (SPOBs) led by Major General James E. Chaney was established in London and Admiral Ghormley was redesignated Special Naval Observer. The observer title was a cover name for the real task of these missions, which was to conduct coordination with the British on potential US military and naval activities when and if the United States entered the war and to provide the nucleus for a wartime US headquarters in Britain.[74]

The ABC-1 talks also started combined planning for possible US entry into the war. Military leaders of the three countries agreed on a US–British Commonwealth Joint Basic War Plan that called for a concentration of effort to defeat Germany, with initial defensive operations in the Pacific if Japan entered the war. The plan identified a requirement to capture bases from which the offensive against Germany could be launched. After talks in Singapore with British Commonwealth and Dutch authorities in April 1941, an August 1941 US–British summit conference, and mobilization planning in September, the Rainbow 5 plan was revised. The new plan envisioned a two-ocean war, with the principal US effort to be in the Atlantic and Europe while the United States conducted defensive operations in the Pacific. The plan identified the boundaries of the US land and sea defense commands and provided a troop list of forces to be sent to Britain and Northern Ireland, Hawaii, Iceland, and the west coast of South America during the first 3 months of deployment.[75] Although planning had assumed there would be no reinforcements for the Philippines, the escalation of tensions with Japan had caused a relook at Western Pacific defense requirements. In July 1941 General MacArthur, then serving in retirement as commander of the Philippine Commonwealth Army, was recalled to Active Duty and assigned as Commander of United States Army Forces in the Far East (USAFFE). By the end of the year, US Army forces had increased to nearly 19,000, augmented by a newly mobilized Philippine Army, and 35 modern B-17 bombers and 159 fighter planes had been dispatched to the Philippines.[76]

Amphibious training continued throughout this period, although there were a number of obstacles to developing an effective Army amphibious force. The Army was expanding rapidly and it was difficult to keep together a trained force capable of conducting amphibious operations. The 1st Infantry Division was the best trained and equipped Army force and was, therefore, identified as the Army element of various task forces being considered for deployment. Both the 1st and 3d Infantry Divisions did their best to carry out amphibious training, but both units were repeatedly stripped of experienced officers and soldiers to serve as cadre for new units being activated. Neither unit was able to bring an entire division together for training during those hectic days. Furthermore, Major General Lesley J. McNair, GHQ Chief of Staff, was concerned that such specialized training, if carried too far, would interfere with the unity of the Army and its ability to carry out its fundamental ground combat mission. In early 1941 McNair cautioned the commanding general of the 3d Infantry Division that basic training was more important than the amphibious training, warning, "Even though landing is the first step, success presumably will come only from skill in combat."[77]

Early in 1941 an Engineer School committee examined the role of "engineer troops in an amphibious assault," studying Marine Corps and British doctrine and recent German and Japanese tactics. They proposed using engineers as assault troops to destroy beachhead fortifications ahead of the first wave of infantry and stressed the importance of overall Army engineer control of beach and shore operations. (Under doctrine current at that time, the Navy beach party removed underwater obstacles and provided temporary docks and ramps, while the Army shore party constructed emergency roads, removed mines and obstacles, and prepared hasty defensive positions against counterattacks, with the Navy beach party controlling the overall operation.) The committee recommended that the Army develop craft suitable both for river crossings and to augment Navy landing craft if necessary, and that engineer combat units be trained to handle small boats in rough seas and for transferring materiel from ships to shore (lightering). In June 1941 the Army published its own amphibious field manual, FM 31-5, *Landing Operations on Hostile Shores*, and while most of it was taken almost verbatim from the Navy/Marine Corps manual, FM 31-5 also incorporated some of the conclusions from the engineer study.[78]

Army forces once again participated in FLEX 7 in February 1941 in the Caribbean, where three battalions of General H.M. Smith's 1st Marine Division were joined by a two-battalion task force of the 1st Infantry Division. In June 1941 the Joint Board issued a plan (the Carib Plan) for amphibious training on the east coast. The 1st Infantry Division and the 1st Marine Division were organized into the landing force component of the 1st Joint Training Force, subsequently renamed Amphibious Force, Atlantic Fleet, which conducted further exercises at New River, North Carolina, in August 1941. The Pearl Plan of September 1941 designated the 3d Infantry Division and the 2d Marine Division as the landing force of the 2d Joint Training Force (later, Amphibious Force, Pacific Fleet) at

San Diego, California. GHQ exercised responsibility for the Army forces in these organizations, while the Navy had overall control, and the landing forces were commanded by Marine Corps Major General H.M. Smith for the 1st Joint Training Force and Major General Clayton B. Vogel for the 2d Joint Training Force.[79]

Development of Landing Ships and Craft

A crucial element in the conduct of effective amphibious operations was the production of suitable ships to transport troops and equipment to the objective and landing craft to transfer them from the ships to the beach. Although some expeditionary transports had been built for the Marine Corps after World War I, warships had generally been used to transport landing forces, which were then delivered to the shore by beetle boats (a covered motor launch with a primitive ramp system), cumbersome artillery lighters, whaleboats, and motor launches. In the late 1930s the Navy converted several World War I four-stack destroyers into fast transports (APDs) by removing some of the boilers to provide troop space and adding davits for landing craft. One APD could carry a company of troops and its 4-inch guns provided fire support. First tested during FLEX 7, they were particularly useful for transporting raider units to seize special objectives. Eventually, 36 destroyers and 98 destroyer escorts would be converted to APDs and several of the destroyer escort types would serve in the Korean War.[80]

The Navy also began converting some troop transports (AP) and cargo ships (AK) by modifying the davits and other gear to carry landing craft. Initially called combat loaders, they were later designated attack transports (APA) and attack cargo ships (AKA). One APA could carry a battalion landing team; four could carry a regimental landing team, with its heavy gear and supplies carried aboard an AKA. The establishment in 1936 of the US Maritime Commission facilitated the arrival of combat loaders on the amphibious scene. Intended to revitalize the American Merchant Marine, the Commission also explicitly planned for the expansion of the US Navy fleet of auxiliaries and so several of its standard merchant ship types were designed to be easily converted to combat loaders.[81]

Both the Army and the Navy searched for improved landing craft during the 1930s, but it was the Marine Corps that took the lead in identifying and testing the Eureka boat, a fast, durable, spoon-bowed 30-footer designed by Louisiana boat builder Andrew Jackson Higgins. A 36-foot version was adopted as the landing craft, personnel (large) (LCP[L]), which became the progenitor of the World War II fleet of landing craft. The next version, the landing craft, personnel (ramped) (LCP[R]), had a narrow bow ramp that allowed troops to run directly onto the beach rather than climbing over the sides. The installation of a wider ramp to accommodate trucks and other light vehicles resulted in the optimum landing craft, the 36-foot landing craft, vehicle, personnel (LCVP)—the most widely used American World War II landing craft. The LCP(R) with its narrow bow had excellent sea-keeping qualities particularly useful for beach reconnaissance and raiding missions, so it continued in service aboard APDs for use by raiders and underwater demolition teams (UDTs). To get tanks and heavy equipment ashore, a 50-foot craft originally called a tank lighter and then designated landing craft, mechanized (LCM), was also put into service.[82] The third platform for ship-to-shore movement introduced before the war was an amphibious tractor based on a vehicle developed for rescue work in the Florida Everglades. The Marines saw in it a way to get cargo onto the shore and then inland, reducing congestion at the beachhead, as well as a way to cross the coral reefs that ringed Pacific atolls. By July 1941 the first military version, the landing vehicle, tracked (LVT[1]), was in production. In December 1941 Food Machinery Corporation (FMC) and Borg–Warner began work on improved cargo-carrying LVTs as well as an Army-sponsored armored version that could mount a 37-mm gun turret to provide an amphibious assault and fire support capability.[83]

On the other side of the Atlantic, the British had established an Inter-Service Training and Development Center (ISTDC) in 1937 to study the techniques and equipment for amphibious warfare on a joint basis. By 1939 the British had produced small numbers of LCMs and landing craft, assault (LCA), an armored equivalent of the US LCP(R) and LCVP, designed to be carried aboard landing ships, infantry (LSIs), the British equivalent of the American combat loaders. The tiny British amphibious fleet first saw action during the battles on the Norwegian fjords around Narvik in 1940. That year, a Combined Operations Headquarters (COHQ) was established to continue the development of amphibious doctrine and to carry out amphibious commando raids on the coast of Europe. The landing craft, tank (LCT), a 150-to-200-foot-long tank lighter that could carry three to six 40-ton tanks, entered British service in 1940. By 1941 the British were experimenting with the conversion of shallow-draft tankers into ocean-going tank landing ships and had entered into talks with the Americans concerning production of an Atlantic-crossing tank carrier that would become known as the landing ship, tank (LST), as well as a landing ship, dock (LSD), that could carry landing craft and LVTs in a floodable well deck and launch them from the stern. Early operations at Dakar and North Africa had convinced the British that warships made poor command posts for amphibious operations: firing the guns interfered with radio communications and the warships were likely to be called away from the landing area to deal with hostile naval units. Accordingly, the British developed a headquarters ship for amphibious operations.[84]

World War II[85]

By December 1941 Britain had been standing against the Axis powers of Germany and Italy for 2 years. The Germans occupied all of Northern Europe except neutral Sweden, Switzerland, and Spain. The southern part of France remained nominally independent under a government at Vichy that also controlled the French North African colonies of Morocco, Algeria, and Tunisia. British forces in Egypt faced German and Italian forces in Libya. Germany had invaded Russia in June 1941, pushing nearly to Moscow. Japan, at war with China since 1937, controlled the China coast and, with the acquiescence of the Vichy Government, had occupied French Indochina.

The Japanese attacks on Pearl Harbor and the Philippines in December 1941 and the subsequent German declaration of war brought the United States into the conflict. The Rainbow 5 plan with its "Germany first" strategy was put into effect immediately, but the rapid Japanese advance into Southeast Asia and the threat to Australia meant that much of the flow of US troops and materiel in the early months of the war went to the Pacific. At an initial US–British strategy conference in Washington (ARCADIA), the Allies agreed to try to hold the "Malay Barrier"—the line running through Malaya and the Netherlands East Indies (now Indonesia) north of Australia—and to reestablish the line of communication to the Philippines. However, by May 1942 the Japanese had defeated US, Australian, British, and Dutch forces; occupied Burma, Malaya, the Indies, and the Philippines, as well as Wake Island, Guam, and Rabaul in the Bismarck Archipelago; and had established footholds on the northeast coast of New Guinea and the Solomon Islands. Allied strategy shifted from trying to stop the Japanese advance to securing the island chain along the line of communication to Australia, developing bases, and building up forces to defend Australia and prepare for a counteroffensive.[86] (See map 1.)

The Japanese offensive began to falter in May 1942 when the Japanese launched an amphibious operation to capture Port Moresby on the southeastern coast of New Guinea for use as a base from which to threaten Australia. In the ensuing naval battle of the Coral Sea, the Japanese sank the US aircraft carrier *Lexington,* but lost one of their own small carriers and canceled the Port Moresby operation. In June 1942 US naval forces sank four Japanese aircraft carriers for the loss of the carrier *Yorktown* in

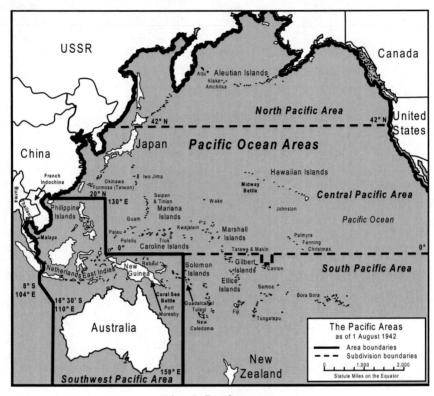

Map 1. Pacific areas.

the Battle of Midway, ending the Japanese threat to Hawaii. In a secondary operation that same month, Japanese forces attacked the Aleutians, occupying the islands of Kiska and Attu, and beginning a strange and deadly campaign among the craggy islands, icy waters, fogs, and williwaw winds of the thousand-mile-long Aleutian chain.

In the summer of 1942, the Allies prepared to go on the offensive. In accordance with the agreed-on strategy, Army Chief of Staff General George C. Marshall and the US Army leadership argued for a concentration of effort in Europe, a buildup of forces in Britain, and preparation for an invasion of the continent across the English Channel in 1943. The Army Special Observers mission in London had been redesignated United States Army Forces in the British Isles (USAFBI) after Pearl Harbor and its mission expanded from prewar planning for strategic air bombardment to command of the growing US ground force in Northern Ireland and preliminary planning for the invasion of Europe. In mid-April 1942, General Marshall made an agreement with Vice Admiral Lord Louis Mountbatten, the British Chief of Combined Operations, for a small cadre of American Army officers and noncommissioned officers to be assigned to Mountbatten's COHQ to assist in amphibious planning and to participate in commando raids to gain combat experience. The mission, led by Colonel Lucian K. Truscott, arrived in London in May. Truscott's team also recruited men from the forces in Northern Ireland to form a US commando-type force—the First Ranger Battalion.[87]

Admiral Ernest J. King, commander in chief of the US Fleet and Chief of Naval Operations, and the US Navy leadership, while agreeing to the "Germany first" approach, wanted to assure sufficient forces were available in the Pacific to stop the Japanese advance and to permit an early counteroffensive. The strategic debate in the Pacific was whether to begin the Central Pacific offensive envisioned in the prewar Orange Plan, as the Navy desired, or to adopt a proposal by General MacArthur for an offensive to capture Rabaul (the main Japanese base in the Southwest Pacific) as a step toward recapture of the Philippines. In March 1942 the US Joint Chiefs of Staff (JCS), which had replaced the Joint Board as the senior joint military-naval policy and strategy body, had established two unified commands in the Pacific. Admiral Chester W. Nimitz, the commander in chief of the US Pacific Fleet, was given command of the Pacific Ocean Areas (POA) encompassing the area north of Formosa (Taiwan), east of the Philippines, north of New Guinea, and east of a line through the central Solomon Islands. The southern part of the POA was designated as a subordinate unified command, the South Pacific Area, under Vice Admiral Ghormley. General MacArthur, who had been ordered from the Philippines to Australia that same month, became Supreme Commander of the Southwest Pacific Area (SWPA) encompassing Australia, the Netherlands East Indies, the Philippines, New Guinea, and the northwestern Solomon Islands.[88]

Given the forces then available, the Central Pacific drive was not yet feasible. On 2 July 1942 the JCS issued a directive to Nimitz and MacArthur giving them three tasks. Task One, seizure of Tulagi Island in the Solomons (where the Japanese had established a sea plane base), was to be carried out by Ghormley's Navy and Marine Corps forces. Task Two, for MacArthur, was to seize the northern Solomon Islands and to clear the Japanese from Papua (the eastern part of New Guinea). Task Three, also for MacArthur, was to occupy Rabaul and the adjacent island of New Ireland.[89] (See map 2.)

The events that took place in the summer of 1942 affected the plans for Europe and the Pacific. In North Africa, Axis forces began an offensive in late May that pushed British forces back nearly to Alexandria in Egypt. This

33

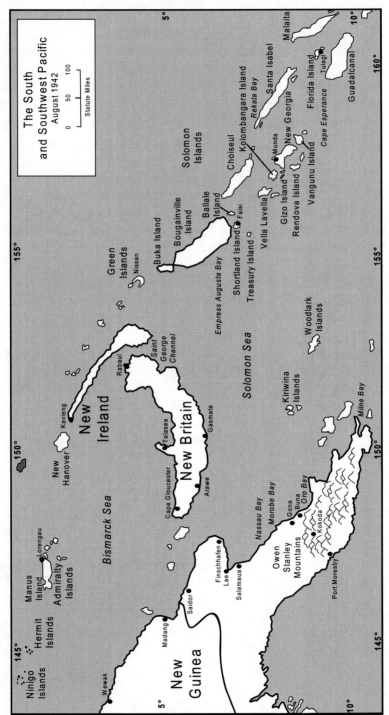

Map 2. The South and Southwest Pacific.

34

crisis diverted shipping and ruled out an early cross-channel attack. In July the JCS reluctantly agreed to a landing in North Africa as an alternative.[90] That same month, aerial reconnaissance and intelligence reports revealed that the Japanese were building an airfield on Guadalcanal. This led to the identification of that island as the specific objective of Task One of the 2 July directive.[91] These two circumstances set the stage for the first two Allied amphibious operations of the war: the landing in August 1942 of the 1st Marine Division on Guadalcanal and the landing in November 1942 of US and British forces in North Africa. While the preparations for these operations were underway, changes were taking place in the amphibious forces.

Amphibious Developments in 1942

The Army Amphibious Training Center and Engineer Amphibian Command

Training for the two amphibious forces in the Atlantic and Pacific continued after the war began, although the Amphibious Force, Atlantic Fleet moved its training area from the North Carolina coast to Chesapeake Bay because of the threat of German submarines. In March 1942 the two forces were renamed Amphibious Corps, Atlantic and Pacific Fleet. By this time the Army leadership had become dissatisfied with the amphibious training being conducted under the Navy and Marine Corps leadership. Complaints specified inadequate and poorly trained shore parties, poor coordination between beach and shore parties, and inadequate communication between the Navy and the landing forces resulting in troops being put ashore at the wrong place. There were also complaints of friction between the Services, some of which may have had to do with the personality of General H.M. Smith—a passionate advocate for amphibious warfare and the Marine Corps—who did not soft pedal his criticisms of the Navy and Army. Furthermore, the Army was now focused on the invasion across the English Channel planned for 1943 and believed that this very large shore-to-shore operation would involve a scale of forces and techniques quite different from the Pacific island landings for which Marine Corps doctrine was designed. Army leaders considered that doctrine useful, but best suited for the seizure of small islands by specialized assault forces that would subsequently be relieved by garrison forces and then carry out repeated landing operations in cooperation with the Navy. The Army saw an amphibious operation as a way to put forces ashore to conduct sustained operations on land. Because Army forces believed they would only conduct one amphibious landing and then carry on with the overarching land mission, it was not seen as desirable to develop specialized amphibious forces. Instead, standard Army units would be trained to carry out the initial landing. After the beachhead was seized, support of the Army force would become a matter of large-scale seaborne logistic sustainment that would no longer require the use of specialized naval amphibious ships. There was also a widely held belief in the Army that Marine Corps officers and staffs did not have the expertise and capacity to organize and command corps, army, and larger operations on the scale envisioned in Europe.[92]

The Army, and the British, also saw differences between landing on islands where the choice of landing sites was limited, tactical surprise was unlikely, and enemy reinforcements from off the island could be interdicted; and landing on continental land masses with many potential landing sites, the possibility of tactical surprise, the threat of massive enemy reinforcement of the forces defending the beachhead, and the likelihood of large-scale counterattacks. The Navy and Marines considered that in island landings, the better coordination and control inherent in a daylight assault outweighed the value of surprise but required extensive air and naval gunfire destruction of enemy defenses and suppression of enemy fire during the landing. The Army, thinking in terms of continental assaults, firmly believed that tactical surprise was paramount. This meant night landings with no extensive preliminary bombardment that would alert the enemy as to the location of the landing. In light of these differences, the Army proposed splitting the amphibious training and preparation, with the Army preparing with the Navy on the Atlantic coast for the European cross-channel invasion and the Marines moving to the Pacific to conduct the island operations along with such Army forces as might be necessary. Left for the future was the issue of who would conduct and control the operations against the larger Pacific land masses—New Guinea, the Philippines, and Formosa (Taiwan). These discussions coincided with Army–Navy talks in which the Navy indicated it did not have the capacity to man large numbers of landing craft while also mobilizing to fill the crews of new combatant ships coming into service. Thus, it was tentatively agreed that the Army, with assistance from the Coast Guard, would take responsibility for crewing many of the landing craft.[93]

With these factors in mind, the Army Ground Forces (AGF), which had replaced GHQ as the organization responsible for training, preparation, and deployment of ground forces, began considering the establishment of an Army amphibious training program to prepare 12 divisions (in addition to the 1st, 3d, and 9th Divisions, which were already carrying out amphibious training under the existing system) for operations in Europe.

The training was to be conducted by an Amphibious Training Command (ATC—later renamed the Amphibious Training Center) at Camp Edwards on Cape Cod, Massachusetts, beginning in July 1942, with additional facilities to be established at Carrabelle, Florida, and Fort Lewis, Washington. The mission of organizing and training the shore parties, landing craft crews, and boat maintenance units was given to the Services of Supply, which established an Engineer Amphibian Command (EAC), also at Camp Edwards, in June 1942, and began recruiting watermen, fishermen, yachtsmen, and others with small boat and maritime experience.[94]

The commander of the EAC, Colonel Daniel Noce, and his chief of staff, Lieutenant Colonel Arthur Trudeau, developed an organization for an engineer shore regiment that would combine the roles of the Navy beach party and Army shore party with two near shore companies to load and dispatch landing craft and two far shore parties to bring troops, equipment, and supplies across the beach and handle logistical support until the beachhead had been established. Noce and Trudeau anticipated that each shore regiment would be integrated with a boat regiment to operate the landing craft and other service elements, thus forming an engineer amphibian brigade (EAB). Their initial guidance was to organize and train eight of these brigades. The first two units were activated in June 1942.[95] The next month the 45th Infantry Division arrived at Camp Edwards to begin training at the ATC, which also began a program of amphibious commando training.[96] Coast Guard Commandant Vice Admiral Russell R. Waesche gave whole-hearted support to the effort, assigning a Coast Guard element to assist in the training.[97]

The EAC and ATC pressed on with training and self-invention throughout the rest of 1942 and into 1943, but the situation kept changing. On 1 July the AGF objective was changed from 12 to 8 divisions. Two weeks later the number of engineer amphibious brigades was reduced from eight to five. For a while it appeared that the Army engineers would operate the larger LCTs, but then the decision was made that the Navy would crew and operate all large landing vessels and the Army would operate the smaller landing craft. The 1st EAB completed its organization in mid-July and prepared to take up duties with the ATC when it was alerted for movement overseas. When it arrived in England, it found that the decision had been made to land in North Africa, which would mean a transoceanic ship-to-shore operation instead of a cross-channel shore-to-shore landing. General Dwight D. Eisenhower had agreed to put the Navy in charge of all amphibious training in the European Theater of Operations (ETO) and the Navy saw no use for the engineer boat regiments or any other Army amphibious organization larger than a battalion. The 1st EAB thus lost all its boats and would spend the war as a shore party organization for the landings in North Africa, Sicily, Normandy, and Okinawa. In August the EAC was advised that only three brigades would be required and Admiral King recanted his decision to have soldiers man landing craft. It appeared that all the EABs would be shore party units only, until events in September and October altered the situation.[98]

In September Noce and Trudeau had recommended reorganizing the brigades by combining the boat and shore units into three engineer boat and shore regiments (EB&SR), each with one boat and one shore battalion. This would facilitate the tactical division of the brigade to support the three regimental combat teams (RCTs) in a division.[99] The brigade would also include a headquarters and headquarters company, a boat maintenance battalion, and other service elements. At about this time, General MacArthur requested amphibious support for his planned operations in the SWPA. The Navy had proved reluctant to share its own meager amphibious resources with MacArthur (or to risk aircraft carriers and other fleet units in the narrow and dangerous waters off New Guinea). They were willing to send landing craft to SWPA for MacArthur's use, but the space available on the decks of cargo ships and transports would limit the shipments to about 60 a month. At that rate it would take a year to provide enough amphibious lift for one division. However, Trudeau calculated that large numbers of 36-foot LCVPs could be shipped disassembled in bulk and reassembled in theater by Army engineers. While this discussion was taking place, MacArthur requested EABs, including boats and operators, because those units would be ideal for the kind of shore-to-shore operations he envisioned for SWPA. In October the Navy approved the scheme, and the 2d EAB and the 411th Engineer Base Shop Battalion (augmented by specialists from the Higgins, Chris-Craft, and other boat assembly yards) were alerted for movement to the Southwest Pacific.[100]

Ultimately, the 2d, 3d, and 4th Brigades, now renamed Engineer Special Brigades (ESBs) since the Navy had assumed the amphibious mission, went to SWPA, while two other brigades, the 5th and 6th, consisting of shore party only, would participate along with the 1st ESB at Normandy. Before closing its doors, the EAC produced a body of doctrinal literature on boat and shore operations and the logistic support and sustainment of amphibious operations.[101] The AGF ATC trained three divisions, the 45th, 36th, and 38th, at Camp Edwards and at Camp Gordon Johnson in Carrabelle, Florida, before it, too, shut down in March 1943. The Amphibious Corps, Atlantic Fleet was reconstituted in March 1942 at Camp Pickett, Virginia, and trained the 3d and 9th Infantry Divisions and 2d Armored Division under Navy control before closing in October 1942.

Thereafter, the Amphibious Force, Atlantic Fleet at Little Creek, Virginia, and the Amphibious Force, Pacific Fleet at Coronado, California, conducted the amphibious training with additional small facilities elsewhere, including a Scout and Raider School at Fort Pierce, Florida.[102]

Amphibious Ships, Craft, and Vehicles

The first LST was launched in September 1942.[103] Before the end of the year, 23 of a total wartime production of 1,054 would be commissioned, with the first ships entering combat in 1943. The keel of the first LSD was laid in June and the first of 25 entered service in 1943. The LCVP was first tested in October 1942 and small numbers were used in North Africa the following month. Over 23,000 would be built before the war ended. In 1942 the Services settled on the Higgins version of the LCM, which went into large-scale production as the LCM(3). A US version of the LCT, smaller than the British designs and capable of being carried on the deck of an LST, was produced as the 105-foot LCT(5). A modified drive-through version, the LCT(6), had a gate at the stern that could be opened to allow vehicles to drive off an LST ramp, through the LCT, and onto the beach in situations where the LST could not get close enough to the shore. An alternative arrangement was developed using pontoons that could be lashed to the sides of the LSTs and then bolted together to form a long causeway from the LST ramp to the shore. These, too, entered service in 1943.[104]

Early in 1942 the British Combined Operations Headquarters approached the Americans about a "raiding" ship that could carry an infantry company at least 200 nautical miles, approach shore quietly, and land the troops directly onto the beach. The Army leadership saw merit in such a vessel as a way to get troops across the channel. Eventually, the ship would be produced as the 153-foot landing craft, infantry (large) (LCI[L]). The early versions had gangways on either side of the bow, but later versions had a bow ramp. The LCI(L) was widely used in the Mediterranean, at Normandy, and in the Solomons and Southwest Pacific where it was particularly useful for shore-to-shore operations. It also proved to be quite adaptable. A gunboat version, the landing craft, infantry (gunboat) (LCI[G]), was later developed into the landing craft, support (large) (LCS[L]). Others were used as salvage vessels, barrage balloon tenders, and control ships to guide landing craft ashore. They were not well suited for the Central Pacific, however, because they could not cross coral reefs and, because they had to beach to unload troops, could not transfer troops into LVTs at the reef line, like the LSTs and LCTs. At the end of the war, the Pacific Fleet recommended the type be discontinued and they quickly disappeared.[105] An increase in the size and weight of tanks and the poor sea-keeping qualities of the LCTs led to yet another amphibious ship in 1943, the 203-foot landing ship, medium (LSM). Smaller, faster, and more maneuverable than an LST, the LSM could carry five medium tanks and operate on steeper beaches than the LCT. With the addition of a 5-inch gun and rockets, it became the landing ship, medium (rocket) (LSM[R]), a handy fire support vessel.[106]

During 1942 the Army began testing and procuring LVTs, including an armored version. They also experimented with amphibious trucks, beginning with a small vehicle called the Ford General Purpose Amphibian (GPA), an amphibious version of the ¼-ton utility truck, widely known as the jeep. The GPA (also known as the sea-going jeep or seep) was not particularly useful, but an amphibious version of the ubiquitous General Motors 2½-ton CCKW truck proved to be a key element of over-the-shore supply operations. Designated DUKW (D = 1942 model, U = amphibious, K = all-wheel drive, and W = dual rear wheels) and commonly known as the "Duck," it could be loaded with supplies, driven aboard an LST or LSD, then launched off shore and driven through the surf and across the beach to the supply dumps. With a small modification, a 105-mm howitzer could be carried and some DUKWs had light cranes installed to unload the howitzer (or other heavy cargo). The DUKW could also be used as the prime mover for the artillery piece until the regular artillery trucks were brought ashore. DUKWs quickly became the standard vehicle for bringing light artillery ashore. In the Southwest Pacific, Army amphibious engineers rigged DUKWs with rocket launchers, and at Normandy, the Rangers installed extensible fire ladders in DUKWs as a way to assist in scaling the cliffs west of Omaha Beach. Over 21,000 of these versatile vehicles were built by the end of the war.[107]

Amphibious Operations in 1942[108]

General MacArthur was anxious to start operations toward Rabaul, which would be the beginning of his return to the Philippines. First, the Japanese offensive in Papua had to be halted. Having been stymied in their attempt to take Port Moresby by amphibious assault, the Japanese sent their forces across the Owen Stanley Mountains. On 18 September when they were within 30 miles of Port Moresby, they stopped, having been ordered by the Japanese Command to concentrate at Buna on the north coast of Papua for possible redeployment to Guadalcanal. MacArthur then began his counteroffensive to retake Buna. The Australians and some elements of the US 32d Division began the difficult task of crossing the mountains, while other 32d Division units were airlifted to the north coast of Papua.

In the absence of any Navy support in these early days, the Buna operation depended on the use of captured Japanese landing craft (the only boats available with ramps that could be used to land light armored vehicles over the beach) and small Australian coastal freighters generically known as luggers. These circumstances led MacArthur to request the engineer amphibious units. The Allies would finally secure the Buna–Gona area in January 1943 (see map 2).[109]

On 7 August 1942 Major General Alexander A. Vandegrift's 1st Marine Division landed on Guadalcanal and the nearby small islands of Tulagi and Gavutu-Tanambogo. The Guadalcanal landing was initially unopposed and the small islands were secured after 2 days of fierce resistance by Japanese naval infantry. However, Japanese air and naval forces reacted quickly and on 9 August, after a night attack that sank four US and Australian heavy cruisers, Rear Admiral Richmond Kelly Turner, the amphibious force commander, withdrew the partially unloaded transports. For the next 4 months, the Japanese challenged the Americans in a series of air and naval battles and sent naval infantry and army reinforcements to try to wrest the island from the Marines. With air support from Marine, Navy, and Army aircraft flown into the Guadalcanal air strip, Henderson Field, the Marines held on. In October they were joined by a regiment of Major General Alexander Patch's newly-formed Americal Division. On 18 October Admiral William F. Halsey Jr. replaced Admiral Ghormley as Commander, South Pacific and on 9 December, Patch replaced Vandegrift in command of operations on Guadalcanal when the 1st Marine Division was relieved by Patch's Americal Division and elements of the 2d Marine Division.[110]

The Guadalcanal operation, mounted hastily under severe pressure and without control of the air and sea that would become essential for such operations, provided many lessons for future landings. This first amphibious landing demonstrated the need for prelanding rehearsals and proved that intelligence about beach conditions was as important as information about enemy forces. Unloading over the beach was too slow due to limitations of the early landing craft, excessive nonessential supplies and equipment, and failure to provide enough manpower for the shore party. The new amphibious tractors (LVTs) demonstrated their value in bringing supplies over the beach, as well as in river crossing and as light combat vehicles. Disagreement between Vandegrift and Turner raised questions about the system of command relations in which the Navy amphibious force commander retained overall control of the operation, including postlanding operations ashore. Eventually, the Americans adopted a system based on the prewar concept of "paramount interest" in which the naval commander of the amphibious task force commanded the operation until the landing force was established ashore, then the commander of the landing force would take command of operations on land and give general direction to the naval commander on matters directly related to support of the land operations. This system worked well throughout the war, although it left room for controversy on precisely when the transfer of authority would take place and who would make the decision.[111]

Three smaller amphibious operations also took place in August 1942. On 18 August, 18 marines from the 2d Raider Battalion landed by submarine on Butaritari Island in the Makin Atoll of the Gilbert Islands. Although the marines forced the defenders to withdraw, killing 86 of them, the Japanese quickly sent reinforcements by flying boat and the marines withdrew, losing 21 killed and 9 inadvertently left behind to be executed by the Japanese. The operation was hardly worth the cost, especially as it may have caused the Japanese to improve the defenses of the Gilbert Islands, to the later cost of marines landing on Tarawa.[112]

On 19 August 1942 a force of 9,800 British and Canadians, accompanied by 60 US Army Rangers, carried out a dress rehearsal for the cross-channel attack by conducting a large-scale raid at the French seaport of Dieppe. To achieve surprise, there had been no preliminary bombardment, but a coastal German convoy came across some of the inbound landing craft, alerting the German defenders. Naval gunfire support was limited to that of a few destroyer guns, and the Germans soon sank 33 landing craft and 1 destroyer and disabled all of the 33 tanks that accompanied the landing force. Although the raiders managed to capture one of their objectives, a coast defense battery, they lost some 4,500 killed, wounded, or captured. The cost was high, but it was argued that many useful lessons were learned (or relearned) about the necessity of air superiority, the value of naval gunfire support, the importance of intense preliminary air and naval bombardment, the value of close-in fire support craft, the need for dedicated amphibious command ships, and the importance of getting enough tanks onto the beach and through the beach defenses. It also appears to have convinced the Germans to concentrate their defenses on ports, while the Allies concluded that the best approach for the cross-channel invasion would be to land across open beaches, sustain the operation over-the-shore initially, and then capture ports through land operations.[113]

On 30 August 1942 the Americans took the first step toward recapturing the lost Aleutian Islands when Army forces occupied Adak, halfway along the Aleutian chain and about 250 miles from Kiska. In spite of fog,

Japanese submarines, and a storm that struck the beach just as the troops landed, Major General Eugene M. Landrum's 4,500-man Adak Landing Force went ashore quickly and began construction of an airfield to support further operations.[114]

On 8 November 1942 British and American forces under the overall command of Eisenhower made simultaneous landings in North Africa at Casablanca on the Atlantic coast of French Morocco; Oran, 280 miles east of Gibraltar; and Algiers, 220 miles east of Oran. The forces for the Oran and Algiers landings came from England, but Major General George S. Patton's western task force was carried to Casablanca across the Atlantic from the east coast of the United States by an amphibious task force under the command of Rear Admiral Henry Keith Hewitt, commander of Amphibious Force, Atlantic Fleet. Patton's troops got ashore successfully at three beaches north and south of Casablanca in spite of initial resistance from the French, but there were many problems and lessons to be learned. To achieve tactical surprise, the landings were to be made before dawn. The first waves touched down before daylight, but delays in disembarking the troops meant that most landed in broad daylight. Inexperienced crews and high surf led to many wrecked landing craft. The shore party was too small to clear the beach efficiently, and the Americans relearned the lesson that warships do not make good amphibious command ships. Hewitt's flagship, the cruiser *Augusta,* had to leave the landing area to engage French warships just as Patton was preparing to disembark, and the shock and vibration of the guns disabled his tactical radios. Overall, however, the amphibious doctrine proved to be sound.[115] (See map 3.)

Amphibious Operations in 1943

The first 6 months of 1943 were a time of preparation for amphibious operations. At the Casablanca Conference in January 1943, American and British leaders concluded they were still unprepared for the major cross-channel attack and agreed that the next step after the Germans and Italians were cleared from North Africa would be the invasion of Sicily. Forces were already in position in North Africa to continue operations in the Mediterranean and the seizure of Sicily would reduce the air threat to shipping and provide an advance base from which to invade Italy. The buildup in Britain for the cross-channel invasion would continue and the initiative would be maintained against the Japanese through offensives in the South and Southwest Pacific and across the Central Pacific.[116]

Lieutenant General Mark W. Clark's newly-activated US Fifth Army established an Invasion Training Center on the Algerian coast to "develop

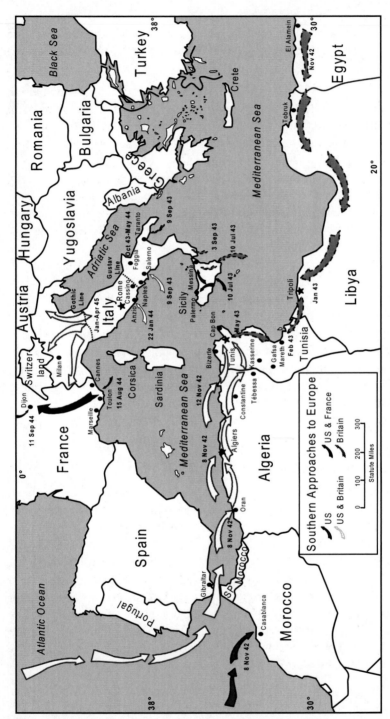

Map 3. Southern approaches to Europe.

44

doctrines, technique, and instruction for invasion and to build up a reserve of trained troops for invasion operations."[117] The name "invasion," rather than "amphibious," was chosen for the training center to emphasize that the purpose was not just to deal with the assault landing, "the water and craft phase," but also with the action after landing that would be the major mission of the Army forces that trained there.[118] This reflected the Army view that its role was to conduct sustained operations on land and that an amphibious operation was just the first phase of an invasion. Under the command of Brigadier General John W. O'Daniel, and with support of Navy, Army, Air Force, and 1st Engineer Amphibian Brigade [later, 1st ESB] elements, the Fifth Army Invasion Training Center prepared for the Sicily operation (Operation HUSKY) by providing amphibious and follow-on operations instruction for the 3d and 45th Infantry Divisions, the 2d Armored Division, and the 1st Ranger Battalion.[119]

Army Amphibious Tank and Tractor Battalions

The Army had quickly become convinced of the value of LVTs and in 1943 began a program to train amphibious tank and tractor battalions (ATTBs) at Monterey, California. This training was carried out by Colonel William S. Triplet's 18th Armored Group (Amphibious). Triplet, who had been a sergeant in World War I and had extensive infantry and armor experience, developed techniques for using the LVTs in heavy surf, collaborated with Marine amphibious tank and tractor experts from Coronado, and constantly sought ways to improve the capabilities of the vehicles and the survivability of the crews (often clashing with the Navy Bureau of Ships and the AGF in the process). Among his many achievements was the development of an improved amphibious tank, the LVT(A)4, that mounted a turret from an M-8 75-mm howitzer motor carriage on an LVT chassis. By the time Triplet left in 1944 to take over an armored division combat command in Europe, he had supervised the training and deployment of nine ATTBs, all but two of which served in the Pacific.[120]

South and Southwest Pacific Operations

On Guadalcanal, the Americal Division and the lead elements of the 2d Marine Division were joined in January 1943 by the 25th Division and the rest of the 2d Marine Division to form the XIV Corps under General Patch. By the end of February, the last of the Japanese defenders escaped by sea from the island and the long battle of Guadalcanal ended. In the Southwest Pacific, MacArthur prepared to clear the Japanese from Papua and to continue the advance to Rabaul. MacArthur's ability to conduct amphibious operations improved in the early months of 1943 with the arrival of Lieutenant General Walter Krueger and the Sixth Army Headquarters; Rear Admiral Daniel E. Barbey's Navy amphibious force (including the first LSTs and LCTs seen in SWPA); and Brigadier General William F. Heavey's 2d ESB.[121] The first task of the amphibious engineers was to assist the 411th Engineer Base Shop Battalion in constructing the facility for the assembly of landing craft. In April the first of thousands of LCVPs was completed and the 2d ESB began amphibious training with the US 41st and Australian 9th Divisions.[122] (See map 4.)

In March 1943 the JCS sent a new directive to MacArthur, Nimitz, and Halsey, ordering them to establish airfields on Woodlark and Kiriwina Islands and to capture the Huon Peninsula area of New Guinea, western New Britain, and the Solomon Islands as far north as southern Bougainville. Halsey and MacArthur met in April to refine their plan for these operations, dubbed Operation CARTWHEEL, and the offensive against the Japanese resumed on 30 June 1943, with unopposed landings on Woodlark and Kiriwina, landings by Admiral Halsey's forces at several places on the island of New Georgia, and the first landing conducted by the Army's amphibious engineers on the coast of New Guinea.[123] The latter was a small-scale operation compared to those that would follow: 29 LCVPs, 1 LCM, and 3 captured Japanese landing craft manned by the boat battalion of the 532d EB&SR loaded a task force of the 41st Division at Morobe Bay, about 75 miles west of Buna, and landed them at Nassau Bay, 50 miles up the coast. Many of the landing craft broached in the heavy surf, the Japanese quickly counterattacked, and the amphibious engineers found themselves fighting as infantry to defend the beachhead. The Japanese were repulsed, and for the next month and a half, the engineers supported the operation by hauling ammunition and supplies up the coast, back-hauling casualties, and establishing additional beaches for over-the-shore supply operations. In late August Admiral Barbey's ships landed the 9th Australian Division near Lae, while the amphibious engineers traveled along the coast to support the operation by delivering supplies and reinforcements over the shore. On 22 September 2d ESB scouts went in with the first wave of Australian troops at Finschhafen, on the north shore of the Huon Peninsula, to mark the beaches and routes through the coral reefs for the Navy's LSTs and LCTs. On 11 October the amphibian engineers once again found themselves defending a beachhead, this time from a Japanese amphibious landing at Finschhafen. By November 1943 MacArthur's Australian and US forces had secured the Huon Peninsula and Halsey's Army and Marine forces had fought their way up the Solomon chain to Bougainville. In December the 1st Marine Division landed at Cape Gloucester at the western tip of New Britain,

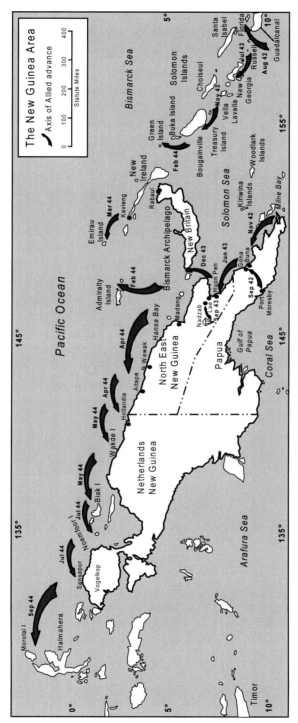

Map 4. New Guinea area.

47

while the Army's 112th Cavalry Regiment landed on the southern side of the cape at Arawe aboard landing craft of the 2d ESB carried in the davits of one of Barbey's transports.[124]

The Arawe operation saw the introduction of a new unit and weapon: the 2d ESB Support Battery equipped with rocket DUKWs mounting 120 4.5-inch rocket tubes each. The support battery was developed to deal with the 1,000 yard or 4 minute gap, so called because, to prevent friendly fire from hitting friendly troops, the naval bombardment was halted or shifted inland when the first waves of the landing force were 1,000 yards from the beach—a distance it took the landing craft about 4 minutes to travel—giving the enemy a chance to come out from cover and begin firing before the troops hit the beach. The answer was to begin a barrage of rockets against enemy positions as soon as the naval gunfire was lifted. The support battery equipped with rocket DUKWs, as well as heavily armed LCVPs, LCMs, and LVTs, was formed experimentally in July 1943 and went into action at Arawe. It was so successful that the 2d ESB Support Battery (Provisional) was activated in February 1944 with the mission of providing neutralization fire during the 4-minute gap, to neutralize enemy strongpoints from the water or from the land, to provide antiaircraft protection, and to provide fire support for coastal boat patrols. The 220-man unit consisted of a headquarters section, a maintenance platoon, and two combat platoons, each equipped with two rocket DUKWs; two LVT(A)s; two rocket LCVPs; and two flak LCMs equipped with 37-mm, 20-mm, .50-caliber, and .30-caliber machineguns as well as rockets. The composition and armament of the support battery was constantly modified and eventually a fire support platoon was organized within each boat battalion. The support battery and its successor fire support platoons operated with the 2d ESB in every operation until the end of the war.[125]

The Aleutians

In the Aleutians, US forces occupied Amchitka Island, only 40 miles from Kiska, on 5 January 1943. The next step was an amphibious assault on Attu. Major General Albert Brown's 7th Infantry Division, originally a mechanized unit trained for desert warfare, was selected to conduct the amphibious landing. Two regiments of the 7th Infantry Division landed on 11 May 1943, but soon bogged down, stymied by the Aleutian weather and terrain and the Japanese defense. Four days into what they had hoped would be a 3-day operation, the Alaska commanders called for General Landrum to come up from Adak and take over. By the time Landrum arrived on 16 May, the situation had already begun to improve, but 2 weeks of tough fighting still lay ahead, including a final Japanese counter-attack that overran the American front line before Attu was secured. On

15 August the 7th Infantry Division, now commanded by Major General Charles H. Corlett, landed on Kiska to find that the Japanese had already evacuated the island.[126]

Mediterranean Operations

The Sicily landing on 10 July 1943 was the largest to date and was successful in spite of bad weather and determined German and Italian counterattacks against the beachheads. Army respect for naval gunfire support was heightened when Navy ships helped stop an Axis armor counterattack at Gela.[127] Sicily saw the first use in Europe of purpose-built LSTs (rather than converted tankers), LCI(L)s, and DUKW 2½-ton amphibious trucks, and the first large-scale use of LCVPs. All of these ships, craft, and vehicles proved their worth, as did the first of the new amphibious force flagships, *Ancon* (AGC-4).[128] Coordination of air support was poor however, and there was some difference of opinion between Army and Navy commanders as to when the landing force commander was to take command of operations ashore. There were also still problems with shore party operations, but overall, it was clear that the Allies were improving their amphibious warfare skills.[129]

Following the defeat in Sicily of Axis forces (many of which escaped across the Strait of Messina in a large-scale amphibious withdrawal), the Allies determined to land on the Italian mainland in conjunction with an Italian offer of surrender. It was hoped that this would pin down large numbers of German forces and prevent reinforcement of the Eastern Front during the Soviet offensive and in northern France during the cross-channel attack the next spring. The seizure of southern Italy would also provide air bases for the strategic air offensive against Germany. On 3 September British forces crossed the Strait of Messina to the Calabrian Coast and landed at the port of Taranto in the southeast. British and American forces of General Clark's Fifth Army landed at Salerno, south of Naples, a landing site largely determined by the range of fighter aircraft flying from Sicily. The Germans immediately counterattacked, but after a difficult battle were repulsed by the Fifth Army, supported by air and naval gunfire and reinforced by additional forces, including airborne troops landed in the beachhead. After a link up with British forces coming up from the south, Fifth Army captured Naples on the west coast and the British occupied the airfield complex at Foggia in the east.[130]

Central Pacific Operations

Wartime strategy conferences in Washington in May 1943 (TRIDENT), in Quebec in August (QUADRANT), and in Cairo and Tehran in November

(SEXTANT-EUREKA) established Allied strategy for the last half of 1943 and 1944, including decisions to conduct the cross-channel invasion in the spring of 1944 and to carry out the Pacific offensive against Japan along two lines of operation: through the Southwest Pacific and across the Central Pacific. In the Southwest Pacific, Rabaul was to be isolated and neutralized rather than captured in a costly amphibious operation. MacArthur was then to continue his advance along the New Guinea coast to the Vogelkop (the large round peninsula at the westernmost end of New Guinea) and then prepare to land on Mindanao in the southern Philippines. For Nimitz's forces, these decisions set the stage for the Central Pacific campaign envisioned in War Plan Orange. First, islands in the Gilberts chain would be captured to provide air bases to support the next step, seizure of islands in the Marshalls Group. Then Saipan, Tinian, and Guam in the Marianas would be captured and used as bases for the air attack and blockade of the Japanese home islands. These operations beyond the range of land-based fighter aircraft would be supported by a new generation of fast aircraft carriers, carried out by the latest amphibious ships, and sustained by fleets of logistic ships. It was the beginning of a new phase of amphibious warfare in the pattern originally conceived by the Marines.[131]

The Central Pacific thrust began in November 1943 with Operation GALVANIC, landings in the Gilbert Islands at Betio in the Tarawa Atoll by Major General Julian C. Smith's 2d Marine Division, and at Butaritari in the Makin Atoll by the 165th RCT of Major General Ralph C. Smith's 27th Infantry Division. The overall commander of the Central Pacific Force was Vice Admiral Raymond A. Spruance. The amphibious assault force, commanded by Turner, was divided into a northern attack force commanded by Turner himself and including General Ralph Smith's RCT, and a southern attack force commanded by Rear Admiral Harry W. Hill and including General Julian Smith's marines. Major General H.M. Smith, commander of V Amphibious Corps, was responsible for training and preparation of the Army and Marine Corps troops, but his position during the operation was ambiguous. He was directed to be aboard Turner's flagship and to advise him on the operation, but the chain of command ran directly from Turner to Generals Ralph Smith and Julian Smith, who would take command ashore when directed by Turner.[132]

The landings took place on 20 November. For the first time, LVTs were not used just as logistical support vehicles, but carried the first waves of troops to the beach. The 165th RCT was supported by 48 LVTs operated by a provisional company of the 193d Tank Battalion. They proved to be priceless, because a peculiarity of the tide prevented landing craft from crossing the reef at both islands, while the LVTs took the coral reefs in stride. Unfortunately, there were not enough of them. At Betio, Japanese resistance was fierce. Many of the LVTs in the first waves were destroyed and so most of the marines had to disembark from LCVPs at the reef and wade ashore, taking heavy casualties. Three days of fighting at Tarawa cost the marines over 3,000 casualties, more than 1,000 of whom were killed or died of wounds.[133]

Complicating the Makin attack was a decision to land on two widely separated beachheads, poor communications that made coordination between the two assault forces difficult, and the same dodging tide that had plagued the marine landing on Betio. But Butaritari was far more lightly defended, and the soldiers took far fewer casualties than the marines (66 killed and 152 wounded). However, it took 4 days before General Ralph Smith could report "Makin taken," sparking criticism of the Army's slow advance by General H.M. Smith. The official Army historians concluded: "Considering the size of the atoll, the nature of the enemy's defenses, and the great superiority of force enjoyed by the attacking troops [Smith's], criticism seems justified."[134]

Nonetheless, both landings provided important lessons. The preparatory naval gunfire bombardment was insufficient. Air support was poorly coordinated with the landings and the naval aviators did not provide adequate close air support. There were communications problems in the coordination among infantrymen, tanks, artillery, flame throwers, and demolitions. The problem of using a warship as the amphibious flagship was once again demonstrated when gunfire from Hill's flagship, the battleship *Maryland,* disabled General Julian Smith's communications off Betio. A proposal to land artillery on nearby islands to support the Betio landing had been rejected, a mistake that would not be made again. On the positive side, the LVTs had proven their value as troop carriers for the first waves of the assault, although there had not been enough of them, and an armored version was needed to improve survivability. The Army units at Makin had put most of their supplies on wooden pallets that could be dragged over the beach and coral, a technique first used in the Aleutians. This cut the landing craft unloading time to one-twelfth and was a technique adopted for all future amphibious operations by both the Army and the Marines. All of these "lessons learned" were quickly disseminated to the units preparing for the next offensive—the Marshall Islands in January 1944.[135]

Amphibious Operations in 1944

The pace of amphibious operations had quickened in the second half of 1943 and continued to do so throughout 1944 as the Allies closed in on the Axis powers in both Europe and the Pacific. The year opened with a series of amphibious landings in rapid succession in the Southwest Pacific, the Mediterranean, and the Central Pacific.

The first, and smallest, of these operations took place in the SWPA with the landing of the 32d Infantry Division's 126th RCT on Saidor, New Guinea, on 2 January 1944, completing the conquest of the Huon Peninsula. The operation was conducted on short notice, but by now Krueger's soldiers, Barbey's Navy amphibians, and Heavey's amphibious engineers had become a well-coordinated team. The initial landing was carried out by 9 APDs and 16 landing craft, infantry (LCI) carrying the 126th RCT and the shore battalion of the 542d EB&SR with 15 destroyers providing naval gunfire support and protection from Japanese submarines. On D+1, six LSTs towing the LCMs of the 542d's Boat Battalion arrived with additional troops and equipment, after which the amphibious engineers set up the now-routine over-the-shore sustainment operation.[136]

In Italy an amphibious landing was seen as a way to bypass German defenses (the Gustav Line) that had stalled Allied forces of the 15th Army Group (US Fifth Army in the west and British Eighth Army on the Adriatic coast) south of Rome. The plan for Operation SHINGLE envisioned US and British forces of Major General John P. Lucas's VI Corps landing behind the German lines at Anzio, 33 miles south of Rome, while 15th Army Group conducted a general offensive, including a breakthrough by Fifth Army to link up with VI Corps.[137] The 22 January 1944 amphibious landing went smoothly, but before Lucas's forces could secure the high ground overlooking the beachhead, the Germans counterattacked, nearly driving VI Corps into the sea. Only a tenacious defense, massive and effective naval gunfire support (at the cost of several ships lost to German air attacks), and close air support prevented a disaster. Furthermore, the offensive from the south failed to break through, leaving the beachhead isolated. It was not until late May that VI Corps finally broke out of the Anzio beachhead to link up with the advancing Fifth Army. For 2½ months, the situation in the Anzio beachhead resembled, in the words of one veteran, the Western Front in World War I.[138]

The Central Pacific offensive continued with Operation FLINTLOCK, landings on Kwajalein Atoll in the Marshall Islands on 31 January 1944.[139] By now, the amphibious warfare techniques had been honed and the lessons of Operation GALVANIC had been passed on quickly to the units that would conduct the landings, the Army 7th Infantry Division and the 4th Marine Division. Corlett's 7th Infantry Division, veterans of the Aleutian landings, had the added advantage of training in Hawaii as the operation was being planned and so could review the operational plans and use them in their final rehearsals (the 4th Marine Division trained at Camp Pendleton in California, making such coordination difficult). This time, small offshore islands near the objective would be captured before the main assault to provide artillery support bases. The 708th Provisional Amphibian Tractor Battalion had enough LVTs, including 56 of the armored versions, to put the entire first wave ashore and a company of LVT(A)1s would provide additional support with their 37-mm guns, both during the landing and on the beach. In rehearsals, the Army armored amphibians developed a technique of stationing the LVT(A)1s on the flanks of the leading wave of transport LVTs so that they wouldn't mask the fire of the transport LVTs' own machineguns, a procedure that would become standard for amphibious operations. Over 100 DUKWs were made available to keep supplies flowing across the beach. Another Army innovation was the establishment of repair stations on unoccupied islets and the conversion of some LSTs to support vessels to service LVTs and DUKWs and provide amenities for the crews, reducing attrition of the amphibians. Other innovations for Operation FLINTLOCK included underwater demolition teams to reconnoiter the beach and destroy obstacles and a provisional Joint Assault Signal Company (JASCO) assigned to the 7th Infantry Division to ensure good communications between ships and the shore and to coordinate naval gunfire and close air support.[140] All the training and preparation paid off in the landings at Kwajalein Atoll on 31 January 1944, followed by the seizure of Eniwetok Atoll at the western edge of the Marshalls in February. Admiral Turner called Operation FLINTLOCK "the perfect one" that established the pattern of subsequent Pacific amphibious operations.[141]

Southwest Pacific Area Operations

In the Southwest Pacific, MacArthur had planned to secure the Admiralty Islands in April 1944, but in February Nimitz's carrier forces raided the Japanese stronghold of Truk in the Caroline Islands, ending the air and naval threat from that area, and aircraft flying from SWPA bases reported a lack of activity in the Admiralties. In spite of conflicting intelligence reports, General MacArthur decided to send a reconnaissance force to the islands immediately. On 29 February 1944, a 1,000-man force of the 1st Cavalry Division, accompanied by MacArthur and Vice Admiral Thomas C. Kinkaid, the Seventh Fleet commander, landed from three APDs escorted by a small naval force. The Japanese attacked the next day, but the reconnaissance force held until reinforcements could be sent to clear the island. The Admiralties operation provided an excellent harbor and air base for future operations and, with the capture by Halsey's forces of Emirau to the north, completed the isolation of Rabaul.[142]

The early seizure of the Admiralties led MacArthur to recommend to the JCS that the Japanese forces at Hansa Bay and Wewak be bypassed in a bold operation that would leapfrog to the Hollandia region of New Guinea 400 miles to the west. On 12 March 1944 the JCS issued a directive confirming that MacArthur was to capture Hollandia and Aitape in April with the support of one of Nimitz's aircraft carrier task forces. Nimitz was then to move into the Marianas in June to seize Saipan, Tinian, and Guam and then into the Palaus in September. In November MacArthur was to land on Mindanao in the southern Philippines and then to plan for the invasion of Luzon in early 1945 while Nimitz planned for the invasion of Formosa.[143]

On 22 April MacArthur's forces had grown to the point that he could send a force of 217 ships and 80,000 men to make three simultaneous landings—at Tanahmerah Bay and at Humboldt Bay in Hollandia, and at Aitape 140 miles to the east. All three landings were unopposed. MacArthur had cut the Japanese Army in New Guinea in half, isolated most of the forces to the east, and secured an important airfield complex. MacArthur's amphibious engineer capability was expanded with the arrival in New Guinea of the 3d ESB in February 1944 and the 4th ESB in May. The fast pace of operations continued with a landing at Wakde–Sarmi, 115 miles to the west of Hollandia, on 17 May; at Biak, 300 miles west of Hollandia, on 27 May; at Noemfoor Island on 2 July; and at Sansapor on the Vogelkop Peninsula on 30 July—the end of a 1,500 mile journey completed in 1 year.[144]

By the summer of 1944, the unique character of the SWPA was apparent. Much of this difference was driven by the geography of the New Guinea coast and the nearby islands, but it was also influenced by the character of General MacArthur, with his strong determination to return to the Philippines and his sense of competition for strategic priority and resources with the Central Pacific Theater. The command structure in SWPA also differed from that in other theaters. Unlike Admiral Nimitz, who commanded the Pacific Fleet as well as the POA, and Eisenhower, who after the Normandy invasion acted as the ground component commander as well as Supreme Commander of Allied Forces in Europe, MacArthur was not granted authority to command any national force operationally and had to relinquish command of USAFFE on assumption of the supreme command of SWPA. Since the majority of ground combat forces in the theater were initially Australian, and for logical political reasons, an Australian general was appointed Commander, Allied Land Forces. The re-establishment of USAFFE in February 1943 gave MacArthur administrative control of US Army forces, but operational control still rested with Australian General Sir Thomas Blamey, the Allied Land Forces commander. When General

Krueger arrived and Sixth Army was activated, MacArthur bypassed the binational command structure by giving Krueger command of a task force (*Alamo Force*) that came directly under GHQ, SWPA. *Alamo Force* had most of the same staff and troop units as Sixth Army, but was not under Blamey's control. Sixth Army was the US Army component of Allied Land Forces and had administrative control of US Army forces, while *Alamo Force* was the operational force. In the words of one Army historian, the organization of SWPA ground forces was "somewhat complicated."[145]

MacArthur refused to appoint a single commander at the operational level with overall authority over the planning and conduct of joint operations. Below MacArthur, SWPA relied on the principle of cooperation rather than unity of command. Krueger had authority to coordinate planning for the ground, naval, and air forces, but his position was one of first among equals rather than as a joint force commander.[146] Krueger would have preferred a system of unity of command, but he made the arrangement work by establishing joint planning groups with representatives of the Navy and Air Force headquarters; through planning conferences among the commanders; and through constant informal coordination visits and consultation among the headquarters. This system overcame the problems of personal and Service cultural differences and the great geographical separation of the Service headquarters.[147] It seems likely that MacArthur used Krueger's joint planning groups as the model for the Joint Strategic Plans and Operations Group (JSPOG) that he later established at his Far East Command Headquarters in Tokyo before the Korean War.[148]

SWPA was also different from any other theater in the number and pace of its operations. After the Admiralties, Krueger recalled, "Operations now followed one another with little intermission, and Headquarters Alamo Force had to prepare plans for a number of impending ones while two or three were actually in progress."[149] The pace was driven by a need to stay ahead of the Japanese and not give them time to redeploy forces and establish defenses, but also because of MacArthur's sense that he had to show that the SWPA provided the best and fastest way to get to the China–Formosa–Luzon area so that his theater would not be bypassed in favor of Nimitz's Central Pacific offensive.[150] These multiple, fast-paced operations were possible because of the effective planning and coordination system and because all of the staffs and forces involved were now amphibious veterans. At GHQ, at Krueger's Sixth Army/Alamo Force Headquarters, and at Barbey's amphibious headquarters, it was normal to have three teams working simultaneously on three consecutive operations, and it was routine to plan, organize, and pull together the forces for hastily conceived amphibious operations. It was very different from the

Europe/Mediterranean and Central Pacific theaters, where the operations took place at intervals of months rather than weeks or days, as they did in SWPA.[151]

SWPA was also unique in having the use of three Army ESBs to provide a quick reaction capability through their multiple skills and capabilities. The amphibious engineers provided landing craft and crews trained and equipped for assault landings; carried out shore party tasks during those landings and then provided sustainment through over-the-shore resupply; conducted beach reconnaissance; provided coastal transportation services; carried out offshore security and combat patrols; and performed such varied tasks as port operation, road and facility construction, earth moving, machinery repair and maintenance, and infantry combat. All within a single organization that was immediately responsive to the Sixth Army commander and trained to work well with the other Services.

Central Pacific Operations

As SWPA operations followed one after the other across the northern coast of New Guinea, Admiral Nimitz's forces prepared for the next step in the Central Pacific. On 15 June Marine and Army forces of General H.M. Smith's V Amphibious Corps landed on the large island of Saipan in the Mariana Islands. The initial landings were made by the 2d and 4th Marine Divisions, a substantial number of which were carried ashore in 196 LVTs of the Army's 708th, 715th, and 773d Amphibious Tractor Battalions and supported by 138 Army LVT(A)1s and LVT(A)4s. The 311th and 539th Army Transportation Port Companies came ashore early to assist in organizing the beachhead and found themselves fighting off Japanese infiltrators while bringing in supplies on D-Day.[152]

Japanese resistance at the beachhead was heavy and on D+1 General H.M. Smith brought in the lead elements of his reserve, Major General Ralph Smith's 27th Infantry Division, the unit that H.M. Smith had criticized at Makin.[153] The fighting on Saipan was bloody and difficult. It would take 3 weeks to secure the island and, in the middle of the battle, General H.M. Smith once again became displeased with what he perceived as the slow advance of the 27th Division. On 24 June he relieved General Ralph Smith of command, a controversial action that caused a long-lasting bitter feeling between the two Services. Soon after the Saipan campaign ended, Lieutenant General Robert C. Richardson Jr., Commanding General, Army Forces, Central Pacific Area, convened a board composed entirely of Army officers to investigate the incident. The board concluded that although H.M. Smith had the authority to relieve Ralph Smith, he had not been fully informed of the conditions in the 27th Infantry Division zone and the relief was not justified by the facts. The unbalanced composition of the board called its findings into question and no further action was taken at the Washington level, other than to remove Ralph Smith from the theater (he was initially given command of another division and then sent to Europe as liaison officer to the French military forces) and to reassign H.M. Smith as Commander, Fleet Marine Force Pacific, a position where his expertise and leadership would be of value, but where he would no longer directly command Army forces. One side effect was that Army officers in Washington reviewing the material presented to the board found what they saw as evidence that H.M. Smith's V Amphibious Corps' staff work was below acceptable standards, reinforcing a preconceived view that marines did not have the training and experience to command above division level—an argument that would influence Army views during the postwar inter-Service struggles over defense unification, roles, and missions.[154]

In any event, the US advance westward continued with the capture of Guam by the 3d Marine Division and 77th Infantry Division from 21 July to 8 August 1944, and by a very smooth and efficient operation to capture the island of Tinian, near Saipan, from 25 July to 1 August. In the Tinian operation, over half of the LVTs and LVT(A)s were provided by the Army, which also provided the shore party, while XXIV Corps provided artillery support from Saipan.[155]

Operations in Europe

On 6 June 1944, a week before the Saipan landing, the long-awaited cross-channel invasion of Europe began with Operation OVERLORD, the landing of Allied forces at Normandy between the Cotentin Peninsula and the city of Caen (see map 5). The landing site had been selected because it was within range of Britain-based fighter aircraft, was near the port of Cherbourg, and was not quite as heavily defended as the Pas de Calais area directly across the English Channel from Dover, which would otherwise have been the ideal location.[156] It was a huge undertaking with five reinforced divisions in the initial amphibious assault and three airborne divisions making preliminary landings behind the beaches. More than 30 divisions would then be funneled through the beachhead. Because Cherbourg would not be available for some weeks after the landing, huge floating harbors were fabricated in secrecy and pre-positioned on the English coast so they could be towed into place to sustain the operation ashore. Three ESBs and a quartermaster port would support the US beaches. The use of LVTs for the initial assault waves was not contemplated. Instead, conventional tanks were fitted with folding waterproof

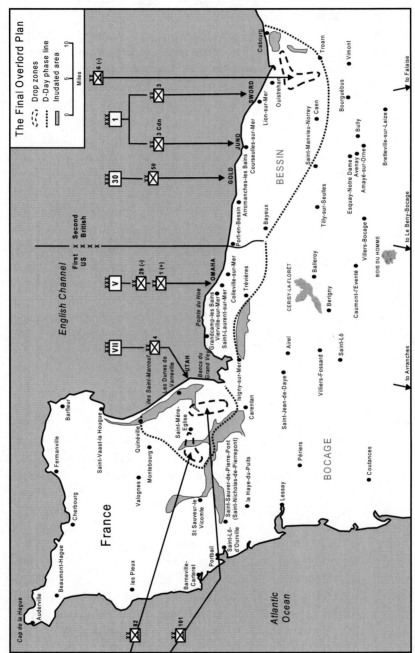

Map 5. Final Overlord plan.

58

screens that permitted them to float in calm seas and propellers so they could be driven to shore. The resulting vehicle was called a duplex drive tank.[157] The issue of day versus night landings and long, heavy preparatory bombardment versus tactical surprise was settled by a compromise. The landings would take place just after dawn to provide good visibility for coordination and fire direction. Instead of an extended prelanding bombardment, there would be a short, intense, naval gunfire bombardment followed by air strikes on beach fortifications and obstacles by heavy and medium bombers just before the landing.[158]

The landings were successful, but the costs and consequences varied among the invading forces. On the British beaches to the east, the first waves were across the beach and moving inland within an hour of landing, in spite of a pile up of supplies due to delayed landing craft arrivals and heavy initial German defensive fires. At Utah Beach in the west, currents swept the incoming landing craft off course and to a lightly defended stretch of beach. Within 3 hours, the US 4th Infantry Division had secured the beachhead at a cost of 197 Army casualties out of 23,000 men who landed on D-Day. Among those 23,000 was a regimental commander in the 4th Infantry Division, Colonel James A. Van Fleet, who would later command Eighth Army in Korea. His D-Day experience gave him a positive impression of amphibious operations. At Omaha Beach, it was very different. Many of the landing craft were swamped by heavy seas that also sank over half of the duplex drive tanks. The heavy bombers overshot the beach and most of their bombs landed 3 miles inland. Most of the radios of the gunfire direction teams were on board the sunken landing craft, making it difficult to adjust the naval fires. The beach obstacles were particularly dense on that stretch of beach and a veteran German division had unexpectedly arrived in the area just before the landing. Nonetheless, by nightfall 34,000 men were ashore and holding a lodgment on Omaha Beach at a cost of 2,500 killed and wounded. By the end of June, two Allied armies had come ashore with nearly a million men, over a million tons of supplies, and 177,000 vehicles in spite of the destruction of one of the artificial harbors and heavy damage to another by a storm on 19 June.[159] The main reason the destruction of the artificial harbor did not delay the logistical buildup was the versatility of the LSTs. Experimentation showed that LSTs could be beached and then "dried out"—allowed to remain sitting on the beach when the tide went out—without damage to the hulls. This permitted them to be unloaded between the tides and then refloated on the incoming tide. Thus, vast quantities of supplies and equipment could be brought ashore over the beach without a requirement for an artificial harbor.[160]

Two months later, on 15 August 1944, the last large-scale amphibious operation in Europe was carried out in Southern France by Lieutenant General Jacob L. Devers' Allied Sixth Army Group. Meant to occur simultaneously with Operation OVERLORD, Operation DRAGOON had been postponed because of a shortage of amphibious shipping and controversy within the Allied war councils. It was a hastily mounted operation, but one that was conducted smoothly because many of the planners and forces involved were Mediterranean amphibious warfare veterans.[161]

By 1944 the Fifth Army Invasion Training Center, now under Brigadier General Henry C. Wolfe, had been relocated near Naples. The 36th and 45th Divisions trained there for the Southern France operation, while the 3d Division, veteran of four major amphibious operations, conducted its own training. In each case, the preparations included a full-scale rehearsal of the landing.[162]

The landing was made in daylight, the decision having been made that improved visibility was worth the risk. The landing forces advanced quickly (Major General Lucian Truscott, the assault force commander, had been at Anzio and did not want to repeat the disastrous results of the delay in capturing the high ground) and by 28 August the Allies had captured the ports of Toulon and Marseilles that, along with the roads and rail lines of the Rhone Valley, provided a valuable additional line of communication for Allied forces in France. During the remainder of the war in Europe, amphibious assets and techniques would be used by US forces in the major river crossings and by the British to capture the island of Walcheren on the Dutch coast in November 1944.

Advance to the Philippines

On 15 September 1944 MacArthur's forces took the first step toward the Philippines by landing on the large island of Morotai, between New Guinea and the southern Philippine island of Mindanao. On the same day, Admiral Nimitz's forces invaded the Palau Islands, with Marines landing on Peleliu and Army forces landing on Angaur, to the south. On 23 September an Army RCT made an unopposed landing at Ulithi Atoll, between the Palaus and the Philippines. The opposition on Angaur was light, but the fighting on Peleliu was bloody and difficult, dragging on until November. However, these landings completed the twin advances through New Guinea and across the Central Pacific. There was still debate through September as to whether the next step should be the seizure of the main Philippine Island of Luzon or Formosa, which would set the stage for securing a port on the coast of China from which to support air operations against Japan. Councils in Washington were divided. Admiral Nimitz argued for the Formosa invasion, but his senior commanders and staff favored Luzon, and Nimitz had directed his staff to prepare alternate plans for the seizure of Okinawa rather than Formosa. MacArthur argued vigorously for Luzon. He intended to land in Mindanao in mid-November and conduct the major assault at Leyte in December, with movement into Luzon in early 1945.[163]

Circumstances would advance that timetable and lead to the decision to take Luzon rather than Formosa. In September the Japanese conducted a major offensive in China, overrunning the area where the United States planned to build airfields, and the capture of the Marianas provided bases from which long-range bombers could attack Japan more easily than from China, removing much of the rationale for the Formosa option. Furthermore, airmen flying over the southern Philippines from Pacific Fleet carriers reported a lack of naval activity or air opposition, leading MacArthur to propose scrapping the Mindanao operation and moving directly to Leyte in October 1944 with an invasion of Luzon in December. For these operations, he would only need Pacific Fleet aircraft carrier support until air bases could be established in the Philippines. Consequently, Nimitz recommended that instead of Formosa his forces capture Iwo Jima, 650 miles south of Tokyo, in late January 1945, and then take Okinawa and the other Ryukyu Islands, 850 miles southwest of Tokyo, in March. On 3 October 1944 the JCS directed MacArthur to begin the Luzon invasion on or about 20 December and directed Nimitz to execute the Iwo Jima and Okinawa operations on the schedule he had proposed. (See map 1.)

The Leyte landing, the biggest amphibious operation in the Pacific to date, took place on 20 October 1944 (see map 6). For this invasion, additional elements from the Central Pacific Area reinforced General MacArthur's SWPA forces, including an amphibious task force. However, Admiral Halsey's Third Fleet, which provided supporting fast aircraft carrier and battleship task forces, remained under the command of Admiral Nimitz. In a preliminary operation, the 6th Ranger Battalion was landed on outlying islands by an amphibious force commanded by Rear Admiral Arthur D. Struble, who had arrived in the theater from Europe, where he had participated in the Normandy invasion. Struble would conduct several amphibious operations in the Philippines and would command the Seventh Fleet during the Korean War landings. The main assault force consisted of General Krueger's Sixth Army, with two corps of two divisions each in the initial landing.[164] The X Corps was transported from Hollandia and the Admiralties by Admiral Barbey's Seventh Amphibious Force. There was

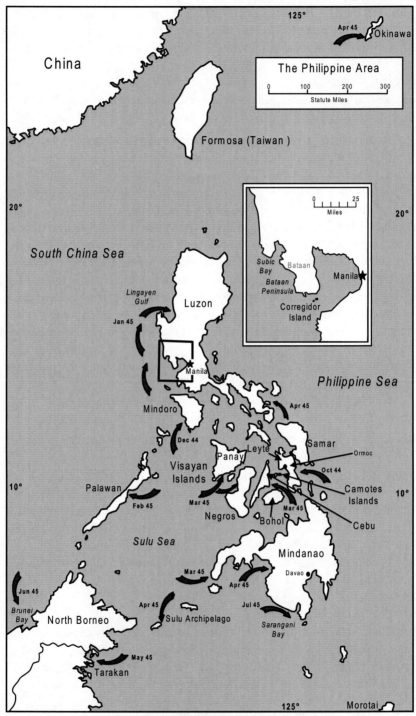

Map 6. Philippine area.

no way that the 2d ESB's many landing craft could make the 1,200-mile journey, so Barbey's ships off loaded their own landing craft and used the 2d ESB landing craft for the assault. The engineers' boats then remained to support the operation in the Philippines and Barbey's transports picked up their own boats on subsequent trips.[165] The Japanese reacted quickly and in force, but during the resulting Battle of Leyte Gulf, from 23 to 26 October, much of the Japanese fleet was destroyed. However, the division of command between MacArthur and Nimitz led to a dangerous situation in which a major Japanese surface force nearly broke through a screen of small aircraft carriers and destroyers to threaten the amphibious force while Admiral Halsey's main battle force engaged Japanese aircraft carriers to the north.[166]

A tenacious Japanese defense, poor weather, and difficult terrain made the ground operations on Leyte difficult. The fighting continued into 1945 and involved several additional amphibious operations, the largest being the landing of the 77th Infantry Division by Struble's ships at Ormoc, on the west coast of Leyte. The 2d ESB supported these operations and, in the case of landings on the Comotes Islands off the west coast of Leyte, all of the craft involved were those of the 2d ESB (rocket and flak LCMs for fire support, 30 landing craft, and 48 LVTs in the assault) with no Navy assistance. The amphibious engineers also provided coastwise logistics support, operated ports, transported Philippine guerrilla units, and conducted armed coastal patrols, for which the flak and rocket landing craft were particularly useful. On 15 December 1944 Struble's amphibians landed two RCTs on the island of Mindoro, south of Luzon. Several Navy landing ships and 2d ESB landing craft were sunk by Japanese suicide aircraft, but the landing itself was easy. The amphibious engineers remained to provide over-the-shore supply, resupply of radar stations on outlying islands, coastal patrol, and other duties, including pulling five stranded patrol torpedo (PT) boats off a reef.[167]

Amphibious Operations in 1945

On 9 January 1945 two Sixth Army corps landed at Lingayen Gulf on the main Philippine island of Luzon. The 4th ESB, reinforced with two regiments of the 3d ESB, provided the usual amphibian engineer support. The flat beach gradient, poor weather, and heavy surf impeded shore party operations, which were also complicated by differences in procedures between the SWPA and Central Pacific amphibious forces. Nonetheless, the landings and the beach clearing operations were successful. In his report on the Luzon operation, Admiral Barbey said that the "Engineer Special Brigade as organized in the Southwest Pacific Area is now the most efficient

Shore Party organization now functioning in amphibious warfare . . . the permanent organization of these [brigades has] contributed in large measure to the success of amphibious operations in this theater."[168]

After the Lingayen Gulf landing, most of the Japanese Army forces withdrew into the mountains to conduct a protracted delay and defense, but naval units in Manila held the city with fanatical determination and systematically demolished the port as they withdrew, sinking ships at their piers and in the approach channels, blowing up docks and wharves, destroying unloading facilities, and burning down buildings. Manila was essential to sustain operations in the Philippines, and so a major effort was made to rehabilitate the devastated port. On 26 February units of the 4th ESB, reinforced with Navy LCTs, two amphibian truck companies, two port companies, and engineer maintenance and ordnance elements arrived at Manila Harbor to begin the rehabilitation of the port and to assist in unloading and lightering operations. The first ships arrived to be unloaded on 11 March and by the end of the month, the 4th ESB, assisted by 11 port companies and 3 DUKW companies, were unloading nearly 5,000 tons of cargo a day.[169]

The many islands and convoluted coastline of the Philippines made amphibious and over-the-shore logistic operations essential, and dozens of landings were carried out before the islands were declared secure. In February Lieutenant General Robert Eichelberger's Eighth Army, supported by the 2d and 3d ESBs, began a campaign to occupy the southern Philippine islands. On 28 February 1945 two regiments were landed at Palawan and on 10 March another regiment landed in southwestern Mindanao. These were followed by a series of landings in the Sulu Archipelago, the Visayan Islands, and at several places on the coast of Mindanao. Eichelberger finally declared the southern islands cleared on 30 June 1945.[170]

While these operations were taking place in the Philippines, two Marine divisions with a few Army troops, including two amphibious truck companies, landed on Iwo Jima on 19 February 1945. The amphibious landing operation was carried out smoothly, but the strong Japanese defenses in over a month of hard fighting caused severe casualties that required the commitment of a third Marine division. On 26 March the 77th Infantry Division landed on the Kerama Islands north of Okinawa in preparation for the main assault on 1 April 1945. Admiral Spruance was the overall commander of the operation; Vice Admiral Turner was Commander, Joint Expeditionary Force; and Army Lieutenant General Simon Bolivar Buckner Jr. commanded the Tenth Army, which provided the expeditionary troops. With the 1st ESB providing the shore party support, two Army and two Marine divisions went ashore almost unopposed, but then ran into extremely strong and tenacious Japanese defenses inland. Buckner committed two more Army divisions and an additional Marine regiment. On 16 April the 77th Infantry Division made another landing at Ie Shima Island, west of Okinawa. By the time the island was secured on 10 June 1945, some 50,000 US and British Commonwealth soldiers, sailors, and marines had been killed or wounded, including General Buckner who was killed on 18 June, and 79 ships had been sunk or damaged beyond repair by Japanese suicide attacks.[171]

The last amphibious operations of the war were carried out in the Southwest Pacific. On 1 May 1945 Australian troops landed on Tarakan, northeast of Borneo, in LCMs of the 3d ESB that had been carried aboard a Navy LSD and several Australian merchant ships or towed behind LSTs. Australian troops also carried out the final amphibious operation, landing on 10 July 1945, at Brunei Bay in Borneo, in landing craft manned by US Army amphibious engineers.[172]

Amphibious Doctrine, Planning, and Training, 1945–50

The Postwar Amphibious Establishment

When World War II ended, the Pacific-based ESBs were preparing for the invasion of Japan. Instead, they helped land the occupation forces in Japan and Korea and then spent a few months conducting port operations and general engineering duties. The immense amphibious forces developed during the war were quickly demobilized. Because of their extraordinary value and versatility, General MacArthur recommended incorporating the ESBs into the postwar Regular Army force structure. The 2d ESB was selected to become the single postwar Regular Army ESB, with all the other brigades and all of the ATTBs to be inactivated. On 15 October 1945 the 2d ESB turned over its port operation duties in Yokohama to a newly-formed port command and began moving in increments to its new home base at Fort Ord, California. The 5th and 6th ESBs returned from Europe to be inactivated at their old training center at Camp Gordon Johnson in Carrabelle, Florida, in October 1945. In January 1946 the 1st ESB was inactivated in Korea and the 3d ESB was inactivated in California. The 4th ESB remained in Japan on occupation duty for a few more months before it, too, was inactivated in April 1946.[173]

The Navy also underwent a substantial demobilization. Of the nearly 3,000 large amphibious warfare ships (LCI[L] and larger) in commission at the end of the war, only 158 were on Active Duty in 1948, with 611 in the Navy Reserve.[174] The Navy retained a small amphibious force on each coast after the war, as well as the nucleus of its amphibious training capability. The ATC, Pacific remained in operation at Coronado, California, and the ATC, Atlantic, which had been inactivated in May 1945, was reactivated at Little Creek, Virginia, in February 1946. Each command included a Marine Corps troop training unit (TTU) to provide amphibious warfare instruction for Army and Marine Corps units. A few Army officers were assigned to the two Navy establishments as liaison officers and instructors.[175]

As the great amphibious force was dispersed, some attempts were made to capture the Army's wartime experience. The ETO produced an extensive after action report on the Normandy landing and river crossing operations. The AGF published a series of studies on all aspects of its operations, including the wartime amphibious training. General officers who had commanded amphibious operations wrote and spoke widely.[176] The Army's amphibious expertise, and interest in promulgating an Army perspective on amphibious operations, lay with the Headquarters, AGF, commanded by Devers and officially designated as the War Department Operational Representative for Amphibious Training of Army Ground Units within the United States in June 1946.[177] At the tactical level, the Army's amphibious expertise rested with the amphibious engineer and armor units in the Active and Reserve Components.

During the first year after the war, the two remaining EB&SRs and the boat maintenance battalion of the 2d ESB were stationed at three Army posts in southern California. In 1946 they participated in an amphibious exercise with the 2d Infantry Division. In December 1946 the unit was reduced to the Brigade Headquarters and Headquarters Company; Headquarters Company, Company B (Boat), and Companies D and E (Shore) of the 532d EB&SR; and Company A, 562d Boat Maintenance Battalion. In 1947 the unit relocated to Fort Worden, Washington, at the entrance to Puget Sound, where it was joined briefly by the 75th Amphibian Tank Battalion (ATB), a Reserve unit stationed at nearby Camp Casey. The brigade remained at Fort Worden for the remainder of the decade, maintaining the Army's amphibious expertise, participating in amphibious exercises, and, in 1947 taking part in the atomic tests at Eniwetok Atoll. In 1949 the 56th Amphibious Tractor Battalion, 50th Port Construction Company, and 501st Transportation Harbor Craft Platoon were activated from the General Reserve, where they had been on inactive status. The 56th was reorganized as a composite ATTB and all three units were attached to the 2d ESB.[178]

A small amphibious capability was also maintained in the Army Organized Reserve Corps, beginning with the 75th ATB, activated in 1946 and inactivated the following year. The 409th ESB was organized in December 1946, with its headquarters in Los Angeles, California, and its subordinate units, the 369th, 370th, and 371st EB&SRs; the 425th Medical Battalion; the 380th Engineer Boat Maintenance Battalion; the 356th Ordnance Maintenance Company; and the 409th Quartermaster Company based along the Pacific Coast in Los Angeles; Portland and Salem, Oregon; and Seattle, Washington. In January 1947 the 302d Amphibious Tractor Battalion was activated on the Gulf Coast of Mississippi. The 747th Amphibian Tank Company was organized in 1949 at Gainesville, Florida, and nearby small towns and reorganized the following year as an ATTB. All of these units were at greatly reduced strength, but they helped to maintain some amphibious force structure for the Army and several would be mobilized during the Korean War.[179]

Resumption of Amphibious Exercises

The first postwar amphibious exercise took place within General MacArthur's command in the Far East. In April 1946 Eighth Army in Japan began planning a large-scale exercise in coordination with the Amphibious Force, Pacific Fleet now commanded by Rear Admiral Struble, who had commanded several amphibious operations in the Philippines. As the exercise was originally conceived, 13 RCTs would receive amphibious training culminating in a division-size landing exercise. Rapid demobilization led to a reduction in the scope of the exercise to four RCTs by July, when a TTU from the Amphibious Force, Pacific Fleet arrived in Japan to begin 18 days of shore training for each RCT. The ships scheduled for the exercise were diverted to Operation MAGIC CARPET (the return of US troops to the United States) and were not available until October. After 7 days during which one RCT conducted three landings, further training was canceled because of a shortage of personnel.[180]

On 21 January 1946 the AGF announced resumption of Army amphibious training in the United States. On the east coast, ATC, Atlantic developed a program that included a demonstration landing exercise for West Point cadets and Annapolis midshipmen. The first Cadets-Midshipmen (CAMID) exercise took place in August 1946 and continued as an annual event in late summer for the rest of the decade and through the Korean War years.[181]

On the west coast, Major General George P. Hayes's Sixth Army was tasked as the AGF agency responsible for Pacific Coast amphibious training, with the 12th Air Force representing the Tactical Air Command (TAC). On 1 July 1946 Sixth Army and ATC, Pacific began planning for the first large-scale west coast exercise, Operation DUCK/OILSKIN/ MOUNTAIN GOAT. The 2d Infantry Division, then stationed at Fort Lewis, provided the landing force and the other participating Army units included the 2d ESB and the 41st ATB. After preliminary training at San Diego, Fort Lewis, Coronado, and San Clemente Island, the landings took place on 25 and 26 November at Aliso Canyon near San Diego. Time constraints prevented exercise of the follow-up phase: landing of supplies and equipment after D+5, operation of the beaches after the beachhead was secured, and initiation of base development.[182]

Hayes noted in his after action report, "By agreement with the Army Ground Forces, the Navy utilized the Mid-Pacific doctrine as a basis of instruction." The Mid-Pacific doctrine assumed the withdrawal of the landing force, including the shore parties, and its replacement by a garrison force once the beachhead was established. Hayes recommended the doctrine be revised "to include operations against continental land masses as well as small islands." He explained that in continental operations, Army units are landed with the intention of conducting sustained land operations and shore parties are not integral parts of the landing forces, but are "advance elements of the Service of Supply which is built up progressively to provide logistical support for a large military force." To accommodate this type of operation, Hayes argued that "Mid-Pacific doctrine should include provisions for the employment of ESBs, DUKW companies, Port companies, Truck companies, QM service companies, Gas Supply companies, and Ordnance companies, none of which are contemplated in the present doctrine."[183]

The Unification and Roles and Missions Struggle

General Hayes's critique of "Mid-Pacific doctrine" reflected an issue that would persist over the next 4 years. Those Army officers with a passionate interest in amphibious warfare would fight a running battle with both the Army leadership and the Navy over the nature of amphibious doctrine and the Army's role in amphibious operations. Their complaint to the Army Staff was that the leadership was paying insufficient attention to amphibious doctrine and allowing by default an inappropriate doctrine to be promulgated by the Navy, which had taken control of the amphibious training program. Their argument to the Navy generally followed Hayes's comments—techniques and procedures suited to the kind of large-scale operations the Army expected to conduct were being ignored.

Three major bodies of amphibious experience had emerged from the war. The Mid-Pacific doctrine adopted by the Navy and promulgated in its postwar training and exercises was derived from the campaigns among the islands of the Central Pacific. The postwar Army view of amphibious operations drew largely on the Mediterranean and Normandy experience, which generally conformed to the prewar views on continental amphibious operations, and that of MacArthur's SWPA: principally shore-to-shore operations against undefended or lightly defended areas, bypassing enemy force concentrations, and with a major contribution by ESBs that included boat as well as shore party units.

There was a dichotomy in the Army attitude toward amphibious operations. Some, like General Omar Bradley whose experience was in Europe, remembered Salerno, Anzio, and Omaha Beach at Normandy and saw amphibious operations as inherently dangerous, risky, and unnecessary except when needed to establish an initial lodgment. Others, especially those who served in the Southwest Pacific and looked at the coastlines, rivers, and inland waterways, were convinced that amphibious warfare would continue to be an essential military capability.[184] Some saw the atomic bomb as making large-scale amphibious operations obsolete, because amphibious task forces and beachheads would be vulnerable to atomic destruction, but if amphibious operations of division or larger size *were* to be conducted, then the Army should conduct those operations. The Marines might have invented the doctrine for landing on hostile shores, but the Army had developed the techniques for large-scale operations and had conducted more amphibious operations during the war.[185] All of these Army attitudes would come into play during the postwar struggle over Service unification, roles, and missions.

During the war, the Army leadership became convinced that the Services should be unified into one military department with a single chief of staff to improve the efficiency of decisionmaking and reduce the duplication of effort and competition for resources.[186] As the war neared its end, Army Chief of Staff George C. Marshall raised the issue within the JCS. As part of this overall position, the Army leadership also argued for a separate Air Force with control over all land-based aircraft and for a reduction in the size and role of the Marine Corps. The Navy leadership opposed this approach, preferring to adhere to existing *JAAN* arrangements under which the war had been fought successfully. To some extent, the Navy concerns reflected a fear that the Army, as the largest Service, would dominate any unified organization. The Marines, now at unparalleled strength and prestige and proud of their wartime service and sacrifice, saw a renewed threat to their existence and to their role as amphibious experts.[187]

The Marine concerns were not without foundation. Prior to World War II there had never been a Marine Corps unit larger than brigade size. Many Army officers, who saw warfare as an activity that was conducted at the corps, army, or higher level, believed the Marine experience of division and higher command was too short for them to have developed the experience and understanding to command above the division level. Furthermore, the Marine Corps, which had grown to six divisions and two amphibious corps headquarters, and had garnered much public adulation for its Pacific victories, would now compete with the Army for manpower and resources in the postwar world of constrained budgets. Added to this, and less easy to measure, was the antipathy many Army officers felt for what they generally saw as an elitist and disdainful attitude on the part of Marines. They particularly resented General H.M. Smith's frequent criticism of the performance of Army troops and leaders, and they remained angry about H.M. Smith's relief from command of General Ralph Smith on Saipan, which they saw as unjustified.[188]

During a 1946 internal JCS exchange of views on postwar missions of the Services, Army Chief of Staff Dwight Eisenhower argued that the Marine Corps should be restricted to units no larger than regiments and its role confined to the initial phase of landing operations and guard duty, with all major amphibious operations carried out by the Army. Air Force Chief of Staff General Carl Spaatz supported Eisenhower in this. Admirals Leahy and Nimitz, the Navy members of the JCS, objected strongly to this recommendation. The Navy view was that amphibious operations were essentially naval in character until after a beachhead had been established and sustained combat operations began on land. The Marines, organized into divisions and including armor and artillery, should be assigned the responsibility for the amphibious phase. The members of the JCS were unable to resolve this impasse and in June 1946 agreed to suspend further consideration of the Services missions. The JCS did not discuss the "roles and missions" issue again until 1948.[189]

In parallel with this internal JCS debate, Congress had begun hearings on the unification issue. In congressional testimony, in the media, and in behind the scenes debate, the Services engaged in a harsh war of words, intensified by deeply held beliefs on all sides.[190] The Marines had strong and influential support within Congress, and the National Security Act as enacted in 1947 stated:

> The Marine Corps shall be organized, trained, and equipped
> to provide fleet marine forces of combined arms, together
> with supporting air components, for service with the fleet

in the seizure or defense of advanced naval bases and for the conduct of such land operations as may be essential to the prosecution of a naval campaign. It shall be the duty of the Marine Corps to develop, in coordination with the Army and the Air Force, those phases of amphibious operations which pertain to the tactics, technique, and equipment employed by landing forces.[191]

The Marines thus had their existence and amphibious mission written into law. Nonetheless, some disagreements over Service roles and missions remained. When President Truman signed the National Security Act, he also promulgated an Executive order setting forth the Service functions. It did not specify Marine Corps operational responsibilities beyond assigning the Navy the mission of seizing shore positions by "such landing forces as may be comprised within the fleet organization," but it assigned to the Army the mission of seizing, occupying, and defending land areas through airborne and *joint* amphibious operations.[192] The Army view, supported by the Air Force, was that in such *joint* amphibious operations (as opposed to operations incidental to naval campaigns), the Army should provide the landing force. For the Navy to develop Marine units of division, corps, or larger size capable of joint amphibious operations would be an unnecessary duplication of effort, as well as a violation of the principles of Service integration and unity of command.[193]

At the insistence of Secretary of Defense James V. Forrestal, the JCS met at Key West, Florida, in March 1948 to address this and other roles and missions issues. The resulting Key West Agreement stated that the Marine Corps functions as stated in the National Security Act did not "contemplate the creation of a second land army" but otherwise set no limit on the size of the corps. The agreement also specified, "The Marine Corps shall have primary interest in the development of those landing force tactics, techniques, and equipment which are of common interest to the Army and the Marine Corps."[194] The Army was given primary interest in the development of airborne doctrine, procedure, and equipment, but was also to "develop, in coordination with the other Services, tactics, techniques, and equipment of interest to the Army for amphibious operations" not otherwise provided for in the Marine Corps' amphibious function.[195] The Key West Agreement also set forth a definition of amphibious operations that would later be contested by Army officers who argued for a unique Army style of amphibious warfare:

Amphibious Operations—An attack launched from the sea by naval and landing forces embarked in ships or craft involving a landing on a hostile shore. An amphibious operation includes final preparation of the objective area for the landing and operations of naval, air and ground elements in over water movements, assault, and mutual support. An amphibious operation may precede a large-scale land operation in which case it becomes the amphibious phase of a joint amphibious operation. After the troops are landed and firmly established ashore the operation becomes a land operation.[196]

Army critics saw the definition as misleadingly narrow in its restriction to "naval and landing forces," which ignored the kinds of purely Army shore-to-shore operations carried out in SWPA, and in its limitation of the definition to "final" preparation of the objective. They also objected to the distinction between an amphibious operation (which the Navy argued was quintessentially a *naval* operation and must be commanded by a naval officer) and a land operation because, in their view, an amphibious operation might be a phase in a land operation under the overall command of an Army officer.[197] However, Army leadership had accepted the definition and the voices of the critics were temporarily stilled or ignored.

Post-National Security Act, Army Amphibious Doctrine and Training

The National Security Act and the Key West Agreement led to a revision of Service doctrine taking into account the new separate US Air Force and the newly defined missions and functions of the Services. Post-1947 amphibious exercises were conducted in this new environment and in the context of strategic war planning, which assumed that in a war against the United States and Britain, the Soviet Union would overrun most of continental Europe, Turkey, Iran, Korea, Manchuria, and North China, requiring amphibious operations in any counteroffensive.[198] The 1949 plan (OFFTACKLE) anticipated that, although Allied forces would try to maintain a lodgment in Europe, perhaps at the line of the Pyrenees, evacuation of forces to Britain and North Africa would likely be required. The United States and its allies might then conduct limited offensives to seize footholds on Sicily, Southern Italy, Sardinia, and/or Corsica, eventually reentering Western Europe through a two-pronged operation, with northern landings between Cherbourg and the base of the Jutland Peninsula as far to the east as possible and a southern thrust from North Africa into Southern France and up the Rhone Valley. The last plan developed before the Korean War (DROPSHOT) included several alternative schemes for the counteroffensive, with amphibious operations on the North Sea and Black Sea coasts. Thus, even in the atomic era, there was a need to train joint forces in the conduct of amphibious operations.[199]

The first joint exercise held after the unification of the armed forces, Exercise *Seminole*, took place in October and November 1947 near Panama City, Florida. Combat Command A of the 2d Armored Division provided the landing force. The objectives were to train air, naval, and ground personnel for landing operations; to practice high-level amphibious planning; and to develop techniques for loading and landing armored forces and other heavy equipment. The exercise provided valuable experience that would later be incorporated into instructional material and an amphibious study produced by the Armor School at Fort Knox, Kentucky.[200] The following year, the Puerto Rican 65th Infantry participated with Marine Corps units in a 1st Marine Division exercise at Vieques Island, serving both as a floating reserve and as part of the amphibious assault force.[201]

In early 1949 the 2d ESB stepped up its training in preparation for major exercises planned for the next 2 years. Company E, 532d EB&SR served as the shore party for an Antilles Command amphibious exercise at Vieques Island in January. In April Company B (Boat), 532d EB&SR and watercraft of the 501st Harbor Craft Platoon carried out a 21-day, 1,114-mile cruise on the Columbia River. The first of the big exercises was Joint Army–Navy Exercise *Miki*, held on the west coast and in Hawaii from 20 September to 25 November 1949. The scenario for the exercise, which was strictly an Army–Navy affair with no Marine Corps or Air Force participation, simulated the invasion of a large enemy-held island (Oahu, Hawaii). It was a substantial operation. General Clark, Commanding General of Sixth Army and soon to replace General Devers as Commanding General of Army Field Forces (AFF), was the maneuver director.[202] The Navy amphibious task force that transported the landing force from the west coast to Hawaii included 40 major amphibious ships escorted by two aircraft carrier divisions sailing under simulated combat conditions. The 2d Infantry Division, minus one regiment, was the landing force. Company C, 56th ATTB provided support for the landing in Hawaii and the 2d ESB (minus the boat elements) provided the shore party. The boat company did not participate, as postwar Navy policy was to exclude ESB boat units from exercises (very different from the days when Admiral Barbey carried ESB landing craft aboard his own transports in SWPA). Although dangerously heavy surf prevented the use of some of the planned beach on Oahu, all of the troops and 1,700 vehicles were ashore by D+2 and most of the exercise objectives (training in all phases of an amphibious operation) were judged to have been met. It was the largest and most complex amphibious operation since World War II, and would not be exceeded until the Incheon landing the following year.[203]

While not as large as *Miki*, the next joint amphibious exercise was still substantial. Puerto Rican Exercise (*PORTREX*) took place at Vieques Island in the Caribbean from 25 February to 11 March 1950, with preliminary training in January and February. While *Miki* was an Army–Navy exercise, *PORTREX* was directed by the JCS to provide training in the planning and execution of a joint operation and to test actual contingency plans. The scenario was one of invasion of an island by means of a coordinated airborne and amphibious attack to establish a lodgment for subsequent operations of the kind envisioned in the war plans. The attacking force included a battalion combat team of the 82d Airborne Division and a landing force consisting of major elements of the 3d Infantry Division plus some 17,000 marines, with Company D, 56th ATTB, in support and the 532d EB&SR (less boat elements) providing the nucleus of the shore party. The 65th RCT simulated the enemy defenders.[204]

Thus, both of the Active Army divisions that deployed from the Continental United States to Korea during the Korean War, the 2d and 3d Infantry Divisions, had participated in large-scale amphibious exercises within a year of deployment. Although General MacArthur requested the 2d Infantry Division to be part of the landing force for the Incheon operation, circumstances caused the early commitment of the division into ground combat and neither of the amphibious-trained Army divisions was ever actually used in an amphibious assault operation.[205]

While these exercises provided the opportunity for amphibious planning and operations, the intellectual work took place at AGF/AFF, the US Army Command and General Staff College, and the Service schools. At the Command and General Staff College, Lieutenant Colonel William B. Rosson, a veteran of the North Africa, Sicily, Salerno, Anzio, and Southern France amphibious operations, developed a course in 1947 designed to teach amphibious staff planning techniques and tactical principles at the infantry division level. The Armor School developed amphibious doctrine specifically related to landing armor forces, and Brigadier General David Ogden, who had commanded the 3d ESB in World War II and the 2d ESB after the war, lectured at the Engineer School, as well as at other venues, and wrote about the Army-unique perspective on amphibious operations.[206] AFF monitored the information collected from exercises and reports from the Army liaison officers serving with the Navy ATCs, and served as an advocate for Army involvement in amphibious doctrine development.[207]

Since 1946 advocates for Army amphibious operations had complained about certain aspects of the Navy's training program. An underlying concern was that, based on the wartime agreements that gave the Navy responsibility for amphibious training, the Navy had developed its postwar training program with very little, if any, Army input. The fault did not lie entirely with the Navy. In 1946 Admiral Nimitz had proposed the assignment of Army officers and enlisted men to fleet amphibious forces, amphibious groups, and ATCs. The unification struggle had already begun by then and some Army general staff officers were concerned that the assignment of such officers might be used by the Navy as an argument against unification, arguing that their presence "might lead to the conclusion that the staffs are joint, thereby indicating a lessening of the necessity for unification, whereas, in effect, those staffs will merely contain liaison officers."[208] The officers were assigned, ranging in rank from lieutenant colonel to staff sergeant, but they rarely received guidance from the Army and had no authority to speak for the Army on policy recommendations.[209]

Specific issues raised by Army advocates primarily concerned the Navy emphasis on Mid-Pacific doctrine and the focus on operations against islands that assumed the landing force and the shore party would withdraw once the beachhead was secured. The Army anticipated that it would be involved in large-scale operations of corps size or larger. ("The Army does not fight small wars," General Ogden said in his critique of the 1946 exercise and repeated frequently thereafter.) In such a case, the landing force troops would not depart after the beachhead was secure, but would continue to conduct sustained operations on land. The shore party in these operations would be the lead element of a major sustainment effort.

The Army advocates also objected to the Navy assumption that all amphibious operations were primarily naval operations of such a technical nature that the joint expeditionary force commander had to be a naval officer who must remain in overall command until the landing force was established ashore. Pointing to the SWPA experience, the Army advocates noted that a shore-to-shore operation might be conducted entirely by Army forces and that even in the case of ship-to-shore operations, the landing was likely to be part of the initial phase of a land operation. In such cases, the Navy would be the supporting force and the Army commander should have overall command throughout the operation. A related issue was the importance to Army forces of control over landing craft *after* the landing for support of operations ashore through over-the-shore logistics; coastal and inland waterway transportation; and such follow-on operations as subsidiary shore-to-shore landings, river crossings, and waterborne patrol and intelligence operations. Furthermore, in the post-National Security Act era, Army advocates argued that the *joint* operations envisioned in the Act, the Executive order, and the Key West Agreement required that *joint* doctrine be developed jointly by the Services and not unilaterally by a single Service. They also argued for a truly joint amphibious training establishment.[210]

At the Army staff level, there was not universal agreement about the importance of amphibious operations. In 1947 Lieutenant General J. Lawton Collins, Deputy Chief of Staff of the Army, expressed concern that the curriculums of Army schools included too much time on amphibious operations at the expense of airborne operations. The subject would arise again over the next 2 years, and in 1949 the Army Staff considered changing the organization and mission of the ESBs to reduce the amphibious beachhead shore party responsibilities and add responsibility for operating airheads during airborne operations.[211] Nonetheless, the Army staff supported an effort by AFF to develop an agreed Army position on amphibious operations. In September 1948 General Devers appointed a board of officers led by Lieutenant General Truscott to "define the position of the Department of the Army on basic doctrine, policies, and procedures on joint matters pertaining to joint amphibious operations."[212] Ogden was a member of the panel that heard testimony from a large number of officers with amphibious experience, including General Krueger, Sixth Army commander in SWPA, and Lieutenant General John R. Hodge, who had commanded XXIV Corps in the Central and Southwest Pacific amphibious operations.

Among the panel's principal conclusions were that unilateral development of amphibious doctrine had resulted in "narrow concepts and arbitrary views"; that all of the Services must participate actively in the development of amphibious doctrine and techniques; that an amphibious operation "is essentially an assault of any size to achieve an objective on land in which the landing force is dependent on waterborne means for transport and for tactical and logistical support"; that when "the objective of a joint amphibious operation is within the field of normal land combat operations, Army responsibility is dominant" and the amphibious assault is "only an initial step in the development of land combat"; and that the Army should have in its peacetime establishment "an organization to develop and train shore parties and other special purpose amphibious units."[213] Based on these conclusions, the panel recommended the establishment of a joint agency to supervise the development of joint amphibious operations. The panel argued that all the Services should recognize that, although an amphibious operation might be conducted to seize a base for naval operations, it could also be a phase of land combat. For this reason, the panel recommended one of the primary functions of the Army be "to conduct such amphibious operations as are necessary for the seizure of objectives in a land campaign." The panel also proposed a new definition of an amphibious operation to replace the one in the Key West Agreement:

> An attack launched from the sea by forces embarked in ships or craft involving a landing on a hostile shore. An amphibious operation includes preparation of the objective area for the landing, and operations of these forces in over water movements, assault, and support. The amphibious operation is a joint amphibious operation when the assigned forces are composed of elements of more than one Service of the National Military Establishment.[214]

Other recommendations provided for greater Army control of amphibious assets and operations when the land campaign was the dominant element. There were also recommendations for unilateral Army actions, including the maintenance of some equivalent of the ESB to train shore parties and other special purpose amphibious units. The panel did not insist that the Army own its own landing craft, but that there be "sufficient army-controlled landing craft (Army or Navy operated) to ensure minimum maintenance of army logistics and minimum support of minor operations of an amphibious nature."[215] The report was forwarded to the Army Staff and became the basis for the Army position on amphibious operations. Shortly thereafter, in August 1949, Army General and Service School instructors met at the Engineer School at Fort Belvoir.[216] Among the topics discussed was the Army role in amphibious operations, the findings of the Truscott Panel, and the Army's view of inter-Service amphibious doctrinal differences. As the Army officers perceived the basic difference, the Navy based its thinking on limited operations ashore, while the Army had to plan for extensive operations on land, for which the amphibious landing was only the first phase. As one participant put it, "The Navy looks at [the amphibious assault] primarily from the standpoint of a beachhead and the Army looks at it from the standpoint of invasion."[217]

The Navy and Marine Corps and the Army also approached shore party operations differently. Because the Marine Corps trained all of its combat units to conduct amphibious operations, the Navy and Marine Corps believed that shore parties could be organized quickly from the landing force units. Army divisions, however, were organized, trained, and equipped for sustained operations on land. Units selected for an amphibious assault could be given the required training prior to the operation, but the key to an effective amphibious operation was a well-trained and equipped shore party capable of moving large quantities of supplies and large numbers of troops over the beach and inland. As one of the conference participants put it, "The Marine idea is you take all your divisions and train them for amphibious operations and you don't need a [specially trained] shore party. . . . The Army's position is that we should be able to take any Army division and with a little bit of training in climbing in and out of boats, put it ashore in amphibious operations. But the key to the whole situation is the existence of a well-trained shore party."[218]

The instructors also discussed the ESB units, noting the value of engineer boat and shore units in the Southwest Pacific. The 2d ESB, which retained the Army's amphibious expertise, was organized after the Southwest Pacific pattern, although there was some move toward expanding its mission to include the logistic support of airborne airheads as well as amphibious beachheads. The discussants noted that the Army had no objection to relinquishing to the Navy the responsibility for operating landing craft, so long as the Army's continuing requirements for shore-to-shore, coastal, and inland waterway transportation were met. However, the conference participants were not sanguine that the Navy would be prepared to meet those requirements.[219]

The Truscott Panel report served as the basis for the Army position during coordination of *Joint Action Armed Forces* published in 1951 to replace the old *JAAN* document. Some of the recommendations would later be reflected in the language of Army amphibious doctrine published in the early 1950s. The 1952 draft of the Army's capstone operational doctrine publication, Field Manual 100-5, *Field Service Regulations: Operations*, adhered closely to the AFF panel recommendations. The final version, published in 1954, reverted to the phrase, "a joint amphibious operation is essentially an attack launched from the sea *by naval and landing forces* embarked in ships or craft" (emphasis added). But it also identified certain fundamentals. One of these was that "[l]arge amphibious operations are usually joint in nature [and all] large amphibious operations involving Army landing forces will be joint operations." The field manual noted that small amphibious operations might be "unilateral Navy operations," but the Army might conduct small shore-to-shore operations unilaterally. Another fundamental was that control of the joint force involved in an amphibious operation "must be vested in one commander," leaving open the possibility that it might be an Army commander. The manual also noted that amphibious shore-to-shore techniques might be used for "subsidiary interisland or coastal flanking operations," on navigable rivers and lakes, and the crossing of wide or swift rivers.[220]

By the time these manuals were published, Army forces had participated in actual amphibious operations in Korea. The preparations for those operations had begun while the panel was deliberating. In the Far East, General MacArthur was arguing and planning for a large-scale amphibious training program to prepare his command for war.

The Situation in the Far East on the Eve of the Korean War

In 1947 the JCS had established two unified commands in the Pacific. Admiral Arthur W. Radford, then commander in chief of the US Pacific Fleet, was named Commander in Chief Pacific Command (CINCPAC) with responsibilities in the Central Pacific. MacArthur, then commanding the occupation of Japan as Supreme Commander of the Allied Powers (SCAP) and Commanding General, USAFFE, was named Commander in Chief, Far East (CINCFE) with responsibilities in the Western Pacific. At that time the chain of command ran from the President and Secretary of Defense through the JCS, who designated specific Service chiefs as executive agents for the various unified commands. Strategic direction and guidance was communicated to Radford through the Chief of Naval Operations, Admiral Forrest P. Sherman; and to General MacArthur through the Chief of Staff of the Army, General Collins. The Far East Command (FEC)[221] initially encompassed Japan; Korea; the Ryukyu Islands (Okinawa); the Philippines; and the Mariana, Bonin, and Volcano Islands. However, from 1947 until the start of the Korean War, Korea was removed (at General MacArthur's request) from the FEC area of responsibility (AOR). The commander of US forces in Korea reported directly to the Army Chief of Staff.[222]

The JCS intention was that unified commands would have balanced, joint staffs. General MacArthur's approach was to re-designate GHQ USAFFE as GHQ FEC. As a result, there was no joint staff and no Army Service Component Command. Because MacArthur did not establish a separate staff for Army Forces Far East, each major Army command in the theater reported directly to CINCFE.[223] To aid in carrying out his joint responsibilities, in 1949 MacArthur established the JSPOG under Brigadier General Edwin K. Wright, who was also the GHQ FEC chief of operations (G3). Consisting of three Army, three Navy, and two Air Force general and flag officers, JSPOG was the primary joint planning element throughout the Korean War, including responsibility for planning amphibious operations.

The most significant Army command in the Far East was Lieutenant General Walton H. Walker's Eighth US Army (EUSA), which acted as the Army Service Component Command. On the eve of the war, Eighth

Army, with its headquarters in Yokohama, Japan, consisted of four under-strength divisions (1st Cavalry and 7th, 24th, and 25th Infantry Divisions), the 40th Antiaircraft Artillery (AAA) Brigade with seven AAA battalions, and service and logistic support units. Two battalions of the 29th Infantry Regiment and two AAA battalions were located on Okinawa. The nearest units outside the theater were the 5th RCT in Hawaii; the 1st Marine Division and 1st Marine Air Wing at Camp Pendleton, California; and the 2d Infantry Division at Fort Lewis, Washington. The only American soldiers stationed in Korea at the start of the war were the 492 members of the United States Military Advisory Group to the Republic of Korea (KMAG).[224]

Lieutenant General George Stratemeyer commanded the Air Force component command, Far East Air Forces (FEAF). FEAF included three numbered air forces (Major General Earle E. Partridge's Fifth Air Force in Japan consisting of air defense fighters and light bombers, 13th Air Force in the Philippines, and 20th Air Force responsible for the air defense of Okinawa), the 19th Bombardment Group (B-29s) in the Marianas, and a FEAF Materiel Command.[225]

Vice Admiral C. Turner Joy commanded the Navy component command, Naval Forces, Far East (NAVFE). NAVFE included small naval forces in the Philippines (TF 93) and the Marianas (TF 94), but its main strength was in Japanese waters and was provided by TF 96 (Naval Forces Japan): a cruiser, several destroyers, a submarine, and a few minesweepers. Admiral Joy also had operational control over the Shipping Control Administration, Japan (SCAJAP). SCAJAP in June 1950 consisted of 12 ex-US Navy freighters and 39 LSTs manned by Japanese but controlled by SCAP. These ships had been used to repatriate Japanese from the continent following the war and continued to be used for FEC logistic support and as interim transport in the Japanese islands until the war-destroyed Japanese Merchant Marine could be reconstituted.[226] By 1949 NAVFE had come to see the constant repair and maintenance of these old ships to be a liability and recommended they be scrapped. Wright, the FEC G3, and officers of the G4 (Logistics) section, argued that the ships should be kept operational "as an amphibious capability in the event of an emergency." Within a year, the value of these LSTs would become clear.[227]

As SCAP, MacArthur also had operational control of Lieutenant General H.C.H. Robertson's British Commonwealth Forces (BCOF); No. 77 Squadron Royal Australian Air Force (RAAF); the 3d Battalion, Royal Australian Rifles; and the Australian frigate *Shoalhaven,* which served with TF 96 as Task Unit (TU) 96.5.3, Commonwealth Support Element. In the FEC AOR, but not under MacArthur's control, were Struble's Seventh Fleet at Subic Bay in the Philippines, which was under CINCPAC, and the British Far East Fleet commanded by Rear Admiral Sir William G. Andrewes. Struble's force included an aircraft carrier, a heavy cruiser, eight destroyers, four submarines, and a small force of auxiliaries. Andrewes' force included an aircraft carrier, cruiser, and several destroyers and escort ships.[228]

The primary responsibility for water transportation, other than Rear Admiral James H. Doyle's amphibians and the SCAJAP fleet, rested with the MSTS, a unified organization within the Navy Department that was established in October 1949, absorbing both the Naval Transportation Service (the Navy's nonamphibious transports and cargo ships) and the sea-going ships and functions of the Army Transportation Corps. MSTS had primary responsibility for water transportation for the military. It operated its own fleet of ships, chartered civilian ships, and scheduled shipping. In January 1950 Navy Captain Alexander F. Junker arrived in Tokyo, to prepare to assume his duties as the deputy commander for MSTS in the Western Pacific (DepComMSTS WestPac) effective 1 July 1950. By the time his office began operation, Junker would be faced with the challenge of orchestrating the shipping resources in support of the Korean War.[229]

GHQ FEC Amphibious Training Program

When reading accounts of the Incheon landing, one sometimes receives the impression that the FEC staff was totally ignorant of amphibious warfare. An examination of the GHQ FEC records for the period prior to the war tells a somewhat different story. It is true that most of the amphibious expertise lay with the Navy and Marine amphibious forces, but General MacArthur had initiated a vigorous amphibious training program in 1949 that was about to come to fruition when the North Koreans attacked.

US forces in Japan had spent the first years after the end of World War II focused primarily on occupation duty to the detriment of their combat readiness. However, as the occupation proceeded peacefully, the Japanese regained increasing control over their own affairs, and tensions increased between the United States and the Soviet Union, MacArthur began to refocus the effort toward regaining combat proficiency. On 10 June 1949 GHQ FEC announced a new joint training program with RCT-level amphibious landing exercises to be conducted by 31 July 1950.[230] That month MacArthur requested a commitment from the Navy for instruction and shipping to conduct amphibious training for one battalion landing team (BLT) from each of the four divisions in Japan. By December he had increased the scope of the program to training for 10 battalions culminating in a division-size landing exercise (LEX) in Okinawa. By February 1950 MacArthur notified the Army Staff that his planning for a "large scale joint amphibious-air transportable exercise" was progressing satisfactorily, but there had been no commitment from the Navy for the essential shipping support. The Navy's response later that month was that other commitments would limit Navy support to the four-BLT program originally planned.[231]

A disappointed MacArthur accepted that the training planned for May to August 1950 would have to be limited, but he then proposed a major amphibious training program, arguing that he considered "amphibious training to have unusual significance and importance in the Far East Command since the nature of troop dispositions and geography of the theater are such that a continuous requirement exists for the training of troops in over-water movement." His new program would begin in 1951 with the training of a division headquarters and three RCTs and a divisional LEX in Okinawa. He proposed a similar program for the next 3 fiscal years. He also advised that a reconnaissance of the Okinawa beaches revealed a requirement for LVTs, since LCVPs and LCMs could not pass over the offshore reefs. Additionally, he requested consideration of temporary assignment of the 2d ESB to participate in the LEX and the establishment of a permanent amphibious training center in the Far East.[232]

While awaiting a response (and receiving generally discouraging signals from the Navy), GHQ FEC pressed ahead to do as much as possible from within its own resources. Funds were provided to Eighth Army for the construction of an amphibious training center at Camp McGill, about 75 miles southwest of Tokyo. Soldiers with amphibious or maritime experience were recruited to form a provisional ATC within Eighth Army. Navy LST crews were requested to man SCAJAP LSTs to form a nucleus of an FEC amphibious training force. When the Navy failed to respond, a search began for potential civilian or military mariners of whatever Service. Plans were made to convert one or more SCAJAP cargo ships into makeshift assault transports by fitting them with Welin davits and other amphibious gear taken from SCAJAP LSTs.[233] Meanwhile, Major General Edward M. Almond, GHQ FEC Chief of Staff, peppered the staff with queries on the status of the program, amphibious warfare doctrine, and the conduct of amphibious operations in SWPA in World War II.[234]

By the spring of 1950, Eighth Army had established an amphibious training center at Camp McGill, on the east coast of Sagami Bay southwest of Tokyo, and near a suitable beach for landing exercises (Chigasaki

Beach), and on 1 April 1950 had activated a 50-man unit of Army engineers and others with amphibious and related expertise as the 8206th Army Unit (AU), ATC.[235] In April Doyle's Amphibious Group One arrived to add Navy ships and expertise to the training program. Designated as Task Force 90 (Amphibious Force, Far East) upon its assignment to Naval Forces Far East, Amphibious Group One consisted of Doyle's flagship, the amphibious flag ship *Mount McKinley* (AGC-7), the attack transport *Cavalier* (APA-37), the attack cargo ship *Union* (AKA-106), the tank landing ship LST-611, and the fleet tug *Arikara* (ATF-98). Doyle was one of the most experienced amphibious officers in the US Navy. During World War II he had been the operations officer of Amphibious Force, South Pacific during the Guadalcanal and Solomon Islands Campaigns; served in the Amphibious Section of the staff of the commander in chief, US Fleet; served on the Joint Amphibious Warfare Committee; and commanded a light cruiser during the Okinawa campaign. After service with the United Nations Military Committee, he had returned to amphibious warfare. He was highly respected by MacArthur's staff and commanders and acknowledged as an expert on amphibious warfare.[236]

On 27 April Marine Colonel Edward H. Forney's Mobile Training Team (MTT) Able and an Air and Naval Gunfire Liaison Company (ANGLICO) arrived from the Coronado, California, amphibious training base.[237] The training program began with the arrival in May of the 35th Infantry Regiment of the 24th Infantry Division, soon followed by the 5th Regiment of the 1st Cavalry Division. Forney's MTT was to conduct the first few cycles of pre-afloat (on-shore) training; then the 8206th would take over. The pre-afloat training was to be followed by battalion-size landing exercises at nearby Chigasaki Beach carried out by Doyle's TF 90.[238] On 29 April 1950 lead elements of the 35th Infantry Regiment arrived at Camp McGill. The amphibious training school opened on 1 May and training began on 1 June. The first landing exercise coincided almost exactly with the North Korean attack that began the Korean War.

Notes

1.   A useful summary of British amphibious operations in the colonial period is Herbert Richmond, *Amphibious Warfare in British History* (Exeter, UK: A. Wheaton & Company, 1941). A description of Phips's bloodless capture of Port Royal and his disastrous expedition against Quebec is in the biography of Sir William Phips in *Dictionary of Canadian Biography Online*, biographica/EN/ ShowBio.asp?BioId=34586 (accessed 15 June 2005). For Vernon's Caribbean operations, see Richard Harding, *Amphibious warfare in the eighteenth century: the British expedition to the West Indies, 1740–1742* (Suffolk, UK: Boydell Press, 1991).

2.   For the Louisburg and Quebec operations, see Brook Nihart, "Amphibious Operations in Colonial North America," in Merrill L. Bartlett, ed., *Assault from the Sea: Essays on the History of Amphibious Warfare* (Annapolis, MD: Naval Institute Press, 1983), 46–48; John Creswell, *Generals and Admirals: The Story of Amphibious Command* (New York, NY: Longmans, Green, 1952), 63–84; William M. Fowler Jr., *Empires at War: The French and Indian War and the Struggle for North America, 1754–1763* (New York, NY: Walker and Company, 2005), 163–172; and Douglas Edward Leach, "The Colonial Period," in John E. Jessup and Louise B. Ketz, eds., *Encyclopedia of the American Military* (New York, NY: Charles Scribner's Sons, 1994), Vol. 1, 507–544. For MacArthur's comparison of the Incheon landing to the Quebec operation, see Douglas MacArthur, *Reminiscences* (New York, NY: McGraw-Hill Book Company, 1964, Second Printing), 349–350. For Pocock's Havana expedition, see Francis Russell Hart, *The Siege of Havana 1762* (Boston and New York: Houghton Mifflin Company, 1931).

3.   Glover's Regiment, which included African–American soldiers, became known as the amphibious regiment after its river crossing operations in the evacuation of Long Island and at the Battle of Trenton. David Hackett Fisher, *Washington's Crossing* (New York, NY: Oxford University Press USA, 2004), 21–22; *Glover's Marblehead Regiment,* gloversregiment.org/history.html (accessed 5 May 2007).

4.   Charles Dana Gibson and E. Kay Gibson, *The Army's Navy Series, Vol. I, Marine Transportation in War: The U.S. Army Experience, 1775–1860* (Camden, ME: Ensign Press, 1992), 7–8, 31–33; Fisher, *Washington's Crossing,* 21–24, 101, 110, 215–220; Allan R. Millett, *Semper Fidelis: The History of the United States Marine Corps* (New York, NY: The Free Press, 1991), 9–10; James Kirby Martin and John Morgan Dederer, "The War of the Revolution," in *Encyclopedia of the American Military*, Vol. 1, 545–594; and George E. Buker, *The Penobscot Expedition: Commodore Saltonstall and the Massachusetts Conspiracy of 1779* (Annapolis, MD: Naval Institute Press, 2002).

5.   James Ripley Jacobs, *The Beginning of the U.S. Army, 1783–1812* (Princeton, NJ: Princeton University Press, 1947), 149, 153; Gibson & Gibson, *Marine Transportation,* 41–44.

6.   William S. Dudley, "The War of 1812 and Postwar Expansion," in *Encyclopedia of the American Military*, Vol. 1, 629–676. A particularly useful

study of the history of joint operations and command and control in US Armed Forces is Lawrence J. Legere, "Unification of the Armed Forces," PhD diss., Harvard University, 1950. Pages 14 through 26 cover joint command relations in the War of 1812.

7.　Letter, Captain Oliver H. Perry to Secretary of the Navy Jones, 7 October 1813, and letter, Major General William Henry Harrison, USA, to Secretary of War Armstrong, 9 October 1813, in William S. Dudley, ed., *The Naval War of 1812: A Documentary History*, Vol. II (Washington, DC: Naval Historical Center, 1992), 570–576.

8.　Letter, Commodore Isaac Chauncey to Major General Jacob Brown, USA, 10 August 1814, in Dudley, ed., *The Naval War of 1812*, Vol. III, 2002, 584–585.

9.　Gibson & Gibson, *Marine Transportation,* 45–66; Dudley, "The War of 1812 and Postwar Expansion"; George E. Buker, *Swamp Sailors: Riverine Warfare in the Everglades, 1835–1842* (Gainesville, FL: University Presses of Florida, 1975), 136–140. Buker argues that the concepts of riverine warfare developed in the Second Seminole War and later used in the Mexican and Civil Wars were essentially the same as those used by Army riverine forces in the Mekong Delta during the Vietnam War.

10.　K. Jack Bauer, *Surfboats and Horse Marines, U.S. Naval Operations in the Mexican War, 1846–48* (Annapolis, MD: US Naval Institute, 1969); Henry W.T. Eglin, "General Scott's Landing at Vera Cruz, March 9, 1897," in *The Coast Artillery Journal,* Vol. 68, No. 3 (March 1928): 244–247; John Fleming Polk, "Vera Cruz, 1847," in Bartlett, ed., *Assault from the Sea,* 74–78; Cornelius C. Smith Jr., "Our First Amphibious Assault," *Military Review,* Vol. XXXVIII, No. 11 (January 1959): 18–28; and Gibson & Gibson, *Marine Transportation,* 87–94.

11.　The impact of the operation on Army engineers is discussed by Rowena Reed, *Combined Operations in the Civil War* (Annapolis, MD: Naval Institute Press, 1978), xii–xiii.

12.　Reed, *Combined Operations,* 3–10; Kevin J. Weddle, *Lincoln's Tragic Admiral: The Life of Samuel Francis DuPont* (Charlottesville and London: University of Virginia Press, 2005), 106–124. Weddle argues that the Blockade Board was the first (and only Civil War) body that systematically formulated joint naval and military strategy.

13.　Charles Dana Gibson and E. Kay Gibson, *The Army's Navy Series, Vol. II, Assault and Logistics: Union Army Coastal and River Operations, 1861–1866* (Camden, ME: Ensign Press, 1995), 3–23; Reed, *Combined Operations*, 11–32; Weddle, *Lincoln's Tragic Admiral,* 125–137.

14.　Robert W. Daley, "Burnside's Amphibious Division," in Bartlett, ed., *Assault from the Sea*, 88–94; Gibson & Gibson, *Assault and Logistics,* 24–33.

15.　These operations are described in Gibson & Gibson, *Assault and Logistics;* and Reed, *Combined Operations.*

16.　Chester G. Hearn, *Ellet's Brigade: The Strangest Outfit of All* (Baton Rouge, LA: Louisiana State University Press, 2000). I am indebted to David Keough of MHI for bringing this unit and this book to my attention.

17. "Reports of Lieutenant Colonel Barton S. Alexander, US Army, Engineer Officer of Operations from April 20 to July 12" (Washington, DC, 28 January 1863), *Official Records of the Rebellion*, Vol. 11, Chapter 23, Part 1: "Peninsular Campaign, Reports," 134–139; Reed, *Combined Operations*, 149–160. I am indebted to Dr. James B. Batholomees of the US Army War College for bringing this operation to my attention.

18.   Gary J. Ohls, "Fort Fisher: Amphibious Victory in the American Civil War," *Naval War College Review*, Vol. 59, No. 4, Autumn 2006, 81–99; Joseph E. King, "The Fort Fisher Campaigns, 1864–65," in Bartlett, ed., *Assault from the Sea,* 95–104; Reed, *Combined Operations,* 321–383.

19.   Graham T. Cosmas makes this point in "Joint Operations in the Spanish–American War," in James C. Bradford, ed., *Crucible of Empire: The Spanish–American War & Its Aftermath* (Annapolis, MD: Naval Institute Press, 1993), 104.

20.   Bruce E. Bechtol Jr., *Avenging the General Sherman: The 1871 Battle of Kang Hwa Do* (Quantico, VA: Marine Corps University Foundation, 2002).

21.   Brian McAllister Linn, "America's Expeditionary War Transformation," *Naval History*, Vol. 19, Issue 5, October 2005, 58.

22.   Jack Shulimson, "Marines in the Spanish–American War," in Bradford, ed., *Crucible of Empire*, 127–157; Millett, *Semper Fidelis*, 131–134.

23.   David F. Trask, *The War With Spain in 1898* (New York, NY: Macmillan, 1981), 213–214, 353–358; Cosmas, "Joint Operations," in Bradford, ed., *Crucible of Empire,* 115–116; Jonas L. Goldstein, "*Cuba Libre!* Army–Navy Cooperation in 1898," *Joint Force Quarterly*, Summer 2000, 116–121. Graham T. Cosmas discusses the Army's attempts to procure landing craft for the operation and the use of the ship's lifeboats, Navy steam launches, and other small craft for the Daiquirí and Siboney landings in *An Army for Empire: The United States Army in the Spanish–American War,* 2d ed. (Shippensburg, PA: White Mane Publishing Company, 1994), 180–182, 192, 207–208, 233–234.

24.   Cosmas, *An Army for Empire,* 235. The communications between General Miles and the Secretary of War and other correspondence during the Puerto Rico landings are particularly informative on the technical aspects of the landing operations. These are collected in *Correspondence Relating to the War With Spain including the Insurrection in the Philippine Islands and the China Relief Expedition, April 15, 1898, to July 30, 1902*, Vol. 1 (Washington, DC: Center of Military History, United States Army, 1993), 285–338.

25.   Cosmas, *An Army for Empire*, 240; Trask, *The War with Spain,* 382–388.

26.   Trask, *The War with Spain,* 96–107; Brian McAllister Linn, *The U.S. Army and Counterinsurgency in the Philippine War, 1898–1902* (Chapel Hill, NC: University of North Carolina Press, 1989), 99, 113, 115, *et passim.*

27.   Erna Risch, *Quartermaster Support of the Army: A History of the Corps, 1775–1939* (Washington, DC: GPO, 1962), 551–555, 566–569, 609–610, 715–716. The Navy took over the fleet of transports and the US Shipping Board from 1917 to 1920. Thereafter, the Army Quartermaster Corps continued to operate

the ATS until the creation on 31 July 1942 of the Transportation Corps, which operated the ATS until it was absorbed into the MSTS in 1950. Chester Wardlow, *United States Army in World War II: The Transportation Corps: Responsibilities, Organization, and Operations* (Washington, DC: Office of the Chief of Military History, 1951), 32–33, 55; James A. Field Jr., *History of United States Naval Operations, Korea* (Washington, DC: GPO, 1962), 71–74.

28.   Vernon E. Davis, *The History of the Joint Chiefs of Staff in World War II, Organizational Development, Vol. I, Origin of the Joint and Combined Chiefs of Staff* (Washington, DC: Historical Division, Joint Secretariat, Joint Chiefs of Staff, 1972), 6–10.

29.   Legere, "Unification of the Armed Forces," 60.

30.   Jack Shulimson, *The Marine Corps Search for a Mission: 1880–1898* (Lawrence, KS: University Press of Kansas, 1993).

31.   Kenneth J. Clifford, *Progress and Purpose: A Developmental History of the United States Marine Corps, 1900–1970* (Washington, DC: History and Museums Division, US Marine Corps, 1973), 1–15; Millett, *Semper Fidelis,* 138–144, 271–276.

32.   William F. Atwater, "United States Army and Navy Development of Joint Landing Operations, 1898–1942," PhD diss., Duke University, 1986, 52–53; citing for the landing manual, War Department, *United States Army Transport Service Regulations, 1908* (Washington, DC: GPO, 1908), (Atwater notes there was an even more rudimentary section on landing operations in the 1905 version); and, for the landing exercise, "Field Exercise in Massachusetts," *Army and Navy Journal* 52 (28 August 1909): 1474–1478.

33.   Robert E. Quirk, *An Affair of Honor: Woodrow Wilson and the Occupation of Veracruz* (Lexington, KY: University of Kentucky Press, 1962), 85–155; James H. Alexander, "Roots of Deployment—Vera Cruz, 1914," in Bartlett, ed., *Assault from the Sea,* 132–141; Jack Sweetman, *The Landing at Veracruz, 1914* (Annapolis, MD: US Naval Institute, 1968).

34.   Charles B. Burdick, *The Japanese Siege of Tsingtau* (Hamden, CT: Archon Books, 1976); W.J. Davis, "Japanese Operations at Tsing Tao, 1914," in *Monographs of the World War* (Fort Benning, GA: US Army Infantry School [1923?]; Clifford Jones, "Japanese Landing at Tsing-tao," *Coast Artillery Journal,* Vol. 68, No. 6 (June 1928): 145–149.

35.   Lathrop B. Clapham, "The Gallipoli Expedition Until May 6, 1915"; and Charles E. Speer, "From Battle of Sari Bair, August 10, 1915, to include Third Phase of the Gallipoli Campaign Evacuation, January 9, 1916," in *Monographs of the World War* (Fort Benning, GA: US Army Infantry School [1923?]; Shepard L. Pike, *Landing and Operations at Gallipoli, Apr 25, 1915: Study* (Washington, DC: Army War College, 1929); and Ned B. Rehkopf, "The Landing at Gallipoli," *Coast Artillery Journal,* Vol. 68, No. 6 (June 1928): 475–491, and Vol. 69, No. 1 (July 1928): 19–35.

36.   Michael B. Barrett, *Operation ALBION: The German Conquest of the Baltic Islands* (Bloomington, IN: Indiana University Press, 2008); Robert Foley, "Ösel & Moon Islands: Operation ALBION, September 1917, The German Invasion

of the Baltic Islands," Tristan Lovering, ed., *Amphibious Assault: Manoeuvre from the Sea* (Rendlesham, Woodbridge, Suffolk, UK: Seafarer Books, 2007), 23–36.

37. Deborah Lake, *The Zeebrugge and Ostend Raids 1918* (Barnsley, South Yorkshire, UK: Leo Cooper, 2002); Barrie Pitt, *Zeebrugge* (New York, NY: Ballantine Books, 1958). This overview of World War I amphibious operations is also based on Army War College studies in the Curricular Archives at the US Army Military History Institute, Carlisle, PA, hereafter, MHI.

38. An excellent overview of amphibious warfare developments in the United States, Great Britain, and Japan is provided by Allan R. Millett, "Assault from the Sea: The Development of Amphibious Warfare Between the Wars: The American, British, and Japanese Experiences," in Williamson Murray and Allan R. Millett, eds., *Military Innovation in the Interwar Period* (Cambridge, UK: Cambridge University Press, 1996), 41–95. See also Kenneth J. Clifford, *Amphibious Warfare Development in Britain and America from 1920–1940* (New York, NY: Edgewood, 1983). Army activities are summarized in John T. Greenwood, "The U.S. Army and Amphibious Warfare During WWII," *Army History* PB-20-93-4, No. 27 (Summer 1993): 1–10. More detailed information is provided in Atwater, "Development of Joint Landing Operations." For Marine Corps developments, see Jeter A. Isely and Philip Crowl, *U.S. Marines and Amphibious War: Its Theory and Practice in the Pacific* (Princeton, NJ: Princeton University Press, 1951); Millett, *Semper Fidelis*, 319–343; and Clifford, *Progress and Purpose,* 25–59. British developments are covered by Bernard Fergusson, *The Watery Maze: Story of Combined Operations in World War II* (New York, NY: Collins, 1961), and L.E.H. Maund, *Assault from the Sea* (London: Methuen, 1949).

39. Edward S. Miller, *War Plan Orange: The U.S. Strategy to Defeat Japan 1897–1945* (Annapolis, MD: Naval Institute Press, 1991), 19–38; H.P. Willmott, *Empires in the Balance: Japanese and Allied Pacific Strategies to April 1942* (Annapolis, MD: Naval Institute Press, 1982), 106–118.

40. Brian McAllister Linn, *Guardians of Empire: The U.S. Army and the Pacific, 1902–1940* (Chapel Hill & London: The University of North Caroline Press, 1997), xii–xiii, 239–242, 254.

41. Steven T. Ross, *American War Plans, 1890–1939* (London: Frank Cass, 2002), 128–137. One of the plans for Mexico essentially recapitulated the 1847 operation, anticipating a landing at Vera Cruz followed by a march to Mexico City.

42. Davis, *History of the Joint Chiefs of Staff,* 14–15.

43. JPC Report in Joint Board Serial No. 19, "Joint Operations of Army, Navy, and Marine Corps," quoted in Legere, "Unification of the Armed Forces," 73.

44. US Joint Board of the Army and Navy, *Joint Action of the Army and the Navy (JAAN)* (Washington, DC: GPO, 1927), 4–6, and (1935 Revision), 56.

45. Change No. 2 (30 November 1938) to *JAAN,* 1935. Legere, "Unification of the Armed Forces," 149–150, describes the discussion of this issue, citing the relevant correspondence.

46. Ross, *American War Plans, 1890–1939*, 154–156.

47. Ross, *American War Plans, 1890–1939*, 164–166.

48. Leo J. Daugherty III, "Away All Boats: The Army–Navy Maneuvers of 1925," *Joint Force Quarterly*, Autumn/Winter 1998–99, 107–113.

49. US Joint Board of the Army and Navy, *Joint Overseas Expeditions* (Washington, DC: GPO, 1933).

50. Millett, "Assault from the Sea," in Murray and Millett, eds., *Military Innovation in the Interwar Period,* 72. The most detailed account of Ellis's development of the advanced base force study is Dirk Anthony Ballendorf and Merrill Lewis Bartlett, *Pete Ellis: An Amphibious Warfare Prophet, 1880–1923* (Annapolis, MD: Naval Institute Press, 1997), 119–125.

51. Clifford, *Progress and Purpose,* 30.

52. *JAAN,* 1927, 3, 12.

53. Clifford, *Progress and Purpose,* 46; Anthony A. Frances, *History of the Marine Corps Schools* (Quantico, VA: Marine Corps Schools, 1945).

54. US Navy, *The Landing-Force and Small-Arms Instructions,* 1905 and 1907 (with corrections to pages 293–352 of 1910 and 1911 versions), 1912, and 1915. In 1918 the document was reissued with a new title, *Landing-Force Manual, United States Navy.* This was the first major revision with much more detail on tactics, conduct of fire, and field fortifications, but the flotilla of boats with line of columns of towed boats was essentially unchanged from 1905. The 1920 version contained a new chapter on "Minor Warfare," but otherwise had few changes. The 1927 version was revised to be in agreement with US Army Training Regulations for Infantry, machinegun units, and combat principles, but was unchanged with regard to the actual movement of troops from ship to shore. This was the version still in effect when the 1933 Marine Corps schools' study began. A whaleboat was a large, long, narrow, highly maneuverable rowing or motor boat carried aboard US warships. It was similar to the 19th century boats used to hunt whales.

55. Isely and Crowl, *U.S. Marines and Amphibious War,* 35–44. The final prewar version was published on 25 November 1938 as Fleet Training Publication 167, *Landing Operations Doctrine, U.S. Navy* (FTP-167). Clifford provides a chronology in *Progress and Purpose,* appendix F, 139–140.

56. Millett, "Assault from the Sea," in Murray and Millett, eds., *Military Innovation in the Interwar Period,* 76–77.

57. Greenwood, "The U.S. Army and Amphibious Warfare During WWII," 1–10; Henry G. Gole, "War Planning at the U.S. Army War College, 1934–40, 'The Road to Rainbow'," *Army History* 25 (Winter 1993): 13–28.

58. See, for example, Pike, *Landing and Operations at Gallipoli;* and Clapham, "The Gallipoli Expedition Until May 6, 1915," in *Monographs of the World War,* 92–108.

59. Atwater, "Development of Joint Landing Operations," 44–45.

60. R.G. Kirkwood, "Artillery Loads for Navy Lighter for Landing Heavy Artillery" (Fort Leavenworth, KS: The General Service Schools, 20 June 1928), MHI Archives, Box: CGSC Curricular Material 1927–28.

61. US Army War College, "Course at the Army War College, 1929–1930, G1"; Report of Committee No. 8: "Joint Army and Navy Landing Operations;

Modification in Training, Equipment, and Supply for Long Overseas Expeditions, and Operations in Specific Theaters; and Principles Governing the Construction of War Plans, Including Joint Army and Navy War Plans," 26 October 1929. No. 361-8, MHI Archives, Box: AWC Curricular Archives, 1929–30, G1 Course, Files No. 361, 1–8 to File No. 361A, 1–5.

62. These reports are in the Curricular Archives at MHI. See also General Eli K. Cole and Major Watkins, *Joint Overseas Operations, Overseas Expedition: A Compilation of Joint Articles by General Cole, Major Watkins* (Fort Humphreys, VA: US Army Engineer School, 1932). In 1929 Cole had published an article on joint overseas operations envisioning Army troops as the landing force. In the 1930s George S. Patton, examining ways to defend Hawaii against amphibious invasion, studied the Gallipoli operation in depth. The knowledge of amphibious warfare he gained in this study was one of the reasons he was selected to command an Army landing force in the 1942 North Africa landings. Martin Blumenson, *The Patton Papers, 1885–1940,* Vol. 1 (Boston, MA: Houghton Mifflin, 1972), 819–820, 912–916.

63. US Army War College, "Course at the Army War College, 1939–1940, Analytical Studies: Report of Committee No. 8, Joint Operations of the Army and the Navy," 6–1940-8, 28 February 1940, MHI Archives, Box: AWC Curricular Archives, 1939–40, Analytical Course, File No. 6–1940–7 to 6–1940–9, File No. 6–1940A, 1–14.

64. US War Department, The Adjutant General's Office, "Notes on Fleet Landing Exercise No. 2, Culebra, P.R.," AG 354.23 (3–24–36), 30 March 1936, copy at MHI.

65. Millett, "Assault from the Sea," in Murray and Millett, eds., *Military Innovation in the Interwar Period,* 76; Isely and Crowl, *The U.S. Marines and Amphibious War,* 46, 52.

66. Atwater, "Development of Joint Landing Operations," 109–110.

67. Atwater, "Development of Joint Landing Operations," 5; Blanche D. Coll, Jean E. Keith, and Herbert H. Rosenthal, *United States Army in World War II, The Corps of Engineers: Troops and Equipment* (Washington, DC: Historical Division, Department of the Army, 1958), 356–357; John B. Dwyer, *Commandos from the Sea: The History of Amphibious Special Warfare in World War II and the Korean War* (Boulder, CO: Paladin Press, 2002), 5.

68. This account is based on Ross, *American War Plans, 1941–1945,* 3–18; Mark Skinner Watson, *United States Army in World War II, The War Department, Chief of Staff; Prewar Plans and Preparations* (Washington, DC: Department of the Army Historical Division, 1950); Maurice Matloff and Edwin M. Snell, *United States Army in World War II, The War Department, Strategic Planning For Coalition Warfare: 1941–1942* (Washington, DC: Historical Division, Department of the Army, 1953), 5–8, 12–13, 24–28, 43–47; Legere, "Unification of the Armed Forces," 184–201.

69. Anne Cipriano Venzon, *From Whaleboats to Amphibious Warfare: Lt. Gen. "Howling Mad" Smith and the U.S. Marine Corps* (London and Westport, CT: Praeger, 2003), 67–68.

70. Atwater, "Development of Joint Landing Operations," 122–126. The Army did provide observers to the Navy–Marine Corps exercise that year.

71. Dwyer, *Commandos from the Sea,* 5.

72. Kent Roberts Greenfield, Robert R. Palmer, and Bell I. Wiley, *United States Army in World War II, The Army Ground Forces, The Organization of Ground Combat Troops* (Washington, DC: Historical Division, Department of the Army, 1947), 32, 85; Atwater, "Development of Joint Landing Operations," 127–129.

73. The Coast Guard would ultimately man large numbers of amphibious ships and craft and would participate in every major amphibious operation of World War II. Gary J.E. Thornton, *The U.S. Coast Guard and Army Amphibious Development,* US Army War College Military Studies Program Paper (Carlisle Barracks, PA: US Army War College, 1987), 5, 6, handle.dtic.mil/100.2/ ADA180972 (accessed 11 February 2008). The Thornton monograph is a well-documented and valuable summary of Coast Guard involvement in amphibious operations that makes use of primary sources from the Coast Guard files. See also, Malcolm F. Willoughby, *The U.S. Coast Guard in World War II* (Annapolis, MD: United States Naval Institute, 1957), 8–9, for prewar Coast Guard activities.

74. The establishment and operation of General Chaney's Special Observers is described in Charles L. Bolte, "History of First Days in England, 1941–1942" [1945?], ii–iv, 4, 27–35, copy in the Charles L. Bolte Papers, Box 3, MHI Archives; US Department of the Army, Office of Military History, *The Administration and Logistical History of the ETO, Part I, The Predecessor Commands: SPOBS and USAFBI,* 1945, copy at MHI in Box, "OCMH IIIA, Drafts, WWII, Admin & Log Hist ETO, Part I," 1–44, MHI Archives; Gordon A. Harrison, *United States Army in World War II, The European Theater of Operations, Cross-Channel Attack* (Washington, DC: Historical Division, Department of the Army, 1951), 1–2. The operation of the Army Special Observers group is also described retrospectively by General Bolte, who was Chaney's plans officer and later chief of staff, in his oral history, *Conversations Between General Charles L. Bolte, USA, Ret., and Mr. Arthur J. Zoebelein,* 3 vols., US Army Military History Research Collection, Senior Officers Debriefing Program (Carlisle Barracks, PA: Military History Institute, 1972), Vol. 1, Section 1, 72–80, and Vol. I, Section 2, 6–13, 55–61, copy in the Charles L. Bolte Papers, Box 17, "Oral History Interview" Part I, MHI Archives.

75. Ross, *American War Plans 1941–1945,* 16–17.

76. Linn, *Guardians of the Empire,* 244–245.

77. Letter, Major General Lesley J. McNair to Major General C.F. Thompson, 10 March 1941, quoted in Greenfield, Palmer, and Wiley, *Organization of Ground Combat Troops,* 38.

78. Coll, Keith, and Rosenthal, *The Corps of Engineers: Troops and Equipment,* 357–358; Headquarters, Department of the Army, Field Manual (FM) 31-5, *Landing Operations on Hostile Shores* (Washington, DC: GPO, 1941).

79. Greenfield, Palmer, and Wiley, *Organization of Ground Combat Troops,* 85; Atwater, "Development of Joint Landing Operations," 130–136. Two Coast Guard cutters had participated in FLEX 6 and five of the Navy assault transports

used in FLEX 7 carried temporarily assigned Coast Guard landing craft crews. During this exercise, the Coast Guard also took over the operation of three Army transports previously manned by civilian crews that refused to operate under simulated combat conditions. Thornton, *Coast Guard and Army Amphibious Development,* 6–7, 9; Robert Erwin Johnson, *Coast Guard-Manned Naval Vessels in World War II,* US Coast Guard Historian's Office, www.uscg.mil/hq/g-cp/history/h_cgnvy.html (accessed 9 February 2008).

80.   Norman Friedman and A.D. Baker, *U.S. Amphibious Ships and Craft: An Illustrated Design History* (Annapolis, MD: Naval Institute Press, 2002), 33–35, 195–197; James C. Fahey, *Ships and Aircraft of the United States Fleet, 1945* (New York, NY: Ships and Aircraft, 1945, reprinted Annapolis, MD: Naval Institute Press, 1976), 26–30, 64, 76. APD was the Navy designation for auxiliary (A) transport (P) destroyer (D), but the ships were universally known as fast transports or high-speed transports. Jon T. Hoffman relates the development of the APDs, initially in conjunction with the formation of the Marine Raider battalion in *From Makin to Bougainville: Marine Raiders in the Pacific War* (Washington, DC: Marine Corps Historical Center, 1993); and in "The Legacy and Lessons of WW II Raids," *Marine Corps Gazette* (September 1992): 62–65.

81.   Friedman and Baker, *U.S. Amphibious Ships and Craft,* 3, 37–65; Frederic L. Lane, *Ships for Victory, A History of Shipbuilding Under the U.S. Maritime Commission in World War II* (Baltimore, MD: The Johns Hopkins University Press, 1951), *passim.*

82.   Friedman and Baker, *U.S. Amphibious Ships and Craft,* 67–101; John W. Mountcastle, "From Bayou to Beachhead: The Marines and Mr. Higgins," *Military Review* 60 (March 1980): 20–29; Jerry E. Strahan, *Andrew Jackson Higgins and The Boats That Won World War II* (Baton Rouge, LA: Louisiana State University Press, 1994).

83.   Friedman and Baker, *U.S. Amphibious Ships and Craft,* 99–100; Victor J. Croizat, one of the Marine Corps LVT pioneers, describes the development and operational use of the LVTs, and provides a fine account of amphibious operations in World War II, in *Across the Reef: The Amphibious Tracked Vehicle at War* (Quantico, VA: Marine Corps Association, 1989, reprinted London: Blandford, 1992), 31–32.

84.   Maund, *Assault from the Sea,* 9–19, 24–59, 65–82, 112–113 (Admiral Maund was the Director of the ISTDC); *ONI 226 Allied Landing Craft and Ships* (Washington, DC: Office of Naval Intelligence, Navy Department, 1944), reprinted as *Allied Landing Craft of World War II* (Annapolis, MD: Naval Institute Press, 1985); Friedman and Baker, *U.S. Amphibious Ships and Craft,* 111–120. See also, Fergusson, *Watery Maze.*

85.   Williamson Murray and Allan R. Millett provide an excellent single-volume account of World War II: *A War to be Won; Fighting the Second World War, 1937–1945* (Cambridge, MA: Belknap Press of Harvard University Press, 2000). Still useful for an Army-focused concise account with emphasis on strategy is Maurice Matloff, *World War II: A Concise Military History of America's*

All-Out, Two-Front War (New York, NY: Galahad Books, 1982) (extracted from his *American Military History* [Washington, DC: GPO, 1988]).

86. Allied strategy for the Pacific during this period is described in Grace P. Hayes, *The History of the Joint Chiefs of Staff in World War II: The War Against Japan*, Vol. 1 (Washington, DC: Historical Section, Joint Chiefs of Staff, 1953), 45–186; Willmott, *Empires in the Balance*, 181–197, 218–238, and 255–282; and Matloff and Snell, *Strategic Planning For Coalition Warfare: 1941–1942*, 120–164.

87. Bolte, "History of First Days in England," 84; Lucian K. Truscott, *Command Missions: A Personal Story* (New York, NY: E.P. Dutton and Company, 1954), 17–72. Truscott would later participate in every amphibious operation in the Mediterranean, commanding a regimental task force in the Morocco landing at Port Lyautey; the 3d Division at Sicily, Salerno, and Anzio; and the VI Corps in Southern France. He ended the war as a lieutenant general and was promoted to full general in 1954. MHI biographical file.

88. A unified command was (and is) a command with a broad continuing mission under a single commander and composed of significant assigned components of two or more military departments. The Pearl Harbor attack had revealed the problems with Service coordination through mutual cooperation at the geographical theater level and the unified commanders established in 1942 had authority over the assigned forces of both Services. In June another unified command, the European Theater of Operations, was established under the command of Lieutenant General Dwight D. Eisenhower. Matloff and Snell, *Strategic Planning For Coalition Warfare: 1941–1942*, 168–169, 196–197.

89. Matloff and Snell, *Strategic Planning For Coalition Warfare: 1941–1942*, 256–263.

90. Matloff and Snell, *Strategic Planning For Coalition Warfare: 1941–1942*, 244–255, 265, 279–286.

91. John Miller Jr., *United States Army in World War II, The War in the Pacific, Guadalcanal: The First Offensive* (Washington, DC: Historical Division, Department of the Army, 1949), 19.

92. Coll, Keith, and Rosenthal, *The Corps of Engineers: Troops and Equipment*, 538–359. These views were expressed, among other places, in a study of 3d Infantry Division amphibious training by Lieutenant Colonel Floyd L. Parks, deputy chief of staff of Army Ground Forces (AGF), and in a memorandum by Major General John P. Lucas, then commander of the 3d Infantry Division (and later commander of VI Corps at the February 1944 Anzio landing) to the Commanding General of AGF, quoted in Marshall O. Becker, *The Amphibious Training Center*, Study No. 22 (Washington, DC: Historical Section, Army Ground Forces, 1946), 1–2. General H.M. Smith's life and personality are described in Venzon, *From Whaleboats to Amphibious Warfare*. General Smith tells his own story in Holland M. Smith, *Coral and Brass* (New York, NY: Scribner's, 1949).

93. Becker, *The Amphibious Training Center*, 1–3; Coll, Keith, and Rosenthal, *The Corps of Engineers: Troops and Equipment*, 357–359; Thornton,

Coast Guard and Army Amphibious Development, 9–10, 16–17. In September 1941 the Commandant of the Coast Guard had agreed to provide over 2,000 Coast Guard officers and men to operate as part of the Navy, including the operation of four transports, with their assigned landing craft, as well as the landing craft aboard 22 other Navy transports and other ships.

94. Becker, *The Amphibious Training Center,* 3–7; Coll, Keith, and Rosenthal, *The Corps of Engineers: Troops and Equipment,* 359–362. AGF and Services of Supply (later renamed Army Service Forces) were established in March 1942 as part of a reorganization of the War Department. Ray S. Cline, *United States Army in World War II, The War Department, Washington Command Post: The Operations Division* (Washington, DC: Office of the Chief of Military History, Department of the Army, 1951), 93. See also, US Army Recruiting, Publicity Bureau, "Put 'em Across! That is the Slogan of the Army Engineer Amphibian Command," *Army Life and United States Army Recruiting News,"* Vol. XXIV, No. 8, August 1942, 2, 3, 14.

95. Coll, Keith, and Rosenthal, *The Corps of Engineers: Troops and Equipment,* 361–365; William F. Heavey, *Down Ramp! The Story of the Army Amphibian Engineers* (Washington, DC: Infantry Journal Press, 1947, reprinted, Nashville, TN: Battery Press, 1988), 1–13. (Brigadier General Heavey commanded the 2d Engineer Amphibious (later Special) Brigade during its entire World War II service.)

96. Becker, *The Amphibious Training Center,* 10; Merle T. Cole, "Cape Cod Commando Training," *Military Collector & Historian,* Vol. 58, No. 2 (Summer 2006): 95–101.

97. Thornton describes the Coast Guard participation in *Coast Guard and Army Amphibious Development,* 16–27.

98. Becker, *The Amphibious Training Center,* 10–17; Coll, Keith, and Rosenthal, *The Corps of Engineers: Troops and Equipment,* 369–372, 376–379.

99. A regimental combat team was an infantry regiment reinforced with a field artillery battalion (FAB), a combat engineer company, and other combat and support elements capable of operating as a self-contained combat unit.

100. Arthur G. Trudeau, *Engineer Memoirs,* "Oral History of Lieutenant General Arthur G. Trudeau," EP 870–1–26 (Fort Belvoir, VA: US Army Corps of Engineers, Office of the Chief of Engineers, 1986), 75–111; Coll, Keith, and Rosenthal, *The Corps of Engineers: Troops and Equipment,* 376–387.

101. Copies of the manuals are in RG 337 (Records of Headquarters, Army Ground Forces), Entry 32A (G4 Administrative Division Decimal File 1947), Box 67, National Archives and Records Administration, Modern Military Records, College Park, MD, hereafter, NACP.

102. Becker, *The Amphibious Training Center,* 4–17; "Unit History of Amphibious Training Command, U.S. Atlantic Fleet," attached to Letter, Commander Amphibious Training Command, US Atlantic Fleet, to Chief of Naval Operations, same subject, 5 November 1953, copy provided to the author by Captain Patrick H. Roth, USN (Ret), Center for Naval Analyses. The Fort Pierce facility was initially organized by the G2 of Amphibious Corps, Atlantic

Fleet, Lieutenant Colonel Louis B. Ely, who would later organize an amphibious special operations force in the early days of the Korean War. "Louis Brainard Ely," biography at Arlington National Cemetery Web site, arlingtoncemetery.net/lely.htm (accessed 10 July 2006); West Point *Register of Graduates and Former Cadets, Class of 1919*; Dwyer, *Commandos from the Sea*, 8, 243. Ely's correspondence on scout and raider operations is in the *Lloyd E. Peddicord Papers*, Box 14, MHI Archives.

103. The Army had contributed to the development of these ships. A key issue was ventilation of the tank deck so tanks could warm up their engines prior to a landing without suffocating the crews. In the spring of 1942, Army carpenters built a structure at Fort Knox, Kentucky, that duplicated the interior of an LST. Using actual tanks, a Navy design group tested various systems before deciding on large exhaust fans that effectively kept the tank deck clear of fumes. Paul W. Urbahns, "Ft. Knox's Ark: The LST Building," www.aths.com/history-ftknox.html (accessed 28 February 2008). I am indebted to David Keough of MHI for bringing this interesting sidelight to my attention.

104. Friedman and Baker, *U.S. Amphibious Ships and Craft*, 120–121, 130–139, 207, 483, 485.

105. Friedman and Baker, *U.S. Amphibious Ships and Craft*, 138–148.

106. Friedman and Baker, *U.S. Amphibious Ships and Craft*, 202–205, 246–249.

107. Timothy J. Kutta, Don Geer, and Perry Manley, "DUKW in Action," *Armor* Number 36 (Carrollton, TX: Squadron/Signal Publications, 1996).

108. For a good one-volume account of World War II amphibious operations, see John A. Lorelli, *To Foreign Shores: U.S. Amphibious Operations in World War II* (Annapolis, MD: Naval Institute Press, 1995). Gordon L. Rottman covers amphibious tactics in *US World War II Amphibious Tactics: Army & Marine Corps, Pacific Theater*, Elite No. 117 (Botley, UK: Osprey Publishing, 2004), and *US World War II Amphibious Tactics: Mediterranean & European Theaters*, Elite 144 (Oxford, UK: Osprey Publications, 2006). Jon T. Hoffman wrote a series of excellent analyses of all the major World War II Army and Marine Corps amphibious operations that appeared in *Marine Corps Gazette* between 1992 and 1995 (see the bibliography). Richard B. Frank provides a useful compressed history of the development of amphibious warfare in World War II (but almost completely ignores the Southwest Pacific Area and the ESBs) in "The Amphibious Revolution," *Naval History*, Vol. 19, No. 4, August 2005, 20–26. Amphibious operations in the Mediterranean Theater are well covered in Barbara Brooks Tomblin, *With Utmost Spirit: Allied Naval Operations in the Mediterranean, 1942–1945* (Lexington, KY: University Press of Kentucky, 2004). See also the series of case studies in Lovering, ed., *Amphibious Assault*.

109. Samuel Milner, *United States Army in World War II, The War in the Pacific, Victory in Papua* (Washington, DC: Historical Division, Department of the Army, 1957); Charles R. Anderson, *The U.S. Army Campaigns of World War II: Papua*, CMH Pub 72-7 (Washington, DC: GPO, 1992). On the use of coastal shipping, see Harry A. Gailey, *MacArthur Strikes Back: Decision at Buna New*

Guinea 1942–1943 (Novato, CA: Presidio Press, 2000), 73–74; D. Clayton James, *The Years of MacArthur, Vol. II, 1941–1945* (Boston, MA: Houghton Mifflin Company, 1975), 211–220.

110. The official accounts of Guadalcanal are Frank O. Hough, Ludwig E. Verle, and Henry I. Shaw, *History of the United States Marine Corps Operations in World War II, Vol. I, Pearl Harbor to Guadalcanal* (Washington, DC: Historical Branch, G3 Division, Headquarters, United States Marine Corps, 1958), and Miller, *Guadalcanal: The First Offensive.* See also, Charles R. Anderson, *The U.S. Army Campaigns of World War II: Guadalcanal,* CMH Pub 72-8 (Washington, DC: GPO, n.d.); Lorelli, *To Foreign Shores,* 43–57; Richard B. Frank, *Guadalcanal* (New York, NY: Random House, 1990); and Isely and Crowl, *U.S. Marines and Amphibious War,* 109–165.

111. Isely and Crowl, *U.S. Marines and Amphibious War,* 153–162; Creswell, *Generals and Admirals,* 159–160.

112. Hoffman, *From Makin to Bougainville,* 6–9.

113. Address by Commodore J. Hughes-Hallett (Naval Force Commander at Dieppe) and Address by Major General Hamilton Roberts (Military Force Commander in the Dieppe Operation) at the Assault Training Center Conference, 26 May 1943, 7 June 1943, in *Conference on Landing Assaults, 24 May–23 June 1943,* US Assault Training Center, European Theater of Operations, United States Army, 1943; Fergusson, *Watery Maze,* 168–185. Lorelli provides a concise summary of the Dieppe operation, *To Foreign Shores,* 58–60. For a critical account of the planning for the raid that assesses it as a tragic "failure of decision making," see Brian Loring Villa, *Unauthorized Action: Mountbatten and the Dieppe Raid* (Oxford, UK: Oxford University Press, 1989). For an argument that the "useful lessons" of the operation have been overstated, see Stephen Prince, "The Raids on St. Nazaire and Dieppe: Operation CHARIOT, March 1942 and Operation JUBILEE, August 1942," Lovering, ed., *Amphibious Assault,* 123–125, 130–144.

114. Stetson Conn, Rose C. Engelman, and Byron Fairchild, *United States Army in World War II, The Western Hemisphere, Guarding the United States and its Outposts* (Washington, DC: Historical Division, Department of the Army, 1960), 270–272; Samuel Eliot Morison, *History of United States Naval Operations in World War II, Vol. 7, Aleutians, Gilberts and Marshalls, June 1942–April 1944* (Boston, MA: Little, Brown and Company, 1960), 12–13; Brian Garfield, *The Thousand-Mile War: World War II in Alaska and the Aleutians* (Garden City, NY: Doubleday, 1969), 151–161.

115. The official Army account is George F. Howe, *United States Army in World War II, The Mediterranean Theater of Operations, Northwest Africa: Seizing the Initiative in the West* (Washington, DC: Historical Division, Department of the Army, 1957). A concise account is Charles R. Anderson, *The U.S. Army Campaigns of World War II: Algeria-French Morocco,* CMH Pub 72-11 (Washington, DC: GPO, n.d.). Rick Atkinson provides a thoroughly researched and lively account in *An Army at Dawn: The War in North Africa* (New York, NY: Henry Holt & Co., 2002). See also Samuel Eliot Morison, *History of United States Naval Operations*

in World War II, Operations in North African Waters, October 1942–June 1943 (Boston, MA: Little, Brown, & Company, 1989); Tomblin, *With Utmost Spirit,* 23–80; Lorelli, *To Foreign Shores,* 61–84; Jon T. Hoffman, "The Legacy and Lessons of Operation TORCH," *Marine Corps Gazette,* December 1992, 60–63.

116. Maurice Matloff, *United States Army in World War II, The War Department, Strategic Planning For Coalition Warfare: 1943–1944* (Washington, DC: Historical Division, Department of the Army, 1959), 36–37.

117. *Fifth Army History, Part I, From Activation to the Fall of Naples* (Florence, Italy: Headquarters, Fifth Army, 1945), 6.

118. John W. O'Daniel, Memorandum, "Invasion Training Center," 1 November 1943, copy in the John W. O'Daniel Papers, Box 4, "WWII Operation 'Husky' 3d and 45th Div, 1942–1943," MHI Archives, 1.

119. O'Daniel, Memorandum, 1, 2; Truscott, *Command Missions,* 182–185.

120. William S. Triplet, *A Colonel in the Armored Forces: A Memoir, 1941–1945,* ed. Robert H. Ferrell (Columbia, MO: University of Missouri Press, 2001), 45–93. The *William S. Triplet Papers* in the MHI Archives includes Triplet's lively and detailed journal, as well as other documents on the 18th Armored Group (Amphibious). The LVT1, LVT2, LVT3, and LVT4 were various types of personnel and cargo carrying amphibious tractors. The designation LVT(A), or "armored amphibian," generally referred to amphibious tanks mounting a 37-mm gun, the LVT(A)1; or a 75-mm howitzer, the LVT(A)4; but was also used for the Army's armored version of the cargo/personnel amphibious tractor, the LVT(A)2. The final version of the armored amphibian, the LVT(A)5, had a gyro-stabilized howitzer that could be fired accurately even while moving. It was introduced at the end of the war and served in Korea. Croizat, *Across the Reef;* Robert J. Ickes, *Landing Vehicles Tracked* (Windsor, UK: Profile Publications, n.d.); Steven J. Zaloga, Terry Hadler, and Mike Badrocke, *Amtracs: US Amphibious Assault Vehicles,* New Vanguard 30 (Oxford, UK: Osprey Publications, 1999).

121. General Krueger's own account of the war in SWPA is Walter Krueger, *From Down Under to Nippon: The Story of Sixth Army in World War II* (Washington, DC: Combat Forces Press, 1953); for an account of Krueger's leadership, see Kevin Holzimmer, *General Walter Krueger: Unsung Hero of the Pacific War* (Lawrence, KS: University of Kansas Press, 2007). Admiral Barbey has described the operations of his amphibious force in Daniel E. Barbey, *MacArthur's Amphibious Navy: Seventh Amphibious Force Operations, 1943–1945* (Annapolis, MD: US Naval Institute, 1969). General Heavey tells the story of the amphibious engineers in *Down Ramp!;* see also, Karl C. Dod, *United States Army in World War II, The Corps of Engineers: The War Against Japan* (Washington, DC: Historical Division, Department of the Army, 1966).

122. US Army Forces, Pacific, General Headquarters, Office of the Chief Engineer, *Engineers of the Southwest Pacific, Vol. IV, Amphibian Engineer Operations* (Washington, DC: GPO, 1959), 38–48.

123. John Miller Jr., *United States Army in World War II, The War in the Pacific, Cartwheel: The Reduction of Rabaul* (Washington, DC: Historical Division, Department of the Army, 1959), 19–27.

124. William F. Heavey, "Amphibian Engineers in Action," *Military Engineer,* Vol. XXXVI, No. 223, May 1944, 145–151; Miller, *Cartwheel;* Edward J. Drea, *The U.S. Army Campaigns of World War II: New Guinea,* CMH Pub 72-9 (Washington, DC: GPO, n.d.); Stephen J. Lofgren, *The U.S. Army Campaigns of World War II: Northern Solomons,* CMH Pub 72-10 (Washington, DC: GPO, n.d.); Douglas T. Kane and Henry I. Shaw, *History of the United States Marine Corps Operations in World War II, Vol. II, Isolation of Rabaul* (Washington, DC: Historical Branch, G3 Division, Headquarters, United States Marine Corps, 1958).

125. US Army Forces, Pacific, *Amphibian Engineer Operations,* 146, 156, 723–729.

126. These operations are described in Garfield, *The Thousand-Mile War;* Conn, Engelman, and Fairchild, *Guarding the United States and its Outposts;* and Morison, *Aleutians, Gilberts and Marshalls.*

127. The official Army account is Albert N. Garland and Howard McGaw Smyth, *United States Army in World War II, The Mediterranean Theater of Operations, Sicily and the Surrender of Italy* (Washington, DC: Historical Division, Department of the Army, 1965). See also, Carlo D'Este, *Bitter Victory: The Battle for Sicily* (New York, NY: E.P. Dutton, 1988); Tomblin, *With Utmost Spirit,* 148–194; Lorelli, *To Foreign Shores,* 123–133.

128. Friedman and Baker, *U.S. Amphibious Ships and Craft,* 264. AGC stood for Miscellaneous Auxiliary (AG), Command (C), but the ships were always referred to as "Amphibious Force Flagships." Although *Ancon* was the fourth AGC built, it was the first to see service.

129. Tomblin, *With Utmost Spirit,* 138–139; Lorelli, *To Foreign Shores,* 132–133.

130. The official Army account is Martin Blumenson, *United States Army in World War II, The Mediterranean Theater of Operations, Salerno to Cassino* (Washington, DC: Historical Division, Department of the Army, 1969). See also, Tomblin, *With Utmost Spirit,* 241–267; Lorelli, *To Foreign Shores,* 133–155.

131. Matloff, *Strategic Planning for Coalition Warfare, 1943–1944,* 133–139, 234–235, 374–377; Croizat, *Across the Reef,* 97–99; Philip A. Crowl and Edmund G. Love, *United States Army in World War II, The War in the Pacific, Seizure of the Gilberts and Marshalls* (Washington, DC: Historical Division, Department of the Army, 1955, reprinted 1985, 1989, 1995); Morison, *History of United States Naval Operations in World War II, Aleutians, Gilberts and Marshalls;* Henry I. Shaw, Bernard C. Nalty, and Edwin C. Turnbladh, *History of the United States Marine Corps Operations in World War II, Vol. III, Central Pacific Drive* (Washington, DC: Historical Branch, G3 Division, Headquarters, United States Marine Corps, 1966).

132. Crowl and Love, *Seizure of the Gilberts and Marshalls,* 34–36.

133. Joseph H. Alexander, *Utmost Savagery: The Three Days of Tarawa* (Annapolis, MD: Naval Institute Press, 1995). The Makin Operation is covered in Crowl and Love, *Seizure of the Gilberts and Marshalls,* 75–126.

134. Crowl and Love, *Seizure of the Gilberts and Marshalls,* 126. General H.M. Smith appears to have developed a very critical attitude toward the 27th

Infantry Division that began with the Makin Operation. While the 165th RCT's capture of the island was not particularly speedy, historian Harry A. Gailey, after studying the records of the operation, noted that the 165th accomplished all of its objectives on the island on time. Harry A. Gailey, *"Howlin' Mad" vs. The Army: Conflict in Command, Saipan 1944* (Novato, CA: Presidio Press, 1986).

135. This discussion of lessons learned is taken from Lewis Bernstein, *Learning and Transmitting Lessons in the Pacific War: From GALVANIC to FLINTLOCK, November 1943–February 1944,* unpublished paper prepared for the Conference of Army Historians, 13–15 July 2004. Copy provided to the writer by Dr. Bernstein. On pallets, see Crowl and Love, *Seizure of the Gilberts and Marshalls,* 48–49.

136. Miller, *Cartwheel,* 295–302; Heavey, *Down Ramp!,* 110–111.

137. US Department of the Army, Office of Military History, *Anzio Beachhead, 22 January–25 May 1944* (Washington, DC: GPO, 1948).

138. Clayton D. Laurie, *The U.S. Army Campaigns of World War II: Anzio,* CMH Pub 72-19 (Washington, DC: GPO, n.d.), 23.

139. Crowl and Love, *Seizure of the Gilberts and Marshalls,* 219–332; Robert D. Heinl and John A Crown, *The Marshalls: Increasing the Tempo* (Washington, DC: Historical Division, Headquarters, United States Marine Corps, 1954).

140. Bernstein, *From GALVANIC to FLINTLOCK,* 14–15; Crowl and Love, *Seizure of the Gilberts and Marshalls,* 172–180, 183–193; Alfred D. Bailey, *Alligators, Buffaloes and Bushmasters: The History of the Development of the LVT Through World War II,* Occasional Paper (Washington, DC: History and Museums Division, Headquarters, US Marine Corps, 1986), 100–105, 129–135; A.V. Arnold, "Preparation for a Division Amphibious Operation," *Military Review,* Vol. XXV, No. 2 (May 1945): 3–11; George C. Dyer, *The Amphibians Came to Conquer: The Story of Admiral Richmond Kelly Turner, Vol. 2* (Washington, DC: GPO, 1972), 743–748; Shaw, Nalty, and Turnbladh, *History of the United States Marine Corps Operations in World War II, Vol. III,* 134, 175.

141. Dyer, *The Amphibians Came to Conquer,* 733.

142. John Miller Jr., "MacArthur and the Admiralties," in Kent Roberts Greenfield, ed., *Command Decisions* (New York, NY: Harcourt, Brace, 1959), 287–302; concerning the intelligence picture, see Edward J. Drea, *MacArthur's ULTRA: Codebreaking and the War Against Japan, 1942–1945* (Lawrence, KS: University of Kansas Press, 1992), 97–104.

143. Robert Ross Smith, *United States Army in World War II, The War in the Pacific, The Approach to the Philippines* (Washington, DC: Historical Division, Department of the Army, 1953), 11–12.

144. Smith, *United States Army in World War II,* 53–83; Drea, *New Guinea,* 18–25; Barbey, *MacArthur's Amphibious Navy,* 215; US Army Forces, Pacific, *Engineers of the Southwest Pacific, Vol. IV, Amphibian Engineer Operations,* 141, 450–451.

145. Louis Morton, *United States Army in World War II, The War in the Pacific, Strategy and Command: The First Two Years* (Washington, DC: Historical Division, Department of the Army, 1962), 247–248, 403–408.

146. Miller, *Cartwheel,* 26.

147. Kevin Holzimmer describes this process in *General Walter Krueger* and, more specifically, in "Joint Operations in the Southwest Pacific, 1943–1945," *Joint Force Quarterly,* Issue 38, 102–108. He ascribes the success of the system to the seminar system of cooperation in planning developed and inculcated at the Army and Navy War Colleges in the interwar years.

148. The writer has found no specific document making this link, but the record indicates that MacArthur's GHQ FEC staff frequently examined the SWPA experience: RG 554 (Records of GHQ FEC), Entry 50, ACofS G3, Training Division Memorandums (Action File), NACP.

149. Krueger, *From Down Under to Nippon,* 75.

150. Stephen R. Taaffe makes this argument in *MacArthur's Jungle War: The 1944 New Guinea Campaign* (Lawrence, KS: University of Kansas Press, 1998), 27–28.

151. Admiral Barbey describes this three-fold planning system in *MacArthur's Amphibious Navy,* 179–182. John A. Lorelli quotes from the oral history of an officer on Barbey's staff who describes the system and notes the contrast between SWPA and the Central Pacific in *To Foreign Shores,* 211–212.

152. Philip A. Crowl, *United States Army in World War II, The War in the Pacific, Campaign in the Marianas* (Washington, DC: Historical Division, Department of the Army, 1960), 81–83, 96; Russell A. Gugeler, *Army Amphibian Tractor and Tank Battalions in the Battle of Saipan, 15 June–9 July 1944,* US Army Center of Military History, army.mil/cmh-pg/documents/WWII/amsai.htm (accessed 25 October 2006). The official Marine Corps account is Shaw, Nalty, and Turnbladh, *Central Pacific Drive.* See also Carl W. Hoffman, *Saipan: The Beginning of the End* (Washington, DC: Historical Division, Headquarters, United States Marine Corps, 1950, reprinted Nashville, TN: Battery Press, 1988).

153. Crowl, *Campaign in the Marianas,* 99–101.

154. The official Army historian's account is in Crowl, *Campaign in the Marianas,* 149–151, 178–179, 191–201. Crowl's conclusion is "that Holland Smith had good reason to be disappointed with the performance of the 27th Infantry Division . . . whether the action he took to remedy the situation was a wise one, however, remains doubtful," 201. To get the full flavor of the situation on Saipan and the immediate aftermath of the incident, the reader should begin with the official Army and Marine Corps accounts by Crowl and Carl W. Hoffman. Harry A. Gailey provides a well-researched account that is sympathetic to Ralph Smith in *Howlin' Mad vs. the Army.* The series of *Infantry Journal* articles and letters to the editor cited in the bibliography are also essential reading on this complex and controversial incident. H.M. Smith's own account is in *Coral and Brass,* 171–173. Anne Cipriano Venzon gives a good account of the aftermath of the incident in *From Whaleboats to Amphibious Warfare,* 111–115. Harold J. Goldberg provides a thoughtful account of the entire Saipan campaign and the "Smiths" episode in *D-Day in the Pacific: The Battle of Saipan* (Bloomington and Indianapolis: Indiana University Press, 2007).

155. Crowl, *Campaign in the Marianas,* 285–303 (Tinian), 339–437 (Guam);

Charles R. Anderson, *The U.S. Army Campaigns of World War II: Western Pacific,* CMH Pub 72-29 (Washington, DC: GPO, n.d.).

156. The literature on the Normandy invasion is immense. The official Army account is Harrison, *Cross-Channel Attack.* William M. Hammond provides a concise account in *The U.S. Army Campaigns of World War II: Normandy,* CMH Pub 72-18 (Washington, DC: GPO, n.d.). A recent compilation of articles by various historians is Jane Penrose, ed., *The D-Day Companion* (Oxford, UK: Osprey Publishing, 2004).

157. Gordon Rottman explains that there were not enough LVTs for both the Pacific and European theaters and the Pacific had priority because the LVTs were essential to cross the broad reefs that fringed the Pacific atolls and islands. Furthermore, he suggests that the surf conditions in the Mediterranean and Europe were too rough for LVTs (*US World War II Amphibious Tactics,* 24). But Richard B. Frank notes that 300 LVTs were available in England (Frank, *The Amphibious Revolution,* 25). Army LVT battalions trained in Monterey, California, in very difficult surf conditions. Colonel William Triplet, commanding the 18th Armored Group (Amphibious), noted the excellent sea-keeping qualities of the amphibious tractors (*William S. Triplet Papers*), while during the Normandy landings, many of the duplex drive tanks with their frail flotation screens and low freeboard sank in the rough seas on the way to the beach.

158. Adrian Lewis, who has written extensively on the Normandy landing, discusses and criticizes these decisions in *Omaha Beach: A Flawed Victory* (Chapel Hill & London: University of North Carolina Press, 2001).

159. These figures on men, supplies, and vehicles are from Maurice Matloff, ed., *American Military History* (Washington, DC: GPO, 1988), 488.

160. Omaha Beach handled considerably more cargo than the port of Cherbourg until the fall of 1944. The performance of the LSTs at Normandy raises the question as to whether the enormous effort and resources put into the fabrication of the artificial harbors might better have been spent on more LSTs. Harrison, *Cross-Channel Attack,* 426; Roland G. Ruppenthal, *United States Army in World War II, The European Theater of Operations, Logistical Support of the Armies, Volume I: May 1941–September 1944* (Washington, DC: Historical Division, Department of the Army, 1953), 392, 414–415.

161. The official Army history of the Southern France operation is Jeffrey J. Clarke and Robert Ross Smith, *United States Army in World War II, The European Theater of Operations, Riviera to the Rhine* (Washington, DC: Historical Division, Department of the Army, 1993). Jeffrey J. Clarke also provides concise accounts in *The U.S. Army Campaigns of World War II: Southern France,* CMH Pub 72-31 (Washington, DC: GPO, n.d.), and "The Champagne Campaign," *Military History Quarterly,* Vol. 20, No. 2, Winter 2008, 37–45.

162. Truscott, *Command Missions,* 400–401.

163. This discussion is based on Robert Ross Smith, "Luzon Versus Formosa," in Greenfield, ed., *Command Decisions,* 461–477.

164. The official Army account is M. Hamlin Cannon, *United States Army in World War II, The War in the Pacific, Leyte: The Return to the Philippines*

(Washington, DC: Historical Division, Department of the Army, 1954). Charles R. Anderson provides a concise account in *The U.S. Army Campaigns of World War II: Leyte,* CMH Pub 72-27 (Washington, DC: GPO, n.d.). Naval operations are covered in Samuel Eliot Morison, *History of United States Naval Operations in World War II: Leyte, June 1944–January 1945* (Boston, MA: Little, Brown and Company, 1958).

165. Heavey, *Down Ramp!,* 132.

166. In addition to Morison, *Leyte,* two classic and still valuable accounts of the naval Battle of Leyte Gulf are James A. Field, *The Japanese at Leyte Gulf: The Sho Operation* (Princeton, NJ: Princeton University Press, 1947), and C. Vann Woodward, *The Battle for Leyte Gulf* (New York, NY: The Macmillan Co., 1947), reprinted with an introduction by Evan Thomas (New York, NY: Skyhorse Publishing, 2007). Two authoritative recent accounts are Thomas Cutler, *The Battle of Leyte Gulf: 23–26 October 1944* (Annapolis, MD: US Naval Institute Press, 2001), and H.P. Willmott, *The Battle of Leyte Gulf: The Last Fleet Action* (Bloomington, IN: Indiana University Press, 2005). A dramatic account that focuses on the actions of two Japanese and two American commanders during the battle is Evan Thomas, *Sea of Thunder: Four Commanders and the Last Great Naval Campaign 1941–1945* (New York, NY: Simon & Schuster, 2006).

167. Heavey, *Down Ramp!,* 133–142. Samuel Eliot Morison, *History of United States Naval Operations in World War II: The Liberation of the Philippines: Luzon, Mindanao, the Visayas, 1944–1945* (Boston, MA: Little, Brown and Company, 1959), 17–51. A patrol torpedo (PT) boat was a fast 80-foot Navy motor torpedo boat.

168. "VII Amphibious Force Report Luzon" quoted in Robert Ross Smith, *United States Army in World War II, The War in the Pacific, Triumph in the Philippines* (Washington, DC: Historical Division, Department of the Army, 1963, reprinted 1968, 1984, 1991), 128.

169. US Army Forces, Pacific, *Engineers of the Southwest Pacific, Vol. IV, Amphibian Engineer Operations,* 571–577.

170. Smith, *Triumph in the Philippines,* 583–648.

171. The official Army account is Roy E. Appleman et al., *United States Army in World War II, The War in the Pacific, Okinawa: The Last Battle* (Washington, DC: Historical Division, Department of the Army, 1948). 1st ESB operations are in *Engineers of the Southwest Pacific, Vol. IV, Amphibian Engineer Operations,* 682–691. Naval operations are covered in Samuel Eliot Morison, *History of United States Naval Operations in World War II: Victory in the Pacific, 1945* (Boston: Little, Brown & Company, 1960). The British Commonwealth casualties were those from the British Pacific Fleet (Task Force 57), an aircraft carrier task force composed of British, Australian, Canadian, and New Zealand ships and aircraft.

172. US Army Forces, Pacific, *Engineers of the Southwest Pacific, Vol. IV, Amphibian Engineer Operations,* 659–682.

173. US Army Forces, Pacific, *Engineers of the Southwest Pacific, Vol. IV, Amphibian Engineer Operations,* 697–682; Heavey, *Down Ramp!,* 186–188.

174. Fahey, *Ships and Aircraft of the United States Fleet, 1945,* 61–64, 76–79, 96, and 1948 Addendum; Friedman and Baker, *U.S. Amphibious Ships and Craft,* 288.

175. "Unit History of Amphibious Training Command, U.S. Atlantic Fleet," 2–4; "Report of Amphibious Troop Training Operations in the Pacific During Calendar Year 1946," Commander, Amphibious Forces, Pacific Fleet, 21 June 1947, RG 337, Entry 55, Army Ground Forces General Correspondence 1942–1948, Box No. 695, NACP; Army Ground Forces G1 Memo, 5 September 1947, "Amphibious Experience," list of officers at Coronado and Little Creek and officers at HQ AGF with amphibious experience, RG 337, Entry 9, Box 63, Folder 353 (Amphibious) (Training), Action 1, NACP.

176. US Forces European Theater, General Board, *Report of the General Board, United States Forces, European Theater,* Study No. 22: "Control of the Build-up of Troops in a Cross-channel Amphibious Operation as Illustrated in Operation Overlord"; Study No. 72: "Engineer Tactical Policies"; Study No. 129: "Mounting the Operation 'Overlord'," 1945, 1946; Becker, *The Amphibious Training Center.* For some key examples of the postwar retrospectives on amphibious operations, see, for example, Jacob L. Devers, "OPERATION DRAGOON: The Invasion of Southern France," *Military Affairs,* Vol. X, No. 2, Summer 1946, 2–41; Jacob L. Devers, "Major Problems Confronting a Theater Commander in Combined Operations," address at the Armed Forces Staff College, 8 October 1947, copy at MHI; Arnold, "Preparation for a Division Amphibious Operation"; Arthur G. Trudeau, *Doctrine and Techniques in Amphibious Operations* (Washington, DC: Army Services Forces, 1946). A series of articles analyzing World War II amphibious operations was published throughout 1946 and into 1947 in *Military Affairs.*

177. War Department Memorandum WDGS G3 for Commanding General Army Ground Forces, 12 June 1946, "Amphibious Training," RG 337, Entry 55, Box 712, Action 100, NACP.

178. *Historical Report, 2d Engineer Special Brigade, 1949,* 28 March 1950, I-3, V-5, and Appendixes 1–4 (activation orders for units from General Reserve), RG 407, Entry 429, Box 4665, NACP.

179. *Unit History, Hq & Svc Co, 302d Amphibious Tractor Battalion, 1949,* Box 4599; *Command Report, Headquarters, 409th Engineer Brigade, September 1951,* Box 5119; *Unit History, 747th Amphibian Tank Battalion,* Box 4599, all in RG 407, Entry 429, NACP. The 75th Amphibian Tank Battalion is identified as a Reserve unit activated in 1946 in Mary Lee Stubbs and Stanley Russell Connor, *Army Lineage Series, Armor-Cavalry, Part I: Regular Army and Army Reserve* (Washington, DC: Office of the Chief of Military History, US Army, 1969), 76. The 2d ESB history does not identify it as a Reserve unit and refers to it as an ATTB, but it seems likely it is the same unit identified in Stubbs and Connor.

180. *Report of Amphibious Troop Training Operations in the Pacific during Calendar Year 1946* (San Diego, CA: Office of the Commander, Amphibious Force, US Pacific Fleet, 21 June 1947), RG 337, Entry 55, "Army Ground Forces

General Correspondence 1942–48," Box 695, File "353/12 Amphib (Separate Enclosure)," NACP.

181. "Unit History of Amphibious Training Command, US Atlantic Fleet," 9–10.

182. US Army, Sixth Army, *Sixth Army Report on Amphibious Training Program, 1946* (Presidio of San Francisco, CA: Headquarters, Sixth Army [1946?]); Jean R. Moenk, *A History of Large-Scale Army Maneuvers in the United States, 1935–1964* (Fort Monroe, VA: Historical Branch, Office of the Deputy Chief of Staff for Military Operations and Reserve Force, US Continental Army Command, December 1969), 110–114; US Pacific Fleet, *Operation DUCK: Operation Plan (Training) No. A109-46* (San Diego, CA: Amphibious Forces, Pacific Fleet, Commander Amphibious Group One, and Commander Task Group 13.12, 25 October 1946), MHI Archives, Box: "Operation Duck Observer Reports 1946."

183. *Sixth Army Report*, Annex 7, "Critique of 'OPERATION DUCK' Covering West Coast Amphibious Training Exercises held by Commander, Amphibious Forces, US Pacific Fleet at Naval Amphibious Base, Coronado, 1 December 1946," 2.

184. D. Clayton James points out this difference in perspective, and the impact of Anzio in particular, on Generals Omar N. Bradley and J. Lawton Collins (future chairman of the JCS and chief of staff of the Army at the time of the Incheon landing in Korea) in *The Years of MacArthur, Vol. III, Triumph and Disaster 1945–1964* (Boston, MA: Houghton Mifflin, 1985), 464–466 and (with Anne Sharp Wells) in *Refighting the Last War: Command and Crisis in Korea 1950–1953* (New York, NY: The Free Press, 1993), 165. Although neither general was directly involved in Anzio, both had read the analyses of the operation.

185. These views are set forth in a 1948 historical study by Albert N. Garland, *Amphibious Doctrine and Training*, AGF Study No. 6, and in an unpublished essay by Major General Clark L. Ruffner titled "What are they trying to do to the Marines?" 16 June 1947. Both documents are in the Historical Manuscript File at the US Army Center of Military History. I am indebted to Mr. Frank R. Shirer for bringing these documents to my attention. In World War II, General Ruffner had served as Deputy Chief of Staff, US Army Forces, Central Pacific in 1943, and Chief of Staff, US Army Forces, Pacific Ocean Areas and Middle Pacific in 1944–45. He had assisted in the planning for the Gilberts operation, had participated in the Makin and Leyte assaults, and had been involved in the planning for the amphibious invasion of Japan. (See "Biographical File, General Clark L. Ruffner, USA," MHI.) The number of amphibious operations conducted is difficult to pin down, since there were many small-scale landings of less than regimental size, but the numbers developed by the US Army Center of Military History for assault landings of regimental size or larger are 42 Army, 10 Marine, and 6 that involved both Army and Marine units. The list was "based on readily available sources and is not an official definitive statement on the subject." See "Major U.S. Amphibious Operations—World War II and Korea," 27 July 1964, CMH File 228.01 HRC 370.03 Invasions, Amphibious Operations. *Engineers of*

the Southwest Pacific, Vol. IV, Amphibian Engineer Operations, identifies 148 "combat landings" in which the 2d, 3d, and 4th ESBs participated, 698.

186. Ray S. Cline and Maurice Matloff, "Development of War Department Views on Unification," *Military Affairs,* Vol. XIII, No. 2 (Summer 1949): 66–68.

187. The debate within the JCS in 1946 is described in James F. Schnabel, *The History of the Joint Chiefs of Staff: The Joint Chiefs of Staff and National Policy, Vol. I, 1945–1947* (Wilmington, DE: Michael Glazier, Inc., 1979), 227–247.

188. These views are summarized in Demetrios Caraley, *The Politics of Military Unification: A Study of Conflict and the Policy Process* (New York, NY: Columbia University Press, 1966), 66–68.

189. The JCS debate came to be known as the "JCS 1478 Papers" when it became public knowledge during the congressional hearings. "JCS 1478" was the number assigned to the topic by the Joint Staff. Schnabel, *The Joint Chiefs of Staff and National Policy, Vol. I,* 227–247; Legere, 320.

190. Caraley and Legere describe the activities of the Services during the congressional debate on unification. For Marine Corps activities, see Gordon W. Keiser, *The U.S. Marine Corps and Defense Unification, 1944–47* (Baltimore, MD: Nautical and Aviation, 1966). Jon T. Hoffman provides an excellent account of the activities of Brigadier General Merritt A. Edson, one of the key players on the Marine Corps side, in *Once a Legend: "Red Mike" Edson of the Marine Raiders* (Novato, CA: Presidio, 1994). See also Hoffman's "The Roles and Missions Debate," *Marine Corps Gazette,* December 1994, 16–19. David Jablonsky describes the imbroglio from the Army perspective in his forthcoming *War by Land, Sea and Air: Dwight D. Eisenhower and the Concept of Unified Command* (unpublished manuscript).

191. Public Law 253–80th Congress, as amended by Public Law 36–81st Congress and Public Law 216–81st Congress.

192. Executive Order 9877, 26 July 1947. "Joint" amphibious operations would be those in which forces of two or more Services participate. The Army leadership anticipated these would be much larger operations than the seizure of advanced naval bases as set forth in the Marine Corps mission in the National Security Act.

193. Kenneth W. Condit, *The History of the Joint Chiefs of Staff: The Joint Chiefs of Staff and National Policy, Vol. II, 1947–1949* (Wilmington, DE: Michael Glazier, Inc., 1979), 165–184.

194. Departments of the Army and the Air Force, "Functions of the Armed Forces and the Joint Chiefs of Staff" (Key West Agreement), *Joint Army and Air Force Bulletin No. 18* (Washington, DC: Departments of the Army and the Air Force, 13 May 1948), Section V copy in MHI Archives, Adjutant General AGO Letters 1950.

195. Departments of the Army and the Air Force, *Joint Army and Air Force Bulletin No. 18,* Section IV.

196. Departments of the Army and the Air Force, *Joint Army and Air Force Bulletin No. 18,* Section VII.

197. *Report of Army Advisory Panel on Joint Amphibious Operations* (Fort

Monroe, VA: Office of the Chief of Army Field Forces, 18 January 1949), RG 337, Entry 38 (Development and Testing Section Decimal File 1942–50), Box 11, NACP, Annex B to Appendix A, A-B-1–A-B-6.

198. Michael A. Palmer, *Origins of the Maritime Strategy: American Naval Strategy in the First Postwar Decade* (Washington, DC: Naval Historical Center, 1988), 15, 29–30. I am indebted to David Keough of the MHI for bringing this rationale for postwar amphibious operations to my attention.

199. Steven T. Ross, *American War Plans, 1945–1950* (New York & London: Garland Publishing, Inc., 1988), 115–119, 130–131. Frank Pace, Secretary of the Army during this period, recalls reconnoitering the Pyrenees line to assess whether a foothold could be retained in Europe. *Frank Pace Oral History,* 21–22, MHI Archives.

200. *Exercise Seminole: Report of Joint Amphibious Training Exercises, November 1947.* Fleet Post Office (New York, NY: Commander Amphibious Force, United States Atlantic Fleet, Commander Joint Expeditionary Force, 1947), (I)(A)-1; J.C. Kennedy, *Planning Amphibious Operations* (Fort Knox, KY: Instructor Training Division, General Instruction Department, US Army Armored School, 27 April 1948); LTC Alva T. McDaniel et al., *The Armored Division as an Assault Landing Force*, Research Report (Fort Knox, KY: US Army Armored School, 1951–52).

201. Gilberto Villahermosa, "The 65th Infantry Regiment: Prelude to Inchon: The Puerto Rican Exercises of 1950," valerosos.com/PreludetoInchon.html (accessed 25 June 2006).

202. AFF replaced AGF in March 1948 as the agency responsible for the training of Army forces in the Continental United States.

203. Commander First Task Fleet, *Control Order No. 2-49, Exercise MIKI,* 1 August 1949; *Observer's Report, Exercise MIKI, After Action Report, Joint Army–Navy Exercise, FY 49, MIKI,* 25 November 1949; all in The William Lawton Papers, MHI Archives; *2d ESB Historical Report 1949,* IV-3–IV-7; Moenk, *History of Large-Scale Army Maneuvers,* 128–135.

204. US Army, Second Army, *Report on Joint Puerto Rican Exercise (PORTREX),* Fort George G. Meade: Headquarters, Second Army, 1 July 1950, copy at MHI; *2ESB Historical Report 1949,* II-7, IV-8; Villahermosa, "Prelude to Inchon"; Moenk, *History of Large-Scale Army Maneuvers,* 136–143. The 3d Infantry Division did participate in the amphibious withdrawal from northeast Korea in December 1950.

205. Moenk, *History of Large-Scale Army Maneuvers*, 150.

206. US Army Command and General Staff College, "Infantry Division in Amphibious Operations," Subject 3503A (Fort Leavenworth, KS: US Army Command and General Staff College, 31 March 1948). Box: "CGSC Curricular 1940s," MHI Archives; Kennedy, *Planning Amphibious Operations;* "Amphibious Operations Manual," Command and General Staff College (Fort Leavenworth, KS: 1 September 1948); David A. Ogden, *Amphibious operations: lecture before the Engineer School, Fort Belvoir, Virginia—March 15, 1949* (Fort Belvoir, VA: US Army Engineer School, The Engineer Center, 1949); David Ogden, *Amphibious*

Operations of Especial Interest to the Army (Fort Belvoir, VA: US Army Engineer School, The Engineer Center, 1951).

207. Garland, *Amphibious Doctrine and Training*. RG 337, Entry 55 series (Army Ground Forces/Army Field Forces General Correspondence) contains the record of these reports and studies.

208. War Department G3 Memorandum WDGCT 353 Amph, 4 February 1946, to Chief of Staff of the Army, "Army Personnel for Post-War Amphibious Staff Organization," RG 337, Entry 55, Box 712, NACP.

209. Letter, Office of Chief of Army Field Forces, GNGCT-22 319.1, 1 May 1948, to Senior Army Officer, Troop Training Unit, Amphibious Training Command, Amphibious Force, Pacific Fleet, "Report on TTU Amphibious Force, Pacific Fleet," RG 337, Entry 55H, Box 16, File 535 (Amph), NACP.

210. Garland, *Amphibious Doctrine and Training,* summarizes these arguments on pages 90–134. The arguments are also set forth in the various exercise after action reports, in General Ogden's writings, in Army comments on proposed US Fleet doctrinal publications USF-6, 63, and 66 published in 1946 and 1947 (RG 337, Entry 31A, Box 26, NACP), and in the testimony and discussion contained in *Report of Army Advisory Panel.*

211. Letter, War Department General Staff G3, 29 December 1947, to Commanding General, Army Ground Forces, "Amphibious and Airborne Instruction" and other correspondence in Action 353/5006, Office of the Chief, Army Field Forces, 12 January 1948, "Amphibious and Airborne Instruction," RG 337, Entry 55, Box 714, Action 353/5008, NACP; Ogden, *Amphibious Operations,* 50.

212. *Report of Army Advisory Panel on Joint Amphibious Operations.*

213. *Report of Army Advisory Panel on Joint Amphibious Operations,* 14–16.

214. *Report of Army Advisory Panel on Joint Amphibious Operations,* 17–21.

215. *Report of Army Advisory Panel on Joint Amphibious Operations,* 17–21.

216. US Army, Engineer School, "Abstract of Proceedings, Conference of General and Special Service School Instructors, 15–18 August 1949" (Fort Belvoir, VA: US Army Engineer School, The Engineer Center, and Fort Belvoir, 1949), copy in the Engineer School Collection, MHI Archives.

217. Engineer School, "Abstract of Proceedings, Conference of General and Special Service School Instructors," 27–28, 73–76. The quotation is on page 73.

218. Engineer School, "Abstract of Proceedings, Conference of General and Special Service School Instructors," 28–29.

219. Engineer School, "Abstract of Proceedings, Conference of General and Special Service School Instructors, 27, 30, 73–76.

220. Department of the Army, *Draft Field Service Regulations: Operations,* 1953; 299–323; Headquarters, Department of the Army, FM 100-5, *Field Service Regulations: Operations* (Washington, DC: GPO, 1954).

221. The acronym for the Far East Command used in Washington was

FECOM; however, within the Far East Command itself, the preferred acronym was FEC.

222. This discussion of FEC command relations is based on Ronald H. Cole et al., *The History of the Unified Command Plan 1946–1993* (Washington, DC: Joint History Office, Office of the Chairman of the Joint Chiefs of Staff, 1995), 11; James F. Schnabel and Robert J. Watson, *The History of the Joint Chiefs of Staff: The Joint Chiefs of Staff and National Policy, Vol. 3, The Korean War, Part One* (Washington, DC: Office of the Chairman of the Joint Chiefs of Staff, 1998), 29, 49–52, 56.

223. In June 1950 these were Eighth Army; GHQ Headquarters and Service Group; Ryukyus Command; and the Marianas-Bonins Command.

224. Donald W. Boose Jr., *U.S. Army Forces in the Korean War 1950–1953*, Battle Orders No. 11 (Oxford, UK: Osprey Publishing, 2005), 63. The 1st Cavalry Division was organized as an infantry division.

225. Robert Frank Futrell, *The United States Air Force in Korea, 1950–1953* (Washington, DC: Office of Air Force History, US Air Force, 1983), 1–4.

226. Field, *History of United States Naval Operations, Korea,* 46, 54, 71.

227. Letter, Major General E.K. Wright, USA Retired, to Colonel Robert Heinl, USMC, 27 April 1967, 35, copy in the Robert D. Heinl Papers, Box 42, PCC277, folder, "Victory at High Tide 1967/2," Marine Corps University Archives, hereafter, MCUA.

228. Field, *History of United States Naval Operations, Korea*, 44–48.

229. Field, *History of United States Naval Operations, Korea*, 72.

230. General Headquarters, Far East Command, *Annual Historical Report, 1 January 1950–31 October 1950,* 6, RG 409, Entry 429, Box 346, NACP.

231. GHQ FEC G3 Memo for Chief of Staff, FEC, Subject: "Department of the Army Message WX 99128, Relative to Amphibious Training," 6 February 1950; Letter, GHQ FEC to Director, Organization and Training, General Staff, US Army, "Informal Quarterly Report, 7 February 1950"; GHQ FEC G3 Training Memorandum for the Record, "Amphibious Training for FEC, 1950," 18 February 1950, RG 554, Entry 57, Box 1, NACP. A battalion landing team was an infantry battalion specially reinforced by additional combat and service elements and was the basic unit for planning an assault landing.

232. GHQ FEC letter to ACofS, G3, Operations, Department of the Army, "Advance Amphibious Planning, Far East Command," 3 April 1950, RG 554, Entry 57, Box 1, NACP.

233. GHQ FEC 1st Indorsement to Eighth Army letter, "New Construction for Amphibious Training Center, Camp McGill," 28 March 1950; GHQ FEC G3 Memorandum, "Troop Housing for Amphibious Training," 20 April 1950; GHQ FEC G3 3d Indorsement (Check Note) to G1, "Request for Permanent Augmentation of NAVFE Strength by Crews for 5 LSTs," 5 May 1950; GHQ FEC G3 Training Memorandum for the Record Brief, "Request for Permanent Augmentation of NAVFE, 27 May 1950; GHQ FEC letter, "Permanent Assignment of an Attack Transport to Naval Forces," 5 June 1950; GHQ FEC G3 Memo for

Chief of Staff, "Use of SCAJAP Liberty Ship, JOHN W. WEEKS, in Far East Command Amphibious Training Program," 15 June 1950, RG 554, Entry 57, Box 1, NACP. A Welin davit (a type of crane for lowering boats into the water from ships) is designed to accommodate three LCVPs or LCPRs on an amphibious ship. For the location of Camp McGill and other bases in Japan, see map 8.

234. These documents are located in RG 554, Records of GHQ FEC, Entry 50 (ACofS G3 Training Division Memorandums—Action File, 1950), Box 1, NACP.

235. US Army, 8206th Army Unit, Amphibious Training Center, *Unit History* [1951?], hereafter, ATC History, 3–5. A photographic copy of this document is at MHI. For the locations of Camp McGill and Chigasaki Beach, see map 8.

236. Dyer, *The Amphibians Came to Conquer*, 266, 606, 1054,1123; James F. Schnabel, *United States Army in the Korean War, Policy and Direction: The First Year* (Washington, DC: GPO, 1972), 145 and note 5.

237. MTT Able was a detachment of Marine Brigadier General William S. Fellers' Troop Training Unit (TTU) of the Training Command, Amphibious Forces, Pacific Fleet, based at Coronado, California, with the mission of training Marine and Army forces in amphibious warfare techniques and procedures.

238. ATC History, 3–5; Field, *History of United States Naval Operations, Korea*, 45, 46; US Marine Corps Board, *An Evaluation of the Influence of Marine Corps Forces on the Course of the Korean War (4 Aug 50–15 Dec 50)*, hereafter, Marine Corps *Evaluation*, Vol. I, Part 3, III-B-1, MCUA.

Chapter 3

Initial Operations and Planning

North Korean Attacks and ROK and US Evacuations

The Korean War began on 25 June 1950 when the North Korean People's Army (KPA) invaded the Republic of Korea (ROK). The initial North Korean attacks included small-scale amphibious operations on the east coast while, in the west, the ROK conducted a regimental-size amphibious evacuation from the Ongjin Peninsula and US civilians were evacuated by sea from the port of Incheon. (See map 7.)

Evidence indicates that the North Koreans established two naval infantry units (*Yukjeondae*: literally, land combat unit) under the KPA Naval Headquarters (599th Unit) at Jinnampo (Chinnamp'o) in July 1949. The 956th Naval Infantry Unit was based at Jinnampo in the west and the 945th at Wonsan on the east coast, where it received amphibious training by Soviet advisors.[1] Another unit, the 766th Independent Unit, a guerrilla force established under the direction of future Democratic People's Republic of Korea (DPRK) defense minister O Jin U, also received amphibious training at Wonsan before the outbreak of war. On 22 June the 766th Independent Unit moved to the port of Yangyang, where it was joined by the 945th Naval Infantry Unit and several small separate guerrilla units, bringing the size of the combined organization to 1,200 to 1,500 amphibious troops. Their mission was to support the KPA 5th Division's attack by landing at beachheads along the South Korean east coast behind the defending ROK Army forces and to disrupt the line of communications by destroying railroad tracks, bridges, tunnels, and telephone and telegraph facilities. The forces that had conducted the amphibious landings would then join with the nonamphibious elements of the 766th that had remained behind to participate in the KPA 5th Division's land attack. The reconstituted unit would serve as a reconnaissance and ranger force supporting the 5th Division and infiltrating guerrilla teams through the mountains to the west and south toward Busan (Pusan) and Daegu (Taegu).[2]

The first three battalions of the 766th Independent Unit and elements of the 945th Naval Infantry Unit loaded aboard small coastal cargo ships, fishing boats, and motor launches at the port of Yangyang. The other units, joined by several hundred more guerrillas, moved to various coastal ports to embark in assorted small ships and craft, including sail boats. These motley flotillas sortied between 22 and 25 June and headed south, some of them escorted by motor torpedo boats of the 2d Naval Squadron. The North Korean attack began in the predawn hours of 25 June along the

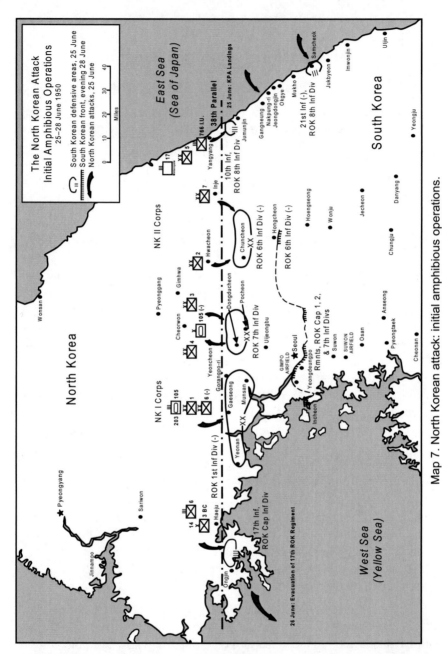

Map 7. North Korean attack: initial amphibious operations.

38th Parallel. In the east, following a preparatory artillery barrage, the KPA 5th Division, reinforced by the 1st Border Guard Brigade (*Gyeongbi Yeodan)* and elements of the 766th Independent Unit, crossed the border around 0400 and moved down the narrow coastal plain toward Gangneung (Kangnung). Opposing them were the ROK 8th Division, commanded by

Colonel Lee Song Ga, with its headquarters at Gangneung. Lieutenant Colonel Ko Kung Hong's 10th Infantry Regiment was in defensive positions near the border, just north of the little port of Jumunjin (Chumunjin). One battalion of Lieutenant Colonel Kim Yong Bae's 21st Regiment was based at the coastal town of Samcheok (Samch'ok); the other two battalions were conducting counterguerrilla operations in the mountains to the west.[3]

Soon after the attack began, ROK police and military units began receiving reports of sightings of North Korean soldiers along the coast. Shortly after 0500, Major Gerald E. Larson, the US advisor with the ROK 8th Division, was notified that enemy troops were landing in two locations near Samcheok. Larson, Lieutenant Colonel Kim Yong Bae, and the 21st Regiment operations officer drove by jeep up the coast, where they saw junks and sampans circling off shore and about a battalion of North Korean troops on the beach.[4] They saw a similar scene south of Samcheok and villagers at other locations along the coast reported groups of North Korean soldiers moving inland. One attempted landing north of Nakpung-ri (Nakp'ung-ni) was driven off by soldiers of the 21st Regiment, who sank at least two of the boats with 57-mm antitank guns. However, some 1,300 KPA troops landed successfully at various places on the coast between Gangneung and Uljin (Ulchin), with most of the landings concentrated around the coastal towns of Jeongdongjin (Chongdongjin), south of Gangneung, and Imwonjin, north of Uljin.[5]

The North Koreans had planned another landing, probably by the 3d Battalion of the 766th Independent Unit and/or elements of the 945th Naval Infantry Unit, at Busan. This would have had serious implications, as the city was essentially undefended and was the primary port of debarkation for US reinforcements and materiel coming into Korea. However, a small ROK Navy force successfully intercepted the North Korean ship. On Sunday evening, 25 June, the ROK Navy submarine chaser PC-701 (*Baekdusan*) and motor minesweepers YMS-512 and YMS-518 were patrolling north of Busan under the tactical control of the captain of PC-701, Commander Choi Yong Nam.[6] Just after sunset lookouts sighted smoke on the horizon. PC-701 steamed toward the smoke and discovered an unidentified 1,000-ton cargo ship. After repeatedly challenging the ship by blinker light with no response, Commander Choi brought PC-701 to within 600 yards and illuminated the suspicious vessel with a searchlight. He could clearly see North Korean soldiers in uniform crowding the deck of the unmarked ship, which was armed with a 76-mm gun and four machineguns. Choi radioed ROK Navy Headquarters in Busan, reported his sighting, and was granted permission to shoot. PC-701 commenced 20 rounds of rapid fire with its 3-inch gun, damaging the North Korean ship, which came to a stop and returned fire, sending a 76-mm shell crashing through PC-701's wheelhouse, killing an officer and a sailor. PC-701 fired 20 more rounds until its 3-inch gun jammed, but by then the armed transport was listing to starboard with its mast toppled. A few moments later, it plunged bow-first beneath the waves as the ROK sailors cheered their Navy's first battle and first victory at sea.[7]

As these events were taking place in the east, the North Korean assault was continuing in the Ongjin Peninsula on the west coast. There, ROK Army Colonel Paik In Yup's 17th Regiment was cut off from reinforcement or escape by land and in danger of being overwhelmed by the KPA 14th Regiment and 3d Border Guard Brigade. Fortunately, one ROK Navy and two ROK Merchant Marine landing ships, tank (LSTs) were able to sail to the area. In the late 1940s, several LSTs that had been in use by the US Government in Korea had been transferred to the ROK Merchant Marine along with some small freighters. However, at the beginning of the war, the ROK Navy had only one such ship, LST-801, commanded by ROK Navy Lieutenant Kim Ok Gyeong. The Merchant crews were not trained in beaching and retraction techniques, but the LST-801 had an effective commander and crew fully capable of amphibious operations. On 26 June the three LSTs, along with fishing boats carrying 20 to 50 men each, evacuated about 1,750 survivors of the regiment.[8]

That same day plans to evacuate American military dependents and embassy, business, and missionary families were put into effect. Fifth Air Force fighters provided overhead cover and US destroyers *Mansfield* and *De Haven* steamed to Incheon to provide protection to the Norwegian freighter *Reinholt,* hastily cleaned up from its previous cargo of fertilizer, to accommodate the evacuees.[9] Among these was a professional geographer who would later be employed by General Douglas MacArthur's headquarters in Japan. Years later she recollected that the evacuation was affected by the same hydrographic conditions that would later shape the amphibious landing at Incheon. "In time-honored fashion," she recalled, "we were poled—slowly-slowly—in barges over the mud flats [and] my barge experienced a few shots from two enemy planes overhead to scare us." The *Reinholt* was packed with some 300 people, most of them women and children, who cheered loudly when one of the Navy destroyers met them at sea during the night.[10]

As these first amphibious combat moves of the war were taking place in Korea, the amphibious training program that had been under development by the General Headquarters (GHQ) Far East Command (FEC) was underway in Japan (see map 8). By coincidence, on 25 June 1950, the same day that the North Koreans began their attack, Admiral James H. Doyle's amphibious ships were underway from Yokosuka with one battalion landing team of the 35th Infantry Regiment on board. The battalion went ashore at Chigasaki Beach on 26 June. The second landing exercise began as scheduled on 28 June, but all the Fifth Air Force units, Far East Air Force (FEAF) observers, tanks, and destroyers were withdrawn, and once the landing was completed, the ships returned to port to debark the troops. The subsequent exercises were canceled, and on 30 June Doyle's amphibious group was placed on 4-hour notice to sail.[11]

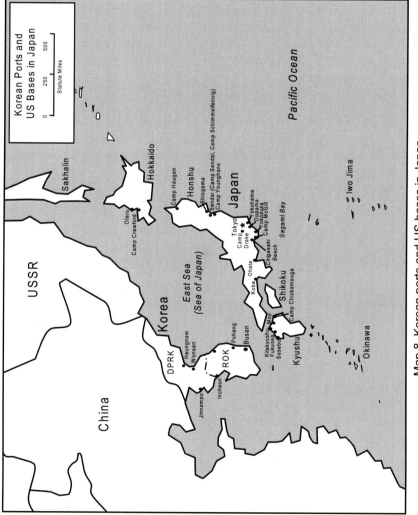

Map 8. Korean ports and US bases in Japan.

Command Relationship Changes and Arrival of US/UN Forces

On the outbreak of hostilities, the US Joint Chiefs of Staff (JCS) returned Korea to MacArthur's FEC area of responsibility (AOR). Formosa (Taiwan) and surrounding waters and islands were also added to MacArthur's AOR. On 27 June the JCS advised MacArthur that President Harry S. Truman had removed all restrictions on the use of FEC naval and air assets and directed that these be used to "offer fullest possible support" to ROK forces.[12] Two days later, the JCS transferred the Seventh Fleet to MacArthur's operational control, and directed Admiral Arthur W. Radford, Commander in Chief, Pacific Command and Pacific Fleet to provide support and reinforcement "as necessary and practicable." MacArthur further delegated operational control of the Seventh Fleet to Admiral C. Turner Joy. In the same message, the JCS authorized MacArthur to extend his operations into "Northern Korea against air bases, depots, tank parks, troop columns, and other such purely military targets" when MacArthur judged these attacks to be essential to carry out his mission or to avoid unnecessary casualties to US forces.[13]

The North Korean advance continued. By the end of June, the KPA had captured the ROK capital of Seoul and all the territory north of the Han River. In the central part of the country, the KPA were advancing toward the crucial transportation hub at Wonju, and in the east ROK forces had been pushed south of Gangneung.

On 30 June General MacArthur was authorized to use US ground troops to support the South Koreans.[14] The next day, Admiral Joy issued Commander, United States Naval Forces, Far East (COMNAVFE) Operation Order (OPORD) No. 7-50, directing Admiral Doyle to use his Task Force (TF) 90 amphibious ships to move the 24th Infantry Division from Fukuoka and Sasebo, Japan, to Korea, and assigning 16 Shipping Control Administration, Japan (SCAJAP) LSTs to expand the lift capability of Doyle's small amphibious force. Doyle arrived at Sasebo on 3 July to find that the 24th Infantry Division had already begun moving by locally available shipping and air. His ships were retained at Sasebo and Doyle flew to Tokyo for a meeting with MacArthur concerning his next mission—an amphibious operation.[15]

On 1 July the lead element of the 24th Infantry Division, a reinforced infantry battalion designated TF *Smith*, flew to Korea, moving forward the next day to engage the advancing North Koreans. TF *Smith* went into action near the town of Osan, about 30 miles south of the ROK capital of Seoul, on 5 July. It was able to do little to delay the KPA, but additional forces were on the way.[16] The rest of the 24th Infantry Division was in Korea by 6 July and the lead elements of the 25th Infantry Division began loading on leased *Marus* (Japanese merchant ships) at Moji, Japan, on 8 July. The movement of Army forces to Korea was the first major task of Captain Alexander Junker's newly formed Western Pacific Office, Military Sea Transportation Service (MSTS). Doyle's amphibious group was an operational unit of COMNAVFE with no connection to MSTS, but Doyle's staff coordinated with that of Junker, and MSTS (and SCAJAP) ships were often assigned to Doyle to provide sufficient shipping for amphibious operations.[17]

Other nations were also providing support to the effort in Korea. On 25 June, 27 June, and 7 July, the United Nations Security Council passed three resolutions that condemned the North Korean attack, called on UN member states to assist the ROK to "repel the armed attack and to restore international peace and security in the area," asked UN states to make forces available "to a unified command under the United States," and requested the United States designate a force commander. President Truman designated MacArthur to be commander in chief of the United Nations Command (CINCUNC) as well as commander in chief of the FEC.[18]

The United Kingdom and Australia immediately put their naval forces in Far Eastern waters (an aircraft carrier, two cruisers, destroyers, and frigates) under MacArthur's operational control. New Zealand, the Netherlands, and Canada deployed ships to the Far East, and Australia made No. 77 Squadron (the one Commonwealth combat air unit that was still in Japan) available for combat operations in Korea. Eventually, the ROK and 15 UN nations, in addition to the United States, contributed combat forces to the United Nations Command (UNC), while 5 other nations sent medical units. On 3 July the United States declared a naval blockade of the Korean coast, aircraft from the USS *Valley Forge* and H.M.S. *Triumph* attacked the North Korean capital of Pyeongyang (P'yongyang), and No. 77 Squadron Royal Australian Air Force (RAAF) began conducting air strikes in support of ROK ground troops.[19]

On 13 July 1950 General Walton H. Walker moved his headquarters to Korea, establishing Eighth United States Army in Korea (EUSAK). On 14 July President Syngman Rhee gave operational control of all ROK military forces to MacArthur, who designated Walker as the UNC Ground Component Commander with operational control of all US, ROK, and UN ground forces. Walker initially had to commit forces piecemeal to delay the North Koreans until he could form a coherent line to stop the North Korean attack and defend until enough forces could be assembled to begin a counterattack.

Amphibious Planning and Operation BLUEHEARTS[20]

At the beginning of July 1950, a week after the North Korean attack, the concerns of the US JCS over amphibious operations focused not on attack but withdrawal. On 1 July the Secretary of Defense had asked for a military estimate of the situation in Korea. The next day, the Joint Strategic Plans Committee presented the JCS with the results of their deliberations. One of the questions the Secretary asked was "Is there any possibility that Korea could be another 'Dunkirk'?" The planners concluded that the chances of a forced withdrawal from Korea were "negligible," so long as only North Korean forces were involved and would be increased only slightly if Chinese or Manchurian forces intervened. If evacuation became necessary, Russian air and submarine forces would be a serious threat, but the United States could probably maintain air and naval superiority at the evacuation area and could, therefore, conduct a successful withdrawal. The planners concluded that the United States had available "adequate lift for a withdrawal of a force of two divisions" within 10 days for an orderly withdrawal of equipment and personnel, or within as little as 1 day if all equipment and supplies were abandoned or destroyed and only personnel were evacuated.[21]

While the Joint Staff planners were deliberating on the likelihood of another Dunkirk, General MacArthur, whose success in World War II was based on a series of amphibious operations across the Southwest Pacific and into the Philippines, was thinking in terms of another Hollandia or Leyte. It is impossible to determine the exact moment when the Incheon amphibious operation was conceived, but given MacArthur's experience and the emphasis within the FEC on amphibious training, it is possible that the idea of an amphibious counterthrust was on the minds of the commander in chief, his chief of staff, and his G3 immediately following the North Korean attack. On 26 June, the day after the attack, General Edward M. Almond, the GHQ FEC Chief of Staff, had directed General Edwin K. Wright's Joint Strategic Plans and Operations Group (JSPOG) to begin preparing plans "with regard to the present emergency in Korea."[22]

As early as 1948, the Army G4 Plans Division had conducted a series of strategic studies to determine logistic requirements in potential theaters of operations. One of these studies, SL-17, was based on a scenario involving an invasion of South Korea, with friendly forces withdrawing to a defensible perimeter, then conducting a breakout in conjunction with an amphibious landing in the vicinity of Incheon. The study had been approved and distributed to the Army technical services the week of 19 June 1950. According to the staff officer who wrote the strategic concept for SL-17, GHQ FEC requested 50 copies of the study the week of 26 June.[23]

On 29 June MacArthur flew to Korea accompanied by General George Stratemeyer, General Almond, Major General Charles A. Willoughby (FEC G2), General Wright, and Brigadier General Courtney Whitney (Chief of the Supreme Commander Allied Powers [SCAP] Government Section). From a hill overlooking the Han River, MacArthur observed ROK Army forces withdrawing to the south amidst throngs of refugees. Later that day, in reporting the situation to the JCS, he recommended immediate commitment of a US regimental combat team (RCT) and the buildup of a two-division US force in Korea for a counteroffensive.[24] In his retrospective account, MacArthur says that it was while he stood watching the refugees and ROK soldiers streaming south that he conceived his "desperate" plan to "throw my occupation soldiers into this breach" and "rely upon strategic maneuver to overcome the odds against me." It was here, MacArthur later claimed, that "the genesis of the Inchon operation began to take shape."[25]

On 1 July Major General Alonzo P. Fox, the SCAP Chief of Staff, announced that General Almond would hold a meeting with Admiral Doyle and the principal FEC staff officers the next day to discuss "plans for possible use of amphibious forces, plus requirements for lifting such forces." He noted that Admiral Joy estimated that in the theater lift was available for 1,600 men and equipment.[26] That same day the officers of the 8206th Army Unit, Amphibious Training Center (ATC), were brought to the headquarters to assist in amphibious planning and ATC teams were sent to begin teaching basic amphibious techniques (preparation of vehicles and equipment, embarkation procedures, and the technique of climbing down nets into landing craft) at camps across Japan.[27]

Following Almond's preliminary meeting on 2 July, General Wright's JSPOG began developing a plan, BLUEHEARTS, for an amphibious assault at Incheon, using the 1st Cavalry Division and a Marine Corps RCT to cut the North Korean line of communications and seize the crucial Seoul area as the 24th and 25th Infantry Divisions attacked from the south. MacArthur sent a message to the JCS requesting the Marine RCT. Also, Colonel Edward H. Forney's Mobile Training Team (MTT), which had been attached to Eighth Army while conducting the amphibious training at Camp McGill, was attached to Admiral Doyle's amphibious group and Forney was brought up to the FEC staff to serve as advisor on amphibious operations. On 3 July MacArthur told the Department of the Army that he urgently needed trained US personnel "to man and operate 13 LST, 20 LCM [landing craft, mechanized], and 20 LCVP [landing craft, vehicle, personnel]." He recommended they be airlifted to Japan to arrive no later than 15 July. That same day the JCS advised him that they had approved the "earliest practicable dispatch" of the Marine RCT and an escort carrier with supporting tactical aircraft.[28]

Unaware that GHQ had other plans for the 1st Cavalry Division, General Walker suspended the 5th Cavalry Regiment's amphibious training at Camp McGill on 1 July and on 2 July directed Major General Hobart R. Gay, the division commander, to prepare plans for movement to Korea.[29] On receiving an information copy of Walker's message to Gay, General Almond asked, "What started this? We are not going to move 1st Cav to Pusan!" The FEC G3 Plans Chief, in his response to Almond, noted that General Walker's directive was sent "prior to any knowledge on the part of anyone in Eighth Army that the C-in-C had directed the preparation of a plan for the amphibious assault by the 1st Cav Div against the northwest coast of South Korea."[30]

Thus, planning for BLUEHEARTS was well underway when, on 4 July 1950, MacArthur called a conference to discuss the amphibious operation. Among those attending were Generals Almond and Wright, Marine Brigadier General William S. Fellers (Commanding General of the Troop Training Unit [TTU], Training Command, Amphibious Force, Pacific Fleet, who was visiting Korea to observe the amphibious training program), Admiral Doyle, and Colonel Forney. Wright explained the concept of the operation. One Marine RCT and the 1st Cavalry Division would land at Gunsan (Kunsan) or, preferably, Incheon. They would then seize Seoul and cut the KPA line of communication through the city.[31] Doyle was directed to work up a detailed plan for the landing, reactivate landing craft then in storage, and convert MSTS ships to be suitable for amphibious operations. Forney was assigned as G5 (Plans) of the 1st Cavalry Division with selected Marine Corps officers in planning billets.[32]

On 5 July MacArthur requested the amphibious trained 2d Infantry Division, then stationed at Fort Lewis, Washington; the 2d Engineer Special Brigade (ESB) at Fort Worden, Washington; and one airborne RCT be sent to Japan for possible amphibious operations. He also requested armor and antiaircraft artillery battalions.[33] The JCS approved these requests and on 9 July the 2d ESB, with the attached 56th Amphibious Tank and Tractor Battalion (ATTB), 50th Engineer Port Construction Company, and 501st Transportation Harbor Craft Platoon, was alerted for movement to the Far East.[34] Apparently, even at this early date, consideration was being given to the use of the southeast coast port of Pohang as a site for bringing in US forces, as the ATC Deputy Commander, Lieutenant Colonel John B.

Gibbons, flew to Pohang with representatives of the Navy underwater demolition team (UDT) assigned to Admiral Doyle's amphibious force and the Marine MTT. The reconnaissance party examined the port and nearby beaches, then returned to Japan.[35]

On 6 July MacArthur called General Gay and a few members of his staff to FEC headquarters for a briefing on the plan to land his division at Incheon. There was still an expectation that US Army forces would make short work of the North Koreans. In the office of the G2, Gay was told to expedite his preparations "because if the landing is delayed all that the 1st Cavalry Division will hit when it lands will be the tail end of the 24th Division as it passes north through Seoul." Three years later, Gay recollected, "This prophecy did not prove to be correct. The 1st Cavalry Division did hit the tail end of the 24th Division on the 20th of July 1950, but the [24th] Division was not moving north."[36]

While General Gay and his staff were being briefed on the operation, the 8206th Army Unit, ATC, was attached to the 1st Cavalry Division to assist in planning and training for the operation. An embarkation-planning group was established at FEC headquarters to develop the plan for loading the troops and equipment aboard ship and a subordinate group went to work at the 1st Cavalry Division Headquarters at Camp Drake (about 20 miles northwest of the center of Tokyo). To prepare the division for the operation, teams from the ATC and detachments of marines from MTT Able were sent to each of the 1st Cavalry Division camps. Platforms with landing nets were installed and the marines and ATC soldiers began intensive, if abbreviated, amphibious training, including how to debark from ships into landing craft, DUKW operations, vehicle and signal equipment waterproofing, and communications.[37]

Lieutenant Colonel Gibbons of the ATC was designated commander of the 1st Cavalry Division shore party, the organization that would control the flow of logistic support over the beach. The officers and soldiers of the ATC were to serve as the nucleus of the shore party, with most of the personnel provided by the 8th Engineer Combat Battalion (the 1st Cavalry Division's engineer battalion) augmented by members of the 13th Engineer Combat Battalion (temporarily detached from the 7th Infantry Division) and two separate units, the 14th Engineer Combat and 43d Engineer Construction Battalions.[38]

On 8 July D-Day was set for 18 July, allowing 10 days to "prepare all plans, waterproof vehicles, procure [equipment to replace shortages], load completely the entire landing force and sail to Korea."[39] The planning process proceeded at the same time as the division was moving to the embarkation ports. So units could move to the ports on time, some annexes to the plan were distributed before the entire plan was completed. The plan was finished the night of 13 July, about the same time the division had finished loading and the first ships sailed. Beginning on 9 July, 1st Cavalry Division units began moving from their home stations to the embarkation ports of Yokosuka, Yokohama, and Oppama (south of Yokohama). Detachments of the 7th Infantry Division arrived from their bases in Japan to the 1st Cavalry Division bases to take over security and occupation functions of the departing forces.[40]

Meanwhile, shipping was being assembled for the operation. Admiral Doyle's small amphibious force was insufficient to transport the assault echelon of the division, so 15 of the Japanese-manned SCAJAP LSTs and two MSTS cargo ships were assigned to TF 90, as were seven landing ships, utility (LSUs) that had been brought out of storage. US Navy signalers and quartermasters (petty officers responsible for steering the ships) were put aboard the SCAJAP LSTs to provide for communications and assist in beaching and retracting the ships. Because the 120-foot LSUs were to be towed behind LSTs, towing gear had to be installed.[41]

The two MSTS ships, *Oglethorpe* and *Titania,* were still designated as AKAs, but much of their amphibious equipment had been removed and they had no landing craft aboard. During the short time remaining, they were fitted with the appropriate boat fittings, slings, skids, nets, and other gear to turn them back into combat loaders. Meanwhile, 36-foot LCVPs (the primary landing craft for putting troops and light vehicles on the beach) and 56-foot LCMs (for landing larger vehicles) were reactivated. Some landing craft crews were recruited from the ATC and Army engineer and transportation units, and additional Navy crews were flown from the United States.[42]

The division was to be moved to Korea in three lifts or echelons. The first lift was the assault force consisting of the division headquarters, the 5th and 8th Cavalry Regiments each organized into two battalion landing teams, an artillery group of three 105-mm howitzer field artillery battalions (FABs) and an amphibian truck company, and the divisional reconnaissance company.[43] The second lift would bring in the 7th Cavalry Regiment, two more artillery battalions, the rear echelons of the two lead regiments, and other units. Support units and the rest of the division's supplies and equipment would come in on the third lift. On 9 July the support elements of the 5th Cavalry joined the regiment at Camp McGill, from where it would move to Yokosuka, its embarkation location. On 10 July the 8th Cavalry began moving to its embarkation port of Yokohama and the artillery units traveled to the LST port at Oppama.[44]

As preparations for the landing were taking place, the ROK Army and US 24th Infantry Division had been withdrawing. As the front line moved south, the likelihood of success of a landing at Incheon diminished. On 7 July GHQ FEC had notified Admiral Doyle's and General Gay's planners that Gunsan should be considered as an alternate landing site and this was incorporated into the planning. By 8 July General MacArthur had decided that a landing at Incheon was not feasible and the issue became how to get the 1st Cavalry Division into Korea at all, since Busan Harbor was clogged with shipping. On 10 July Doyle suggested landing the division at the southeast coast port of Pohang, which had piers capable of handling shallow-draft ships and beaches suitable for LSTs and landing craft. Another reconnaissance team had surveyed the port and beaches on 9 July, finding them suitable for such an operation. Although the North Korean advance threatened Pohang, the ROK 3d Division was still holding the line to the north. A US Air Force contingent was guarding the nearby airfield of Yeongil (Yongil), and ground crews and equipment of the 35th Fighter Group were being landed by LST.[45]

The Air and Naval Gunfire Liaison Company (ANGLICO) that was at Camp McGill for the prewar amphibious training program was assigned to the 1st Cavalry Division. ANGLICO teams were sent to the 5th Cavalry Regiment at Camp McGill, the 7th Cavalry Regiment at Camp Drake, and the 8th Cavalry Regiment at Camp Zama to provide those regiments naval gunfire and naval air support.[46]

Embarkation began on 11 July. At Yokohama, Gay and the 1st Cavalry Division command group boarded Doyle's flagship, the *Mount McKinley,* and the 8th Cavalry Regiment loaded onto the APA *Cavalier,* AKA *Oglethorpe,* and three LSTs. At Yokosuka, the 5th Cavalry loaded aboard the AKAs *Union* and *Titania.* At Oppama, the 61st, 77th, and 99th Field Artillery Battalions, the 6 M-24 light tanks of the 16th Reconnaissance Company, 66 DUKWs of the 8062d Army Unit (Amphibious Truck Company), and the personnel and equipment of the shore party that were not still assisting the embarkation at the other ports began loading onto LSTs.[47] The use of DUKWs to move light artillery ashore was a technique developed during World War II amphibious operations. Each howitzer was loaded into a DUKW. One DUKW per firing battery had an A-frame to unload the howitzers once ashore. The DUKWs would then serve as prime movers to tow the artillery pieces until trucks were brought ashore, then the amphibian trucks would revert to the shore party.[48] At Oppama, the lower deck of each LST was covered with ammunition, and then the DUKWs were driven aboard and parked on top of the ammunition boxes. The division's light aircraft were to be flown to the Busan airfield to be available when the division landed, but the artillerymen of the 77th FAB disassembled their L-4 (military version of the Piper Cub) and loaded it aboard an LST with their guns.[49]

On 12 July Admiral Joy issued his order for BLUEHEARTS, Commander, United States Naval Forces, Far East (COMNAVFE) OPORD No. 9-50, identifying the landing area as Pohang. Admiral Doyle's TF 90 was designated as the attack force, and the 1st Cavalry Division was designated as the landing force. If the North Koreans captured Pohang before the force arrived, the division was prepared to make an assault landing. A gunfire support group (the light cruiser *Juneau;* the US destroyers *Kyes, Higbee,* and *Collett;* and the Australian destroyer *Bataan*) would bombard the beach and Admiral Arthur D. Struble's Seventh Fleet would provide air cover and close air support.[50]

Admiral Doyle issued his own operation order on 13 July. It was based on the assumption that the landing would take place at Pohang, but that the time and place could be changed at any time. The order stated: "Amphibious Group ONE has been ordered to land the First Cavalry Division in Korea at a place and time to be designated. The landing is designed as an amphibious assault but may take place against no opposition. In either case the division will be placed ashore as a division organized for immediate operations against the enemy."[51]

Amphibious shipping for the assault would consist of a Transport Group (TG 90.1 consisting of Admiral Doyle's flagship, *Mount McKinley*; the APA *Cavalier*; the AKA *Union*; and the two MSTS ships converted into AKAs, *Titania* and *Oglethorpe*) and a Tractor Group (TG 90.3 consisting of US Navy LST-611; 15 SCAJAP LSTs; six LSUs, which were to be towed to the objective area behind LSTs; two fleet tugs, *Lipan* and *Cree;* and a salvage ship, *Conserver*). A Protective Group of seven minesweepers (TG 90.4) would ensure the approaches to Pohang were clear of mines. Beach reconnaissance, control of the landing craft, and organization of the beach would be the responsibility of the fast transport *Diachenko* (APD-123), the tug *Lipan,* and a detachment of UDT-3.[52] Follow-up shipping for the second and third lifts would consist of three MSTS transports (*Fred C. Ainsworth, David C. Shanks*, and *General Edwin D. Patrick*), 12 SCAJAP LSTs, and four chartered Japanese merchant ships (*Marus*).[53]

On 13 July, the same day Doyle issued his operation order, the ships carrying the 8th Cavalry Regiment sailed from Yokohama and the LSTs and LSUs with the artillery, tanks, and shore party sailed from Oppama. On 14 July the 7th Cavalry Regiment and other elements of the second lift began boarding *Ainsworth, Shanks,* and *E.D. Patrick* at Yohohama, and an advance party flew to Korea to await the division's arrival at Pohang. Also on 14 July, the minesweepers of the Protective Group began sweeping Yeongil Bay and the approaches to Pohang. On 15 July the 5th Cavalry Regiment on the *Mount McKinley* sailed from Yokosuka.[54]

The transports and LSTs linked up outside Yeongil Bay on the morning of 18 July. The 1st Cavalry troopers were unaware that ROK forces still held the line north of Pohang and expected an opposed landing. But there was no opposition, and the ships of the gunfire support group remained off shore in watchful silence as the LSUs cast off from the LSTs that had towed them across the East Sea, landing craft were lowered from the APA and AKAs, troops were boated (clambered down landing nets into the LCVPs), and light vehicles and equipment were winched over the sides into LCMs. At 0559 Admiral Doyle signaled "Land the Landing Force," and the landing craft formed into waves and headed for the beach. The 8th Cavalry troopers splashed ashore at 0610, the 5th Cavalry at 0630, and the LSTs and LSUs nosed onto the beach at 0730. It was not necessary for the DUKWs to swim ashore. Nine of the LSTs dropped their ramps at the Pohang jetty or along the gently curving beach of Yeongil Bay. Because of congestion in the harbor, seven of the LSTs were diverted around the peninsula 35 miles south of Pohang to the little port of Guryeongpo-ri (Kuryongp'o-ri). As each unit landed, it moved to a previously-designated assembly area. The lead element of the division headquarters set up an advance command post near the Yeongil air strip at 1430. By midnight more than 10,000 troops, 2,000 vehicles, and nearly 3,000 tons of cargo had been discharged.[55]

General Gay took command ashore at noon on 19 July as unloading of the LSTs continued. The entire first echelon was unloaded by 1700 and began the move inland toward Daejeon (Taejon) by rail and truck to link up with the 24th Infantry Division. As predicted, the 1st Cavalry did run into the 24th Infantry Division, but the 24th was not attacking to the north; it was withdrawing to the east under enemy pressure. Since the 1st Cavalry Division moved west out of range of naval gunfire, the ANGLICO was detached on 19 July and returned to Yokohama the next day aboard *Cavalier.* On 22 July the 1st Cavalry Division assumed responsibility for blocking the enemy advance.[56]

The second lift was scheduled to arrive on 21 July, but the remnants of Typhoon Grace with 50-mile-an-hour winds came up the coast, delaying their arrival and forcing the ships of Admiral Doyle's attack force to seek safer heavy-weather anchorages in deeper water. The MSTS ships of the second lift arrived on 23 July and the Japanese *Marus* arrived the next day. Doyle headed back for Yokosuka on 23 July, leaving the captain of LST-611 as the senior officer present afloat. The LSTs of the third lift arrived on 26 and 29 July. The unloading of the follow-on ships was a much slower process than that of the attack force. The shore party was tiring after days of intense labor, the MSTS transports were short of personnel and unloading gear, and there were no trained hatch crews for the Japanese merchant ships.[57] By 30 July unloading was complete and all the shipping had cleared the harbor except for the 7 LSUs, which were left behind to be turned over to the ROK Navy, and the 11 LCMs of the 8206th Army Unit, ATC. The 14th Engineer Combat Battalion moved out to the front lines, the other engineers returned to their units, and only Lieutenant Colonel Gibbons' Korea element of the ATC remained as the sole defenders of Pohang Harbor.[58]

Delay and Reinforcement

During the last 2 weeks of July 1950, ROK and US forces continued to withdraw under North Korean pressure. The ROK Army fought mostly in the mountainous central and eastern part of the country and along the west coast, while the US Army forces delayed along the broad valley running southeast from Daejeon toward the city of Daegu. The American ground force now consisted of the remnants of the 24th Infantry Division (whose commander, Major General William F. Dean, was captured by the North Koreans near Daejeon), the 25th Infantry Division, and the newly-arrived 1st Cavalry Division. By 29 July General MacArthur realized he had to increase the combat force in Korea if he were to stop the North Korean advance. On that date he advised the JCS that, although he still hoped to carry out an amphibious landing, for now both the 1st Marine Provisional Brigade and the 2d Infantry Division (the units that were to have conducted the landing) would have to be committed to the ground fighting in Korea.[59]

The aircraft of Marine Air Group 33 (MAG-33), the air element of the Marine brigade, flew into Japan on 1 August from the deck of the escort carrier *Badoeng Strait* and the 5th Marines (the RCT that was the brigade's ground element) arrived at Busan on 2 August.[60] The 2d Infantry Division arrived in Korea in increments between 1 and 20 August.[61]

By the end of July substantial naval reinforcements had arrived in Korean waters, including Rear Admiral Charles C. Hartman's Cruiser Division 3 with the heavy cruisers *Helena* and *Toledo*. On 25 July Hartman took command of Task Group 96.5, the Japan–Korea Support Group, with four subordinate elements. Royal Navy Rear Admiral Sir William G. Andrewes commanded the West Coast Support Element and all non-US naval forces of the UNC. Royal Navy Captain A.D.H. Jay commanded the Escort Force, protecting shipping between Japan and Korea. There were two East Coast Support Elements that would rotate on station off the east coast of Korea, bombarding the coastal line of communication and supporting UNC forces with naval gunfire. Admiral Hartman commanded one element, consisting of the *Helena* and a destroyer division, while Rear Admiral John M. Higgins commanded the other, consisting of the *Toledo* and another destroyer division.[62]

Doyle's amphibious force had also been greatly strengthened with the arrival of the ships that had brought the Marine brigade to the Far East: two LSDs (*Fort Marion* and *Gunston Hall*), three AKAs (*Alshain, Achernar,* and *Whiteside*), three APAs (*George Clymer, Henrico,* and *Pickaway*), and the transport *General A.E. Anderson.*[63]

The Pusan Perimeter[64]

General Walker had to hold Busan (Pusan) (see map 9), the only deepwater port in South Korea, and enough territory west and north of Busan to provide depth to the defense. The Nakdong (Naktong) River was the obvious location for a main line of resistance. The river runs south for about 80 miles from the mountain town of Nakdong-ri (Naktong-ni), 40 miles northwest of Daegu (Taegu), to within 10 miles of the south coast before turning east to empty into the Korea Strait near Busan. Sixty miles of mountainous terrain from Nakdong-ri to the east coast town of Yeongdeok (Yongdok) provided a northern anchor for the defense. During the first week of August 1950, Eighth Army forces withdrew behind the line of the Nakdong and finally halted the North Korean offensive at what came to be known as the Pusan Perimeter. Throughout August and the first 2 weeks of September, Eighth Army held the perimeter against a series of North Korean attacks along four lines of operation: down the east coast toward the port of Pohang, toward Waegwan and Daegu, toward the town of Miryang via a bend in the river on the west side of the perimeter called the Naktong Bulge, and along the south coast of Korea toward the city of Masan.[65]

Over-the-Shore Logistics: The Jindong-ri (Chindong-ni) Operation

After the landing of the 1st Cavalry Division had been completed on 30 July, Lieutenant Colonel Gibbons' element of the 8206th Army Unit, ATC remained at Pohang, Korea. Admiral Doyle's TF 90 had left seven LSUs behind for the ROK Navy, but since there were no ROK crews available, the ATC took them over, thus acquiring its largest amphibious craft.

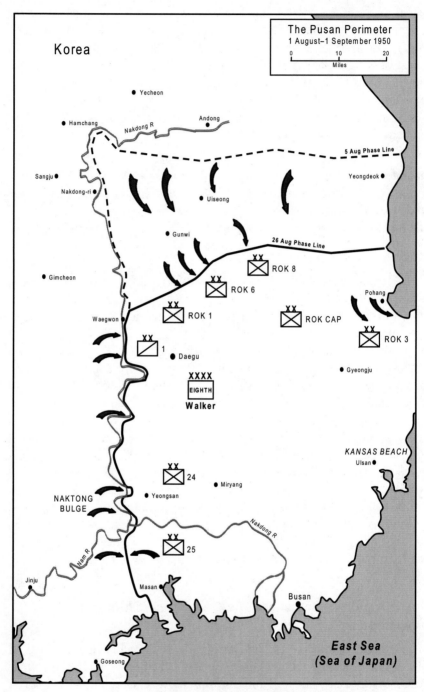

Map 9. Pusan Perimeter.

At noon on 30 July the unit was ordered to move to Busan.[66] On the morning of 31 July, the ATC's 11 LCMs and 7 newly-acquired LSUs sortied from Pohang Harbor into the teeth of a storm. Battered by rain squalls and high winds that drove one LCM onto a reef, the rest of the convoy sailed 30 miles down the coast, arriving at a sheltered area called KANSAS Beach by 2000. There, they put in for the night. They off-loaded two jeeps so that Gibbons and the executive officer, Lieutenant Colonel Frank Spier, could drive up the coast to recover the crew of the wrecked LCM. The next morning was bright and fair. The sea-going soldiers resumed their journey, arriving by 1000 at Busan. Since landing craft were at a premium, they were immediately pressed into service off-loading the ships anchored in the harbor.

During the first week in August, the Korea-based element of the ATC operated as a boat company, moving men, ammunition, and rations ashore and evacuating the wounded to hospital ships *Hope* and *Consolation* anchored off shore. The men of the ATC were fundamentally Army engineers, albeit sea-going engineers, and their skills were put to various uses, including assistance in the construction of an airfield by the unit's heavy equipment operators. On 8 August two officers and eight enlisted men were sent back with a few landing craft to Pohang, now threatened by the advancing KPA, to help evacuate US Air Force personnel from Yeongil Airfield. On the same day, another ATC contingent was attached to an ad hoc over-the-shore logistics force created to support the first allied counteroffensive of the war.

Once the front was stabilized and the North Korean advance checked, General Walker had ordered an attack against the enemy's southern thrust toward Masan. For this purpose, he formed TF *Kean* under Major General William B. Kean, commanding general of the 25th Infantry Division. The task force was made up of the 25th Infantry Division, less the 27th RCT, and reinforced by the Army 5th RCT and 5th Marine RCT, an ROK Army unit called the Min Force, and a Korean Marine Corps battalion. TF *Kean* began its attack on 7 August 1950 with the 5th Marine RCT advancing along the southern coast. To provide them with logistical support, the Navy organized a group of ships and landing craft dubbed TF *Keen*, consisting of three SCAJAP LSTs, ROK Navy submarine chaser PC-501, and Colonel Gibbons' 33-man ATC contingent with two LCMs and LSU-1042. TF *Keen* sailed before dawn on 8 August to Jindong-ri (see map 10). Finding that the Marines had not yet captured the town, they lay off shore until the area was secure. Then, using Jindong-ri as a base, the Army/Navy floating supply dump moved along the coast, evacuating

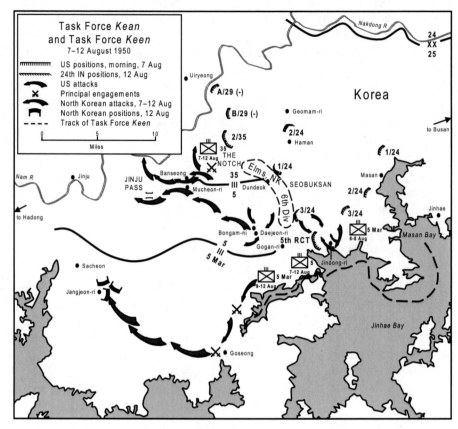

Map 10. Task Force *KEAN* and Task Force *KEEN*, 7–12 August 1950.

casualties and providing supplies to the Marines as they advanced toward the coastal town of Goseong (Kosong).[67]

By 11 August the Marines had taken Goseong and were continuing the attack when North Korean threats to other parts of the perimeter caused General Walker to recall TF *Kean*. By 14 August the Marines had withdrawn to Jindong-ri, where TF *Keen* outloaded the casualties and heavy equipment that could not be taken by road to Masan. Last to leave was SCAJAP LST-Q019, which retracted from the beach as North Korean soldiers entered the burning town. The 5th Marine RCT would be called on to deal with a North Korean penetration of the perimeter in the vicinity of Yeongsan (Yongsan) at the Naktong Bulge (see map 9). Meanwhile, another North Korean thrust down the east coast had imperiled the ROK 3d Infantry Division north of Pohang, resulting in the next amphibious operation of the war when, in August 1950, ROK and US naval forces, with some assistance from the 8206th Army Unit (AU), ATC, successfully evacuated the ROK 3d Division, which was cut off by KPA forces north of Pohang.

Evacuation of ROK 3d Division, 13–17 August 1950 (Map 11)

The 3d (*Baekgol* or Skeleton) Division originally consisted of two infantry regiments, a 12-gun battalion of 75-mm howitzers, and support elements. At the start of the war, it had been conducting counterguerrilla operations in southern Korea. After the North Korean attack, the 22d

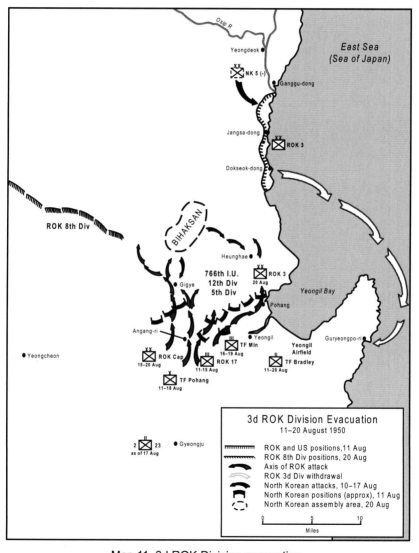

Map 11. 3d ROK Division evacuation.

Regiment, the divisional engineer battalion, and an antitank company were sent to Seoul to assist in the defense, but were badly mauled by the KPA. The division, now consisting of one regiment, the artillery battalion, and support troops, was sent north to Uljin on 29 June to block the east coast road against the KPA 5th Division, which was attempting to push down the coast road to capture the port of Pohang and nearby Yeongil Airfield (K-3), while the KPA 12th Division advanced inland to the city of Andong, which it captured on 1 August. The 3d Division conducted a delay back to Yeongdeok, about 25 miles north of Pohang. During the first week of August, the division commander was relieved and replaced by Brigadier General Kim Suk Won.[68]

At Yeongdeok, the division was reinforced by the remnants of the 22d Regiment, the 2d Yeongdeungpo (Yongdungp'o) Separate Battalion, and the 1,200-man Korean National Police Kangwon Battalion. Supported by a US 105-mm artillery battalion, naval gunfire support from Rear Admiral Hartman's cruiser-destroyer force, and F-51 fighter-bombers of the US 35th Fighter Group flying from Yeongil Airfield, the 3d Division held off the attacking North Koreans until 8 August, when the US artillery battalion was withdrawn to assist in the defense of Daegu and the division was pushed further south, to the town of Ganggu-dong (Kanggu-dong) at the mouth of the Osip River.[69]

Forced out of Ganggu-dong on 9 August, the division managed to hold the south bank of the Osip and a 6,000-yard wide strip of coast running south for 11 miles to the village of Dokseok-dong (Toksokdong or Toksong-ni) and including the small port of Jangsa-dong (Changsa-dong). On 10 August the KPA captured the town of Heunghae (Hunghae), cutting the east coast road that connected the division to its rear headquarters and other UNC forces in the vicinity of Pohang. The division's American advisor, Lieutenant Colonel Roland S. Emmerich, requested a helicopter from Admiral Hartman's flagship, *Helena,* and flew to Yeongil Airfield to confer with General Walker, Lieutenant General Earle E. Partridge (Fifth Air Force commander), and Brigadier General Francis Farrell, Chief of the Korean Military Advisory Group (KMAG). Walker told Emmerich to request General Kim Suk Won to hold the road as long as possible to delay the KPA north of Pohang, and General Farrell directed that the division be resupplied by LST.[70]

On 11 August elements of the KPA 766th Independent Unit (which had participated in the east coast amphibious landings on 25 June) cut the road west of Pohang and the KPA 12th Division entered the city. With Yeongil Airfield threatened and the possibility that the KPA would break through toward Busan, Walker established a task force under Brigadier General Joseph S. Bradley (assistant division commander of the US 2d Division) consisting of a battalion of the 9th Infantry Regiment, a tank company, a combat engineer battalion, an artillery battery, an antiaircraft automatic weapons battery, and supporting mortar, signal, and medical units. TF *Bradley* moved to protect the airfield and the avenue of approach to the south.[71] In the north, enemy pressure caused the 3d Division to contract its perimeter. The division command post was moved to Jangsa-dong and then further south to Dokseok-dong, where there was a narrow channel through a rocky reef leading to a beach suitable for landing an LST. On 12 August Admiral Hartman sent two helicopters from the *Helena* to transfer medical supplies and gasoline to the beleaguered division. A tactical air control party (TACP) under US Air Force First Lieutenant Russell L. Rodgers coordinated close air support, while the KMAG artillery advisors, First Lieutenant John W. Airsman and Sergeant First Class Nicholas Reuland, directed naval gunfire.[72]

During the night of 12 August, an ROK LST arrived at Jangsa-dong with ammunition and other supplies, but due to the rocky reefs and heavy seas, it could not come close enough to unload supplies directly onto the beach. After several failed attempts to build ramps with wrecked fishing boats and sand-filled rice bags, the Korean soldiers and KMAG advisors contrived a pulley and cable device to haul supplies from the ship to the shore. Gasoline drums were tied together in sets of 6 to 10 and floated ashore, being guided through the heavy surf by KMAG noncommissioned officers (NCOs) and enlisted advisors and ROK soldiers. Helicopters from the *Helena* were used to evacuate the seriously wounded and transport food from the ships. A second LST arrived on 13 August and was successfully beached and unloaded at Dokseok-dong. The first LST took 313 wounded on board at Jangsa-dong, then moved down the coast to Dokseok-dong to pick up rations for the wounded. However, as it pulled away from the beach it struck the submerged rocks and was seriously damaged. Water poured into the hull, shutting down the diesel engines. A walkway was jury-rigged between the two LSTs and most of the wounded were carried over the rickety swaying bridge above the pounding surf. One of the LSTs had two DUKW amphibious trucks aboard, and these were used to transfer 86 of the wounded to an ROK Navy hospital ship that had arrived and anchored 500 yards offshore. The rest of the wounded were carried to Busan aboard the second LST.[73]

On 14 August Air Force ground personnel and heavy equipment were withdrawn from Yeongil Airfield by three LSTs (an operation in which part of the 8206th AU, ATC, participated).[74] The *Helena* and two destroyers had been diverted to shell the coastal railroad at Sinchang (Sinch'ang), northeast of Heungnam (Hungnam), on the 14th, but as the situation at Pohang and Jangsa-dong worsened, Admiral Hartman curtailed the bombardment mission and returned with his ships at high speed. On 15 August General Walker ordered the 3d Division to be evacuated and relocated to Guryeongpo-ri, about 20 miles south of Jangsa-dong. One ROK and three SCAJAP LSTs were sent north from Busan. Concerned that the evacuation LSTs might not arrive in time, Admiral Hartman developed a plan for removing the soldiers by rafts towed by whaleboats to the ships offshore.[75] Meanwhile, the KMAG advisors developed a plan to coordinate the evacuation. First Lieutenant Mario Paglieri flew out to the *Helena* to coordinate the rescue shipping. Major Perry Austin, who had flown up from Pusan with details on the LST arrival, flew back to Guryeongpo-ri to meet the first of the LSTs from Busan and to send it on to Dokseok-dong. While these preparations were underway, Air Force C-119s dropped 75-mm artillery ammunition for the 3d Division's howitzers. In spite of the small beachside drop zone, just 800 yards long and 200 yards wide, every one of the artillery rounds was recovered.[76] On 16 August aircraft of the carriers *Philippine Sea* and *Valley Forge* joined the fight. In spite of some difficulties with communications, the Navy aircraft usefully added their ordnance to the naval gunfire support and the division's own artillery.[77]

The first of the four LSTs from Busan arrived at Dokseok-dong on 16 August. It beached successfully and took on board the divisional support troops and headquarters personnel. The badly-worn Korean Army vehicles didn't have enough power to drive through the sand and up the ramp of the LST, so a ¾-ton weapons carrier was secured at the top of the ramp and its front bumper winch was used to assist the vehicles aboard. By the end of the day, the LST was loaded. It retracted from the beach and waited off shore for the arrival of the other three LSTs. Preparations were made to blow up the wrecked LST with the 1,200 rounds of artillery ammunition that were still on board. However, two US Navy salvage tugs and five South Korean vessels arrived on the 16th and were able to pull the damaged ship off the beach and tow it south to Busan.[78]

Three more LSTs arrived during the night of 16 August. The destroyer *Wiltsie* led the ships through the darkness to Dokseok-dong beach, where the KMAG advisors guided them to shore through the rocky channel using jeep headlights. General Kim Suk Won had ordered each battalion to have one company conduct an attack at 2100 as the rest of the troops withdrew to the beach. He also deployed jeeps to flash their lights out to sea at various locations so as to confuse the enemy as to the exact location of the evacuation site.[79] The ships were beached with ramps down at 2130 and the loading began, with a certain amount of confusion and delay due to the soft beach sand that mired the vehicles, inexperience of the soldiers with amphibious ships, and language problems. Nonetheless, the loading took place steadily, as the ships offshore, the divisional artillery, and the last detachments of ROK soldiers kept up a heavy fire. The ROK artillerymen fired as they withdrew to the ships and continued to do so until the very end as enemy forces closed on the beachhead. One KMAG team with an SCR 300 walkie-talkie radio went aboard each LST to maintain communications. By 0700, 17 August, the last LST retracted from the beach as Fifth Air Force fighter-bombers, aircraft from the carriers, and Admiral Hartman's cruiser and destroyers, in the words of two of the American advisors, "laid down a curtain of fire completely around the beach area. Automatic weapons and heavy machineguns of the 3d Division were mounted on the top deck [of the LST] adding their fire power to the protective curtain of fire around the area."[80] Escorted by Admiral Hartman's ships and with a Navy and Air Force fighter umbrella overhead, the four LSTs steamed south to Guryeongpo-ri packed with some 9,000 3d Division troops, 1,200 Korean National Police, and over 1,000 civilian laborers. By 1030 the division began debarking. Resupplied and reorganized, the division rejoined the battle to hold the line south of Pohang and to prepare to recapture the city, which was back in UNC hands by 18 September.[81] The successful evacuation of the ROK 3d Division again demonstrated the value for operational maneuver of an amphibious capability, including ships and craft capable of beaching.

The Tongyeong Amphibious Operation

While these operations were taking place on the east coast, the ROK Navy was involved in the evacuation by sea of refugees along the south coast in the face of advancing North Korean forces. Following the conclusion of the TF *Kean* operations, an ROK Marine battalion known as the Kim Sung-eun Unit, which had participated in the capture of Jindong-ri, had returned to its base at the Jinhae (Chinhae) Naval Headquarters. On 16 August the unit was alerted for action to deal with a North Korean threat to the coastal town of Tongyeong (T'ongyong) south of Goseong. While the North Korean 6th Division attacked toward Masan, elements of the KPA 7th Division were pushing south toward Tongyeong. If they were to consolidate their hold on the town, they could cross the narrow Gyeonnaeryang (Kyonnaeryang) channel separating the Tongyeong Peninsula from the large island of Geojedo (Koje-do), from where they could threaten Masan and Jinhae.[82] (See map 12.)

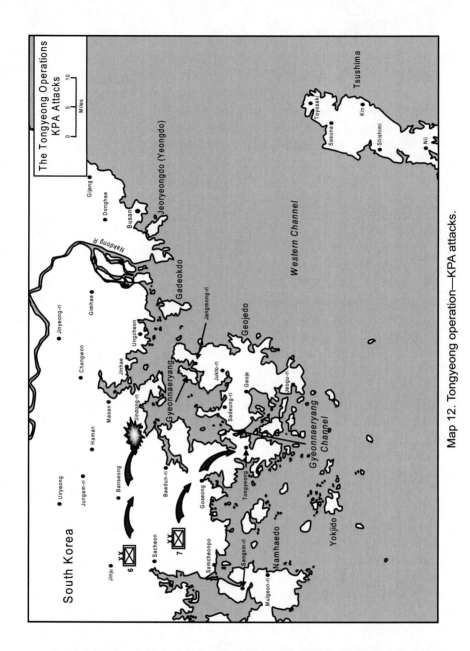

Map 12. Tongyeong operation—KPA attacks.

On 16 August Admiral Sohn Won-il, ROK Chief of Naval Operations (CNO), ordered the Kim Sung-eun Unit to land on the east coast of Geojedo Island to block and annihilate enemy forces attempting to seize the island by attacking south from Tongyeong. The force of about 600 ROK Marines sailed that day aboard motor minesweeper YMS-512 and the patrol boat *Pyongtaek*. They landed at an island off the coast of the Tongyeong Peninsula, set up a command post, and sent reconnaissance teams to the west coast of Geojedo Island and the headland northeast of Tongyeong. The Tongyeong reconnaissance team reported that the KPA had occupied Tongyeong City with about 600 troops armed with mortars and heavy weapons. Based on this information, the Marine commander recommended to the ROK CNO that, rather than just defend Geojedo Island, his troops land on the Tongyeong Peninsula and seize the high ground (Wonmun Hill) that controlled the narrow neck of the peninsula, thus blocking any attempt by the KPA to move south, and trapping the enemy forces in Tongyeong City. At around noon on 17 August, Commander Lee Song Ho (Yi Seong-ho), captain of ROK Navy submarine chaser PC-703, provided additional information on the disposition of KPA forces, advising that the North Koreans were deployed along the south coast of Tongyeong, with strong defenses in and near the city. (See map 13.)

At 1700 on 17 August, Admiral Sohn Won-il approved the plan and gave the Marine commander operational control over all naval forces in the vicinity of Tongyeong (the *Pyongtaek*, PC-703, and four motor mine-sweepers) for the purpose of conducting the amphibious landing. Jinhae Naval Command also requested air support from the Republic of Korea Air Force (ROKAF), which sent a flight of F-51 fighters and six machine-gun armed T-6 trainer/observation aircraft that had been conducting training near Jinhae. The aircraft strafed a KPA artillery unit that was moving to assist the forces in Tongyeong while the warships shelled the enemy positions near Tongyeong City and conducted an amphibious demonstration designed to deceive the KPA into believing the landing would take place in Tongyeong Harbor.

At 1800 on 17 August, the 2d Company of the Marine Kim Sung-eun Unit landed on the coast of the Tongyeong peninsula opposite Geojedo Island and established a beachhead. The 3d and 7th Companies, the Heavy Weapons Company, and Headquarters Company landed as the follow-on force. The Marines seized Wonmun Hill and the adjacent high ground. They resisted a KPA counterattack with the help of ROKAF air support and naval gunfire and, after being resupplied with ammunition, the ROK Marines continued the attack south, entering Tongyeong City and mopping up the remaining North Korean forces. Two of the motor minesweepers, YMS-513 and YMS-504, destroyed three wooden junks that were sailing north toward Goseong and sent landing parties ashore to cut off the KPA escape routes. Following this action, Commander Lee Song Ho headed north with PC-703 for other missions among the islands west of Incheon.

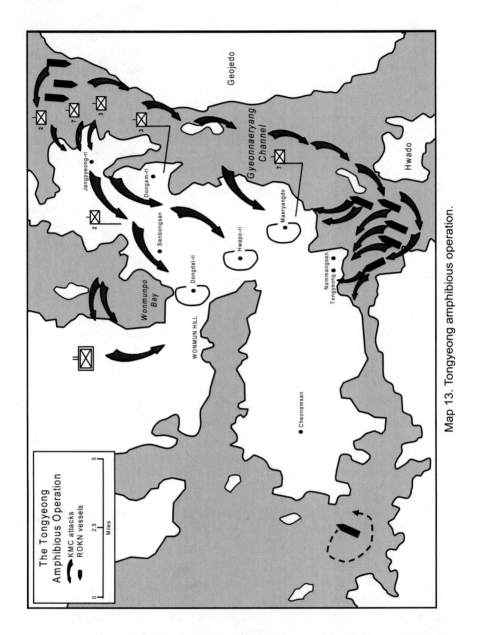

Map 13. Tongyeong amphibious operation.

Over the next 3 days, the marines and sailors, assisted by air and naval gunfire support, fought off repeated North Korean attempts to recapture Wonmun Hill. On 8 September the KPA made one more battalion-size attack in a concerted but unsuccessful attempt to overcome the ROK defenses. On 20 September the ROK 11th Naval Reserve Coast Defense Unit took over the defense of the Tongyeong Peninsula and the Marine

Kim Sung-eun Unit was withdrawn to become part of the Korean Marine Corps Regiment for the Incheon landing.

So ended the first independent ROK amphibious landing in modern times. The operation was notable for the flexibility demonstrated by the Marines and the Navy headquarters, the rapidity with which the operation plan was developed, the granting of operational control over Navy warships to the Marine landing force commander, and the effective cooperation between the ROK Navy and Marine forces and the fledgling ROKAF in a genuine joint operation.

Amphibious Special Operations, July–August 1950

In the early months of the Korean War, as US and ROK forces were pushed south by the North Korean attack, efforts were made to use American air and sea power to slow the Communist offensive. The long Korean coastline was vulnerable to incursions from the sea, while the proximity to the ocean of the east coast North Korean railroad line made it a tempting target. Naval gunfire was one weapon that could be used against railroad bridges near the coast. However, until Admiral Hartman's heavy cruisers arrived, the heaviest firepower available to Naval Forces Far East lay with the 5-inch guns of Admiral Higgins' antiaircraft cruiser *Juneau* and the 6-inch guns of H.M.S. *Belfast* and *Jamaica*. Accordingly, during the first 2 weeks of July, these ships and their accompanying destroyers struck railroad lines and roads along the Korean east coast.[83]

On 10 July Admiral Joy directed Higgins to extend the blockade as far north as possible and to do his best to damage railway tunnels along the line running from the Soviet border south to the major port and industrial complex of Wonsan. *Juneau* and the US destroyer *Mansfield* steamed north to attempt to destroy a railroad tunnel between the little coastal ports of Seongjin (Songjin) and Dancheon (Tanch'on). Gunfire had little effect against tunnels, so Higgins ordered a demolition party to destroy the tunnel with explosive charges. This would be the first US amphibious raid of the war, and the first landing in North Korea. It was strictly a Navy–Marine Corps affair and more closely resembled the landings of the 18th and 19th centuries than the recent World War II amphibious assaults. (See map 14.)

On the evening of 11 July, four marines and four sailors led by Commander William B. Porter, the *Juneau's* executive officer, transferred from the cruiser to the *Mansfield*, which then sailed close to shore and debarked the raiding party in a whaleboat. Porter's team landed unobserved, scrambled over the rugged terrain, and planted two 60-pound

Map 14. Amphibious special operations, July–August 1950.

charges in the tunnel, set to detonate when a train came through. They withdrew without incident, although they were unable to observe whether any explosion took place. This was the first of many such anti-railroad operations that the Navy would carry out during the war.[84]

Maritime special operations began to gather momentum at the end of July and the first weeks of August. On 27 July Admiral Joy directed Admiral Doyle to conduct harassing and demolition raids against military objectives on the east coast of North Korea.[85] The next day he ordered small craft to be seized along the west and south coasts to deny the North Korean forces advancing along the coast their use. On 1 August Joy directed UNC surface units and the ROK Navy to interdict land and water movement along the south coast, particularly in the vicinity of Namhaedo Island, where KPA forces were threatening Eighth Army's southern flank.

ROK Navy forces were active in assisting refugees and establishing guerrilla bases in the islands off the coast near Incheon and in sinking North Korean small craft off the west coast. On 9 August ROK Navy LST-801 established a supply base at the island of Eocheongdo (Och'ong-do), 40 miles west of Gunsan, to support the coastal interdiction and guerrilla operations.[86]

Meanwhile, Doyle, in response to Admiral Joy's directive to conduct raids, established a small Navy special operations force. The assets available to him for such missions consisted of an 11-man detachment from UDT-3, commanded by Lieutenant (jg) George Atcheson, and Marines of MTT Able, including Major Edward P. Dupras, who had been a company commander in the 1st Marine Raider Battalion at Tulagi and Guadalcanal and had much experience with rubber boats and beach reconnaissance.[87] The Marines and Atcheson's detachment were in Japan as part of the prewar amphibious training program. They had been joined soon after the war started by the high-speed transport *Diachenko*, which arrived at Sasebo flying the flag of Captain Selden C. Small. Small commanded Transport Division (TRANSDIV) 111, which was based in San Diego and consisted of four high-speed transports (APDs), the *Diachenko* (APD-123), *Harold A. Bass* (APD-124), *Wantuck* (APD-125), and *Begor* (APD-127). The Korean War era APDs were destroyer escorts that had been converted to carry four landing craft and were capable of carrying a UDT or a company-size force of 162 troops that could be landed over the beach in the landing craft or, when stealth was required, in rubber boats. Their single 5-inch gun, six 40-mm guns, and six 20-mm guns gave them a naval gunfire support capability. The APDs were primarily used for beach reconnaissance and other special operations and as control ships to guide landing craft to the beach in amphibious operations.[88] They usually carried two standard 36-foot LCVP landing craft and two landing craft, personnel (ramped) (LCP[R]). The older LCP(R) had a narrow ramp and could not carry vehicles. It had been superseded by the wide-ramped LCVP for most amphibious operations, but was faster and had better sea-keeping qualities than the LCVP and so was preferred for UDT and clandestine operations.[89]

Another of Small's APDs, the *Horace A. Bass,* arrived at Sasebo on 2 August carrying an advance element of the 1st Marine Division Reconnaissance Company and UDT-1, which absorbed Atcheson's frogmen. On 6 August Admiral Doyle activated the Navy Special Operations Group (SOG), consisting of the two APDs, the UDT, and the Reconnaissance Marines. Captain Small had overall command of the force, while Major Dupras commanded the Marine element. The rest of UDT-3 arrived from the west coast at mid-month to join the SOG.[90]

Even before the SOG was activated, the *Diachenko* had set sail with Atcheson's detachment for its first operation. The objective was a small railway bridge near the town of Yeosu (Yosu) on the south coast. On the night of 5 August, the *Diachenko* arrived off Yeosu and under a full moon launched the LCP(R)s, one of which then towed a rubber boat to within a mile of shore. From there, the team paddled closer to shore. Then Atcheson and Boatswain's Mate Warren Foley swam to the beach, where they discovered a 20-foot tall embankment that had not been revealed on aerial photographs. They scrambled up, did a brief reconnaissance, and signaled the rubber boat to come ashore. As the UDT prepared to set their charges, a squad of North Korean soldiers arrived on a railroad handcar and drove off the raiders with small arms fire, wounding Foley. Atcheson's team returned to the *Diachenko* without any further casualties and the APD bombarded the Yeosu railroad yard for 40 minutes before departing, thus bringing an end to the second US Navy amphibious raid of the war.[91] There would be many more.

On 8 August the Navy SOG was strengthened by the arrival of the transport submarine *Perch* (ASSP-313). The *Perch* could carry 160 troops and had a 16-by-36-foot-long watertight cylinder mounted on its afterdeck. The cylinder was designed to hold an amphibious tractor (LVT), but this had been replaced by a motor launch nicknamed the *Skimmer* that was better suited to towing rubber boats. Recommmissioned after these modifications in 1948, the *Perch* had trained on the west coast for 18 months with Company B of the 5th Marine Regiment and with members of UDT-3. The crew of the *Perch* had anticipated that they would operate in the Far East with the Marines they had trained with, but Company B had been thrown into the Pusan Perimeter fight along with the rest of the 5th Marines. The *Perch* embarked with UDT-1, but after a week's training the UDT was flown off for another mission.[92]

The Navy SOG undertook another series of railway-busting missions in mid-August. This time, it was the *Horace A. Bass* that took aboard the Marine reconnaissance company and members of the UDT and headed to the northeast coast of Korea. Between 12 and 15 August, the *Bass* bombarded the rail line by day, and the SOG raiders landed at night three times to blow up tunnels and bridges from north of Hamheung to an area north of Seongjin. During these raids, the Marines provided beach security while the UDT placed the demolitions. The *Horace A. Bass* team would set sail again later in the month to conduct beach reconnaissance missions at Gunsan and Asan Bay between 21 and 25 August in preparation for the Incheon landing. During the last of these missions, once again under a nearly full moon, the Marines and UDT came under automatic weapons fire. The mission was aborted and all the members of the team were recovered, although three were wounded.[93]

As these raids and reconnaissance missions were taking place, a new unit was being formed by GHQ FEC. It would be the only Army amphibious special operations unit of the war. On 6 August the Headquarters and Service Command, GHQ FEC, was directed to organize a Provisional Raider Company from personnel assigned to the command. One writer has suggested that this was General Almond's idea and that he was inspired by the exploits of Civil War Confederate General John Moseby's Raiders.[94] This may be true, but there were many scout, raider, ranger, commando, and other amphibious special operations groups in World War II that were likely to have been in the minds of the FEC planners. The unit with the closest identification with General MacArthur would have been the Alamo Scouts.

The Alamo Scouts were formed in 1943 in MacArthur's Southwest Pacific Area (SWPA) by Lieutenant General Walter Krueger, commanding general of Sixth Army. They were organized in six-man teams that conducted reconnaissance ahead of Sixth Army amphibious operations. In 106 missions in New Guinea, the Bismarck Islands, and the Philippines, including participation in two prison camp rescues, the Alamo Scouts killed 84 Japanese and captured 24 without the loss of a single man. They were usually inserted by rubber boat, paddling ashore from PT boats, but they also made use of landing craft, flying boats, submarines, and light aircraft.[95]

Whatever its inspiration, the GHQ Provisional Raider Company was to be trained in scouting and raider tactics and was intended to provide "direct assistance to the combat effort in Korea." When the call for volunteers went out to Army service units in the Tokyo–Yokohama area, over 700 applied and many of the 125 selected had World War II combat experience, some with special operations and airborne units.[96] Under the command of Major James H. Wear, the Raiders were sent to Camp McGill on 9 August. There they were trained by the Marine MTT in rubber boat and amphibious reconnaissance techniques, demolitions, and physical conditioning.[97]

Two other maritime special operations units joined the Raiders at Camp McGill. In mid-August MacArthur accepted an offer by the British Government of a Royal Marine Commando to conduct amphibious raids against North Korean supply lines. Under the command of Acting Lieutenant Colonel Douglas B. Drysdale, a veteran of Royal Marine Commando operations in the Far East during World War II, the 200-man unit, the 41 Independent Commando Royal Marines, was flown to Japan and established at the FEC ATC at Camp McGill.

Another small group of 10 British sailors and 6 marines recruited from the shipboard detachments of the British Far East Fleet and commanded by Lieutenant Derek Pounds, Royal Marines, arrived at about the same time. Known as the Fleet Volunteers, the unit was the brainchild of Admiral Sir Patrick Brind, the commander in chief of the Royal Navy's Far East Station in Hong Kong, who responded to a request from Admiral Joy for Royal Navy volunteers to form a small raiding force under US command. The Fleet Volunteers trained on weapons, demolitions, and rubber boats at Camp McGill, alongside the GHQ FEC Provisional Raider Company. Some of the Fleet Volunteers were attached to 41 Commando, while 10 of them served with the Army Raider Company.[98]

On 22 August the *Perch* docked at Camp McGill, where Major Wear and 67 men of the GHQ Raider Company went aboard to begin training in submarine-launched coastal insertion techniques. A week later, *Perch* returned to Camp McGill to embark Captain D.H. Olson and the remaining 56 Raiders. The Raiders' submarine training concluded at the end of the month, when they were informed they would not be serving with the *Perch*. They awaited word on how, where, and when they would be employed against the enemy.[99]

The FEC originally intended that the GHQ Raider Company, the Royal Marine Commando, the Fleet Volunteers, and the Marine Reconnaissance Company be combined to form a Special Activities Group (SAG) under the command of Colonel Louis B. Ely. From June 1941 to August 1943, Ely had served on the staff of the Amphibious Force, Atlantic Fleet, where he established an amphibious Scouts and Raiders School and experimented with the use of rubber boats for amphibious operations. From August 1943 to January 1944, he served at the US Assault Training Center in Bideford, England. During the Okinawa Campaign, he was the G2 of Tenth Army. After the war, he served at Headquarters, Army Ground Forces (renamed

Army Field Forces in 1948) and participated in a study of amphibious doctrine.[100]

The SAG was established on 7 September, but General Oliver P. Smith, 1st Marine Division commanding general, would not release the reconnaissance company and the Royal Marine Commando was diverted to coastal raiding missions. Ely had to be content with Wear's GHQ Raider Company, reinforced by the small contingent of Fleet Volunteers. Its future missions would be preliminary to the Incheon landing, which was being planned throughout July and August 1950.

There were other maritime special operations forces in the Far East during the war. The Air Force used crash rescue boats and other vessels for intelligence collection and other special operations, and the Central Intelligence Agency (CIA) had a large clandestine operation that included the insertion of agents, raiders, and guerrilla teams by boat, including the Navy APDs and the *Perch*, as well as Korean fishing boats and other craft. However, these operations are beyond the scope of this study.[101]

Notes

1.   Joseph S. Bermudez Jr., *North Korean Special Forces* (Annapolis, MD: Naval Institute Press, 1998), 34–37, 51, and "Korean People's Army Guerrilla and Unconventional Warfare Units, June 1950–September 1950," Part 3, updated material posted on the Internet by Bermudez in March 2000, korean-war.com/ Archives/2000/03/msg00016.html (accessed 20 January 2007). In the 1930s the Soviets had developed amphibious doctrine building on their experiences in World War I and the subsequent Civil War and had organized naval infantry units up to brigade size. During World War II they conducted over 100 amphibious operations, including several major operations in the Baltic, Crimea, and Far East. Soviet doctrine did not differentiate between river crossings and landings from the sea; they classified both as amphibious operations. These operations were seen as flank support to land operations, with the army generally in overall command. While their doctrine was well-thought out and effective, they were hampered throughout the war by a lack of specialized amphibious ships and craft and thus had to make expedient use of warships, small combatant vessels, merchant ships, fishing boats, and small craft to transport landing forces. In August 1945 they carried out three amphibious assaults at ports on the northeast Korean coast, as well as several landings on the coast of Sakhalin and the Kurile Islands. The largest Soviet waterborne operations were crossings of the Amur, Ussuri, and Aigun Rivers in Manchuria. The North Korean amphibious operations in June 1950 were very similar to those conducted by Soviet naval infantry in August 1945. Charles B. Atwater Jr., *Soviet Amphibious Operations in the Black Sea, 1941–1943,* www. globalsecurity.org/military/library/report/1995/ACB.htm (accessed 12 February 2008); Raymond L. Garthoff, "Soviet Operations in the War With Japan, August 1945," *United States Naval Institute Proceedings*, Vol. 92, No. 5, (May 1966): 50–63; David M. Glantz, *August Storm: The Soviet 1945 Strategic Offensive in Manchuria* (Fort Leavenworth, KS: Combat Studies Institute Press, 1983), 71–77, 139–153, 167–168, 170–189.

2.   Bermudez, *North Korean Special Forces*; Bermudez, "Korean People's Army Guerrilla and Unconventional Warfare Units"; Republic of Korea Ministry of National Defense, *6.25 Jeonjaengsa, 2, Bukhan ui Jeonmyeonnamchim gwa Bangeojeontu* (*The Korean War, Vol. 2, The North Korean All-out Southern Invasion and the Early Defensive Battles*) (Seoul: Ministry of National Defense Military History Compilation Research Institute, 2005), 554–560, 598.

3.   This account is based on *6.25 Jeonjaengsa,* 597–601, 605–606; and Roy E. Appleman, *United States Army in the Korean War: South to the Naktong, North to the Yalu* (Washington, DC: GPO, 1961), 27–28.

4.   *6.25 Jeonjaengsa,* 606.

5.   Appleman, *South to the Naktong,* 27; Bermudez, *North Korean Special Forces*, 35–38, and Internet updates; Kim Sang Mo, "The Implications of the Sea War in Korea from the Standpoint of the Korean Navy," *Naval War College Review*, Vol. XX, No. 1 (Summer 1967): 105–139; *6.25 Jeonjaengsa,* 549–553, 597–601, 605–606.

6. Classified as submarine chasers, the ships provided to the ROK Navy were 173-foot steel hulled patrol craft armed with one 3-inch deck gun and six .50-caliber machineguns. Later in the war, the armament varied. *Ships of the Republic of Korea Navy: Pak Tu San PC-701*, Naval Historical Center, history. navy.mil/photos/sh-fornv/rok/roksh-mr/paktusn.htm (accessed 20 June 2006). The "Motor Minesweepers" (YMS) were 136-foot ships armed with one 3-inch gun and machineguns. James C. Fahey, *Ships and Aircraft of the United States Fleet, 1945* (New York, NY: Ships and Aircraft, 1945; reprinted, Annapolis, MD: Naval Institute Press, 1976), 36.

7. James A. Field Jr., *History of United States Naval Operations, Korea* (Washington, DC: GPO, 1962), 51; Walter Karig, Malcolm W. Cagle, and Frank A. Manson, *Battle Report: The War in Korea* (New York, NY: Rinehart and Company, 1952), 29, 30; and Joseph S. Bermudez Jr., "Korean People's Army—766th Independent Unit—revision," militaryphotos.net/forums/showthread.php?t=41529 (accessed 28 February 2007) (this is a further revision of Bermudez's book posted on the Internet).

8. *6.25 Jeonjaengsa*, 135–139, 152–157; Appleman, *South to the Naktong*, 22.

9. Field, *Naval Operations, Korea,* 52.

10. Dr. Patricia M. Bartz, letter to Colonel (Retired) Donald W. Boose Jr., 10 February 2007.

11. Field, *Naval Operations, Korea,* 53–54.

12. Teletype transcript CA TT 3426, "Korea Situation," of teletype conference between JCS (plus the Secretaries of the Army and Air Force) and CINCFE, 27 June 1950, RG 218, UD 7, Entry 7, CCS 383.21 Korea (3–19–45) Sec. 21, Correspondence from 2–21–50 through 7–1–50, National Archives and Records Administration, Modern Military Records, College Park, MD, hereafter, NACP.

13. JCS Messages 84681 and 84718 to CINCFE, 29 and 30 June 1950, in Teletype transcript CA TT 3426. The Pacific Command, with its headquarters in Hawaii, was responsible for the Central Pacific area. Although the Seventh Fleet was based in the Far East, before the war it was under the operational control of CINCPAC rather than CINCFE.

14. JCS Message 84718 to CINCFE, 30 June 1950, RG 218, UD 7, Entry 7, CCS 383.21 Korea (3–19–45) Sec. 21, Correspondence from 2–21–50 through 7–1–50, NACP.

15. Field, *Naval Operations, Korea,* 54.

16. Appleman, *South to the Naktong*, 59–76.

17. Field, *Naval Operations, Korea,* 72–74.

18. Donald W. Boose Jr., "The United Nations Command in the Korean War: A Largely Nominal Connection," paper presented 8 June 2000 at the 2000 Conference of Army Historians, 7–13. The quotations are from UN Security Council Resolutions S/1511 and S/1588, in *Yearbook of the United Nations, 1950*, 223–224, 230.

19. Boose, "The United Nations Command," 9–10; JCS Message 84622 to CINCFE, 29 June 1950, Sec. 21, Correspondence from 2–21–50 through

7–1–50; Naval Blockade: JCS Message 84885 to CINCFE, 3 July 1950, CCS 383.21 Korea (3–19–45) Sec. 22, Correspondence from 7–2–50 through 7–7–50, both in RG 218, UD-7, Entry 7, Box 38, CCS 383.21 Korea (3–19–45), NACP.

20.   Recent concise overviews of the planning and conduct of amphibious operations during the first 3 months of the war include Stephen L.Y. Gammons, *The Korean War: The UN Offensive, 16 September–2 November 1950*, CMH Pub 19-7 (Washington, DC: Center of Military History, 2000), 1–19; Curtis A. Utz, *Assault from the Sea: The Amphibious Landing at Inchon*, in Edward J. Marolda, ed., *The U.S. Navy in the Korean War* (Annapolis, MD: Naval Institute Press, 2007), 52–109; Edward Howard Simmons, USMC (Retired), *Over the Seawall: US Marines at Inchon* (Washington, DC: History and Museums Division, Headquarters, US Marine Corps, 2000); and Gordon L. Rottman, *Inch'on 1950: The Last Great Amphibious Assault* (Oxford, UK: Osprey Publications, 2006). The most useful and authoritative of the more detailed secondary accounts are Field, *Naval Operations, Korea*, 102–108 (Pohang) and 171–218 (Incheon); Malcolm W. Cagle and Frank A. Manson, *Sea War in Korea* (Annapolis, MD: Naval Institute Press, 1957), 39–44 (Pohang) and 75–106 (Incheon); Appleman, *South to the Naktong*, 195–196 (Pohang) and 488–514 (Incheon); Lynn Montross and Nicholas A. Canzona, *US Marine Operations in Korea, 1950–1953, Vol. II, The Inchon–Seoul Operation* (Washington, DC: Historical Branch, G3, 1955); James F. Schnabel, *United States Army in the Korean War, Policy and Direction: The First Year* (Washington, DC: GPO, 1972; reprinted 1992), 85–86 (Pohang) and 139–177 (Incheon); Robert Debs Heinl, *Victory at High Tide: The Inchon–Seoul Campaign* (Annapolis, MD: Nautical & Aviation Pub. Co. of America, 1979); and Shelby L. Stanton, *America's Tenth Legion, X Corps in Korea, 1950* (Novato, CA: Presidio Press, 1989), 21–93. An excellent analysis of all of the US amphibious operations in Korea that focuses on command relationship issues is Donald Chisholm, "Negotiated Joint Command Relationships," *Naval War College Review*, Vol. 53, No. 2 (Spring 2000): 65–124.

21.   JCS 1776/12, "Report by the Joint Strategic Plans Committee to the Joint Chiefs of Staff on Military Estimate of the Present Korean Situation," 2 July 1950, 77–78, RG 218, UD-7, Entry 7, Box 38, CCS 383.21 Korea (3–19–45), Sec. 22, Correspondence from 7–2–50 through 7–7–50, NACP. By 25 July the joint planners estimated that in the event of Soviet intervention, the United States had the capability of withdrawing three US divisions with their equipment, plus the personnel of two US divisions and 35,000 ROK forces in 7 to 10 days. JSPC 853/26, "Withdrawal from Korea," 25 July 1950, CCS 383.21 Korea (3–19–45) Sec. 26, Correspondence from 7–22–50 to 7–31–50, RG 218, UD-7, Entry 7, Box 39, NACP.

22.   Memorandum from JSPOG (Lt Col Warren AO) to JSPOG, 26 Jun 50, "Korea Emergency Planning," RG 554, Entry 50, GHQ FEC ACofS, G3, Planning Division; Memorandums ("Action File") 1949–50 (290/48/16/4, Containers 1–2), Box 1, December 1949–September 1950, NACP. JSPOG was a group of senior

Army, Navy, and Air Force officers established to conduct strategic joint planning for the FEC. General Wright was also the GHQ FEC Chief of Planning and Operations (G3).

23. Donald McB. Curtis, "Inchon Insight," letter to the editor, *Army*, Vol. 35, No. 7 (July 1985): 5.

24. *History of the Korean War, Chronology, 25 June 1950–31 December 1951* (Tokyo: Military History Section, Far East Command, 1952), 11, hereafter, *Korean War Chronology*; CINCFE Message C 56942 to JCS, 30 June 1950, quoted in Schnabel, *Policy and Direction*, 77–78. The RCT was an infantry regiment reinforced with a field artillery battalion (FAB), a combat engineer company, and other combat and support elements capable of operating as a self-contained combat unit.

25. Douglas MacArthur, *Reminiscences* (New York, NY: McGraw-Hill Book Company, 1964, Second Printing), 333.

26. Memorandum from A.P.F. C/S, ROK, to G3, G1, G2, G4, 1 July 1950, Subject: "Chief of Staff Conference, 1730, 2 Jul 50," RG 554, Entry 50, GHQ FEC ACofS, G3, Planning Division; Memorandums ("Action File") 1949–50 (290/48/16/4, Containers 1-2), Box 1, December 1949–September 1950, NACP.

27. US Army, 8206th Army Unit, ATC, *Unit History* [1951?], hereafter, ATC History, 7.

28. Marine Corps *Evaluation*, III–B–1; CINCFE C 57061 (CM IN 9291), 2 July 1950, to JCS; CINCFE CX 57149 (CM-IN 9573), 3 July 1950, to DEPTAR; and JCS 84876, 3 July 1950, to CINCFE, all in JCS Geographic File 1948–50, CCS 381 Far East (7–2–50), "Emergency Reinforcements to C-in-C Far East," Sec 1: Correspondence from 7–2–50 through 7–23–50, RG 218, UD 7, Entry 7, Box 22, NACP.

29. Headquarters, 1st Cavalry Division, Activities Report for the Month of July (1950), hereafter, 1CavDiv AR July 1950, "First Cavalry Division Command Reports 1949–1954," RG 407, Entry 429, Box 429, NACP.

30. Memorandum from Colonel Armstrong to G3 and CofS, ROK [A.P. Fox], 3 July 1950, "CofS Query Re Eighth Army Msg #EX 33362 FB, A Planning Directive to CG, 1st Cav Div," RG 554, Entry 50, GHQ FEC ACofS, G3, Planning Division; Memorandums ("Action File") 1949–50 (290/48/16/4, Containers 1–2), Box 1, December 1949–September 1950, NACP.

31. Schnabel, *Policy and Direction*, 139.

32. Colonel Edward H. Forney, USMC, *Transcript of Special Report* [1951?], hereafter, Forney Special Report, 1, copy in RG 127, Entry 17 (Quantico Schools Files, 1947–70), Box 1, NACP; Chisholm, "Negotiated Command Relations," 72 (Chisholm's account is based on the COMPHIBGRU 1 War Diary, 24 June to 15 July 1950).

33. CINCFE CX 57218 (CM IN 9974), CX 57243 (CM IN 9994), and CX 57248 (CM IN 9997), all 5 July 1950, all to DEPTAR, CCS 383.21 Korea (3–19–45) Sec. 21, Correspondence from 2–21–50 through 7–1–50, RG 218, UD-7, Entry 7, Box 38; Forney, *Transcript of Special Report*.

34. *Korean War Chronology,* 11; Headquarters, 2d Engineer Special Brigade, Unit Activities Report, 9 July 1950 to 1 October 1950, hereafter, 2ESB UAR, 1, RG 407, Entry 429, Box 4665, NACP.

35. ATC History, 6.

36. Letter, Hobart R. Gay to Roy E. Appleman, 24 August 1953, RG 319, Records of OCMH 2–3.7A BA2, Box 746, NACP.

37. 1CavDiv AR July 1950; 1st Cavalry Division War Diary, July 1950, hereafter, 1CavDiv WD, "Summary," 1, RG 407, Entry 429, Box 429, "First Cavalry Division Command Reports 1949–1954," NACP; Marine Corps *Evaluation,* III–B–2.

38. ATC History; 1CavDiv AR July 1950.

39. ATC History, 5.

40. 1CavDiv AR July 1950.

41. On 10 April 1949 the landing craft, tank (LCT) was redesignated landing ship, tank (small) (LST[S]). It was redesignated LSU in late 1949 and this was the designation it carried during the first 2 years of the Korean War. It was redesignated landing craft, utility (LCU) on 15 April 1952. Norman Friedman and A.D. Baker, *U.S. Amphibious Ships and Craft, An Illustrated Design History* (Annapolis, MD: Naval Institute Press, 2002), 383.

42. Field, *Naval Operations, Korea,* 104–105. During World War II the 50-foot LCM(3) had been superseded by the 56-foot LCM(6), which was the type used during the Korean War. The LCM had originally been intended for landing tanks, but tanks had now become too large and heavy for the LCMs and had to be carried in LSUs or LSTs. Friedman and Baker, *U.S. Amphibious Ships and Craft,* 290–295.

43. At that time, the regiments of the 1st Cavalry Division had only two infantry battalions and no regimental tank companies. As explained below, the amphibious trucks were used to carry the artillery and serve as prime movers (vehicles to tow the artillery pieces) until regular trucks were brought ashore.

44. 1CavDiv WD, 7–10 July 1950.

45. Field, *Naval Operations, Korea,* 103; Chisholm, "Negotiated Command Relations," 72; ATC History, 6.

46. Marine Corps *Evaluation,* III–C–1.

47. 1CavDiv WD, 11 September 1950; Marine Corps *Evaluation,* III–B–3; ATC History, 6.

48. *Amphibious Operations Instructional Notes,* T 18, Oct 55, Department of Tactics and Combined Arms, The Artillery and Guided Missile School, Fort Sill, Oklahoma, Artillery School Files, Box: "Artillery, Artillery School, Curricular 1950–1955," MHI Archives.

49. Letter, Colonel W.A. Harris (Commander of the 77th FAB at the time of BLUEHEARTS) to Roy E. Appleman, 18 May 1954, RG 319, Records of OCMH 2–3.7A BA2 "South to the Naktong," Box 746, Folder: "Korea 1951—Chs I–XX," NACP, hereafter, Harris letter, 18 May 1954. Colonel Harris would be involved in several of the amphibious operations during the Korean War. During World War

II, he was the Chief of Special Plans Section, First US Army Group, in charge of planning for the American contribution to Operation FORTITUDE, which was intended to deceive the Germans into believing first that the Allies were going to invade Norway and then that they were to invade France via the Pas de Calais. During the Normandy invasion, Harris was in charge of a deception operation at Utah Beach. Thaddeus Holt, *The Deceivers: Allied Military Deception in the Second World War* (New York, NY: Scribner, 2004), 502–504, 519, 522–523, 575–576, 637.

50. Chisholm, "Negotiated Command Relations," 74.

51. ComPhibGru ONE OPORD No. 10-50, 13 July 1950, RG 407, Entry 429, Box 4405, 1CavDiv WD, NACP.

52. ComPhibGru ONE OPORD No. 10-50, 13 July 1950, RG 407, Entry 429, Box 4405, 1CavDiv WD, NACP. The terms "transport group" for APAs and AKAs and "tractor group" for LSTs and other landing ships was the standard terminology. Tractor group originated because the assault echelons usually went ashore in amphibious tractors (LVTs) carried in the landing ships. There were no LVTs available at the time of the BLUEHEARTS operation, but the term "tractor group" remained.

53. Field, *Naval Operations, Korea,* 104; 1CavDiv WD, 14 July 1950.

54. 1CavDiv WD, 13–15 July 1950; Field, *Naval Operations, Korea,* 107.

55. 1CavDiv WD, 18 July 1950; Field, *Naval Operations, Korea,* 107; ATC History, 6; Annex I (Ship to Shore Movement), of ComPhibGru ONE OPORD No. 10-50.

56. 1CavDiv WD, 19–22 July 1950; Marine Corps *Evaluation,* III–C–2.

57. Field, *Naval Operations, Korea,* 108. Hatch crews are military, naval, or civilian personnel responsible for unloading ships through the hatches (openings into the cargo space).

58. ATC History, 7–8.

59. Schnabel, *Policy and Direction,* 144–145. The 5th Marine Regiment and Marine Air Group 33 (MAG-33) together formed the 1st Provisional Marine Brigade commanded by Brigadier General Edward A. Craig. Brigadier General Thomas H. Cushman, commander of MAG-33, was Brigade Deputy Commander, and Lieutenant Colonel Raymond L. Murray commanded the 5th Marines.

60. Lynn Montross and Nicholas A. Canzona, *U.S. Marine Operations in Korea, 1950–1953, Vol.1, The Pusan Perimeter* (Washington, DC: Historical Branch, G3, 1954), 89–91.

61. Donald W. Boose Jr., *U.S. Army Forces in the Korean War 1950–1953,* Battle Orders No. 11 (Oxford, UK: Osprey Publishing, 2005), 40.

62. Field, *Naval Operations, Korea,* 125.

63. Field, *Naval Operations, Korea,* 85. A landing ship, dock (LSD) was a 475-foot ship that could carry landing craft, amphibious tractors, or amphibious trucks in a well deck that could be flooded to allow the craft to be launched under their own power through stern gates (see appendix B).

64. Although Korean geographic names are rendered here in the National

Institute of the Korean Language style, some widely used terms (Pusan Perimeter, Naktong Bulge) and those that were part of the names of military units (Pusan Base Command) are spelled in the style in use during the Korean War.

65. Appleman, *South to the Naktong,* 252–255.

66. This account is from the ATC History, 6–7.

67. ATC History, 8–10 (which says TF *Keen* also provided support to elements of the 24th and 25th Divisions during the operation); Field, *Naval Operations, Korea,* 145.

68. Major Perry Austin and Captain Mario Paglieri (KMAG advisors with ROK 3d Div), "It Can Be Done: A Lesson in Tactics," undated manuscript, also in the RG 319 OCMH records, Box 746, Folder: "Korea 1950—Chs I–XX"; Korea Institute of Military History, *The Korean* War, *Vol. 1* (Lincoln and London: University of Nebraska Press, 2000), 494–495; Colonel Roland S. Emmerich and Captain Mario Paglieri (KMAG advisors with ROK 3d Div), "Notes on the ROK 3d Division in August," n.d., in the collection of documents relating to the writing of Roy E. Appleman's *South to the Naktong, North to the Yalu* in RG 319, "Records of OCMH 2–3.7 BA2, Box 743, Folder: "August 1950," NACP, 1.

69. *Hanguk Jeonjang Sa* [History of the Korean War], Vol. 3 (Seoul: Ministry of National Defense, 1970), 388–389.

70. Austin and Paglieri, "A Lesson in Tactics," 2.

71. Appleman, *South to the Naktong,* 325.

72. Austin and Paglieri, "A Lesson in Tactics," 4.

73. Austin and Paglieri, "A Lesson in Tactics," 5.

74. Appleman, *South to the Naktong,* 329–330; ATC History, 10.

75. Field, *Naval Operations, Korea,* 148–149.

76. Austin and Paglieri, "A Lesson in Tactics," 7.

77. Field, *Naval Operations, Korea,* 148–149. Austin and Paglieri, "A Lesson in Tactics," say that air support came from the aircraft carrier USS *Leyte,* but that ship did not arrive in Korean waters until October 1950.

78. Austin and Paglieri, "A Lesson in Tactics," 8. The detachment from the 8206th AU, ATC, which had been sent to Pohang to assist in the evacuation of Yeongil Airfield provided their expertise to the salvage operation. ATC History, 10.

79. *Hanguk Jeonjang S,* 395–396; *Baeggol Sadan Yeoksa, 1947 nyeon 12 wol 1 il buto, 1980 nyeon 10 wol 31 il ggaji* [History of the Skeleton Division from 1 December 1947 to 31 October 1980] (Seoul: ROK 3d Division, 1980), 159.

80. Austin and Paglieri, "A Lesson in Tactics," 10.

81. *Baekgolsadan Yeoksa,* 158–161. Both the history of the 3d Division and the Austin and Paglieri account give these figures; but Field, *Naval Operations, Korea,* says that 5,800 ROKs, 1,200 civilian refugees, the KMAG advisors, and some 100 vehicles were evacuated, 149. Field, *Naval Operations, Korea,* says that three of the LSTs that made the evacuation on the 16th and 17th were SCAJAP and one was ROK. None of the accounts specifically identify the ROK LSTs as

ROK Navy or Merchant Marine. It seems likely that one of them was the very active ROK Navy LST-801.

82. This description of the Tongyeong operation is based primarily on *Saryukjeonsa* [History of Amphibious Operations] (Daejeon, ROK: *Haeguntaehak* [Navy War College], 2004), 463–473; see also *Korean War Chronology*, 39–40, and Field, *Naval Operations, Korea,* 154.

83. Field, *Naval Operations, Korea,* 99.

84. Field, *Naval Operations, Korea,* 99–100. There never was any confirmation that the charge ever detonated.

85. Naval Historical Center, Selected Documents: Korean Conflict, Korean War: Chronology of US Pacific Fleet Operations, June–December 1950, July, history.navy.mil/wars/korea/chron50.htm#jun (accessed 21 June 2005).

86. Field, *Naval Operations, Korea,* 137.

87. A UDT was a "naval unit organized and equipped to perform beach reconnaissance and underwater demolition missions in an amphibious operation" (Department of the Army Field Manual 17-34, *Amphibious Tank and Tractor Battalions* (Washington, DC: GPO, 1950). The nickname "frogmen" became attached to the UDT members during World War II. The Marine Raider battalions were developed in 1941 and 1942 as light strike forces capable of landing in rubber boats from high-speed transports converted from destroyers. The Raider concept was also somewhat influenced by the experience of British Commando forces. Jon T. Hoffman, *From Makin to Bougainville: Marine Raiders in the Pacific War* (Washington, DC: Marine Corps Historical Center, 1993), 1–5; Gordon L. Rottman, *US Special Warfare Units in the Pacific Theater 1941–45: Scouts, Raiders, Rangers and Reconnaissance Units,* Battle Orders No. 12 (Oxford, UK: Osprey Publications, 2005), 46–49.

88. As described in chapter 2, the first APDs were converted from World War I-era four-stack, flush-deck destroyers specifically to carry Marine Raiders. They were so useful that 35 old destroyers and 98 destroyer escorts were converted to APDs during World War II, Friedman and Baker, *U.S. Amphibious Ships and Craft,* 195–197; Fahey, *Ships and Aircraft,* 26, 76; Department of the Navy, Naval Historical Center, *Dictionary of American Naval Fighting Ships,* hereafter, *DANFS, Diachenko,* www.history.navy.mil/danfs/d4/diachenko.htm (accessed 10 October 2006).

89. John B. Dwyer, *Commandos from the Sea: The History of Amphibious Special Warfare in World War II and the Korean War* (Boulder, CO: Paladin Press, 2002), 239–240; Friedman and Baker, *U.S. Amphibious Ships and Craft,* 86.

90. Joseph H. Alexander, *The U.S. Navy and the Korean War, Fleet Operations in a Mobile War: September 1950–June 1951* (Washington, DC: Department of the Navy, Navy Historical Center, 2001), 9; Montross and Canzona, *The Inchon–Seoul Operation,* 47–48; Michael E. Haas, *In the Devil's Shadow: U.N. Special Operations During the Korean War* (Annapolis, MD: Naval Institute Press, 2000), 133–134, 144–146.

91. Field, *Naval Operations, Korea,* 137; Dwyer, *Commandos from the Sea,*

237–239. Field says the raid was the night of 4/5 August, but Atcheson's first-person account in Dwyer says that the *Diachenko* got underway from Sasebo the morning of 5 August.

92. Haas, *Devil's Shadow*, 136–140; Field, *Naval Operations, Korea,* 147; *DANFS, Perch*, history.navy.mil/danfs/p5/perch-ii.htm (accessed 20 July 2006). ASSP stood for auxiliary (A) submarine (SS) transport (P) and was the hull number of *Perch* in 1950. Over the years, *Perch* was variously designated SS-313, SSP-313, ASSP-313, APSS-313, and LPSS-313, and IX-313, "Haze Gray and Underway: Naval History and Photography: Perch," hazegray.org/danfs/submar/ss313.txt (accessed 20 July 2006).

93. Field, *Naval Operations, Korea,* 146–147; Dwyer, *Commandos from the Sea,* 240–242; Haas, *Devil's Shadow,* 146–147, Alexander, *Fleet Operations in a Mobile War,* 9.

94. Dwyer, *Commandos from the Sea,* 243.

95. Rottman, *US Special Warfare Units in the Pacific Theater*, 43–45.

96. *GHQ UNC/FEC Command Reports 1950*, "Staff Section Reports, Annex XIV Headquarters & Service Command—GHQ, FEC 1 Jan–31 Oct 1950," Adjutant General Section Report, 9, and G1 Section Report, 6, RG 407, Entry 429, Box 361, NACP.

97. Marine Corps *Evaluation*, III–B–7; Dwyer, 243.

98. Fred Hayhurst, *Green Berets in Korea: The Story of 41 Independent Commando Royal Marines* (Cambridge, MA: Vanguard, 2001), 19–21, 27, 28–33; Dwyer, *Commandos from the Sea,* 243; Marine Corps *Evaluation*, III–B–7.

99. Haas, *Devil's Shadow,* 139.

100. "Louis Brainard Ely," biography at Arlington National Cemetery Web site, arlingtoncemetery.net/lely.htm (accessed 10 July 2006); West Point, *Register of Graduates and Former Cadets, Class of 1919*, 1919. Dwyer, *Commandos from the Sea,* 243, says that Ely also served as police chief of the National Defense Force of Korea.

101. These Air Force and CIA operations are addressed by Haas, *Devil's Shadow;* also, Ed Evanhoe, *Dark Moon: Eighth Army Special Operations in the Korean War* (Annapolis, MD: Naval Institute Press, 1995). Evanhoe, 8, says that the *Horace A. Bass* was sent to Korea in response to a CIA request.

Chapter 4

CHROMITE: The Incheon Landing

Planning

Throughout July and August 1950, as the Pohang Landing, the defense of the Pusan (Busan) Perimeter, and operations on the Korean south and east coasts were taking place, planning continued for a west coast amphibious landing. General Douglas MacArthur's vision was not confined to an assault at Incheon; if he had had enough forces to do so, he would have liked to carry out a double envelopment with landings at Incheon in the west and Wonsan in the east. He directed General Edwin K. Wright to assemble information on the beaches and terrain near Wonsan, but shortage of personnel and shipping meant that only one landing could be conducted at a time. Nonetheless, MacArthur still considered Wonsan a suitable landing site and the Wonsan plan remained in the Joint Strategic Plans and Operations Group's (JSPOG) files to be resurrected at an opportune time.[1]

In Washington, the Joint Chiefs of Staff (JCS) and the Services grappled with the problems of quickly reinforcing the Far East while balancing the needs of the active war in Korea against the potential requirement to defend Europe and other areas against possible Soviet aggression. On 9 July Admiral Arthur W. Radford advised the Chief of Naval Operations, Admiral Forrest P. Sherman, that two-thirds of the US Pacific Fleet was directly supporting or committed to support of Commander in Chief, Far East (CINCFE), and the rest of his command was being made ready to assist. He anticipated a requirement for a much larger ground, air, and naval force to deal with the North Korean offensive and recommended that combat ships and aircraft be activated, the Marine regimental combat team (RCT) already committed to Korea be built up to full division strength, and "amphibious and other shipping be activated to carry and logistically supply these forces." Sherman concurred and proposed to the JCS that they recommend a partial mobilization.[2]

At that time the JCS and the Services were also discussing a CINCFE request for the 1st Marine Division and an airborne RCT. On 10 July, the day the BLUEHEARTS Incheon operation was canceled, MacArthur met with Lieutenant General Lemuel C. Shepherd, Commanding General, Fleet Marine Force, Pacific. Recalling the 1st Marine Division's service in the Southwest Pacific Area, MacArthur told Shepherd that if he had the 1st Marine Division again, he could conduct an amphibious operation at the earliest possible opportunity. With Shepherd's encouragement, MacArthur amended his 3 July request for a Marine RCT, now asking the JCS for a full Marine division "with appropriate supporting air components."[3]

On 13 July, a few days after Shepherd's visit, MacArthur met with Army Chief of Staff General J. Lawton Collins and Air Force Chief of Staff General Hoyt S. Vandenberg. He told them he intended to conduct an amphibious landing at Incheon, including an airborne landing north of the Han River using the airborne RCT he had requested. Collins was skeptical about the Incheon landing site because of the extreme tides and pointed out that limited numbers of specially trained airborne troops were available. The 82d Airborne Division was the only effective infantry unit left in the strategic reserve, while the 11th Airborne Division could field a single half-strength regiment—the 187th Airborne Infantry.[4]

During their deliberations on these requests, the JCS agreed that the 1st Marine Division at Camp Pendleton, which was badly understrength and had been further sapped of troops to fill the 1st Provisional Marine Brigade, should be built up to war strength. They recommended the President put the Selective Service Law into effect to make this possible and to replace the forces being sent to the Far East. On 19 July the President announced to the nation that he was increasing military service personnel limits using the Selective Service Law as necessary; on 20 July mobilization of the Reserves, including the Marine Corps Reserve, began.[5] The official Navy historian has called this one of a set of "interlocking circumstances" that made it possible for MacArthur to plan for a mid-September amphibious operation. The other circumstances were the availability of enough amphibious ships to transport the marines and confidence on the part of the Marine Corps that an "expedited arrival" of Marine forces to the Far East was "both desirable and feasible," thus producing an advanced departure date for the 1st Marine Division.[6] One could argue that equally important circumstances were MacArthur's strategic vision, the prewar development of the amphibious training program in Japan with the concomitant predisposition of the Far East Command (FEC) headquarters for amphibious operations, and the availability of both the Shipping Control Administration, Japan (SCAJAP) landing ships, tank (LSTs) and a much-reduced but very well trained 2d Engineer Special Brigade (ESB) capable of serving as a nucleus of a shore party, boat unit, and logistical support establishment.

In spite of the presidential action, a full-strength Marine division was not yet on its way to Korea. On 20 July the JCS advised MacArthur that it would not be possible to bring the division to full strength before November or December. Over the next few days, MacArthur and the

JCS exchanged messages and in a teleconference MacArthur urgently requested reconsideration, because the presence of the Marine division by 10 September was "an absolutely vital element to accomplish a decisive stroke." On 23 July, in response to a JCS query, MacArthur described his planned operation as a two-division corps amphibious landing behind enemy lines to envelop and destroy enemy forces in conjunction with an attack from the south by Eighth Army. The requested airborne RCT would be flown from Japan and air dropped in the Incheon objective area "as soon after D-Day as the situation will warrant" to seize a "key communication center immediately ahead of [the] troops advancing out of [the] beachhead area."[7] Finally, on 25 July the JCS advised that, after further consideration, the Navy had determined it could deploy a second Marine RCT (the 1st Marines), a division headquarters, and reinforcing elements that, added to the 1st Provisional Marine Brigade already en route, would provide MacArthur with a full-strength division minus one RCT. The third RCT, the 7th Marines, would be built from the nucleus of marine forces then based in the Mediterranean, but it would not arrive in Korea until after the Incheon assault had taken place. Furthermore, by filling the 187th Airborne RCT with airborne-qualified volunteers from other units, it could be brought up to strength and deployed to the Far East. The unit was alerted for movement, but it, too, would not arrive in Korea until just after the Incheon landing.[8]

Meanwhile, planning for the amphibious operation continued. On 20 July, with the original BLUEHEARTS plan overtaken by events and the 1st Cavalry Division no longer available, MacArthur directed JSPOG to develop another plan for an amphibious assault using the 5th Marine RCT and the 2d Infantry Division. Wright's team developed three outline plans—100-B for a landing at Incheon, 100-C for a landing at Gunsan, and 100-D for a landing at Jumunjin on the east coast—and sketched out the concepts for alternative landings at Jinnampo on the west coast near Pyeongyang and Wonsan on the east coast. On 23 July General Wright distributed these outline plans to key members of the General Headquarters (GHQ) staff for review and comment. Although there were several alternatives, MacArthur made it clear he favored a landing at Incheon. On 25 July MacArthur advised the Army Staff that one of the two corps headquarters he had requested 6 days earlier would be used to control the planned amphibious operation. By 29 July the desperate situation in Korea forced MacArthur to divert the inbound 5th Marine RCT and 2d Infantry Division to Eighth Army in Korea.[9] When MacArthur notified the JCS of this action, he also signaled that he still hoped to conduct the amphibious assault, even if he had to launch it from within the Pusan (Busan) Perimeter, and advised that he intended to commit the last division remaining in Japan, the 7th Division, to Korea.[10] Three days earlier he had alerted General Walton H. Walker to begin rebuilding the now half-strength 7th Division through intensive training and reequipping.[11]

With the two units intended for the amphibious landing no longer available and the 7th Division gutted to provide fillers for the units deployed to Korea, Wright and the planning staff urged MacArthur to postpone the Incheon operation to October. MacArthur remained steadfast. He wanted to relieve the pressure on the Pusan (Busan) Perimeter as soon as possible and also realized that the optimum conditions at Incheon would occur between 15 and 18 September, when the spring tides would be high enough to allow LSTs and landing craft to go in over the mud flats.[12] High tides would come again in mid-October, but then the autumn weather was likely to cause heavy surf and the onset of winter would affect the breakout and pursuit phases of the operation.[13] Furthermore, by the first week of August the North Korean advance had finally been halted with Eighth Army's establishment of the Pusan (Busan) Perimeter. The North Korean People's Army (KPA) would continue their attacks, but the Eighth Army delay and withdrawal had ended and from this point on, its strength inside the perimeter would grow steadily, while that of the KPA, at the end of a long line of communication repeatedly hit by United Nations Command (UNC) air and naval forces, diminished.[14]

On 4 August MacArthur directed Walker to have the 7th Division ready for deployment by 15 September and had 1,700 replacements, originally intended to provide a third battalion to the depleted 29th RCT on Okinawa, diverted to the 7th Division.[15] The next day he provided Walker with the "Strategic Concept for the Destruction of the North Korean Forces in the Field." At a date to be determined, "an amphibious force of not less than two divisions, to be known as the GHQ Reserve, will be landed at X and will establish a beachhead from which a rapid advance can be made to area Y. This area will be seized and secured as a base for operations towards the East and South against the enemy." Eighth Army was "to launch an offensive, in conjunction with the amphibious attack, in the direction of the PUSAN [BUSAN]–TAEGU [DAEGU]–TAEJON [DAEJEON]–Ascom City–SUWON rail and highway line." The forces identified as available for the amphibious landing included the 1st Marine Division, the 7th Infantry Division, one airborne RCT of the 11th Airborne Division, the 2d ESB, an artillery group of two 155-mm field artillery battalions (FAB), one antiaircraft automatic weapons (AAA AW) battalion, and an engineer group of three battalions, plus Navy lift and support elements and "[s]uch Service and Supply elements as required."[16]

Immediately after the strategic concept was sent to Walker, another high-level delegation arrived in Tokyo, giving MacArthur one more chance to argue his case for the Incheon operation and for more reinforcements. The visitors were Ambassador W. Averell Harriman, accompanied by Lieutenant General Matthew B. Ridgway, Army Deputy Chief of Staff for Plans, and Lieutenant General Lauris Norstad, Acting Vice Chief of Staff of the Air Force. They had been sent by President Harry S. Truman to "discuss the Far East political situation" and ensure MacArthur's understanding of and commitment to the policy of neutralization of Formosa after some disquieting public statements MacArthur had made after visiting the island on 31 July.[17] During his meetings with Harriman's delegation, MacArthur described his plans for the Incheon landing and made a plea that the rest of the 1st Marine Division and the 3d Infantry Division be sent to arrive in the Far East no later than 15 September, with the 2d Marine Division to be sent by 15 October.[18] On their return to Washington, Harriman and the two generals endorsed MacArthur's Incheon plan and recommended approval of his request for additional forces. It would be impossible to bring the 2d Marine Division to combat strength within the timeframe MacArthur desired, but the understrength 3d Infantry Division could be filled out by assigning the 65th Infantry Regiment from Puerto Rico as the third divisional RCT (the 65th itself would be brought up to strength by assigning to it the 33d Infantry Battalion, then stationed in the Panama Canal Zone). Because this action and the measures needed to provide a third RCT for the 1st Marine Division would further reduce the general reserve, the JCS took the issue to the President, who approved both actions on 10 August.[19]

Sometime between 10 and 15 August, MacArthur decided that General Edward M. Almond would command the GHQ Reserve (referred to as Force X during the early stages of planning and later designated X Corps) for the Incheon operation. On 12 August JSPOG issued the next revision of Operation Plan (OPLAN) 100-B, which identified the Incheon–Seoul area as the objective and set the date of the amphibious assault for 15 September. On 15 August Almond directed that a "Special Planning Staff, GHQ" be established to develop a plan, CHROMITE, based on the 100-B concept of a landing at Incheon. Major General Mark L. Ruffner, who had arrived on 6 August, was put in charge of this group. During World War II Ruffner had served as Deputy Chief of Staff, US Army Forces, Central Pacific in 1943 and then as Chief of Staff, US Army Forces, Pacific Ocean Areas and Middle Pacific in 1944–45. He had helped plan the Army part of the Gilberts operation, participated in the Makin and Leyte assault landings, and was involved in the planning for the amphibious invasion of Japan.

Marine Colonel Edward H. Forney, the commander of the Marine Mobile Training Team (MTT) who had served as the amphibious planner for the 1st Cavalry Division's Pohang operation, was assigned as Ruffner's deputy. Nine other Marine and two Navy officers of Forney's MTT were assigned to the planning staff.[20]

As Ruffner's group began working out the operational details of CHROMITE, another Washington delegation arrived to confer with General MacArthur. CINCFE had provided Washington with no additional information about his plans since the late July exchange of messages, so the JCS decided to send General Collins, Admiral Sherman, and Lieutenant General Idwal H. Edwards representing General Vandenberg, to Japan to discuss the operation. They arrived on 21 August and were soon joined by Admiral Radford and General Shepherd from Hawaii. On 23 August MacArthur met with Admiral Sherman, General Collins, General Edwards, Admiral Radford, General Almond, General Doyle O. Hickey, Admiral C. Turner Joy, Admiral Arthur D. Struble, Admiral James H. Doyle, General George Stratemeyer, and General Ruffner at his headquarters for briefings on the proposed operation. Doyle's staff described the concept and pointed out the problems inherent in making an amphibious landing in a built-up area with a convoluted approach channel and extreme tides. In Doyle's opinion, the best he could say was that an Incheon landing would not be impossible. MacArthur acknowledged the Navy objections as "substantial and pertinent," but pointed out that those very obstacles would assure surprise, because the enemy would be convinced that no such landing was possible. He likened the situation to that of Major General James Wolfe's use of a seemingly impossible route for his successful amphibious attack on Quebec in 1757 and expressed complete confidence in the Navy's ability to overcome the obstacles. He dismissed the Gunsan alternative as too shallow an envelopment that would be indecisive and ineffective, arguing that the Seoul–Incheon complex was the key area where the enemy's supply line could be cut, sealing off the peninsula. The alternative to Incheon, he argued, was to continue the "savage sacrifice" in the Pusan (Busan) Perimeter with no end in sight. He concluded by expressing complete confidence that CHROMITE would not fail.[21]

In spite of MacArthur's persuasive rhetoric, the Navy and Marine Corps officers still had reservations. Major General Oliver P. Smith, commander of the 1st Marine Division, had arrived in Tokyo on 22 August and found that Doyle remained skeptical about Incheon because of the tidal mud flats, lack of beaches suitable for landing craft, docks and sea walls along the waterfront, and the large urban area at the landing site. His underwater demolition team (UDT) had examined other west coast sites, including Gunsan and Poseungmyeon (Posung Myon) at Asan Bay, about 20 miles south of Incheon and due west of Osan. The Navy UDT and Marine amphibious scouts operating from the fast transport *Horace A. Bass* surveyed Poseungmyeon between 22 and 25 August and reported that the beach was much better for landing craft and could be used without regard to tides, thereby eliminating any restriction on the date or hour of the assault. Furthermore, the area was not built up. General Shepherd became quite enthusiastic about Poseungmyeon as an alternative and both he and Doyle tried to persuade Almond and MacArthur. However, MacArthur was determined to land at Incheon and would not accept the Poseungmyeon alternative, although Almond said it might be used for a subsidiary landing.[22]

MacArthur's confidence in the operation, in spite of the problems inherent in the Incheon landing site, were no doubt the product of his experiences in the Southwest Pacific Area (SWPA) in World War II where he had seen such problems repeatedly overcome. In the debates over CHROMITE and in postwar discussion and analyses, one can see a number of factors that influenced the perceptions of the various players. Smith, Doyle, and other Marine Corps and some Navy writers have stressed not only the challenges of Incheon as a landing site and the obduracy of MacArthur and Almond, but also the short planning time for the Incheon operation. Doyle and Smith had gained their amphibious experience in the Central Pacific where amphibious operations took place at intervals of months with a long planning time, systematic development, and a large Commander in Chief, Pacific Command (CINCPAC)/Commander in Chief, Pacific Ocean Areas (CINCPOA) staff to work out the details. MacArthur's memory, and the historical information imparted to Almond and the staff, was of the SWPA, where the majority of the landings were shore-to-shore, conducted on a fast time schedule, with little planning time and multiple simultaneous operations. Struble also came from this environment, where he had conducted half a dozen landings ranging from battalion to division size, most on very short notice, and under some of the most intense air attacks of the war.

General Oliver Smith was frequently exasperated at what he saw as Almond's lack of appreciation of the complexity and risks of an amphibious operation, which Almond on at least one occasion dismissed as technical matters. While it is true that Almond had no amphibious experience, he had studied amphibious doctrine and operations during the development of the GHQ amphibious training program. His confidence in the success of CHROMITE no doubt derived in part from MacArthur, but he was also looking at the operation from a different perspective than Smith.

The Marine general, perhaps reflecting the Mid-Pacific mindset, saw the amphibious landing as his most important challenge, while to Almond it was a preliminary action: a necessary precondition to his overarching mission to conduct sustained operations on the Korean Peninsula after the landing.[23]

The Plan

With General Oliver Smith now in Japan, detailed planning for Operation CHROMITE began in earnest. On 21 August MacArthur had requested Department of the Army approval to activate Headquarters, X Corps as the command element of the CHROMITE operation and on 26 August he issued GHQ Order 24 formally activating X Corps with Almond in command and Ruffner as chief of staff. The corps-level planning focused on the post-landing, exploitation, phase of the operation. Doyle and Smith's staffs worked together on board the *Mount McKinley* to develop the fire support and landing plans. The advance party of the 2d ESB had arrived in Japan on 30 July, with the rest of the brigade arriving in company with the 56th Amphibious Tank and Tractor Battalion (ATTB), 50th Engineer Port Construction Company, and 501st Transportation Harbor Craft Platoon at Yokohama on 14 August. The 2d ESB staff joined in the CHROMITE planning, coordinating with X Corps and the Navy/Marine team in the process.[24] One individual who was particularly helpful during the planning was Army Warrant Officer W.R. Miller, a transportation corps watercraft specialist who had lived on Wolmido and operated Army boats in Incheon Harbor before the war. Now stationed in Yokohama, he was brought in to add his expertise on tides and the details of the harbor.[25]

Admiral Struble was given overall command of the amphibious phase of the CHROMITE operation, for which Joint Task Force (JTF) 7 was established. Struble's chain of command ran through Admiral Joy from General MacArthur. His mission was to transport the landing forces, seize a beachhead in the Incheon area, and transport and land the follow-on forces on the beachhead. Once Almond assumed command ashore, JTF 7 would provide naval air, gunfire, and logistical support until relieved of this responsibility.[26]

The first major component of JTF 7 was Doyle's Task Force (TF) 90, the attack force, which would consist of the amphibious ships, a support force of small aircraft carriers, cruisers, destroyers, fire support ships, escorts (including British, New Zealand, French, and Republic of Korea [ROK] Navy ships), and US and ROK minesweepers. Of the 47 LSTs in TF 90, 30 would be Japanese-manned SCAJAP ships. The second echelon group that would bring the 7th Infantry Division in on D+3 and the third echelon group that would bring in the X Corps support elements consisted largely of Navy and Military Sea Transportation Service (MSTS) transports and civilian cargo ships.

Admiral Sir William G. Andrewes' TF 91, the blockade and covering force, was composed of a British aircraft carrier; a British cruiser; and eight British, Australian, Canadian, and Dutch destroyers. Rear Admiral G.R. Henderson's TF 99, the patrol and reconnaissance force, would be made up of US and British maritime reconnaissance aircraft and seaplane tenders. Rear Admiral E.C. Ewen's TF 77, the fast carrier force, would be comprised of up to four aircraft carriers and escorting destroyers. Captain B.L. Austin's TF 79, the service squadron, would be made up of oilers, tenders, supply ships, and rescue and salvage ships.

The major land component of JTF 7 was Almond's X Corps, designated as TF 92 while it was embarked on the ships of Doyle's attack force. It would include the 1st Marine Division, the 7th Infantry Division, and Corps Troops—which consisted of the Corps Artillery (Headquarters and Headquarters Battery, 5th Field Artillery Group, 92d and 96th FABs, and the 50th AAA AW Battalion) and the 19th Engineer Group.

The first challenge facing those planning the assault landing was the convoluted, island-strewn channel from the West Sea (Yellow Sea) to the entrance of Incheon Harbor (see map 15). The next challenge was the fortified island of Wolmido that lay just off Incheon Harbor. The guns on Wolmido would have to be destroyed and the island captured before the landing force could go ashore at Incheon. The third challenge was the 32-foot tide and the impenetrable mud flats at low tide. Between 15 and 18 September the high spring tide would allow LSTs to enter the harbor and unload at the sea wall along the shore. After those dates, LSTs could only use a single channel through the harbor at high tide; otherwise, troops and supplies would have to be lightered ashore in landing craft, mechanized (LCM) and landing craft, vehicle, personnel (LCVP). A tidal basin normally permitted full-size ships to dock during high tide and to remain within the basin during the low tide period, but the entrance gates to the lock had been disabled during the withdrawal in June 1950. Until the gates were repaired, only landing craft could use the basin. A much larger tidal basin was under construction, but was not yet usable. There was no actual beach. Most of the waterfront consisted of a stone sea wall. The initial waves of troops would have to use ladders to get over the sea wall and holes would have to be blasted to allow LSTs and landing craft to unload over their ramps.

Because Wolmido had to be secured first, the D-Day assault would take place in two phases. On the morning of D-Day, while the tide was high, one battalion of the 5th Marines, supported by tanks, would seize

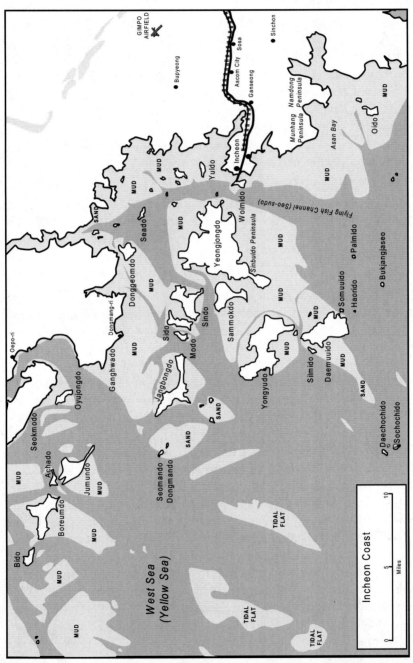

Map 15. Incheon coast.

Wolmido. They would land on the side of the island facing the West Sea (Yellow Sea), which was designated as GREEN Beach (see map 16). The battalion would have to hold the island during the low tide period, during which they would be cut off from the sea by the mud flats. During the evening high tide, the rest of the 5th Marines would land on RED Beach,

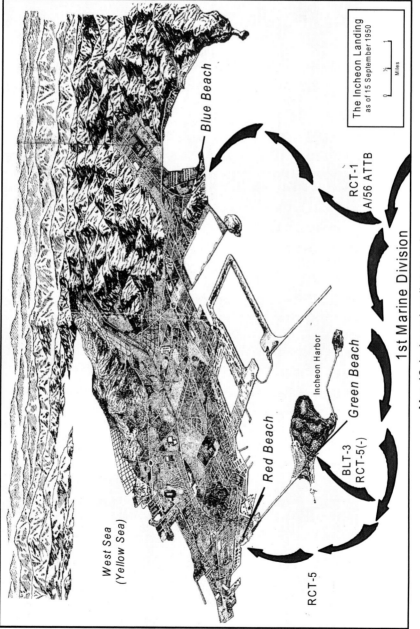

Map 16. Incheon Landing overview.

just north of the narrow causeway that connected Wolmido to the city of Incheon. Once the tide receded, the 5th Marines would again be cut off from reinforcements or supplies; therefore, six LSTs loaded with ammunition and other supplies and two LSTs loaded with medical and surgical facilities would be brought in to RED Beach and remain overnight as supply dumps and aid stations. They would retract on the morning tide and be replaced by more LSTs. Simultaneous with the 5th Marines landing on RED Beach, the 1st Marines would land south of the city at an area designated as BLUE Beach. Because the water at BLUE Beach would be shallow, even at high tide, the assault waves of the 1st Marines would come in aboard LVTs, with the follow-on forces landing in LCVPs. The 1st Marine Division amphibious tank battalion could not be used for the operation because all of the division's 17-year-old marines had been transferred into that unit after receipt of a Secretary of the Navy directive that no marine under 18 years of age was to be sent into combat. US Army Captain James D. O'Donnell's Company A, 56th ATTB was, therefore, attached to the 1st Marines for the operation.[27]

After securing Incheon, the Marines were to move inland to seize the city of Seoul and the high ground to the east and protect the corps left flank. The ROK 17th Regiment would occupy Seoul as the Marines continued the attack (on 3 September the 1st Korean Marine Corps (KMC) Regiment was substituted for this mission). The 7th Infantry Division would land administratively after D-Day to expand the beachhead to the south and protect the corps right flank, providing one regiment for the corps reserve. The 187th Airborne RCT was to be prepared for airborne or ground operations or to act as the corps reserve.[28]

The 1st Marine Division would be responsible for logistics at Incheon until it was relieved of that responsibility by an organization designated as Inchon (Incheon) Base Command. The 2d ESB, which was designated as the X Corps shore party, would be attached to the Marine division until the Inchon (Incheon) Base Command was activated. On D-Day, the marines would provide their own shore party for the assault landings. A 2d ESB reconnaissance team from the brigade's intelligence section would accompany the 5th Marines onto RED Beach on D-Day to survey the port facilities. On order, 2d ESB would assume operational control of the Marine shore party elements and take responsibility for all port operations. The marines would operate RED and GREEN Beaches under 2d ESB direction, while the 532d Engineer Boat and Shore Regiment (EB&SR), with the 50th Engineer Port Construction Company attached, would operate the inner harbor, designated as YELLOW Beach, and the tidal basin. As the marines moved inland, the 2d ESB would take over their beaches and the

Inchon (Incheon) Base Command would assume shore party and harbor defense responsibilities once it was established ashore.[29]

A full-strength ESB was capable of supporting a corps-size amphibious landing with two divisions landing simultaneously. However, the 2d ESB was far from a full-strength organization and required augmentation to carry out its mission. Officers of the technical services were attached to the 2d ESB staff during the planning and initial phase of the operation. Naval Beach Group 1, the 104th Naval Construction Battalion, the 1st Marine Division Shore Party Battalion, the 1st Combat Service Group and 7th Motor Transport Battalion (Fleet Marine Force Pacific units), the Army 73d Combat Engineer Battalion, and other smaller units would be attached to the brigade effective on D-Day. In addition, Japanese and Korean workers were recruited to serve as stevedores and hatch crews to assist in loading and unloading the ships. The 532d EB&SR was reorganized to include a provisional boat battalion and a provisional shore battalion to provide command and control for the organic boat company, the two organic shore companies, the Marine shore party battalion, and the 50th Engineer Port Company, which would initially operate as an ad hoc shore party unit. A group of Air Force elements, an Army aviation engineer battalion (an airfield construction and repair unit), and an AAA AW battery were designated as TF *Kimpo*, with the mission of putting the airfield into operation after it was captured.[30]

In planning for fire support, the old issue of tactical surprise versus destruction of enemy fortifications arose again. The compromise was that Navy and Marine aircraft would strike a range of targets on the Korean west coast, increasingly focusing on the Incheon area and culminating in napalm attacks on Wolmido a few days prior to the landing to burn off the vegetation that might conceal fortifications. Naval gunfire bombardments would be carried out at various places on both coasts as a deception measure and an amphibious raid at Gunsan on 13 September was intended to further confuse the enemy as to the actual objective. The plan called for only 1 day of preparatory bombardment on D-1. However, on 10 September Admiral Struble decided on a 2-day operation beginning on D-2. On 13 September a cruiser-destroyer force would steam up the channel to bombard Wolmido and Incheon to destroy as much of the fortifications as possible and to draw enemy fire so that coastal defense guns could be located and destroyed during a second bombardment on 14 September. Navy and Marine Corps aircraft flying from carriers would conduct strikes on both days. Final preparatory fires would precede the landings on D-Day.[31]

Although General Stratemeyer desired to have control of all aviation during the operation, General MacArthur's decision was that Navy and

Marine aircraft would support the landing and conduct all air operations within the amphibious objective area (AOA)—a radius of approximately 60 miles around Incheon—beginning on D-3 and would conduct attacks against airfields within 150 miles of Incheon. Far East Air Force (FEAF) would be responsible for interdiction operations to isolate the Seoul–Incheon area, support of Eighth United States Army in Korea (EUSAK), and other air operations outside the AOA. Aircraft of Marine Air Group (MAG) 33, providing preliminary air strikes and close air support would initially fly from the two small carriers of Rear Admiral R.W. Ruble's Carrier Division 15 and be under Ruble's operational control until their headquarters and planes were established ashore. Then the commanding general of MAG 33 of the 1st Marine Air Wing would become the X Corps Tactical Air Commander, controlling all air operations within the X Corps operational area with the option of calling on Fifth Air Force (FEAF's tactical air force) for air support.[32]

On 30 August MacArthur issued UNC/FEC Operation Order (OPORD) No. 1, giving X Corps the mission to "Land over beaches in the INCHON [INCHEON] area, seize and secure INCHON, KIMPO [GIMPO] AF and SEOUL and block enemy forces south of the line: SUWON-ICH'ON. Sever enemy communications in SEOUL Area." Smith, 1st Marine Division commander, was to command the landing force and Major General David Barr, 7th Infantry Division commander, was to command the follow-up force. The 3d Infantry Division and 187th Airborne RCT were designated as GHQ Reserve with the 187th prepared to "Execute air drop or landing in area when ordered." Eighth Army was to initiate its offensive on D+1 and was to release the 1st Marine Brigade, the 73d Tank Battalion, and the ROK 17th Regiment (all amphibiously combat loaded) to the 1st Marine Division by 4 September. Although D-Day was not specified in the order, the day was set as 15 September 1950.[33] At Kobe and Yokohama, the troops were preparing to embark. Loading of the cargo ships had already begun, although it had been interrupted when Typhoon Jane swept across Japan on 3 September. Another storm was brewing at GHQ over the release of the 5th Marines.

5th Marines Issue

On 30 August, the day UNC/FEC OPORD No. 1 was issued, Smith asked for the return of the 1st Provisional Brigade to 1st Marine Division control by 1 September. GHQ FEC ordered Walker to make the brigade available on 4 September, but on 31 August the North Koreans began another major offensive in an attempt to break through the Pusan (Busan) Perimeter. With desperate fighting taking place in Korea, the order was rescinded. Almond offered to provide the 32d Infantry Regiment of the 7th Division as an alternative, but Smith refused arguing that to send in an untrained Army regiment for the initial assault would be unfair both to the soldiers and to his marines. He also doubted that the substitution could be made, since the ship was already en route to Korea to pick up the 5th Marines and would have to return to Japan to load the 32d Infantry. The issue was finally resolved on 3 September when Struble proposed that one of 7th Division's regiments be sent to Busan to serve as a floating reserve offshore. The Marine brigade could then be released to the 1st Marine Division and, if the floating reserve regiment was not used in the perimeter, it could later rejoin the 7th Division.[34] The 17th Infantry was alerted for movement that same night.[35] General Wright flew to Korea the next day to explain the situation to General Walker. The Marine brigade was to be pulled off the line no later than the night of 5/6 September and sent immediately to Busan. The 17th Infantry was to arrive off Busan no later than 7 September to serve as the floating reserve. The lead regiment of the incoming 3d Division, the 65th Infantry, would also be sent to Busan between 18 and 20 September and assigned to Eighth Army. Once the 65th Infantry arrived, the 17th Infantry (if it had not been committed to combat by that time) would be sent on to Incheon to join the 7th Division.[36]

Decision in Washington

There was still some disquiet in Washington following the JCS visit to Tokyo. On 28 August the JCS had sent MacArthur a message concurring in an amphibious landing on the west coast, but with only conditional approval of the Incheon landing site:

> 1. After reviewing the information brought back by General Collins and Admiral Sherman we concur in making preparations and executing a turning movement by amphibious forces on the west coast of Korea either at Inchon in the event that enemy defenses in vicinity of Inchon prove ineffective or at a favorable beach south of Inchon if one can be located. We further concur in preparation, if desired by CINCFE, for an envelopment by amphibious forces in the vicinity of Kunsan [Gunsan]. We understand that alternate plans are being prepared in order best to exploit the situation as it develops.
>
> 2. We desire information as becomes available with respect to conditions in the possible objective areas and timely information as to your probable intentions and plans for offensive operations.[37]

On 5 September the JCS asked MacArthur to inform them of any changes that might have been made to his plans for the mid-September amphibious assault.[38] MacArthur replied the next day that the general outline of the plan had not changed and he was dispatching a courier who would arrive in Washington approximately 11 September with a copy of the GHQ campaign plan and the OPORDs of the major subordinate commands. On 7 September the JCS concurred in launching a counteroffensive as early as feasible, but expressed concern over recent events, clearly a reference to the North Korean offensive and the commitment of practically all of Eighth Army's reserves. They reminded MacArthur that all available trained reserves except the 82d Airborne Division had been allocated to the Far East and, even though National Guard divisions were being mobilized, they could not reach Korea for at least 4 months in the event the linkup of Eighth Army and X Corps could not be effected quickly. It would appear that the ghost of Anzio hung over the JCS as they asked for MacArthur's estimate of the "feasibility and chance of success" of the planned operation. MacArthur responded at once, reassuring the JCS that there was no question in his mind as to the feasibility of the operation, downplaying the significance and impact of the recent KPA attacks, and pointing out that the success of the operation did not depend on an early EUSAK—X Corps linkup, since both forces were "completely self-sustaining because of our absolute air and naval supremacy." He noted pointedly that the "embarkation of troops and preliminary air and naval preparations" were already underway. On 8 September the JCS radioed that, in view of MacArthur's 7 September message, "we approve your plan and President has been so informed."[39]

As these final messages were crossing the Pacific, the embarkation and preliminary activities MacArthur mentioned were taking place. On 5 September the 1st Provisional Marine Brigade reverted to 1st Marine Division command and moved to Busan to begin outloading. It was met there by Lieutenant Colonel Kim Sung Eun's 3,000-man 1st KMC Regiment, which had conducted the Tongyeong operation the previous month, and had now been substituted for the ROK 17th Regiment as the Incheon occupation force. The two units began loading aboard the transports. They would join the division at sea en route to Incheon.[40] That same day, Colonel Herbert B. Powell's 17th RCT began loading aboard two large MSTS transports (*General W.M. Black*, T-AP-113, and *General John Pope*, T-AP-110) and a leased civilian freighter. Heavy cranes lifted the tank company vehicles and the regimental trucks, combat loaded with ammunition, onto the freighter. Powell was aboard one of the transports, but the senior Navy captain in charge of the little convoy was aboard the other transport, complicating coordination. The three ships sailed at 0200 on 6 September.[41]

The ships carrying the 17th RCT arrived at the crowded Busan Harbor the next day (7 September), anchoring 3 miles off shore. Powell went ashore to check in with the Eighth Army chief of staff and the G3, Colonel John Dabney, who were unclear as to exactly what orders Powell had been given or how much authority Eighth Army had over its floating reserve. However, later that day Eighth Army received a message from GHQ FEC confirming the verbal instructions that sent the 17th RCT to Busan. Powell's RCT would spend the next 17 days floating off Busan. To be ready for deployment, the vehicle drivers turned their engines over each day and Powell received permission to bring one of the transports into port every other day so that groups of soldiers could debark for a 5-mile march to keep them in shape for combat. They also got some impromptu amphibious training, as they debarked and re-embarked by climbing landing nets thrown over the sides of the ships.[42]

The rest of the 7th Division had begun embarkation at Yokohama on 6 September. It had undergone a quick course of amphibious training and was still absorbing huge numbers of replacements. Because the 7th Division had been so badly depleted by providing fillers to the divisions deploying to Korea, extraordinary measures had to be taken to bring it up to strength. In addition to the replacements diverted from Okinawa, all of the infantry and artillery replacements going to the Far East from the end of August to the end of the first week of September had been sent to the 7th Division. These 390 officers and 5,400 enlisted replacements were still not enough to bring the unit up to war strength, so General MacArthur had directed General Walker to send South Korean civilian volunteers to Japan to be hastily trained and assigned to the division. Over 8,600 of these men of various ages had arrived over a 3-day period, "stunned, confused, and exhausted," to undergo an intense training regime, be outfitted in American uniforms, and folded into the 7th Division. Every rifle company and artillery battery received 100 of these men, each of which was assigned an American "buddy" for training and control. It was not an ideal system, but it worked well enough to be adopted for all US Army units as the Korean Augmentation to the US Army (KATUSA) Program.[43]

On 10 September Lieutenant Colonel Lynn D. Smith, the courier MacArthur had promised to send to JCS, left Tokyo with a copy of the CHROMITE plan. Concerned that the JCS would try to meddle with the operation if they were given too much advance notice, MacArthur told Lieutenant Colonel Smith, "Don't get there too soon." He also advised

Lieutenant Colonel Smith that, if the JCS said the operation was too big a gamble, "tell them I said this is throwing a nickel in the pot after it has been opened for a dollar. The big gamble was Washington's decision to put American troops on the Asiatic mainland." Lynn Smith would arrive in Washington just before midnight on 13 September and report to the JCS the next morning. At 1100 on 14 September (15 September Korea time) Smith entered the JCS briefing room. General Collins said, "This is D-Day, isn't it, Colonel?" and asked when H-hour was. When Smith replied that the landing on Wolmido would begin in 6 hours, Collins said, "Thank you. You'd best get on with the briefing." The Chiefs listened to the briefing and asked questions for 2 hours without any criticism of the concept of the operation or of any of the details. Smith noticed that as they left the briefing room, they each glanced at the clock on the wall, realizing that the 5th Marines would hit the Wolmido sea wall in 4 hours.[44]

On 9 September the LSTs carrying the 1st Marines and A/56th ATTB shoved off from the pier at Kobe. Captain O'Donnell's armored amphibians, which would constitute the first wave going into BLUE Beach, were distributed among four LSTs. On 11 September the 1st Marine Division (less the 5th and 7th Marines) sailed from Kobe, and the 7th Division sailed from Yokohama into heavy seas caused by approaching Typhoon Kezia. Admiral Doyle was counting on the typhoon curving north, away from the route of his attack force, as indeed it did.[45] The next day, the 5th Marines sailed from Busan. On 13 September Admiral Struble's cruiser-destroyer force steamed up the Flying Fish Channel to begin the preparatory bombardment of Wolmido and Incheon. Watching their approach were an ROK Navy commander and a US Navy lieutenant who with a group of young guerrillas had ensured the offshore islands were in friendly hands and had reconnoitered the approaches to Incheon.

Special Operations in Preparation for CHROMITE

Operations LEE and TRUDY JACKSON

In the month before the Incheon landing, ROK Navy patrol and landing craft, supported by warships of the Royal Navy and Royal Canadian Navy, carried out reconnaissance probes, raids, and landings on the islands along the approaches to Incheon. These activities were collectively called Operation LEE, after Commander Lee Sung Ho whose submarine chaser PC-703 had played a key role in the opening stage of the Tongyeong operation on the south coast. Lee had tactical control of the ROK operations that began on the night of 17 August 1950, as PC-703 arrived from southern waters and joined two motor minesweepers and LST-801, supported by the Canadian destroyer *Athabaskan*, which landed 110 ROK sailors on Deokjeok (Tokchok-do), the largest of a string of islands southwest of Incheon. (See map 17.)

On 19 August they secured the island of Yeongheungdo (Yonghung-do), about 14 miles southwest of Incheon. The next day, Canadian sailors from the *Athabaskan* landed on the island of Palmido at the mouth of Incheon Harbor and disabled the navigation light and radio in the Palmido lighthouse. On 1 September Commander Lee was joined by US Navy

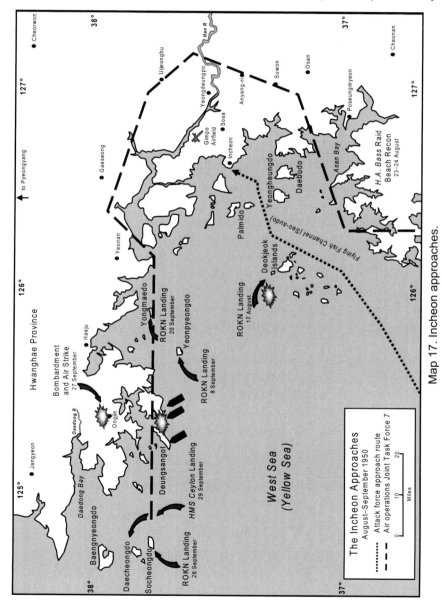

Map 17. Incheon approaches.

Lieutenant Eugene F. Clark, who had been sent by Far East Command Joint Special Operations, and two Korean officers to gather intelligence on the tides and beach conditions in preparation for the landing. Clark, a former Navy enlisted man, had been commissioned in 1943 and served as a Japanese linguist and amphibious warfare officer. He had commanded an LST and an attack transport and had been involved in intelligence operations on the China coast before the war; thus, he was well suited to the task ahead.[46]

Clark's mission, code named Operation TRUDY JACKSON, was a special project of the Joint Special Operations Staff, which had been set up by GHQ FEC to coordinate intelligence efforts. The FEC G2 representative for the operation was retired Major General Holmes E. Dager. In addition to Clark and his two Korean colleagues (ROK Navy Commander Youn Joung, who operated under the alias "Yong Chi Ho," and ROK Army counterintelligence Colonel Ke In-Ju, who operated under the alias "Kim Nam Sun"), the TRUDY JACKSON team included a US Army major, a civilian intelligence analyst, and two signal corps lieutenants.[47]

In the 2 weeks prior to the Incheon operation, Clark, Youn, and Ke, supported by Commander Lee's forces, set up a base on the island of Yeongheungdo. There they recruited a force of men and teenage boys to serve as a security and reconnaissance force and acquired a small fleet of machinegun-armed sailing junks, sampans, and one motorized junk. To collect intelligence for the upcoming operation, they questioned local fishermen and conducted personal explorations of Palmido (where Clark determined that the light could be put back into operation), Incheon, and even the outskirts of Seoul, where they made contact with other resistance groups. On 8 September Clark's armed fishing boats fought off an attempted North Korean landing, but on 14 September the North Koreans mounted a more determined attack. Clark evacuated his base island and set off for Palmido, where he reignited the light to help guide the approaching UNC invasion force. Back at Yeongheungdo, the North Koreans rounded up and shot 50 of the men, women, and children left behind.

GHQ FEC Raider Company Demonstration at Gunsan

Other operations were taking place in preparation for the landing. From 21 to 24 August Navy UDT frogmen and Marine reconnaissance company members of the Navy Special Operations Group operating from the APD *Harold A. Bass* reconnoitered the beaches at Gunsan to the south and at Poseungmyeon in the Asan Bay. These operations provided intelligence about alternative beaches and, equally important, were part of a deception plan to confuse the North Koreans about the actual landing site.

Major James H. Wear's GHQ Raider Company also contributed to the deception operation, but at a cost. On 12 September the Raider Company and 10 of the Royal Navy Fleet Volunteers boarded the British frigate *Whitesand Bay*, accompanied by Colonel Louis B. Ely. On 13 September they arrived off the coast near Gunsan, where they paddled ashore in rubber boats to a small island at the mouth of Gunsan Bay (see map 18). After moving a short distance inland, they came under machinegun fire. Having no hand grenades, they had to engage with rifle fire. In the course of the

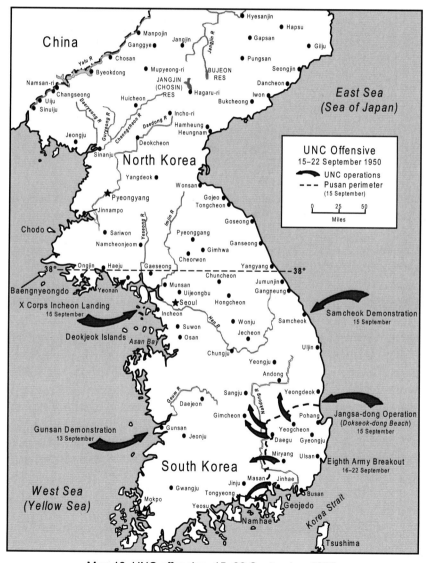

Map 18. UNC offensive, 15–22 September 1950.

firefight, two of the Raiders were killed: First Lieutenant James W. Clance, a veteran of the 82d Airborne Division, and Corporal John W. Maines. Corporal Raymond E. Puttin was seriously wounded. As they withdrew, the Raiders came under artillery fire and were unable to bring the two bodies of their comrades with them. Corporal Puttin died of his wounds aboard the *Whitesand Bay*.[48] The frigate then headed north for the Raiders' next mission.

Operational Execution

On 13 and 14 September Admiral Struble's cruisers and destroyers and Admiral Ewen's aircraft bombarded Wolmido and Incheon, destroying most of the coast defense guns at a cost of one officer killed and eight men wounded. They had also detonated several mines, but the North Koreans had fortuitously only emplaced a few of their large stockpile. Admiral Doyle's attack force arrived before dawn on D-Day, 15 September. Doyle's flagship (the *Mount McKinley*, anchored in the channel) and the fire support ships, destroyers, and LSMRs moved into position. At 0520 Doyle ordered, "Land the landing force." Three APDs— *Horace A. Bass*, *Diachenko*, and *Wantuck*—carried Lieutenant Colonel Robert D. Taplett's 3d Battalion, 5th Marines, who now boarded LCVPs and headed for GREEN Beach as the three landing ships, medium (rocket) (LSM[R]s) each fired a barrage of 1,000 5-inch rockets and Marine F4U *Corsair* fighter-bombers strafed the shoreline. At 0633 Taplett's marines went ashore against light opposition and by 0655 had raised an American flag on the 325-foot peak of Radio Hill, the highest ground on the island. Taplett's battalion was reinforced by 10 tanks that had been brought ashore in 3 landing ships, utility (LSUs), which had made the journey from Kobe in the well deck of the *Fort Marion*. The battalion reserve came in behind the tanks. After several firefights with bypassed North Koreans, the 3/5th Marines secured the island by 0800. Now the tide receded and Taplett's marines waited for the next act to begin. General MacArthur sent a message to the JCS: "Landing first phase successful with losses light. Surprise apparently complete. All goes well and on schedule." He commented on the noteworthy cooperation between the Services, and pointed out that the "natural obstacles, combined with the extraordinary tidal conditions, demanded a complete mastery of the technique of amphibian warfare." During the day Struble took MacArthur, Almond, and Shepherd aboard his barge for a cruise along GREEN Beach and to within 1,000 yards of the still-hostile RED Beach. The Navy construction battalion that had landed at Wolmido spent the day building a pontoon causeway to facilitate unloading LSTs.[49] (See map 19.)

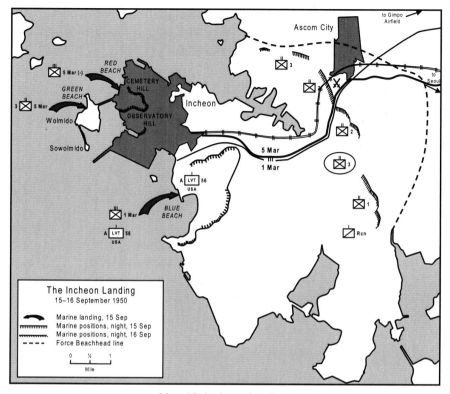

Map 19. Incheon landing.

The cruisers, destroyers, and Navy and Marine Corps aircraft continued their bombardment of Incheon throughout the day, increasing in intensity as the attack transports *Cavalier* (APA-37) and *Henrico* (APA-45) carrying Lieutenant Colonel Raymond L. Murray's 5th Marines (minus the 3d Battalion, which had made the Wolmido assault) and the LSTs carrying Colonel Lewis B. Puller's 1st Marines and Captain O'Donnell's A/56th ATTB approached Incheon with the rising tide. At 1445 Doyle once again signaled "Land the landing force." Off RED Beach, the LCVPs and LCMs carrying the 1st and 2d Battalions of the 5th Marines followed the guide ship, APD *Horace A. Bass*, to the line of departure. The LSM(R)s fired a final barrage of some 6,500 rockets as the landing craft raced toward the beach. At 1732 the 5th Marines, carrying scaling ladders, hit the sea wall at RED Beach with two battalions abreast. Resistance was moderate, and by 2000 the 5th Marines had secured the high ground behind the beach. The eight supply and hospital LSTs came in between 1830 and 1900. Some damage and casualties were caused aboard the LSTs by enemy fire, but otherwise the operation went smoothly. The eight landing ships remained aground during the night, providing ammunition, rations, and medical care to the marines. Lieutenant Claude L. Roberts Jr. and the 2d ESB reconnaissance team that had come ashore on D-Day with the 5th Marines picked their way through the rubble to survey the piers along YELLOW Beach and the tidal basin in preparation for the arrival of the brigade the next morning.[50]

The landing of the 1st Marines on BLUE Beach was set for the same time as that of the 5th Marines on RED Beach. At 1630 O'Donnell's landing vehicles, tracked (armored) (LVT[A]s) rumbled down the ramps of the LSTs and into the water. They formed up and, assisted by UDT guide boats, crossed the line of departure at 1705 and headed for the shore. Behind them came the LVTs carrying the 2d and 3d Battalions of the 1st Marines. The Army LVTs soon disappeared from the marines' view into a yellow and gray haze caused by the intense preparatory fires. Brigadier General Edwin H. Simmons, then a major commanding the Weapons Company, 3/1st Marines, recalled that the "soldiers had the compasses and seamanship to pierce the smoke and reached the beach on time. The second and following waves did not do so well." Some of the Marine LVTs strayed off course, and the leading wave of the regimental reserve (BLT 1/1) initially landed along some salt flats to the left of BLUE Beach before reaching the assigned landing area.[51]

BLUE Beach, like RED Beach, was fronted by a 15-foot high sea wall. O'Donnell's LVT(A)s sought a way past the wall, some of them trundling back into the water to move around to the flank. Eventually, all of his armored amphibians managed to get on line beyond the sea wall, where they engaged enemy automatic weapons and snipers with their 75-mm howitzers. In spite of the initial confusion, the marines quickly came ashore, disembarked from their LVTs, and climbed over the sea wall, moving inland past the Army LVT(A)s. Throughout the night, O'Donnell's howitzers periodically answered calls for indirect fire from the marines.[52]

Incheon D+1 Operations

By 0730 on 16 September, the 1st and 5th Marine RCTs had linked up and continued the attack inland toward the Force Beachhead Line (see map 20). On BLUE Beach, O'Donnell moved the 18 amphibious tanks of Company A, 56th ATTB, 1,000 yards inland. There, they established a perimeter defense, set up a fire direction center, and ran telephone wire to Puller's command post so that the company no longer had to rely on the SCR 300 walkie-talkies for communications with the 1st Marine RCT. When Puller displaced his headquarters forward, he ordered O'Donnell's company to stay in place and stand by for indirect fire missions. Although gunfire support from the ships offshore and from the 11th Marines on Wolmido and RED Beach continued throughout the day, no fire missions came for Company A.[53]

The 1st KMC Regiment landed on D+1 and took over responsibility for the security of the Incheon area, initially reporting to 1st Marine Division Headquarters and then to the 2d ESB as the Marines moved inland. Colonel Joseph J. Twitty, the brigade commander, and his headquarters came ashore later in the day.[54] On Wolmido, Team 3 of the 1st Marine Shore Party Battalion Group A continued unloading operations while the 104th Naval Construction Battalion completed the first pontoon pier on the west side of the island, began work on a second pier on the east side, and continued to improve the LST ramps. The eight LSTs at RED Beach retracted with the morning tide and eight more arrived. Six made it to shore safely to be unloaded during the day by the Naval Beach Group, the Shore Party Battalion Headquarters and Service Company, and Shore Party Group A (reinforced by a team from Group B), but two of the ships grounded too far out to be unloaded and had to wait for the next tide. On

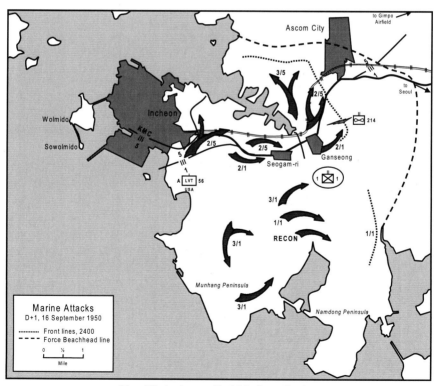

Map 20. Incheon: D+1 Marine attacks.

179

BLUE Beach, the supply LVTs that had been prevented from landing the previous evening by the outgoing tide now came ashore to be unloaded. As the marines moved inland, they could be supplied from the other beaches. The small and unsatisfactory BLUE Beach was therefore closed down on the evening of D+1 and Shore Party Group B (-) moved to Wolmido.[55]

The 532d EB&SR, with the 50th Engineer Port Construction Company and the Headquarters and Company A of the 73d Engineer Combat Battalion attached, was scheduled to take responsibility for the Incheon inner harbor area on arrival. The inner harbor was collectively designated YELLOW Beach (see map 21), with specific areas designated as NORA and OPAL Beaches on the eastern shore of Wolmido; GRACE, FANNY, WANDA, and CAROL Beaches between the Wolmido causeway and the tidal basin; and BETTY Beach south of the tidal basin. The field order called for the 532d and other 2d ESB units to come ashore over RED Beach on D+1. However, the brigade reconnaissance team that had come ashore on RED Beach with the marines on D-Day had scouted the waterfront during the night and determined that, in spite of widespread destruction and damage to the lock, the channel leading to the tidal basin was open and BETTY Beach to the south was clear. Knowing that RED Beach would be unusable in a few days when the spring tides waned, Lieutenant Colonel E.C. Adams, the regimental commander, decided to bring the brigade units in over BETTY Beach, reducing the congestion on RED Beach.[56]

The four SCAJAP LSTs carrying the brigade and its attached units arrived at BETTY Beach with the morning tide. LST-Q067, with the brigade headquarters and the 50th Port Construction Company aboard, beached successfully, but LST-Q099 grounded short, leaving Company B (the boat company), Shore Company D, most of the 287th Signal Company, and a contingent of the Navy Beach Group temporarily stranded by 150 yards of deep sticky mud between the ramp and the beach. LST-Q090, with the 73d Combat Engineers aboard, and LST-Q075, carrying the headquarters companies of the 532d Regiment and the Provisional Shore Battalion, as well as Shore Company E, arrived after the tide had begun to ebb, forcing both LSTs to stand offshore and wait for the next high tide. The regimental and battalion commanders, along with small staffs and an eight-man team from the 287th Signal Company, climbed aboard LCVPs and, as the falling tide once again isolated Incheon, motored toward the tidal basin to set up a command post near the brigade headquarters and to take charge of YELLOW Beach unloading operations.[57]

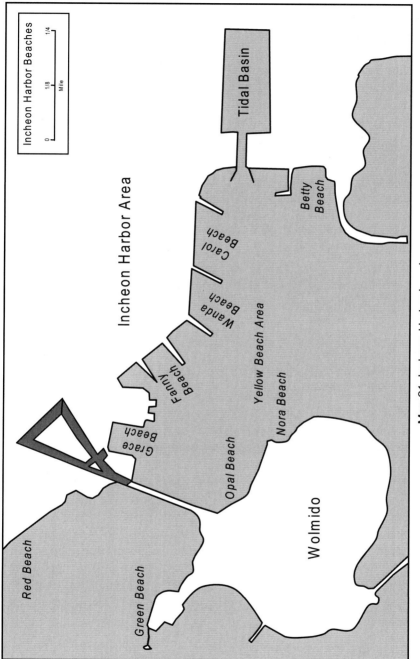

Map 21. Incheon Harbor beaches.

Since little could be done without civilian laborers to supplement the understrength engineer units, the brigade contracting officers headed to city hall and the Chinese Chamber of Commerce, which represented Chinese companies holding construction and stevedoring contracts in Incheon. Within 2 hours of landing, they had hired nearly 800 civilian workers. The 50th Port Construction Company used some of this contract labor to build a log causeway over the mud so that Boat Company B, Shore Company D, and the others on board LST-Q099 could come ashore.[58]

Company B's landing craft, along with dozens of Japanese powered barges to be used as harbor lighters, were still in Japan awaiting follow-on shipping. Until these vessels arrived, the boat company operated Navy landing craft, a few DUKWs the brigade had brought with it, and local Korean barges and harbor craft that had survived the bombardment. Company D's engineers set to work along the waterfront between the tidal basin and the Wolmido causeway, breaking gaps in the seawall and bulldozing LST ramps. Since Shore Company E was still afloat, the 50th Port Engineers took on the additional and unaccustomed task of cargo discharge at BETTY Beach and the tidal basin, using some cranes unloaded from its beached LST and others borrowed, along with their crews, from the Marine shore party battalion. With the assistance of the Marine crane operators, Company D and the 50th Port emptied 50 LCM loads of cargo when the evening high tide once again allowed landing craft to come into the harbor.[59]

The amphibious engineers also went into the railroad business, making initial repairs to the tracks that serviced the piers. The brigade had no trained railway men, but its troops were accustomed to making machinery operate under difficult conditions. By midnight on D+1, they had a switch engine and six freight cars in operation and 3 days later, a train carried 1,200 marines from Incheon to Ascom City and daily cargo runs began, all organized by an ad hoc 2d ESB rail transportation section. As seemed always to happen in amphibious operations, many of the trucks intended for clearing the beach dumps disappeared inland, commandeered to haul troops and supplies to the forward areas. The ability of the amphibious engineers to make the trains run long before the regular transportation railway engineers arrived was fortuitous and helped compensate for the severe shortage of trucks.[60]

The convoy of ships carrying the 7th Infantry Division (less the 17th RCT, which was still afloat off Busan as Eighth Army Reserve) dropped anchor in Incheon Harbor the evening of D+1.[61] By that time, the marines had pushed to the Force Beachhead Line, so the harbor was now out of enemy artillery range. At 1800 General Oliver Smith opened his command post east of Incheon, assuming command of operations ashore and ending the amphibious assault phase of CHROMITE.[62]

Excursions and Alarms

While the marines fought their way to the Force Beachhead Line and the Army amphibious engineers and the marines and sailors of the beach and shore parties unloaded cargo and sent it inland, other dramas were playing out elsewhere on the peninsula.

The Miryang Battalion's Jangsa-dong Operation

On the same day as the Incheon landing, but on the opposite coast, an attempt was made to put an ROK Army guerrilla battalion ashore.[63] Eighth Army had planned to land the force to block the eastern coastal road north of Pohang in preparation for the Incheon landing and the breakout from the perimeter. The intent was to tie up North Korean forces during the west coast amphibious operation and facilitate a ROK 3d Division attack to recapture Pohang. Dokseok-dong, where the 3d Division had been evacuated the previous month, offered a good location because the narrow coastal plain behind the town was a natural chokepoint and the nearby Jangsa-dong beach was suitable for an amphibious landing in spite of some offshore rocky shoals. Eighth Army originally intended to use the newly formed Eighth Army Ranger Company for this mission, but the unit had not yet completed its training. The task was passed to the ROK II Corps, which directed the ROK 3d Division to provide a battalion for the operation. Since the division was fully committed at that time, its commander recommended the mission be given to an irregular force commanded by Captain Yi Myeong-heum and variously known as the 1st Independent Mobile Unit, the Miryang Guerrilla Battalion, or the Myeong (Lustrous) unit. This was a group of young high school student volunteers and North Korean defectors then training at the town of Miryang. They were armed with captured Soviet and Japanese weapons and dressed in an assortment of Korean peasant clothing, school uniforms, and military battle dress.[64] This guerrilla band was to be transported to Dokseok-dong by an ROK Merchant Marine LST escorted by an ROK Navy frigate and landed during the night of 14/15 September. Admiral Charles C. Hartman's cruiser-destroyer force, which was scheduled to conduct a bombardment and demonstration at Samcheok, about 80 miles north of Dokseok-dong, would provide a prelanding bombardment. The ROK 3d Division Headquarters requested a US tank company and combat engineer platoon to reinforce the guerrillas and assist in the landing. The UNC turned down the request and canceled the prelanding bombardment, causing Hartman to conclude that the entire operation had been called off.[65] (See map 18.)

In fact, the US planners had left the decision up to ROK Army Headquarters. There it was decided that the benefits of the operation would be worth risking the inadequately trained irregulars. After discarding a plan to infiltrate the guerrillas by fishing boats, the planners reverted to the original idea of transporting the entire unit on one LST. The landing was to be made at 0230 on 15 September, with the ROK Navy frigate providing naval gunfire support and illumination of the landing area. However, since star shell rounds were in short supply, the illumination mission was canceled and the time of the landing was changed to 30 minutes before dawn.[66]

ROK Merchant Marine LST-667, *Munsan-ho*, escorted by the US destroyer-minesweeper *Endicott* (DMS-35) in lieu of the ROK Navy frigate, departed on 14 September carrying the 772-man guerrilla battalion and its two American advisors, First Lieutenant William Harrison and Sergeant Frederick D. Cooper, who carried the unit's only radio, an SCR-300 walkie-talkie.[67] En route, they encountered heavy weather from Typhoon Keizia. The ships, slowed by 10-foot waves, arrived off Jangsa-dong well after dawn. Rather than landing clandestinely at night, the LST stood in toward the beach in broad daylight, in 20 to 30 knot winds and heavy seas, and under the eyes of the 12th Regiment of the KPA 5th Division, which was garrisoned in a village overlooking the beach, having been sent there to recuperate after its battles with the ROK 3d Division the previous month.

As the LST approached the shore, the captain dropped a stern anchor intended to keep the ship perpendicular to the beach and to assist in retraction after the landing. However, the anchor cable immediately parted. As the bow hit the beach, the waves and wind caused the ship to broach and dragged it sideways over a rocky shoal that tore open a gash beneath the waterline. The LST settled to the bottom in shallow water just offshore. Several of the guerrillas plunged into the surf and swam ashore to tie ropes between the sunken ship and trees behind the beach. The rest of the battalion struggled through the breaking waves, clinging to the ropes, and quickly moved into the hills, supported by fire from the *Endicott's* 5-inch guns. After a 4-hour gun battle, the KPA drove the guerrillas back to the beach, where they established a defensive perimeter in the sand dunes near the wrecked LST. Cooper then made radio contact with the *Endicott*, whose commander reported the situation to Admiral Hartman.[68]

Hartman, who had not been informed that the Jangsa-dong operation was still on, was astonished to get this news. His cruiser-destroyer force, Task Group 95.2, had been reinforced by the battleship *Missouri* and was in the midst of the Samcheok bombardment. Hartman ceased fire and turned his ships south to help the beleaguered guerrillas. For the next 4 days, the Miryang Battalion held off its attackers with the help of naval gunfire from Hartman's ships and close air support from Air Force and Navy aircraft. Hartman brought Captain Yi out to his flagship by helicopter to coordinate the support and rescue effort. Navy helicopters also evacuated the most seriously wounded, including Harrison and Cooper, and carried ammunition and food to the soldiers ashore. It was only by chance that Hartman's flagship, the cruiser *Helena*, was able to provide ammunition for the Miryang Battalion's Russian weapons. During the previous few weeks, Hartman's ships, which had been operating in support of ROK Army units on the east coast, had provided ammunition, spare parts, rations, and comfort items (including ice cream) to the Korean Military Advisory Group (KMAG) ashore. They, in return, had sent out captured weapons (including swords, as well as submachineguns and pistols) as war souvenirs. They also sent out captured ammunition that had been stored in the *Helena's* magazines, and this was now used to replenish the beleaguered guerrillas.[69]

On 16 September Lieutenant Colonel Frank Spier, the executive officer of the 8206th Army Unit (AU), Amphibious Training Center (ATC), arrived off Jangsa-dong aboard Army tug LT-636. He and the tug's civilian captain, Charles Roy, went ashore in a rubber boat to assess the situation and determined that the *Munsan-ho* was unsalvageable. Spier, who had considerable amphibious, and specifically LST, experience, assisted with the evacuation efforts over the next few days. On 19 September ROK Merchant Marine LST-665, *Chochiwon-ho*, arrived at Jangsa-dong. The civilian captain was unwilling to risk his ship by running it up onto the beach, but with Spier's advice and encouragement, he brought the LST close enough that the guerrillas could come out through the surf, again using ropes strung between the ship and the shore.[70] The operation ended on 20 September when the *Chochiwon-ho* returned to Busan with the survivors of the guerrilla battalion and the crew of the wrecked LST, including 110 wounded. Of the young student-soldiers, 39 had been killed or had drowned and 39 were left behind.[71]

In spite of the bravery of the young guerrillas and the professionalism of their commander, Admiral Hartman's team, Spier, and others, it is difficult to find any salutary aspect to this operation. There is no evidence that the North Koreans were seriously inconvenienced and the rescue operation diverted Hartman's task group from its mission of bombardment and deception. Admiral Joy radioed to Rear Admiral Allan E. Smith, commander of the UNC blockading and escort force (TF 95), who had operational control of the ROK Navy, that any such missions in the future should be conducted by people experienced in amphibious operations.[72]

The Raiders Attempt at Gimpo

The GHQ Raider Company conducted the other Incheon-related special operation. It was also unsuccessful, although there were no casualties. During the planning for the Incheon operation, General Almond and Colonel Ely had proposed that, after the Gunsan raid, the Raider Company would move up to Incheon, paddle ashore during the night of 16 September, and make an early capture of Gimpo Airfield. General Oliver Smith had argued against the mission, anticipating confusion and the possibility of friendly-fire casualties, even if it were successful, which Smith thought unlikely. Almond canceled the raid, but Ely either did not get the word or made the decision to proceed independently.[73]

Whatever the reason, Ely and Major Wear's Raider Company sailed north aboard *Whitesand Bay* after the Gunsan raid and, in the approaches to Incheon, transferred to an ROK Navy frigate that then carried them into the Han River estuary. On the evening of 16 September, they prepared to make a 3-mile paddle in their rubber boats and then march overland for 12 miles to take possession of the airfield in the face of over 500 North Korean defenders. However, it proved impossible to paddle the boats against the strong tides and the attempt was abandoned.[74] The Raiders then joined the invasion fleet and went ashore on 19 September to report to the X Corps Advance Command Post for further orders. The failed mission was to be the Raiders last amphibious operation of the war.[75]

Morning Alarms

Sunday morning, 17 September (D+2), opened with an unexpected flourish as, just before 0600, a pair of North Korean fighter-bombers flew in over the anchored transports, dropped eight 100-pound bombs near Struble's flagship, and machine-gunned the British cruiser *Jamaica*. Although straddled by the bombs, one of which bounced off the ship without exploding, the *Rochester* was undamaged, but one sailor was killed and two more were wounded aboard the *Jamaica*, whose guns brought down one of the aircraft.[76]

The Incheon Build-Up, D+2 to D+4

Later that morning, General MacArthur came ashore to view the battlefield as the marines continued the attack inland toward the town of Sosa and the Gimpo Airfield (see map 22). The Army's 96th Field Artillery Battalion brought its 155-mm howitzers ashore that day and was placed

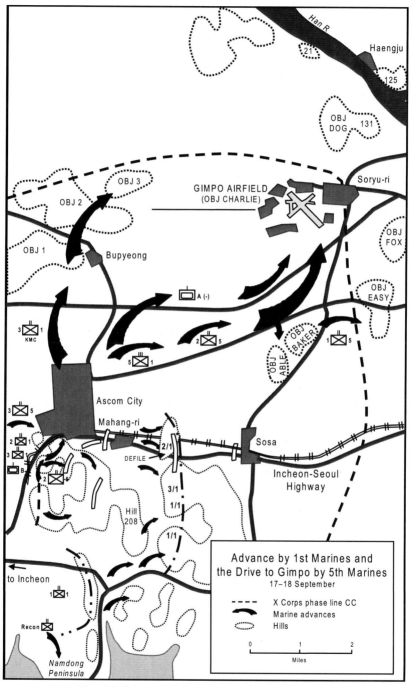

Map 22. Advance by 1st Marines, 17 September.

in support of Puller's 1st Marines for the drive inland. Company A of the 56th ATTB was detached from the 1st Marines at 1000 and attached to the 11th Marines. During the day, the 11th Marines moved their howitzers from Wolmido to the A/56th position inland from BLUE Beach. With their wheeled vehicles still aboard the LST, the Army amphibious tankers borrowed a DUKW from the 2d ESB to haul water, and then they waited. Over the next 2 days, they stood ready to add their 75-mm howitzer fire to the support of the marines, but no calls for fire broke the silence until the evening of 19 September when the company was called forward to support the first Han River crossing.[77]

On D+2 Rear Admiral Lyman A. Thackrey, commander of Amphibious Group 3, arrived aboard his amphibious command ship, *Eldorado* (AGC-11), to take charge of Incheon port operations. His Army counterpart was Brigadier General George C. Stewart, who would assume duties initially as the Incheon base commander and then as the commanding general of the 3d Logistical Command.[78] Over the next 3 months, Stewart would play a key role in supporting operations in northwestern Korea. During World War II, he had served as chief of transportation for the Mediterranean Theater and had supervised over-the-shore logistic operations for the Sicily, Salerno, Anzio, and Southern France amphibious operations. After the war, he organized the Transportation Center at Fort Eustis and was the assistant division commander of the 10th Infantry Division when the Korean War broke out.[79]

SCAJAP LST-Q075 carrying Company E of the 532d EB&SR had waited for the evening tide on D+1, but had again failed to make it to shore. It finally beached on the morning of 17 September. Company E relieved the 50th Port Construction Company at BETTY Beach and the tidal basin. The 50th Port now focused its efforts on getting the huge lock of the tidal basin into operation. Until that was accomplished, only shallow draft landing craft could make use of the basin.[80]

LST-Q090, carrying the Headquarters and Company A of the 73d Engineer Combat Battalion, arrived on D+2. It was the first LST to land at OPAL Beach on the east side of Wolmido. The combat engineers unloaded themselves, bulldozed LST ramps, and, under the direction of an officer from the 532d EB&SR staff, set up operations as cargo handlers on that beach until D+10, when they were detached from the regiment and sent forward to assist in river crossings.[81]

At midnight on 17 September, Colonel Twitty assumed operational control of the 1st Marine Division's 1st Shore Party Battalion, which was still operating GREEN and RED Beaches, and the Fleet Marine Force 1st

Combat Service Group and 7th Motor Transport Battalion.[82] The brigade was responsible for operating beach dumps (unloading supplies, transporting them to the dumps, storing them, and issuing them to the combat units at the dump sites). The Army controlled the ammunition and engineering material dumps, while 1st Combat Service Group operated all the others. The Army engineers and the marines worked well together, although differences in operating procedures sometimes had to be worked out.[83]

In addition to its primary task of operating the port, Twitty's brigade was responsible for Incheon security. The KMC regiment moved out of Incheon on 18 September to join the 1st Marine Division, but it left the KMC 2d Battalion to assist in the port security mission until D+4. For civilian law and order, Korean National Police Lieutenant Park Song Wook was installed as the acting chief of police with an initial force of about 200 police officers. (General Smith, having been directed to establish civil government in Incheon, and acting on the advice of Admiral Sohn Won il, the ROK Chief of Naval Operations, had earlier appointed Mr. Pyo Yang-moon, a recent holder of the office, to be acting mayor of Incheon.)[84]

At 0800 on the 18th, the 2d ESB also took control of some 700 prisoners of war (POWs), including 94 wounded, who had been held by the marines in hastily-constructed compounds on the beach. A brigade survey party examined the Incheon prison and found it to be suitable and large enough for the task. A platoon of the versatile Company A of the 73d Combat Engineers was brought in from Wolmido to operate the prison until a X Corps Military Police (MP) Company arrived 5 days later.[85] The POW mission entailed setting up cooking, sanitation, and medical facilities and the hiring of local Korean doctors, nurses, and workers, in addition to the stevedores, supply dump laborers, craftsmen, and unskilled workers needed to operate the port. By 18 September over 2,300 civilians were on the payroll. By the end of the month, nearly 10,000 civilians and the Japanese contract workers brought over to work as hatch crews aboard the transports and cargo ships were on the payroll.[86]

Brigadier General Henry I. Hodes, the Assistant Division Commander of the 7th Infantry Division, had come ashore on 17 September with the Division G2, G3, and a small staff to establish the division advance command post. On 18 September the first combat elements of the division landed. These were the Headquarters and the 1st and 2d Battalions of Colonel Charles E. Beauchamp's 32d RCT, the 7th Reconnaissance Company, and the Headquarters and Company A of the 73d Tank Battalion. Because of the tides, the transports and cargo ships could not tie up to the pier and had to unload in the stream—troops and equipment being transferred onto

LSTs and landing craft and then brought ashore. The ships were all MSTS transports without the special gear for handling landing craft, and the transfer process damaged some of the vehicles and equipment.[87]

By the time the 7th Division began arriving in Incheon, the marines had captured Gimpo Airfield. The first aircraft, a Marine helicopter carrying General Shepherd, landed at 1000 on 18 September. The next day, Marine F4U *Corsair* fighter-bombers and F7F *Tigercat* night fighters arrived, Major General Field Harris set up the X Corps Tactical Air Command, and General Thomas J. Cushman's Marine Air Group 33 began operating out of Gimpo.[88]

On the morning of 19 September, the X Corps Deputy Chief of Staff established an advance command post (CP) at the 1st Marine Division Headquarters and General Barr activated his 7th Division Headquarters ashore.[89] (See map 23.) The GHQ Raider Company provided security for the X Corps advance CP until noon, when Marine MPs replaced them. The Raiders were then attached to the 1st Marine Division and moved forward to assist the KMC regiment in providing security in the area west of Gimpo. The Fleet Volunteers were now detached from the Raider Company and returned to Japan, where they were assigned to 41 Independent Commando Royal Marines.[90]

The 7th Division's 31st Infantry came ashore on 19 September and began operations south of Incheon toward Suwon. The 32d Infantry moved forward on that day to take responsibility from the 1st Marines for the area south of the Incheon–Seoul Highway as part of a complex series of maneuvers in preparation for the first Han River crossing.[91] General Smith and General Almond had conferred that morning and decided that a ferry site north of Gimpo Airfield and across the river from the town of Haengju was most suitable for the river crossing operation.

To align the forces for the crossing and subsequent operations, the 2d Battalion, 32d Infantry moved to an area southeast of the town of Sosa, relieving the 1st Battalion, 1st Marines, which then moved by truck to the west and north to replace the 1st Battalion, 5th Marines on the high ground northwest of the industrial suburb of Yeongdeungpo opposite Seoul on the south bank of the Han River. The 1st Battalion, 5th Marines moved back to the vicinity of Gimpo Airfield to join the 3d Battalion, 5th Marines and other units preparing for the river crossing. The 2d Battalion, 5th Marines moved to secure the south bank of the river at the proposed crossing site. The Marine 1st Amphibian Tractor Battalion, which had been supporting the 1st Marines, was now attached to the 5th Marines.[92]

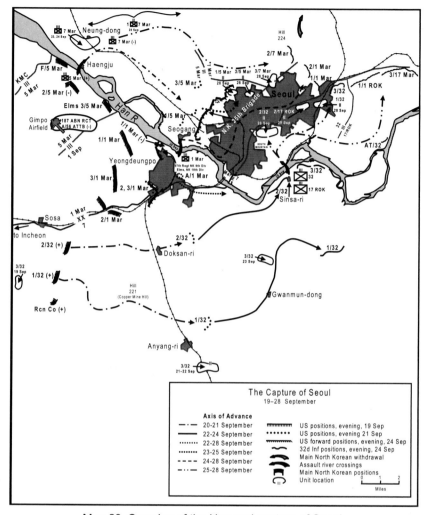

Map 23. Crossing of the Han and capture of Seoul.

Back at Incheon, Company A, 56th ATTB was also directed to support the river crossing. They were attached to the 5th Marines, displaced to an assembly area south of the river, refueled, issued rations, dug in, and prepared to provide artillery preparation fires and to participate in the crossing. The 1st Marine Shore Party Battalion reverted to 1st Marine Division control for the crossing and at 0915 began moving inland to the crossing site.[93] The withdrawal of this unit, which had been operating GREEN Beach, had an impact on operations, but the 104th Navy Construction Battalion remained at Wolmido and took over unloading operations at OPAL Beach, freeing up the 73d Combat Engineers for construction work, including a DUKW ramp and approach road.[94]

The 2d Battalion of the KMC regiment, which had been providing port security under Colonel Twitty's direction, was also pulled out on 19 September, moving inland to join the 5th Marines. Since there were no MPs in the understrength 2d ESB, Twitty called on the 73d Combat Engineers (who had supplied hatch crews aboard the ships, had been operating OPAL Beach, and were constructing and repairing roads) to provide two companies to serve as provisional MPs until the X Corps MP units arrived. A security platoon of Company A, 562d EB&SR Maintenance Battalion was organized to set up traffic checkpoints throughout the city, and quick reaction teams were established to deal with snipers and civil disturbances.[95]

Considerations of a Landing at Gunsan

While these activities were taking place ashore, General MacArthur, aboard the *Mount McKinley,* had become concerned about the lack of progress on the Eighth Army front and was considering another amphibious operation on the west coast.

The Incheon landing was a turning movement, intended to seize key terrain deep behind the enemy forces attacking the Eighth Army perimeter, threaten the enemy's rear, and cause the enemy to turn to meet that threat.[96] Anticipating that the North Koreans would be aware of the threat to their rear, the Eighth Army offensive was scheduled to begin the day after the Incheon landing. On 16 September Eighth Army units began the attack, but the North Korean defenses were still unshaken. Furthermore, Walker's forces had to cross the Nakdong River and, because priority for bridging equipment had gone to X Corps, he had limited resources to do so. "I have a river across my whole front," Walker told FEC Acting Chief of Staff Hickey, "and the two bridges I have don't make much."[97]

It was not until 18 September that the first Eighth Army unit, a battalion of the 2d Division's 38th Infantry, made the first crossing of the Nakdong River. Two regiments of the 24th Division crossed the next day, but the 5th RCT and the 1st Cavalry Division were still fighting their way to the river and in some places, the KPA were still attacking. By that time MacArthur had begun to fear that Eighth Army would not be able to break through and conduct a timely linkup with X Corps.[98]

General Shepherd left a record of the initial deliberations by key members of MacArthur's staff. On 19 September Shepherd had concluded that, with the assault phase of the operation completed, it was time for him to leave, but MacArthur asked him to stay on for another day or so. Aboard the *Mount McKinley* that evening, MacArthur invited Shepherd to sit in on a staff conference. There he found MacArthur; Admirals Struble and Doyle; and Generals Almond, Alonzo P. Fox, Courtney Whitney, and Wright seated at a table with a large map of Korea in front of them. Shepherd now learned of MacArthur's concern about Eighth Army's lack of progress and his growing belief that the North Koreans were not going to quit even after Seoul was captured.[99]

MacArthur proposed using two of Walker's US divisions and one ROK division for an amphibious landing at Gunsan, one of the sites for which Wright's JSPOG staff had prepared alternative plans before Incheon was decided on. This Gunsan landing would be an immediate threat to the enemy rear and, MacArthur believed, would cause the southern front to collapse. The Gunsan forces could then link up with both X Corps and the advancing Eighth Army. Struble assured MacArthur that there was enough shipping to carry out the landing. Doyle confirmed that nonamphibious shipping could support X Corps by 1 October, freeing up his amphibious ships for the operation. Doyle saw Gunsan as a suitable landing site and did not expect any enemy resistance at that location. The others concurred in the scheme, although Shepherd argued that the 1st Marine Division should be used for the landing and Struble, with strong support from Shepherd, proposed Poseungmyeon, the site the Navy and Marines had argued for so strongly during the CHROMITE planning, as a more suitable alternative to Gunsan.

MacArthur wanted the Marine division, his strongest division, to continue the attack toward Seoul, which he still considered the most critical objective. Doyle had studied the Poseungmyeon area since the earlier arguments about the CHROMITE landing sites and had since concluded that it was not suitable, as there were rice paddies in the area where unloading would take place and no roads led inland from the beach.[100]

MacArthur ordered Wright to develop a plan for a Gunsan landing. Wright radioed Hickey to begin planning based on CINCFE OPLAN 100-C, which had been one of the Incheon alternatives developed the previous month. Hickey advised Walker of the concept on 22 September. Walker objected to giving up any of his divisions, and by then North Korean resistance had begun to collapse and Eighth Army was surging forward.[101] The 5th RCT and the 2d and 24th Divisions had crossed the Nakdong River in strength, the 2d Division had thrown a bridge across the river, the 25th

Division had broken through in the southwest, and in the east the ROK 3d Division had recaptured Pohang (see map 18). By 23 September the KPA were in retreat all along the Eighth Army front.[102]

Han River Crossing[103]

The 5th Marines, with the participation of Company A, 56th ATTB, crossed the Han River at the Haengju ferry site west of Seoul on 20 September after an unsuccessful attempt the night before (see map 24). The forces, including Captain O'Donnell's Army amphibious tank company (A/56th ATTB) had formed up on the south bank of the river on the evening of 19 September. A reconnaissance team swam across the river without incident, reaching the north bank at 2040. They then signaled that they had no enemy contact and the reconnaissance company commander ordered his troops to cross in nine LVTs. However, the amphibious tractors came under heavy fire as they crossed the river and were forced to turn back.[104]

After this failed attempt at a hasty crossing, plans were made for a deliberate assault the next morning. After a 15-minute artillery preparation, the 3d Battalion, 5th Marines crossed the river in LVTs at dawn and successfully occupied high ground on the north side (Objectives ABLE, BAKER, and CHARLIE). At 1000 the 2d Battalion crossed in LVTs, followed by the 2d Battalion of the KMC regiment riding in DUKWs and accompanied by A/56th ATTB. The 2/5th Marines and KMC 2d Battalion passed through the 3d Battalion while still mounted, turned east, and moved on Objectives DELTA and EASY. A group of North Korean soldiers who were dug in on Objective EASY surrendered after the Army amphibious tanks fired a few 75-mm rounds at them. O'Donnell's company then dug in and prepared for indirect fire missions.[105]

The next day, the Headquarters, 1st, and 2d Platoons of A/56th recrossed the river to assist in the security of Gimpo Airfield, while the five LVT(A)s of the 3d Platoon remained north of the river in general support of the 1st Marine Division.[106]

The Conclusion of the Incheon–Seoul Operation

As the 5th Marines crossed the Han River on 20 September, most of the X Corps Headquarters and Headquarters Company came ashore from the *Buckner* (like the 7th Division troops, they transferred from the MSTS transport to an LST that brought them to the beach) and took over the headquarters area vacated by the 1st Marine Division when General Smith displaced his CP to Gimpo Airfield. General Almond arrived from the *Mount McKinley* at 0900 on 21 September. During the day he visited General Barr, Colonel Puller, and General Smith at their CPs. In the afternoon, he met with General MacArthur at Gimpo Airfield just before the

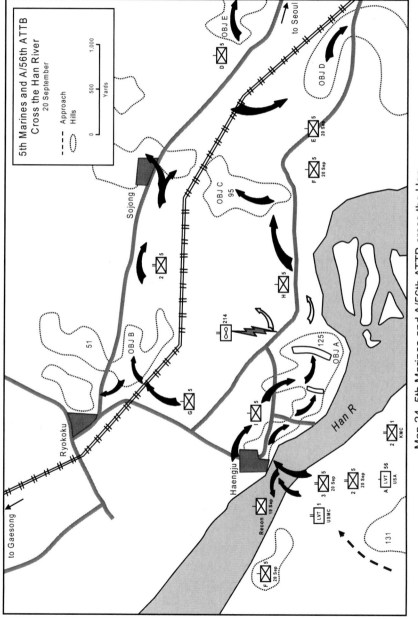

Map 24. 5th Marines and A/56th ATTB cross the Han.

commander in chief returned to Tokyo, and at 1700 he assumed command ashore in a ceremony at the X Corps CP.[107] At the same time, Stewart activated the Inchon (Incheon) Base Command and took over the responsibility for shore party operations and defense of Incheon from Colonel Twitty. The next day, X Corps Headquarters displaced to Ascom City.[108]

The next day the 7th Marines and the 3d Battalion, 11th Marines arrived at Incheon. The 3d and 2d Battalions moved inland to join the division north of the Han River while the 1st Battalion unloaded the transports before also joining the division.[109] The 7th Infantry Division continued its debarkation on 21 September. The necessity of using LSTs and landing craft to lighter troops and equipment ashore from transports anchored in the stream, the inability to move within the harbor except at high tide, and the limited beach facilities all made this a slow process. The shortage of trucks also hampered the clearing of the beach dumps. General Hodes halted the unloading until the backlog on the beach was reduced, and General Stewart agreed to provide additional trucks to haul the division's petroleum, oils, and lubricants (POL) and other supplies inland.[110]

As the 5th Marines consolidated their position north of the river and began moving toward Seoul, and the 1st Marines began the fight for control of Yeongdeungpo, the two regiments of the 7th Division secured the area south of Seoul. On 21 September the 32d Infantry captured the town of Anyang-ri, cutting the Seoul–Suwon Highway. The division reconnaissance company and an armored task force, TF *Hannum*, probed south toward Suwon, engaging KPA tank and infantry units, and reaching the town around midnight. They secured the Suwon Airfield the next day and were relieved by the 31st Infantry Regiment. North of the Han River, the 1st Marine Division began advancing toward Seoul, hitting the main line of KPA resistance and beginning the battle for the city.[111]

On 22 September General Smith alerted the 7th Marines that they were to cross to the north side of the Han River the next day and join the 5th Marines in the fight for Seoul. Smith's plan was to have the 1st Marines cross the Han River west of Yeongdeungpo and move into position on the right (southeastern) flank of the 5th Marines. The 7th Marines would secure the left flank and prevent KPA forces from escaping to the north. The entire division with three regiments on line would then move into Seoul. Almond approved this approach in a meeting with Smith that afternoon, but directed that the KMC regiment and the ROK 17th Infantry Regiment (due to arrive on 24 September) take part in the liberation of Seoul.[112] (See map 25.)

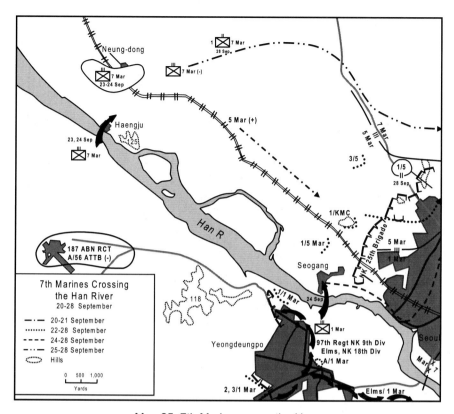

Map 25. 7th Marines cross the Han.

Colonel Homer L. Litzenberg's 7th Marines began crossing the Han on the morning of 23 September. His Headquarters and Service Company and the 3d Battalion were shuttled across by LVTs of the Marine 1st Amphibian Tractor Battalion. By 1710 he had opened his regimental CP north of the river. Meanwhile, the 3d Platoon of A/56th ATTB, which was supporting the 5th Marines on the northeast side of the river, re-crossed back to Gimpo Airfield, where it was put in support of the 2d Battalion, 7th Marines.[113]

Generals Almond and Smith met again on 23 September, at which time the 5th Marines were still fighting against stiff opposition. Almond proposed to have the 1st Marines cross the Han River east of Yeongdeungpo, taking "advantage of the possibility of maneuver from the south and east against a position which was being stubbornly defended by the enemy." Smith did not want to have his division split by the Han River, and Almond agreed with his request to have the 1st Marines cross to the west of Yeongdeungpo as planned.[114] (See map 26.)

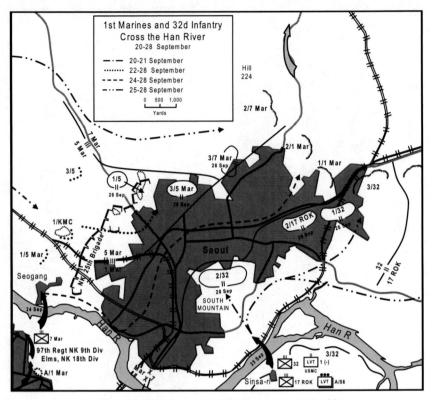

Map 26. 1st Marines and 32d Infantry cross the Han.

On the morning of 24 September, after a tough 4-day fight for posses-sion of Yeongdeungpo, the 1st Marines crossed the Han River at Seogang. A reconnaissance party and assault force of the 2d Battalion crossed at 0800 after an hour delay while mines were cleared at the crossing site, and the rest of the regiment crossed in LVTs and DUKWs over the next 2 hours.[115] The 3d Battalion, 187th Airborne RCT was airlifted from Ashiya, Japan, to Gimpo Airfield. They took over the Gimpo security mission from the 2d Battalion, 7th Marines, which then made the crossing of the Han, followed by the 1st Battalion, which had finished its task of unloading the ships. The 3d Platoon of A/56th ATTB was relieved of its mission of sup-port of the 2/7th Marines and commenced support of the 187th Airborne RCT.[116]

At 1230 General Almond met with General Smith in Yeongdeungpo and presented his plan to change the boundary between the 1st Marine Division and the 7th Infantry Division and to have the 32d Infantry and the ROK 17th Regiment (then debarking at Incheon) cross the Han River east of Yeongdeungpo in LVTs of the Marine 1st Amphibian Tractor Battalion. The 32d and 17th would then capture and "take the enemy resistance then confronting the 1st Marine Division in reverse and by maneuver from the south and southeast capture the dominant terrain feature of South Mountain [Namsan, the prominent high ground south of Seoul]."[117] General Smith disagreed both with the planned use of the 32d Infantry and with its use of Marine LVTs, but, in the words of the official Marine Corps historian, "Differences between commanders are not remarkable, and it is noteworthy that Corps and Division usually managed in the Inchon–Seoul operation to reach an acceptable solution. Such was the case [when Almond agreed to allow Smith to keep his division together north of the river and used the 32d Infantry in place of the 1st Marines as the maneuver element to the southeast]."[118]

The 32d RCT had already been alerted for the river crossing at 1115 that morning. When General Almond made the final decision on the afternoon of 24 September, the Marine 1st Amphibian Tractor Battalion (less one company) and the 1st and 2d Platoons of Company A, 56th ATTB were attached to the 32d RCT to support the crossing (Headquarters and 3d Platoon of the 56th ATTB remained at Gimpo in support of the 187th Airborne RCT). The amphibious tanks and tractors road marched to the 32d's position south of the river, and at 2200 that night, the ROK 17th Regiment was also attached to the 32d RCT.[119]

At dusk on the evening of 24 September, the transports carrying the 17th RCT steamed into Incheon Harbor after cruising "through a sea of glass under a bright blue sky."[120] As they dropped anchor, the battleship *Missouri* was firing its 16-inch main battery in support of the troops inland while the Japanese stevedores, brought over to unload the ships, watched the show from atop the hatch covers. By midnight, the tide was high enough for the regimental commander, Colonel Herbert B. Powell, to go ashore in a launch to the assigned beach and coordinate with the Navy beach master and the amphibious engineers from the 532d EB&SR. The troops went over the rails of the transport and into LSTs while the regiment's equipment and vehicles were loaded onto the LSTs by cranes. Most of the regiment was ashore by 0400 on 25 September. During the day, they moved by train and foot to the vicinity of Anyang-ri, where the 1st Battalion was designated the corps reserve, the 3d Battalion was designated the division reserve, and the 2d Battalion was moved north to the Han River to occupy part of the area held by the 32d Infantry as that unit crossed the Han.[121]

As the 17th RCT was coming ashore before dawn, the 32d RCT was preparing to cross the Han River at the Sinsa-ri ferry site, across from the

900-foot high mass of Namsan (South Mountain). At 0600 the 48th Field Artillery Battalion and the regimental heavy mortars began a 30-minute artillery preparation, and at 0630 the assault company of the 2d Battalion, 32d Infantry entered the river in amphibious tractors. By 0730 the entire battalion and the 2d Platoon of A/56th ATTB were across the river without any casualties and the battalion was moving toward Namsan. The 1st Platoon of A/56th ATTB remained south of the river to provide artillery support. By 0830 the 1st Battalion of the 32d Infantry was across the river and moving to the east, followed by the 3d Battalion a little after noon. The ROK 17th Regiment followed the 3d Battalion. The 2d Battalion had secured Namsan by 1500. During the night, 2/32d Infantry repelled a KPA counterattack and the ROK 17th Regiment attacked through the night toward the high ground 4 miles east of the city, which they secured the next day. By nightfall on 26 September, the 32d Infantry and the ROK 17th Regiment had cleared the enemy from their zones and the 2/32d Infantry had made contact with the marines west of Namsan.[122]

The 2d ESB also played a role in the 32d Infantry's Han River crossing. First Lieutenant Claude L. Roberts's DUKW Platoon of Company B (the boat company), 532d EB&SR, helped carry troops across the river and the 73d Combat Engineer Battalion, released from duty at OPAL Beach on Wolmido, came up to construct a 50-ton ferry at the crossing site.[123]

By 26 September the 1st Marine Division, elements of the 7th Infantry Division, the ROK 17th Regiment, and ROK marines occupied substantial parts of Seoul, although heavy fighting continued. The next day, lead elements of the 1st Cavalry Division (TF 777, 7th Cavalry) met elements of the 7th RCT, 7th Division, south of Suwon Airfield, near Osan, accomplishing the linkup of Eighth Army and X Corps at almost the same spot where TF *Smith* had been overrun on 5 July 1950.[124]

On 28 September enemy resistance in Seoul ended, although combat was still taking place north of the city. That same day, Company A, 56th ATTB, finally began operating again as a single unit. For the last several days, the company had been thoroughly dispersed. The Headquarters Platoon had remained at Gimpo. The 1st Platoon on the south bank of the Han River had provided indirect fire in support of the 32d Infantry and ROK 17th Infantry while the 2d Platoon had crossed the river with the 32d, providing direct fire. The 3d Platoon had been attached to the 187th Airborne RCT. Now the entire unit was brought together and attached to the 187th as it cleared the area northwest of Gimpo. Captain O'Donnell attached one tank from the Headquarters Platoon to each of the other platoons, so there were now three six-gun firing batteries. O'Donnell noted on 29 September, "all guns were firing" and that morale was high.[125]

ROK Operations

Elsewhere in Korea, on 20 September the ROK 3d Division captured the port of Pohang.[126] In the week following the Incheon landing, ROK Navy coastal forces cleared islands along the west coast from Gunsan to the islands in the West Sea (Yellow Sea) west of the Ongjin Peninsula. In the south, ROK Navy and Marine forces cooperating with Eighth Army captured Namhae Island on 27 September and the port of Yeosu on 29 September. On 3 October Commander Lee with PC-703 and several smaller craft supported a landing by ROK marines to secure the southwestern port of Mokpo (see map 18).[127]

On 24 September Eugene Clark (now promoted to lieutenant commander) returned to Korea with orders to liberate major islands south of the 38th Parallel (see map 17). His guerrillas augmented a KMC battalion and ROK Navy LST-801. Landings were made on Yongmaedo Island, southeast of Haeju on 20 September and on Socheongdo (Soch'ong-do), west of Ongjin on 26 September. Royal Navy units were active in support of these ROK operations. The cruiser *Manchester* and four destroyers bombarded enemy troop concentrations on Deungsangot (Tungsan-got), a peninsula south of Ongjin, on 27 September, and on 29 September the cruiser *Ceylon* put a landing party ashore on Daecheongdo (Taech'ong-do), another of the islands west of Ongjin, finding it deserted. On 2 October Clark's mission was expanded to include liberating West Sea (Yellow Sea) islands north of the 38th Parallel off the coast of North Korea's Hwanghae province, the largest of these being Baengnyeongdo (Paengyong-do), which would become a base for guerrilla and other special operations against North Korea later in the war. Clark concluded his mission on 14 October and his irregulars returned to their home islands and disbanded.[128]

Incheon Port and Logistic Support Operations

While these combat actions were taking place, the vital logistic sustainment operation continued at Incheon and along the lines of communication to the front line forces. On 23 September the 8206th AU, ATC, which had been conducting logistical support operations along the southern Korean coast, arrived at Wolmido, having been transported with their LSU and LCMs aboard the landing ships, dock (LSDs) *Gunston Hall* and *Fort Marion*. The unit was placed in direct support of the 2d ESB and began assisting in the lighterage operations. Some of its personnel were assigned to the railroad repair mission, some were assigned temporarily to the POW security task, and one contingent was sent up the Han River with landing craft to assist the 1st Marine Shore Party Battalion in the ferrying operations at the Haengju ferry site.[129] There, the Marine 1st Engineer Battalion had assembled a raft within 6 hours of the 19 September assault crossing so that tanks could be brought across. They assembled another raft the next day and had three rafts in operation by 25 September, when the ferry operation was taken over by the 1st Shore Party Battalion, assisted by Army engineers of the 532d EB&SR and the ATC detachment.[130] The 73d Engineers were also detached from the 2d ESB on 25 September and sent forward to assist in the river crossings.[131]

On 25 September the 50th Engineer Port Construction Company finished repairing one of the tidal basin lock gates so it could be manually opened and closed. The first ship to enter was a small Japanese coastal freighter.[132] It was a significant first step, but the process of manually operating the lock was difficult and time-consuming. On 3 October an engineer team arrived from Tokyo to repair the electric motors and machinery. By 9 October three of the four locks could be operated electrically, reducing the time for locking ships into or out of the basin from more than 3 hours to 15 minutes. The fourth lock had to be worked manually, but overall, the tidal basin operation was enormously improved.[133]

On 26 September the rest of the 3d Logistical Command, the advance party had arrived on 18 September, landed at Incheon. General Stewart put the command into operation on that date, replacing the Inchon (Incheon) Base Command as the Army organization responsible for unloading, receiving, storing, and forwarding supplies in support of X Corps.[134] Also on 26 September, the 532d EB&SR took over the duties of the Navy beach master unit (control of LSTs and landing craft, direction of lighterage operations, provision of pilotage for ships entering the harbor, the operation of aids to navigation, and operations of the harbor communications system) and also took control of the Navy boat unit. That same day, the 14th Transportation Port Battalion, consisting of the headquarters and the 155th Port Company, arrived. Initially, it conducted port operations under the direction of the 532d EB&SR pending the withdrawal of the regiment and the assumption by the battalion of responsibility for operating the port. A second port company, the 153d, would arrive on 10 October, by which time the 2d ESB had turned over responsibility for operating the port of Incheon to the 14th Transportation Port Battalion.[135]

On 1 October the 3d Logistical Command took over the railroad operation from the 2d ESB, which was now preparing for the next amphibious operation.[136] On 3 October the ATC turned its LSUs over to the Navy and the following week the unit was transferred from the 2d ESB and assigned by the 3d Logistical Command to assist in the operation of Incheon Port.[137]

The Incheon amphibious operation had concluded. The operation of Incheon Port was now a logistical operation to support combat forces conducting sustained combat operations on land. However, another amphibious operation was in the offing. On 27 September Admiral Thackrey relieved Admiral Doyle, who sailed back to Japan to prepare for that operation.[138] On 29 September General MacArthur conducted a ceremony in which he returned the city of Seoul to Syngman Rhee. Shortly before the ceremony, MacArthur had met with his commanders and informed them of his plan for the next phase of operations: an offensive by Eighth Army into North Korea and another amphibious operation by X Corps to capture the east coast port of Wonsan.

Notes

1. James F. Schnabel, *United States Army in the Korean War, Policy and Direction: The First Year* (Washington, DC: GPO, 1972; reprinted 1992), 187, based on a July 1955 letter from General Wright to Schnabel.

2. JCS 1776/25, Memorandum by the Chief of Naval Operations for the Joint Chiefs of Staff, "Recommendations of Commander in Chief, Pacific Fleet, Concerning Support of Commander in Chief, Far East," 9 July 1950, RG 218, Entry UD7, CCS 383.21 Korea (3–19–5) Section 23, Box 38, National Archives and Records Administration, Modern Military Records, College Park, MD, hereafter, NACP.

3. General Shepherd records that his motivation for encouraging MacArthur to request the Marine division was to "ensure that the Marine Units in Korea would be under command of a Marine General officer of sufficient rank to protect the interests of the Corps" in light of "attempts by the Army and Air Force to dismember the Marine Corps and reduce its roles and missions during discussion of the recently enacted 'Unification of the Services' [legislation]," Lemuel C. Shepherd, *Korean War Diary covering period 2 July to 7 December 1950,* copy provided to the writer by Professor Allan R. Millett (a copy is also available in the Lemuel C. Shepherd Papers at the Marine Corps University Archives), 3–5; CINCFE Message C-57553 (CM IN 11150) to Department of the Army for JCS, 10 July 1950, RG 218, Entry UB7, CCS 381 Far East (7–2–50), Section 1, Box 22, NACP.

4. J. Lawton Collins, *War in Peacetime: The History and Lessons of Korea* (Boston, MA: Houghton Mifflin, 1969), 82–85.

5. JCS Action 2147, "Reinforcement to Commander in Chief, Far East," 11 July 1950, RG 218, Entry UB7, CCS 381 Far East (7–2–50), Section 1, Box 22; JCS 1776/34, "Note by the Secretaries to the Joint Chiefs of Staff on Increase in Strength of the First Marine Division," 14 July 1950, RG 218, Entry UD7, CCS 383.21 Korea (3–19–45) Sec 24, Box 39, both at NACP; James F. Schnabel and Robert J. Watson, *The History of the Joint Chiefs of Staff: The Joint Chiefs of Staff and National Policy, Vol. 3, The Korean War,* Part 1 (Washington, DC: Office of the Chairman of the Joint Chiefs of Staff, 1998), 77–78.

6. James A. Field Jr., *History of United States Naval Operations, Korea* (Washington, DC: GPO, 1962),171–172.

7. CINCFE Message CX 58239 (CM IN 13725) to JCS, 19 July 1950; JCS 86511 to CINCFE, 20 July 1950; CINCFE Message CX 58327 (CM IN 14303), 21 July 1950 [decisive stroke]; JCS 86511 to CINCFE, 20 July 1950; CINCFE Message CX 58327 (CM IN 14303), 21 July 1950; CINCFE CX 58473 (CM IN 14839) to JCS, 23 July 1950 [description of the operation], RG 218, Entry UB7, CCS381 Far East (7–2–50), Section 1, Box 22, NACP.

8. Schnabel, *Policy and Direction,* 168–171.

9. Schnabel, *Policy and Direction,* 141–145, 159–171; Schnabel and Watson, *Joint Chiefs of Staff and National Policy, Vol. 3, The Korean War*, Part 1, 80, 81; Lynn Montross and Nicholas A. Canzona, *U.S. Marine Operations*

in Korea, 1950–1953, Vol. II, The Inchon–Seoul Operation (Washington, DC: Historical Branch, G3, 1955), 18–34, 56–57; Roy E. Appleman, *United States Army in the Korean War: South to the Naktong, North to the Yalu* (Washington, DC: GPO, 1961), 489.

10. Summary of 29 July 1950 personal message from General MacArthur to General Collins, contained in a Letter, Department of the Army G3 to Commandant, Army War College, 30 December 1954, 2, copy in MHI Archives.

11. Schnabel, *Policy and Direction,* 165–166.

12. A spring tide is an exceptionally high tide that occurs during a full or new moon, when the sun, moon, and earth are approximately aligned. A neap tide is the lowest level of high tide, occurring twice each month during the first and third quarters of the moon.

13. Schnabel, *Policy and Direction,* 143–144.

14. The Pusan (Busan) Perimeter battles are described in Uzal W. Ent, *Fighting on the Brink: Defense of the Pusan Perimeter* (Paducah, KY: Turner Publishing Co., 1996), and in Appleman, *South to the Naktong,* 289–487.

15. Schnabel, *Policy and Direction,* 166.

16. "Strategic Concept for the Destruction of the North Korean Forces in the Field," 5 August 1950, copy in the *Ridgway Papers*, Series 2 Correspondence, Box 8, MHI Archives.

17. D. Clayton James, *The Years of MacArthur, Vol. 3, Triumph and Disaster 1945–1964* (Boston, MA: Houghton Mifflin, 1985), 452–456, provides the background on the Harriman mission. President Truman's concern was that MacArthur had exceeded his authority in coordinating with Republic of China (Taiwan) President Chiang Kai-shek's generals and planning to send fighter aircraft to the island, actions that should have had prior Washington approval.

18. Memorandum, "Conference in Office of CINCFE," 8 August 1950, and Memorandum, "Notes on 081035–081255 Conference with General MacArthur," 8 August 1950, *Ridgway Papers*, Series 2 Correspondence, Box 8, MHI Archives.

19. JCS Action 2147/4, 10 August 1950, "Reinforcement of the Far East Command," RG 218, Entry UB7, CCS 381 Far East (7–2–50), Section 2, Box 22, NACP; Schnabel and Watson, *Joint Chiefs of Staff and National Policy, Vol. 3, The Korean War,* Part 1, 81–84.

20. Edward M. Almond, "How Inchon Korea was Chosen for the X Corps Amphibious Landing There on 15 Sept. 1950," *The Edward M. Almond Papers*, Box 75, MHI Archive; "Biographical File, General Clark L. Ruffner, USA," MHI; Montross and Canzona, *The Inchon–Seoul Operation,* 58.

21. There was no transcript of MacArthur's remarks, but the various observers agree on the key points. MacArthur's own version appears in Douglas MacArthur, *Reminiscences* (New York, NY: McGraw-Hill Book Company, 1964, Second Printing), 349–350. Schnabel, *Policy and Direction,* provides a similar summary, 149–151. Schnabel and Watson provide background on the JCS visit in *Joint Chiefs of Staff and National Policy, Vol. 3, The Korean War,* Part 1, 87.

22. Schnabel, *Policy and Direction,* 148–150; Montross and Canzona, *The Inchon–Seoul Operation,* 43–44, 48; Field, *Naval Operations, Korea,* 175;

Shepherd Diary, 21 and 24 August 1950. Several weeks later, during the Incheon operation, Admiral Doyle took another look at Poseungmyeon and determined that, because of the configuration of the terrain behind the beach, it was not very suitable for an amphibious operation. Shepherd Diary, 19 September. See map 17 for the location of Poseungmyeon in relationship to Incheon.

23. There were also personality issues that are beyond the scope of this study. Admirals Sherman and Struble were not well liked by Admiral Doyle and many other naval officers because they were not believed to have been sufficiently passionate Navy advocates during the unification struggles. There may have been some professional jealousy between Doyle and Struble, both of whom had strong amphibious backgrounds (although postwar Navy writers rarely mention Struble's extensive amphibious experience). Almond and Smith did not get along well. Smith seems to have viewed Almond as condescending, arrogant, and stubborn, while Almond saw Smith as an overly cautious naysayer. Colonel (later Brigadier General) Forney and Lieutenant Colonel (later Lieutenant General) William J. McCaffrey, two officers who worked closely with both Almond and Smith in 1950, had a high regard for both generals and saw their mutual antipathy as unfortunate. The unification struggles clearly affected attitudes of the various Service leaders, especially early in the war, and it seems likely that the scars from the Smith-vs-Smith episode had not yet completely healed. In this regard, it should be noted that Almond was a close friend of Ralph Smith, who visited Almond in Italy following his relief from command by H.M. Smith. Ruffner was the Chief of Staff of Army Forces in POA at the time of the incident. For various perspectives on the personality issues, see Robert Debs Heinl, *Victory at High Tide: The Inchon–Seoul Campaign* (Annapolis, MD: Nautical & Aviation Pub. Co. of America, 1979); Thomas B. Buell, "Naval Leadership in Korea: The First Six Months," in Edward J. Marolda, ed., *The U.S. Navy in the Korean War* (Annapolis, MD: Naval Institute Press, 2007), 110–174; and Donald Chisholm, "Negotiated Joint Command Relationships," *Naval War College Review*, Vol. 53, No. 2 (Spring 2000): 65–124. Some of the tensions among these strong personalities played out in correspondence with Heinl during his research on *Victory at High Tide*: letters from Almond, Struble, Doyle, Smith, Ruffner, and others are available in The Robert D. Heinl Papers, PC 277, Box 42, Marine Corps University Archives. Forney's comments on Smith and Almond are in his "Special Report." McCaffrey's assessment is contained in his correspondence with Roy Appleman, available in the *Roy Appleman Collection, 1945–1989*, Box 20, MHI Archives.

24. *History of the Korean War, Chronology 25 June 1950–31 December 1951* (Tokyo: Military History Section, Far East Command, 1952), 29, 38, hereafter, *Korean War Chronology;* Schnabel, *Policy and Direction*, 156–157; Appleman, *South to the Naktong*, 489; Montross and Canzona, *The Inchon–Seoul Operation*, 55–62; Headquarters, 2d Engineer Special Brigade, Unit Activities Report, 9 July 1950 to 1 October 1950, hereafter, 2ESB UAR, 1, RG 407, Entry 429, Box 4665, NACP.

25. Heinl, *Victory at High Tide*, 34.

26. UNC/FEC OPORD No. 1, Annex A, Task Organization, Annex E, Command Relations; Field, *Naval Operations, Korea,* 179–181.

27. Kenneth W. Estes, *Marines Under Armor: The Marine Corps and the Armored Fighting Vehicle, 1916–2000* (Annapolis, MD: Naval Institute Press, 2000), 139; Company A, 56th Amphibious Tank and Tractor Battalion, Diary Report of "A" Company, 56th Amphibious Tank and Tractor Battalion to Cover the Period from 26 August to 15 January 1950–51, RG 338, Entry 37042, ATTB Cmd Rpts Jan 51, Box 28, NACP, hereafter, A/56th ATTB Diary Report, 1.

28. This description of the CHROMITE plan is from X Corps OPORD No. 1, 28 August 1950, RG 554, Entry 48, Box 5, NACP.

29. X Corps OPORD No. 1; 2d Engineer Special Brigade *Field Order 1-50,* 2 September 1950, RG 407, Entry 429, Box 4665, NACP, hereafter, 2ESB FO 1-50; 2ESB UAR; *After Action Report, Inchon Operation, 532d Engineer Boat & Shore Regiment,* 3 November 1950, copy in the Office of the Engineer Command Historian, hereafter, 532d Inchon AAR.

30. 2ESB UAR; 2ESB FO 1-50; X Corps OPORD No. 1.

31. Field, *Naval Operations, Korea,* 179, 186–187, 191–193.

32. Annex F, "Coordination of Air Operations," to *UNC/FEC Operation Plan No. 1*; Robert Frank Futrell, *The United States Air Force in Korea, 1950–1953* (Washington, DC: Office of Air Force History, US Air Force, 1983), 151–152; Field, *Naval Operations, Korea,* 179; Montross and Canzona, *The Inchon–Seoul Operation,* 67–71. Ruble's carriers would be part of Admiral Doyle's TF 90, not under Admiral Ewen's TF 77.

33. *GHQ FEC Operations Order No. 1,* 30 August 1950, RG 218, Entry UD7, CCS 383.21 Korea (3–19–45), Box 43, NACP.

34. Schnabel, *Policy and Direction,* 164–165; Appleman, *South to the Naktong,* 496–497.

35. Herbert B. Powell, "Conversations between General Herbert B. Powell and Lieutenant Colonel Philip J. Stevens and Others," *Vol. I, Senior Officer Debriefing Program* (Carlisle Barracks, PA: US Army Military History Institute Research Collection, 1972), 52, hereafter, Powell Oral History.

36. Schnabel, *Policy and Direction,* 165.

37. Message JCS 89960, JCS to CINCFE, 28 August 1950, RG 218, UD-7, CCS 383.21 Korea (3–19–45) Entry 7, Section 29, Box 40, NACP. General MacArthur invariably referred to the Incheon operation as an "envelopment" or a "deep envelopment," while the JCS referred to it as a "turning movement." In terms of the contemporary doctrine, the Incheon operation *was* a turning movement, "an enveloping maneuver which passes around the enemy's main forces to strike at a vital point deep in the hostile rear" in which the "force making the maneuver usually operates so far from the secondary attack that the principal tactical groupings may be beyond mutual supporting distance." An envelopment was a shallower maneuver: an attack "directed against the flank or rear of the initial disposition of the enemy's main forces and toward an objective in rear of his front lines." Department of the Army Field Manual (FM) 100-5, *Field Service*

Regulations: Operations (Washington, DC: GPO, 1949), 82–83. These definitions appeared in the 1923 edition of *Field Service Regulations* and remain essentially the same in current Army doctrine (see United States War Department, *Field Service Regulations, United States Army,* Washington, DC: GPO, 1923, 88–89, and, for current doctrine, FM 3-90, *Tactics* (Washington, DC: GPO, July 2001), 3-12 to 3-19). They do not appear in the earlier doctrinal manuals (*Field Service Regulations, United States Army* [Washington, DC: GPO, 1905 and 1910], for example); raising the possibility that MacArthur was not particularly conversant with the term "turning movement," which would have been familiar to the younger members of the JCS and Army Staff.

38. Message JCS 90639, JCS to CINCFE, 5 September 1950, RG 218, Entry UD7, CCS 383.21 Korea (3–19–45), Section 30, Box 40, NACP.

39. Message CINCFE C 62213 (CM IN 8572), to Department of the Army (DEPTAR) for JCS, Personal for General Collins, 6 September 1950; JCS Message 90908, Personal for MacArthur, 7 September 1950; CINCFE Message C 62423, DEPTAR for JCS, 8 September 1950; JCS Message 90958, to CINCFE, 8 September 1950, all in RG 218, Entry UD7, CCS 383.21 Korea (3–19–45) Section 31, Correspondence from 9–6–50 to 9–14–50, Box 40, NACP.

40. *Korean War Chronology*, 48; Edwin Howard Simmons, *Over the Seawall: U.S. Marines at Inchon* (Washington, DC: History and Museums Division, Headquarters, US Marine Corps, 2000), 22; Montross and Canzona, *The Inchon–Seoul Operation,* 73–74.

41. Powell Oral History, 53; 7th Infantry Division, *War Diary, 1 September to 30 September 1950,* hereafter, 7th Div WD, RG 407, Entry 429, Box 3171, NACP, 5 and 6 September 1950.

42. Powell Oral History, 53–54; 7th Div WD, 6 and 7 September 1950. Powell does not identify the Eighth Army chief of staff, but it would have been either Colonel Eugene M. Landrum or Brigadier General Leven C. Allen, who replaced Landrum at about this time.

43. 7th Div WD, "Narrative Summary," 1; *Address by Major General David G. Barr, USA, Before the Army War College, Fort Leavenworth, KS, 21 February 1951,* AWC R-201, MHI Archives, hereafter, Barr Lecture, 3; "stunned, confused, and exhausted," Appleman, *South to the Naktong,* 492.

44. GHQ UNC Letter to JCS, 9 September 1950, "United Nations Command Operational Plans and Orders," RG 218, Entry UD7, CCS 383.21 Korea (3–19–45) Section 31, Correspondence from 9–6–50 to 9–14–50, Box 40, NACP; Lynn D. Smith, "A Nickel After a Dollar," *Army* (September 1970): 25, 33–34.

45. Field, *Naval Operations, Korea,* 188–190; A/56th ATTB Diary Report, 9 and 10 September 1950; 7th Div WD; Barr Lecture.

46. This account of Clark's activities and Operation LEE is based primarily on Clark's own memoir, written in 1951 and published posthumously: Eugene Franklin Clark, *The Secrets of Inchon: The Untold Story of the Most Daring Covert Mission of the Korean War* (New York, NY: Putnam's, 2002). Other sources include Field, *Naval Operations, Korea,* 178, 183–185, 190, and 202; and Heinl, *Victory at High Tide,* 66–69, 89.

47. Clark, *Secrets of Inchon*, 8; Charles Adam Willoughby, *MacArthur: 1941–1951* (New York, NY: McGraw-Hill Book Company, 1954), 372–373. Willoughby was the GHQ FEC G2. Since Clark mentions only the two ROK officers as accompanying him on the mission, presumably the others operated from Tokyo. Major Norberg's first name and background are unknown.

48. This account is based on John B. Dwyer, *Commandos from the Sea: The History of Amphibious Special Warfare in World War II and the Korean War* (Boulder, CO: Paladin Press, 2002), 243–244; Fred Hayhurst, *Green Berets in Korea: The Story of 41 Independent Commando Royal Marines* (Cambridge, MA: Vanguard, 2001), 43–44; and an on-line summary by Ed Evanhoe, "GHQ 1st Raider Company," korean-war.com/ghqraiders.html (accessed 10 July 2006). The accounts differ. Hayhurst quotes one of the Fleet Volunteers who says there were two Raiders killed and who suggested they were killed by friendly fire, possibly by Ely himself, who got separated from the main body and reported engaging North Koreans. Dwyer's account, which is based on letters from Colonel (Retired) James H. Wear and Lieutenant Colonel Albert T. Noreen, only mentions two killed (Clance and Maines). Evanhoe's account, for which no sources are given, says the landing was on an island and that Corporal Puttin died of wounds.

49. Field, *Naval Operations, Korea,* 191–198; Curtis A. Utz, *Assault from the Sea: The Amphibious Landing at Inchon* (Washington, DC: Naval Historical Center, Department of the Navy, 1994), 80–87; Simmons, *Over the Seawall*, 26–29; Montross and Canzona, *The Inchon–Seoul Operation,* 87–96; 1st Marine Division, FMF, Special Action Report for the Inchon–Seoul Operation, 15 September–7 October 1950, Volume III, Annex QueenQueen, 5th Marines, hereafter 5th Marines SAR. MacArthur's message: CINCUNC Message, C 63153 (CM IN) 15 September 1950, to JCS, RG 218, Entry UD7, CCS 383.21 Korea (3–19–45), Box 41, Section 32, NACP.

50. 5th Marines SAR, 4–7; 2ESB UAR; Lynn Montross and Nicholas A. Canzona, "Large Sedentary Targets on RED Beach," *Marine Corps Gazette,* Vol. 44, No. 9 (September 1960): 44–50; Claude L. Roberts Jr., "2d Engineer Special Brigade," Barry W. Fowle and Jon C. Lonnquest, eds., *Remembering the "Forgotten War": U.S Army Engineer Officers in Korea* (Alexandria, VA: Office of History, Headquarters, US Army Corps of Engineers, 2005), 109; Utz, *Assault from the Sea*, 87–88; Simmons, *Over the Seawall*, 33–36.

51. A/56th ATTB Diary Report, 15 September 1950; US Marine Corps, 1st Marine Division, FMF, *Special Action Report for the Inchon–Seoul Operation*, 15 September–7 October 1950, Volume II, Annex PeterPeter, 1st Marines, 12 November 1950, hereafter, 1st Marines SAR, 5; Simmons, *Over the Seawall*, 38–42 (quote is on page 41); Montross and Canzona, *The Inchon–Seoul Operation,* make a similar statement about seamanship and compasses with regard to the UDT, 115.

52. A/56th ATTB Diary Report, 15 September 1950.

53. A/56th ATTB Diary Report, 16 September 1950; Montross and Canzona, *The Inchon–Seoul Operation*, 131–136.

54. Appleman, *South to the Naktong*, 504; 2ESB UAR, 8, 10.

55. 1MarDiv, 1st SPBn SAR, 5; 2ESB UAR, 14.

56. This description of D+1 activities is based on 2ESB UAR; 532d Inchon AAR; and Frank L. Mann, "Operation Versatile: Korean Saga of the 2d Engineer Special Brigade," *Military Engineer*, Vol. XLIV, No. 299 (May–June 1952): 168–169.

57. 532d Inchon AAR, 9.

58. 2ESB UAR, 12; 532d Inchon AAR, 9.

59. 532d Inchon AAR, 7, 11; 1MarDiv, 1st SPBn SAR, 5.

60. Trucks of the Marine 1st Combat Service Group (36 2½-ton trucks), the 120 trucks of the FMF 7th Motor Transport Battalion, and the brigade's own organic transportation were all pooled under the 2d ESB (2ESB UAR, 11–12). The vehicle shortage was made worse when most of the 85 DUKWs of the 1st Marine Division, which the 2ESB boat company had counted on for off-loading ammunition at Wolmido GREEN Beach, were taken inland to be used to transport the 1st Marines (532d Inchon AAR, 10; Simmons, *Over the Seawall*, 55).

61. 7th Div WD, 16 September 1950.

62. Montross and Canzona, *The Inchon–Seoul Operation*, 142.

63. The most complete English language account of this episode is in Walter Karig, Malcolm W. Cagle, and Frank A. Manson, *Battle Report: The War in Korea* (New York, NY: Rinehart and Company, 1952), 243–255. Former ROK Chief of Naval Operations, Admiral Ham Myong-su, described the operation in a series of articles in a Korean newspaper (Ham, Myong-su. *"Badaro! Syegyero!"* ["To the sea! To the world!"], *Kukbang Ilbo [Korea Defense Daily]*, 22, 27, 28, 29 March, 3 April 2006). Ed Evanhoe, who served with the Eighth Army special operations staff, describes the operation based on interviews with survivors of the Miryang Battalion in *Dark Moon: Eighth Army Special Operations in the Korean War* (Annapolis, MD: Naval Institute Press, 1995), 25–30. There are also brief, mutually consistent accounts in Kim Sang Mo (who cites the ROKN *Naval History*) in "The Implications of the Sea War in Korea from the Standpoint of the Korean Navy," *Naval War College Review*, Vol. XX, No. 1 (Summer 1967): 127; Cagle and Manson, *Sea War in Korea*, 298–299; Field, *Naval Operations, Korea*, 212; and Montross and Canzona, *The Inchon–Seoul Operation*, 145.

64. Evanhoe, *Dark Moon*, 27; Ham, *Korea Daily Defense*, 22 March, 27 March, and 3 April 2006 installments. The 27 March installment includes a photograph of the young irregulars of the Miryang Battalion. There is some confusion about the name of the battalion commander: Ham refers to him as Captain Yi Myeong-heum (later known as Yi Chong-hun); Karig refers to him as Captain Choi Byung Chen.

65. Evanhoe, *Dark Moon*, 27–28; Ham, *Korea Daily Defense*, 27 March 2006 installment.

66. Evanhoe, *Dark Moon*, 28. Evanhoe suggests that ROK Army Headquarters considered the Miryang Battalion, with its large contingent of North Korean defectors, to be expendable.

67. Karig, *Battle Report*, 244, 246; Ham, *Korea Daily Defense*, 27 March 2006 installment. Admiral Ham says the LST departed Busan at 1600; Evanhoe

says it departed from Jinhae at noon. It seems likely that the LST sortied from the Jinhae naval base and embarked the guerrilla battalion at Busan.

68. Evanhoe, *Dark Moon*, 29; Karig, *Battle Reports*, 245, 246; and Ham, *Korea Daily Defense*, 27 March 2006 installment.

69. Karig, *Battle Reports*, 247–251; Evanhoe, *Dark Moon*, 30; Ham, *Korea Daily Defense*, 22 and 27 March 2006 installments.

70. The nature of Spier's encouragement is reported differently in the various accounts. The Karig narrative has Spier holding a pistol to the head of the LST captain. Admiral Ham's account simply says the civilian LST skipper "had no intention of willingly damaging his ship."

71. Karig, *Battle Reports*, 251–255; Ham, *Korea Daily Defense*, 29 March installment. Ham says the men were left behind because the LST was in danger of being destroyed by enemy fire; Karig says they refused to enter the dangerous surf.

72. Malcolm W. Cagle and Frank A. Manson, *Sea War in Korea* (Annapolis, MD: Naval Institute Press, 1957), 299.

73. In a letter to Robert Debs Heinl, Almond recollected 16 years after the event that, "The plan, when analyzed by General Smith, and his staff, was considered impractical [and] an order was immediately issued to recall the project. . . . If Ely took any steps after the cancellation, . . . he did it because of failure in communication or as you intimate, enthusiastic over indulgence." Letter, Almond to Heinl, 31 August 1966, Heinl Papers, Box 42, MCUA.

74. Forney, "Special Report," 4–6, MHI Archives.

75. "GHQ Raider Company," korean-war.com/ghqraiders.html (accessed 21 November 2005); Hayhurst, *Green Berets in Korea*, 47.

76. Heinl provides a vivid account based on the *Rochester* and *Jamaica* action reports (*Victory at High Tide*, 141). The incident was also reported in the 7th Div WD, 17 September 1950.

77. A/56th ATTB Diary Report, 17–18 September 1950; MacArthur's visit, the arrival of the 96th FAB, and the drive inland toward Sosa and Gimpo are described in Simmons, *Over the Seawall*, 48–55; Montross and Canzona, *The Inchon–Seoul Operation*, 131, 143–183; and Appleman, *South to the Naktong*, 509–513.

78. Field, *Naval Operations, Korea*, 204; Headquarters, X Corps, *Operation CHROMITE, X Corps Command, 15 Aug to 30 Sep 1950*, RG 407, Entry 429, AG Command Reports, X Corps, Box 1968, NACP, hereafter, *X Corps Command*; George Craig Stewart, "Korea: August, 1950–December 15, 1950," unpublished manuscript in the Blair Collection, Box 83, "Forgotten War, Alphabetical File S-V," MHI, hereafter, Stewart MS.

79. Biography of Major General George Craig Stewart, MHI; Obituary of General Stewart in *Assembly*, Vol. LIV, No. 1, September/October 1995, 159.

80. 532d Inchon AAR, 9.

81. 532d Inchon AAR, 10.

82. 1st Shore Party Bn SAR, 6; 2ESB UAR, 6. By 18 September the tides were no longer high enough to allow LSTs to reach the shore at RED Beach, so the marines closed that beach and consolidated their operations on Wolmido.

83. On 24 September the 1st Combat Service Group was attached to the newly-established Inchon (Incheon) Base Command and the 2d ESB was relieved of responsibility for the dump operations. 2ESB UAR, 17; Montross and Canzona, *The Inchon–Seoul Operation*, 129.

84. 2ESB UAR, 9–10; Incheon City Government Web site, http://incheon. go.kr/inpia_en/servlet/html?pgm_id=INPIA_EN000019 (accessed 6 June 2006); Montross and Canzona, *The Inchon–Seoul Operation*, 143–144.

85. Apparently, the X Corps MPs took little interest in the POW mission. Later, when the 3d Logistical Command was given responsibility for the POWs, General Stewart was shocked to find 16,000 people living at the prison unguarded and in squalor. He relocated the prisoners to an old factory complex and arranged for locally-procured food to be supplied until proper arrangements could be made for clothing, bedding, and food to be delivered from Japan. Stewart MS, 6–8.

86. 2ESB UAR, 5, 8.

87. 7th Div WD, 17 and 18 September 1950; Comments by Colonel Charles E. Beauchamp, Commanding Officer, 32d Infantry, on draft manuscript of *South to the Naktong*, attached to letter of 19 January 1954, RG 319, Records of OCMH, 2-3.7A BA2, Box 746, NACP; Barr Lecture, 3.

88. Shepherd Diary, 18 September 1950; Simmons, *Over the Seawall*, 51–52.

89. *X Corps Command*, 19 September 1950; 7th Div WD, 19 and 20 September 1950.

90. The Raiders' amphibious career was now behind them. They provided flank security for the marines at Gimpo and after the capture of Seoul were transferred from GHQ FEC to X Corps, later being designated the 8245th Army Unit, X Corps Raider Company. They performed reconnaissance and intelligence missions with X Corps in Northeast Korea and, according to one source, were part of TF *Drysdale*, a force built around the British 41st Independent Company Royal Marines, which took heavy casualties at the Jangjin (Chosin) Reservoir in November 1950. The Raider Company was disbanded in April 1951 along with the Ranger Airborne Infantry companies then serving in the Far East. "GHQ Raider Company," korean-war.com/ghqraiders.html (accessed 21 November 2005); Hayhurst, *Green Berets in Korea*, 47.

91. 7th Div WD, 19 September; X Corps WD, 12.

92. Montross and Canzona, *The Inchon–Seoul Operation*, 184–185, 206.

93. 1st Shore Party Bn SAR, 6; A/56th ATTB Diary Report, 19 September 1950.

94. The 2ESB boat company (B/532d EB&SR) made use of this ramp to unload an ammunition ship, a slow process since eight of the brigade's DUKWs had to do the work of 85 Marine Corps DUKWs that had been deployed inland to transport the 1st Marines and to support river crossings; 532d Inchon AAR, 10. On 22 September General Almond directed General Smith to send 15 DUKWs back to Incheon temporarily to help with the ammunition unloading. Edward M. Almond Personal Notes, 31 August 1950–15 July 1951, hereafter, Almond Diary, 21 September 1950, Edward M. Almond Papers, Box 64, MHI.

95. 2ESB UAR, 9–10.

96. For a discussion of the Incheon operation as a "turning movement," see note 37, above.

97. Quoted in Schnabel, *Policy and Direction*, 176.

98. Appleman, *South to the Naktong*, 551–554.

99. Shepherd Diary, 19 September 1950.

100. Shepherd Diary, 19 September 1950. Doyle's rejection on 19 September of the Poseungmyeon landing site raises questions about the original proposal to land there, for which the Navy and Marines had argued so vociferously. The issue seems to have been the suitability of the area behind the beaches for rapid exploitation of the initial landing. The UDT reconnaissance party apparently determined that the beaches were favorable for an initial landing, but Doyle's second thoughts had to do with the exits from the beach for follow-on and sustainment operations.

101. Schnabel, *Policy and Direction*, 176.

102. Schnabel, *Policy and Direction*, 176; Appleman, *South to the Naktong*, 554–559, 569–572.

103. Appleman, *South to the Naktong*, 515–516 (3/5 Marines), 527–530 (32d Inf); Montross and Canzona, *The Inchon–Seoul Operation*, 183–197 (3/5 Marines), 251–255 (RCT-1, ROK 17th Regiment, and 32d Inf); 7th Div WD, and 32d Div WD.

104. 5th Marines SAR, 9.

105. A/56th ATTB Diary Report, 20 September 1950; 5th Marine SAR, 9–10; Montross and Canzona, *The Inchon–Seoul Operation*, 196–197.

106. A/56th ATTB Diary Report, 21 September 1950.

107. Almond Diary, 21 September 1950.

108. *X Corps Command*, 21–23 September 1950; X Corps OPORD No. 1, paragraph 3l, "Inchon Base Command."

109. Montross and Canzona, *The Inchon–Seoul Operation*, 201.

110. 7th Div WD, 21 September 1950. Lightering is the transfer by barges or landing craft of personnel and/or cargo between the shore and ships anchored off shore (in the stream).

111. TF *Hannum* was commanded by Lieutenant Colonel Calvin S. Hannum, Commander of the 63d Tank Battalion, and consisted of Hannum's advance command group and Company B of the 63d Tank Battalion, Company K of the 32d Infantry, and Battery C of the 48th Field Artillery Battalion. 7th Div WD, 21 and 22 September 1950; X Corps WD, 15, 16; Montross and Canzona, *The Inchon–Seoul Operation*, 519–523; Appleman, *South to the Naktong*, 520–523.

112. Because of the problems the engineer boat company was having in getting ammunition unloaded, Almond also directed Smith to send back 15 DUKWs with the assurance that they would be returned by midnight on 24 September for the 1st Marines' river crossing. Almond Diary, 22 September 1950; Montross and Canzona, *The Inchon–Seoul Operation*, 243; Appleman, *South to the Naktong*, 519–520.

113. 7th Marines Special Action Report, 10–12RR; A/56th ATTB Diary Report, 23 September 1950.

114. Almond Diary, 23 September 1950. The matter of how best to accomplish the capture of Seoul was a contentious one, with disagreement between General Almond and General Smith. At issue were differences in approach, a desire on the part of Almond to capture Seoul by 25 September (3 months after the North Korean attack), and an apparent desire on the part of Smith to have the city captured by his division alone. It is likely that a contributing factor was the underlying Army–Marine antipathy that dated back at least to the beginning of World War II, was made worse by Marine General H.M. Smith's relief of Army General Ralph Smith on Saipan in 1944, and was intensified by the post-World War II unification and roles and missions struggles. Some sources say that at the 23 September meeting, Almond gave Smith a 24-hour deadline to make progress or else he would change the boundaries and bring in part of the Army 7th Division to conduct the desired maneuver from the southeast. Almond's diary and Smith's account make no mention of such a deadline, but it seems likely that Almond had this plan (which he put into effect on 24 September) in mind at least as early as the 23 September meeting. In any event, these matters are beyond the scope of this study. Heinl corresponded extensively with all the concerned parties when writing his book, *Victory at High Tide*, and provides a thorough discussion, 210–213.

115. 1st Marines Special Action Report (1MarDiv SAR, Annex PP), Box 8–6, MCUA.

116. 7th Marines SAR; A/56th ATTB Diary Report.

117. Almond Diary, 24 September 1950.

118. Montross and Canzona, *The Inchon–Seoul Operation*, 244.

119. 7th Div WD, 24 September 1950; A/56th ATTB Diary Report, 24 September 1950.

120. Letter, Herbert B. Powell (RCT 17 Commander) to Beryl King Powell, 24 September 1950, Herbert B. Powell Collection, Series I; Papers, Box 9, Correspondence to Beryl King Powell, 1926–1951," MHI Archives.

121. 7th Inf Div WD, 24, 25 September 1950; Powell Oral History, 56–57.

122. 7th Div WD, 25 September 1950; A/56th ATTB Diary Report, 25 September 1950; Appleman, *South to the Naktong*, 529–530.

123. *Remembering the "Forgotten War,"* 110; 532d Inchon AAR, 10.

124. *Korean War Chronology*, 56–57.

125. A/56th ATTB Diary Report, 29 September 1950.

126. *Korean War Chronology*, 54.

127. UNC Command Report; Field, *Naval Operations, Korea,* 216–217; *Korean War Chronology*, 61.

128. Field, *Naval Operations, Korea,* 217–218; Evanhoe, *Dark Moon*, 38. See map 17 for the location of these operations.

129. US Army, 8206th Army Unit, Amphibious Training Center, *Unit History* [1951?], hereafter, ATC History, 10.

130. 1st MarDiv SAR, Annex NN (1st Engineer Battalion), 6; ATC History, 10.

131. 532d Inchon AAR, 10.

132. 532d Inchon AAR, 11.

133. 2ESB UAR, 14; 532d Inchon AAR, 11; Memorandum, 1st Lt Albert Krause, Utilities Branch, GHQ FEC Engineer Section, to Colonel Medding, 20 October 1950, Subject: "Repair of Locks at Inchon and Power Situation in the Seoul–Inchon Areas," copy in File XII-9-13, Office of the Engineer Command Historian.

134. Headquarters, US Army Forces Far East and Eighth US Army (Rear), *Logistics in the Korean War*, Vol. I, 1 December 1955, copy at the Office of the Engineer Chief Historian.

135. 532d Incheon AAR, 10, 11.

136. 2ESB UAR, 13.

137. ATC History, 12.

138. Field, *Naval Operations, Korea*, 218.

Chapter 5

Operations in North Korea, October–December 1950

The Invasion of North Korea

Strategic Setting

The decision to invade North Korea ran on parallel tracks in Tokyo and Washington. During his 13 July meeting with Generals J. Lawton Collins and Hoyt S. Vandenberg, General Douglas MacArthur made clear that he saw his mission as not just to restore the 38th Parallel, but to destroy the North Korean forces and, if necessary, occupy all of North Korea.[1] His plans for amphibious operations included potential landings at Jinnampo (Chinnamp'o) and Wonsan, although at the time of the planning he had no authorization to conduct operations in North Korea.[2] In Washington, the decision to invade North Korea had been under consideration from the opening days of the war. Initial United Nations Command (UNC) objectives established by the 27 June 1950 UN Security Council Resolution were to "repel the armed attack and to restore international peace and security in the area." This clearly required driving the attacking forces back to the 38th Parallel, but both US policy and earlier UN General Assembly resolutions identified the long-range goal as a free, united, and independent Korea. Republic of Korea (ROK) President Syngman Rhee and some of President Harry S. Truman's advisors saw the war as an opportunity to achieve that goal.[3]

On 17 July 1950, even as US and ROK forces were being pushed south by the North Koreans, Truman ordered a formal study to determine if the UNC should conduct operations north of the 38th Parallel. The National Security Council (NSC) secretly debated this issue and on 11 September President Truman approved policy paper NSC 81, which recommended postponing a decision, but anticipated that the president would decide to approve operations in North Korea unless the Soviets or Chinese intervened first. MacArthur was to be ordered to prepare plans to occupy North Korea, but not to execute those plans without explicit presidential approval. The Joint Chiefs of Staff (JCS) informed MacArthur of the gist of the decision on 15 September, the same day the Incheon landing took place. On 27 September President Truman made the decision to invade North Korea. Also, on that date the JCS informed MacArthur that his objective was now the destruction of the North Korean Armed Forces, authorized him to conduct operations north of the 38th Parallel so long as the Soviets or Chinese had not intervened or threatened to intervene, and directed him to submit plans for invading and occupying North Korea.[4]

MacArthur immediately directed General Edwin K. Wright and the Joint Strategic Plans and Operations Group (JSPOG) staff to develop a plan that would include an amphibious operation well north of the 38th Parallel in conjunction with an overland attack by Eighth Army. He wanted two alternatives, one in which Eighth Army would make the main effort in the west, attacking toward Pyeongyang (P'yongyang), while X Corps landed at Jinnampo or another suitable location. The other was for an Eighth Army attack toward the east coast and a simultaneous X Corps landing at Wonsan. With the plan for a Wonsan landing already in existence, Wright suggested a combination of the two alternatives: an Eighth Army main attack to capture Pyeongyang with a X Corps landing at Wonsan. Several characteristics of Wonsan recommended it as the amphibious objective. There were suitable beaches for the landing, it was far enough north to provide a basis for encircling the North Korean field force, and the Wonsan–Hamheung (Hamhung)–Heungnam (Hungnam) complex was the east coast transportation nexus. There was a good avenue of approach to Pyeongyang to the west across the narrow waist of Korea, which would facilitate operations by X Corps to link up with Eighth Army. Furthermore, a large east coast port would be necessary to sustain the advance into North Korea. Neither Incheon (Inch'on) with its strong tides and small capacity, nor Busan (Pusan) at the beginning of a long line of communication to the north, would be adequate for that purpose.[5]

MacArthur submitted his plan to the JCS on 28 September, advising them that he would issue a surrender proclamation on 1 October and, if he received no response, would then enter North Korea to accomplish his objectives. Eighth Army would continue the attack across the 38th Parallel to seize Pyeongyang; X Corps would make an amphibious landing at Wonsan, then link up with Eighth Army; the 3d Infantry Division would initially remain in Japan as General Headquarters (GHQ) Reserve; and ROK forces would attack north along the east coast toward Heungnam. ROK forces only would operate north of Heungnam. After obtaining President Truman's authorization, the JCS advised MacArthur on 29 September that his plan was approved. An hour after the JCS message was dispatched, Secretary of Defense George C. Marshall sent a personal message to General MacArthur noting a report that ROK divisions would halt at the 38th Parallel "for regrouping," and advising that "[w]e want you to feel unhampered tactically and strategically to proceed north of 38th Parallel."[6]

On 29 September, just before the ceremony in Seoul to return the city to President Rhee, MacArthur met with Generals Walton H. Walker, Edward M. Almond, and George Stratemeyer, and Admiral C. Turner Joy to inform them of the plan, with a tentative date for the Wonsan amphibious landing of 20 October. Almond was directed to turn over control of Seoul to Walker by 7 October, to move the 7th Division to Busan for embarkation, and to mount out the Corps Troops and the 1st Marine Division from Incheon.[7]

MacArthur broadcast his surrender message on 1 October, and lead elements of the 3d ROK Division crossed the 38th Parallel on the east coast of Korea (see map 27). UNC Operation Order (OPORD) No. 2, issued on 2

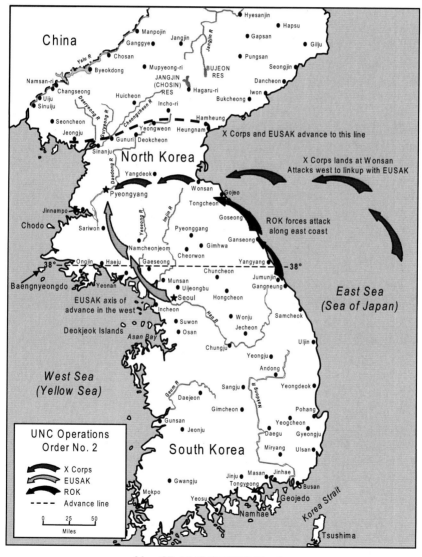

Map 27. UNC OPORD No. 2.

October, directed Eighth Army to attack north toward Pyeongyang on a line of operation Gaeseong (Kaesong)–Sariwon–Pyeongyang, while X Corps conducted an amphibious turning movement, landing at Wonsan with a subsequent attack westward to link up with Eighth Army. Together, Eighth Army and X Corps would destroy North Korean People's Army (KPA) forces south of a line Jeongju (Chongju)–Gunu-ri (Kunu-ri)–Yeongwon (Yongwon)–Hamheung–Heungnam. Naval Forces Far East (NAVFE) was to outload X Corps Headquarters and the 1st Marine Division (the assault force) from Incheon and the rest of X Corps (including the 7th Infantry Division, the follow-on force) from Busan. The 187th Airborne Regimental Combat Team (RCT) was to assemble in the Gimpo (Kimp'o) area as GHQ Reserve and be prepared to carry out an airdrop or air landing as required. The 3d Division (minus the 65th RCT, which had been sent directly to Korea and was operating with Eighth Army) was to be prepared to ship out from the port of Sasebo. The 65th RCT would outload at Busan and revert to control of the 3d Division when directed. Admiral Joy would command all the forces engaged in the amphibious assault through Admiral Arthur D. Struble's Joint Task Force (JTF) 7. Control of the landing force would pass from the commander, attack force (Admiral Doyle), to the commander, landing force "at such time as Landing Force has been landed ashore, the beachhead secured and Commander Landing Force, informs the Commander Attack Force, that he is ready to assume responsibility for further operations ashore" [punctuation as in the original].[8]

X Corps Mount Out

On 4 October amphibious shipping began to assemble at the ports of Incheon and Busan and the 1st Marine Division began to assemble in the Incheon area. The next day, the 7th Infantry Division, which had already assembled in the Incheon–Suwon area, began moving by rail and road to Busan in preparation for outloading. Its tanks and heavy equipment were loaded aboard Shipping Control Administration, Japan (SCAJAP) landing ships, tank (LSTs) at Incheon and transported to Busan, where the rest of the division would be loaded aboard transports and cargo ships. On 7 October X Corps was relieved of responsibility for the Seoul area by Eighth Army and reverted to GHQ Reserve. That same day, the 1st Marine Division closed Incheon Harbor and on 8 October began loading aboard assault shipping under the direction of Admiral Lyman A. Thackrey, commander of Amphibious Group 3.[9]

On 10 October General George C. Stewart's 3d Logistical Command was transferred from X Corps to Eighth United States Army in Korea (EUSAK), which in turn attached it to the 2d Logistical Command (headquartered in Busan). The command would continue to operate the Seoul–Incheon advance base in support of the Eighth Army operations in North Korea.[10] On 11 October Thackrey was relieved of his Incheon Port responsibilities and sailed aboard the *Eldorado* to Busan to direct the 7th Infantry Division mount out.[11]

The 2d Engineer Special Brigade (ESB) had been ordered to assist in outloading the 1st Marine Division and X Corps troops at Incheon and then to outload itself. As was the case during the landing and subsequent port operations, the tides and inability to bring the transports and cargo ships up to the piers complicated the loading. In a reverse process, LSTs and landing craft lightered the troops out to the transports. Vehicles were carried out on LSTs and then loaded by cranes onto the ships. While the outloading took place, the 2d ESB continued to operate the Incheon Port. Once the LSTs and most of the landing ships, utility (LSUs) were combat loaded, they were no longer available for lightering duty. With 1,100 vehicles (two-thirds of the total) still to be loaded, the 532d Engineer Boat and Shore Regiment (EB&SR) made use of barges and floating cranes to supplement the few remaining LSUs and landing craft, mechanized (LCMs) to get the vehicles on board the ships. By 16 October the marines and X Corps troops, vehicles, and equipment were all embarked. The 2d ESB turned the port operation mission over to the 14th Transportation Port Battalion on that day and began its own embarkation. The plan at this time was that the 1st Marine Division would make the initial assault into Wonsan using its own shore party assets. The 2d ESB was to follow them in and then operate the port. Since they were not expected to be part of the assault landing, the brigade was ordered to load administratively so that it could unload at Wonsan as quickly and efficiently as possible to put the port into operation. At twilight, 21 October, the last LCM carrying Colonel Joseph J. Twitty, the rest of the brigade command and staff personnel, and the last group of boat crews locked out of the tidal basin, and the amphibious engineers went aboard their transport, the Military Sea Transportation Service (MSTS) T-AP-154, *General Leroy Eltinge*. The outloading was complete.[12]

Also on board the *Eltinge* were Captain James D. O'Donnell with 4 officers, 1 warrant officer, and 71 enlisted men of Company A, 56th Amphibious Tank and Tractor Battalion (ATTB), which had been attached to the 2d ESB for the move to North Korea. The tanks, drivers, assistant drivers, and maintenance section remained in Incheon to be brought forward later by turn-around shipping. O'Donnell's outfit was finding itself to be something of an orphan. The troops had not been paid since August, nor had repair parts been delivered. O'Donnell asked a Navy officer who was on his way to Japan to contact the 56th ATTB commander and pass on a list of parts needed to keep the tanks running. In spite of these trials, O'Donnell reported that morale was high.[13]

The move of the 7th Infantry Division units to Busan over poor roads and damaged rail lines was a difficult operation. The roads and railways were overloaded by the two-way traffic of Eighth Army supplies and reinforcements moving north at the same time the 7th Infantry Division was moving south. It was also a dangerous journey because of attacks by North Korean forces that had been bypassed by Eighth Army in its advance north after the breakout. By 12 October, however, all of the 7th Infantry Division units were in the Busan area and preparing to embark.[14]

Logistics presented additional problems. UNC OPORD No. 2 had specified that X Corps was responsible for logistic support of all UN forces in its area of responsibility (AOR) and that Eighth Army was responsible for logistic support of all UN forces in Korea except for those in the X Corps AOR. Thus, while X Corps was responsible for logistic support of its own assigned and attached units, Eighth Army was responsible for supporting X Corps. The X Corps had been requisitioning its supplies directly from the Japan Logistical Command (JLC) in Yokohama and had established detailed supply plans with that agency. Those arrangements were now disrupted and another level added between X Corps and the JLC just as the division was outloading.[15] Furthermore, X Corps had required the 2d Logistical Command in Busan to provide 10 days supply of clothing and construction material and 15 days of all other classes of supply to be delivered to Wonsan by D+8. Stocks in the Busan area, especially of winter clothing, were soon depleted and the supplies had to be requisitioned from Japan.[16] In spite of these difficulties, the troops and equipment of the division were aboard ship and ready to sail by 17 October.[17] Other complications had arisen, however, and the sailing date was to be postponed.

Eighth Army Moves into North Korea[18]

Since 1 October Brigadier General Kim Paik-il's ROK I Corps had been advancing rapidly up the east coast, resupplied over the beach from time to time by LSTs. By 9 October they were approaching Wonsan. This rapid movement and the likelihood that General Kim's forces would capture Wonsan before the amphibious force had even finished outloading caused General MacArthur to consider a change in plans. He requested General Wright's staff prepare an alternative to UNC OPORD No. 2 in which the 7th Infantry Division would land administratively just north of Wonsan, and the 1st Marine Division would conduct an assault landing at Heungnam, some 50 miles further north. X Corps would then attack to the west, across the peninsula, toward Pyeongyang. Wright presented a proposed Commander in Chief, Far East (CINCFE) Operation Plan (OPLAN) 9-50 (Alternate) to MacArthur on 8 October, but Admiral Joy persuaded the commander in chief that it would be unwise to split the two divisions and pointed out the limited time available to change the plan for amphibious assault. He also doubted that the approaches to both Wonsan and Heungnam could be cleared of mines in time for the proposed operation. On 10 October MacArthur directed that the original plan be carried out. That same day, General Kim Paik-il's ROK I Corps forces entered Wonsan, securing the port city on 11 October. Walker notified MacArthur that Wonsan was secure and requested the harbor and approaches be swept clear of mines so that resupply operations could begin. MacArthur advised that Wonsan sweeping operations, which had begun on 10 October, would continue, but that no LSTs would be available for ROK resupply until X Corps landed. He also advised that X Corps would take over operational control of ROK I Corps.[19]

On 13 October Major General Field Harris, commander of the 1st Marine Air Wing and the X Corps Tactical Air Command (TAC), arrived by air to inspect the airfield, after which he ordered his squadrons to begin flying in. On 16 October General Almond sent his deputy chief of staff, Lieutenant Colonel William J. McCaffrey, to Wonsan to establish an advance command post and to make contact with General Kim and with Captain Richard T. Spofford, commander of the minesweeper task group. On 18 October a survey party from the 2d ESB flew in to reconnoiter the port facilities.[20]

Spofford's minesweepers had uncovered a serious problem that would significantly delay the X Corps landing. The sweepers started finding mines as soon as they began their operation on 10 October. Helicopters flying ahead of the sweepers spotted five lines of mines planted in an exceptionally dense pattern. By the end of the day, Spofford reported that there were at least 2,000 mines of various types blocking the approaches to Wonsan. A substantial, difficult, and dangerous sweeping effort would be required before Admiral James H. Doyle and Admiral Thackrey's ships could enter the port.[21]

Meanwhile, Eighth Army was on the move. An unintended consequence of the decision to re-embark X Corps for an amphibious operation was that the outgoing forces blocked Eighth Army's lines of communication and Walker was logistically incapable of beginning his attack north. Not only was the line of communication from Busan clogged, unloading at Incheon had virtually stopped as the 1st Marine Division, X Corps

Headquarters, and the 7th Division's tracked vehicles and heavy equipment outloaded. By 7 October, however, Walker was ready to move and asked his chief of staff to advise GHQ Far East Command (FEC). General Doyle O. Hickey, the acting FEC chief of staff, immediately responded that MacArthur had given the go-ahead, and patrols from the 1st Cavalry Division began to slip across the 38th Parallel that night. On 9 October MacArthur transmitted a second surrender message and Walker gave orders to Eighth Army "to strike out for Pyongyang [Pyeongyang] without delay." Later that day, the 1st Cavalry Division, the British 27th Brigade, the ROK 1st Division, and elements of the US 24th Division crossed the 38th Parallel in force.[22]

Yeseong Resupply Operation

The 1st Cavalry Division moved north, with the 7th Cavalry RCT on its left flank pushing toward the Yeseong River, west of Gaeseong (Kaesong) (see map 28). As the 7th Cavalry approached the river, the G4 advised Colonel William A. Harris, the regimental commander, that the division could not provide fuel and ammunition support. Harris sent the regimental assistant S3, Captain Arthur Westburg, back to Incheon to request support from the 3d Logistical Command. On 9 October General Stewart ordered the 8206th Army Unit (AU), Amphibious Training Center (ATC), to support the 7th Cavalry. The men of the ATC loaded 500 tons of supplies into 13 LCMs and, escorted by an ROK Navy gunboat and under Marine Corps air cover, the convoy motored up the coast through the West Sea (Yellow Sea), the Ganghwa (Kanghwa) Channel between the Gimpo Peninsula and Ganghwa Island, the Han River estuary, and the Yeseong (Yesong) River to the 7th Cavalry positions, arriving late on the afternoon of 10 October at a destroyed bridge site.

After unloading supplies, the ATC used its LCMs to ferry tanks of Company C, 70th Tank Battalion across the river while I Corps engineers constructed a pontoon ferry at the bridge site. Then they headed back to Incheon for more supplies, returning on 13 October with five LCMs and an LSU. The Army watermen remained in the area, conducting a ferry service across the Yeseong River until 17 October, when they returned to Incheon and continued to assist in port operations.[23]

Opening of Jinnampo Port

To keep Eighth Army supplied, the rail lines, bridges, and highways damaged or destroyed by air attacks during the defense phase of operations now had to be repaired or replaced. As an interim measure to supplement the ground line of communication, an LST beach for over-the-shore operations was established at the port of Haeju. The Haeju LST beach was helpful, but insufficient. The port of Jinnampo also had to be put into service. Jinnampo, at the mouth of the Daedong (Taedong) River, was the seaport for Pyeongyang, as Incheon was the seaport for Seoul. Like Incheon, Jinnampo suffers from huge tides, a long island-clogged approach channel, 3-to-5 knot tidal currents, and broad mud flats at low tide. By the time Eighth Army crossed the 38th Parallel, the North Koreans had heavily mined the approaches to Jinnampo. But because of the configuration of

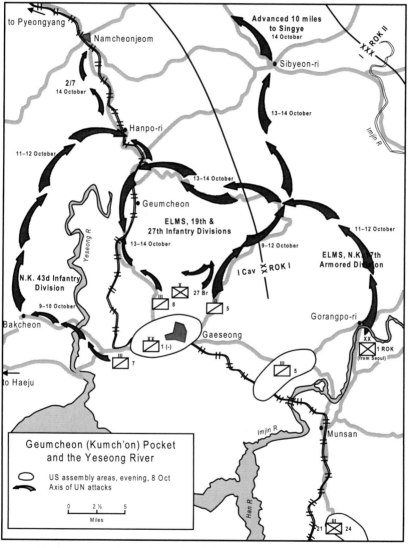

Map 28. Geumcheon (Kumch'on) Pocket and the Yeseong River.

the northwest Korean coast and lack of suitable LST beaches elsewhere, Jinnampo was the only port capable of supporting Eighth Army's military operations in the north and it had to be made usable. The first step was to clear the mines from the channel. The Navy began a major minesweeping effort on 21 October and by 6 November the first ships (small Japanese cargo ships and a SCAJAP LST) arrived at the port. Soon thereafter, an element of the 7th Transportation Medium Port and the 501st Harbor Craft Platoon arrived by LST to operate the port facilities, and by the end of the month nearly 5,000 tons of cargo were being unloaded daily.[24] The city was without power, but Lieutenant Commander Henry J. Ereckson's destroyer escort, the USS *Foss* (DE-59), was sent to assist. The *Foss*, a turbo-electric powered ship that had been equipped with ship-to-shore power conversion equipment in 1946, tied up at the Jinnampo wharf and generated electric power for the city. The ROK Navy established a Jinnampo Naval Base Command and provided port and harbor security with a shore patrol and three motor launches.[25]

TAILBOARD (Wonsan/Iwon), 29 October–4 November 1950

While X Corps was mounting out, General MacArthur was meeting with President Truman at Wake Island. During this 15 October 1950 meeting, MacArthur outlined his plan. With Wonsan already in UNC hands, he intended to land X Corps at the captured seaport and then cut across Korea to link up with Eighth Army. He anticipated that North Korea would collapse soon thereafter and he could begin sending troops back to the United States. There was "very little" chance of Chinese intervention, he said in reply to a question. However, he qualified this by stressing that his opinion was only speculation, since the issue of whether or not other nations would enter the war was in the realm of political intelligence and should be dealt with by the Central Intelligence Agency (CIA) and State Department intelligence groups, rather than by the theater commander's intelligence staff.[26]

At Wonsan, Captain Spofford's multinational task force of US and ROK Navy and Japanese civilian minesweepers worked their way through the dense minefield. On 12 October two US minesweepers were sunk, and on 17 October one of the Japanese contract minesweepers was sunk. Although most of the amphibious attack force had already sailed from Incheon by 13 October (the 2d ESB would not sail until 26 October), Admiral Joy ordered Admiral Thackrey at Busan to delay the 7th Infantry Division's sailing until more progress was made with the minesweeping. Those transports that had already loaded remained anchored in Busan Harbor to await developments.[27]

Meanwhile, General Walker's lead forces were nearing Pyeongyang in the west. On 17 October 1950 General MacArthur issued UNC OPORD No. 4, to become effective if Pyeongyang was captured before X Corps was in position to advance to the west (see map 29). On order, the boundary between Eighth Army and X Corps was to follow the 38th Parallel from the east coast to west of Majeon-ri (Majon-ni), then north through the Jangjin (Changjin/Chosin) Reservoir to the border. Instead of clearing North Korea south of the Jeongju (Chongju)–Heungnam line (the narrow waist), Eighth

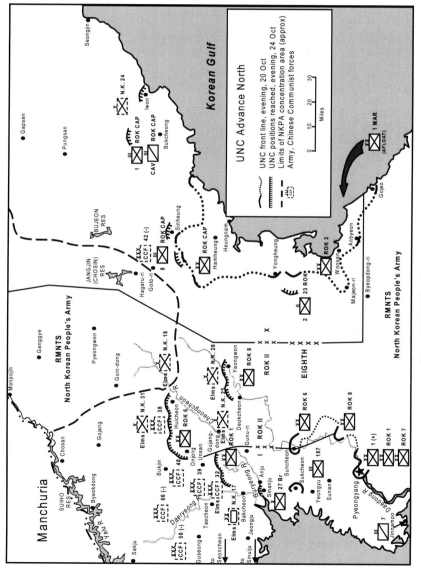

Map 29. UNC advance north.

Army in the west and X Corps in the east would make a general advance to the north to a line making an arc from Seoncheon (Sonch'on) on the west coast to Seongjin (Songjin) on the east coast. The 3d Division was to assemble in the Wonsan area as GHQ Reserve and the 187th Airborne RCT was to prepare to parachute into Suncheon (Sunch'on) and Sukcheon (Sukch'on), north of Pyeongyang to try to trap KPA forces escaping to the north and to liberate UNC prisoners of war (POW).[28]

Unknown to the UNC, the Chinese leadership had decided to intervene in Korea. On 19 October as the 1st Cavalry Division and 1st ROK Division entered Pyeongyang and UNC OPORD No. 4 was put into effect, Chinese forces began crossing the Yalu River into Korea.[29] On 20 October the 187th Airborne RCT made its jump north of Pyeongyang. That same day, General Almond established his X Corps Headquarters in Wonsan and took command of all forces in its new zone.

Offshore, minesweeping operations continued while the 21 transports and 15 LSTs carrying the 1st Marine Division steamed north and south off the coast, in what the marines called Operation YO-YO. It was not until 25 October that the channel was declared clear and the ships were allowed to enter the port. That evening, the five LSTs carrying the marine shore party, combat service group, and Navy engineers beached on the south shore of the peninsula that forms the southern boundary of Wonsan Bay. The next day, the main ship-to-shore landing began with the first of 39 waves of landing craft, LSTs, and LSUs coming ashore, where the marines were welcomed by X Corps Headquarters, the 1st Marine Air Wing, and the ROK forces occupying Wonsan. Unloading would continue until 31 October.[30]

In the west, Eighth Army advanced rapidly north of Pyeongyang, crossing the Cheongcheon (Ch'ongch'on) River on 23 October. Since the rail and vehicle bridges over the river had been bombed out, General Stewart carried out an aerial reconnaissance to locate a suitable site for an LST beach for over-the-shore supply delivery.[31] The Eighth Army advance came to an abrupt end on 25 October, when a large force of Chinese People's Volunteers (CPV) hit Walker's lead elements and pushed the Eighth Army center and right flank back to the Cheongcheon River. By 6 November the Chinese attacks ended and their forces withdrew.[32] By that time X Corps was established ashore in the east and was advancing north.

With the 1st Marine Division at Wonsan, Almond no longer saw any benefit to landing the 7th Infantry Division in their wake. Instead, he decided to land them further north to be better able to carry out MacArthur's orders for a rapid advance. He flew along the coast, looking for suitable landing sites, and settled on the beach at Iwon, about 105 miles north of Wonsan. On 26 October he issued X Corps Operations Instruction No. 13, directing General Kim's I Corps to advance north rapidly in multiple columns and to form a "flying column" of at least one RCT supported by one LST for logistic support to advance along the coastal road as rapidly as possible. The 1st Marine Division was to relieve ROK forces at Wonsan and at the coastal town of Gojeo (Kojo) to the south, concentrate one RCT in the Hamheung–Heungnam area, and advance rapidly to the northern border, being prepared to use one battalion landing team (BLT) for amphibious movement to outflank pockets of KPA forces. The 7th Infantry Division was to land over the beaches at Iwon and advance rapidly to the northern border.[33]

On 26 October Admiral Thackrey, who had directed the outloading of the 7th Infantry Division and X Corps troops at Busan, arrived at Wonsan aboard the *Eldorado*. Learning of the change in plans, he now sailed to Iwon to inspect the landing site and supervise the 7th Infantry Division landing. En route he issued an order advising that the approaches to Iwon had been swept and the beach surveyed by the underwater demolition team (UDT) to establish a new landing site "to expedite the landing of the 7th Infantry Division." The 17th RCT would be the first unit to be landed over the Iwon beaches. The division (still anchored in Busan Harbor) was embarked on an MSTS transport (*General Weigle,* T-AP-119), an AKA (*Thuban,* AKA-19), and several chartered merchant ships. Only the *Thuban* carried landing craft, so the SCAJAP LSTs carrying the vehicles and heavy equipment and three LSUs being carried aboard the LSD *Colonial* would be used as lighters after they were unloaded and would ferry troops and equipment from the ships to the shore.[34] Colonel Herbert B. Powell's 17th Infantry, as the first unit to go ashore and secure the beach, had to be able to land immediately, so while Powell flew north with the assistant division commander, Brigadier General Henry I. Hodes, to reconnoiter the beach and get instructions from X Corps Headquarters, his executive officer supervised the debarkation of the RCT from its transports and cargo ship and reloading aboard SCAJAP LSTs.[35]

The 2d ESB was at sea, off Incheon, when it got the word on 26 October that instead of landing administratively at Wonsan to operate the port, the engineers would land over the beach at Iwon, prepare the beach for over-the-shore operations, and assist in the landing of the 7th Division. The ships carrying the brigade sailed for the northeast, arriving at Iwon on 29 October to find eight LSTs already on the beach unloading the 17th RCT. Colonel Powell, who had earlier flown to Wonsan from Busan, was standing on the shore when the LSTs arrived. The Japanese LST commanders brought their ships in as close as possible to the beach, which still left a gap with water about 5 feet deep between the end of the ramps and the shore. The loose sand provided very little traction for vehicles, so Powell ordered his tanks off the LSTs first and used them as impromptu tractors to haul the trucks and artillery ashore. Korean Augmentation to the US Army (KATUSA) soldiers, who formed a human chain to pass the boxes to the beach, unloaded rations and other supplies.[36] (See map 30.)

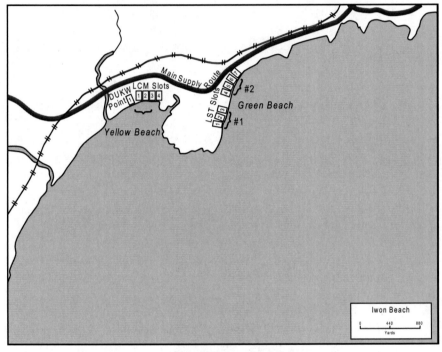

Map 30. Iwon Beach.

The 2d ESB aboard the *Eltinge* and the merchant ship *Luxembourg Victory,* which carried the brigade's heavy equipment, arrived offshore at 1215 along with the 3 LSUs, brought to Iwon by the LSD *Colonial*, and 10 LCMs. These 13 craft provided the only lighterage until the SCAJAP LSTs were unloaded. The 532d EB&SR sent their shore party in with bull-dozers to assist the final stages of unloading the 17th RCT, then one of the LSTs was used to bring equipment ashore from the *Luxembourg Victory*. Powell initially provided security for the beach before moving inland. On the morning of 30 October, the 2d ESB took control of beach opera-tions, using the dismounted armored amphibians of Captain O'Donnell's Company A, 56th ATTB for beach security after the 17th RCT departed. First priority was to get bulldozers ashore so vehicles being brought in by the LSTs, LSUs, and LCMs could be towed through the surf and loose sand. A storm that struck later that day caused unloading of the rest of the division to be postponed, giving the 2d ESB time to prepare the beach. The biggest problem was the soft sand, but the engineers found suitable fill soil inland, which they used to stabilize the bulldozed sand ramps that would permit the LSTs to unload directly onto the beach. The engineers contracted for local labor, bought materials from a nearby lumberyard, and purchased huge quantities of rice straw sacks that proved to be better than sandbags for trimming the LST ramps.[37]

Unloading resumed on 31 October. The 3d Battalion, 31st Infantry Regiment, 7th Infantry Division, landed at Iwon on 3 November 1950 and the rest of the regiment and lead elements of the 32d Infantry came ashore the next day. It was a slow process, but by 8 November the 7th Infantry Division and its supporting elements had been landed and the division was moving inland and preparing to advance to the north. On 17 November one final late-arriving LST was unloaded by a rear detachment of the brigade. After completion of 7th Infantry Division debarkation, the 2d ESB moved via LST, LSD, train, and truck to Heungnam to operate the port there beginning on 19 November 1950. In total, the brigade unloaded some 14,000 tons of supplies and equipment, nearly 5,000 vehicles, and 21,000 troops over the beach, not including the men, vehicles, and equipment of the 17th RCT, which had unloaded itself.[38]

On 2 November the 7th Marines and ROK I Corps units advancing north were hit by the Chinese at the town of Sudong about 20 miles northwest of Hamheung. A fierce battle ensued, but during the night of 6/7 November the Chinese broke contact and withdrew.[39] Between 5 and 15 November, X Corps had been bolstered by the arrival at Wonsan of the 3d Infantry Division. With the ROK 26th Regiment attached, the 3d Infantry Division relieved the 1st Marine Division of responsibility for securing the port areas and took up blocking positions to deal with North Korean forces moving up from the south while the 1st Marine and 7th Infantry Divisions pushed inland to the north.[40]

Special Operations in Support of Operations in the North

During the time that Eighth Army and X Corps were advancing into North Korea, British commandos were carrying out more coastal interdiction raids. On 20 September General MacArthur approved the use of Lieutenant Colonel Douglas B. Drysdale's 41 Independent Commando Royal Marines for raids against North Korean lines of communications. The commandos had been training aboard the transport submarine *Perch,* which set sail on 25 September for their first mission. On 30 September they made their first tunnel destruction attempt near Dancheon (Tanch'on). However, the engine of their motor launch (the *Skimmer*) failed, the distance to shore was too far for paddling, radar detected a North Korean patrol boat in the area, and lights began flickering ashore, so the mission was aborted. On 1 October, with the *Skimmer's* engine repaired, the Royal Marines went ashore at a secondary target in the Dancheon area and successfully detonated explosives in a culvert and railway tunnel with one casualty. The next day, the *Perch* put the Royal Marines aboard two US destroyers that later transferred them to the APDs *Horace A. Bass* and *Wantuck*. *Perch* returned to Yokosuka on 5 October and, after an assessment of the risks and problems with these missions, Admiral Joy decided to end submarine raids.[41] (See map 31.)

After a brief period of training with the two APDs, the commandos were dispatched on another mission. Escorted by the US destroyer *DeHaven*, they conducted a successful tunnel destruction raid near Cheongjin (Ch'ongjin) on the night of 5/6 October, and then landed again to destroy a tunnel and bridge near Seongjin on the night of 6/7 October. This would be their last raid for many months, since in mid-October the Commando was reorganized and re-equipped for sustained operations ashore and served on operations in North Korea as an additional reconnaissance company of the 1st Marine Division.[42]

Amphibious Withdrawals, December 1950

The Chinese attacks during 25 October to 6 November raised the possibility of a major Chinese intervention. Even as Eighth Army and X Corps forces continued their advance deeper into North Korea, Admiral Joy decided to take precautionary measures in the event a large-scale withdrawal was required. He recommended ships that were released for return to the United States be recalled and on 13 November issued NAVFE OPLAN No. 116-50, which established procedures for the emergency evacuation of UN forces from Korea. The plan, which would be put into effect either as a result of a "general emergency" or the outbreak of a world war, covered circumstances ranging from "controlled withdrawal of forces with ships being loaded from docks" to a "Dunkirk type evacuation conducted under attack conditions from beachheads, utilizing any or all available shipping." It directed that plans be flexible enough to provide for concurrent evacuations from both the east and west coasts of Korea and be based on the principle of an "assault in reverse."[43]

Annexes provided estimates of the UN and ROK troop strength over the next 4 months, the specific ships likely to be available and their characteristics, and information on the hydrography and capacity of Korean

Map 31. Amphibious Special Operations, October–November 1950.

and Japanese ports.[44] Admiral Doyle (Commander, Task Force [CTF] 90) would control all naval and air operations in the embarkation areas (identified as the area within a 35-mile radius of each designated evacuation port), while Admiral Struble's Seventh Fleet would control the aircraft carrier groups and coordinate air operations, including the "activities of any Far East Air Force (FEAF) planes assisting."[45] TF 95, the blockading and escort force, would provide escorts, gunfire support ships, minesweepers, antisubmarine operations, and ships for the evacuation as required.

233

On 21 November 7th Infantry Division elements reached the Yalu River near Hyesanjin, the furthest X Corps penetration of North Korea. Three days later, Eighth Army, then generally north of the Cheongcheon River, began a coordinated attack toward the Manchurian border. But on the night of 26 November the Chinese began their Second Phase Offensive with attacks against Eighth Army forces that badly mauled ROK II Corps and the US 2d Infantry Division. On 27 November the Chinese struck the 1st Marine Division west of the Jangjin (Changjin/Chosin) Reservoir and the 31st RCT of the 7th Infantry Division east of the reservoir.[46]

On 28 November General Walker and General Almond flew to Tokyo to meet with General MacArthur. At that time, Walker said that he believed he could hold a line north of Pyeongyang, and Almond expressed confidence that he could continue his advance north in spite of the Chinese attack. Nonetheless, MacArthur ordered X Corps to withdraw from its advance positions and concentrate at Heungnam. At the time, there still seemed to be a possibility of holding an enclave in the Heungnam area.[47] MacArthur radioed a report to the JCS, advising them that with the intervention of the Chinese the United States and the UNC faced "an entirely new war." His immediate strategic plan was "to pass from the offensive to the defensive with such local adjustments as may be required by a constantly fluid situation."[48]

While MacArthur's Tokyo meeting was taking place on 28 November, Admiral Doyle arrived at Heungnam aboard his flagship, the *Mount McKinley*, in time to receive an alert from Admiral Joy that there was a possibility of a general emergency. The next day, Doyle issued CTF 90 OPORD No. 19-50. Half of TF 90, most ships of which were located at Sasebo in Japan, was to deploy to the west coast and come under Rear Admiral Thackrey, commander of Amphibious Force 3, which would become the Western Deployment Force (TG-90.1). This force would be prepared to evacuate Eighth Army forces from Jinnampo and Incheon. The other half of TF 90 would deploy to the Wonsan–Heungnam area for the amphibious evacuation of X Corps forces from Heungnam, Wonsan, and Seongjin in the northeast.[49]

On 29 November, on his return to Korea from Tokyo, Almond directed his forces to discontinue the attack and withdraw. X Corps OPORD No. 8 ordered the 1st Marine Division to concentrate initially at Hagaru-ri, south of the reservoir, the 7th Infantry Division to concentrate in the Hamheung–Heungnam area, the ROK I Corps to protect the east flank, and the 3d Infantry Division to attack to the west from Yeongheung (Yonghung) to assist Eighth Army. The 3d Infantry Division was also to establish a task force based on one US battalion with the Korean Marine Corps (KMC) 1st

Regiment attached to protect Wonsan port and airfield.[50] On the morning of 30 November, Eighth Army Movements Control Branch ordered all the ships taking on cargo at Pusan (Busan) Port to stop loading. All of the LSTs and other vessels that were discharging cargo were ordered to be unloaded as quickly as possible and to stand by for instructions.[51] That afternoon, General Almond traveled to the 1st Marine Division Headquarters at Hagaru-ri to meet with his US commanders, Generals Oliver P. Smith and David Barr, and other senior officers to advise them of the situation and the plan for withdrawing to Heungnam. That same day, he issued orders to General Kim Paik-il to stop the ROK I Corps advance and move south, protecting the X Corps right flank and the east coast road.[52]

Admiral Doyle, anticipating seaborne evacuation from both coasts, ordered half his combat loaders (four APAs and two AKAs) to Incheon and the other half to Wonsan. Nonamphibious shipping was also mobilized for the withdrawal, but because of the difficulty of loading large transport and cargo ships out of the west coast ports with their smaller tide-beset harbors, Doyle sent two-thirds of the LSTs, LSDs, and other beaching ships and craft to the west to augment Thackrey's Amphibious Group 3, operating as TG 90.1. Thackrey himself had flown to Incheon on 29 November with General Walker to inspect the port facilities while members of his staff flew to Jinnampo. On 1 December Thackrey's flagship the *Eldorado*, an additional APA, 2 LSDs, the destroyer-transport *Horace A. Bass*, and 10 SCAJAP LSTs were sent to the west coast to join the amphibious and other shipping already there.[53]

Also on 30 November, the JCS approved MacArthur's intention to pass to the strategic defensive and asked for his plan to coordinate the operations of X Corps and Eighth Army. MacArthur explained that the terrain between X Corps and Eighth Army made a continuous defensive line across the peninsula impracticable and pointed out that in its current position, X Corps threatened the flank of the Chinese and forced them to commit several divisions that would otherwise be available to join the attack on Eighth Army. He advised that X Corps would contract its position into the Hamheung–Wonsan area, avoiding entrapment by the Chinese. The JCS, still concerned about the progressively widening gap between Eighth Army and X Corps, suggested that X Corps be extricated from what seemed to them to be an exposed position. The next day, the JCS advised MacArthur that General Collins was flying out to the Far East for discussions on the situation.[54]

On 1 December MacArthur directed that the 3d Infantry Division move to Wonsan for movement south to reinforce Eighth Army. This would disrupt Almond's plans for the withdrawal and risk the 1st Marine

Division's being cut off and destroyed. Therefore, Almond sent two officers, Marine Colonel Edward H. Forney and the X Corps G2, Lieutenant Colonel William Quinn, to Tokyo to try to persuade the FEC to leave the division with X Corps. After they met with Acting Chief of Staff Hickey, the order was reversed and the 3d Infantry Division was ordered to move from Wonsan to Heungnam to secure the concentration area and to assist the 1st Marine Division and 7th Infantry Division as they withdrew.[55]

Evacuation of Jinnampo

After the defeat of Eighth Army forces at the Cheongcheon River, Walker pulled his forward elements back to a line running from Sukcheon near the west coast, through Suncheon to Seongchon. He had hoped to establish a defensive perimeter around Pyeongyang, but concluding that he did not have enough troops to form a coherent perimeter, he decided to withdraw further south. To provide time to empty the Army and Air Force supply points in Pyeongyang and the west coast port of Jinnampo, he intended to delay at a line about 20 miles north of Pyeongyang. The evacuation of the supply points began on 1 December.[56] Although most of the material in and around Pyeongyang was removed overland by rail and truck (and much of it destroyed), some supplies were transferred by rail from Pyeongyang to the Jinnampo port for evacuation by surface shipping.[57] The withdrawal came just as Jinnampo was beginning to reach its capacity after the approach channel had been swept of mines and the 7th Medium Port had begun operations. (See map 32.)

Eighth Army forces reached the line north of Pyeongyang on 3 December and Walker immediately ordered a withdrawal further to the south, moving with his command post from Pyeongyang to Seoul on that day. With Jinnampo now unprotected, Eighth Army sent an urgent message to NAVFE requesting that the ships of Transport Squadron One, then en route to Incheon from Japan, be sent to evacuate the port. NAVFE signaled Admiral Thackrey's headquarters (CTG 90.1), but Thackrey was still ashore and there was a delay in his staff's responding. However, the Transport Squadron One commander, Captain Samuel G. Kelly, intercepted the signal. Kelly waited for 5 hours and when he still received no orders, changed course on his own initiative and headed for Jinnampo. Six hours later the orders came from CTG 90.1, but by that time Kelly and his squadron—his flagship (the attack transport *Bayfield*), two other APAs (*Bexar and Okanogan*), and two AKAs (*Algol* and *Montague*)—were well on their way to Jinnampo.[58]

Commander Ereckson's destroyer escort, *Foss,* was continuing to provide electrical power to Jinnampo. At approximately 0300 on 4 December,

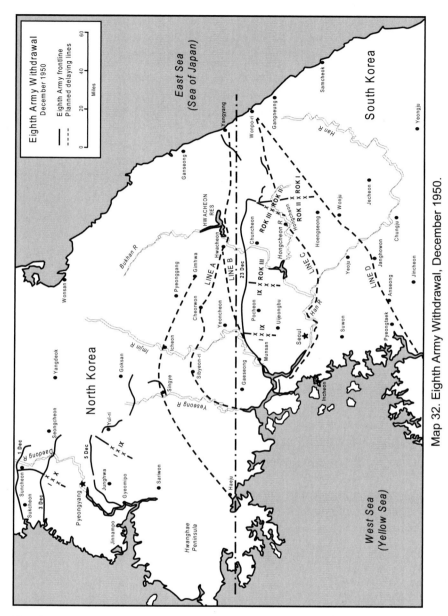

Map 32. Eighth Army Withdrawal, December 1950.

Ereckson was notified that the ROK naval base commander had been ordered to leave. At about the same time, Kelly received a message from Rear Admiral Allan E. Smith, commander of Task Force (TF) 95, the UN blockading and escort force, that Task Element (TE) 95.12, a force of Australian, Canadian, and US destroyers under Captain Jeffrey V. Brock, Royal Canadian Navy (RCN), was sailing to his assistance and that Royal Navy cruiser *Ceylon* was also sailing from Sasebo. In addition, Royal

Navy Rear Admiral Sir William G. Andrewes, commander of the West Coast Support Group (TF 95.1), was also steaming toward the west coast with British aircraft carrier *Theseus* and four destroyers.[59]

At 0930 on 4 December, when Kelly and his transports arrived at the end of the channel that had been swept by the UNC minesweepers, he assumed command of the Jinnampo evacuation. Ordering his ships to man their guns, lower their boats, and keep steam up, he commenced loading. After his hazardous journey up the Daedong River, Kelly was disappointed to find that the only remaining personnel to be transported were the 1,700 soldiers of the 7th Medium Port and 501st Harbor Craft Platoon, who had their own shipping, and about 7,000 wounded ROK soldiers, government workers, military and civilian prisoners, and police. Two of Captain Brock's destroyers, *HMCS Sioux* and *HMAS Warramunga*, had run into problems navigating the dark, narrow channel, but the *HMCS Cayuga, HMCS Athabaskan, HMAS Bataan,* and *USS Forrest Royal* arrived at Jinnampo at 0230 the next morning and trained their guns on the Jinnampo waterfront.[60] Loading continued throughout 5 December, with Royal Navy aircraft of the *Theseus* arriving overhead around noon, the *Foss* continuing to provide power, and the ROK Navy shore party and motor launches guarding the waterfront. About 100 civilian sailing junks carrying some 20,000 refugees, all they could hold, slipped down the channel, leaving about 30,000 refugees behind to head south over land. Kelly's transports began to sail independently a little after noon on 5 December and the beach was clear by 1630. An additional 3,000 refugees showed up, but they were accommodated by an MSTS ship that arrived late in the day. At 1730 the *Bexar*, the last of the transports to leave the harbor, stood down the channel escorted by the *Foss*. The LSTs with the 7th Medium Port personnel aboard anchored for the night in Jinnampo Harbor while the destroyers bombarded the oil storage facilities, railroad equipment, and dockyard cranes. In spite of the ad hoc nature of the operation, the evacuation was carried out quickly and efficiently, and when the destroyers and LSTs sailed away on the morning of 6 December, very little was left behind and only negligible quantities of supplies and equipment had to be destroyed.[61]

Evacuation of Wonsan and Seongjin

On 2 December X Corps published Operations Instruction No. 21 ordering the 3d Division, less the 7th Infantry, to concentrate at Wonsan to protect the port and Yonpo Airfield. The KMC 1st Regiment was to move to Hamheung to cover the withdrawal of troops from the Jangjin (Changjin/Chosin) Reservoir.[62]

Admiral Doyle sent Transport Division 11 to Wonsan to lift the 3d Division to Heungnam and to evacuate the remaining personnel and equipment. The heavy cruiser *St. Paul* (CA-73) arrived at Wonsan on 3 December, escorting four APAs and one APD. Most of the 3d Division moved from Wonsan to Heungnam by rail on 4 December, but elements of the 1st Marine Division, one battalion of the 3d Division, Company B of the 64th Tank Battalion, and the KMC 1st and 3d Battalions loaded aboard the ships. By 7 December some 4,000 troops, 12,000 tons of material, 1,146 vehicles, and over 7,000 refugees had been removed by sea and only a KMC battalion remained in the port. A Victory ship loaded the ROK marines and 7,000 refugees on 9 December. The next day the last ships departed, protected by a US destroyer.[63]

On 5 December Captain Michael J. Flaherty steamed north to the small port of Seongjin with his ship, the *USS Noble* (APA-218), and two merchantmen to outload General Kim's ROK I Corps (Headquarters and ROK 3d and Capital Divisions). Flaherty's ships were joined at Seongjin by one SCAJAP LST and one ROK LST. The little port had a 1,800-foot quay with a water depth of more than 27 feet, so the ships were able to tie up to take the ROK soldiers aboard beginning on 7 December. The operation was completed by 1600 on 9 December and the ROK troops were unloaded at Heungnam, from where they would be further evacuated south along with the rest of X Corps.[64]

Washington Deliberations

In Washington the JCS continued to monitor the situation in Korea. As General Collins flew to the Far East, the Army Chief of Transportation directed an urgent study of the feasibility and requirements to evacuate UN forces from North Korea. The Transportation staff assumed that 60,000 US, 2,000 UN, and 50,000 ROK troops would have to be withdrawn and that all equipment would be destroyed. As of 5 December, the "E-Day" on which they assumed the withdrawal would begin, 100 Victory-type ships, 10 smaller C1MAV1 cargo ships, 8 to 10 troop transports, and 50 operable LSTs were known to be within the FEC area, in addition to the Navy APAs and AKAs.[65] The study, presented on 6 December, concluded that sufficient shipping was available to remove the troops within 5 days. However, FEC, X Corps, NAVFE, and Admiral Doyle were already in action. When it was completed, the evacuation of Northeast Korea redeployed about the number of troops anticipated by the Washington study, but also over 100,000 civilian refugees and almost all of the X Corps and ROK I Corps vehicles, equipment, and supplies.

The Heungnam Evacuation

On 5 December X Corps issued OPORD No. 9 for the concentration of the corps forces in the Hamheung–Heungnam area. By separate instruction, Almond ordered the 3d Division to establish a task force (TF *Dog*) based on Lieutenant Colonel Thomas A. O'Neil's 1st Battalion, 7th Infantry, and Lieutenant Colonel Leon Lavoie's 92d Armored Field Artillery Battalion (155-mm self-propelled howitzers) reinforced with a company of combat engineers and other elements. Its mission was to help the 1st Marine Division, the attached Army elements (including a composite battalion dubbed "31/7" consisting of the survivors of RCT-31's action east of the Jangjin Reservoir), and Drysdale's Royal Marine Commandos withdraw from the reservoir area. TF *Dog* was alerted on 7 December and moved to the northwest of Heungnam to establish a blocking position.[66] Meanwhile, on 6 December, General Collins arrived in Tokyo to confer with General MacArthur. On 7 December Collins and MacArthur met in Tokyo with General Stratemeyer, Admiral Joy, Admiral Struble, and General Lemuel C. Shepherd. There was agreement that UNC forces should withdraw from North Korea, with the seaborne evacuation of the Heungnam enclave and withdrawal to successive positions by Eighth Army. On its return from North Korea, X Corps would be subordinate to Eighth Army, which would attempt to hold a line across the peninsula north of Seoul. Consideration was also given to withdrawing UNC forces from Korea out of a beachhead at Busan. The next day, MacArthur issued the order for the evacuation from Heungnam.[67]

General Almond issued X Corps Operations Instruction No. 27 on 9 December. It called for the withdrawal of X Corps by air and water from Heungnam to the Busan–Pohang area (see map 33). A control group under Colonel Forney was established to provide overall coordination of the evacuation of personnel, equipment, and supplies. The 2d ESB, with the Marine 1st Shore Party Battalion, the 58th MP Company, the 79th Combat Engineer Battalion, and Company A, 56th ATTB (minus the tanks) attached, was to be responsible for loading the ships, operating the port facilities, stocking the ships with rations for the voyage, and operating the final staging area where the troops awaiting evacuation would be fed and sheltered. X Corps OPORD No. 10, issued on 11 December, provided for a defensive perimeter around the Heungnam area that would be reduced in size by phases until the final evacuation took place. Initially, the perimeter would be manned by the 3d Division (with the KMC 1st Regiment attached) and the 7th Division while the 1st Marine Division embarked. Then the 7th Division would embark on order, after which the 3d Division would hold the perimeter. The last combat force on the perimeter would be

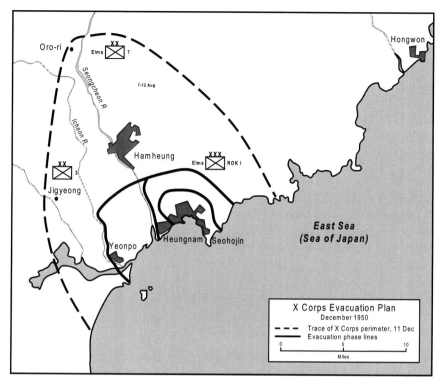

Map 33. X Corps evacuation plan, December 1950.

an RCT of the 3d Division. Naval gunfire would supplement, and eventually replace, artillery and carrier air would provide overhead cover.[68]

On the night of 11 December, the last Marine and Army forces arrived at the Heungnam perimeter, followed by TF *Dog*, which was then disbanded. The Chinese attack appeared to have reached a culminating point, and pressure on the withdrawing forces had eased considerably. The UN forces had now completed their concentration within the Heungnam evacuation area. Amphibious shipping, MSTS ships, and chartered merchant ships had also begun to arrive. That same day, General MacArthur flew to the Heungnam airfield to meet with General Almond. Almond explained the disposition of the corps, the plans for outloading and for the defense of Heungnam, and the plans for phasing out X Corps as a separate force.[69] The challenge facing X Corps, Doyle, the 2d ESB, and Forney was that 105,000 troops, over 18,000 vehicles, and some 350,000 tons of bulk cargo would have to be moved. Between 10 and 15 December, 3,000 troops, 200 vehicles, 500 tons of bombs, and some refugees were airlifted out of the Heungnam airfield. The rest went out by ship.[70]

The outloading operations by the 2d ESB and its attached units began on 9 December. Until that time, the brigade had been unloading incoming ships and to some extent continued this effort even as troops and material were being outloaded, since ammunition, medical supplies, and other critical items were still needed by the defending forces. An added complication was that the electrical power source for the city lay well outside the perimeter, and on 7 December the Chinese cut off the power. This had been anticipated, however, and Commander Ereckson's "electric" destroyer escort *Foss* was brought in to provide power during the evacuation.

Because the order for evacuation was expected, the brigade had made a preliminary plan and it was put into effect. An assembly area for staging outbound units was cleared and a tent city built in the area behind the LST beach. Six berths capable of handling Victory-type cargo ships were made ready, and sunken barges and other debris were cleared from alongside another pier so that it too could be used. The 532d EB&SR was designated the shore party for outloading ships from alongside the piers. To load the LSTs and ships in the stream, a provisional shore party was established under the command of the brigade S4, using troops from the brigade headquarters company, the boat maintenance battalion, the quartermaster company, the marine shore party battalion, the 73d Combat Engineer Battalion, and an antiaircraft battery. Company A of the 7th Infantry Division provided security until it was outloaded. Thereafter, Captain O'Donnell's amphibious tankers became the security force, using landing vehicles, tracked (armored) (LVT[A]s) found in the Corps Ordnance Depot to replace their own vehicles, which were still at Incheon and had been pressed into service in the defense of that port. Colonel Forney maintained a list of all shipping as it arrived, allocated shipping among the units, and coordinated with the commander of each unit or the officer responsible for the cargo to be loaded. Each unit to be embarked was required to designate a transportation quartermaster (TQM) to coordinate with the control group and supervise the loading.

Civilian hatch crews hired in Japan worked throughout the evacuation living aboard their barracks ship the *Shinano Maru*. It became increasingly difficult to hire Korean civilian laborers as the evacuation proceeded, thus requiring a levy of military personnel from the remaining units to assist in loading the ships. A further complication occurred when General Almond ordered that the civilian refugees crowding the harbor be embarked to the maximum extent possible consistent with the mission. Korean LSTs and coastal freighters were primarily used for this task, although other ships also took refugees on board. All were filled with as many people as possible. Normally, LSTs had berthing and mess facilities for up to 250 troops, with a capacity of 550 for short voyages. But they were essentially large hollow boxes, and so in an emergency, could squeeze in much larger numbers. One LST, for example, embarked over 10,000 refugees during the Heungnam evacuation.[71]

By 14 December most of the 1st Marine Division had been loaded aboard the transports and the 7th Division began embarking. On 19 December the commanding general of the 3d Division assumed command of the remaining forces at Heungnam and General Almond and the X Corps staff went aboard the *Mount McKinley*. A small X Corps staff element remained on shore until the end of the operation, but responsibility for the evacuation passed to Admiral Doyle. On 20 December the 7th Division completed loading and sailed at first light the next morning. Seven LSTs and many landing vehicles, tracked (LVTs) lined the beach in preparation for the final departure. On 23 December the 3d Division withdrew to the final perimeter. From 0930 to 1100 the 3d Division and some remaining elements of the 7th Division loaded out. The 39th Field Artillery Battalion covered the loading and then boarded the LSTs. At 1230 the last 7th Division troops left the beach in LVTs. The 65th RCT departed at 1237, the 15th Infantry at 1400, and the 3d Division command post closed ashore and opened aboard the USS *Bayfield*.[72] The 2d ESB had begun to withdraw its landing craft, equipment, and personnel as loading of the outbound units was completed. At 1 hour before midnight on the 23d, the headquarters and all of the 532d EB&SR went aboard the LSD *Fort Marion* and the MSTS transport *General David I. Sultan*. The last amphibious engineers to leave the beach were the men of Company D, 532d EB&SR, who assisted in a final effort to load remaining ammunition until 0600 on 24 December, when they went aboard an LST and shoved off from the shore.[73]

D-Day was 24 December. By 1405 all the beaches were clear. At 1410 Admiral Doyle ordered the UDT to destroy the facilities and seawall and by 1436, all US personnel were off the beach and afloat.[74] MacArthur radioed to the JCS:

> The Tenth Corps accomplished its withdrawal from the Hungnam perimeter at 1436 hours and all elements are at sea or landed in the Pusan–Pohang concentration area. . . . The outloading of this Command, commenced on 12 December and completed 11 days later, has embraced withdrawal of 105,000 troops, including ROK units, approximately 100,000 refugees, 17,500 vehicles,

350,000 tons of organizational equipment and supplies, 1,500 tons of which were evacuated by air. There has been no abandonment of equipment or supplies. The smoothness of loading out of this base is a tribute to the troops and the Navy alike and the final withdrawal today, and for the past three days, has been executed brilliantly by the Third Division under cover of masterful supporting fire provided by Naval guns and aircraft.[75]

Notes

1. J. Lawton Collins, *War in Peacetime: The History and Lessons of Korea* (Boston, MA: Houghton Mifflin, 1969), 82–83.

2. James F. Schnabel, *United States Army in the Korean War, Policy and Direction: The First Year* (Washington, DC: GPO, 1972; reprinted 1992), 140, 187.

3. James I. Matray develops this argument in "Truman's Plan for Victory," *Journal of American History* (September 1979): 314–333.

4. Donald W. Boose Jr., "The Decision to Cross the 38th Parallel," in Spencer C. Tucker, ed., *The Encyclopedia of the Korean War* (New York, NY: ABC Clio, 2000); JCS Message 92801, Personal for MacArthur, 27 September 1950, RG 218, Entry UD 48, Box 9, Folder 5, National Archives and Records Administration, Modern Military Records, College Park, MD, hereafter, NACP.

5. Schnabel lays out these arguments based on his conversations with General Wright in *Policy and Direction,* 187–188.

6. CINCFE Message C-64805 (CM IN 16170), to Department of the Army for JCS, 28 September 1950; Chairman, JCS, Memorandum for the Secretary of Defense, 29 September 1950, "Future Korean Operations"; JCS Message 92975, to CINCFE, 29 September 1950; JCS Message (SECDEF Sends) 92985, Personal for General of the Army Douglas MacArthur, 29 September 1950, all in RG 218, Entry UD7, Box 41, Section 34, NACP.

7. Schnabel, *Policy and Direction,* 188; X Corps War Diary, Monthly Summary, 1 October 1950 to 31 October 1950, "Wonsan–Iwon Landings," 1, RG 319, Records of the OCMH 2-3.7 BA2, Box 743.

8. GHQ UNC, OPORD No. 2, 2 October 1950, RG 218, Entry UD7, Box 42, Section 42, NACP.

9. X Corps War Diary; Seventh Infantry Division, *War Diary, 1 September to 30 September 1950,* 5 October 1950, hereafter, 7ID WD; *History of the Korean War, Chronology 25 June 1950–31 December 1951* (Tokyo: Military History Section, Far East Command, 1952), 62, hereafter, *Korean War Chronology*; James A. Field Jr., *History of United States Naval Operations, Korea* (Washington, DC: GPO, 1962), 224.

10. US Army Forces, Far East. *Logistics in the Korean Operations* (Camp Zama, Japan: Headquarters, US Army Forces Far East and Eighth US Army (Rear), APO 343, 1955), Vol. 1, 24.

11. Field, *Naval Operations, Korea,* 225.

12. *After Action Report, Inchon Operation, 532d Engineer Boat & Shore Regiment,* 3 November 1950, copy in the Office of the Engineer Command Historian, hereafter, 532d Inchon AAR; X Corps OPORD No. 1; 2d Engineer Special Brigade *Field Order 1-50,* 2 September 1950, RG 407, Entry 429, Box 4665, NACP, hereafter, 2ESB UAR, October 1950.

13. Company A, 56th Amphibious Tank and Tractor Battalion, Diary Report of "A" Company 56th Amphibious Tank and Tractor Battalion to Cover the

Period from 26 August to 15 January 1950–51, RG 338, Entry 37042, ATTB Cmd Rpts Jan 51, Box 28, NACP, hereafter, A/56th ATTB Diary Report, 5–19 October 1950.

14. 7ID WD, 7–12 October 1950; X Corps War Diary, 2.

15. Schnabel, *Policy and Direction,* 207–208; UNC OPORD No. 2, Annex D, Logistics.

16. Roy E. Appleman, *United States Army in the Korean War: South to the Naktong, North to the Yalu* (Washington, DC: GPO, 1961), 632–633.

17. 7ID WD, 12–17 October 1950.

18. Richard W. Stewart provides a concise account of operations in North Korea prior to the Chinese intervention in *The Korean War: The Chinese Intervention, 3 November 1950–24 January 1951,* CMH Pub 19-8 (Washington, DC: Center of Military History, 2000), 1–11. For more detailed discussions, see Billy C. Mossman, *United States Army in the Korean War: Ebb and Flow, November 1950–July 1951* (Washington, DC: Office of the Chief of Military History, 1990), 61–64; Appleman, *South to the Naktong,* 654–774; Roy E. Appleman, *Disaster in Korea: The Chinese Confront MacArthur* (College Station, TX: Texas A&M University Press, 1989), 34–59; Roy E. Appleman, *Escaping the Trap, The US Army X Corps in Northeast Korea, 1950* (College Station, TX: Texas A&M University Press, 1990), 44–58; Lynn Montross and Nicholas A. Canzona, *U.S. Marines Operations in Korea, 1950–1953, Vol. III, The Chosin Reservoir Campaign* (Washington, DC: Historical Branch, G3, 1957), 61–150; Schnabel, *Policy and Direction,* 274–330; and Shelby L. Stanton, *America's Tenth Legion, X Corps In Korea, 1950* (Novato, CA: Presidio Press, 1989), 167–206.

19. *Korean War Chronology,* 63; Schnabel, *Policy and Direction,* 206.

20. Montross and Canzona, *The Chosin Reservoir Campaign,* 31–34; X Corps War Diary; *After Action Report of Iwon Operation, 532d Engineer Boat & Shore Regiment,* 31 December 1950, hereafter, 532d EB&SR Iwon AAR, copy at Office of the Engineer Command Historian, XII-16b-12.

21. Montross and Canzona, *The Chosin Reservoir Campaign,* 208–209; Field, *Naval Operations, Korea,* 232–233. For a detailed account of the Wonsan mine sweeping operations, see Arnold S. Lott, *Most Dangerous Sea: A history of mine warfare and an account of U.S. Navy mine warfare operations in World War II and Korea* (Annapolis, MD: Naval Institute Press, 1959).

22. Schnabel, *Policy and Direction,* 195, 202.

23. US Army, 8206th Army Unit, Amphibious Training Center, *Unit History* [1951?], hereafter, ATC History, 10–15; Appleman, *South to the Naktong,* 628, citing Ltr, (LtCol James B. Webel, 7th Cav S3, Oct 50) to author, 13 Apr 54; Ltr, Harris to author, 7 Apr 54; 7th Cav Regt WD, 10–11 Oct 50; 3d Log Comd Hist Opn Rpt, G4 Sec (Hist Memo: Yeseong River Supply and Ferry Mission), 10–12 Oct 50. See also Letter, William Harris to Roy E. Appleman, 18 May 1954, in RG 319, Records of OCMH, 2-3.7A BA2, Box 746, NACP.

24. Field, *Naval Operations, Korea,* 237–242; Appleman, *Disaster in Korea,* 306.

25. Field, *Naval Operations, Korea,* 272–273; *Dictionary of American Naval Fighting Ships,* hereafter, *DANFS, Foss,* www.history.navy.mil/danfs/f4/foss.html (accessed 15 January 2007).

26. Schnabel, *Policy and Direction,* 210–214; D. Clayton James, *The Years of MacArthur, Vol. III, Triumph and Disaster 1945–1964* (Boston, MA: Houghton Mifflin, 1985), 508.

27. Field, *Naval Operations, Korea,* 233–237, 243.

28. CINCUNC Message CX 66705, to CG Eighth Army, CG FEAF, COMNAVFE, X Corps, 17 October 1950, RG 218, Entry UD7, Box 42, Section 36, NACP.

29. For the Chinese decision to intervene in the Korean War see Jian Chen, *China's Road to the Korean War: The Making of the Sino-American Confrontation* (New York, NY: Columbia University Press, 1994); William Stueck, *The Korean War: An International History* (Princeton, NJ: Princeton University Press, 1995); and Zhang Shu Guang, *Mao's Military Romanticism: China and the Korean War, 1950–1953* (Lawrence, KS: University of Kansas Press, 1995).

30. Appleman, *South to the Naktong,* 648–658; Montross and Canzona, *The Chosin Reservoir Campaign,* 38–42.

31. George Craig Stewart, "Korea: August, 1950–December 15, 1950," unpublished manuscript in the Blair Collection, Box 83, "Forgotten War, Alphabetical File S-V," MHI, hereafter, Stewart MS, 12.

32. Appleman, *South to the Naktong,* 653–715. The Chinese forces were called Chinese Communist Forces (CCF) by the UNC; however, the English equivalent of the name that the Chinese used for the forces that intervened in Korea was the Chinese People's Volunteers (CPV).

33. X Corps Operations Instruction No. 13, 26 October 1950, in X Corps War Diary, October 1950.

34. Commander, Amphibious Group 3 OPORD No. 4-50, 28 October 1950, RG 407, Entry 429, Box 3172, NACP.

35. Herbert B. Powell, "Conversations between General Herbert B. Powell and Lieutenant Colonel Philip J. Stevens and Others," *Vol. I, Senior Officer Debriefing Program* (Carlisle Barracks, PA: US Army Military History Institute Research Collection, 1972), Section 3, 70, 71; Section 4, 1–2, hereafter, Powell Oral History.

36. Powell Oral History, 20–22.

37. This description of 2d ESB operations at Iwon is based on 2ESB *Activities Report,* October 1950, and 352d EB&SR Iwon AAR. See also Frank L. Mann, "Operation Versatile: Korean Saga of the 2d Engineer Special Brigade," *Military Engineer,* Vol. XLIV, No. 299 (May–June 1952): 168–173.

38. Field, *Naval Operations, Korea,* 246, says that 29,000 troops were unloaded, but this number seems too high. Based on the engineer after action reports, the total number, including the 17th RCT, seems likely to have been between 26,000 and 27,000 men. 2ESB UAR; 532d EB&SR Iwon AAR; Appleman, *South to the Naktong,* 733.

39. Montross and Canzona, *The Chosin Reservoir Campaign,* 99–120.

40. Appleman, *Escaping the Trap,* 275.

41. Michael E. Haas, *In the Devil's Shadow: U.N. Special Operations During the Korean War* (Annapolis, MD: Naval Institute Press, 2000), 148–150, 152–156; Fred Hayhurst, *Green Berets in Korea: the Story of 41 Independent Commando Royal Marines* (Cambridge, MA: Vanguard, 2001), 53–58; Field, *Naval Operations, Korea,* 217; *DANFS, Perch,* history.navy.mil/danfs/b3/bataan-i.htm (accessed 26 January 2007).

42. Hayhurst, *Green Berets in Korea,* 63–77, 89; Field, *Naval Operations, Korea,* 226.

43. COMNAVFE OPLAN No. 116-50, CNFE/A4-3(9), 13 November 1950, copy in RG 127, Entry 17 170/A/54/07 Box 1 (Quantico Schools, 1947–1970) NACP; Donald Chisholm, "Negotiated Joint Command Relationships," *Naval War College Review,* Vol. 53, No. 2 (Spring 2000): 103; Field, *Naval Operations, Korea,* 265.

44. Hydrography refers to the characteristics of bodies of water or to the mapping of bodies of water.

45. In an interview with Robert Debs Heinl, Admiral Doyle said he told Admiral Joy that he "could not and would not come under Struble again." Quoted in Chisholm, "Negotiated Command Relations," 103.

46. For the Chinese attack and Eighth Army and X Corps operations, see Stewart, *The Chinese Intervention,* 11–27. For more detailed discussions, see Mossman, *Ebb and Flow, November 1950–July 1951,* 61–148; Appleman, *Disaster in Korea,* 77–389; Appleman, *Escaping the Trap,* 59–373; Montross and Canzona, *The Chosin Reservoir Campaign,* 151–335; and Stanton, *America's Tenth Legion,* 207–288.

47. Appleman, *Escaping the Trap,* 119–121, 267–268.

48. CINCFE Message C 69953 to JCS, 28 November 1950, RG 218, Entry UD7, Box 42, Section 39, NACP.

49. Field, *Naval Operations, Korea,* 265; Chisholm, "Negotiated Command Relations," 105–106.

50. Summary of OPORD No. 8, 30 November 1950, in *November War Diary Summaries, Headquarters X Corps: 1 November 1950 to 30 November 1950,* V. "Catalog of Plans and Orders," copy in *The Edward M. Almond Papers,* Box 75, "War Diary 1950–1951, Command Report January to March 1951," MHI; Appleman, *Escaping the Trap,* 121. The 3d Division attack to the west was later canceled and the division was given the mission of securing the Heungnam enclave.

51. Monthly Action Reports, 2d Logistical Command (C), Nov 30, Transportation, Water Division in Folder, "1 Dec 1950," Box 22 (Chronological Files), *Roy Appleman Collection 1945–1989,* MHI. Appleman's handwritten comment: "evacuation possibility already in minds of high command."

52. Edward M. Almond, "Personal Notes Covering Activities of Lt. Gen. E.M. Almond During Military Operations in Korea 31 August 1950–15 July 1951" (Almond Diary), Box 64: Personal Notes on the Korean Operation, *The Edward*

M. Almond Papers. MHI Archives Collection. Almond Diary, 30 November 1950; Mossman, *Ebb and Flow, November 1950–July 1951*, 129.

53. Field, *Naval Operations, Korea,* 269.

54. JCS Message 97592 to CINCFE, 29 November 1950; CINCFE Message 50095 (CM IN 15673) to JCS, 30 November 1950; JCS Message 97772 to CINCFE, 30 November 1950; JCS Message 97804 to CINCFE, 1 December 1950, all in RG 218, Entry UD7, Box 43, Section 40, NACP.

55. Appleman, *Escaping the Trap*, 278; see also comments by General William McCaffrey in the Appleman Collection, Box 20, "Correspondence w/ Gen. Ridgway and Gen. McCaffrey," MHI. On 2 December Admiral Doyle had advised COMNAVFE that TF 90 was prepared to move the 3d Infantry Division from Wonsan to either Hamheung or Busan, as required. Field, *Naval Operations, Korea,* 265; Chisholm, "Negotiated Command Relations," 105–106.

56. A concise description of the Eighth Army withdrawal is in Stewart, *The Chinese Intervention,* 20–22. For more detailed discussions, see Mossman, *Ebb and Flow, November 1950–July 1951,* 149–157; and Appleman, *Disaster in Korea,* 294–330.

57. Eighth US Army, *Logistical Problems and Their Solutions (25 August 1950–31 August 1951): Monograph,* compiled by personnel of the Historical Section, EUSAK and the Eighth Army Historical Service Detachment (Prov.) (Seoul: Headquarters, Eighth US Army, Korea (EUSAK) [1950–52?], copy at MHI.

58. Roy E. Appleman, *Ridgway Duels for Korea* (College Station, TX: Texas A&M University Press, 1990), 333; Field, *Naval Operations, Korea,* 272.

59. Field, *Naval Operations, Korea,* 333–334.

60. Field, *Naval Operations, Korea,* 273.

61. *Command Report*, 2d Logistical Command, December 1950, The Roy E. Appleman Collection, Box 22 (Chronological Files), Folder, "5 Dec 1950," MHI, 6; Field, *Naval Operations, Korea,* 273–274; Appleman, *Ridgway Duels for Korea*, 334.

62. X Corps Operations Instruction No. 21, X Corps War Diary, December 1950.

63. Chisholm, "Negotiated Command Relations," 109; Appleman, *Escaping the Trap*, 279; see also Field, *Naval Operations, Korea,* 286–287.

64. Field, *Naval Operations, Korea,* 287.

65. Office of the Chief of Transportation memorandum TCMPI-SP 1838(TS), 6 December 1950, "Withdrawal of UN Forces from Northeast Korea. The study group used the term "Victory-type" to cover all Maritime Commission ship types of roughly equivalent capacity (10,000 deadweight tonnage), including EC-2 (Liberty ships), VC-2 (Victory ships), and C-2 and C-3 cargo ships. The characteristics of these ships, and the smaller C-1 types (such as the C1MAV1), are set forth in Frederic L. Lane, *Ships for Victory, A History of Shipbuilding Under the U.S. Maritime Commission in World War II* (Baltimore, MD: The Johns Hopkins University Press, 1951), 28.

66. X Corps OPORD No. 9, 5 December 1950, RG 127, Entry 17, 170/

A/54/07 Box 1, NACP; Appleman, *Escaping the Trap*, 282–283. For details on the 31/7 composite battalion, see Changjin Journal 02.28.03 and 05.01.03, library-automation.com/nymas/changjinjournalTOC.html (accessed 21 August 2008).

67. X Corps War Diary, December 1950; Mossman, *Ebb and Flow, November 1950–July 1951,* 158–160; Chisholm, "Negotiated Command Relations," 106; Appleman, *Escaping the Trap*, 383; Lemuel C. Shepherd, *Korean War Diary covering period 2 July to 7 December 1950,* copy provided to the writer by Professor Allan R. Millett (a copy is also available in the Lemuel C. Shepherd Papers at the Marine Corps University Archives), hereafter, Shepherd Diary, 7–8 December.

68. X Corps Operations Instruction No. 27, 9 December 1950; X Corps OPORD No. 10, 11 December 1950, copies in the Edward M. Almond Papers, Box 75, MHI; 2d Engineer Special Brigade, Command Report, 1 December to 31 December 1950, RG 407, Entry 429, Box 4665, NACP.

69. Almond Diary, 11 December 1950; Appleman, *Escaping the Trap*, 316–318, 322–323.

70. X Corps War Diary, December 1950.

71. This description of the work of the 2d ESB is based on the 2ESB Command Report for December and After Action, Hungnam, Korea, 532d Engineer Boat & Shore Regiment, n.d., copy in the Office of the Engineer Command Historian, hereafter, 532d EB&SR Heungnam AAR.

72. X Corps War Diary, December 1950; Appleman, *Escaping the Trap*, 331; *Korean War Chronology*, 85–86; Chisholm, "Negotiated Command Relations," 109–110.

73. 532d EB&SR Heungnam AAR, 6.

74. Field, *Naval Operations, Korea,* 304–305; Appleman, *Escaping the Trap*, 331.

75. CINCFE Message C-52020 (CM IN 3838), 25 Dec 50, To: DEPTAR for JCS, RG 218, Entry UD 48 Chairman's File—General Bradley, 1949–53, Messages Relating to Operations in the Far East, 1950–1953, Box 1, Folder 2, NACP.

Chapter 6

The War of Movement, December 1950–November 1951

Evacuation of Incheon

On 23 December 1950 General Walton H. Walker was killed in a jeep accident north of Seoul. Three days later Lieutenant General Matthew B. Ridgway arrived in Korea to take command of Eighth Army. Ridgway, who had been serving as the Army Deputy Chief of Staff for Operations and Administration at the time of Walker's death, was a distinguished airborne commander in World War II. In that conflict he had been involved with three major amphibious operations—commanding the 82d Airborne Division during the Sicily and Salerno landings and jumping with this division at Normandy. But his participation was always with the airborne forces, rather than those landing across the beach.[1]

With the completion of the evacuation of northeast Korea on 26 December, X Corps lost its independent status and became part of Eighth Army. That same day the Chinese resumed their attack, beginning a general offensive (their Third Phase Offensive) (see map 34) across a 44-mile front from east of Gaeseong (Kaesong) in the west to northeast of Chuncheon (Ch'unch'on) in the east, with their main effort directed south toward Seoul, Gapyeong (Kap'yong), and Wonju.[2]

Between 30 December 1950 and 3 January 1951, Far East Command (FEC) and Eighth Army considered the possibility of conducting a small-scale diversionary landing in the vicinity of Haeju.[3] However, Eighth Army was forced to pull back, initially to a line along the Han River north of Seoul. On 3 January 1951 Ridgway, concerned that the I and IX Corps forces in western Korea would be cut off and surrounded, ordered the evacuation of Seoul.[4]

Based on Admiral C. Turner Joy's guidance, Rear Admiral Lyman A. Thackrey, commander of TG 90.1, had been preparing for the evacuation of the Seoul–Incheon area since early December. On 7 December 1950 Thackrey requested carrier support and began preparations for the removal of Army supplies from Incheon making use of the immediately available ships: his flagship the *Eldorado*; 1 attack cargo ship; 2 attack transports; 2 landing ships, dock (LSDs); 1 APD; and 11 landing ships, tank (LSTs) (two US Navy ships and 9 Shipping Control Administration, Japan [SCAJAP] vessels). The Military Sea Transportation Service (MSTS) held an additional 15 empty cargo ships in Japan as a reserve to supplement Thackrey's amphibians. Six additional SCAJAP LSTs and other ships were made available after the completion of the Heungnam (Hungnam) evacuation.[5]

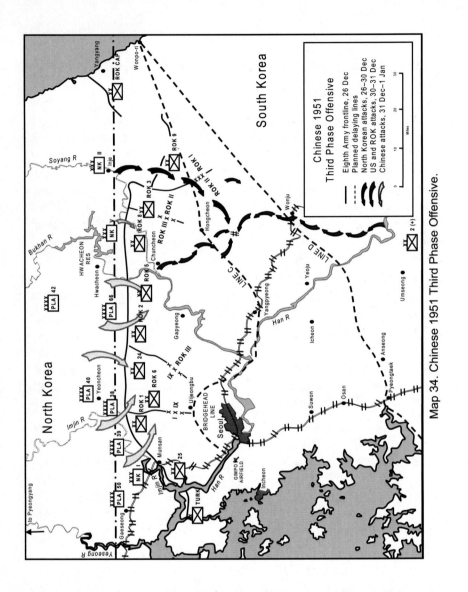

Map 34. Chinese 1951 Third Phase Offensive.

Thackrey had initially contemplated the use of the Deokjeok (Tokchok) Islands, about 30 miles southwest of Incheon, as a temporary refuge for some 135,000 troops. However, this became unnecessary as much of the personnel and equipment from Seoul, Gimpo (Kimp'o), and Incheon (Inch'on) were withdrawn by land and the Chinese attack was delayed long enough for the seaborne evacuation to proceed smoothly. During December TG 90.1 ships transported 32,000 military personnel, over 1,000 vehicles, and 55,000 tons of cargo to Busan (Pusan) or Japan.[6]

During the evacuation, the 8206th Army Unit (AU), Amphibious Training Center (ATC) had continued to provide yeoman service. On 1 December the unit of about 40 men had been assigned a defensive sector at Incheon along a ridge east of the city, overlooking the Seoul–Incheon Highway. In the event of attack, the ATC was to delay, then cross the causeway to Wolmido. On 11 December the ATC had been ordered to leave Incheon and deploy to Busan. They made the journey aboard SCAJAP LST-Q043, towing LSU 1381 loaded with three smaller craft, arriving on 23 December. Additional equipment was loaded at Busan and on Christmas Day, the LST sailed for Pohang, where the ATC troops prepared that port for the arrival of the 1st Marine Division as it returned from North Korea.[7]

Admiral Thackrey continued loading troops and equipment as the Chinese approached Incheon. On 4 January he received an order from Admiral Joy to destroy the port facilities. Colonel John G. Hill's 3d Logistical Command ceased port operations at noon that day and at 1800, the 50th Engineer Port Construction Company began the demolition, including destruction of the huge tidal locks, which significantly reduced Incheon's capability as a deep-water port. Since the United Nations Command (UNC) had complete control of the waters off Korea, this destruction was unnecessary and would soon be regretted when Incheon was reoccupied the next month.[8]

As Chinese forces entered the outskirts of the city on 5 January 1951, the last elements of the 50th Engineer Port Construction Company loaded aboard the transports and Thackrey sortied his shipping from Incheon. During the first 5 days of January, TG 90.1 had transported an additional 37,000 military personnel and over 64,000 civilian refugees.[9]

With Incheon now in enemy hands, a port was needed to support Eighth Army forces in the west. In September 1950 an underwater demolition team (UDT) operating from the submarine *Perch* had reconnoitered the beaches at Daecheon (Taech'on) 25 miles north of Gunsan (Kunsan) at the mouth of Cheonsu (Ch'onsu) Bay as an alternative to Incheon for the CHROMITE landing. In December 1950 Thackrey, anticipating the withdrawal from Incheon, had the approaches to Daecheon swept. As the evacuation LSTs left Incheon in January, he sent two minesweepers back in to check sweep to ensure no mines had been planted, and then sent the LSTs from Incheon to discharge their cargo on the beach at the small port. On 8 January 1951 more LSTs brought the 3d Division's tanks and artillery up to Daecheon. Over the next 2 days, SCAJAP LSTs brought petroleum, oils, and lubricants (POL) and other cargo up from Busan to Daecheon and Gunsan.[10]

Planning for Evacuation of Korea and the Defense of Japan

After withdrawing from Seoul, Eighth Army pulled back to a line running from Pyeongtaek (P'yongt'aek) on the west coast, through Wonju in the center of the country, to the town of Wonpo-ri (Wonp'o-ri) on the east coast. Ridgway prepared to bring on line the X Corps, now consisting of the US 2d and 7th Infantry Divisions, and the remnants of three ROK divisions. On 7 January 1951 the North Koreans captured Wonju, which turned out to be the high water mark of their offensive.

General Douglas MacArthur and the Washington community considered the possibility of UNC forces being ejected from Korea.[11] Admiral Joy's Naval Forces Far East (NAVFE) Headquarters began planning for the evacuation by sea of US, UN, and Republic of Korea (ROK) military forces; ROK police and government officials and their families; and prisoners of war (POWs). Admiral James H. Doyle's Task Force (TF) 90 preparations for this large-scale evacuation included the conduct of hydrographic surveys of Korean and Japanese beaches to identify those suitable for amphibious use. These surveys were conducted by the underwater demolition unit (UDU) (consisting of UDT-1, UDT-3, and part of Naval Beach Group One) and continued through June 1951.[12]

The FEC Operation Plan (OPLAN) No. 1-51 envisioned the relocation of the ROK Government, a substantial number of ROK forces, and others (up to a million people) to the island of Cheju-do and the continuation of military operations through guerrilla, commando, and covert operations.[13] A later plan, OPLAN No. 4-51, provided for the evacuation of ROK personnel to ports in Japan and then, as shipping became available, to Saipan and Tinian.[14] Unlike the situation in July and August 1950, when possible evacuation of US and ROK military forces was seen as a precursor to an amphibious re-entry to the peninsula, there was little or no talk now of such a return by means of another "Normandy."[15]

Nonetheless, Ridgway did not ignore the possibility of using the strong Navy TF 90 amphibious force and the amphibious-trained marines for smaller scale operations. After their return from the north, the 1st Marine Division was detached from X Corps and, after a brief period refitting near Masan, had been relocated in mid-January to the Pohang area, traveling by road and LST. There they served as Eighth Army Reserve and provided rear area security protecting the 75-mile Pohang to Andong railway line from North Korean guerrillas.[16] Ridgway flew to Pohang to confer with General Oliver P. Smith. During this conversation, Ridgway raised the possibility of using Doyle's amphibious ships and marine forces to conduct landings along the east coast to block the southward advance of Chinese forces along the coastal avenue of approach. Smith argued that any amphibious operations should be made in strength, and Ridgway did not pursue the idea further at that time.[17]

In an attempt to provide some ground combat force for the defense of Japan, in January 1951 MacArthur withdrew the 34th Infantry Regiment and the 63d Field Artillery Battalion from the 24th Infantry Division in Korea. Brought up to full strength and augmented by the 56th Amphibious Tank and Tractor Battalion (ATTB), this small force prepared to defend the Kanto Plain near Tokyo.[18] Company A of the 56th ATTB had been detached from the 2d Engineer Special Brigade (ESB) on 12 January and returned to Japan by LST on 16 January, bringing the entire battalion together again. A shortage of tanks prevented the unit from reorganizing as a light tank force. Instead, attached to the 34th Infantry, the 56th ATTB prepared to assist in the defense of Japan with their amphibious tractors and 75-mm howitzer-armed landing vehicles, tracked (armored) (LVT[A]s).[19]

Beginning in January, the amphibious ships of Doyle's TF 90 were divided into three roughly equal groups. At any time, one-third of the force was conducting amphibious training for Army units in Japan, one-third was on call for transportation and other services (including amphibious demonstrations) for forces in Korea, and one-third was conducting upkeep and maintenance at Yokosuka. In addition to its hydrographic survey work and in the absence of amphibious missions, TF 90 was tasked on 15 January with carrying refugees and POWs to the Korean islands of Geojedo (Koje-do) and Jejudo (Cheju-do). The first AKA fitted with makeshift cells and loaded with POWs departed from Busan on 20 January. This was Doyle's last mission in the Far East, and he transferred his flag to Vice Admiral Ingolf N. Kiland on 24 January.[20]

During January 1951 the 2d ESB, with an ordnance detachment and a petroleum distribution platoon attached, operated the port of Ulsan, initially to offload LSTs carrying ammunition from the Heungnam evacuation. Later, Ulsan became a rations and POL unloading and distribution facility. Colonel Joseph J. Twitty was designated by 2d Logistical Command as the commander of the Ulsan Port Command Area, with responsibility for operating the port, maintaining the roads, and providing logistical support to units in the area. The Ulsan operation was strengthened during the month by the addition of the 558th Transportation Amphibious Truck Company and the 60th Transportation Truck Company.[21]

On 13 January 2d Logistical Command directed the brigade to establish an ammunition unloading facility at Suyeong (Suyong), a fishing village at the head of a small bay about 8 miles north of Busan. Turning the Ulsan operation over to the 532d Engineer Boat and Shore Regiment (EB&SR), Twitty moved his Brigade Headquarters and Headquarters Company by LST to Suyeong, accompanied by Company A of the 562d Engineer Boat Maintenance Battalion; a platoon from Company D of the 532d EB&SR; and small signal, ordnance, and quartermaster elements. There, using the Suyeong beaches and a small pier, he established a facility for unloading ammunition. The 532d EB&SR commander took over the Ulsan Port Command Area responsibilities. The Suyeong Group was reinforced soon after its arrival by the rest of Company D of the 532d EB&SR with its landing craft, mechanized (LCM) and about a dozen Navy landing ships, utility (LSUs). The Navy stationed an LSD near Suyeong to provide for maintenance of the watercraft. The 3d Transportation Amphibious Truck Company put its DUKWs into action in early February. Using the LSUs, LCMs, DUKWs, and appropriated barges as lighters, the brigade was able to offload several hundred tons of ammunition and other cargo a day. Two Victory-type ships could be offloaded at the same time from the pier, while LSTs landed their cargo directly over the beach. Ships could also be offloaded from the harbor anchorage (in the stream) by LSUs that brought the cargo to the piers and by DUKWs that landed over the LST beach. During the first 10 days of February, the brigade unloaded an average of 400 tons a day at the little seaport.[22]

The troops of the 8206th AU, ATC, after assisting in preparing Pohang Port for the reception of the 1st Marine Division, redeployed to Gunsan via Busan aboard SCAJAP LST-Q030, arriving on 10 January 1951. After a week of stevedoring duties, unloading fuel from LSTs and then reloading the LSTs with rice, they returned briefly to Busan. On 20 January the peripatetic outfit again mounted out by LST, this time to the island of Geoje, where they would spend the next several months working as stevedores and construction engineers, assisting in the building of a large POW camp, billets, and dock facilities.[23]

Thus, throughout the early months of 1951, as Eighth Army withdrew, halted the Chinese attack, and then began a counteroffensive to the north, all the Army amphibious forces in the Far East, as well as the 1st Marine Division, were committed to other than amphibious activities.

Special Operations: Irregulars in the Northwest Islands in January–February 1951

But while the Army conventional amphibious troops were otherwise occupied, Eighth Army was about to become involved in unconventional warfare, including ad hoc and irregular amphibious operations, that would play out along the rugged coastline and offshore islands of North Korea's Hwanghae province. The population of Hwanghae was culturally and politically aligned with Seoul and had resisted the imposition of the North Korean regime as early as 1947. When UNC forces invaded the north in the fall of 1950, armed Hwanghae irregulars made contact with the advancing forces, protected the UNC lines of communication, and harried the retreating North Koreans. When the Chinese attacked, these guerrillas were forced to flee, along with thousands of refugees and irregular forces from other parts of North Korea. Some carried on the resistance from the mountains, some established strongholds along the Hwanghae coast, and others took refuge on the offshore islands. Many fled from the coast southwest of Jinnampo (Chinnamp'o) by way of the village of Wolsa-ri ("a Korean Dunkirk") to the island of Chodo (Ch'odo). Others escaped to the southwest through the town of Jangyeon (Changyon) into the small Jangsangot (Changsan-got) peninsula and then south to the string of islands: Baengnyeongdo (Paengyong-do), Daecheongdo (Taech'ong-do), and Socheongdo (Soch'ong-do).[24] (See map 35.)

The flood of escapees traveling to the islands in sampans and junks continued throughout December 1950, with some assistance from ROK Navy ships. During the first weeks of January 1951, ROK Navy, including the merchant marine LST *Tangyang*, evacuated refugees from the southwest coast of Hwanghae province as the partisans delayed the advancing Chinese and North Korean forces. KPA forces in northwest Hwanghae province cut off and attacked a second group of irregulars. On 19 January the group in northwestern Hwanghae province, which called itself the Pyeongyang Partisan Regiment, fought its way out to the coast and was withdrawn by sea from the mainland to Chodo Island. In all, on 19 January the ROK Navy evacuated some 13,000 North Korean refugees and guerrilla fighters from the northwest Korean coast, covering the operation with a heavy bombardment and an amphibious landing south of Jinnampo.[25]

Although the FEC and Eighth Army knew about the exodus, they were unaware that guerrilla fighters were among the civilian refugees until 8 January, when TG 95.7, the ROK Navy group that was assisting the refugees, reported that some 1,000 volunteers armed with Japanese weapons were operating in Hwanghae province and asked if Eighth Army had any Japanese ammunition that could be made available.[26] The plea for help found a willing and informed ear in Colonel John McGee of the Eighth Army Staff. McGee had conducted a successful guerrilla campaign in the Philippines during World War II and had tried to persuade Eighth Army to arm and equip a behind-the-lines guerrilla force in July 1950.

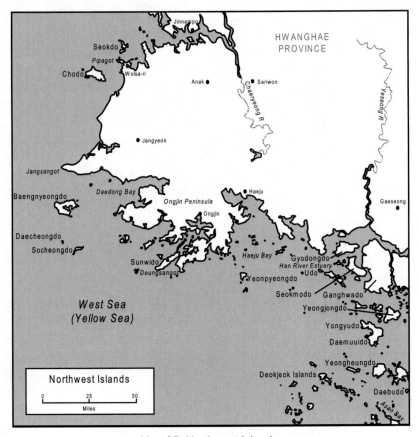

Map 35. Northwest Islands.

That plan had been abandoned, but now McGee found support for establishing an organization to assist, organize, and direct the Hwanghae irregulars. Believing that they could be turned into an organized guerrilla force to disrupt North Korean and Chinese supply lines and support a future offensive, the Eighth Army G3 Miscellaneous Division, which had been coordinating special operations in Korea, established on 15 January 1951 an Attrition (Partisan) Section to direct the efforts of the North Korean irregulars. McGee arranged to make contact with the partisans and to supply them with food and other supplies from civil relief resources.[27]

On 23 January Eighth Army published a plan drafted by McGee called "Plan Able," to train and equip the partisans and then infiltrate them back onto the mainland from the offshore islands. The plan called for an initial phase in which cadres would be trained on the islands. The teams of partisans were to carry out intelligence collection and sabotage missions and assist in the recovery of downed UNC aircrews. In the second phase of the operation, the partisan force was expected to be of sufficient size, organization, and training to be able to make a major contribution to a renewed Eighth Army offensive. Throughout the spring and summer, there was still some hope that such an offensive would actually take place.[28]

On 15 February 1951 a base of operations for the partisans was established on the west coast island of Baengnyeongdo (already in use by the Central Intelligence Agency (CIA), the South Korean Government, and the US Air Force for their own clandestine operations). Two other operational units were formed: *Baker* Section, with its headquarters and training camp near Busan, to conduct airborne training and insertions; and TF *Redwing*, an American-led company of ROK Marines that carried out intelligence, sabotage, and commando operations along the coasts and among the islands off North Korea. Originally code-named *William Able*, the Baengnyeongdo base was renamed *Leopard* in March and the partisan units adopted the nickname "Donkey" with a number to indicate the identity of the team.[29]

The *William Able* and *Leopard* operations were planned, directed, and supplied (sometimes meagerly) by Eighth Army, and they were amphibious in that the partisans infiltrated by sea from islands off the coast, largely with a fleet of motorized junks (some modified with an additional powerful engine, hidden radio antennas, and concealed recoilless rifles), as well as smaller craft (including sailing junks and little boats powered by a single oar sculled over the stern and referred to in English as "wiggle sticks" or "wiggle boats" from the motion of the oar). Supported from time-to-time by ships of the Royal Navy, they conducted raids against Chinese and North Korean forces and carried out intelligence collection, aircrew rescue, sabotage, and assassination missions until the end of the war.[30] They were tactically effective in terms of producing enemy casualties. However, the partisan operations were essentially limited to Hwanghae province. If the large-scale UNC offensive into the north had materialized, the partisans were unlikely to have had much effect in the crucial interior areas. Nevertheless, they might have had an important effect in disrupting that part of the North Korean transportation and communications network that ran through the west coast.

Eighth Army Counteroffensive

By mid-January the Chinese offensive had stalled, the North Korean V Corps began withdrawing from Wonju, and the 9th RCT of the 2d Infantry Division cautiously moved into the city.[31] On 15 January Ridgway began aggressive patrolling and large-scale reconnaissance-in-force operations to regain contact and probe the Chinese front line. On 25 January he began a full-scale counteroffensive with two operations called THUNDERBOLT, an attack by I and IX Corps in the west that was expanded on 11 February by Operation ROUNDUP by X Corps and the ROK III and I Corps in the east (see map 36). By 11 February Eighth Army had reached a line from just south of Seoul in the west to just south of the port city of Gangneung in the east.[32]

When Ridgway attacked, he did so aggressively, but with deliberation and caution, using phase lines to control forward movement and ensure that units maintained contact with the forces on their flanks. In a memorandum to MacArthur at the height of the THUNDERBOLT operation and on the eve of ROUNDUP, Ridgway described his operation as "a coordinated, phased advance under Army control for the purpose of developing the enemy situation in their front; inflicting maximum losses with minimum sustained; and prepared to exploit on army order up to the Han, and there to hold."[33]

Ridgway pointed out that an advance to the line of the Han River was "a sound operation, with a high potential payoff, providing resistance does not stiffen to the point where our losses would cancel out military gains." However, an advance beyond the river would offer "little of military value commensurate with the risks incurred, unless Communist China should elect to withdraw north of the 38th Parallel." He also argued that retaking Seoul would put his forces on the enemy side of an unfordable obstacle and would risk destruction of those forces. He therefore considered recapture of Seoul to be unsound, although he was prepared to capture the city if the opportunity arose to do so safely.[34]

MacArthur concurred with Ridgway's views. He believed that the reoccupation of Gimpo Airfield and of the Incheon Harbor would "unquestionably be of marked value, and if they present easy prey they should be taken." Although he had argued the previous fall that Seoul was the key to a successful counteroffensive, he now said that while the "occupation of Seoul itself would, of course, present certain diplomatic and psychological advantages which would be valuable . . . its military usefulness is practically negligible."[35]

US intelligence indicated that the North Koreans and Chinese feared another amphibious attack. There were neither Army nor Marine forces available to conduct large scale amphibious operations at this time, but to take advantage of these fears, Commander in Chief, United Nations Command (CINCUNC) ordered a series of amphibious demonstrations to cause the enemy to reinforce Incheon and other coastal areas and draw forces from the front.[36] At the same time, a major effort was underway to interdict the enemy's lines of communication. Naval forces contributed to this interdiction effort through air operations; through naval gunfire; and through a resumption of amphibious raids against bridges, tunnels, and other transportation facilities along the coastal routes. Rear Admiral Allan

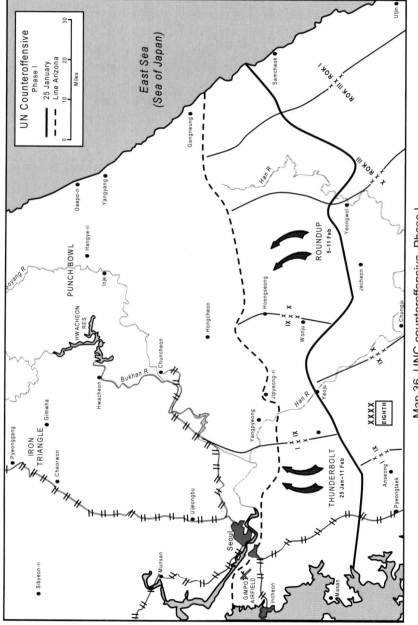

Map 36. UNC counteroffensive, Phase I.

E. Smith, commander of TF 95, developed an operational concept that included the seizure of islands off the North Korean coast as observation posts, areas from which coastal interdiction operations could be mounted, bases for irregular operations against the vulnerable road and rail lines along the coasts, and staging areas for future operations. The most important objective was the blockade of Wonsan, which was not only North Korea's major east coast port, but also a key transportation node. Control of Wonsan Harbor would prevent Soviet resupply of North Korean and Chinese forces through that port. Admiral Joy and General MacArthur approved Admiral Smith's concept, which included the bombardment of Incheon and Wonsan and possible seizure of islands in Wonsan Harbor. Joy also approved the capture of Wolmido in Incheon Harbor. All of the island seizures were to be done by ROK Navy and Marine forces, which began training in early February.[37]

Amphibious Demonstrations and the Reoccupation of Incheon

The ROK 4th Marine Battalion, supported by the American and Canadian ships of TG 95.1 providing gunfire support, conducted a brief landing and raid at Incheon on 27 and 28 January. Commander, United States Naval Forces, Far East (COMNAVFE) ordered TF 95 to conduct demonstrations, including bombardments and amphibious demonstrations, on the east coast. The first of these, Operation ASCENDANT, was conducted on 30 and 31 January near Ganseong (Kansong) (see map 37) and Goseong (Kosong). Rear Admiral Smith, aboard his flagship—the destroyer tender *Dixie* (AD-14), directed the demonstration, which included a bombardment, mine sweeping, and simulated landing activities by two attack cargo ships, several LSTs, and some landing ship, medium (rocket) (LSM[R]) rocket-firing ships (perhaps the only time such an operation had ever been led by a destroyer tender). Another such demonstration was planned for 10 February at Incheon with two AKAs and an LSD under the same Captain Samuel G. Kelly who had played a prominent role in the evacuation of Jinnampo the previous December, supported by air and naval gunfire from a combined British–American force that included the battleship USS *Missouri*, the aircraft carrier H.M.S. *Theseus,* cruisers, and destroyers. Kelly's small amphibious force arrived off Incheon on 8 February and the next day the *Missouri* began its bombardment of the beaches. However, before the amphibious ships could stand in to simulate a landing on 10 February, the enemy evacuated the city. Consequently, ROK marines were able to land at Incheon unopposed later that afternoon.[38]

On 10 February Ridgway acknowledged the value of the amphibious demonstrations in a message to Admiral Joy in which he noted the apparent

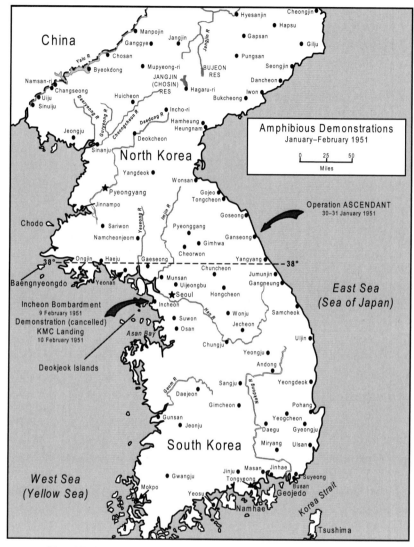

Map 37. Amphibious demonstrations, January–February 1951.

disappearance of the enemy forces that had recently been opposing
I Corps. The realism of the prelanding operations had the desired effect.
He concluded that the "Wholehearted cooperation and expeditious manner
in which this [operation] was effected are fully appreciated."[39]

The Siege of Wonsan

As the bombardments, amphibious demonstrations, and reoccupation of Incheon were taking place on the west coast, Admiral Smith's east

coast plan went into effect (see map 38). The ROK Navy had activated two Korean Marine Corps (KMC) units, the 41st and 42d Companies, trained specifically for the capture and garrison of the offshore islands. On 7 February Second Lieutenant Shim Hee T'aek's 42d Company sailed aboard ROK Navy LST-801 and headed for Yeongheung Bay. On 12 February minesweepers check-swept the approaches to Wonsan and Yeongheung Bay to ensure they had not been re-mined. Two days later, Lieutenant Shim's marines conducted a raid on Wonsan and occupied the islands of Yodo and Ungdo. On 16 February two US destroyers stood into the harbor to bombard the port, beginning a continuous naval and air bombardment of the port that would last for months. Two days later, the destroyers returned. During the bombardment, USS *Ozbourn* (DD-846) was hit by artillery fire from one of the offshore islands, which was subjected to an air strike by TF 77 carrier aircraft. On 19 February the H.M.S. *Belfast* added its weight of metal to the bombardment; and on 24 February, two destroyers, a frigate, and the LST-801 carrying 110 Korean marines of the 42d Company entered the harbor. The marines then went ashore on Sindo and Daedo Islands. On 27 February the Korean marines conducted another raid on Wonsan. A detachment then sailed south on ROK Navy minesweeper AMS-501 and on 4 March transferred to two US Navy landing craft, vehicle, personnel (LCVPs) to land on and occupy the island of Hwangtodo.[40]

Rehabilitation of Incheon Port

With Incheon now back in friendly hands, the badly damaged port had to be returned to working order as quickly as possible. Admiral Thackrey, who had returned to Yokosuka after the evacuation, was put in charge of the rehabilitation operations. The 2d ESB was ordered to turn over the Ulsan and Suyeong operations to the 7th Medium Port, which had been operating Pusan (Busan) Port, and to move to Incheon to bring their special skills and expertise to put the port back into operation. Thackrey sailed from Yokohama on 10 February with *Eldorado* leading an amphibious task group (TG 90.1) consisting of five LSTs, two LSDs (*Tortuga* and *Catamount)*, and one APA (*Okanogan*). Newly promoted Brigadier General Twitty and one of his staff officers joined Thackrey aboard the *Eldorado,* and the *Tortuga* transported an advance element of the 532d EB&SR to Incheon on 12 February. The rest of the 532d EB&SR (less Company D, which was at Suyeong) and the 558th Transportation Amphibious Truck Company loaded out from Ulsan from 12 to 15 February and embarked on the *Catamount*. The Brigade Headquarters and Company D of the 532d EB&SR left Suyeong via two LSTs on 17 February. The 50th Engineer

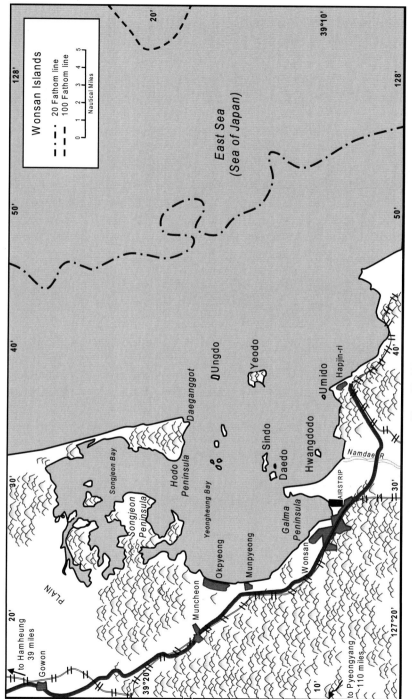

Map 38. Wonsan Islands.

265

Port Construction Company and the 5th KMC Battalion were attached to the brigade and deployed to Incheon from Busan aboard LSTs. Because indigenous labor was unlikely to be available at the newly liberated city of Incheon, the brigade also recruited 1,400 Korean laborers at Busan and brought them to Incheon aboard four LSTs.[41]

Admiral Thackrey and General Twitty arrived at Incheon on 15 February, followed a day later by the advance detachment of the 532d EB&SR and the 5th KMC Battalion, which immediately established a security perimeter. The rest of the 532d EB&SR and the 50th Engineer Port Construction Company arrived on 17 February and began work. The DUKW ramp at Incheon and the causeway to Wolmido were found to be heavily mined. Thus, the first project for the amphibious engineers was to clear the ramp and the road. On 18 February a representative from Eighth Army G4 arrived to clarify the mission and the situation. General Twitty had previously been directed to get the port up to 1,000 tons per day as soon as possible. However, even though Eighth Army was now pushing north, the danger of another Chinese attack meant that the brigade had to be ready to evacuate the port once again. In this situation, it was undesirable to have large stockpiles of incoming cargo at the port, and lack of transportation in the area would make it difficult to clear 1,000 tons a day. Therefore, the initial requirement was reduced to 500 to 600 tons a day. Twitty decided to reload onto the LSTs all but the troops and equipment necessary to meet that requirement. Thackrey was opposed to leaving these LSTs to dry out on the beach during the low tides and ordered them to anchor offshore and to come into port only to unload equipment when required.[42]

On 19 February Thackrey received a message from Eighth Army advising him that in light of a possible enemy counterattack, I Corps might withdraw from the Incheon area at any moment. Based on this, Twitty decided to leave only elements of two companies of the 532d EB&SR and the 5th KMC Battalion ashore and to move the brigade's campsite to Wolmido. The port remained under 48-hour evacuation warning for the rest of the month, but unloading and port rehabilitation continued. On 24 February the 558th Amphibious Truck Company was unloaded. The next day, the 50th Engineer Port Construction Company was also unloaded and went to work on the repair of the docks and movement of the huge tidal lock gates to the open position. It would be some time before the tidal lock was put back into operation, but with the gate open the basin could be used by LCMs, LSUs, and other lighterage.[43]

On 20 February Eighth Army had begun its next offensive, Operation KILLER, which would take the IX and X Corps to a line (LINE ARIZONA) some 15 miles north of Wonju. When the 1st Cavalry Division operating east and north of the Han River found high water and flooded fords impeding its line of communication, two platoons from the 558th were sent to help get supplies across the river with their DUKWs. The amphibious trucks would also be used to evacuate wounded across the river and to provide logistic support to the 25th Infantry Division and other units during the offensive.[44]

Amphibious Raids, Demonstrations, and Special Operations to Support the Offensive

To support the Operation KILLER offensive, Eighth Army once again asked for amphibious demonstrations to fix enemy forces. Admiral Sir William G. Andrewes, the British commander of the west coast force, began his deception efforts on 27 February. The light carrier, USS *Bataan* (CVL-29), conducted air strikes in the vicinity of Jinnampo and 2 days later, US and Korean mine sweepers, escorted by a British frigate, swept a channel up the Daedong River. (See map 39.) On 3 March three APAs and two AKAs appeared offshore escorted by two destroyers and steamed toward Chodo before reversing course back to Incheon.[45]

On 1 March TF *Leopard* (the partisans operating from the Northwest Islands) were instructed to initiate partisan operations as soon as possible to support Eighth Army's operations. This first insertion of partisan teams was named Operation SHINING MOON. The first of the TF *Leopard* teams to go in, code name Donkey 1, consisted of 38 partisans commanded by a former merchant named Chang Chae Hwa. First Lieutenant William Harrison, who had been the advisor to the Miryang Battalion in its ill-fated landing at Jangsadong on 15 September 1950, had trained the unit in communications and demolitions. Chang's partisans successfully landed over the beach on the Jangsangot peninsula the night of 3/4 March and moved up into the hills to make contact with locals who were willing to join forces with the partisans. On the night of 20/21 March, during a meeting of local Communist party officials, Donkey 1 conducted a raid on a police station killing 27 men and women and capturing weapons and ammunition. After other successful attacks on truck stops and warehouses, the team gained adherents until it was more than 100 strong. It continued its operations on the mainland for 4½ months. By mid-July the team had engaged in many actions: claimed to have assassinated or killed in battle some 500 soldiers, police, and Communist officials; blown up bridges; rescued prisoners; raided warehouses; and, in the words of a former member of the Eighth Army Attrition Section, "generally, raised hell." They had also taken many casualties, and on the night of 23 July the 20

Map 39. Raids, demonstrations, and special operations, March–April 1951.

survivors waded through the low tide to a friendly-held island ending their operation. Other Donkey teams infiltrated during this time, but Donkey 1's operation was the most successful.[46]

The ROK marines were also active in the Northwest Islands during this time. On 28 March ROK Navy LST-801 carrying the KMC 41st Company, commanded by First Lieutenant Lee Tong Ho, sailed to the islands off the northwest coast. On 2 April they landed on the island of Gyodongdo (Kyodong-do), just west of the mouth of the Yeseong (Yesong) River in the

Han River estuary, and made contact with friendly guerrilla forces. They also recruited about 100 young men from a group of 700 refugees on the island and organized them into a guerrilla unit. After training by the ROK marines, the new guerrilla force was infiltrated by sea into the Haeju area of mainland North Korea. Having completed its mission on Gyodongdo, Lieutenant Lee's marines moved up to the island of Baengnyeongdo, the hub of special operations activity in the northwest. There they took over defense of the island and then sent a detachment north to the island of Seokdo (Sok-do), northeast of Chodo near the mouth of the Daedong River. Landing on 7 May, the Korean marines established a base camp and recruited another 100 young men for intelligence and harassment operations.[47]

In April and May 1951, the effort was extended to the east coast with the organization of a partisan operation called TF *Kirkland* with its main base at Jumunjin (Chumunjin). East coast operations posed some difficulties. There were far fewer suitable offshore islands than in the west and the CIA, which was conducting clandestine operations from islands further north, insisted that the partisan activities be confined to the coastal area south of Wonsan. Eventually, forward bases for TF *Kirkland* were established on the small islands of Namdo (Nan Do) and Solseum (Sol-sum) southeast of Wonsan.[48] (See map 40.)

Recruitment of partisans posed another problem. Unlike the situation in the northwest, there was no large pool of anti-Communist North Koreans in the east. Initially, Eighth Army gave some thought to deploying teams of the Hwanghae partisans to TF *Kirkland*. However, the success of the Hwanghae guerrillas depended on their knowledge of and familiarity with their operating area. With no knowledge of the east coast and no contacts there, they were unsuitable for the *Kirkland* mission. Therefore, Eighth Army recruited the east coast partisans from among North Korean defectors already in the south, principally from the survivors of the Miryang Battalion that had conducted the unsuccessful landing at Jangsa-dong on 15 September 1950. Colonel McGee, who was in charge of the partisan operation, asked the ROK Army for permission to recruit 200 guerrillas from the battalion. ROK Army Headquarters had always mistrusted the loyalty of the former North Koreans of the Miryang Battalion and were glad to transfer the entire battalion to Eighth Army control. First Lieutenant Harrison, then serving as advisor to Donkey 1, was given command of TF *Kirkland*. The east coast partisans were infiltrated by sea or land behind Communist lines to support Eighth Army offensive operations by collecting intelligence, recovering downed aircrews, and disrupting enemy lines of communication beyond the range of naval gunfire.[49]

Map 40. Eighth Army Offshore Partisan Bases, August 1951.

During this period, the 41st Independent Commando Royal Marines resumed their operations as coastal raiders. On 6 and 7 April Special Task Force 74, consisting of 274 Royal Marines aboard the USS *Fort Marion* (LSD-22) and a UDT aboard the fast transport *Begor* (APD-127), escorted by the heavy cruiser *St. Paul* (CA-73) and the destroyers *Lind* (DD-703) and *Massey* (DD-778), conducted a raid at Soryedong near Seongjin, south of Cheongjin. Coming ashore in LVTs carried aboard the *Fort Marion*, they secured a beachhead without enemy opposition and blew up 100 feet of track at a key railway bridge, leaving 8-foot deep craters.[50]

Hwacheon (Hwach'on) Reservoir Operation, 9–11 April 1951

Operation KILLER had brought Eighth Army forces to the Han River by the end of February 1951. The next operation, RIPPER, began on 7 March and continued the advance to the north all across the front. Seoul was liberated on 14 and 15 March. By 22 March Chuncheon, in the central part of the country, was in friendly hands and that same day paratroopers of the 187th Airborne RCT and the 2d and 4th Ranger Infantry Companies (Airborne) dropped just south of the Imjin River near Munsan-ni. At the end of March, Eighth Army was close to the 38th Parallel. In the face of indications that a Chinese counterattack was imminent, General Ridgway recommended, and General MacArthur and President Harry S. Truman approved, a further advance across the 38th Parallel to disrupt the enemy's offensive preparations and to secure defensible terrain further north.[51]

Ridgway's plan was to conduct an attack, Operation RUGGED, to a line from the Imjin River to the Hwacheon Reservoir and east to the sea (LINE KANSAS) (see map 41). A second operation, DAUNTLESS, would push I and IX Corps 20 miles further north in the central sector to a line, WYOMING, just south of the towns of Cheorwon (Ch'orwon) and Gimhwa (Kumhwa). These two towns and the town of Pyeonggang (P'yonggang) outlined an area of rugged terrain and a transportation and logistic nexus known as the Iron Triangle. LINE WYOMING would be heavily fortified and, when the Chinese attacked, Eighth Army would, if necessary, conduct a slow withdrawal under pressure to LINE KANSAS, inflicting as much damage and as many casualties as possible.[52]

The first phase of the operation began on 1 April. By 6 April Major General William M. Hoge's IX Corps, consisting of the 27th Commonwealth Brigade on the left, the ROK 6th Division in the center, and the 1st Cavalry Division with the 7th Marines attached, on the right flank, had reached LINE KANSAS almost everywhere. In the east of the corps zone, however, the 7th and 8th Cavalry Regiments, slowed by the difficult terrain and Chinese resistance, were still some 3 miles south of the Hwacheon Reservoir (see map 42). General Ridgway was concerned that the Chinese were fighting hard to keep the cavalry away from the reservoir because they wanted to let the water rise behind the Hwacheon Dam sluice gates and then release it to flood the Bukhan River Valley to the south.[53]

The irregularly shaped Hwacheon Reservoir was 13 square miles in area. Its southern shore constituted 16 miles of LINE KANSAS. It was created by a dam across the Bukhan River at the northwest corner of the reservoir that held back 19 billion cubic feet of water. The 275-foot high

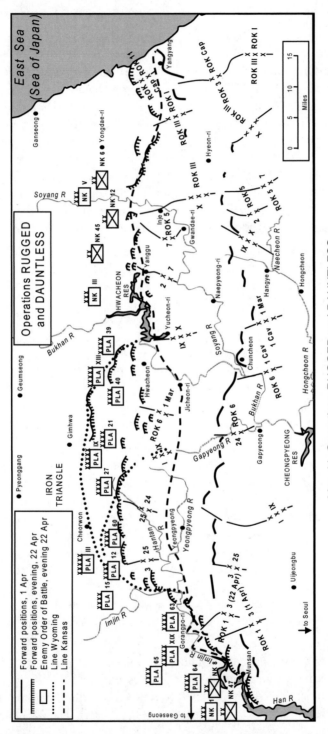

Map 41. Operations RUGGED and DAUNTLESS.

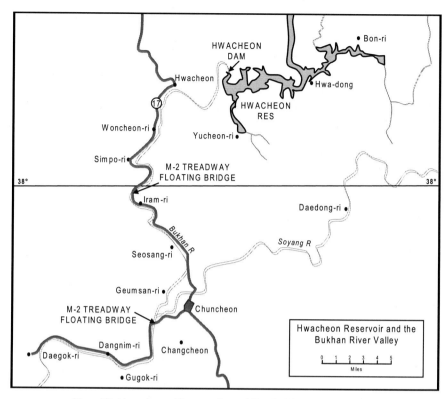

Map 42. Hwacheon Reservoir and the Bukhan River Valley.

dam had a concrete spillway 826 feet wide with 18 sluice gates across the top that could raise the water level an additional 32 feet.[54] In February, before Operation RIPPER, General Ridgway had considered destroying the dam to release the water, and then beginning the attack after the water had subsided. With this in mind, he asked Eighth Army engineer Colonel Paschal N. Strong what effect "bomb demolition" of the dam would have on friendly and enemy operations. Strong replied that "instantaneous demolition" of the dam would cause a 60-foot high flood immediately below the dam flattening to a 15-foot rise at the confluence of the Bukhan and Han Rivers and further flattening to 7 feet where the Han River ran through Seoul. This would create an impassable water barrier along the length of the Bukhan River that would last for 48 hours and make river crossing "difficult but not impossible" in the vicinity of Seoul for 36 hours. Offensive operations north of Cheorwon would be impossible until the water subsided. The engineer pointed out, however, that it was nearly impossible to destroy the dam with conventional bombs and that destruction of the sluice gates alone would not release enough water to make the Bukhan River impassable.[55]

Since the danger of flooding appeared slight, Ridgway did not pursue the matter and did not include the dam among the RUGGED and DAUNTLESS objectives. However, on 4 April after Operation RUGGED began, the IX Corps engineer conducted an appraisal that came to different conclusions. He argued that if the reservoir was filled to capacity and all the sluice gates and penstocks were opened simultaneously, the Bukhan River would rise immediately 10 to 12 feet in the river gorge near LINE KANSAS, flooding the Chuncheon Plain to a depth of 5 feet, disrupting lateral movement in the corps zone, and obstructing traffic along the corps' main line of communication. That line of communication ran from below Chuncheon to Hwacheon along Route 17, which crossed the Bukhan River on two floating treadway bridges. If these bridges were to be flooded out, logistical sustainment of IX Corps would be severely hampered.[56]

Based on this new assessment, Ridgway kept the dam under aerial observation and on 6 April moved the trace of LINE WYOMING slightly to the north, including the dam as an objective of Operation DAUNTLESS. He also shifted the boundary between IX and X Corps so that the dam and its approach from the south were both in the IX Corps sector, while most of the reservoir remained within the X Corps sector (see map 43). The 1st Marine Division, with the KMC 1st Regiment attached, was scheduled to relieve the 1st Cavalry Division as the right flank of IX Corps front line unit once the Corps reached LINE KANSAS, so the mission of capturing the dam logically would have fallen to the marines. However, after the Munsan-ni airborne operation, Eighth Army released Captain Dorsey B. Anderson's 4th Ranger Company from the 187th Airborne RCT and attached it to IX Corps. General Hoge decided that this unit, which arrived on 7 April, would be ideally suited to conduct a raid to put the sluice gates out of commission. Accordingly, he attached the Rangers to the 1st Cavalry Division and instructed the division commander, Major General Charles D. Palmer, to use the Ranger Company against the dam before the division was pulled out of the line. Hoge did not, however, specify precisely how the operation was to be conducted.[57]

There were only two ways to approach the dam from the south. One was by way of a 2½-mile long peninsula formed by a horseshoe bend in the Bukhan River and forming the west shore of the reservoir. The other approach could only be made by crossing the water to another mile-long peninsula that jutted south into the reservoir east of the dam. Hoge's concept was that the Rangers would infiltrate along the west shore of the reservoir (the eastern side of the western peninsula); destroy the gate machinery, thus immobilizing the sluice gates in the closed position; and then withdraw. Hoge anticipated that the operation would take 2 to 4 hours.[58]

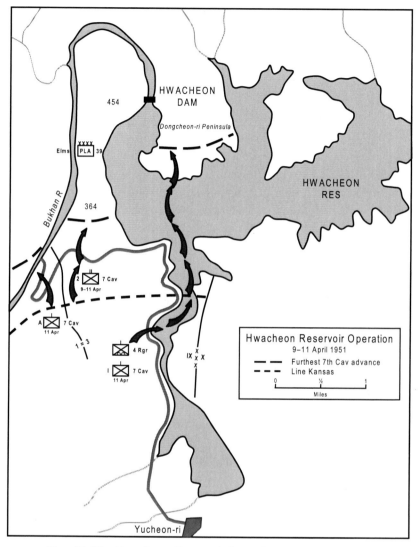

Map 43. The Hwacheon Reservoir Operation, 9–11 April 1951.

Palmer, commanding general of the 1st Cavalry Division, apparently unaware of Hoge's concept for a raid, attached the Rangers to the 7th Cavalry Regiment, and directed the regimental commander, Colonel William A. Harris, to capture the dam and immobilize the sluice gates. Harris further attached the Rangers to his 2d Battalion, commanded by Lieutenant Colonel John B. Callaway, to whom he assigned the dam mission.[59] The battalion jumped off at 0730 on 8 April in an attempt to get closer to the dam. Moving up from their reserve position, they skirted

275

the IX Corps right flank, entering the X Corps zone to pass through the 23d Infantry Division and the French Battalion (the left flank units of the US 2d Infantry Division). With Company G in the lead, the battalion moved slowly forward without meeting much initial resistance, although its patrols came under attack later in the day and received mortar fire. By nightfall, the 2d Battalion and the Rangers had arrived just south of the base of the western peninsula.[60]

While Callaway's battalion and the Rangers moved forward on 8 April, Captain Anderson and Major Russell J. Wilson, the commander of the 8th Engineer Combat Battalion (the 1st Cavalry Division Engineer Battalion), visited another dam across the Bukhan River at Cheongpyeong (Chungp'yong) to examine the sluice gate machinery, which was presumed to be similar to that of the Hwacheon Dam. They determined that if the cogs on the wheel that controlled the sluice gates were destroyed, the gates would be immobilized.[61]

Given the slow rate of advance toward LINE KANSAS by the 1st Cavalry Division, Colonel Harris did not expect the dam operation to take place for several days, but two events now increased the pace of operations. Late on 8 April, General Palmer ordered his two assault regiments, the 7th and 8th Cavalry, to press the attack to LINE KANSAS the next day. At midnight on 8 April, the Chinese soldiers and North Korean dam employees began opening the sluice gates. Because the central electrical power system was not working, the gates had to be opened manually or with auxiliary power, a slow process, and only 10 gates were opened to varying degrees. Early in the morning of 9 April, pilots flying over the dam reported that about half of the gates had been opened and a crest of water was moving down the river. At 0715 debris pushed down the river ahead of the water surge damaged the northernmost of the floating bridges before it could be swung out of the way. Engineers cut the southern bridge loose and swung it to the east side of the river before the surge of water hit so it was not damaged. Although the water level reached 7 feet in the Bukhan River Valley, IX Corps was able to keep its supplies flowing across the river using ferries constructed of assault rafts. The flood surge soon passed and both bridges were put back into operation.[62]

As the sluice gates were opened, the Chinese opposing the 7th and 8th Cavalry Regiments withdrew behind the river to avoid being cut off by the flood. This left the way open for a 1st Cavalry Division advance, and by 1200 on 9 April Palmer's two assault regiments had reached LINE KANSAS. General Ridgway, who had made an aerial reconnaissance of the flood damage, was at the IX Corps command post (CP) at the time, and ordered Hoge to carry out the planned raid to close the open sluice gates and immobilize the machinery to prevent them from being reopened. Hoge ordered Palmer to carry out the dam operation immediately. Callaway's 2d Battalion, with the Ranger Company and a platoon of engineers attached, was designated as TF *Callaway* for this operation.[63]

The plan was for the 2/7th Cavalry (which during the morning had advanced to the high ground south of the western peninsula) to advance north to seize Hill 454, overlooking the dam. Once Hill 454 was secured, the Rangers and engineers would slip forward along the west bank of the reservoir to the dam, close the opened sluice gates, destroy the gate mechanism, then cross the dam and secure the high ground overlooking the dam on the eastern peninsula.[64] The hastily-planned attack began at 1330. At about 1500 the lead unit, Company F, 2/7th Cavalry, reached the road at the base of the western peninsula. As soon as they crossed the road, Company F came under small arms, automatic weapons, and mortar fire from an estimated company of Chinese that held a line across the narrow neck of the peninsula and who were supported by fire from Hill 364 and from the high ground west of the Bukhan River.

Artillery and air support for the task force was limited. The 7th Cavalry's line of communication was a narrow, twisting road that came up from the south through the 2d Infantry Division sector and then ran from the village of Yucheon-ri (Yuch'on-ni) to the reservoir. It was a mountain track, impassable by anything larger than a jeep, thus preventing the 105-mm direct support artillery battalions from being brought within range. Artillery support was limited to that of the divisional 155-mm howitzer battalion (the 82d Field Artillery Battalion) firing at extreme range.

Poor weather hindered air support; however, one close air support mission made it through the clouds at about 1700. Colonel Callaway called it in based on reports from Company F, which had misreported its position so the air strike fell on unoccupied ground with little impact on the Chinese. Soon thereafter, Company F called for six stretchers and reported that its commander had been killed. Callaway took this to mean that the company had sustained heavy casualties although, in fact, only one other soldier had been hit. As darkness fell, with its lead company pinned down by enemy fire, Callaway called in artillery fire, withdrew his force back behind the road at the base of the peninsula, and prepared to resume the attack the next morning.[65]

During the morning of 9 April, prior to TF *Callaway's* attack, Captain Anderson of the Rangers made an aerial reconnaissance of the reservoir and concluded that, while an overland approach was limited by the terrain to a narrow frontal attack, it would be possible for the Rangers to cross the reservoir under cover of darkness, land on the eastern peninsula, and make a surprise attack on the dam while the Chinese were diverted by the attack up the western peninsula. Colonel Harris had reached a similar conclusion and directed his staff to get 20 assault boats from the 8th Engineers. The engineers, anticipating a requirement to cross the Bukhan River, had earlier acquired boats and material for an amphibious operation; but before Harris's request reached them, and anticipating the 1st Cavalry Division's relief by the 1st Marine Division on 10 April, they had returned most of the gear to the depots at Chuncheon and turned the rest over to the marines.[66]

In any event, there was to be one more attempt to reach the dam over land. Before dawn on the morning of 10 April, Callaway and Anderson discussed the plans for the attack. Anderson proposed the amphibious operation, but believing that the Chinese had withdrawn from the critical terrain (as they had consistently done during the previous days' actions), Callaway sent his men forward at 0730 in another frontal attack based essentially on the same plan as the previous day, this time with Company G in the lead.[67] Once again, they were stopped by small arms, automatic weapons, and mortar fire as soon as they crossed the road. Some 2 dozen soldiers were killed or wounded. Low on ammunition, unable to push through the enemy troops dug in along the half-mile wide neck of land, and expecting to be relieved by the KMC 2d Battalion that evening, Callaway halted the attack and broke contact with the enemy at 1530.[68]

The relief of the 1st Cavalry Division had already begun with the 8th Cavalry moving off the line to be replaced by the 1st Marine Division and the KMC regiment. By 1730 the relief was completed and the 8th Cavalry moved south into a reserve position. The 7th Cavalry remained in place, however. General Hoge, who had visited the 1st Cavalry Division command post at 1000, was displeased with the efforts so far. Based on the light casualties, Hoge concluded that the Chinese resistance was not great. He insisted that the 7th Cavalry conduct a bona fide attack on the dam before it left the front line. Callaway received word at 1830 that his task force would not be relieved and would "take the dam." Thinking that they might continue the attack that night, the battalion sent forward ammunition and communications equipment.[69]

General Hoge's verbal order was confirmed by a IX Corps message to General Palmer received by the 1st Cavalry Division at 2245 on 10 April: "Take immediate steps to deny by fire enemy access to dam at CT9319. Dispatch force to dam to close flood gates and to execute such work as will reduce enemy capability to release additional water from reservoir."[70]

General Palmer told Colonel Harris that he could commit his entire regiment if necessary. Harris decided to resume the attack before dawn the next morning, making a much more substantial effort involving all four battalions (including the Greek Battalion, which was attached to the 7th Cavalry), as well as the Rangers. The Rangers would cross the reservoir in assault boats and land on the peninsula east of the dam under cover of darkness with a lead element departing the south shore at 0230 and the main body crossing at 0330. This would be the main effort. Meanwhile, the 2d Battalion would make another frontal attack up the western peninsula, jumping off at 0400 to "contain and pin down the enemy." Company C of the 70th Tank Battalion was to move through the 23d Infantry Division and up the road through the 7th Cavalry zone to support the attack. Six DUKW amphibious trucks of the 558th Transportation Amphibious Truck Company were to follow the tanks and then support the amphibious operation. The 3d Battalion would be prepared to support the Rangers, either by crossing the reservoir to reinforce them, by passing through the 2d Battalion, or by securing the western peninsula after it was captured by the 2d Battalion. As a diversion, the 1st Battalion was to send one reinforced company northwest across the Bukhan River and attack the Chinese entrenched on the high ground to the west. The Greek Battalion would be the regimental reserve, prepared for commitment wherever required.[71]

During the afternoon of 10 April, after the TF *Callaway* attack had been called off, the Rangers prepared demolitions, organized teams, and rehearsed various alternative courses of action. At this point, they did not know whether they would be ordered to capture the dam, sneak in to destroy the machinery, or to seize the high ground east of the dam and then move in to immobilize the sluice gates.[72]

Meanwhile, a major effort was being made to retrieve the assault boats, life preservers, and other amphibious gear, including the six DUKW amphibious trucks of the 558th, that had been passed on to the 1st Marine Division. Consideration was even given to air-dropping life boats from air-sea rescue B-17s. Efforts were also made to obtain smoke to obscure the crossing from Chinese observation. The regiment requested Air Force smoke aircraft, smoke pots, and smoke generators to support the operation, but the smoke aircraft mission was refused without explanation and, while an attempt was made to airlift the smoke generating gear, the pots and generators did not arrive until 2 days after the operation was concluded.[73]

During the night of 10/11 April, one battery of 155-mm howitzers of the 4th Battalion, 11th Marines, and two batteries of 8-inch howitzers of the 17th Field Artillery Battalion were brought forward to support the operation. The 1st Cavalry Division Artillery 105-mm howitzers remained out of range.[74] At midnight on 10 April the Rangers were finally told they were to conduct the amphibious crossing of the reservoir to seize high ground east of the dam and then move in to immobilize the machinery. This gave them 2 hours to prepare and move to the embarkation site. Reinforced by a machinegun section from the 3d Battalion, 7th Cavalry Weapons Company (Company M) and artillery and mortar forward observers, the Rangers moved to a cove on the west bank of a narrow inlet protruding south from the reservoir. There were only nine assault boats and six outboard motors, which had been brought forward with great difficulty over the mountain trail by jeeps and trailers or manhandled by Korean porters. Additional boats were on the way, but these nine would be enough to get the Rangers across the reservoir. There were no life preservers, so two inflatable air mattresses were placed in each assault boat.[75]

Lieutenant Michael Healey's 3d Platoon, 4th Ranger Company began paddling across the water at 0345 on 11 April. One squad of Healey's platoon was the "killer" element, armed with knives, hand axes, hand grenades, pistols, and carbines. Their task was to secure the landing site. One assault team of the second squad carried demolitions and was charged with destroying the sluice gate machinery. The other second squad assault team included a 57-mm recoilless rifle. The third squad carried sniper rifles, automatic rifles, and "Ranger-type" rifle grenades: 60-mm mortar rounds rigged to be fired from rifle grenade launchers. The outboard motors were not used for the initial crossing to maintain surprise, so the men paddled quietly across the water through wisps of fog and smoke, reaching the far shore at 0420. Soon Captain Anderson arrived with the 2d Platoon, the machine gunners, and the forward observers. The boats were then sent back for the 1st Platoon while the men of the 3d and 2d Platoons climbed through rain and sleet toward their first objective, a hill some 500 yards north of the landing site.[76]

The Rangers' main objective (Objective 77) (see map 44) was a steep hill just east of the dam. Three finger-like ridges ran south from this hill. The high ground of each of these ridges had been designated from west to east as Objectives 80, 79, and 76. The Rangers initially moved up to Objective 79. Although the hill was occupied by Chinese, the Rangers managed to get to within a hundred yards before they came under rifle and machinegun fire at around 0600. Knocking out one machinegun with fire from the recoilless rifle and the other with grenades, the Rangers seized the hill by 0615. Anderson decided to remain on Objective 79 and to secure Objective 80 rather than move inland to Objective 77, because he

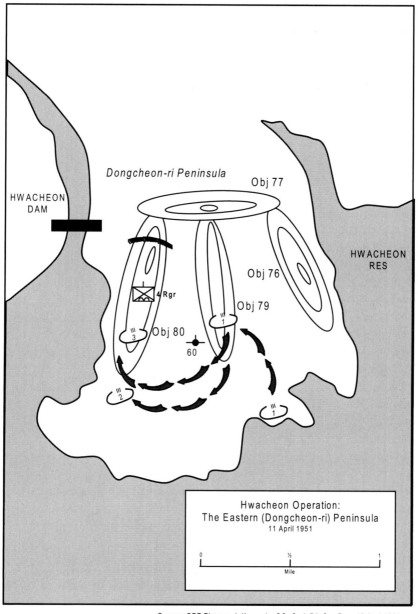

Map 44. Hwacheon Operation: The Eastern (Dongcheon-ri)
Peninsula, 11 April 1951.

feared being cut off by the Chinese and he wanted to cover the landing of the 1st Platoon, which was now paddling across the reservoir and coming under enemy fire. Half of the platoon got across the reservoir and moved to Objective 80, where heavy enemy small arms, automatic weapons, and mortar fire stopped them. The second half of the platoon, including the company executive officer, came under such heavy fire that they returned to the embarkation site, where they joined Company I of the 3d Battalion, 7th Cavalry.[77]

At around 0700 Anderson, with his Rangers unable to advance against the Chinese fire and running out of ammunition, requested permission to withdraw. Colonel Harris refused and ordered Company I of the 3d Battalion, which was assembled at the Rangers' embarkation site, to cross the reservoir to reinforce the Rangers and to resupply them with ammunition. Lieutenant Colonel Charles H. Hallden, commanding officer of the 3d Battalion, 7th Cavalry, had selected Company I to be the lead company if the battalion was committed. He sent Captain Norris M. Teague, his S2 (who had ranger and amphibious experience), to the embarkation site to organize the movement across the reservoir. On the south bank, Teague assisted the Company I commander, Captain Thomas J. Kennedy, to organize his men into 10-man boat teams and platoon-size groups (boat waves) and had the men practice getting in and out of the boats and paddling. Kennedy was alerted at 0900 that he was to reinforce the Rangers. There were only eight boats and two working motors available, but Kennedy and Teague launched the first wave (the 3d Platoon) across at around 1000. It took them 1½ hours to cross the reservoir under small arms and mortar fire, but they arrived on the far shore with no casualties (but some holes in the boats) at around 1130 and moved up to Objective 79 to make contact with the Rangers. By noon, the Rangers, most of which had moved to Objective 80, were still unable to advance and the movement of Company I was going slowly due to the lack of boats and motors. Using the two powered boats to tow up to five additional assault boats, Teague and Kennedy finally got the last of Company I across the reservoir by 1400, but by that time the entire operation was stalled.[78]

The 2d Battalion began its attack on the western peninsula at 0430 with Company E in the lead. Soon after crossing the road at the base of the peninsula, Company E came under heavy fire from a line of Chinese pillboxes that wounded 25 of its men. The Chinese fortifications appeared impervious to the long-range artillery fire. Incoming Chinese artillery fire killed the Company H (Heavy Weapons Company) commander and two other soldiers. Shortly after 0600 tanks from Company C, 70th Tank Battalion tried to move up to support the attack, but couldn't get past craters in the road (the DUKWs of the 558th Amphibious Truck Company that were to follow the tanks and support the operation finally arrived late in the afternoon). Callaway attempted to move Company G around the flank of Company E, but the peninsula was too narrow for maneuver. At 1300 Callaway ordered Company E to prepare to send an element by boat around the flank of the Chinese position. However, all the assault boats were being used to move Company I of the 3d Battalion across the reservoir to reinforce the Rangers.[79] The 1st Battalion's diversionary attack across the river never materialized. Company A sent out patrols to find crossing sites, but came under heavy fire from Chinese emplaced on the high ground on the west bank.[80]

At noon, with neither the Rangers nor the 2/7th Cavalry making any headway, General Palmer called Colonel Harris and asked if he recommended calling off the operation. Harris was still confident that the Rangers could get to the dam if the 3d Battalion could get across the reservoir. At 1300 Palmer called again and gave Harris permission to end the operation. By 1600 the Rangers and Company I were still blocked on the eastern peninsula, and the shortage of boats and operable motors prevented rapid reinforcement of the Rangers by the rest of the 3/7th Cavalry. The 2/7th Cavalry was pinned down on the western peninsula, while the 1/7th Cavalry had made no progress in its attempt to find river crossing sites and was under fire from the Chinese on the western heights. Harris concluded that the losses suffered were more than the operation was worth and at 1800, concerned that the Chinese would attack the force on the far side of the reservoir during the night, he ordered the Rangers and Company I to withdraw. They returned to the landing site, and at 1830 the Rangers paddled back across the reservoir, followed by Company I at 2100. The Chinese did not interfere with the withdrawal. Both units closed the assembly area south of the reservoir by 0130 on April 12.[81]

The Chinese had made a tenacious defense of the approaches to the dam, but other factors affected the outcome of the operation. The configuration of the terrain restricted maneuver room in the attack up the western peninsula. The terrain and the constricted line of communication made resupply difficult and kept much of the divisional artillery out of range. The poor weather hindered air operations. Perhaps more importantly, the attacks were hastily planned and coordination among the attacking and the supporting units was poor. The knowledge that the 1st Cavalry Division was to be relieved on the line on 10 April affected the planning for the operation, including the decision to turn in the assault boats and other amphibious equipment just before the decision was made to use them, and probably reduced the enthusiasm of the 7th Cavalry to press the attack.[82]

Both General Hoge and the Ranger company commander believed that the mission could have been accomplished had the Rangers been sent in initially to infiltrate along the west shore to the dam and conduct a surprise raid. But once the element of surprise was lost and the enemy reinforced his positions on 11 April, Hoge estimated that an entire division would have to be committed to capture the ground dominating the dam. Since Ridgway's orders had been to get the job done without needless casualties and with Operation DAUNTLESS now beginning, Hoge decided to wait until the dam could be captured as part of the IX Corps general advance to LINE WYOMING.[83]

As the 7th Cavalry was making its final, unsuccessful attempt to reach the Hwacheon Dam, the Chinese that were dug in along the south bank of the reservoir began withdrawing to the north. The 23d Infantry Regiment of the 2d Division, X Corps, observed the Chinese making an amphibious withdrawal to the north and called in air strikes that reported sinking 15 boats. On 12 April the 2d Infantry Division reached the area south of the Hwacheon Reservoir as the Chinese continued to withdraw by boat. That same day, the KMC 1st Regiment took over the 7th Cavalry sector. On 13 April the Netherlands Battalion, attached to the 2d Infantry Division, probed along the south bank of the reservoir without making contact with enemy forces and by 16 April it was clear that the Chinese were gone. Elements of the ROK 1st Marine Regiment occupied positions on the west bank of the Hwacheon Reservoir on 16 April and on 18 April they secured the dam.[84]

During the Chinese Spring Offensive, Eighth Army abandoned the dam on 25 April. In late May, Eighth Army had once again crossed the Bukhan River and faced the possibility of another enemy release of water from the dam. To preclude this, Navy *Skyraider* attack aircraft damaged three of the sluice gates with aerial torpedoes. When the ROK 6th Division captured the dam for the final time on 1 June 1951, engineers removed five of the sluice gates so that further water impoundment and release would be impossible.[85]

Amphibious Training, March–May 1951

In March 1951 General MacArthur began to rebuild the FEC's amphibious capability. GHQ FEC requested the 2d ESB, then still operating the port of Incheon, be returned to its amphibious capabilities and mission. General Ridgway agreed that it would be desirable to relieve 2d ESB from port operations to permit overhauling equipment and retraining, but argued that four substitute port facility units would be required to operate Incheon. These were not available from within the FEC resources and, at that time, the relief of the brigade was not considered important enough to warrant a request to Department of the Army for additional transportation port units. Ridgway agreed, however, to have the brigade train as much as possible in its primary amphibious role, consistent with its required use as a port unit, and transferred the 866th Transportation Port Company from Japan to Korea to take over some of the port operations. The eventual relief of the brigade would be at his discretion.[86]

These actions coincided with the establishment of a corps headquarters in Japan with responsibility for the ground defense of the Japanese islands, a mission that soon included the development of amphibious-capable Army forces. During the first 9 months of the war, the FEC referred to combat units in Japan as the GHQ Reserve, although there was no separate headquarters with this function. On 12 March 1951 a corps headquarters, initially designated GHQ Reserve Corps, was assembled at Sendai, Japan, under Major General Roderick Allen. On 1 April 1951 the unit was formally activated with the mission of providing "ground defense and general security for Hokkaido, and for Honshu north and east of the western boundaries of Niigata, Nagano, and Shizuoka prefectures."[87] The corps included the newly arrived 40th and 45th Divisions (California and Oklahoma National Guard units that had been called to Active Federal Service in September 1950), the 34th RCT, the 56th ATTB (now operating as a light tank unit), and the 229th Signal Operations Company, which had been transferred from Korea in April. GHQ Reserve Corps assumed responsibility for the general security of its zone on 20 April.[88]

On 10 May 1951, Headquarters and Headquarters Company, XVI Corps was activated at Sendai, Japan, from the personnel and equipment of the GHQ Reserve Corps.[89] Allen continued in command. Although the primary XVI Corps mission continued to be the defense of Japan, the Corps was about to begin a vigorous amphibious training program to be prepared in the event a landing should be required. By that time Eighth Army in Korea had come under the command of an officer with amphibious experience, an offensive spirit, and a desire to make use of the American amphibious capability.

Van Fleet in Command: Amphibious Plans, April–June 1951

On 14 April 1951 Lieutenant General James A. Van Fleet took command of Eighth Army, replacing General Ridgway, who had succeeded General MacArthur as Commander in Chief, Far East (CINCFE)/ CINCUNC following President Truman's relief of MacArthur from command on 11 April.[90] At this time the mission of Eighth Army was essentially defensive ("to repel aggression against so much of the territory (and the people therein) of the Republic of Korea, as you now occupy") with the goal of "inflicting maximum personnel casualties and materiel losses on hostile forces in Korea." Van Fleet was to "maintain the offensive spirit" of Eighth Army and "retain the initiative, through maximum maneuver of firepower, within the limitations imposed by logistics and terrain, and without undue sacrifice of men or equipment." To this end, Van Fleet was authorized to conduct amphibious and airborne landings, although advance beyond the KANSAS–WYOMING Line running from the junction of the Han and Imjin Rivers, through Cheorwon, the Hwacheon Reservoir, and Daepo-ri (Taep'o-ri) was to be on Ridgway's orders only.[91] (See map 45.)

Van Fleet was an advocate of amphibious operations, both actual assaults to outflank the Communists and deceptive demonstrations to fix their forces in place and disperse their defensive efforts. In World War II, as commander of the 8th Infantry Regiment of the 4th Infantry Division, he had spent months conducting shore-to-shore amphibious training in the United States, followed by intensive ship-to-shore training in England before his regiment landed at Utah Beach on D-Day. Unlike the bitter and bloody situation on adjacent Omaha Beach, the Utah Beach landings went relatively smoothly, reinforcing Van Fleet's positive view of amphibious operations.[92]

His attitude toward amphibious operations was reflected in an anecdote recounted by Rear Admiral George C. Dyer, who replaced Admiral Smith as the commander of TF 95 (the offshore blockade and escort force) in June 1951. Dyer, who had served with amphibious forces in the Sicily and Salerno operations in World War II, commanded a cruiser division in the Mediterranean in 1948, during the Greek Civil War when Van Fleet was Chief of the US Military Mission to Greece. Dyer had pointed out to Van Fleet that Greece was a peninsula, with coasts vulnerable to amphibious assault and naval bombardment. When Dyer arrived in Korea in June 1951, Van Fleet's first words to him were, "Korea is a peninsula!"[93]

A week after Van Fleet took command of Eighth Army, he and Ridgway discussed upcoming operations. Van Fleet agreed with Ridgway that with a new Chinese offensive imminent, Eighth Army should not push beyond its current front line, but he suggested that later in the summer it might be advantageous for Eighth Army to conduct an amphibious operation on the east coast near Wonsan to push north and establish a more favorable defensive line. Ridgway dismissed the idea as too risky.[94]

Van Fleet's next, and more formal, recommendation for an amphibious operation to support a ground offensive came following the Chinese Spring (Fifth Phase) Offensive of 22 April to 20 May 1951. During the first

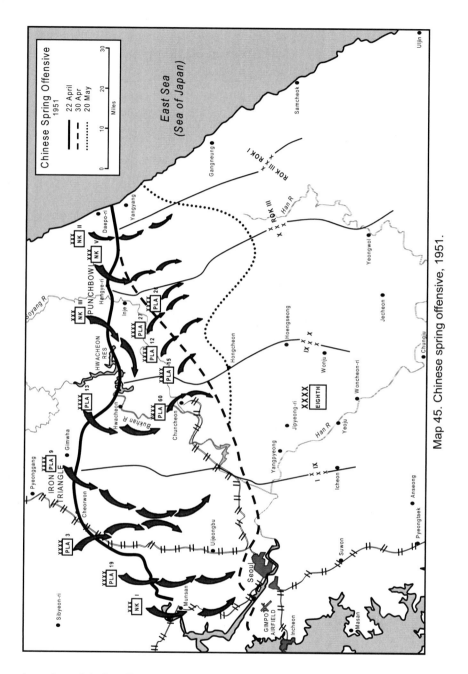

Map 45. Chinese spring offensive, 1951.

impulse of their offensive, from 22 to 30 April, the Chinese broke through the Eighth Army line west of the Hwacheon Reservoir. By 30 April Eighth Army had stabilized its front along a line running from just north of Seoul in the west to a point about 10 miles north of the 38th Parallel in the east.

The Chinese renewed their offensive on 16 May, focusing on the eastern half of the Eighth Army line, pushing the US X Corps and ROK III Corps south and eventually forming a deep salient.[95]

In support of the Eighth Army defense and to fix enemy forces on the east coast, Rear Admiral Kiland's TF 90 (Amphibious Forces Far East) and Rear Admiral Allen E. Smith's TF 95 conducted a series of amphibious demonstrations (see map 46). TF 95 cruisers—the *St. Paul*, *Helena*, and *Manchester*—and four destroyers bombarded Goseong on 24 April. On 29–30 April, the *Helena*, *Manchester*, and two TF 90 APAs and one AKA conducted an amphibious demonstration near Gojeo (Kojo). General Van Fleet requested another such operation for 6–7 May at Ganseong (Kansong). This was carried out by the *Helena* and four destroyers, which opened fire as ROK forces ashore were coming under heavy attack. The Korean Military Advisory Group (KMAG) credited the naval gunfire with saving the ROK unit. On 20 May a small contingent of Royal Marines using landing craft from the LSD *Comstock*, and supported by US and Commonwealth naval units, made a brief incursion on the west coast south of Jinnampo and across from the island of Chodo.[96]

By 20 May the Chinese offensive had been brought to a halt and General Van Fleet immediately went on the offensive (see map 47). The ROK I Corps pushed north along the coast toward Yangyang while X Corps advanced toward the area between the Hwacheon Reservoir and the ROK I Corps boundary. The corps consisted of the 1st Marine Division on the left and the US 2d Division with the ROK 5th Division attached in the center. On the right was the US 3d Division, which had made a fast march across the width of Korea from the Seoul area to reinforce X Corps, with the ROK 9th Division and one regiment of the ROK 8th Division attached. Van Fleet was anxious to capture as many Chinese and North Koreans as possible. Almond, hoping to cut them off by attacking northeast toward the coast, issued orders for Operation CHOPPER on 25 April. The marines were to advance to Yanggu at the eastern tip of the reservoir, the 2d Division was to capture the town of Inje, and the 3d Division was to destroy the enemy in the eastern part of the corps zone. The 187th Airborne RCT, which had also been attached to I Corps, was to form TF *Baker* and strike out to the northeast, all the way to the coast, and capture the seaport of Ganseong.[97]

Van Fleet wanted Ganseong specifically, for he had conceived a bold operation to bag a substantial part of the enemy force. On 28 May he requested approval for an amphibious landing to take place on 6 June (the

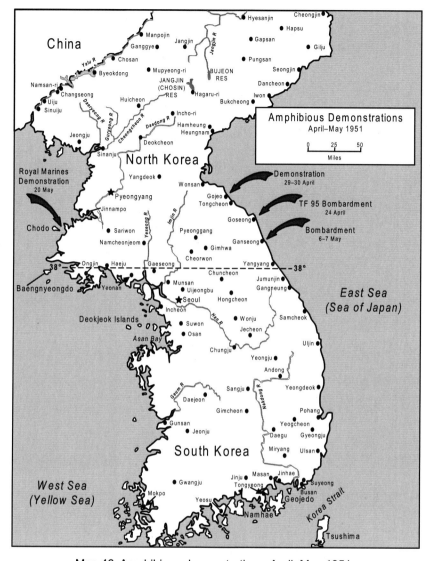

Map 46. Amphibious demonstrations, April–May 1951.

seventh anniversary of his Utah Beach landing) in coordination with an offensive northeast of Hwacheon. The 1st Marine Division was to be withdrawn from the line and replaced by ROK units backed up by the US 2d Division, X Corps Artillery, and additional armor. Part of the marine division would then stage through Ganseong, where they would mount out aboard the amphibious ships of TF 90 and then land 28 miles to the north

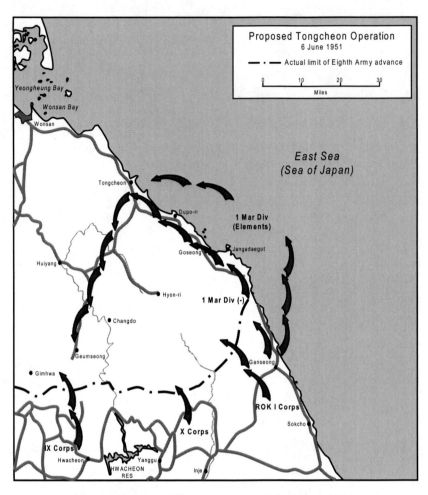

Map 47. Proposed Tongcheon operation, 6 June 1951.

in a shore-to-shore operation at Tongcheon. The rest of the division would move up the coast road. The entire division would then attack to the south-west along the Tongcheon–Gimhwa (Kumhwa) road while the IX Corps, reinforced with the US 2d and ROK 9th Divisions and the 187th Airborne RCT, was to attack from Hwacheon northeast toward Gimhwa. IX Corps and the marines would trap the retreating enemy forces between them and they would then be destroyed by the advancing X Corps.[98]

On 28 May General Almond met with Lieutenant General Lemuel C. Shepherd (Commanding General of the Fleet Marine Force, Pacific), Major General Gerald C. Thomas (who had replaced Oliver P. Smith as command-ing general of the 1st Marine Division on 24 April), and Major General

Clark L. Ruffner (commanding general of the 2d Division). Thomas was enthusiastic about the marines carrying out the kind of amphibious operation for which they were trained.[99] That same day, Ridgway met with Van Fleet at the Eighth Army Tactical Command Post at Pyeongtaek to discuss the next steps, including Van Fleet's proposed amphibious operation. To Van Fleet's disappointment, Ridgway raised objections to the plan.

Ridgway pointed out that since the UN forces were extremely dispersed and the enemy still had an offensive capability, removing the Marine division from the front line would be dangerous. Furthermore, JCS approval would be required for any operation beyond the approved objective line (known as the KANSAS–WYOMING Line). Ridgway saw small rewards to be gained even if the operation was successful and noted the impossibility of clearing all of Korea of enemy forces and the necessity of securing a line that Eighth Army could hold. He reminded Van Fleet of the mission requirement to "effect maximum destruction of the enemy with minimum casualties to our own forces," and the desirability of advancing to, but not beyond, the KANSAS–WYOMING Line.[100]

Ridgway also argued that he could not support the proposed operation from Japan, to which Van Fleet replied that the Chinese Army had been "completely defeated" and that Eighth Army was in the pursuit and so its ammunition requirements would be less than in a deliberate attack.[101] Ridgway was not persuaded. Years later he noted that had the operation taken place, the marines would have been isolated by the mountain spine inland of Tongcheon. "It could have had, again, the makings of the same damn situation that MacArthur had blundered into . . . when he separated the X Corps. So I would have none of it. I thought he would get heavy casualties out of it with little return."[102]

Van Fleet remained convinced that the Chinese Army was so weakened that an amphibious turning movement and push to the north would have been successful and would have put the UNC in a good position for the armistice negotiations that would soon begin. However, the Chinese resistance to the UNC offensive had stiffened by the end of May and, in the central sector, Eighth Army was unable to capture the key logistics and transportation area encompassed by the towns of Cheorwon, Gimhwa, and Pyeonggang known as the "Iron Triangle." Historian Roy E. Appleman, after analyzing the intelligence assessments of the Chinese and North Korean capabilities, concluded that Van Fleet's and Almond's views on the state of enemy forces and the likelihood of success of an amphibious operation in the Wonsan area "were unrealistic and euphoric" and that "General Ridgway's more cautious views were in order." Nonetheless, with the amphibious and other naval assets then available, the Chinese forces in the process of withdrawing, and the enemy coastal defenses not yet consolidated, Van Fleet's arguments for an amphibious operation remain persuasive.[103]

Amphibious Training, May–August 1951

Although Ridgway rejected Van Fleet's proposals for amphibious operations, he recognized the potential value of such operations and as CINCFE continued the reconstitution of an amphibious capability begun by General MacArthur the previous March. From 20 to 28 May, all of the available units of TF 90 began an extensive period of amphibious training in Japan in accordance with Combined Task Force (CTF) 90 Operation Order (OPORD) No. 6-51. The training included landing exercises at Chigasaki Beach in Sagami Bay on 26–27 May. No US Marine or Army units participated in this Navy training, although the British 41st Independent Commando Royal Marines made a landing before dawn on the morning of the 26 May as part of this training.[104]

That same month, Ridgway directed XVI Corps to begin amphibious training at the RCT-level using specialist instructor teams from the Naval Amphibious Training Center at Camp McGill. The 40th Division was scheduled to receive amphibious training from 10 June to 10 September 1951 and the RCTs of the 45th Division would receive their training from September to November. At this time there were no Army amphibious units in Japan. The 56th ATTB was still configured as a light tank unit attached to the 34th RCT for Kanto Plain defense and the 2d ESB could not yet be spared from their duties in Korea.[105]

The goal was for elements of XVI Corps to be combat ready and capable of participating in amphibious operations by 1 September. Preliminary moves toward truce talks had begun in June and Ridgway considered an offensive to keep up the pressure on the Chinese and North Koreans and to establish a suitable defensible front line to serve as a basis for a cease-fire line. On 19 June he directed Van Fleet and the other Service component commanders to prepare an operation plan and "to include an estimate of the feasibility of and requirements for an advance north of the KANSAS–WYOMING Line." The scheme of maneuver was to be a main effort toward Wonsan with the left flank anchored on the Yeseong River and an advance toward Pyeongyang—with the objective of establishing a defensive zone along the line running from Pyeongyang in the west to Wonsan in the east. Ridgway anticipated that, if negotiations were to take place, a demilitarized zone might be established "on the basis of the position of the opposing ground units in combat at the time" of the negotiations. The

PYEONGYANG–WONSAN Line would be an advantageous truce line. Ridgway noted, "The plan should examine the desirability of conducting an amphibious operation in the WONSAN area."[106]

Two RCTs of the 40th Division were scheduled for pre-afloat training at Camp Haugen followed by afloat phases, including landings at Chigasaki and Ohata, in July and August.[107] Amphibious training of the 160th and 223d RCTs of the 40th Infantry Division began on 11 June.[108] From 23 to 27 June the Commander of Transport Division 12 (CTG 90.2) aboard his flagship, the *Calvert* (APA-32), conducted the afloat phase of the training. Troops of the RCTs were embarked at Shiogama, near the Japanese city of Sendai, and landed at Chigasaki Beach.[109]

On 19 June 1951 General Allen visited Camp Younghans to inspect the amphibious training and on 27 June, Allen and Ridgway observed the 223d's amphibious landing at Chigasaki Beach. They expressed satisfaction that the landing was well planned and executed. By the end of June, both RCTs had completed their amphibious training.[110] Amphibious training for other XVI Corps elements at the battalion and regimental level continued in July. The monthly command report noted, "Training was as realistic as possible. Authority was granted to use napalm bombs in the amphibious assaults."[111]

In July XVI Corps requested authority to reorganize the 56th ATTB into a cavalry reconnaissance battalion. The unit had previously been equipped as a light armored unit to supplement the defense of Japan and was currently training as such with emphasis on the battalion in the attack, exploitation and pursuit, delaying actions, and defense, in addition to the mission of reconnoitering the Kanto Plain. CINCFE disapproved the request, because he wished to expand the XVI Corps amphibious capability and was about to direct that the 56th ATTB be reorganized to perform its original function as an amphibious unit.[112]

By August 1951 GHQ FEC believed there were enough transportation corps units in Korea that the 2d ESB, which had been operating the port of Incheon since January, could be returned to Japan "to sharpen its state of readiness to perform its combat mission as an amphibious unit." Ridgway once again asked for Van Fleet's views. Van Fleet said that in September his command would make a detailed study of the port operation requirements and assess whether there was a continuing need for the 2d ESB.[113]

Special Operations, June–August 1951

By June 1951 preliminary moves toward truce talks led to a slowdown in combat operations. The talks began on 10 July 1951, bringing a lull in the war of movement that had taken place during the first 6 months of 1951. However, the siege of Wonsan, partisan operations along the coasts, amphibious raids, intelligence collection missions, and naval bombardments of KPA positions continued.

During this time, the fast transport *Begor* (APD-127) ranged along the northeast coast of Korea, putting South Korean intelligence agents and guerrillas ashore. One of the largest of these clandestine operations took place on the night of 2/3 June, when UDT-3 guided 235 ROK guerrillas to shore on Songdo Island, near Gojeo south of Wonsan (see map 48). That same night an ROK intelligence team was evacuated from the vicinity of Goseong under cover of fire by an ROK Navy submarine chaser and the US destroyer *Rush*. Four days later, the destroyer *Rupertus* (DD-851) put a raiding party ashore at Seongjin. The sailors captured three prisoners and, after coming under small arms fire, returned to the ship without casualties.[114]

In May 1951 Eighth Army revised its organization for partisan operations. Since the beginning of the program in January, these operations had been conducted under the direction of the Attrition Section of the Eighth United States Army in Korea (EUSAK) G3 Miscellaneous Division. This had created the anomaly of a staff section engaging in operations. Accordingly, on 15 May Eighth Army deactivated the Attrition Section and reactivated it as the 8086th AU, Miscellaneous Group.[115] The partisans operating from TF *Leopard* base on the west coast continued their operations during this period and the east coast partisans of TF *Kirkland* were called on in early June to conduct an operation behind the lines in support of the ROK I Corps' final drive to LINE KANSAS. The beginning of the truce talks in July had an impact on partisan operations, however. The prospect of a major Eighth Army offensive faded and the static military situation meant that the partisans could not be used in the optimum fashion, to support conventional military operations as a behind-the-lines auxiliary force. As pressure on the front line eased, North Korean and Chinese forces were freed for increased security measures. The morale of the partisans, who were fighting for a united non-Communist Korea, was also affected by the realization that the liberation of the north was increasingly unlikely. Nonetheless, the west coast partisans continued to carry out their operations, while, with few sources of recruitment, an ever-diminishing TF *Kirkland* force spent the rest of the war on the east coast conducting occasional raids and intelligence collection.[116]

Operations against Wonsan and the surrounding area were stepped up in the summer of 1951. Since the KMC 42d Company had established

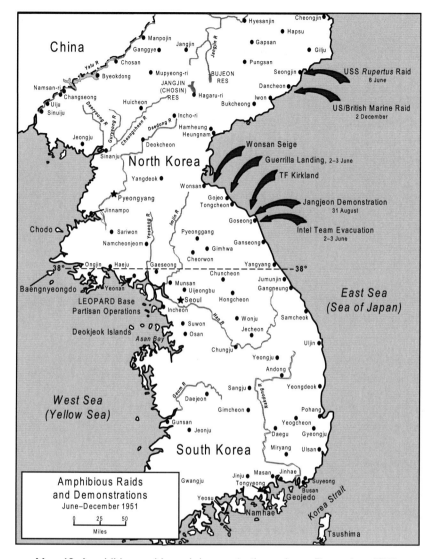

Map 48. Amphibious raids and demonstrations, June–December 1951.

itself on the islands off Wonsan in February and March, a number of intelligence and special operations organizations had begun operating there. On 1 July an advance party of Lieutenant Colonel Douglas B. Drysdale's 41st Independent Commando Royal Marines, accompanied by a Marine Shore Fire Control Party (SFCP), left Camp McGill to establish a base on Yodo, the largest of the islands. The Royal Marines conducted some local small-scale raids before beginning operations along the northeast coast.[117]

Also in July, the UNC established a Senior Military Liaison Office on Yodo to control the various military ground units operating in the Wonsan area, to "supervise ROK Marine garrisons on the islands, and furnish liaison and central authority through which the naval commander in the area would be fully informed." However, the liaison office exercised no control over the multifarious intelligence collections activities of the various groups operating in the Wonsan area.[118]

Amphibious Planning and Training, August–November 1951

On 23 August the North Korean People's Army (KPA)/Chinese People's Volunteers (CPV) side broke off the truce negotiations. With the talks stalled, Eighth Army resumed limited objective attacks to keep pressure on the Communists and to seize terrain to improve its defensive position. In the west, Eighth Army made gains of about 4 miles along the front from the west coast to Cheorwon. Heavy fighting took place in the eastern sector near a terrain feature called the Punchbowl in rugged terrain that came to be known as Heartbreak Ridge and Bloody Ridge.[119] (See map 49.)

Along the east coast, the ROK I Corps pushed north to the outskirts of Goseong. To support this attack, General Ridgway ordered Admiral Joy to conduct a large-scale amphibious demonstration in the vicinity of Jangjeon (Changjon) north of Goseong. On 27 August a minesweeping group and the dock landing ship *Whetstone* moved into the presumed beachhead area. A gunfire support group consisting of the heavy cruiser *Helena*, three destroyers, and an LMS(R) rocket-firing ship followed them. The battleship *New Jersey,* escorted by a destroyer, arrived on 30 August, and on that day the surface ships began bombarding the beach and surrounding area. The bombardment continued through 31 August, when carrier aircraft saturated the beach with rockets and an amphibious transport group moved in. Landing craft were lowered into the water, formed into waves, and churned toward the beach. Then they turned away, returned to the transports, and were recovered. The *New Jersey* and its consorts fired a final bombardment and steamed off, the demonstration complete. It is not clear whether the operation succeeded in persuading the North Koreans to hold forces in the Jangjeon area rather than sending them to reinforce the front line.[120]

The Eighth Army attacks continued into September. While they were taking place, General Van Fleet proposed an operation called TALONS through which he intended to straighten the line along the Eighth Army eastern front by capturing terrain from 1 to 15 miles to the north of

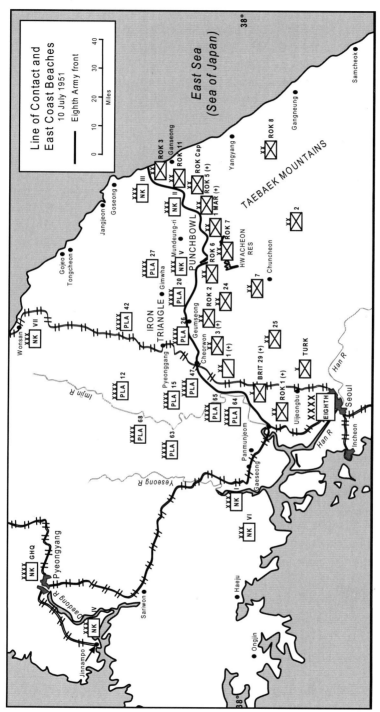

Map 49. Line of contact and east coast beaches, 10 July 1951.

the existing front. However, the heavy casualties incurred during the Heartbreak and Bloody Ridge battles caused Van Fleet to conclude that the casualties would be prohibitive and on 7 September he informed General Ridgway that he was canceling the operation.[121] Ridgway had reached similar conclusions after analyzing casualty projections. He confided to his diary on 5 September, "My feeling is that this estimate of casualties [much more than 4,000] if reasonably correct would substantially exceed the figure which this operation, even if successful, would justify."[122]

Van Fleet was still looking for ways to push forward to a line that would put Eighth Army in a better position to deal with future enemy offensives and improve the UNC's negotiating position when the truce talks resumed. On 17 September he attended a conference called by General Ridgway, who asked for Van Fleet's plans if the enemy "exercised his maximum offensive capability." Van Fleet said that his scheme of maneuver would be to reel with the punch, stop it on or in front of LINE KANSAS, and then launch a counteroffensive. He then described his ideas for operations in October: a limited offensive in the western, west-central, and central sectors in preparation for a larger offensive operation in late October that would include an amphibious operation near Gojeo.[123]

Van Fleet and his staff had drawn up plans for these operations soon after the Punchbowl operations had begun in September. The first phase, CUDGEL, would be a 15-mile drive north of Cheorwon and Gimhwa to force the enemy out of his forward positions and protect the Cheorwon–Gimhwa railroad. The railroad would then be used to provide logistic support to the next phase of the plan, dubbed WRANGLER. This attack in the east was intended to cut off the North Korean forces opposing the US X Corps and ROK I Corps on the Eighth Army right flank and would include an amphibious operation by the 1st Marine Division to establish a beachhead in the Gojeo–Tongcheon area. An ROK division would then follow the marines ashore. An attack to the northeast from Gimhwa by IX Corps would link up with the amphibious force. This was very similar to Van Fleet's May proposal, and while Ridgway approved continuing limited objective attacks as opportunities arose, he would only approve the amphibious operation for planning purposes.[124]

Nonetheless, Ridgway notified the JCS that he was considering the option of an amphibious assault in the Wonsan area with one division in the assault and another in follow-up. The objective would be to seize Wonsan and a lodgment area covering the port in preparation for a rapid advance to the west or southwest to link up with forces launching a major overland attack from the south. An alternative under consideration was

Van Fleet's proposal for an amphibious landing in the area of Tongcheon rather than Wonsan. Another option was a general offensive by Eighth Army, either acting in combination with one of the amphibious assaults or independently, to inflict heavy losses on the enemy and to seize and hold a line along good defensible terrain.[125]

A month later, in October 1951, the JCS responded that they had considered the plan for an amphibious assault and had doubts "as to its feasibility or advantages." If Ridgway still had the plan in mind, they asked him to submit details for JCS consideration.[126] In fact, Van Fleet himself had concluded that the plan was too risky and had submitted an alternative to Ridgway for a more modest 6-mile advance to a new defense line called JAMESTOWN. On 24 October Ridgway advised the JCS that he had decided against the plans for amphibious assaults or an Eighth Army general offensive. The next day, the truce talks resumed.[127]

Even as the negotiators renewed their talks, Van Fleet was still planning offensive operations, including a push north of the Cheorwon–Gimhwa railroad followed by a IX Corps attack to the northeast toward Tongcheon (see map 50). There would be no amphibious assault, but ROK I Corps would strike north along the coastal road to link up with IX Corps at Tongcheon. On 31 October Ridgway told Van Fleet to postpone the operation. The truce talks were making progress toward agreement on a truce line—the Military Demarcation Line (MDL). Ridgway was concerned that the agreed-on MDL might run south of Tongcheon and he did not want to incur casualties to seize territory that would then have to be given up. He was prepared, nevertheless, to resume the offensive if the talks broke down again, and planning continued for major operations that would take Eighth Army to the PYEONGYANG–WONSAN Line, or even north to the Yalu River.[128]

However, agreement on the MDL caused all these plans to be shelved. On 12 November 1951 Ridgway directed Van Fleet to assume the "active defense" and on 27 November the two sides agreed to an MDL running approximately along the line of ground contact. Although subsequent fighting required some minor adjustments, the line remained substantially unchanged until the armistice was signed.[129] The war of movement in Korea was over. Although there would still be 1½ years of conflict, they would be, in the words of one Army historian, "Years of Stalemate."[130]

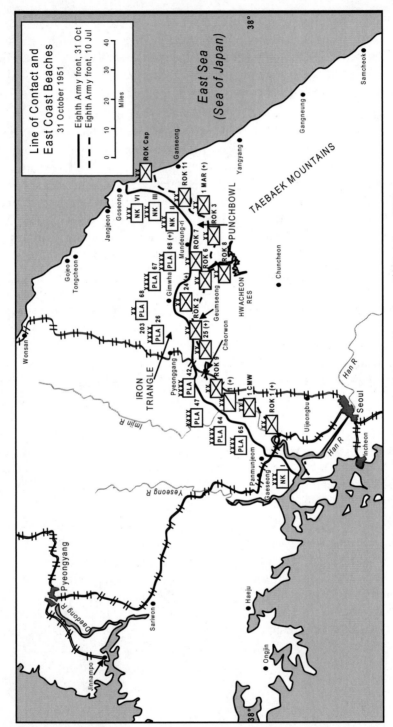

Map 50. Line of contact and east coast beaches, 31 October 1951.

Notes

1.	*History of the Korean War, Chronology 25 June 1950–31 December 1951* (Tokyo: Military History Section, Far East Command, 1952), 88, hereafter, *Korean War Chronology.* A concise account of Ridgway's assumption of command, the Chinese offensive, and the Eighth Army defense is in Richard W. Stewart, *The Korean War: The Chinese Intervention, 3 November 1950–24 January 1951,* CMH Pub 19-8 (Washington, DC: Center of Military History, 2000), 27–33; more detailed accounts are in Billy C. Mossman, *United States Army in the Korean War: Ebb and Flow, November 1950–July 1951* (Washington, DC: Office of the Chief of Military History, 1990), 177–227; and Roy E. Appleman, *Ridgway Duels for Korea* (College Station, TX: Texas A&M University Press, 1990), 3–115.

2.	*Korean War Chronology,* 87; Stewart, *The Chinese Intervention,* 28–29.

3.	James A. Field Jr., *History of United States Naval Operations, Korea* (Washington, DC: GPO, 1962), 314.

4.	CG Eighth Army Message, GX 1-236 KG00, to CG X, IX, and I Corps, 4 January 1951 (confirming "1/3/51 Verbal"), copy in Blair Collection, Box 68, "Forgotten War, Units, High-level Correspondence," MHI Archives; *Korean War Chronology,* 89.

5.	Field, *Naval Operations, Korea,* 308, 311–312.

6.	See map 35 for the location of the Deokjeok Islands.

7.	US Army, 8206th Army Unit, Amphibious Training Center, *Unit History* [1951?], hereafter, ATC History, 17–18.

8.	Mossman, *Ebb and Flow, November 1950–July 1951,* 210–212; Headquarters, Eighth US Army in Korea (EUSAK), *Logistical Problems and Their Solutions: Monograph,* compiled by personnel of the Historical Section, EUSAK and the Eighth Army Historical Service Detachment (Prov) (Seoul: Headquarters, Eighth US Army, Korea (EUSAK)) [1950–52?], 95; US Far East Command, *Command Report.* Separate volumes by month, November 1950–July 1953 (Tokyo: GHQ Far East Command, Military Intelligence Section), January 1951, 1 and 14; Field, *Naval Operations, Korea,* 312.

9.	Field, *Naval Operations, Korea,* 312.

10.	Field, *Naval Operations, Korea,* 313–314. A check sweep is a mine-sweeping operation in which the minesweeping craft tow a wire through an area previously swept, or believed not to have been mined, to verify that no mines are present. For the location of Daecheon and Cheonsu Bay, see map 37.

11.	JCS Message, JCS 80902, Personal for MacArthur, 12 January 1951, RG 218, Entry UD 48 Chairman's File—General Bradley, 1949–1953; Messages relating to Operations in the Far East, 1950–1953, Box 9: Outgoing Messages ("Declassified") 25 June 1950–29 January 1952, Folder 3, "JCS—Declassified Outgoing Dispatches—1/3/51—5/31/51," National Archives and Records Administration, Modern Military Records, College Park, MD, hereafter, NACP.

12.	Field, *Naval Operations, Korea,* 318.

13. FEC, *Command Report*, January 1951, 1.

14. CINCFE Message CX 64845, to Department of the Army, 130423Z June 1951, copy in Blair Collection, Box 68, "Forgotten War, Units, High-Level Correspondence," MHI Archives.

15. See, for example, a State Department "Outline for Discussion with JCS," 9 January 1951, which set forth the case for an evacuation of the ROK Government and military forces to Cheju-do and the conduct of guerrilla, commando, and covert operations by ROK forces and agents, but does not mention the idea of using Cheju-do as a base for an amphibious return to Korea. Nor is such an option addressed in the JCS documents. RG 218, CCS 383.21 Korea (3–19–45) Sec 42, Correspondence from 12–28–50 through 1–23–51, NACP.

16. 1st Marine Division, *Historical Diary for January 1951*, 1 May 1951, Marine Corps University Archives (MCUA), 5–6.

17. Lynn Montross, Hubard D. Kuokka, and Norman W. Wicks, *U.S. Marine Operations in Korea, 1950–1953, Vol. IV, The East-Central Front* (Washington, DC: Headquarters, US Marine Corps, Historical Branch, G3, 1962), 44–45.

18. FEC, *Command Report*, January 1951, 53.

19. FEC, *Command Report,* February 1951, 47; Company A, 56th Amphibious Tank and Tractor Battalion, "Diary Report of "A" Company, 56th Amphibious Tank and Tractor Battalion," *Command Report Narrative Summary, 1–31 January 1951*, RG 407, Entry 429, Box 4826, NACP.

20. Field, *Naval Operations, Korea,* 318–319.

21. This description of the 2d ESB activities is based on Headquarters, 2d Engineer Special Brigade, *Command Report (1 January to 31 January 1951)*, RG 407, Entry 429, Box 5110, NACP.

22. Headquarters, 2d ESB, *Command Report (1 February to 28 February 1951)*, RG 407, Entry 429, Box 5110, NACP, hereafter, 2ESB Command Report.

23. ATC History, 18–21.

24. US Army Forces Far East, *UN Partisan Forces in the Korean Conflict, 1951–52: A Study of Their Characteristics and Operations*, Project MHD-3 (Seoul: 8086th Army Unit [USAFFE Military History Detachment], 1954), hereafter, *Partisan Forces*, 5–6, 71.

25. FEC, *Command Report*, January 1951, 15.

26. *Partisan Forces*, 71.

27. Rod Paschall, "Special Operations in Korea," *Conflict,* Vol. 155, No. 2 (November 1987): 158.

28. Frederick W. Cleaver et al., *UN Partisan Warfare in Korea, 1951–1954*, ORO T-64 AFFE (Baltimore, MD: Johns Hopkins University Operations Research Office, June 1956), hereafter, *UN Partisan Warfare*, 31–32; Ben S. Malcom with Ron Martz, *White Tigers: My Secret War in North Korea* (Washington, DC: Brassey's, 1996), 141–142; Ed Evanhoe, *Dark Moon: Eighth Army Special Operations in the Korean War* (Annapolis, MD: Naval Institute Press, 1995), 72–77; Field, *Naval Operations, Korea,* 422.

29. *UN Partisan Warfare*, 31, 32, 39. The origin of the name "Donkey" for the partisan teams is unclear and is variously attributed to the heavy backpack

loads carried by the partisans and by the posture of a person cranking a portable radio.

30. These operations are described in *Partisan Forces* and *UN Partisan Warfare*. Colonel Ben S. Malcom, USA (Retired), who served as an advisor to one of these partisan bands, provides a first-person account in Malcom with Martz, *White Tigers*. Another useful account is provided by Evanhoe, *Dark Moon*, 36–46.

31. *Korean War Chronology*, 92.

32. A concise account of the first UNC counteroffensive in 1951 is in John J. McGrath, *The Korean War: Restoring the Balance, 25 January–8 July 1951*, CMH Publication 19-9 (Washington, DC: Center of Military History, 2001), 5–9. More detailed accounts are in Mossman, *Ebb and Flow, November 1950–July 1951*, 228–265, and Appleman, *Ridgway Duels for Korea*, 3–115.

33. Letter, Commanding General Eighth United States Army (EUSAK) to Commander in Chief, Far East Command, 3 February 1951, copy in Blair Collection, Box 68, "Forgotten War, Units, High-level Correspondence," MHI.

34. Ltr, CG, EUSAK, to CINCFE, 3 February 1951, copy in Blair Collection.

35. CINCFE Message C-54811, to CG Eighth Army, 4 February 1951, copy in Blair Collection, Box 68, MHI.

36. FEC, *Command Report*, January 1951, 4. In message of 2 March 1951, General Ridgway again noted these enemy fears of amphibious assaults in his rear areas and the value of deception operations to play on this fear and fix enemy reserves. He suggested that the deployment of the 40th and 45th Divisions to the Far East could serve as the basis for a deception operation. CG Eighth Army Message to CINCFE, G 3-245 KGOP (65281), 2 Mar 51, copy in Blair Collection, Box 68, "Forgotten War, Units, High-Level Correspondence."

37. Field, *Naval Operations, Korea*, 326; FEC, *Command Report*, February 1951, 16.

38. Field, *Naval Operations, Korea*, 323–324; James F. Schnabel, *United States Army in the Korean War, Policy and Direction: The First Year* (Washington, DC: GPO, 1972; reprinted 1992), 336; Malcolm W. Cagle and Frank A. Manson. *Sea War in Korea* (Annapolis, MD: Naval Institute Press, 1957), 305; FEC, *Command Report*, January 1951, 15–16, citing COMNAVFE Msg to COM7th Flt and CTF 95, 28 Jan 51 (G-3 TS "I" No. 1708).

39. CG Eighth Army Message, GX-2-1049-KGCO (48592), to COMNAVFE, 10 February 1951, copy in Blair Collection, Box 68, "Forgotten War, Units, High-Level Correspondence," MHI.

40. Korean Institute of Military History, *The Korean* War, *Vol. 2* (Lincoln and London: University of Nebraska Press, 2000), 572–573; Field, *Naval Operations, Korea*, 326–327; FEC, *Command Report*, February 1951, 17.

41. 2ESB Command Report, February 1951, 7.

42. 2ESB Command Report, February 1951, 7–8; FEC, *Command Report*, February 1951, 17.

43. 2ESB Command Report, February 1951, 8–9; Field, *Naval Operations, Korea*, 326.

44.   Appleman, *Ridgway Duels for Korea*, 327, 341, 343.

45.   Field, *Naval Operations, Korea,* 330; *Dictionary of American Naval Fighting Ships,* hereinafter *DANFS, Bataan I,* history.navy.mil/danfs/b3/bataan-i. htm (accessed 26 January 2007).

46.   Evanhoe, *Dark Moon,* 63–66.

47.   Korean Institute of Military History, *The Korean War, Vol. 2,* 574–575.

48.   *UN Partisan Warfare,* 31–34.

49.   *UN Partisan Warfare,* 31–34.; Evanhoe, *Dark Moon,* 72–84 (Evanhoe was an advisor to TF *Kirkland* during the war); Michael E. Haas, *In the Devil's Shadow: U.N. Special Operations During the Korean War* (Annapolis, MD: Naval Institute Press, 2000), 49–51.

50.   Fred Hayhurst, *Green Berets in Korea: The Story of 41 Independent Commando Royal Marines* (Cambridge, MA: Vanguard, 2001), 264–278; Field, *Naval Operations, Korea,* 339–340; Cagle and Manson, *Sea War in Korea,* 305–306; FEC, *Command Report* April 1951, 53; Navy Historical Center, *Korean War: Chronology of U.S. Pacific Fleet Operations, January–June 1951,* www.history. navy.mil/wars/korea/chron51a.htm#apr (accessed 13 December 2006); Eighth Army *Command Report,* G3 Section Report, April 1951; *DANFS, Fort Marion,* history.navy.mil/danfs/f4/fort_marion.htm (accessed 12 October 2006); *DANFS, Begor,* history.navy.mil/danfs/b4/begor-i.htm (accessed 12 October 2006).

51.   Operations KILLER and RIPPER are described briefly in McGrath, *Restoring the Balance,* 9–16. More detailed accounts are in Mossman, *Ebb and Flow, November 1950–July 1951,* 301–350; and Appleman, *Ridgway Duels for Korea,* 307–314 and 334–403. For the decision to cross the 38th Parallel, see Mossman, *Ebb and Flow, November 1950–July 1951,* 344–347; and Appleman, *Ridgeway Duels for Korea,* 409–410. The objectives of the follow-on RUGGED and DAUNTLESS operations are described in Eighth Army Command Report, April 1951, RG 407, Entry 429, Box 1179, NACP.

52.   McGrath, *Restoring the Balance,* 16–17.

53.   Mossman, *Ebb and Flow, November 1950–July 1951,* 353. During World War II, General Hoge had commanded the Provisional Engineer Special Brigade Group that had been responsible for amphibious shore party operations at Normandy (Hoge biography at MHI).

54.   Delbert M. Fowler, "Operations at the Hwachon Dam, Korea," *Military Engineer,* Vol. XLIV, No. 297 (January–February 1952): 7–8. The Hwacheon Dam spillway was formed by the slanting concrete north face of the dam. The sluice gates could be opened to varying degrees to allow controlled release of water over the top of the spillway.

55.   CG Eighth Army Message to Eighth Army Engineer, 280815I February 1951; Eighth Army Engineer Message 7285 to CG Eighth Army, 281450I February 1951, in *Matthew B. Ridgway Papers,* Series 3, Official Papers, Eighth US Army, Special Files, December 1950–April 1951, Box 68, MHI Archives.

56.   "Engineer Study of Hwachon Reservoir and Dam," Annex 1 to IX Corps Periodic Intelligence Report (PIR) 190, 4 April 1951, copy in Eighth US Army Korea, Command Report, 1951, Section IV: After-Action Interviews, Book 3:

Hwachon Dam, interviews by First Lieutenant Martin Blumenson, 3d Historical Detachment, Military History Section, Eighth United States Army Korea (EUSAK), 1951, hereafter *Hwachon Dam Interviews* (a copy of this document is at the Center of Military History); Summary of IX Corps Engineer Report in IX Corps Command Report, 4 April 1951, Box 1797, RG 407, Entry 429, NACP; Fowler, "Operations at the Hwachon Dam, Korea," 7–8. A penstock is a pipe or channel that diverts water to a turbine or around the spillway of a dam. A treadway bridge is a bridge with the travel surface consisting of one track (for a pedestrian bridge) or two tracks (for a vehicular bridge), instead of a complete roadway.

57. Interview with General Hoge, 15 April 1951, in *Hwachon Dam Interviews.*

58. Hoge interview. The following account of the Hwacheon Dam operation is based on the *Hwachon Dam Interviews* and command reports/war diaries of the participating units. The operation is also described in Mossman, *Ebb and Flow, November 1950–July 1951,* 354–362; Appleman, *Ridgway Duels for Korea,* 422–426; Robert W. Black, *Rangers in Korea* (New York, NY: Ballantine Books, 1989), 121–130; and Melbourne C. Chandler, *Of GarryOwen in Glory: The History of the Seventh United States Cavalry Regiment* (Annandale, VA: The Turnpike Press, 1960), 320.

59. 7th Cavalry War Diary, 7 April 1951, Box 4508, RG 407, Entry 419, NACP; Interview with Colonel William Harris, Commanding Officer, 7th Cavalry Regiment, 18 April 1951, in *Hwachon Dam Interviews.* Harris had commanded the 77th Field Artillery Battalion at the time of the BLUEHEARTS operation at Pohang in July 1950 and commanded the 7th Cavalry during the Amphibious Training Center's Yeseong River resupply operation.

60. In interviews conducted soon after the operation, the 7th Cavalry operations officer described the movement of the 2/7th Cavalry on 8 April as a move from their reserve position to a location from where they would be prepared to conduct the attack on the dam, but the battalion operations journal describes the day's activities as a movement to contact. Interview with Major James H. Webel, S3, 7th Cavalry Regiment, in *Hwachon Dam Interviews*; 7th Cavalry War Diary, S2 Journal Summary, 7 April 1951; 2d Battalion, 7th Cavalry War Diary, S3 Journal, 7–8 April 1951, both in Box 4508, RG 407, Entry 429, NACP.

61. Interview with Captain Dorsey B. Anderson, Commanding Officer, 4th Ranger Infantry Company (Airborne), 13 April 1951, in *Hwachon Dam Interviews.*

62. Harris interview, and interview with Captain Arnold Frank, Commanding Officer, IX Corps Engineer Technical Intelligence Team, 15 April 1951, in *Hwachon Dam Interviews*; Eighth Army Command Report, 9 April 1951; War Diary, Office of the Commanding General Eighth Army, 9 April 1951, Box 1180; IX Corps Command Report, G3 Section Report, 9 April 1951, Box 1797, all in RG 407, Entry 429, NACP. See also, Fowler, "Operations at the Hwachon Dam, Korea," 8; Mossman, *Ebb and Flow, November 1950–July 1951,* 358.

63. IX Corps PIR #195, 9 April 1951, copy in *Hwachon Dam Interviews*; War Diary, Office of the Commanding General Eighth Army, 9 April 1951; Eighth

Army Command Report, 9 April 1951; 8th Cavalry Regiment Command Report, April 1951, Box 4517; IX Corps Engineer Section Command Report, 9 April 1951, Box 1798, all in RG 407, Entry 429, NACP. It is not clear whether it was IX Corps, the 1st Cavalry Division, or Colonel Harris who bestowed the TF *Callaway* designation.

64. Anderson interview, in *Hwachon Dam Interviews*.

65. This account of the 9 April combat is based on an interview with Lieutenant Colonel John W. Callaway, Commanding Officer, 2d Battalion, 7th Cavalry, in *Hwachon Dam Interviews;* 2d Battalion, 7th Cavalry War Diary, 9 April 1951; and GHQ FEC Daily Intelligence Summary No. 3135, 10 April 1951, Box 433, RG 407, Entry 429, NACP.

66. 7th Cavalry War Diary, 11 April 1951; Harris and Anderson interviews, and interview with Major Russell J. Wilson, Commanding Officer, 8th Engineer Combat Battalion, 18 April 1951, in *Hwachon Dam Interviews*.

67. Callaway interview in *Hwachon Dam Interviews*. There is some inconsistency among the accounts regarding the availability of assault boats. The 7th Cavalry S3, Major James H. Webel, says that "Despite the effort to bring the boats forward, . . . the 2d Battalion Commanding Officer preferred to advance by land." However, Colonel Harris says that if boats had been available on the 10th, he would have directed the Rangers to conduct the amphibious operation on that date. Captain Anderson, the Ranger company commander, says he presented his amphibious alternative to Callaway's scheme of maneuver but does not say why Callaway chose to continue the overland attack. Major Wilson, the 8th Engineer Battalion commander, says that efforts to get the boats began on the evening of 10 April. Webel, Harris, Anderson, and Wilson interviews. The weight of the evidence indicates that the boats did not arrive in time for the 10 April attack. Although river crossing would seem to be the more accurate term, amphibious is the word used in all of the command reports and interviews, both for the anticipated river crossing and the crossing of the reservoir.

68. Callaway interview; 7th Cavalry War Diary, S2 Journal Summary, 10 April 1951; 2/7th Cavalry War Diary, 10 April 1951; GHQ FEC Daily Intelligence Summary No. 3136, 11 April 1951.

69. 8th Cavalry War Diary, 10 April 1951; Hoge interview; IX Corps Command Report, Chief of Staff Daily Journal Summary, 10 April 1951, Box 1797, RG 407, Entry 429, NACP; "take the dam": 2/7th Cavalry War Diary, 10 April 1951.

70. IX Corps Periodic Operations Report (POR) #579, 10 April 1951; interview with Lieutenant Colonel John Carlson, G3, 1st Cavalry Division, both in *Hwachon Dam Interviews*.

71. Harris and Webel interviews ("contain and pin down": Harris interview); Addendum 1 to 7th Cavalry OPORD No. 11-51, 10 April 1951, copy in *Hwachon Dam Interviews*.

72. Anderson interview, and interview with First Lieutenant John S. Warren, Executive Officer, 4th Ranger Infantry Company (Airborne), 13 April 1951, in *Hwachon Dam Interviews*.

73. Webel interview, and interview with Lieutenant Colonel Thomas M Magness Jr., Chemical Officer, IX Corps, 3 May 1951, in *Hwachon Dam Interviews*. Magness was not informed of the request until the afternoon of 11 April. He claimed that had he been informed of the requirement earlier, the smoke pots and generators could have been sent forward in time to support the operation.

74. Interviews with Major Paul Gray, S3, and Captain William W Cover, Assistant S3, IX Corps Artillery, in *Hwachon Dam Interviews*.

75. Weber and Warren interviews, and interview with Major Dayton F. Caple, Assistant G4, 1st Cavalry Division; and Major Russell J. Wilson, Commanding Officer, 8th Engineer Combat Battalion, 18 April 1951, in *Hwachon Dam Interviews*. Eventually, 35 boats and 20 motors were obtained to support the operation, with an additional 21 boats arriving at Chuncheon the evening of 11 April. The plywood M2 assault boat was 13 feet long, weighed 410 pounds, and could carry 12 troops plus two boat operators. On this operation, see also 7th Cavalry War Diary, 10–11 April 1951; Mossman, *Ebb and Flow, November 1950–July 1951*, 360; Black, *Rangers in Korea*, 124–125; Chandler, *Of Garry Owen in Glory*, 320.

76. Anderson interview, in *Hwachon Dam Interviews*.

77. Anderson and Wilson interviews, and interviews with First Lieutenant James L. Johnson, Platoon Leader, 1st Platoon, 4th Ranger Infantry Company (Airborne); 13 April 1951; and Master Sergeant Donald G. Laverty, Platoon Sergeant, 1st Platoon, 4th Ranger Company, 14 April 1951, in *Hwachon Dam Interviews*.

78. Harris and Anderson interviews, and interviews with Lieutenant Colonel Hallden, Captain Teague, and Captain Kennedy, 16 April 1951, in *Hwachon Dam Interviews*.

79. Callaway interview, and interview with Captain John R. Flynn, S3, 2d Battalion, 7th Cavalry, 17 April 1951, in *Hwachon Dam Interviews*. 7th Cavalry War Diary, S2 Journal Summary, 11 April 1951; and the 2/7th Cavalry War Diary, 11 April 1951.

80. Interview with Captain Carl W. Kueffer, S3, 1st Battalion, 7th Cavalry, in *Hwachon Dam Interviews*.

81. Hoge, Harris, Callaway, Anderson, Hallden, and Teague interviews, in *Hwachon Dam Interviews*; FEC Daily Intelligence Summary No. 3137, 12 April 1951, 7–8, Box 433, RG 407, Entry 429, NACP.

82. Eighth Army G3 chalked up the failure of the 7th Cavalry to take the dam on heavy enemy fire and restricted avenues of approach while the Eighth Army Command Report noted that the dam did not really threaten the main supply route and argued that the operation was hindered by the tenacious enemy defense, bad weather and thus little close air support, and insufficient logistic support (April 1951 command reports). Historian Roy Appleman wonders "whether the 7th Cavalry troops on 11 April made their best effort, in view of the fact that they knew the entire division was to go into reserve that night" (*Ridgway Duels for Korea*, 426). In his personal research notes, Appleman scrawled, "This opn. [operation] a mess." (Roy E. Appleman Papers, Box 24, Chronological Files, Folder: 1–13 April 1951, MHI.)

83. Hoge and Anderson interviews, in *Hwachon Dam Interviews.*

84. 2d Infantry Division Command Report, 11, 12, and 16 April 1951, Box 2526; 23d Infantry Command Reports, 12, 13, and 16 April, Box 2696; X Corps Command Report, 12 April 1951, Box 2006, all in RG 407, Record Group 429, NACP; Eighth Army Command Report, 12 April 1951; IX Corps Command Report, G3 Historical Summary, 12 April 1951 and Chief of Staff Daily Journal Summary, 18 April 1951; *Korean War Chronology,* 106–108.

85. Fowler, "Operations at the Hwachon Dam, Korea," 8; *Korean War Chronology,* 107–108, 115. The issue of dams across the Han River resurfaced in 1986, when North Korea began building a new dam across the Bukhan River north of the DMZ. There was great consternation in South Korea that this "Dam of Aggression" was intended to impound water that would later be released to flood Seoul. The ROK Government began building a "Peace Dam" to protect the city and citizens were asked to contribute to the project. The Peace Dam was never completed, but the North Korean dam was completed in 1999, substantially reducing the flow of water in the river to the detriment of South Korea hydroelectric plans. South Korean concerns about flooding were revived in 2002, when cracks began appearing in the North Korean dam. Aiden Foster-Carter, "Pyongyang Watch: The Dam Nuisance," *Asia Times* on line, 16 May 2003, atimes.com/koreas/DE16Dg03.html (accessed 23 March 2007).

86. FEC, *Command Report,* March 1951, 73–74, citing: G3 Sec GHQ FEC/ UNC Staff Sec Rpt Mar 51 (Annex 4).

87. CINCFE Memorandum for Commanding General, GHQ Reserve Corps, 30 April 1951, copy in *Matthew B. Ridgway Papers,* Series 3, Official Papers, CINC Far East 1951–1952, Box 73, MHI.

88. FEC, *Command Report,* April 1951, 2, 35, and 61; *Korean War Chronology,* 102, 104.

89. The combat units of the XVI Corps in the summer of 1951 were the 40th and 45th Infantry Divisions, the 187th Airborne RCT, the 34th Infantry Regiment, the 63d Field Artillery Battalion, and the 56th ATTB. On 24 October 1951, the 50th Signal Battalion (Corps) was activated to serve as the XVI Corps signal battalion. XVI Corps Command Reports, May and October 1951.

90. Eighth Army Command Report, Office of the Commanding General Narrative, 14 April 1951, RG 407, Entry 429, Box 1180, NACP; *Korean War Chronology,* 106–107.

91. CINCFE Memorandum for Commanding General, Eighth Army, 25 April 1951, copy in *Matthew B. Ridgway Papers,* Series 3, Official Papers, CINC Far East 1951–1952, Box 73, MHI.

92. "James A. Van Fleet Oral History," *James A. Van Fleet Papers, 1892– 1973,* Part 2, 48–56, MHI Archive Collection.

93. Cagle and Manson, *Sea War in Korea,* 388. Dyer, who served on Admiral Ernest King's staff in the first years of World War II and was Admiral Richard L. Connolly's chief of staff during Mediterranean amphibious operations, commanded a cruiser during the Philippine amphibious operations and later wrote a biography of Admiral Richmond Kelly Turner that delves deeply into

amphibious operations in the South and Central Pacific in World War II: George C. Dyer, *The Amphibians Came to Conquer: The Story of Admiral Richmond Kelly Turner,* 2 vols. (Washington, DC: GPO, 1972).

94. Clay Blair, *The Forgotten War: America in Korea 1950–1953* (New York, NY: Times Books, 1987, Reprinted, Doubleday Anchor, 1989), 819. Blair cites a Ridgway Memo of 21 April 1951, located in the Special File, Ridgway Papers, Box 20, MHI. This document is now missing. He also cites a retrospective comment by Ridgway in his Oral History, but that comment may refer to a later proposed landing at Tongcheon. Nonetheless, it is clear from his other comments that Ridgway, while recognizing the value of amphibious operations, was also keenly aware of the risks and potential costs.

95. McGrath, *Restoring the Balance,* 18–22; *Korean War Chronology,* 111.

96. Field, *Naval Operations, Korea,* 351; *DANFS, Comstock,* www.history. navy.mil/danfs/c12/comstock.htm (accessed 12 October 2006).

97. X Corps *Command Report, 1 May to 31 May 1951,* 24–25, copy in the *Edward M. Almond Papers,* Box 67 (Korean War: Command Reports X Corps, May to August 1951), MHI Archives.

98. *Eighth Army War Diary,* Command Report G3 Section, May 1951, RG 407, Box 1197, NACP; Mossman, *Ebb and Flow, November 1950–July 1951,* 485–486, citing CG Eighth Army message to CINCFE, GX-5-5099, 28 May 1951.

99. Montross et al., *The East-Central Front,* 132–133; *Personal Notes Covering Activities of Lt. Gen. E.M. Almond During Military Operations in Korea, 31 August 1950–15 July 1951,* entry for 28 May 1951, copy in the *Edward M. Almond Papers,* Box 64 (Personal Notes on the Korea Operation), MHI Archives.

100. FEC, *Command Report,* May 1951, 43; Memorandum for the Record, 31 May 1951, Subject: Conference between General Ridgway and General Van Fleet, copy in *Matthew B. Ridgway Papers,* Box 73 (Series 3, Official Papers, CINC, Far East 1951–1952), Folder: "Memoranda and Communiqués 1950–1952," MHI Archives.

101. Van Fleet Oral History, Part 4, 28.

102. *Interview with General Matthew B. Ridgway by Colonel John M. Blair,* US Army Military History Institute Senior Officer Debriefing Program, Session 3, 86–87, *Matthew B. Ridgway Papers,* Series 5, Oral Histories 1971–1972, Box 89, MHI Archives.

103. Appleman, *Ridgway Duels for Korea,* 552.

104. Naval Historical Center, *Korean War Naval Chronology, May 1951,* history.navy.mil/wars/korea/chron51a.htm (accessed 23 March 2007). For the location of bases in Japan, see map 8.

105. FEC, *Command Report,* May 1951, 30; XVI Corps *Command Report 1–31 May 1951; Korean War Chronology,* 110.

106. GHQ FEC Letter, AG 381 (19 Jun 51) JSPOG, to Commanding General, Eighth Army; Commander, United States Naval Forces, Far East; and Commanding General, Far East Air Forces, 19 June 1951, copy in *Matthew B. Ridgway Papers,* Series 3, Official Papers, CINC Far East 1951–1952, Box 73, MHI.

107. FEC, *Command Report,* June 1951, 34–35.

108. XVI Corps, *Command Report 1–30 June 1951,* 4.

109. *Korean War Naval Chronology, June 1951.*

110. XVI Corps, *Command Report 1–30 June 1951,* 4.

111. FEC, *Command Report,* June 1950, 77.

112. FEC, *Command Report,* July 1951, 53.

113. FEC, *Command Report,* August 1951, 74–75.

114. *Naval Chronology, June 1951;* Field, *Naval Operations, Korea,* 357; Jack Creamons, "The Role of USS BEGOR (APD-127) in Clandestine Operations in North Korea, 1950–51," USS *Begor* (APD-127) Association Web site, ussbegor. org/seaStories49.htm (accessed 10 March 2007).

115. *UN Partisan Warfare,* 36.

116. *UN Partisan Warfare,* 8–9; Evanhoe, *Dark Moon,* 72–84; Haas, *In the Devil's Shadow,* 49–51.

117. Hayhurst, *Green Berets in Korea,* 296–300; Field, *Naval Operations, Korea,* 419.

118. FEC, *Command Report,* July 1951, 56. One of the holders of the Senior Military Liaison Officer position on Yodo later in the war would be Major Robert Debs Heinl, author of *Victory at High Tide.*

119. These operations are described in Andrew J. Birtle, *The Korean War: Years of Stalemate, July 1951–July 1953,* CMH Pub 19-10 (Washington, DC: Center of Military History, 2000), 1–13; and Walter G. Hermes, *United States Army in the Korean War: Truce Tent and Fighting Front* (Washington, DC: Office of the Chief of Military History, 1966), 73–111.

120. FEC, *Command Report,* August 1951, 16; Field, *Naval Operations, Korea,* 414; Hermes, *Truce Tent and Fighting Front,* 109–110.

121. Hermes, *Truce Tent and Fighting Front,* 86.

122. Ridgway Memorandum for Diary, 5 September 1951, item 70, *Matthew B. Ridgway Papers,* "CINCFE Special File," Part 2 of 4, Box 72, MHI Archives.

123. Ridgway Memorandum for Diary, 17 September 1951, item 77, *Matthew B. Ridgway Papers,* "CINCFE Special File," Part 2 of 4, Box 72, MHI Archives.

124. Hermes, *Truce Tent and Fighting Front,* 86–87, 97–98; Cagle and Manson, *Sea War in Korea,* 391.

125. CINCFE Message C 51424 (DA IN 19478), to JCS, 23 Sep 51, RG 218, Entry UD 48 Chairman's File—General Bradley, 1949–53, Messages Relating to Operations in the Far East, 1950–1953, Box 2: Incoming messages, Folder 3: "JCS—Declassified Incoming Messages 9/1/51–9/30/51," NACP.

126. JCS Message 84810, to CINCFE, 23 Oct 51, RG 218, Entry UD 48, Box 9: Outgoing messages ("Declassified") 25 June 1950–29 January 1952, Folder 5: "JCS—Declassified Outgoing Dispatches 8/2/51–10/31/51," NACP.

127. Hermes, *Truce Tent and Fighting Front,* 97–98; CINCFE Message C 55688 (DA IN 10933), 24 October 1951, to Department of the Army for JCS, Blair Collection, Box 68, "Forgotten War, Units, High-Level Correspondence," MHI Archives.

128. Hermes, *Truce Tent and Fighting Front,* 175–176.

129. Donald W. Boose Jr., "The Korean War Truce Talks: A Study in Conflict Termination," *Parameters*, Vol. XXX, No. 1 (Spring 2000): 107–108.

130. Birtle, *The Korean War: Years of Stalemate.*

Chapter 7

Amphibious Planning and Training
during the Stalemate, 1952–53

During the remaining 18 months of the Korean War there were no more significant amphibious operations, although other amphibious-type operations took place. The United Nations Command (UNC) carried out amphibious demonstrations; units near the coast were supplied by over-the-shore logistic operations; US and Republic of Korea (ROK) forces conducted raids, espionage, and intelligence collection missions from the sea; and battles for control of the offshore islands near Wonsan, the Han River estuary, and the northwest coast of Korea erupted from time to time. However, the stabilization of the front line after the November 1951 agreement on the location of the Military Demarcation Line (MDL), American unwillingness to risk heavy casualties, and greatly increased Communist coast defenses were all deterrents to major amphibious assaults. Nevertheless, during this period, the US Army in the Far East raised its amphibious capability to the highest level of the war by returning the 2d Engineer Special Brigade (ESB) and the 56th Amphibious Tank and Tractor Battalion (ATTB) to their original amphibious missions and through a vigorous amphibious training program in Japan. Also during this period, mobilized Reserve units maintained an amphibious capability in the Continental United States (CONUS), and amphibious engineers and transportation watercraft operators continued to demonstrate their versatility in a variety of roles.

Reserve Amphibious Units

Soon after the outbreak of the Korean War and the alert of the 2d ESB and 56th ATTB for deployment to Korea, a portion of the Army Reserve amphibious force was mobilized to provide an amphibious capability in CONUS. In August 1950 the 747th Amphibious Tank Battalion in Florida was mobilized and sent to Fort Worden, Washington, where it was reconstituted as a composite amphibious tank and tractor battalion. About half of the battalion's enlisted men were levied to fill out the newly mobilized 89th Engineer Port Construction Company.[1] In October 1950 the 409th ESB, located at various places along the coasts of Oregon and California, was mobilized along with most of its subordinate units, most notably the 369th and 370th Engineer Boat and Shore Regiments (EB&SRs) and the 380th Boat Maintenance Battalion. The 371st EB&SR was left in Reserve status. These units joined the 747th ATTB and 89th Engineer Port Construction Company at Fort Worden, where they trained until July 1951. At that time, the Headquarters and Headquarters Company of the 409th ESB was sent to Korea and reorganized as an engineer brigade headquarters with responsibility for supervising engineer construction and maintenance in southern Korea. The 369th and 370th EB&SRs were reorganized as separate engineer amphibious support regiments. The 369th remained at Fort Worden, while the 370th was sent to the Panama Canal Zone. One detachment of the 370th was then sent to Greenland to assist in the construction of an airfield. A detachment of the 369th participated in atomic tests in the desert during 1951, while the rest of the regiment and the 747th ATTB participated in PHIBTEST—the largest wartime amphibious exercise, which was conducted at Coronado, California, from June to October 1952.[2] During their time on Active Duty, these units demonstrated the resourcefulness and adaptability of the amphibious engineers.

Amphibious Training, August 1951–April 1952

The 40th Infantry Division completed its amphibious training in Japan in August 1951. The 45th Infantry Division was then scheduled to begin amphibious training, but that month the Joint Chiefs of Staff (JCS) notified General Matthew B. Ridgway that they wished to see the two National Guard divisions sent to Korea as soon as they completed their ground combat training, raising the possibility that the division's amphibious training would be curtailed or canceled. However, Ridgway objected to sending the Guardsmen to Korea at that time. The Eighth Army summer offensive was taking place and he did not want to move combat-experienced divisions out of Korea so long as there was danger of an enemy counteroffensive. He also feared that a divisional exchange would disrupt the defense of Japan during the 3 months it would take to complete the transfer. With the move to Korea postponed indefinitely, it was decided that the 179th and 279th RCTs of the 45th Division would receive the full course of amphibious training recommended by the Marine Mobile Training Team (MTT) at Camp McGill. This would bring the division up to the fullest possible amphibious proficiency, thus providing two trained divisions if the opportunity arose to conduct a corps-size amphibious assault.[3]

Ridgway's arguments for postponing the division exchange did not find favor in Washington, where it was noted that many of the National Guardsmen would come to the end of their Service obligation the following August. Because of congressional interest and state pride in the units, the Army leadership also disapproved a Ridgway request to use the two divisions as replacement fillers. In September President Harry S. Truman approved a plan to send one of the divisions to Korea and, at a suitable time, rotate one of the combat-experienced divisions back to Japan. This same process could then be repeated later with the other National Guard division. These deliberations increased the likelihood that the two divisions would soon be deployed to Korea after all and may have influenced an October decision to compress the on-going amphibious training from 6 to 4 weeks by extending the daily training from a half to a full day. This turned out to be a sound move, since the JCS ordered Ridgway to begin the deployment of the National Guard divisions to Korea in November, and the 45th Division and 1st Cavalry Division began their rotation cycle at the end of the month. By using the same shipping for both divisions and by exchanging heavy equipment and supplies, the transfer took place smoothly, with the 180th Infantry Regiment arriving in Korea on 5 December and the 5th Cavalry departing for Japan on the same ships 2 days later. By the end of the month, the exchange was complete and the 45th Division was on the front line. In January and February the 40th Division replaced the 24th Division in Korea and the 1st Cavalry and 24th Infantry Divisions were placed on the schedule for amphibious training in Japan.

The 1952 amphibious training cycle would begin with the 29th Separate Infantry Regiment in Okinawa undergoing the pre-afloat phase of amphibious training in January and February 1952 and the afloat phase, including a landing exercise, in April. In preparation, Ridgway directed Commander, United States Naval Forces, Far East (COMNAVFE) to survey the beaches of Okinawa to determine the feasibility of conducting a landing exercise there using landing craft, vehicle, personnel (LCVPs); landing ships, tank (LSTs); and DUKWs. Amphibious training would continue throughout 1952 with one regimental combat team (RCT) completing training and participating in a landing exercise each month from May until October, when the weather would no longer be suitable. By the end of the year, the RCTs of both the 24th Infantry Division and the 1st Cavalry Division would have completed amphibious training.[4]

The Far East Command (FEC) amphibious training and operations capability was expanded with the October 1951 deployment back to Japan of the 2d ESB, which had been operating the port of Incheon since March 1951. The mission of the brigade was to retrain and equip for amphibious operations. In November the 56th ATTB also began converting back from a light armor to an armored amphibious unit. Ridgway ordered the 2d ESB back to Japan over the objections of Lieutenant General James Van Fleet, because of "an urgent requirement for combat units with such amphibious capability to be in Japan in the event of an emergency." Commander in Chief, Far East (CINCFE) directed that the engineers carry out "intensified training" with special emphasis on the operation of landing craft in heavy surf; night operation of landing craft; and weapons, communication, and physical training to bring the unit up to 85 percent proficiency by December. In part this was because the 2d ESB and the 56th ATTB were expected to take part in the Okinawa training and exercises with the 29th Infantry and because of concern that the marines might be removed from the theater, greatly reducing the FEC amphibious capability. But Ridgway was also preparing for a possible amphibious landing in Korea in March when weather conditions would be favorable for such an operation.[5]

On 12 October 1951 the 2d ESB turned Incheon Port operations over to the 21st Transportation Medium Port and boarded ships for Japan a week later, moving into Camp McGill on 19 October to begin the process of re-equipping and re-training. The brigade initially focused on amphibious and infantry combat reorientation, but in November the 532d EB&SR began specialized training with a heavy schedule of practice in pilotage, navigation, control of landing craft in surf, engine maintenance, crane-shovel operation, and communications. Throughout this period, the amphibious engineers also carried out individual and crew-served weapons practice and infantry combat drill. The boat company (Company B) conducted two practice assault-landing exercises and then joined with Navy boats and crews at Chigasaki Beach for more advanced work on assault landing techniques and control of the landing craft, mechanized (LCM) in heavy surf. By December the boat company and one of the shore companies conducted a demonstration of a shore-to-shore operation for the brigade amphibious indoctrination course. At the end of the month, the regiment participated in a joint Army–Navy exercise using Camp McGill as the near shore embarkation and staging point and Chigasaki Beach as the amphibious objective area. The end of the exercise simulated an assault landing of two RCTs abreast with naval personnel and brigade service troops simulating the infantry landing force. In January the brigade successfully conducted an RCT shore-to-shore exercise in spite of severe winter weather. The brigade and the regiment were now ready to take up their roles as trainers and as boat and shore elements for the upcoming Okinawa exercise.[6]

Like the amphibious engineers, the 56th ATTB was also relearning its trade. Since January 1951 the battalion had been organized as a light tank unit, equipped with M24 light tanks and M10 tank destroyers, and attached to various infantry units for the defense of the Kanto Plain. In November they turned in the tanks and tank destroyers and began drawing LVTs and LVT(A)s from the Tokyo Ordnance Depot. The depot had only five of the new LVT(A)5s (with gyro-stabilized howitzers that could be fired effectively from the water en route to the beach), the type the battalion had brought to the Far East, so 25 of the older LVT(A)4s were issued instead, along with 106 LVT4 cargo-personnel carriers. On 23 November the battalion officially reorganized under the 1950 tables of organization and equipment (TOEs) for an amphibious tank and tractor battalion. Companies A and B once again became amphibious tank companies and Companies C and D became amphibious tractor companies. The unit was then detached from the 40th Infantry Division and moved to Camp McGill, where it was attached to the 2d ESB on 6 December. The 2d ESB and the 56th ATTB continued training together.[7]

In March the 532d EB&SR received 21 DUKWs, with which they formed an amphibious truck platoon to be used to land artillery during the upcoming amphibious training cycle. On 15 April the 2d ESB and the 56th ATTB embarked for Okinawa, where the 29th Infantry had been undergoing preliminary shore training for the upcoming landing exercise, Operation CORALHEAD. The LVTs of the 56th and the brigade's rolling stock traveled to Okinawa aboard LSTs, while the rest of the brigade was transported in an APA and an AKA. After 10 days of training with the 29th Infantry, the two units supported the regiment during the landing exercise on 27 April. The amphibious tankers finally had the chance to operate their LVTs in the environment for which they had originally been designed—crossing coral reefs. By the end of the month, the two units were back in Japan, beginning a busy summer of training one RCT after another.[8]

The year 1952 brought changes to the Shipping Control Administration, Japan (SCAJAP) LST fleet. Negotiations were underway to conclude a peace treaty with Japan that would return sovereignty to that nation. Japanese-manned SCAJAP LSTs would no longer be at the call of the FEC, yet the logistic operations of the command, as well as any large-scale amphibious operation depended on those ships. In January 1952, General Headquarters (GHQ) advised the JCS of its continuing need for 38 LSTs for logistic support and possible amphibious operations and noted that operations of units on the front line in the northeast were largely sustained over an LST beach at the coastal port of Sokcho. CINCFE proposed an arrangement whereby the ships could continue to be used under contract for support of operations in Korea; for the redeployment of troops, supplies, and equipment from Korea; and for intra-theater support of the FEC. The final arrangement was that the ships would be returned to the United States. On 31 March 1952, 33 of the LSTs were transferred to the Military Sea Transportation Service (MSTS) and continued to be operated under contract while 5 others were returned to the US Navy. The next day, SCAJAP was dissolved.[9]

Operations in the Offshore Islands

When the truce talks resumed in October 1951, one of the issues was the status of the coastal islands north of the 38th Parallel occupied by UNC forces (see map 35). These included islands off the North Korean Hwanghae province in the northwest, islands off the Han River estuary (HRE) and the mouth of the Imjin River northwest of Seoul, a few islands off the east coast, and the islands in the bay east of Wonsan. A variety of organizations used these islands as bases for special operations, including raids into North Korea by the partisans of Task Force (TF) *Leopard* on the west coast and TF *Kirkland* on the east coast. Some were also used as radar stations, and the islands near Wonsan were part of the siege and blockade of that seaport. The most substantial UNC presence was on three groups of islands to the west of the Ongjin Peninsula (Baengnyeongdo, Daecheongdo, and Socheongdo) and two island groups southeast of the Ongjin Peninsula (Yeonpyeongdo and Udo), referred to collectively as the Northwest Islands.

As the post-armistice status of the islands was discussed at Panmunjom, the North Koreans also began to react to the partisan incursions by mounting amphibious operations to recapture the more vulnerable of the islands. Some of these operations were of substantial size, involving more than a thousand North Korean troops and guerrilla forces. North Korean or Chinese air strikes even supported the attacks on islands furthest to the northwest. In October 1951 a large North Korean force overran a friendly island in the HRE, and in November both North Korean People's Army (KPA) and UNC forces carried out amphibious raids on each other's islands. A small island off Wonsan was overrun by the Communists in November, and on 2 December US and British marines carried out a coastal raid on Dancheon, about 120 miles northeast of Wonsan.[10] On the west coast, some 1,200 North Korean guerrillas succeeded in capturing seven islands off Haeju on the last day of November and the first few days of December. TF 90 LSTs supported by British cruisers brought ROK marines and partisans in to bolster the Northwest Island defenses and to bring out refugees from the lost islands, and a landing ship, dock (LSD) and minesweepers were dispatched to the area to assist in the defense. Nonetheless, during January the KPA captured five more small islands off Hwanghae province. On 6 January 1952 CINCFE gave COMNAVFE the responsibility for defense of designated islands off both coasts and Admiral C. Turner Joy further delegated this responsibility to the commander of TF 95 (the UN blockade and escort force). A West Coast Island Defense Element was formed under a US Marine Corps officer and two battalions of ROK marines were distributed among the islands. Although the North Koreans captured more islands in February, by March the defensive measures had taken hold and partisan forces began recapturing some of the lost islands.[11]

In December 1951 the truce negotiators agreed in principle that on the initiation of an armistice, all coastal islands would revert to the control of the side that held them before the war. There was still disagreement about the islands off the Ongjin Peninsula lying below the 38th Parallel, but on 3 February 1952 the Communists agreed that the UNC would remain in possession of the Northwest Islands. Even though the other occupied islands would have to be evacuated when the truce took effect, UNC forces continued to hold them until that time. For the rest of the war, the North Koreans continued to make periodic attempts, sometimes successful, to wrest control of the islands from the partisans. Periodically, TF 95 manned anti-invasion stations along the northwest coast from the HRE to Jinnampo in support of friendly guerrilla forces and carried out bombardments of North Korean coastal positions and installations. In June 1953, just before the armistice went into effect, TF 90 LSTs evacuated thousands of partisans, their families, and civilians who had been living on the islands off both coasts.[12]

Amphibious Training, May 1952 to the End of the War

On their return from Okinawa, the troops of the 2d ESB continued their participation in the 1952 amphibious training program. In May they worked with the 34th RCT of the 24th Division, which conducted its landing exercise at Chigasaki Beach on 29 May.[13] In June Shore Company E of the 532d EB&SR, along with other elements of the brigade and a Navy beach group, loaded aboard an LST. With their heavy equipment in 2 LSUs carried in the well deck of 1 LSD, and 18 LCMs in the well deck of another LSD, they sailed to Hokkaido in northern Japan to participate with the 7th Cavalry in a landing exercise called Operation SEAHORSE. The regimental boat company (Company B) deployed themselves to the exercise area, sailing 24 LCMs accompanied by a utility boat, a tanker, and a tug, nearly 600 miles up the coast to join the rest of the brigade. This was also the first exercise for the Provisional DUKW Platoon, which traveled to Hokkaido aboard an LST and there practiced landing the howitzers of the 77th Field Artillery Battalion of the 7th Cavalry RCT. There was no suitable beach for the landing exercise on 23 June, so the operation was carried out just like an actual amphibious assault, except that the landing craft did not actually run up onto the shore, but approached a simulated shore line 5,000 yards off the beach.[14]

Elements of the brigade, including one of the 532d's shore party companies (Company D), were back in Hokkaido in July for the 5th Cavalry's landing exercise. Once again lack of a suitable beach led to an exercise with no actual landing. This meant that the shore party's duties were limited to outloading the RCT and had no chance to practice their skills at moving equipment and supplies over the beach. However, the Provisional DUKW Platoon was able to work with the 61st Field Artillery Battalion (FAB), landing their howitzers on a small beach suitable for amphibious truck operations. The boat company, which had remained in Hokkaido, was put to use by the Navy doing lightering and transport work. The experienced Army LCM crews took considerable pride in their seamanship and were happy to demonstrate their skill in front of the Navy.[15]

In August 1952 the 2d ESB was reorganized and redesignated the 2d Amphibious Support Brigade (ASB). The 532d EB&SR was redesignated as an engineer amphibious support regiment (EASR) with one boat battalion and one shore battalion. Six LCMs remained in Hokkaido when the rest of the boat company returned to Camp McGill. They joined Navy craft to support a visit to Hokkaido by the battleship *Iowa* on 9 and 10 August, then returned to Camp McGill in the well deck of an LSD. As the 8th Cavalry RCT began its amphibious training, the shore party company was sent back to Camp McGill leaving a planning group behind, because it was felt that it was a waste of time to keep the entire company in Hokkaido if there was to be no actual landing. In September the 19th RCT of the 24th Division conducted its amphibious training, with a full-scale landing exercise that included back loading the RCT and its tanks and artillery out over the beach after the landing had been completed. The 532d EB&SR shore party was able once again to perform its mission in a "realistic and satisfactory manner."[16]

On 1 October 1952 Company D of the engineer shore battalion traveled to Hokkaido aboard an LSM to assist the 8th Cavalry in its landing exercise. The engineer troops were loaded aboard Navy amphibious ships and given to understand that this time they were going to participate in an actual amphibious assault against the North Korean coast. On 12 October they conducted a rehearsal landing at a beach near Gangneung, Korea. They outloaded the 8th Cavalry from the beach the next day and on the morning of 15 October found themselves off the coast of North Korea in heavy seas and high winds and in the company of several aircraft carriers; cruisers; destroyers; a battleship; and landing ships, medium (rocket) (LSM[R]s) that were conducting preparatory fires on the beach. The amphibious engineers prepared to join the cavalry troopers aboard the landing craft, but then received the order not to load. The empty boats were lowered into the water and headed for the beach, then turned back and were loaded back aboard the transports, which sailed for Pohang to unload the 8th RCT.

At Pohang they assisted in the outloading of the 187th Airborne RCT and two combat engineer battalions that were being returned to Japan.[17] On 7 November 1952 the amphibious exercise program came to an end. Elements of the 2d Amphibious Support Brigade (ASB) had participated in seven regimental-level landing exercises, as well as additional training, and had carried out the wide variety of tasks for which engineers are trained ranging from construction of roads, buildings, piers, and other facilities to repair and maintenance of maritime and other equipment. The amphibious engineers were at the peak of readiness and well prepared if they "should be committed to actual operations again."[18]

In November the FEC submitted its requirements for Navy support to amphibious training for the next 3 years. For 1953 the command intended to train 12 RCTs in Japan, 4 in Korea, and 1 in Okinawa. The following year, anticipating that the war might be over, it reduced the plan to 12 RCTs in Japan and 1 in Okinawa, with 6 RCTs to be trained in Japan and 1 in Okinawa in 1955.[19]

The 2d ASB carried out shore party exercises at Chigasaki Beach in January and the 532d EASR's boat battalion was put to work doing port lightering in February. The first regimental exercise was carried out in May with the 29th Infantry on Okinawa. That same month, the 1st Marine Division was placed in reserve and began amphibious training in Korea using a beach on the west coast near Gunsan for landing exercises. Two such exercises, MARLEX I and II, took place in May and June, but the third, MARLEX III, was canceled as all available shipping was held in readiness for the repatriation of prisoners of war (POWs). All Marine, Army, and Navy landing exercises and afloat training were canceled from June to October 1953.[20]

Amphibious Planning and Operations, 1952–53

During the first week in February 1952, Van Fleet proposed several different operations to Ridgway for his consideration. One of these, BIG STICK, would involve, in the west-central sector, a ground attack as part of an advance to the Yeseong River to destroy Communist supply complexes and capture Gaeseong. In the east, the 1st Marine Division would conduct a simultaneous amphibious demonstration to fix enemy forces that might otherwise reinforce against the ground attack. Another version, HOMECOMING, would use only ROK forces and would not involve an amphibious attack. Neither operation was approved; however, the idea of an amphibious operation on the east coast remained in play, particularly during those times when the truce talks stalled.[21] Although the possibility of a Soviet intervention in the war or of a greatly increased Chinese reinforcement had faded, CINCFE continued to maintain an operation plan for withdrawal from Korea, including detailed lists of shipping requirements.[22]

In March 1952 the 1st Marine Division was transferred from its eastern location to the western flank of the Eighth Army front. Between 17 and 24 March, the division moved by rail and truck, with the heavy equipment and armor loading aboard LSTs and LSDs at the beach at Sokcho for transportation to Incheon. In its new location, the division provided additional security for the Gimpo Peninsula, as well as the main avenue of approach from the north toward Seoul. This move seemed to end serious consideration of an amphibious operation on the east coast, although the XVI Corps with its two divisions in Japan continued to conduct amphibious training in Japan for such an eventuality. Furthermore, the marines were now close to the port of Incheon, from where they could be outloaded if the decision were made to conduct an amphibious assault.[23] Although the FEC continued to maintain that capability, the likelihood of success for such an operation seemed to diminish as the North Koreans steadily improved their coastal defenses at feasible landing sites. An increasing toll on the ships conducting the Wonsan siege, the conduct of anti-invasion exercises by the KPA, and the capture of plans for counteramphibious operations were all indications of the probable high cost of any such operation.[24]

The enemy's concern about an amphibious invasion did cause the diversion of forces from the front lines. Although the military impact during the long period of static warfare is problematic, GHQ continued to see merit in pinning down enemy forces through amphibious demonstrations, which led to the last significant amphibious operation of the war, the Kojo (Gojeo) Feint in October 1952. In July the Commander in Chief, United Nations Command (CINCUNC) directed the 1st Cavalry Division to provide an RCT to Korea for security missions. The 8th Cavalry was selected as the first such unit, and it was decided that "in the interest of economy and realistic training" it would be useful to combine the movement of the regiment to Korea with an amphibious exercise. Vice Admiral Robert P. Briscoe had replaced Admiral Joy as COMNAVFE the previous June. The new naval commander believed the operation would provide an excellent opportunity for training and suggested that it be carried out as if it were an actual landing, including air and naval gunfire preparation of the beach area. It was hoped that enemy forces would be lured into what they believed was an amphibious objective area and that heavy casualties might be inflicted on them by air and surface forces. General Mark W. Clark, who had replaced Ridgway on 12 May 1952, ordered that

COMNAVFE, in coordination with Eighth Army and XVI Corps, submit a plan for the proposed operation. The target date for the demonstration was set for 15 October. The fact that this was a deception operation was kept close hold and known only to the highest-level commanders and staff. Consequently, planning began in September 1952 as if an actual operation was to take place. Two operations were planned: one for a corps-level operation involving two divisions to be landed in column and the other for an RCT-size landing. The final decision was for a regimental-size operation to be carried out in conjunction with the deployment of the 8th Cavalry from Hokkaido to Korea.[25]

Operation Plan No. 5-52 was developed as if for an actual two-division amphibious landing by XVI Corps and naval forces at Gojeo (Kojo), 40 miles southeast of Wonsan and one of the areas previously considered for an amphibious assault. The concept of the operation was for the amphibious assault to be conducted in conjunction with a simultaneous Eighth Army ground attack and an airborne assault to encircle and destroy enemy forces south of a line from Pyeonggang in the Iron Triangle to the coast at Gojeo. Eighth Army and XVI Corps would then continue the attack north to capture Wonsan. Vice Admiral J.J. Clark, Seventh Fleet commander, was designated Commander Joint Amphibious Task Force 7, which was activated on 8 October 1952. As part of the deception measures, the 187th Airborne Regiment was alerted to be withdrawn from the line and prepared for an airdrop.

Operation DOMINO began with the mount out of the 8th Cavalry RCT, a shore party company of the 532d EASR, and other elements of the 2d ASB on 7 October from Hokkaido. On 12 October, in spite of high winds and heavy seas that caused damage to some of the landing craft, they conducted a rehearsal landing near Gangneung on the east coast. While the rehearsal was taking place, a large naval force, which included four aircraft carriers, two escort carriers, a battleship, two heavy cruisers, and destroyers, bombarded Gojeo. The tempo of Air Force operations was also increased, including a simulated airborne drop.

On 13 and 14 October Eighth Army launched a limited objective attack toward Gimhwa (Kumhwa) by two battalions, and on D-Day, 15 October, a force of more than a hundred ships arrived off Gojeo and began what appeared to be a full-scale amphibious landing. However, poor weather conditions delayed the prelanding naval gunfire and air bombardment. Because of 50-knot winds and dangerous sea conditions, the troops were not actually loaded into the boats. Instead, empty landing craft formed up, headed toward shore, and then turned back and returned to the transports.

The ships carrying the 8th Cavalry then proceeded to Pohang. It was one of the largest amphibious operations of the war, but because of the poor visibility, it is unclear whether the North Koreans were aware that it took place. There were no significant troop movements and very little reaction from coastal defenses. It was unclear whether this was because the bad weather prevented the KPA from seeing the extent of the offshore armada or whether they were holding their fire until the troops were ashore. On the UNC side, the deception was so convincing that all but the highest echelons really believed that the UNC was going on the offensive. When it all turned out to be a sham, there was a natural let down. Some of the planners and participants were angry at having been deceived, especially since the preliminary air and naval operations had been conducted with some risk of casualties.[26]

Planning for amphibious operations continued. Clark, on 14 May 1953, facing the possibility that the armistice talks could break down again and another long recess could occur, sent a message to the JCS outlining his plans to put additional military pressure on the Communists. Within his existing directives, CINCUNC could conduct limited objective attacks and expand air, naval, and guerrilla operations. He also suggested breaching operations against a number of irrigation dams not yet attacked; an air attack on the Communist logistic center at Gaeseong; unilateral release of about 35,000 North Korean POWs; and a combined land and amphibious attack in the Toncheon (T'ongch'on)–Geumseong (Kumsong)–Gimhwa area in the fall of 1953 to destroy North Korean forces, shorten the front line, and provide a better base from which to conduct operations toward the narrow waist of Korea.[27] It is unknown whether Washington would have approved these ambitious and costly operations, but the issue became moot on 27 July 1953 when the armistice was signed and the active combat of the Korean War ended.

Notes

1. 747th Amphibious Tank and Tractor Battalion, *Command Report*, 1950, RG 407, Entry 429, Box 4399, National Archives and Records Administration, Modern Military Records, College Park, MD, hereafter, NACP.

2. *Command Reports*, 409th Engineer Special Brigade, 369th and 370th Engineer Boat and Shore Regiments/Engineer Amphibious Support Regiments, 1950, 1951; RG 407, Entry 429, Boxes 4666 and 4667, NACP; Headquarters, Sixth Army, *Report of PHIBTEST*, 19 September 1952, RG 407, Entry 429, Box 6044; Amphibious Force Pacific Fleet, *PHIBTEST*, RG 407, Entry 429, Box 5584, NACP.

3. This discussion of amphibious training and Korea deployment for the two National Guard divisions is based on Walter G. Hermes, *United States Army in the Korean War: Truce Tent and Fighting Front* (Washington, DC: Office of the Chief of Military History, 1966), 202, and Far East Command, *Command Report, s*eparate volumes by month, November 1950–July 1953 (Tokyo: GHQ Far East Command, Military Intelligence Section), September 1951, 74, and October 1951, 76–77.

4. FEC, *Command Report*, September 1951, 74–75, and January 1952, 92.

5. FEC, *Command Report*, September 1951, "urgent requirement," 69, possibility of an amphibious operation in March, 92–93.

6. Headquarters, 532d Engineer Boat and Shore Regiment, *Command Reports* for October, November, and December 1951 and January 1952, RG 407, Box 6045, NACP.

7. Headquarters, 56th Amphibious Tank and Tractor Battalion, *Command Report Narrative Summaries*, November and December 1951, RG 338, Entry 37042, Box 30, NACP.

8. FEC, *Command Report*, January 1952, 82–83; 532d EB&SR Command Reports, February, March, and April 1952.

9. CINCFE Message CX 61516 (DA IN 505), to Department of the Army for JCS, 15 January 1952, "Post-Treaty Operation of SCAJAP Fleet," RG 218, Entry UD48, Box 3, Folder 3, NACP; FEC, *Command Report*, March 1952, 94–95; James A. Field Jr., *History of United States Naval Operations, Korea* (Washington, DC: GPO, 1962), 430. The disposition of the LSTs is summarized in the appendixes to Norman Friedman and A.D. Baker, *U.S. Amphibious Ships and Craft; An Illustrated Design History* (Annapolis, MD: Naval Institute Press, 2002); in the individual ship histories of the US Department of the Navy, Naval Historical Center, *Dictionary of American Naval Fighting Ships,* history. navy.mil/danfs/index.html (accessed 13 February 2008); and in a compilation of information on the disposition of LSTs, www5e.biglobe.ne.jp/~vandy-1/lst2.htm (accessed 10 February 2007).

10. FEC, *Command Report*, December 1951, 21; Field, *Naval Operations, Korea,* 420–423. See maps 49 and 51 for the locations of these islands and forces.

11. FEC, *Command Report*, January 1952, 19–20, February 1952, 27–28, and March 1952, 10, 19; Field, *Naval Operations, Korea,* 423–425; Hermes, *Truce Tent and Fighting Front,* 161.

12. Field, *Naval Operations, Korea,* 430, 457; FEC, *Command Report,* July 1952, 26, June 1953, 13–15; Naval Historical Center, "Korean War: Chronology of U.S. Pacific Fleet Operations," www.history.navy.mil/wars/korea/chron50. htm (accessed 21 November 2007), entries for 1952 and 1953; and Agreement Between the Commander-in-Chief, United Nations Command, on the One Hand, and the Supreme Commander of the Korean People's Army and the Commander of the Chinese People's Volunteers, on the Other Hand, Concerning a Military Armistice Agreement in Korea," Article IIA (a copy of the Armistice Agreement is Appendix C of Hermes, *Truce Tent and Fighting Front*).

13. 532d EB&SR, *Command Report*, May 1952.

14. 532d EB&SR, *Command Report*, June 1952. See map 8 for the various geographical locations in Japan.

15. 532d EB&SR, *Command Report*, July 1952.

16. 532d EB&SR, *Command Report*, August and September 1952.

17. 532d Engineer Amphibious Support Regiment (EASR), *Command Report*, October 1952. The event that the engineers had participated in was Operation DOMINO, an amphibious demonstration.

18. 532d EASR, *Command Report*, November 1952.

19. FEC, *Command Report*, November 1952, 40.

20. 532d EASR, *Command Report*, January–May 1953.

21. Hermes, *Truce Tent and Fighting Front,* 187.

22. FEC, *Command Report,* March 1952, 41.

23. Lynn Montross, Pat Meid, and James M. Yingling, *U.S. Marine Operations in Korea, 1950–1953, Vol. IV, Operations in West Korea* (Washington, DC: Historical Branch, G3, 1972), 9–11.

24. Field, *Naval Operations, Korea,* 433–435.

25. FEC, *Command Report*, August 1952, 5; Hermes, *Truce Tent and Fighting Front,* 328–329.

26. FEC, *Command Report,* October 1952, 5–7; Malcolm W. Cagle and Frank A. Manson, *Sea War in Korea* (Annapolis, MD: Naval Institute Press, 1957), 390–394.

27. FEC, *Command Report*, May 1953, 3–4.

Chapter 8

Postwar Activities, Current Situation, and Lessons Learned

At the end of the Korean War, the Army still had an amphibious infrastructure based on the amphibious support brigade (ASB) and the amphibious tank and tractor battalion (ATTB). The 2d ASB and the 56th ATTB were deactivated in the mid-1950s, with the Transportation Corps inheriting much of the equipment and mission of the amphibious engineers. The 2d Engineer Amphibious Support Command, a new organization, was established a year later and remained in existence for about a decade until its final deactivation. The Army Field Forces, which became the Continental Army Command (CONARC) in 1955, continued to be the Army agency responsible for amphibious training and doctrine. Postwar Army field manuals and publications reflected some of the pre-Korean War doctrinal issues until the Joint Staff began publishing joint amphibious doctrine in the late 1980s. During the Vietnam War, the Army conducted over-the-shore logistics, coastal and riverine transport, and security operations. It also conducted brigade-size riverine combat operations in conjunction with the Navy. After Vietnam, with few exceptions, the Army increasingly focused on the airborne and airmobile aspects of forcible entry operations. Only the Transportation Corps retained the watercraft and other assets for, and an interest in, amphibious and over-the-shore operations.

Doctrine, Force Structure, and Training

In September 1951 all three Services published identical manuals titled *Joint Action Armed Forces (JAAF)* that replaced the old *Joint Action of the Army and Navy (JAAN)*. The new document established the broad principles for doctrine and command of the Armed Forces mutually agreed on by the Services and was generally consistent with the Key West Agreement. It contained a section for each of the Services identifying responsibilities for amphibious operations. The Navy and Marine Corps were charged with organizing naval forces, including naval close air support forces; conducting joint amphibious operations; amphibious training of all forces "as assigned for joint amphibious operations"; developing "in coordination with the other Services" amphibious doctrines and procedures; developing the doctrines and techniques applicable specifically to naval forces in joint amphibious operations and for training those forces; participating in joint amphibious training; and establishing and operating a joint amphibious board with representation from all the Services. Disputes arising in this board were to be resolved through inter-Service consultation and, if irresolvable, presented to the Joint Chiefs of Staff (JCS) for resolution. The board was specifically exempted from dealing with landing force tactics, techniques, and equipment, which were to be the responsibilities of the Marine Corps. The Marine Corps was charged with the development, "[i]n coordination with the Army, Navy, and the Air Force," of the tactics, techniques, and equipment for landing forces in amphibious operations and for establishing, maintaining, and operating a "joint landing force board, with representation from all the Services."[1] The Army's responsibilities were to organize, train, and provide Army forces for joint amphibious operations; to train these forces "in accordance with joint doctrines"; to develop, "in coordination with the other Services, tactics, techniques, and equipment of interest to the Army for amphibious operations" not provided for in the activities of the Marine Corps; and to participate with the other Services in joint amphibious training and exercises "as mutually agreed to."[2]

The year after the Army and Air Force published its statement of amphibious doctrine, the Navy produced its own statement. This document, Naval Warfare Publication (NWP) Number 22, became the basis for the series of Navy publications on amphibious warfare and for Marine Corps landing force manuals.[3] NWP 22 was a unilateral Navy interpretation, not coordinated with or accepted as joint doctrine by the other Services. Nevertheless, the Services generally adopted the broad principles and techniques of amphibious warfare contained in the document, although there were some points of disagreement. For the Army, the contentious issues had to do with Navy insistence on control by a naval officer of all amphibious operations, the range of operations within the rubric "amphibious," the timing of transfer of control from the amphibious task force commander to the landing force commander, and the logistical issues that had been matters of contention before the Korean War. The Army objected to the Navy view that an amphibious operation was complete in itself, arguing that when the effort was the first phase of sustained land operations, the shore party became the lead element of a major logistical effort. The Air Force's principal concern was with control of aviation assets during amphibious operations. A more fundamental issue was the concept of joint doctrine. When the Joint Amphibious Board provided for in *JAAF* convened in 1952, the Navy presented NWP 22 as the solution for joint doctrine. The other Service representatives insisted that for doctrine to be joint, all of the Services had to participate in all phases of its development. The issue was not resolved, the Joint Amphibious Board became dormant in 1954, and the doctrinal issues continued to smolder for the rest of the decade.[4]

New Army amphibious field manuals were published just prior to and during the Korean War. In the early months of 1950, Field Manual

(FM) 60-5, *Amphibious Operations: Battalion in Assault Landings*, and FM 60-10, *Amphibious Operations: Regiment in Assault Landings*, were issued in draft form. They were published during the war, in February 1951 and January 1952, respectively. Reflecting the post-World War II amalgamation of amphibious tanks and tractors into a single composite unit, FM 17-34, *Amphibious Tank and Tractor Battalion*, was issued in draft in 1948 and published in June 1950, the same month as the North Korean attack. The last of the wartime series of amphibious field manuals— FM 60-30, *Amphibious Operations: Embarkation and Ship Loading (Unit Loading Officer)*—was published in September 1952.[5] These doctrinal statements made no significant changes in the methodology for conducting landings on hostile shores developed during World War II and primarily reflected relatively minor changes in technology and organization. They generally followed the doctrine as set forth by the Navy and Marine Corps, with some reflection of the Army-specific viewpoint, particularly in the distinction between amphibious operations intended to capture an island advance base (seizure) and large-scale continental operations that would constitute the first phase of sustained operations on land (invasion). A new series of engineer tables of organization and equipment (TOEs) issued in 1951 and a new FM in 1952 reflected the change from "engineer special brigade" to "amphibious support brigade" and the replacement of the engineer boat and shore regiment with a new amphibious support regiment.[6]

In September 1954 a revised version of FM 100-5, *Field Service Regulations: Operations*, was published. The new Army capstone man-ual on operational doctrine noted the continuing relevance of amphibious operations and the Army's predominant role in joint amphibious opera-tions. It also noted that the Army might conduct small unilateral shore-to-shore operations and that amphibious shore-to-shore techniques were applicable to operations on navigable rivers and lakes, large-scale river crossing operations, and "interisland or coastal flanking operations" that might take place after a major amphibious invasion.[7]

Immediately after the war, a substantial part of the Army's amphibi-ous capability shifted from the Corps of Engineers to the Transportation Corps. The Office of the Chief of Transportation carried out a study in the summer of 1953, as the Korean War was ending. Published in August 1953, the study identified several assumptions, including that in a future war with the threat of atomic weapons, the dispersion of friendly forces and the likelihood that sea ports would be the target of nuclear attack would result in a large and continuing requirement for logistics-over-the-shore (LOTS) and amphibious resupply operations. It noted that during

World War II, Transportation Corps units and personnel were constantly involved in amphibious assault and LOTS operations. As of the time of the study, the Transportation Corps provided boat and boat maintenance elements that were organic to the amphibious support brigade (the Army's shore party organization) and continued to have responsibility for the operation of ports and logistical beach discharge points. The landing craft then being used by the Transportation Corps were designed for amphibious assault operations and were of an expendable nature, not intended for sustained LOTS-type operations. Furthermore, the Transportation Corps doctrine, equipment, and organization were not ideal for either the amphibious assault or LOTS missions, although they were being made to work through ingenuity, hard work, and considerable prior planning. The authors of the study recommended further research to determine the types and numbers of Army landing craft needed to assure the success of Transportation Corps aspects of amphibious operations from the assault to the establishment of a rear boundary. Other recommendations concerned the development of doctrine and training programs.[8]

In the years immediately after the war, boat functions were transferred from the engineers to the Transportation Corps. The 159th Transportation Boat Battalion was activated on 1 September 1953 at Fort Eustis, Virginia, to assume the responsibility for combat landings, LOTS, and terminal (lighterage) operations. It consisted of four light boat companies equipped with 56-foot LCM(6)s—and later with 74-foot LCM(8)s—and two heavy boat companies equipped with 115-foot landing craft, utility (LCU) (the post-Korean War designation of the landing ship, utility [LSU] and the World War II landing craft, tank [LCT]), as well as DUKWs and, eventually, the larger amphibious trucks known as lighter, amphibious resupply, cargo (LARC) and barge, amphibious resupply, cargo (BARC). Lieutenant Colonel Michael D. Isrin, battalion commander from January 1954 to September 1957, gained authorization for the soldiers of the 159th to wear red patches at knee level on their fatigue trousers, the emblem of shore party troops since World War II, and otherwise carry on the traditions of the amphibious engineers. Over the next decade, the 159th would conduct LOTS exercises, including annual training operations on the northern coast of France, and would refine new techniques developed at the Transportation School at Fort Eustis, Virginia, such as the use of aerial tramways (a cable strung between towers) to unload material from DeLong floating piers—sectional, prefabricated piers that could be floated to unimproved sites so that deep-draft berths could be established quickly.[9]

The 56th ATTB and the 2d Engineer ASB were both inactivated at Otawa, Japan, on 24 June 1955.[10] However, there was still a continuing need for engineer amphibious expertise, and in 1956, the 2d Engineer Amphibious Support Command (EASC) was activated at Fort Belvoir, Virginia, for test and evaluation purposes. In March 1958 the unit moved to Fort Lewis, Washington. Composed of the Command Headquarters and the 592d Service Support Battalion (Headquarters, Headquarters and Service Company, 560th Engineer Amphibious Equipment Company, and 793d Engineer Amphibious Company), the 2d EASC had the mission to provide assault transport in amphibious tractors and shore party support for Army units.[11]

From 1950 to 1964 the Transportation Corps continued to practice and improve its LOTS capabilities, conducting Offshore Discharge Exercises (ODEX) and New Offshore Delivery Exercises (NODEX) in northern France to test over-the-shore delivery methods.[12] From 1951 to 1965 the Transportation Corps also supported construction of the Distant Early Warning (DEW) Line in Greenland and in Labrador and Baffin Island, Canada, through LOTS operations. In 1958 another LOTS operation supported the US peacekeeping effort in Lebanon.[13]

During the latter half of the 1950s, Army units also participated in a series of amphibious exercises that diminished in size due to a withdrawal of Navy support and assets. In March 1954 Headquarters, United States Army Forces Antilles (USARFANT) and the Military District of Puerto Rico (MDPR) conducted Exercise *Sentry Box*, which included an amphibious landing exercise.[14] Joint Army–Navy Exercise *Surf Board* took place at the Hunter Liggett Military Reservation from 28 January to 7 April 1955, under the auspices of Sixth Army.[15] Two large-scale exercises were planned for Fiscal Year 1956: joint Army–Air Force Exercise *Sagebrush* and Exercise *High Seas*, a joint Army–Navy amphibious exercise. However, on 1 June 1955 the Navy concluded that it could not support an exercise of the scope and size planned, and *High Seas* was canceled.[16] It subsequently took place the following year as a command post exercise.[17] The Army attempted to have the task organization and command relationships reflect Army doctrine as set forth in its own field manuals, but the Navy insisted that NWP 22 be used.[18] Another large-scale amphibious exercise, *Rocky Shoals*, was planned for the fiscal year 1959 Army exercise program. However, on 27 August 1957 the Chief of Naval Operations once again said that the Navy could not support an exercise of the size contemplated and recommended sealift for the exercise be restricted to a maximum of 11,000 troops. *Rocky Shoals* was subsequently conducted in 1958 with two battle groups participating.[19] The Navy again insisted on applying NWP 22 as the doctrine for the exercise, and the Army had no choice but to agree if it was to have an amphibious exercise.[20]

By this time in the late 1950s, the differences among the Services over amphibious doctrine were narrowing, generally along the lines preferred by the Navy. In 1955 Phillip A. Crowl, a historian at the Office of the Chief of Military History, examined the current statements of Service doctrine to determine exactly where the differences lay. Crowl brought some experience and perspective to this work. He was the coauthor of one of the first comprehensive histories of Marine Corps amphibious operations in the Pacific and had written the official Army histories of the Gilberts, Marshalls, and Marianas operations. Crowl found that much of the previous Army–Navy disagreement had disappeared. Both Services now agreed on the principle of unity of command at all levels of an amphibious operation: when two or more Services participated in an operation, an officer designated from one of the Services would command all of the Service forces during the operation. The Army agreed that the amphibious task force commander should be a naval officer and the amphibious task force commander should coordinate the planning of an amphibious operation, with the landing force and tactical air commanders reporting to the amphibious task force commander during that planning. The Army also agreed that NWP 22 should be the doctrine for the embarkation, rehearsal, movement to the objective area, pre-assault and assault operations, and the early consolidation of the beachhead. In other words, there was agreement on the applicable doctrine for all but the consolidation phase of the amphibious operation. Finally, the Army agreed that the Navy–Marine Corps system of coordination of close air support should be used in joint amphibious operations as it was specifically designed for amphibious operations.[21]

Crowl found only two points of difference between the Army and Navy official positions. The first involved the scope of an amphibious operation, a somewhat pale reflection of the old issue of small-scale "seizure" operations (as in the Mid-Pacific doctrine) and large-scale "invasion" operations. The Army thought a joint amphibious operation should include a final phase that would set the stage for sustained operations on land: a "final phase" in Crowl's interpretation of the Army doctrine, "of logistical build-up, consolidation of the objective, and establishment of facilities for the support of projected operations." The Navy (and Air Force) did not. The Navy defined the "consolidation phase" of an amphibious operation as the final phase of the operation when the "lodgment, or advance base, area, or area to be denied the enemy is made secure."[22] The operation would then be over and the amphibious task force dissolved. Crowl found the only discernable difference between the Services on this issue was an Army desire to have the landing force commander be independent of the amphibious task force commander at some point before the final consolidation and buildup was completed, while the Navy wished to permit relatively early departure of the amphibious shipping. Crowl suggested that it should not be difficult for the Services to establish a set of mutually agreeable principles to govern the timing of dissolution of the amphibious task force.[23]

The other issue concerned command relationships and was, again, an attenuated reflection of the recurring Army view that when conducting an amphibious operation in pursuit of Army objectives, the Army commander should have control over the operation. That view had faded to an Army desire that there be a joint task force headquarters directing the overall joint amphibious operation, as opposed to the Navy view that only a single headquarters—the joint amphibious task force headquarters—would be required. Moreover, the Army also agreed that a naval officer would command the joint headquarters. The Army balanced these concessions, however, by the contention that the overall joint task force commander should be from the Service having "dominant interest in the basic purpose of the over-all operation" (Army Draft Training Circular, paragraph 5a). Crowl saw no reason why the Navy should reject this idea, because that was the approach taken in the Central Pacific in World War II, with Admiral Raymond A. Spruance in the role of joint task force commander (although not with that particular title). However, Crowl saw the determination of dominant interest to be potentially complicated, as most major operations had more than one strategic purpose.[24]

Crowl also found two points of ambiguity between the two Service doctrines. One concerned the transfer of authority from the amphibious force commander to the landing force commander. Army doctrine tended to leave this judgment to the landing force commander, with the transfer occurring as soon as the landing force command was functioning ashore. Navy doctrine tended to give the amphibious force commander leeway on the timing. The other issue was a lack of clarity in both Service doctrines on control of ship-to-shore landing craft after the initial assault. Crowl pointed out that this was a neuralgic issue throughout World War II and was never satisfactorily resolved. He recommended a joint agreement on "an explicit and clear cut doctrine as to who controls what landing craft, and where, and when."[25]

Crowl found one point of strong disagreement between the Air Force on one side and the Army and Navy on the other. The Army and Navy held firmly to the principle of unity of command at all levels, while the Air Force argued for the old principle of mutual cooperation below the level of theater commander with the three Service component commanders "coequal and interdependent." Further, the Air Force doctrine explicitly stated, "The ground forces and the naval forces are joined into an amphibious task force for amphibious operations. The amphibious task force will not include any air forces in its organization. The air commander of the air forces participating in conjunction with the operations is always coequal with the amphibious task force commander."[26]

With some exceptions, these issues were resolved as the Services worked their way toward an agreed on doctrine for amphibious operations. The amphibious warfare proponents at the Continental Army Command were not entirely pleased with the process, which they perceived had a tendency to resolve issues in favor of Navy doctrine. They noted, "The Army has a continuous requirement for joint doctrine covering all aspects of operations involving strategic and tactical mobility and fire support." The study concluded:

> The Army has been the major war time user of amphibious operations. The Army requirements for operations involving amphibious techniques stem from strategic and tactical mobility requirements incident to land warfare. Since the Army requirements include unilateral water barrier crossings and other waterborne operations on restricted coastal and inland waters, the Army cannot rely solely upon development by another Service regardless of proponent responsibility assignments.[27]

The next generation of Army amphibious warfare doctrine, published in the early 1960s, would reflect some of the CONARC views.

The new multi-Service doctrinal statement was published in July 1962 as Army, Navy, and Marine Corps *Doctrine for Amphibious Operations*. At this point, the differences with the Air Force had not been reconciled and the Air Force did not concur with the document.[28] A revision published in 1967 incorporated Air Force views and was published as an Army, Navy, Marine Corps, and Air Force document.[29] Some of the key elements of the document reflected the resolution of the earlier disagreements:

- An amphibious operation is an attack launched from the sea by naval and landing forces embarked in ships or craft involving a landing on a hostile shore [paragraph 101a].

- Combat operations which involve waterborne movement, such as inland-water, ferrying, and shore-to-shore operations in which the landing forces are not embarked in naval ships, waterborne administrative landings on friendly territory, and water terminal and logistics over-the-shore operations possess certain characteristics and employ some of the techniques of an amphibious operation. However, these are not amphibious operations [paragraph 101b].

- The amphibious operation is a complete operation within itself. As an entity, an amphibious operation includes planning, embarkation of troops and equipment, rehearsals, movement to the objective area, final preparation of the objective, assault landing of troops and accompanying supplies and equipment, **and support of the landing force until termination of the amphibious operation** [emphasis added; paragraph 103].

- Except during the planning phase, the amphibious task force commander, **a Navy officer** (emphasis added), is responsible for the operation and exercises that degree of authority over the entire force necessary to ensure the success of the operation [paragraph 213a(1)].

- When Air Force forces are assigned to the amphibious task force they will be organized as a separate force or component under the command of an Air Force officer . . . when the preponderance of tactical aviation is provided by the Air Force . . . an Air Force officer will be designated . . . to direct the total air effort in the amphibious objective area . . . when the preponderance of tactical aviation comes from the Navy or Marine Corps, the overall air effort in the objective area will be directed by a naval aviator under the amphibious task force commander until control is passed ashore [paragraph 226a and b].[30]

During the same general timeframe that this joint doctrine statement was being worked out, the Army published its next generation of doctrinal literature on amphibious operations with the Pentomic Army battle group landing team as the basic element of an Army landing force—soon to be replaced by the brigades and battalions of the Reorganized Army Division (ROAD) force structure. The new publications included FM 31-12,

Army Forces in Amphibious Operations (The Army Landing Force), published in March 1961, followed by FM 31-13, *Battle Group Landing Team, Amphibious,* in September 1961, and FM 60-30, *Embarkation and Loading—Amphibious,* in May 1962. Of these, the key publication setting forth the fundamental Army amphibious doctrine was FM 31-12. The following statements reflect those areas of particular Army interest:

- Amphibious operations may be categorized according to operational purposes as follows: (1) *Invasion.* This category implies initial but large-scale intervention by land combat forces into an enemy controlled territory. . . . Invasion implies intent to enter forcibly a national political area and to occupy captured territory for an indefinite period of time. (2) *Seizure.* This category implies capture of a voluntarily restricted portion of an enemy controlled territory. Capture of an isolated land mass such as an island falls with this category. [Paragraph 8. Italics in the original. The Joint document made no such differentiation.]

- The amphibious operation is a complete operation within itself. **However, when it is conducted by a joint force it is usually one phase or part of a campaign of larger magnitude** [emphasis added; paragraph 9].[31]

The 1960s also saw the publication of new doctrine for the amphibious engineers. Although the Transportation Corps had taken over much of the over-the-shore and amphibious logistics capability, the engineers were still responsible for supporting Army amphibious assaults. FM 5-156, *The Engineer Amphibious Support Command* (Draft), April 1958, was never published, but FM 5-144, *Engineer Shore Assault Units,* was published in October 1963 and replaced by FM 5-144, *Engineer Amphibious Units,* in November 1966. The 1963 manual was based on a unit called an "Engineer Amphibious Command" that would include one or more engineer amphibious groups composed of engineer amphibious companies (shore party units) and engineer amphibian assault companies (equipped with LVTs to provide ship-to-shore movement and inland mobility). The 1966 manual, revised in 1969, envisioned an engineer amphibious brigade headquarters and headquarters company that would provide the command element for two to four engineer amphibious groups, each of which would control a number of engineer amphibious battalions. Each engineer amphibious battalion would consist of a headquarters and headquarters company, two engineer amphibian assault companies (with LVTs), and an engineer amphibious company (shore party company).

These engineer units were designed for large-scale amphibious landings and envisioned the kind of operations conducted 20 years earlier in the Southwest Pacific, the Mediterranean, and Northwest Europe. The engineer amphibious brigade would be assigned to support a field army or independent corps in amphibious or shore-to-shore operations, with each engineer amphibious group of two or three engineer amphibious battalions supporting a corps or multidivision landing. The engineer amphibious battalion would support a brigade landing with two battalion landing teams (BLTs) in the assault, with one engineer amphibian assault company providing LVTs for ship-to-shore, shore-to-shore, or inland movement for one BLT, while the engineer amphibious company would supervise shore parties, amphibious combat support, and signal operations for two BLTs. The assault companies were to be equipped with the then current version of the LVT, the LVTP5 (the personnel carrier) and the landing vehicle, tracked, retriever (LVTR)—a salvage and recovery vehicle. The engineer amphibious company was to be equipped with the successor to the DUKW, the LARC 5-ton amphibious truck.[32]

In 1964 the US Army Engineer School at Fort Belvoir, Virginia, developed an exercise "involving engineer combat support to a hypothetical joint amphibious operation established in an environment of limited war." Operation SUNSET was part of the Engineer Officer Career Course for US Army Reserve engineer officers. The exercise was the major part of a lesson called "Engineers in an Amphibious Assault and Link-Up with Airborne Forces." The objective of the exercise was—

> To provide the student with a general knowledge of an amphibious operation planned to seize a division beachhead, a link-up with airborne forces, and subsequent expansion of control over the initial objective area. Engineer planning and operations, to include employment of elements of Engineer Shore Assault and Amphibian Assault units in assault and shore party operations, will be emphasized.[33]

The scenario posited an "aggressor army" invasion of Cambodia from Laos and a counteroffensive by US Pacific Forces under overall Southeast Asia Treaty Organization (SEATO) command. A composite SEATO corps would enter Cambodia overland from Thailand, while elements of the I US Corps conducted airborne and amphibious landings on the

Cambodian coast. The notional 22d Infantry Division (Reinforced) was to conduct the amphibious assault with three brigade landing teams directing surface and helicopter-borne assaults. Three engineer amphibious assault companies would support the landing, transporting the assaulting forces in their landing vehicles, tracked (LVTs), while an engineer shore assault group would provide shore party support. The students were provided with extensive background information and then asked to play the roles successively as the intelligence staff of the shore assault group, the infantry division staff, and commander of one of the shore assault companies. They were asked to conduct a beach study, evaluate a proposed concept of operation for the landing, evaluate a proposed plan for shore party operations, and develop recommendations for the landing of one of the battalion landing teams and supporting engineers. Considerable effort had been put into the development of this exercise, demonstrating that, as the United States stepped up its involvement in Vietnam, the engineers were preparing officers to conduct major amphibious operations.

However, this immense and powerful organization set forth in the field manuals, the TOEs, and Operation SUNSET existed only on paper. From 1963 to 1965 the Army's actual engineer amphibious establishment consisted of the 2d EASC Headquarters with two companies assigned: the 560th Engineer Amphibian Equipment Company (with three platoons, each operating 10 LVTP5s borrowed from the Marine Corps) and the 793d Engineer Amphibious Company (shore party). The amphibious engineers participated in several exercises, and in August 1964 moved to Fort Story, Virginia. In July 1965 the 2d EASC and its two companies were inactivated, and the story of the amphibious engineers came to an end.[34]

Vietnam and After

In 1960 Army Transportation Corps units participated in a Strategic Army Command (STRAC) mobility exercise, conducted over-the-shore operations in Exercise *Tarheel*, and participated in the first joint Army and Marine Corps landing exercise, JAMLEX, at Camp Lejeune, North Carolina. There would be additional JAMLEX and other exercises involving Army LOTS and water transportation operations throughout the early 1960s, and in 1962 the 159th Transportation Battalion prepared to conduct amphibious operations during the Cuban Missile Crisis.[35]

During the long Vietnam War, the Army conducted no significant amphibious operations as narrowly defined in the joint doctrine, but many Army activities possessed the characteristics and employed the techniques of amphibious operations. The 4th Transportation Command, which had operated ports during World War II and had developed water terminal doctrine and techniques after the war, deployed to Vietnam in August 1965. The 4th Transportation Command initially operated the Saigon port complex and water terminals at Cam Ranh Bay, Cat Lai, Nha Be, Nha Trang, Phan Rang, Qui Nhon, and Vung Tau. In 1966 the 124th Transportation Terminal Command took over the operation of Nha Trang, Cam Ranh Bay, Vung Ro Bay, and Phan Rang. The 5th Transportation Command operated Qui Nhon with lighterage support provided by the 159th Transportation Battalion, while the 125th Transportation Command operated the main port of Saigon. Later in the war, the 4th Transportation Command opened small ports at other locations as they were required.[36] (See map 51.)

In September 1965 large-scale landing ship, tank (LST) operations began, with the landing ships transporting vehicles, supplies, and personnel from Saigon, Cam Ranh Bay, and Okinawa to shallow-water ports such as Qui Nhon, Vung Tau, and Nha Trang. Ramps of crushed coral and sand were constructed at these and other ports to facilitate operations by the LSTs and by LCUs and LCMs lightering cargo ashore from vessels anchored offshore, and DeLong floating piers were installed to provide deep-draft berths.[37]

Units of the 159th Transportation Battalion, which arrived in Vietnam in August 1966, conducted terminal operations in the port of Saigon and operated LST beaches and over-the-shore logistical activities at Cam Ranh Bay, Da Nang, and Qui Nhon, lightering cargo from ships to the shore with LCUs, LCM(8)s, BARCs, and LARCs. In May 1967 a detachment of one of the battalion's boat companies set up a small LOTS operation at Sau Hugynh Beach near the 101st Airborne Division forward supply base at Duc Pho using BARCs and LCMs to bring supplies over the beach. During the Battle of Hue at the time of the 1968 Tet Offensive, Transportation Corps LCUs operated with Navy landing craft to deliver supplies to units fighting along the Qua Viet and Perfume Rivers. In March 1968 the 159th Transportation Battalion set up the largest LOTS operation of the war at Thon My Thuy Beach near the demilitarized zone (DMZ) to provide logistical support for operations in the northern I Corps area. Between March and August 1968, over a thousand tons of cargo a day was brought in over the beach at Thon My Thuy, which was initially called Utah Beach and then dubbed Wunder Beach when the amphibious transporters put up the sign "Welcome to Wunder Beach: The Home of Sunder's Wonders." (Lieutenant Colonel Charles Sunder was the 159th Transportation Battalion commander.) From 1968 to the end of the war,

Army Transportation Corps detachments supplemented Navy and Marine units delivering supplies over the beach in the I Corps Tactical Zone and conducted LOTS operations along the coast of the Mekong Delta.[38]

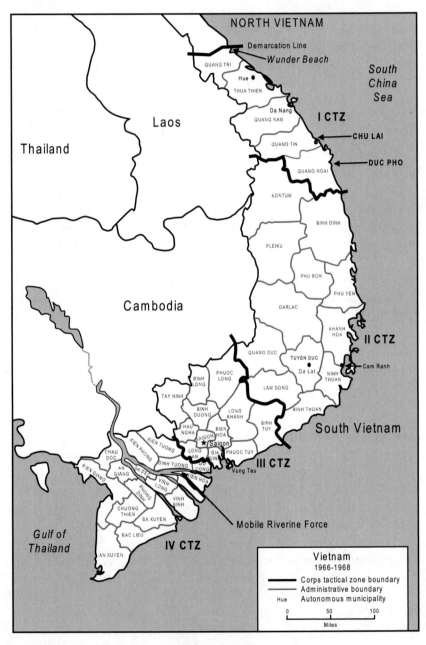

Map 51. Vietnam.

The 10th, 11th, 24th, 71st, and 394th Transportation Battalions (Terminal) operated ports and water terminals, including lighterage and LOTS operations.[39] In July 1967 the 4th Transportation Command formed the US Army Transportation Battalion Vung Tau/Delta (Provisional). This unit, with its two heavy boat companies (LCUs) and one medium boat company (LCMs), operated a terminal at Vung Tau, delivered supplies to small ports and bases along the coast, and provided beaching craft for tactical operations. Throughout the war, other transportation boat companies conducted similar operations.[40]

The 458th Transportation Company deployed to Vietnam in October 1966 as a light amphibious unit equipped with LARC Vs. The unit conducted lighterage and over-the-shore operations until August 1967, when its mission was changed to inland water and port security and it traded its LARCs for Boston Whalers. In 1968 the 458th received Navy armed river patrol boats (PBRs), becoming the only Army PBR unit. Attached to the 92d Military Police (MP) Battalion of the 18th MP Brigade, detachments of the 458th patrolled ports, waterways, and canals at various locations in Vietnam until the unit was inactivated in September 1971.[41]

At various times during the war, US Army advisors accompanied Army of the Republic of Vietnam (ARVN) troops on small-scale amphibious operations along the coasts and broad rivers of the Mekong Delta and elsewhere.[42] But the most significant Army amphibious-type combat operations were those carried out by the Mobile Riverine Force in the Mekong Delta. In 1966 General William C. Westmoreland, commanding general of Military Assistance Command, Vietnam (MACV) conceived the idea of deploying an Army division to the Delta with one of its brigades stationed aboard Navy ships to conduct operations along the extensive navigable waterways. In late 1966 two US Navy barracks ships and a number of landing craft were sent to the Delta, and troops of Colonel William B. Fulton's 2d Brigade, 9th Infantry Division, trained in riverine warfare with Navy units and Army Transportation Corps boat units in an area south of Saigon. By May 1967 Fulton's brigade headquarters and three infantry battalions were established on a man-made island called Dong Tam a few miles west of the Mekong River town of My Tho in Dinh Tuong province, as the Army component of the Mekong Delta Mobile Afloat Force, later redesignated the Mobile Riverine Force. The Navy component was Captain Wade C. Wells' Task Force (TF) 117 (River Assault Flotilla One) with two river assault squadrons, each consisting of 26 assault troop carriers, three command and control boats, five fire support craft (monitors), and a refueling craft, all of them modified LCM(6)s. The Mobile Riverine Force was supported by River Support Squadron Seven, consisting of four modified LSTs, a barge, and a harbor tugboat. The LST *Benewah* served as Wells' flagship and Fulton's headquarters and accommodated the artillery and security troops. Another LST provided quarters for an infantry battalion, while the other two LSTs and the barge provided logistical and maintenance support.[43]

One problem was the provision of artillery support to the riverine force. Captain John A. Beiler and Major Daniel P. Carlton, of the 3d Battalion, 34th Field Artillery, proposed mounting artillery on barges. Existing Navy barges had too deep a draft and were too difficult to move, but standard Navy P-1 pontons could be used to construct a suitable barge. The resulting 90- by 28-foot barge could accommodate two 105-mm howitzers, but was too heavy to be pushed by the Navy LCM(6)s. Captain William G. Pagonis's 1097th Transportation Medium Boat Company was deployed with its larger and more powerful LCM(8)s to the riverine force base at Dong Tam to support the floating artillery. Two batteries of the 3/34th Field Artillery were embarked on the barges. Three barges, each with an Army LCM(8) push boat, could mount a six-tube battery with an additional LCM(8) serving as a fire direction center and command post and another as an ammunition resupply craft. Armor plate was fitted to the sides of the artillery barges, with sections that could be dropped so that the howitzers could fire at zero elevation with antipersonnel "beehive" rounds if the gunners were ambushed as they moved along the waterways. In addition to supporting the 3/34th Field Artillery Battalion, the 1097th also provided logistical support to Fulton's brigade, transporting men and materiel to and from the Dong Tam base. During these artillery and logistical operations, the 1097th frequently came under fire and by the end of its tour in Vietnam had become one of the most decorated units in Transportation Corps history.[44]

The Mobile Riverine Force carried out operations in the Delta until 1969. During this time, some of the old Army–Navy amphibious command and control issues arose once again. General Westmoreland wished to have the force commanded by the assistant division commander of the 9th Division, an Army brigadier general, with a joint Army–Navy staff. The Navy insisted that the joint doctrine, to which the Army had agreed, specified that an amphibious operation would be commanded by a naval officer until the landing force was established ashore, when command passed to the ground commander. The compromise was that there would be no overall commander and the force would operate on the mutual cooperation basis. The senior Army commander would have responsibility for the riverine bases, including the afloat (but anchored) support ships, but once the ships got underway to move to a new location, the senior Navy commander would be in charge until the element anchored again. In combat, the Navy commander took control once the troops were embarked in the landing craft. After they went ashore, the Army commander regained control. When they re-embarked, the Navy commander took charge until they reached the base.[45] The Mobile Riverine Force conducted operations with considerable effectiveness until 1969, when the brigade was withdrawn and the naval assets were either turned over to the Vietnamese as part of the Vietnamization program or incorporated into other Navy coastal and river interdiction forces.[46]

The Navy and Marine Corps carried out amphibious operations throughout the war, beginning with the arrival of one battalion of the 9th Marine Expeditionary Brigade in an administrative landing over the beach (through very heavy surf) at Da Nang on 8 March 1965. In August 1965 Operation STARLIGHT, the first battle of the war in which US forces engaged a large main force Viet Cong unit, began with a helicopter and amphibious assault by a battalion of Marines south of Chu Lai.[47] The Marines carried out several company and battalion-size amphibious operations in 1965, and on 28 January 1966 conducted Operation DOUBLE EAGLE I, with 1,200 Marines of two BLTs landing on the coast of Quang Ngai province.[46] As the Marines became ever more deeply engaged in counterinsurgency and combat operations on land, however, the amphibious operations became the purview of the Seventh Special Landing Force (SLF). This floating mobile contingency force consisted of a regimental staff, a Marine battalion landing team (an infantry battalion reinforced with artillery and other support elements), and a Marine helicopter squadron embarked on the half dozen or so ships of an amphibious ready group (ARG). In 1966 the SLF conducted eight amphibious landings along the entire coast of Vietnam from near Saigon in the south to the DMZ in the north with the objective of trapping enemy forces and interdicting their coastal supply line.[49] A second SLF was established in 1967, but the first operation of the year, in the Mekong Delta area, was the last one conducted outside the I Corps area. The SLF battalions were kept in country for longer and longer periods after each operation and, as the war went on, some came to question the value of these amphibious operations, suggesting that "any combat Marine not ashore and fighting was not being properly utilized."[50] Nonetheless, the operations continued, although more often than not the marines were inserted by helicopter rather than over the beach. In January 1969 the largest amphibious operation of the war, and the largest since CHROMITE, took place south of Chu Lai with two BLTs going ashore in helicopters and LVTs.[51] The last SLF landing took place in September 1969 south of Da Nang with participation by Republic of Korea (ROK) marines.[52]

The United States used amphibious techniques from time to time in the succeeding years to put forces ashore in peacekeeping operations and, on a small scale, in the 1983 Grenada URGENT FURY and 1989 Panama JUST CAUSE operations. From 1987 to 1989, during Operation PRIME CHANCE I, the US Army participation in Operation EARNEST WILL, the reflagging and protection of Kuwaiti oil tankers during the Iran–Iraq War, US Army Special Forces observation and attack helicopters of Detachment 160 using the radio call sign SEABAT, operated from US Navy warships to protect merchant ships transiting the Persian Gulf and to prevent the Iranian Navy from laying mines in the shipping channels.[53]

During Operation JUST CAUSE/NIMROD DANCER, the 1989 US intervention in Panama, the 1097th Transportation Medium Boat Company transported 7th Infantry Division troops by water within Panama; conducted a reinforced company-size amphibious assault at Gamboa Prison on 20 December 1989; assisted Navy special operations forces in coastal security patrols; and ferried cargo, passengers, and prisoners of war across the canal.[54] Operations DESERT SHIELD and DESERT STORM in 1990 and 1991 saw the last large-scale application of an amphibious force in combat, although there was no assault landing, as US Navy and Marine forces offshore in the Persian Gulf during Operation DESERT SHIELD threatened and diverted Iraqi forces.

In 1994 a brigade combat team (BCT) and aviation brigade of the 10th Mountain Division embarked aboard the aircraft carrier USS *Eisenhower* and Special Forces troops and helicopters aboard the USS *America* were prepared to conduct an airmobile assault into Haiti while Marines went in over the beaches. Negotiations precluded the amphibious and airmobile assault, but the ability of Army forces to operate from Navy ships in landing operations was once more demonstrated.[55] In 2001 Special Forces helicopters again operated from US Navy ships when TF *Sword* conducted operations into Afghanistan from the deck of the aircraft carrier USS *Kitty Hawk*.[56]

During the 1980s and 1990s there was increasing emphasis on joint operations and doctrine, a process that was accelerated by the 1986 Goldwater–Nichols Act, which centralized military advice to the President and Secretary of Defense in the Chairman of the Joint Chiefs of Staff and vested operational control of forces in unified commands, with the Services retaining the responsibilities to organize, train, and equip those forces. Joint amphibious doctrine began to appear in the 1990s. The current capstone document, Joint Publication 3-02, *Joint Amphibious Doctrine for Joint Operations*, was published in 2001. It provides a definition of an amphibious operation that is less Service-centric than any of its predecessors:

> A military operation launched from the sea by an amphibious force, embarked in ships or craft with the primary purpose of introducing a landing force (LF) ashore to accomplish an assigned mission. **Types of amphibious operations** [emphasis in original] include assaults, withdrawals, demonstrations, raids, and other amphibious operations in a permissive, uncertain, or hostile environment.[57]

The doctrine continues to evolve. The previously sacrosanct rule that only a naval officer could command an amphibious task force ended in 2004, when Marine Brigadier General Joseph V. Medina assumed command of Expeditionary Strike Group Three.[58] In 2005 the Marine Corps introduced the "Expeditionary Warfare Family of Concepts" that includes "Operational Maneuver from the Sea," "Ship-to-Objective Maneuver" (landing operations), "Sustained Operations Ashore," and "Other Expeditionary Operations."[59] A related concept is "Sea Basing," in which ships and other platforms would be combined to form a base at sea from which Marine or Army forces could conduct and sustain amphibious operations.[60] In 2006 the US Navy announced the organization of riverine forces. As of 2008, the Marine Corps maintained a small number of riverine units,[61] and the Army Transportation Corps had shallow-draft watercraft to conduct riverine logistical support and troop lift operations. In Iraq, Army engineers used bridging boats as ad hoc riverine patrol platforms and Army mariners of the 10th Transportation Battalion trained Army infantrymen to operate and maintain Boston Whalers and Iraqi Fast Assault Boats for riverine operations. However, the Army had no doctrine for the conduct of riverine combat operations.[62]

Department of Defense *Directive 5100.1*, the current manifestation of the Key West Agreement, still requires Army forces to be capable of conducting joint amphibious as well as airborne operations. Since the Vietnam War, however, the Army has focused on airborne and airmobile operations as its forcible entry specialties, essentially leaving the amphibious assault mission to the Marines.[63] The last Army doctrinal publication on amphibious operations, FM 20-12, *Amphibious Embarkation*, was published 25 August 1975. With the deactivation of the 2d Engineer Amphibious Support Command in 1965, the Transportation Corps became the keeper of the Army's amphibious and over-the-shore logistics capabilities and expertise. As of June 2007, those assets resided with the 7th Sustainment Brigade (descendant of the 7th Medium Port that played an important role in the Korean War). The brigade currently includes two terminal battalions with amphibious watercraft. The 10th Transportation Battalion (Terminal) includes a heavy boat company equipped with LCUs, a floating craft company (with tugs, barges, and floating cranes), port operation capabilities, and two of the Army's three Active-Duty Logistic Support Vessels— sea-going ramped ships somewhat reminiscent of Korean War era LSTs. The 24th Transportation Battalion (Terminal) includes floating craft and heavy boat companies, the last remaining medium boat company equipped with LCM(8)s, and a third of the active logistics support vehicles (LSVs). Three other LSVs are in the Reserve component. A third terminal battalion, the 11th, has a LOTS capability and until 2001 its LARC LX Company operated the Army's last LARCs (the only true Army amphibians, because they could operate on both land and sea). The Transportation Corps relinquished its LARCs in October 2001 in anticipation of the acquisition of air cushion vehicles that failed to materialize. Nonetheless, the ramped watercraft and other equipment of the corps continue to provide an ability to deliver troops and cargo over the beach, even if they do not provide a true amphibious capability.[64] At least two other allied nations have Army units with capabilities similar to those of the US Army Transportation Corps. The French 519th Logistics Regiment operates LCMs and LARCs, in addition to other equipment suitable for over-the-beach as well as port operations. The British counterpart is the 17th Port & Maritime Regiment, which operates a fleet of watercraft, including LCUs.[65]

Until the current operations in Iraq became the primary focus of the Army's efforts, there was a renewal of Army interest in, if not amphibious assault, at least the use of seaborne capabilities for operational maneuver. The experience of the First Gulf War and subsequent crises that required the rapid deployment of Army forces led to an examination of the Army's strategic mobility capabilities. In 1999 Secretary of the Army Louis Caldera and Army Chief of Staff General Eric K. Shinseki outlined a concept for Army transformation into a more "responsive, deployable, agile, versatile, lethal, survivable, and sustainable" force.[66] The transformation initiative included restructuring Army forces and a search for ways to make Army combat systems lighter and more easily deployable. A related effort involved improvements in strategic and operational mobility. The wars in Afghanistan and Iraq initially gave further impetus to these efforts, with increasing emphasis on an expeditionary capability as Army transformation developed in the first years of the 21st century. The 2005 *Army Campaign Plan* stated:

> Being expeditionary is far less about deployability than about operational and tactical agility, including the ability to reach routinely beyond organic capabilities for required effects. If in the process the Army can leverage our sister services' mobility, reach, and lethality to satisfy some of those mission requirements, all the better. To achieve that, we must expand our view of Army force design to encompass the entire range of available joint capabilities.[67]

A fundamental requirement for expeditionary operations is strategic mobility based on airlift, sealift, and pre-positioning of military equipment. A limitation of sealift has been that many of the ships available for deployment of Army forces require deep-water ports, hindering rapid and flexible deployment. Attention focused on high-speed sealift platforms that could operate in shallow waters and at austere port facilities. For intertheater sealift, the focus was on a Shallow Draft High Speed Sealift (SDHSS) vessel large enough to carry a substantial number of troops and their equipment to any port with at least a 10-foot depth of water and an offload site.[68] During the East Timor peacekeeping mission, Australian forces made use of high-speed, shallow-draft, catamaran (twin hulled) ships that could carry some 200 troops along with their equipment and light armored vehicles. The US Army leased two of these ships and operated them as HSV-X1 (High Speed Vessel–Experimental) *Joint Venture* and TSV-X1 (Theater Support Vessel–Experimental) *Spearhead,* and subsequently initiated procurement of similar vessels to be used as Theater Support Vessels (TSV) for intratheater lift.[69] Twelve TSVs would be capable of carrying one BCT or Stryker Brigade Combat Team (SBCT), the equivalent of 239 C-17 airlift sorties. There were plans to locate TSVs near BCTs and SBCTs stationed at Fort Lewis, Washington, and Schofield Barracks, Hawaii.[70] However, during 2006, Army funding expired for *Joint Venture* and *Spearhead,* and in 2008 they were returned to the Australian Incat Company. Once again the possibility of the Navy taking over all watercraft operations is under consideration, and the future of Army watercraft is somewhat obscure due to funding and manpower issues.[71]

Conclusions and Lessons Learned

Throughout its long history, the US Army has frequently made use of amphibious techniques to exploit the world's oceans, beaches, and waterways, often in unexpected places and in unanticipated ways. Since the Marine Corps will continue to be the nation's amphibious warfare specialists, future assault landings on hostile shores are likely to be conducted by Marines. But during the Korean War, Army forces had to be prepared to conduct or participate in amphibious operations in the absence of or in conjunction with Marines and may be called on to do so again in the future. It would be prudent for the Army to maintain a small amphibious support element that can develop and test Army-specific doctrine, tactics, techniques, procedures, and equipment and serve as the basis for an Army amphibious-capable force for such situations in which Marine Corps amphibious forces are not available.

Many of the difficult command and control issues that plagued the Services in the past have been overcome or resolved through the development of joint doctrine, the establishment of unified and joint commands, the removal of the Services from the operational branch of the chain of command, and a growing Service mindset attuned to joint operations. No doubt, new issues will arise so long as there are different operating environments and Services optimized to operate in those environments, particularly in times of competition for constrained resources, but it is to be hoped that the kind of counterproductive inter-Service tensions and suspicion that marked some periods of the past will not recur. The question arises whether, in a productive and businesslike joint environment, it is necessary for the Army to control its own amphibious assets, particularly when the large-scale invasions of the type that the Army once saw as its particular forte are unlikely in the foreseeable future.

Some time ago, Lieutenant General Jack C. Fuson, a veteran of the Army's Engineer Amphibious Command, the Camp Edwards Amphibious Training Center, the 2d Engineer Special Brigade in the Southwest Pacific, a port commander during the Korean and Vietnam Wars, Commanding General of Fort Eustis, and Army Deputy Chief of Staff for Logistics, made these points:

> Currently the Army has no capability, no concept, no doctrine, no training, no unit equipment, and no organization to carry out these difficult amphibious operations in combat. The organizations nearest to having such a capability are the Transportation Corps' logistics over-the-shore units, equipped and trained to unload and move cargo. But they are not organized, equipped, or trained to develop lodgment (beachhead) areas with all the engineering requirements that go with such actions. Plans do not exist to marry them up with combat units for assistance

in combat unit landings and their subsequent deployment and unloading over unfriendly beaches in combat. Nor do plans include the even more difficult task of assisting to develop lodgment areas and providing logistics support under combat conditions until normal resupply can be established.

I understand the Army has neither the funds nor the desire to add this capability. It has not been approved as joint doctrine. But if war were to occur, in all probability the Transportation Corps would be called upon to duplicate the actions of the engineer amphibious units in World War II. Therefore, it would be wise for the Transportation Corps, either in its museum or in its school, to acquire all historical information on the Engineer Amphibious Command and its engineer boat and shore regiments of World War II.

They should build a library of manuals, doctrine, organizational information, training literature, and training records. It would certainly be wise to update the information to match the current automated Army supply, maintenance, and transportation doctrine. I'm sure the Army does not believe the need exists; however, filing all the relevant information in the museum and school would make it available should the need ever arise. Looking back on my firsthand experience with the difficulties in learning how to accomplish this mission in World War II, I know that it would be a slow, costly, and difficult job to reinvent such capabilities in the future.[72]

General Fuson's 1994 comments remain valid today. The Army may not have the funds, desire, or personnel to establish the kind of amphibious capability reflected in the past by the Amphibious Training Center or the Engineer Amphibious Support Command, but it should assure that the Army retains its historical memory of doctrine, tactics, techniques, and procedures of amphibious warfare and remains a part of the Marine Corps and Navy efforts to assure that America's amphibious capability remains current and effective.

Notes

1. Departments of the Army, the Navy, and the Air Force, Army Field Manual (FM) 110-5, Navy JAAF, and Air Force Manual (AFM) 1-1, *Joint Action Armed Forces* (Washington, DC: GPO, 1951), 14–16.

2. Army FM 110-5, Navy JAAF, and AFM 101, *Joint Action Armed Forces*, 11.

3. Department of the Navy, Naval Warfare Publication (NWP) 22, *Amphibious Operations* (Washington, DC: GPO, 1952).

4. The Army perspective on this is set forth in a *Chronology and Analysis of the Development of Joint Doctrine for Amphibious Operations* (Fort Monroe, VA: US Army Continental Army Command, 1958). A copy is in the MHI Library.

5. US Army, FM 60-5, *Amphibious Operations: Battalion in Assault Landings*, February 1950 (Draft), 21 February 1951; FM 60-10, *Amphibious Operations: Regiment in Assault Landings*, April 1950 (Draft), January 1952; FM 60-20, *Amphibious Tank and Tractor Battalions*, 24 February 1945 (Superseded by FM 17-34); FM 17-34, *Amphibious Tank and Tractor Battalion*, May 1948 (Draft), June 1950 (Superseded by FM 60-20); FM 60-30, *Amphibious Operations: Embarkation and Ship Loading (Unit Loading Officer)*, 6 September 1952 (Superseded by FM 20-12).

6. FM 60-25, *Employment of the Amphibious Support Brigade*, 8 January 1952; T/O&E 5-511, *Engineer Amphibious Support Regiment*, January 1951; T/O&E 5-512, *Headquarters, Headquarter and Service Company, Engineer Amphibious Support Regiment*, January 1951. The T/O&Es for the Ordnance Maintenance Company (9-97, July 1951) and the Quartermaster Company (10-277, February 1951) also referred to the Amphibious Support Brigade. The field manuals and T/O&Es did not always track precisely. In spite of the name change and appearance of the field manual for the amphibious support brigade, the 1946 Engineer Special Brigade Headquarters and Headquarters Company table of organization and equipment (T/O&E 5-510-1T, January 1946) remained in effect until 1965, when the T/O&E 5-401E series (Engineer Amphibious Brigade) was issued.

7. US Army, *Draft Field Service Regulations: Operations*, 1953, 299–323; US Army, FM 100-5, *Field Service Regulations: Operations* (Washington, DC: GPO, 1954).

8. US Army, Transportation Corps, *Amphibious and Port and Beach Doctrine as it Pertains to the Transportation Corps, United States Army: A Staff Study* (Washington, DC: Office of the Chief of Transportation, 1953).

9. "159th Transportation Battalion (Boat) (Terminal)," unpublished manuscript in files of the Office of the Transportation Corps Command Historian; Norman Friedman and A.D. Baker, *U.S. Amphibious Ships and Craft; An Illustrated Design History* (Annapolis, MD: Naval Institute Press, 2002), 302–303.

10. Department of the Army, Lineage and Honors, Command Headquarters, 2d Engineer Amphibious Support Command, Enclosure 1 to letter, HQDA, OCMH, "Certificate of Lineage and Honors," 30 January 1962, RG 338, Entry

37042, Commands, 2d EASC, Historical Reports, National Archives and Records Administration, Modern Military Records, College Park, MD, hereafter, NACP .

11. Headquarters, The Engineer Center and Fort Belvoir, Virginia, General Orders Number 96, "Activation of Units," 9 November 1956, RG 338, Entry 37042, Commands, 2d EASC, General Orders, NACP; HQDA Message, 211528Z March 1959, "Movement Advice" and "History of the 2d Engineer Amphibious Support Command," n.d., RG 338, Entry 37042, Commands, 2d EASC, Historical Reports, NACP.

12. Richard E. Killblane, "The History of Logistics-Over-The-Shore (LOTS) Operations," unpublished manuscript, n.d., in files of the Command Historian, Fort Eustice, VA.

13. Killblane, "History of LOTS Operations."

14. US Army Forces Antilles and Military District of Puerto Rico, *Sentry Box: USARFANT & MDPR, final report: Vieques Island, 29 March 1954* (Fort Brooke, Puerto Rico: Headquarters, US Army Forces Antilles and Military District of Puerto Rico, 1954).

15. US Sixth Army, *Plan for the Conduct of Exercise Surf Board* (Fort Ord, CA: Headquarters Maneuver Director, Exercise Surf Board, 1955).

16. Jean R. Moenk, *A History of Large-Scale Army Maneuvers in the United States, 1935–1964* (Fort Monroe, VA: Historical Branch, Office of the Deputy Chief of Staff for Military Operations and Reserve Force, US Continental Army Command, December 1969), 203.

17. US Sixth Army, *High Seas: Joint Army–Navy Command Post Exercise: General Plan, Fort Ord, Calif., 16–23 May 1956* (Presidio of San Francisco, CA: Headquarters, Sixth Army, 1956).

18. CONARC, *Chronology and Analysis*, 5. The writer has been unable to locate a copy of the document (Letter, ATTNG-D&R 353 (Amphib)(C), Hq USCONARC, 4 April 1956, "Doctrine Governing Joint Amphibious Operations") that set forth the Army objections, but based on other documentation, it is likely the issue was Army insistence that the unified command concept apply to all phases of the operation, with the Service of the joint amphibious task force commander being determined by paramount interest, as opposed to Navy insistence that command of a joint amphibious task force is a naval function, regardless of the assignment of command above the level of the amphibious task force.

19. Moenck, 222; US Sixth Army, *Rocky Shoals: Army–Navy Amphibious Exercise, California 1958: Observers Handbook* (Presidio of San Francisco, CA: Headquarters Sixth Army, Office of the Commanding General, 1958); Exercise Rocky Shoals Miscellaneous Papers, both in the MHI Archives.

20. CONARC, *Chronology and Analysis*, 6.

21. Philip A. Crowl, Memorandum for the Chief of Military History, "Critique of Proposed Training Circular, 'Doctrines Governing Joint Amphibious Operations' submitted by the Office of the Adjutant General, Department of the Army, 21 December 1954," 21 April 1955. Copy in OCMH, CMH 228.03, HRC 353, "Amphibious Operations."

22. NWP 22, paragraph 1800.

23. Crowl, Memorandum, "Critique of Proposed Training Circular," 6–9.

24. Crowl, Memorandum, "Critique of Proposed Training Circular," 9–11.

25. Crowl, Memorandum, "Critique of Proposed Training Circular," 2–6.

26. Crowl, Memorandum, "Critique of Proposed Training Circular," 12–13; the quoted material is from AFM 1–5, 11.

27. CONARC, *Chronology and Analysis*, 9.

28. US Army, FM 31-11, US Navy NWP 22(A), US Marine Corps LFM 01, *Doctrine for Amphibious Operations* (Washington, DC: Departments of the Army and the Navy, July 1962).

29. US Army, FM 31-11, US Navy NWP 22(A), US Air Force AFM 2-53, US Marine Corps LFM 01, *Doctrine for Amphibious Operations* (Washington, DC: Departments of the Army, the Navy, and the Air Force, 2 August 1967).

30. US Army, FM 3-11, *Doctrine for Amphibious Operations*, August 1967.

31. US Army, FM 31-12, *Army Forces in Amphibious Operations (The Army Landing Force)* (Washington, DC: GPO, March 1961).

32. US Army, FM 5-144, *Engineer Amphibious Units* (Washington, DC: GPO, November 1966, with Change 1, 9 May 1969), 1-1–1-3, 2-1–2-3, 4-1, 4-7–4-11; TOE 5-408G, *Engineer Amphibious Company*, February 1968; TOE 5-407G, *Engineer Amphibian Assault Company*, March 1968; TOE 5-405G, *Engineer Amphibious Battalion*, May 1968.

33. US Army Engineer School, *Operation SUNSET*, USAR ADT Course S.122-117 (Fort Belvoir, VA: The Department of Engineering and Military Science, US Army Engineer School, 1 June 1964), copy in the Engineer School Collection, MHI Archives.

34. *Historical Summary, June 1942 through December 1962,* Headquarters, 2d Engineer Amphibious Support Command, 2 April 1965; *Annual Historical Summary, 2d Engineer Amphibious Support Command, 1 January 1963 to 31 December 1963; Final Historical Report,* Headquarters, 2d Engineer Amphibious Support Command, n.d., RG 338, Entry 37042, Box 1, NACP. "LVTP5s borrowed from the Marines": letter from Mr. David Diels to Colonel (Retired) Donald W. Boose Jr., 8 June 2006. Mr. Diels was a platoon leader in the 560th Amphibian Tractor Company (Engineer Equipment Company) in 1965. The ephemeral nature of these engineer amphibious units is reflected in an Infantry School manual on amphibious operations published in 1962 that makes no mention of the engineer amphibious units or the transportation boat units, but simply states, "The nucleus of the division shore party is the engineer battalion. Other combat service support and naval beach party elements may be assigned as required." *Amphibious Operations Manual* (Fort Benning, GA: US Army Infantry School, September 1962), 21.

35. E-mail message from Richard E. Killblane, Transportation Corps Command Historian, to Colonel (Retired) Donald W. Boose Jr., 16 June 2008.

36. Shelby L. Stanton, *Vietnam Order of Battle* (Washington, DC: U.S. News Books, 1981), 222–223; "A History of the 4th Transportation Command," in *The History of Army Transportation Units in Vietnam,* grambo.us/atav/history. htm (accessed 13 February 2008).

37. Carroll H. Drum, *Vietnam Studies: Base Development in South Vietnam, 1965–1970* (Washington, DC: Department of the Army, 1972), 54–58, 68–69.

38. "159th Transportation Battalion," unpublished manuscript, 5–12; Killblane, "History of LOTS Operations."

39. Stanton, *Vietnam Order of Battle*, 224–227.

40. Richard E. Killblane, "Army Riverine Operations in Vietnam and Panama (What the Navy Won't Tell You)," unpublished manuscript, n.d., copy provided to author by Mr. Killblane; "A Brief History of the VungTau/Delta Transportation Battalion (Provisional)," *History of Army Transportation Units in Vietnam.* For other logistic and tactical boat operations see, for example, "1099th Transportation Company (Medium Boat)," also in *History of Army Transportation Units in Vietnam.*

41. Killblane, "Army Riverine Operations in Vietnam and Panama," 15–17.

42. The writer participated in one such operation in early 1967 as senior advisor to the 1st Battalion, 14th ARVN Infantry, 9th ARVN Division, when several ARVN battalions landed on the coast of Vinh Binh province in LCUs and LCMs.

43. George L. MacGarrigle, *United States Army in Vietnam: Combat Operations: Taking the Offensive, October 1966 to October 1967* (Washington, DC: Center of Military History, 1998), 395–397, 401, 405, 413–414. General Fulton has described the operations of the Mobile Riverine Force in detail in William B. Fulton, *Vietnam Studies: Riverine Operations 1966–1969* (Washington, DC: Center of Military History, 1985); William B. Fulton, *Mobile Riverine Force: America's Mobile Riverine Force Vietnam* (Paducah, KY: Turner Publishing Co., 1998).

44. David Ewing Ott, *Vietnam Studies: Field Artillery, 1954–1973* (Washington, DC: Department of the Army, 1975) 76–80; 1097th Transportation Company (Medium Boat), Unit History Annual Supplement, 1 March 1968, and Headquarters, 1st Logistical Command News Release, 8 July 1968, both reprinted in Douglas R. Magee Jr., "The Striking History of the 1097th Transportation Company" (Panama: USARSO Printing Plant, 1997); Killblane, "Army Riverine Operations in Vietnam and Panama," 17–20.

45. MacGarrigle, *US Army in Vietnam,* 414–415.

46. Killblane, "Army Riverine Operations in Vietnam and Panama," 21; Jim Mesko, *Riverine: A Pictorial History of the Brown Water Navy in Vietnam* (Carrollton, TX: Squadron/Signal Publications, 1985).

47. Jack Shulimson and Charles M. Johnson, *U.S. Marines in Vietnam: The Landing and the Buildup, 1965* (Washington, DC: History and Museums Division, Headquarters, US Marine Corps, 1978), 9–15, 72.

48. Shulimson and Johnson, *The Landing and the Buildup, 1965,* 84–203; Jack Shulimson, *U.S. Marines in Vietnam: An Expanding War, 1966* (Washington, DC: History and Museums Division, Headquarters, US Marine Corps, 1982), 19–28.

49. Shulimson, *An Expanding War,* 297–306.

50. Gary L. Telfer and Lane Rogers, *U.S. Marines in Vietnam: Fighting the North Vietnamese, 1967* (Washington, DC: History and Museums Division,

Headquarters, US Marine Corps, 1984), 150–181; Quotation, "any Marine not ashore": Charles R. Smith, *U.S. Marines in Vietnam: High Mobility and Standdown, 1969* (Washington, DC: History and Museums Division, Headquarters, US Marine Corps, 1988), 297.

51. Telfer and Rogers, *Fighting the North Vietnamese,* 300–301.

52. Graham A. Cosmas and Terrence P. Murray, *U.S. Marines in Vietnam*: *Vietnamization and Redeployment, 1970–1971* (Washington, DC: History and Museums Division, Headquarters, US Marine Corps, 1986), 386.

53. John W. Partin, *Special Operations in Operation EARNEST WILL/PRIME CHANCE I* (MacDill Air Force Base, FL: US Special Operations Command, History and Research Office, 1998), describes these operations. See also Harold Lee Wise, *Inside the Danger Zone: The U.S. Military in the Persian Gulf, 1987–1988* (Annapolis, MD: Naval Institute Press, 2007), 76, 80, 84, 89, 97–102.

54. Edward M. Flanagan Jr., "Battle for Panama: Inside Operation Just Cause" (Washington, DC: Brassey's (US), 1993), 130–131, reprinted in Magee, *The Striking History of the 1097th Transportation Company*; Killblane, "Army Riverine Operations in Vietnam and Panama," 21–22. Operation NIMROD DANCER was the Army deployment to Panama of forces during Operation JUST CAUSE.

55. John R. Ballard, *Upholding Democracy: The United States Military Campaign in Haiti, 1994–1997* (Westport, CT, and London: Praeger, 1998), 91–93, 105–118; Joseph Fischer, Richard Stewart, and Stanley Sandler, *Operation UPHOLD/RESTORE/MAINTAIN DEMOCRACY* (Fort Bragg, NC: US Army Special Operations Command, Directorate of History, Archive, Library and Museums, 1997), 28–32; Walter E. Kretchik, Robert F. Baumann, and John T. Fischel, *Invasion, Intervention, "Intervasion": A Concise History of the U.S. Army in Operation Uphold Democracy* (Fort Leavenworth, KS: US Army Command and General Staff College Press, 1998), 59–79.

56. Benjamin S. Lambeth, *Airpower Against Terror: America's Conduct of Operation Enduring Freedom* (Santa Monica, CA: RAND Corporation, 2005), 65, 123, 146; Rebecca Grant, "An Air War Like No Other," *Air Force Magazine*, Vol. 85, No. 11 (November 2002): 33.

57. US Joint Chiefs of Staff, Joint Publication 3-02, *Joint Doctrine for Amphibious Operations* (Washington, DC: The Joint Staff, 2001).

58. Jared Plotts, "U.S. Marine Corps Brig. Gen. Joseph V. Medina: Marine General Leads Strike Group into History," *Defend America News,* 10 June 2004, defendamerica.mil/cgi-bin/prfriendly.cgi?http://www.defendamerica.mil/ profiles/jun2004/pr0601004a.html (accessed 31 May 2007); Official Biography: Joseph V. Medina, usmc.mil/genbios2.nsf/biographies/DA9C6F9E36A70158852 56D730013425D?opendocument (accessed 31 May 2007).

59. Headquarters, United States Marine Corps, "Expeditionary Maneuver Family of Concepts," *Marine Corps Concepts and Programs,* 2005, hqinet001. hqmc.usmc.mil/p&r/concepts/2005/PDF/Ch2PDFs/CP05%20Chapter%202%20 Warfighting%20Concepts%20pg%20025_Expeditionary%20Maneuver%20Warf are%20Family%20of%20Concepts.pdf (accessed 13 May 2007).

60. Henry B. Cook, "Sea Basing and Maritime Pre-positioning," *Army Logistician*, Vol. 36, No. 3 (May–June 2004): 36–39; Scott C. Truver, "The Sea Base: Cornerstone of the U.S. Tri-Service Maritime Strategy," *Naval Forces*, Vol. XXIX, No. II, 2008; *Seapower for a New Era,* 24–25, 114–130.

61. Amy Klamper, "River War," *Seapower*, Vol. 49, No. 2 (February 2006): 10–12; Patrick Donahoe and Laurence McCabe, "Controlling the Rivers," *U.S. Naval Institute Proceedings,* Vol. 132, No.1 (January 2006): 27; Milan Vego, "Warfare Concepts: Riverine Warfare," *Naval Forces*, Vol. XXIX, No. 11 (2008): 26–33; Edward Wiser, "One Size Does NOT Fit All: A dialogue between industry and government is producing new mount for the riverine cavalry," *U.S. Naval Institute Proceedings,* Vol. 134, No. 6 (June 2008): 26–31. Also see Daniel A. Hancock, "The Navy's Not Serious About Riverine Warfare," *U.S. Naval Institute Proceedings,* Vol. 134, No.1 (January 2008).

62. For the Army Transportation Corps riverine lift capability, I am indebted to Colonel Clark H. Summers, US Army Transportation Corps, former commander of the 385th Transportation Battalion. For Army mariners training infantrymen in riverine techniques, see Richard E. Killblane, "Operation Iraqi Freedom/Enduring Freedom Trip Report 2008," unpublished manuscript, April 2008, copy in the files of the Transportation Corps Command Historian, Fort Eustis, VA.

63. US Department of Defense, *Directive 5100.1,* "Functions of the Department of Defense and Its Major Components" (Washington, DC: Department of Defense, 1 August 2001), 17, paragraph 6.6.1.2.3, dtic.mil/whs/directives/corres/pdf/d51001_080102/d51001p.pdf (accessed 6 April 2006). For the Army emphasis on airborne and airmobile operations, see, for example, James B. Brown, "Joint Amphibious/Air Assault Operations," *Joint Force Quarterly* (Autumn/Winter 1998–99): 48–52; Brian J. Dunn, "Rethinking Army–Marine Corps Roles," *Joint Force Quarterly* (Autumn 2000): 38–42.

64. 7th Sustainment Brigade home page, 7sustainment.forscom.army.mil/default.htm (accessed 13 June 2007); US Army, Office of the Chief of Transportation, "Army Watercraft Master Plan and Theater Support Vessel (TSV) Information Briefing," 22 May 2002, globalsecurity.org/military/library/report/2002/CASCOM_AWMP_and_TSV.pdf (accessed 10 February 2007); Stephen Harding, *Sail Army: A Pictorial Guide to Current U.S. Army Watercraft* (Missoula, MT: Pictorial Histories Publishing Co., 2005); information provided by OCOT Command Historian, 12 June 2007. Information on 309th LARC LX Company: e-mail message, Richard E. Killblane to Donald W. Boose Jr., 16 June 2008.

65. Gunnar Borch and Massimo Annati, "Maritime Sealift—Organizations and Assets." *Naval Forces*, Vol. XXVI, No. VI (2005): 18.

66. "The Army Magazine Hooah Guide to Army Transformation" provides a readable overview of the background of Army Transformation and its status as of 2001, ausa.org/PDFDocs/Hooah_Guide_web.pdf (accessed 6 April 2006).

67. US Army, "Organizing for Conflict," *United States Army: Serving A Nation At War*, army.mil/jec/5_dms.html (accessed 30 June 2005).

68. Kenneth E. Hickins, "Strategic Mobility: The U.S. Military's Weakest Link," *Army Logistician*, Vol. 34, No. 6 (November–December 2002): 34–37;

Shawn M. Callahan, *The Impact of Fastship and High Speed Sealift on Strategic Sealift*, Research Report (Maxwell Air Force Base, AL: Air Command and Staff College, Air University, 1998), fas.org/man/dod-101/sys/ship/docs/99-021.pdf (accessed 25 March 2005); "High Speed Sealift," *Global Security.Org*, globalsecurity.org/military/systems/ship/hss.htm (accessed 25 March 2005); US Army, *United States Army 2003 Transformation Roadmap* (Washington, DC: Headquarters, Department of the Army, 2004), 8–15.

69. *Army 2003 Transformation Roadmap*, 8–15; Harding, *Sail Army: A Pictorial Guide*, 7–17; Huba Wass de Czege and Zbigniew M. Majchrzak, "Enabling Operational Maneuver From Strategic Distances," *Military Review*, May–June 2002, leavenworth.army.mil/milrev/English/MayJun02/wass.htm (accessed 25 September 2007); Stephen R. Trauth et al., "Army Transformation at Sea: The New Theater Support Vessel," *Military Review*, November–December 2005; OCOT, "Army Watercraft Master Plan and Theater Support Vessel (TSV) Information Briefing," 22 May 2002, globalsecurity.org/military/library/report/2002/CASCOM_AWMP_and_TSV.pdf (accessed 30 March 2006); OCOT, "Theater Support Vessel Information Briefing," unpublished PowerPoint presentation, Fort Eustis, VA: US Army Combined Arms Support Command, Directorate of Combat Development for Transportation, 1 September 2003; OCOT, "Theater Support Vessel," unpublished PowerPoint presentation [2003?]; US Army, Office of the Transportation Corps Command Historian, "Interview with General Robert Dail," unpublished manuscript, 5 November 2002; *Army 2003 Transformation Roadmap*, 8–15; Kenneth E. Hickins, "Transforming Strategic Mobility," *Army Logistician*, Vol. 35, No. 3 (May–June 2003), almc.army.mil/alog/issues/MayJun03/MS856.htm (accessed 25 March 2005).

70. Association of the United States Army, "Force Projection Capability for a Transforming Army," May 2002, ausa.org/PDFdocs/tsv.pdf (accessed 31 March 2006); US Department of Defense News Release, "Department of Army Unveils Active Component Brigade Combat Team Stationing," 27 July 2005, army.mil/modularforces/index.htm (accessed 21 February 2006); John M. Brown III, "USARPAC: The Army's Expeditionary Force in the Pacific," *Army*, Vol. 55, No. 10 (October 2005): 115–118.

71. Information provided to the writer by the Transportation Corps Command Historian, 13 June 2007. On return of the ships to Incat: Incat Internet site, www.incat.com/au/domino/incat/incatweb.nsf/v-title/Incat%20Home?OpenDocument (accessed 21 June 2008). Potential use of these vessels continues to be a matter of discussion. See, for example, Edward H. Lundquist, "Fleet Experimentation Lays Groundwork for New Concepts at Sea," *Naval Forces,* Vol. XXIX, No. 11 (2008): 20–25; and Robert K. Morrison and Phillip E. Pournelle, "Widen the Lens for JHSV," *U.S. Naval Institute Proceedings*, Vol. 134, No. 6 (June 2008): 54–58.

72. Jack C. Fuson, *Transportation and Logistics: One Man's Story* (Washington, DC: Center of Military History, 1994), 201.

Glossary

AAA	antiaircraft artillery
ABC-1	American, British, and Canadian Conference
AFF	Army Field Forces
AFM	Air Force Manual
AGF	Army Ground Forces
AKA	attack cargo ships
ANGLICO	Air and Naval Gunfire Liaison Company
ANZAC	Australian and New Zealand Corps
AOA	amphibious objective area
AOR	area of responsibility
APA	attack transport ship
APD	high-speed transport (auxiliary personnel-transport destroyer)
ARG	amphibious ready group
ARVN	Army of the Republic of Vietnam
ASB	amphibious support brigade
ASSP	auxiliary submarine transport
AST	Army Transport Service
ATB	amphibian tank battalion
ATC	Amphibious Training Command/Amphibious Training Center
ATT	Army Training Test
ATTB	amphibious tank and tractor battalion
AU	Army unit
AW	automatic weapon
BARC	barge, amphibious resupply, cargo
BCOF	British Commonwealth Forces
BCT	brigade combat team
BHL	beachhead line
BLT	battalion landing team
CAMID	cadets–midshipmen
CCBP	Combined Communications Board Publication
CCF	Chinese Communist Forces
CCKW	2½-ton truck
CIA	Central Intelligence Agency
C-in-C	commander in chief
CINCFE	Commander in Chief, Far East
CINCPAC	Commander in Chief, Pacific Command/Commander in Chief, Pacific Fleet
CINCPOA	Commander in Chief, Pacific Ocean Areas
CINCUNC	Commander in Chief, United Nations Command
CNO	Chief of Naval Operations
COHQ	Combined Operations Headquarters
COMNAVFE	Commander, United States Naval Forces, Far East
CONARC	Continental Army Command

357

CONUS	Continental United States
CP	command post
CPV	Chinese People's Volunteers
CTF	combined task force/commander, task force
DANFS	*Dictionary of American Naval Fighting Ships*
DEW	Distant Early Warning
DMZ	demilitarized zone
DPRK	Democratic People's Republic of Korea
DUKW	2½-ton amphibious truck
EAB	engineer amphibian brigade
EAC	Engineer Amphibian Command
EASC	engineer amphibious support command
EASR	engineer amphibious support regiment
EB&SR	engineer boat and shore regiment
ESB	engineer special brigade
ETO	European Theater of Operations
EUSA	Eighth United States Army
EUSAK	Eighth United States Army in Korea
FAB	field artillery battalion
FEAF	Far East Air Forces
FEC	Far East Command
FECOM	Far East Command (used in Washington)
FHA	foreign humanitarian assistance
FLEX	Fleet Landing Exercise
FM	field manual
FMC	Food Machinery Corporation
FMF	Fleet Marine Force
GHQ	General Headquarters
GPA	General Purpose Amphibian
GPO	Government Printing Office
HMAS	Her Majesty's Australian Ship
HMCS	Her Majesty's Canadian Ship
HMS	Her Majesty's Ship
HQDA	Headquarters, Department of the Army
HRE	Han River Estuary
HSV-X	High Speed Vessel–Experimental
ISTDC	Inter-Service Training and Development Center
JAAF	Joint Action Armed Forces
JAAN	Joint Action of the Army and Navy
JANAP	Joint Army Navy Air Publication
JASCO	Joint Assault Signal Company
JCS	Joint Chiefs of Staff
jg	junior grade
JLC	Japan Logistical Command
JLFM	Joint Landing Force Manual

JPC	Joint Planning Committee
JSPOG	Joint Strategic Plans and Operations Group
JTF	joint task force
KATUSA	Korean Augmentation to the US Army
KMAG	Korean Military Advisory Group
KMC	Korean Marine Corps
KPA	North Korean People's Army
LARC	lighter, amphibious resupply, cargo
LARC-LX	lighter, amphibious resupply, cargo, 60-ton
LCA	landing craft, assault
LCI	landing craft, infantry
LCI(G)	landing craft, infantry (gunboat)
LCI(L)	landing craft, infantry (large)
LCM	landing craft, mechanized
LCP(L)	landing craft, personnel (large)
LCP(R)	landing craft, personnel (ramped)
LCS(L)	landing craft, support (large)
LCT	landing craft, tank
LCU	landing craft, utility
LCVP	landing craft, vehicle, personnel
LEX	landing exercise
LF	landing force
LFM	landing force manual
LOTS	logistics-over-the-shore
LSD	landing ship, dock
LSI	landing ship, infantry
LSM	landing ship, medium
LSM(R)	landing ship, medium (rocket)
LST	landing ship, tank
LSU	landing ship, utility
LSV	logistic support vessel
LVT	landing vehicle, tracked
LVT(A)	landing vehicle, tracked (armored)
LVTP	landing vehicle, tracked, personnel
LVTR	landing vehicle, tracked, retriever
MACV	Military Assistance Command, Vietnam
MAG	Marine Air Group
MAW	Marine Air Wing
MCUA	Marine Corps University Archives
MDL	Military Demarcation Line
MDPR	Military District of Puerto Rico
MHI	Military History Institute
MP	military police
MSTS	Military Sea Transportation Service
MTO	Mediterranean Theater of Operations

MTT	Mobile Training Team
NAVFE	Naval Forces Far East
NCO	noncommissioned officer
NEO	noncombatant evacuation operation
NODEX	New Offshore Delivery Exercise
NSC	National Security Council
NWP	Navy Warfare Publication
OCOT	Office of the Chief of Transportation
OCMH	Office of the Chief of Military History
ODEX	Offshore Discharge Exercise
OPLAN	operation plan
OPORD	operation order
PBR	river patrol boat
POA	Pacific Ocean Areas
PIR	Periodic Intelligence Report
POL	petroleum, oils, and lubricants
PORTREX	Puerto Rican Exercise
POW	prisoner of war
PT	patrol torpedo
QM	Quartermaster
RAAF	Royal Australian Air Force
RCN	Royal Canadian Navy
RCT	regimental combat team
RGR	ranger
RN	Royal Navy
ROAD	Reorganized Army Division
ROK	Republic of Korea
ROKA	Republic of Korea Army
ROKAF	Republic of Korea Air Force
SAG	Special Activities Group
SBCT	Stryker Brigade Combat Team
SCAJAP	Shipping Control Administration, Japan
SCAP	Supreme Commander of the Allied Powers
SDHSS	Shallow Draft High Speed Sealift
SEATO	Southeast Asia Treaty Organization
SFCP	Shore Fire Control Party
SLF	Special Landing Force
SOG	Special Operations Group
SPOBS	Special Observers
STRAC	Strategic Army Command
SWPA	Southwest Pacific Area
TOE (T/O&E)	table of organization and equipment
TAC	tactical air command
TACP	tactical air control party
TC	Transportation Corps

TE	task element
TF	task force
TG	task group
TM	technical manual
TQM	transportation quartermaster
TRANSDIV	transport division
TSV	Theater Support Vessel
TSV-X	Theater Support Vessel–Experimental
TTU	troop training unit
TU	task unit
UDT	underwater demolition team
UDU	underwater demolition unit
UN	United Nations
UNC	United Nations Command
UNCMAC	United Nations Component of the Military Armistice Commission
US	United States
USAFBI	United States Army Forces in the British Isles
USAFFE	United States Army Forces in the Far East
USARFANT	United States Army Forces Antilles
USMC	United States Marine Corps
USMCR	United States Marine Corps Reserve
WestPac	Western Pacific
WPD	War Plans Division

Bibliography

US Military

US Army

Department of the Army. *Directive for Implementing the Army's Participation in Joint Puerto Rican Exercises, Fiscal Year 1950.* Department of the Army, Office of the Adjutant General. Washington DC, 7 November 1949.

———. HQDA Message, 211528Z March 1959. "Movement Advice" and "History of the 2d Engineer Amphibious Support Command," n.d.

———. Lineage and Honors, Command Headquarters, 2d Engineer Amphibious Support Command. Enclosure 1 to letter, HQDA, OCMH, "Certificate of Lineage and Honors," 30 January 1962.

———. "Organizing for Conflict." *United States Army: Serving A Nation At War.* army.mil/jec/5_dms.html (accessed 30 June 2005).

———. *Summary of messages exchanged between CINCFE and the JCS concerning the Inchon landing conducted in Korea in September 1950.* Washington, DC: Office of the Assistant Chief of Staff, G3, Operations [1954?].

———. *The pre-Inchon North Korean People's Army.* Washington, DC: Office of the Assistant Chief of Staff, G2, 1951.

———. *United States Army 2003 Transformation Roadmap.* Washington, DC: Headquarters, Department of the Army, 2004.

Headquarters, Engineer Center and Fort Belvoir, VA. General Orders Number 96, "Activation of Units," 9 November 1956.

Office of the Chief of Transportation. *Amphibious and Port and Beach Doctrine as it Pertains to the Transportation Corps, United States Army: A Staff Study.* Washington, DC: Office of the Chief of Transportation, 24 August 1953.

———. "Army Watercraft Master Plan and Theater Support Vessel (TSV) Information Briefing." 22 May 2002. globalsecurity.org/military/library/report/2002/CASCOM_AWMP_and_TSV.pdf (accessed 10 February 2007).

———. Command Historian. "Interview with General Robert Dail." Unpublished manuscript. 5 November 2002.

———. "Theater Support Vessel Information Briefing." Unpublished PowerPoint presentation. Fort Eustis, VA: US Army Combined Arms Support Command, Directorate of Combat Development for Transportation, 1 September 2003.

———. "Theater Support Vessel." Unpublished PowerPoint presentation [2003?].

Office of Military History. *Anzio Beachhead, 22 January–25 May 1944.* Washington, DC: GPO, 1948.

———. *The Administration and Logistical History of the ETO, Part I, The Predecessor Commands: SPOBS and USAFBI.* 1945.

————. *The Administration and Logistical History of the ETO, Part II, Organization and Command in the ETO, Vol. I.* March 1946.

Recruiting, Publicity Bureau. "Put 'em Across! That is the Slogan of the Army Engineer Command." *Army Life and United States Army Recruiting News*, Vol. XXIV, No. 8, August 1942.

US Army Armored School. "Loading of Tanks for Assault Landings." Research report prepared by Student Committee 2. Fort Knox, KY: US Army Armored School, April 1952.

————. "The armored division as an assault landing force." Research report prepared by Committee 34, Officers Advanced Course, US Army Armored School, 1951–52; Alva T. McDaniel, et al. Fort Knox, KY: US Army Armored School, 1952.

US Army Caribbean. *Critique Joint Puerto Rican Exercise, FY 1950 Held at Vieques Island, Puerto Rico, 12 March 1950.* Washington DC: National Archives and Records Administration.

————. Headquarters, Army Forces. Exercise PORTREX. *Report on Participation on Exercise PORTREX.* Headquarters, Army Forces, Exercise PORTREX, Fort Benning, GA, 15 April 1950.

US Army Center of Military History. *Correspondence Relating to the War With Spain Including the Insurrection in the Philippine Islands and the China Relief Expedition, April 15, 1898, to July 30, 1902, Vol. 1.* Washington, DC: Center of Military History, US Army, 1993.

US Army Command and General Staff College. Army Forces in Amphibious Operations. The Army Landing Force. Text, October 1960.

————. "Infantry Division in Amphibious Operations." Subject 3503A. Fort Leavenworth, KS: US Army Command and General Staff College, 31 March 1948.

US Army Continental Army Command. *Chronology and Analysis of the Development of Joint Doctrine for Amphibious Operations.* Fort Monroe, VA: US Army Continental Army Command, July 1958.

————. "Doctrinal Guidance for Instruction and Training Literature Concerning the Army Amphibious Land Force." Memo w/3 encl, 7 June 1956. Fort Monroe, VA.

US Army Engineer Amphibious Command. *Engineer Amphibian Troops: Intelligence, Navigation & Communications.* Tentative Training Guide No 5, Camp Edwards, MA, 1943.

US Army Engineer School. "Abstract of Proceedings, Conference of General and Special Service School Instructors, 15–18 August 1949." Fort Belvoir, VA: US Army Engineer School, Engineer Center, and Fort Belvoir, 1949.

————. *Operation SUNSET*, USAR ADT Course S.122-117. Fort Belvoir, VA: Department of Engineering and Military Science, US Army Engineer School, 1 June 1964.

US Army European Theater of Operations. *Conference on Landing Assaults 24 May–23 June 1943.* US Assault Training Center, European Theater of Operations, US Army, 1943.

————. *Report of the General Board, United States Forces, European Theater.* Study No. 22: "Control of the Build-up of Troops in a Cross-channel Amphibious Operation as Illustrated in Operation Overlord"; Study No. 72: "Engineer Tactical Policies"; Study No. 129: "Mounting the Operation 'Overlord'," The General Board, US Forces European Theater of Operations, 1945, 1946.

US Army Forces Antilles and Military District of Puerto Rico. *Sentry Box: USARFANT & MDPR, final report: Vieques Island, 29 March 1954.* Fort Brooke, Puerto Rico: Headquarters, US Army Forces Antilles and Military District of Puerto Rico, 1954.

US Army Forces Far East. *UN Partisan Forces in the Korean Conflict, 1951–52: A Study of Their Characteristics and Operations.* Project MHD-3. Seoul: 8086th Army Unit (USAFFE Military History Detachment), 1954.

US Army Forces, Pacific, General Headquarters, Office of the Chief Engineer. *Engineers of the Southwest Pacific, Vol. IV, Amphibian Engineer Operations.* Washington, DC: GPO, 1959.

US Army Infantry School. *Amphibious Operations Manual.* Fort Benning, GA, September 1962.

US Army Military History Institute. *Photographs, Exercise Miki, 1949.* Maneuver and Training Exercises Photograph Collection.

————. *Photographs, Exercise Seminole.* Maneuver and Training Exercises Photograph Collection.

US Army Training and Doctrine Command. *The U.S. Army; An Unavoidable Challenge: Army Concept Summaries.* Fort Monroe, VA: Headquarters, US Army Training and Doctrine Command, TRADOC Futures Center, Concept Development & Experimentation Directorate, Army Concept Branch, 29 March 2004.

US Army War College. "Amphibious Warfare: To Analyze Current US Amphibious Doctrine and Techniques in Order to Determine Their Adequacy and Effectiveness." Command Report. Fort Leavenworth, KS: Army War College, January 1951.

————. "Course at the Army War College, 1929–1930, G1." Report of Committee No. 8: "Joint Army and Navy Landing Operations; Modification in Training, Equipment, and Supply for Long Overseas Expeditions, and Operations in Specific Theaters; and Principles Governing the Construction of War Plans, Including Joint Army and Navy War Plans," 26 October 1929.

————. *Summary of PISGAH IV Report: Triphibious Operations in Future Limited and General Wars.* Carlisle Barracks, PA: US Army War College, 4 October 1957.

US Second Army. *Report: Joint Puerto Rican Exercise (PORTREX).* Fort George G. Meade, MD: Headquarters, Second Army, 1 July 1950.

US Fifth Army. *Fifth Army History, Part I, From Activation to the Fall of Naples.* Florence: Headquarters, Fifth Army, 1944.

US Sixth Army. Headquarters, Sixth Army. *Report of PHIBTEST,* 19 September 1952.

————. *High Seas: Joint Army–Navy Command Post Exercise: General Plan.* Fort Ord, CA, 16–23 May 1956. Presidio of San Francisco, CA: Headquarters, Sixth Army, 1956.

————. *Plan for the Conduct of Exercise Surf Board.* Fort Ord, CA: Headquarters Maneuver Director, Exercise Surf Board, 1955.

————. *Rocky Shoals: Army–Navy Amphibious Exercise, California 1958: Observers Handbook.* Presidio of San Francisco, CA: Headquarters, Sixth Army, Office of the Commanding General, 1958.

————. *Sixth Army Report on Amphibious Training Program, 1946.* Presidio of San Francisco, CA: Headquarters, Sixth Army [1946?].

US Eighth Army in Korea. Headquarters, Eighth United States Army Korea (EUSAK), Transportation Section. Brochure of TC Activities, 7 April 1951.

————. Command Report, 1951, Section IV: After-Action Interviews, Book 3: *Hwachon Dam.* Interviews by 1st Lt Martin Blumenson, 3d Historical Detachment, Military History Section, Eighth United States Army Korea (EUSAK), 1951.

————. *Logistical Problems and Their Solutions: Monograph.* Compiled by personnel of the Historical Section, EUSAK and the Eighth Army Historical Service Detachment (Prov.), Seoul: Headquarters, Eighth US Army Korea (EUSAK) [1950–52?].

————.*Quartermaster Supply and Services in The Korean Campaign.* Tokyo: Eighth US Army (Forward), Office of the Quartermaster, 25 May 1955.

US X Corps. *Headquarters X Corps operations orders: Inchon Seoul invasion, no. 1-4; Northeastern Korean operations, no. 5-10; Southeastern & central Korean operations, no. 11-* [?]. Headquarters, X Corps, 1950.

————.*X Corps operations orders: Inchon Seoul invasion, no. 1-10; Northeastern Korean operations, no. 11-40; Southeastern & central Korean operations, no. 41-[?].* Headquarters, X Corps, n.d.

————. *X Corps operations instructions.*

————. *X Corps Operation Order No. 1, 28 August 1950.*

————. *Periodic intelligence report.* Headquarters, X Corps, n.d.

————. *Periodic operations reports: Inchon Seoul invasion, no. 1-16; Northeastern Korean operations, no. 17-91; Southeastern & central Korean operations, no. 92-[?].* Headquarters, X Corps [1950?].

————. *Special report on the Hungnam Evacuation, 9–24 December 1950.* Headquarters, X Corps, 1950.

————. X Corps War Diary, Monthly Summary, 1 October 1950 to 31 October 1950.

US XVI Corps. *XVI Corps Command Report.* 1 May 1951–30 April 1953.

US 3d Infantry Division. "3d Infantry Division." US Army Center of Military History, Force Structure and Unit History Branch.

US 7th Infantry Division. US 7th Infantry Division, *War Diary, 1 September to 30 September 1950.*

————. *Bayonet: A History of the 7th Infantry Division* [1951?].

———. *History of the 7th Infantry (Bayonet) Division*. Tokyo, Japan: Dai Nippon Publishing Co., 1967.

———. *Seventh Infantry Division History*. Paducah, KY: Turner Publishing Company, 1991.

———. *The Bayonet: The History of the 7th Infantry Division in Korea*. Public Information Office, 7th Infantry Division for the 7th Infantry Division Historical Council. Tokyo, Japan: Dai Nippon Printing Co, 1953.

US Army, Headquarters, 2d Engineer Special Brigade. Unit Activities Report, 9 July 1950 to 1 October 1950.

US Army, 409th Engineer Special Brigade. Command Reports, 409th Engineer Special Brigade, 369th and 370th Engineer Boat and Shore Regiments/ Engineer Amphibious Support Regiments, 1950, 1951.

US Army, 7th Sustainment Brigade. 7th Sustainment Brigade home page. 7sustainment.forscom.army.mil/default.htm (accessed 13 June 2007).

US Army, 532d Engineer Boat & Shore Regiment. After Action Report, Inchon Operation, 532d Engineer Boat & Shore Regiment, 3 November 1950. Office of the Engineer Command Historian.

———. After Action Report, Iwon Operation, 532d Engineer Boat & Shore Regiment, 31 December 1950. Office of the Engineer Command Historian.

———. After Action Report, Hungnam, Korea, 532d Engineer Boat & Shore Regiment, n.d. Office of the Engineer Command Historian.

———. Headquarters, 532d Engineer Boat and Shore Regiment. Command Reports for October, November, and December 1951 and January 1952.

US Army, Headquarters, 56th Amphibious Tank and Tractor Battalion. Command Report Narrative Summaries, November and December 1951.

US Army, 159th Transportation Battalion (Boat) (Terminal). Unpublished manuscript.

US Army, 747th Amphibious Tank and Tractor Battalion. *747th Amphibious Tank and Tractor Battalion, Camp Cooke, California, 1952*. Baton Rouge, LA: Army and Navy Publishing Company, 1952.

———. 747th Amphibious Tank and Tractor Battalion, Command Report, 1950.

US Army, Company A, 56th Amphibious Tank and Tractor Battalion, Diary Report of "A" Company, 56th Amphibious Tank and Tractor Battalion to Cover the Period from 26 August to 15 January 1950–1951.

US Army, 8206th Army Unit. *Amphibious Training Center, 8206th Army Unit*. Unit history [1955?].

———. Amphibious Training Center, Unit History [1951?].

US Navy

COMNAVFE Operation Plan No. 116-50, CNFE/A4-3(9), 13 November 1950.

Naval Warfare Publication (NWP) 22, *Amphibious Operations*. Washington, DC: GPO, 1952 (with change 5, 1962).

Fleet Training Publication (FTP)-167, "Landing Operations Doctrine, United States Navy," 1938 with C.1, May 1941 (basis for Guadalcanal operation); C.2, 1 August 1942; C.3, August 1943.

Landing-Force Manual, United States Navy, 1918, 1920, 1927, and 1938.

Manual for Naval Overseas Operations, August 1934.

Naval Historical Center. *Dictionary of American Naval Fighting Ships*. history. navy.mil/danfs/index.html (accessed 13 February 2008).

———. *Korean War: Chronology of U.S. Pacific Fleet Operations, January–June 1951*. www.history.navy.mil/wars/korea/chron51a.htm#apr (accessed 13 December 2006).

———. "Republic of Korea Naval Forces & Naval Operations." history.navy.mil/ photos/events/kowar/un-rok/rok-nav.htm and history.navy.mil/photos/ events/kowar/un-rok/rok-nav2.htm (accessed 30 June 2007).

———. "Republic of Korea Naval Ships." history.navy.mil/photos/sh-fornv/rok/ rok-name.htm (accessed 30 June 2007).

———. "Wars and Conflicts of the U.S. Navy, Korean Conflict, 1950–1954." history. navy.mil/wars/index.html#anchor12806 (accessed 13 February 2008).

Naval History Division. *Riverine Warfare: The U.S. Navy's Operations on Inland Waters*. Washington, DC: GPO, 1968.

OPNAV P 34-03, "Landing Party Manual United States Navy," 1960, with C.1, 1 August 1962; C.2, n.d.

OPNAV INST 3800.2, "Intelligence: Joint Landing Force Manual," January 1955. (Also published as FM 110-101, AFM-200-131, and JLFM-1.)

"The Landing-Force and Small-Arms Instructions." Various editions, including 1905 and 1907 (with corrections to pages 293–352 of 1910 and 1911), 1912, and 1915.

USF 6, "Amphibious Warfare Instructions, United States Fleet," 1946.

USF 63, "Amphibious Instructions, Landing Forces," 1947.

USF 66, "Tactical and Operational Instructions, Amphibious Forces," 7 July 1947.

US Navy. *Seapower for a New Era: A Program Guide to the New Navy*. Washington, DC: Department of the Navy, 2007.

US Navy. Director of Naval Intelligence. *ONI 226 Allied Landing Craft and Ships*. Washington, DC: Office of Naval Intelligence, 1944.

US Office of Naval Intelligence. *Allied Landing Craft of World War Two*. Introduction by A.D. Baker. Annapolis, MD: Naval Institute Press, 1985.

US Atlantic Fleet. Amphibious Force. *Exercise Seminole: Report of Joint Amphibious Training Exercises, November 1947*. Fleet Post Office, New York, NY: Commander Amphibious Force, US Atlantic Fleet, Commander Joint Expeditionary Force, 1947.

US Pacific Fleet. Amphibious Forces. *Amphibious Troop Training Operations in the Pacific during Calendar Year 1946*. San Diego, CA: Office of the Commander, Amphibious Force, US Pacific Fleet, 21 June 1947.

———. Commander West Coast Training Group and Commander Amphibious Group One. *Operation DUCK: Operation Plan (Training) No. A109-46*. San Diego. CA: Amphibious Forces, Pacific Fleet, Commander Amphibious Group One, and Commander Task Group 13.12, 25 October 1946.

———. *Amphibious Exercises, November 1947, Conducted by Commander Amphibious Force, Pacific Fleet.* San Francisco, CA: Office of the Commander, Amphibious Force, US Pacific Fleet, 1947.

———. Amphibious Force Pacific Fleet. *PHIBTEST.*

US Marine Corps

Doctrine for Amphibious Operations, 1958 (Tentative Draft).

Headquarters, US Marine Corps. *Concepts and Program 2008.* Washington, DC: Headquarters, US Marine Corps, 2008. www.usmc.mil/units/hqmc/pandr/Documents/Concepts/2008/toc.htm (accessed 20 June 2008).

———. "Expeditionary Maneuver Family of Concepts." *Marine Corps Concepts and Programs*, 2005. hqinet001.hqmc.usmc.mil/p&r/concepts/2005/PDF/Ch2PDFs/CP05%20Chapter%202%20Warfighting%20Concepts%20pg%20025_Expeditionary%20Maneuver%20Warfare%20Family%20of%20Concepts.pdf (accessed 13 May 2007).

———. Direct Reporting Program Manager, Advanced Amphibious Assault. "Expeditionary Fighting Vehicle." efv.usmc.mil/ (accessed 7 May 2007).

———. 1st Marine Division, Fleet Marine Force. *Special Action Report for the Inchon–Seoul Operation, 15 September–7 October 1950.*

———. 1st Marine Division. *Historical Diary for January 1951.* 1 May 1951.

———. US Marine Corps Board. *An Evaluation of the Influence of Marine Corps Forces on the Course of the Korean War (4 Aug 50–15 Dec 50).* 2 vols.

———. Landing Force Manual (LFM)-00, *Amphibious Operations*, 1959 (Tentative Advance Change No. 5 to NWP 22).

———. LFM-01, *Doctrine for Amphibious Operations*, 1962, 1967.

———. LFM-1, *Training, U.S. Marine Corps*, 1956.

———. LFM-2, *Terrain Hydrography & Weather*, 1955.

———. LFM-3, *Landing Force Intelligence (Coordinator, Marine Corps Landing Force Development Activities)*, 1959, 1961 (Tentative Draft Revision).

———. LFM-4, *Ship-to-Shore Movement*, 1952, 1956.

———. LFM-6, *The Battalion Landing Team*, 1956.

———. LFM-7, *Naval Gunfire Tactics, Techniques and Planning*, 1960 (Draft Revision).

———. LFM-8, *Air Operations*, 1952.

———. LFM-11, *Embarkation (Coordinator, Marine Corps Landing Force Development Activities)*, 1959 (Draft Revision).

———. LFM-13 II, *Engineers*, 1957.

———. LFM-14, *Employment of Tanks in the Landing Force*, 1960 (Tentative), 1961.

———. LFM-16, *Medical Service*, 1952, 1956.

———. LFM-17, *The Employment of Amphibious Vehicles*, 1952.

———. LFM-18, *Troop Life and Training Aboard Ship*, 1955.

———. LFM-20, *Logistical Support (Including Personnel)*, 1952.

———. LFM-22, *Coordination of Supporting Arms*, 1960.

———. LFM-23, *Antiaircraft Artillery*, 1954.

—. LFM-25, *The Tactical Air Control Party*, 1955.

—. LFM-27, *Antimechanized Tactics*, 1960.

—. LFM-28, *Landing Force Planning*, n.d.

Tentative Manual for Landing Operations, June 1934. Title changed to *Manual for Naval Overseas Operations*. Department of the Navy, July 1935. Revised 1935. Approved by the Chief of Naval Operations, and published 9 July 1935 as the *Tentative Landing Operations Manual*. Revised and issued 21 June 1937 as *Landing Operations Doctrine, U.S. Navy, 1937*. Superseded 25 November 1938 by Fleet Training Publication 167, *Landing Operations Doctrine, U.S. Navy*, q.v. (Chronology based on Kenneth J. Clifford, *Progress and Purpose: A Developmental History of the United States Marine Corps, 1900–1970*. Washington, DC: History and Museums Division, US Marine Corps, 1973.)

Joint

Chairman, JCS. Memorandum for the Secretary of Defense, 29 September 1950. "Future Korean Operations."

—. JCS Message 92975, to CINCFE, 29 September 1950.

—. JCS Message (SECDEF Sends) 92985. Personal for General of the Army Douglas MacArthur, 29 September 1950.

Combined Communications Board Publication (CCBP) 01. *Combined Amphibious Communications Instructions*, June 1943.

JCS 1776/25. Memorandum by the Chief of Naval Operations for the Joint Chiefs of Staff, "Recommendations of Commander in Chief, Pacific Fleet, Concerning Support of Commander in Chief, Far East," 9 July 1950.

JCS Action 2147. "Reinforcement to Commander in Chief, Far East."

JCS Message 92801. Personal for MacArthur, 27 September 1950.

JLFM-1. *Intelligence: Joint Landing Force Manual*. Washington, DC: GPO, January 1955. (Also published as FM 110-101, AFM-200-131, and OPNAV INST 3800.2.)

Joint Army Navy Air Publication (JANAP) 144, *Joint Amphibious Communications*, May 1948.

"Note by the Secretaries to the Joint Chiefs of Staff on Increase in Strength of the First Marine Division," 14 July 1950.

US Army Far East Command. *Annual Narrative Historical Report, 1 January 1950–31 October 1950*. Tokyo: GHQ Far East Command, Military Intelligence Section, 9 May 1951.

—. CINCFE Message C-57553 (CM IN 11150) to Department of the Army for JCS, 10 July 1950.

—. CINCFE Message C-64805 (CM IN 16170), to Department of the Army for JCS, 28 September 1950.

—. *Command Report*. Separate volumes by month, November 1950–July 1953. Tokyo: GHQ Far East Command, Military Intelligence Section.

———. *Guerrilla Operations Outline, 1952.* Headquarters, Far East Command Liaison Detachment (Korea), 11 April 1952.

———. *Hamhung, Ch'ongjin, Songjin, Munsan, Aoji, Korea.* General Headquarters, Far East Command, Military Intelligence Section, General Staff, Theater Intelligence Division, Geographic Branch, 1951.

———. *History of the Korean War, Chronology 25 June 1950–31 December 1951.* Tokyo: Military History Section, 1952.

———. *Logistics in the Korean Operations.* 4 volumes. Camp Zama, Japan: Headquarters, US Army Forces Far East and Eighth US Army (Rear), APO 343, 1955.

———. *Najin, Hamhung, Unggi, Hoeryong, Sinbuckch'ong Korea.* General Headquarters, Far East Command, Military Intelligence Section, General Staff, Theater Intelligence Division, Geographic Branch, 1951.

———. *Seoul and Vicinity, Korea.* General Headquarters, Far East Command, Military Intelligence Section, General Staff, Theater Intelligence Division, Geographic Branch.

US Far East Command. Japan Logistical Command. *Construction Requirements for Operations in Korea as of 1 Oct. 50.* APO 343: Headquarters, Japan Logistical Command, Office of the Engineer, 13 November 1950.

———. *Logistical Problems and Their Solutions (25 August 1950–31 August 1951).* APO 343: Headquarters, Japan Logistical Command, 1952.

US Joint Board of the Army and Navy. *Joint Action of the Army and Navy in Coast Defense.* Washington, DC: GPO, 1920.

———. *Joint Action of the Army and the Navy.* Washington, DC: GPO, 1927 and 1935.

———. *Joint Overseas Expeditions.* Washington, DC: GPO, 1929 and 1933.

US Joint Chiefs of Staff. "Functions of the Armed Forces and the Joint Chiefs of Staff." Attachment to JCS 1478/23, 26 April 1948, CCS 380 (8-19-45) section 8 (Key West Agreement).

———. Joint Publication 3-02, *Joint Doctrine for Amphibious Operations.* Washington, DC: GPO, 19 September 2001.

———. Joint Publication 3-02.1, *Joint Tactics, Techniques, and Procedures for Landing Force Operations.* Washington, DC: GPO, 11 May 2004.

———. Joint Publication 3-02.2, *Joint Doctrine for Amphibious Embarkation.* Washington, DC: GPO, 16 April 1993.

———. Joint Publication 3-18, *Joint Doctrine for Forcible Entry Operations.* Washington, DC: GPO, 2001.

US Joint Exercise MIKI. *Aggressor Activities, Joint Army–Navy Exercise MIKI.* Fort Shafter, HI: Headquarters Hawaiian Area, Office of the Commander, 1950.

———. *Chief Umpire Report, Joint Exercise MIKI.* Fort Winfield Scott, CA: Headquarters, Umpire Group, Joint Exercise MIKI, 1950.

————. *Chief Umpire's Operation Plan, JSMIKI-03: Joint Exercise MIKI, Army–Navy.* Fort Winfield Scott, CA: Headquarters, Umpire Group, Exercise MIKI, 1949.

————. *Exercise Miki/Commander First Task Fleet.* USS *Curtiss*: TF 130 Western Task Force and ComFirTaskFlt, 1949.

————. *Observer's Report, Joint Exercise Miki, Oct.–Nov. 1949.* 1950.

————. *Maneuver Commander's Control Order 1-49F: Joint Exercise Miki, Army–Navy.* Fort Winfield Scott, CA: Maneuver Commander's Headquarters, Joint Exercise Miki, 1949.

————. *Tactical Study of the Terrain, Island of Oahu.* Oahu, HI: Headquarters, Aggressor Force, Exercise Miki, 1949.

Wendt, James R. *Observer's Report, Exercise Miki.* 1949.

US Merchant Marine

US Maritime Service Veterans. "American Merchant Marine at War." usmm.org/index.html#anchor252856 (accessed 15 January 2008).

Field Manuals

Departments of the Army, the Navy, and the Air Force. Army Field Manual 110-5, Navy JAAF, and Air Force Manual (AFM) 1-1, *Joint Action Armed Forces.* Washington, DC: GPO, 1951.

Departments of the Army and the Navy. Field Manual (FM) 31-11, *Doctrine for Amphibious Operations.* Washington, DC: GPO, July 1962. (Developed by the Navy and Marine Corps and issued as FM 31-11, NWP 22(A), and LFM 01. Revised and reissued 1 August 1967.)

Field Service Regulations, United States Army. 1905, 1910, and 1923.

Headquarters, Department of the Army. FM 1-1, *The Army.* Washington, DC: GPO, June 2005. army.mil/fm1/chapter2.html (accessed 10 July 2007).

————. FM 1-02, *Operational Terms and Graphics.* Washington, DC: GPO, 2004.

————. FM 3-0, *Operations.* Washington, DC: GPO, February 2008.

————. FM 3-90, *Tactics.* Washington, DC: GPO, July 2001.

————. FM 5-5, *Engineer Field Manual: Engineer Troops.* Washington, DC: GPO, 11 October 1943. (Change 1 added new Chapter 8, "Engineer Units with Army Service Forces," Section XV, "Engineer Special Brigade.")

————. FM 5-5, *Engineer Troop Units*, May 1954. (No reference to Engineer Special or Amphibious Brigade, but Chapter 4, "Engineer Combat Support Units," includes Section IX, "Engineer Shore Battalion.")

————. FM 5-144, *Engineer Shore Assault Units.* Washington, DC: GPO, October 1963.

————. FM 5-144, *Engineer Amphibious Units.* Washington, DC: GPO, November 1966.

————. FM 5-156, *Engineer Shore Battalion*. Washington, DC: GPO, August 1954.

————. FM 5-156, *The Engineer Amphibious Support Command* (Draft). Washington, DC: GPO, April 1958.

————. FM 17-34, *Amphibious Tank and Tractor Battalion* (Draft). Washington, DC: GPO, May 1948, June 1950. (Superseded FM 60-20.)

————. FM 20-12, *Amphibious Embarkation*. Washington, DC: GPO, 25 August 1975. (Superseded FM 60-30.)

————. FM 31-5, *Landing Operations on Hostile Shores*. Washington, DC: GPO, 2 June 1941, 13 November 1944.

————. FM 31-5 (Supplement), *Landing Operations on Hostile Shores; Joint U.S. Air—Amphibious Communications Instructions*. Washington, DC: GPO, April 1943, October 1943.

————. FM 31-11, *Doctrine for Amphibious Operations*. Washington, DC: Departments of the Army and the Navy, July 1962. (Also published as US Navy NWP 22(A), US Marine Corps LFM 01.)

————. FM 31-11, *Doctrine for Amphibious Operations*. Washington, DC: Departments of the Army, the Navy, and the Air Force, 2 August 1967. (Also published as US Navy NWP 22(A), US Air Force AFM 2-53, US Marine Corps LFM 01.)

————. FM 31-12, *Army Forces in Amphibious Operations (The Army Landing Force)*. Washington, DC: GPO, March 1961.

————. FM 31-13, *Battle Group Landing Team, Amphibious*. Washington, DC: GPO, September 1961.

————. FM 55-25, *Ports (Overseas) Headquarters and Headquarters Companies*. Washington, DC: GPO, May 1945.

————. FM 55-25, *Ports in Theaters of Operations*. Washington, DC: GPO, September 1952.

————. FM 55-26, *Transportation Inland Waterways Service*. Washington, DC: GPO, March 1953.

————. FM 55-50, *Army Water Transport Operations*. Washington, DC: GPO, September 1976, June 1985.

————. FM 55-50-1, *Transportation Amphibian Operations (Test)*. Washington, DC: GPO, March 1967.

————. FM 55-51, *Army Water Transport Units*. Washington, DC: GPO, August 1972.

————. FM 55-53, *Transportation Amphibious Truck Company*. Washington, DC: GPO, August 1956.

————. FM 55-58, *Transportation Boat Units*. Washington, DC: GPO, December 1959.

————. FM 55-105, *Water Transportation: Ocean Going Vessels*. Washington, DC: GPO, September 1944.

————. FM 55-110, *Transportation Port Company, Military Stevedoring*. Washington, DC: GPO, November 1952.

———. FM 55-130, *Small Boats and Harbor Craft*. Washington, DC: GPO, 31 January 1944.

———. FM 55-130, *The Harbor Craft Company*. Washington, DC: GPO, March 1951.

———. FM 55-501, *Marine Crewman's Handbook*. Washington, DC: GPO, March 1983.

———. FM 55-501-1, *Landing Craft Operator's Handbook*. Washington, DC: GPO, May 1985.

———. FM 55-501-2, *Harbor Craft Crewman's Handbook*. Washington, DC: GPO, December 1984.

———. FM 55-506-2, *Marine Engineman's Electrical Handbook*. Washington, DC: GPO, April 1977.

———. FM 55-509, *Marine Engineman's Handbook*. Washington, DC: GPO, October 1986.

———. FM 55-511, *Operation of Floating Cranes*. Washington, DC: GPO, December 1985.

———. FM 60-5, *Amphibious Operations: Battalion in Assault Landings* (Draft). Washington, DC: GPO, February 1950, 21 February 1951.

———. FM 60-10, *Amphibious Operations: Regiment in Assault Landings* (Draft). Washington, DC: GPO, April 1950, January 1952.

———. FM 60-20, *Amphibious Tank and Tractor Battalions*. Washington, DC: GPO, 24 February 1945. (Superseded by FM 17-34.)

———. FM 60-25, *Employment of the Amphibious Support Brigade*. Washington, DC: GPO, 8 January 1952.

———. FM 60-30, *Amphibious Operations: Embarkation and Ship Loading (Unit Loading Officer)*. Washington, DC: GPO, 6 September 1952. (Superseded by FM 20-12.)

———. FM 60-30, *Embarkation and Loading—Amphibious*. Washington, DC: GPO, May 1962.

———. FM 100-5, *Field Service Regulations: Operations*. Washington, DC: GPO, 1941, August 1949 (Section XII, Joint Amphibious Operations, 233–237); (Draft) 1953 (Section XIII, Amphibious Operations, 299–323); 27 September 1954 (Section XIII, Amphibious Operations, 178–196).

———. FM 101-5, *Staff Officers Manual*. Washington, DC: GPO.

———. FM 110-5, *Joint Action Armed Forces*. Washington, DC: GPO, 1951. (Also published as Navy JAAF and Air Force Manual (AFM) 1-1.)

———. FM 110-101, *Intelligence: Joint Landing Force Manual*. Washington, DC: GPO, January 1955. (Also published as OPNAV INST 3800.2, AFM 200-131, JLFM-1.)

Technical Manuals

Technical Manual (TM) 9-775, *Landing Vehicle Tracked, MK I and MK II*, February 1944.

TM 9-776, *Tracked Landing Vehicle, MK 4 (LVT(4))*, June 1951.

TM 9-2853, *Preparation of Ordnance Material for Deep Water Fording*.

Army Training Tests

Army Training Test (ATT) 17-10, *Amphibious Tank Battalion*, August 1951.

ATT 17-11, *Amphibious Tank Company*, August 1951.

ATT 17-12, *Amphibious Tank Platoon*, August 1951.

ATT 17-13, *Amphibious Tractor Platoon*, August 1951.

ATT 17-14, *Amphibious Tractor Company*, August 1951.

ATT 17-15, *Amphibious Tractor Battalion*, August 1951.

MTP 60-1, *Amphibian Tank or Tractor Battalion*, 27 July 1945 (Mobilization Training Program).

Tables of Organization and Equipment

1-387S, *Air Combat Control Squadron, Amphibious*, September 1944.

5-401E, *Headquarters and Headquarters Company, Engineer Amphibious Brigade*, July 1965.

5-401G, *Headquarters and Headquarters Company, Engineer Amphibious Brigade*, May 1968.

5-402E, *Headquarters and Headquarters Company, Engineer Amphibious Group*, July 1965.

5-402G, *Headquarters and Headquarters Company, Engineer Amphibious Group*, September 1967.

5-405E, *Engineer Amphibious Battalion*, July 1965.

5-405G, *Engineer Amphibious Battalion*, May 1968.

5-406E, *Headquarters and Headquarters Company, Engineer Amphibious Battalion*, July 1965.

5-406G, *Headquarters and Headquarters Company, Engineer Amphibious Battalion*, May 1968.

5-407E, *Engineer Amphibian Assault Company*, July 1965.

5-407G, *Engineer Amphibian Assault Company*, March 1968.

5-408E, *Engineer Amphibious Company*, July 1965.

5-408G, *Engineer Amphibious Company*, February 1968.

5-510-1, *Headquarters and Headquarters Company, Engineer Amphibian Brigade*, July 1942.

5-510-1, *Headquarters and Headquarters Company, Engineer Amphibian Brigade*, September 1942.

5-510-1S, *Headquarters and Headquarters Company, Engineer Special Brigade*, April 1943.

5-510-1S, *Headquarters and Headquarters Company, Engineer Special Brigade*, April 1944.

5-510-1 M-S, *Medical Detachment, Engineer Special Brigade*, April 1943.

5-510-1 M-S, *Medical Detachment, Engineer Special Brigade,* April 1944.

5-510-1T, *Headquarters and Headquarters Company, Engineer Special Brigade*, January 1946.

5-510-1T M, *Medical Detachment, Engineer Special Brigade*, January 1946.

5-510-3, *Maintenance Company, Engineer Amphibian Brigade*, July 1942.

5-511, *Engineer Boat Regiment*, July 1942.

5-511S, *Engineer Boat and Shore Regiment*, April 1943.

5-511S, *Engineer Boat and Shore Regiment*, April 1944.

5-511S-M, *Medical Detachment, Engineer Boat and Shore Regiment*, April 1944.

5-511T, *Engineer Boat and Shore Regiment*, January 1946.

5-511T-M, *Medical Detachment, Engineer Boat and Shore Regiment*, January 1946.

5-511, *Engineer Amphibious Support Regiment*, January 1951.

5-512, *Headquarters and Headquarters Company, Engineer Boat Regiment*, July 1942.

5-512S, *Headquarters and Headquarters Company, Engineer Boat and Shore Regiment*, April 1943.

5-512S, *Headquarters and Headquarters Company, Engineer Boat and Shore Regiment*, April 1944.

5-512T, *Headquarters and Headquarters Company, Engineer Boat and Shore Regiment*, January 1946.

5-512, *Headquarters, Headquarters and Service Company, Engineer Amphibious Support Regiment*, January 1951.

5-513, *Engineer Boat Maintenance Company*, July 1942.

5-514, *Engineer Lighter Company*, July 1942.

5-515, *Engineer Boat Battalion*, July 1942.

5-515, *Boat Battalion, Engineer Amphibian Regiment*, April 1943.

5-515S, *Boat Battalion, Engineer Boat and Shore Regiment*, April 1944.

5-515T, *Boat Battalion, Engineer Boat and Shore Regiment*, January 1946.

5-515, *Engineer Boat Battalion*, January 1951.

5-516, *Headquarters and Headquarters Company, Engineer Boat Battalion*, July 1942.

5-516S, *Headquarters and Headquarters Company, Boat Battalion, Engineer Boat and Shore Regiment*, April 1943.

5-516S, *Headquarters and Headquarters Company, Boat Battalion, Engineer Boat and Shore Regiment*, April 1944.

5-516S-R, *Headquarters and Headquarters Company, Boat Battalion, Engineer Boat and Shore Regiment*, March 1945.

5-516T, *Headquarters and Headquarters Company, Engineer Boat Battalion*, January 1946.

5-516, *Headquarters and Headquarters Company, Engineer Boat Battalion*, January 1951.

5-517, *Engineer Boat Company*, July 1942.

5-517S, *Engineer Boat Company*, April 1943.

5-517S, *Engineer Boat Company*, April 1944.

5-517T, *Engineer Boat Company*, January 1946.

5-517, *Engineer Boat Company*, January 1951.

5-521, *Engineer Shore Regiment*, July 1942.

5-522, *Headquarters and Headquarters and Service Company, Engineer Shore Regiment*, July 1942.

5-525, *Engineer Shore Battalion*, July 1942.

5-525S, *Shore Battalion, Engineer Boat and Shore Regiment,* April 1943.

5-525S, *Shore Battalion, Engineer Boat and Shore Regiment,* April 1944.

5-525T, *Shore Battalion, Engineer Boat and Shore Regiment,* January 1946.

5-525, *Engineer Shore Battalion,* January 1951.

5-525A, *Engineer Shore Battalion,* April 1953.

5-525R, *Engineer Shore Battalion,* March 1955.

5-526, *Headquarters and Headquarters Company, Engineer Shore Battalion,* July 1942.

5-526S, *Headquarters and Headquarters Company, Shore Battalion, Engineer Boat and Shore Regiment,* April 1943.

5-526S, *Headquarters and Headquarters Company, Shore Battalion, Engineer Boat and Shore Regiment,* April 1944.

5-526T, *Headquarters and Headquarters Company, Shore Battalion, Engineer Boat and Shore Regiment,* January 1946.

5-526, *Headquarters, Headquarters and Service Company, Engineer Shore Battalion,* January 1951.

5-526A, *Headquarters, Headquarters and Service Company, Engineer Shore Battalion,* April 1953.

5-526R, *Headquarters, Headquarters and Service Company, Engineer Shore Battalion,* March 1955.

5-527, *Engineer Near Shore Company,* July 1942.

5-527S, *Engineer Shore Company,* April 1943.

5-527S, *Engineer Shore Company,* April 1944.

5-527T, *Engineer Shore Company,* January 1946.

5-527, *Engineer Shore Company,* January 1951.

5-527A, *Engineer Shore Company,* April 1953.

5-527R, *Engineer Shore Company,* March 1955.

5-528, *Engineer Far Shore Company,* July 1942.

5-535, *Engineer Base Shop Battalion, Engineer Amphibian Command,* July 1942.

5-535S, *Engineer Special Shop Battalion,* September 1943.

5-536, *Headquarters and Headquarters Company, Engineer Base Shop Battalion, Engineer Amphibian Command,* July 1942.

5-536S, *Headquarters and Headquarters Detachment, Engineer Special Shop Battalion,* September 1943.

5-537, *Power Plant Repair Company, Engineer Base Shop Battalion, Engineer Amphibian Brigade,* July 1942.

5-537S, *Power Plant Repair Company, Engineer Special Shop Battalion,* September 1943.

5-538, *Hull Repair Company, Engineer Base Shop Battalion, Engineer Amphibian Command,* July 1942.

5-538S, *Hull Repair Company, Engineer Special Shop Battalion,* September 1943.

5-539, *Salvage and Dockage Company, Engineer Base Shop Battalion, Engineer Amphibian Command,* July 1942.

5-539S, *Salvage and Dockage Company, Engineer Special Shop Battalion,* September 1943.

5-547, *Depot Company, Engineer Base Shop Battalion, Engineer Amphibian Command,* July 1942.

5-547S, *Depot Company, Engineer and Special Shop Battalion,* September 1943.

5-550G, *Engineer Dredge Teams,* February 1968.

5-550H, *Engineer Dredge Teams,* December 1974.

5-555S, *Engineer Boat Maintenance Battalion,* April 1943.

5-555S, *Engineer Boat Maintenance Battalion,* April 1944.

5-555T, *Engineer Boat Maintenance Battalion,* January 1946.

5-555, *Engineer Boat Maintenance Battalion,* October 1951.

5-556S, *Headquarters and Headquarters Detachment, Engineer Boat Maintenance Battalion,* April 1943.

5-556S, *Headquarters and Headquarters Detachment, Engineer Boat Maintenance Battalion,* April 1944.

5-556T, *Headquarters and Headquarters Detachment, Engineer Boat Maintenance Battalion,* January 1946.

5-556, *Headquarters, Headquarters and Service Company, Engineer Boat Maintenance Battalion,* October 1951.

5-557S, *Engineer Boat Maintenance Company,* April 1943.

5-557S, *Engineer Boat Maintenance Company,* April 1944.

5-557T, *Engineer Boat Maintenance Company,* January 1946.

5-557, *Engineer Boat Maintenance Company,* October 1951.

5-558T, *Engineer Heavy Maintenance Company, Engineer Boat Maintenance Battalion,* January 1946.

5-559T, *Parts Supply Platoon, Engineer Boat Maintenance Battalion,* January 1946.

5-600T, *Engineer Amphibious Support Command (Tentative),* January 1958.

5-605T, *Service Support Battalion, Engineer Amphibious Support Command (Tentative),* August 1958.

5-606T, *Headquarters, Headquarters and Service Company, Service Support Battalion, Engineer Amphibious Support Command (Tentative),* January 1958.

5-607T, *Composite Direct Support Company, Service Support Battalion, Engineer Amphibious Support Command (Tentative),* January 1958.

5-617T, *Engineer Amphibian Equipment Company, Engineer Amphibious Support Command (Tentative),* January 1958.

5-627T, *Engineer Amphibious Company, Engineer Amphibious Support Command (Tentative),* January 1958.

5-637S, *Engineer Dredge Crew, Hydraulic Suction 21-Inch Cutter Type,* September 1944.

5-638S, *Engineer Dredge Crew, Steam Turbine Powered Suction Dredge, 24-Inch Cutter,* September 1944.

5-647S, *Engineer Dredge Crew, Diesel Electric, Sea-Going Hopper Dredge, 700 Cubic Yards,* September 1944.

5-648S, *Engineer Dredge Crew, Diesel Electric, Seagoing Hopper Dredge, 1,400 Cubic Yards,* September 1944.

5-649S, *Engineer Dredge Crew, Diesel, Seagoing Hopper Dredge, 2,700 Cubic Yards,* September 1944.

8-195, *Medical Battalion, Engineer Amphibian Brigade,* July 1942.

8-195S, *Medical Battalion Engineer Special Brigade,* April 1943.

8-195S, *Medical Battalion Engineer Special Brigade,* October 1944.

8-196, *Headquarters and Headquarters Detachment, Medical Battalion, Engineer Amphibian Brigade,* July 1942.

8-196S, *Headquarters and Headquarters Company, Medical Battalion, Engineer Amphibian Brigade,* April 1943.

8-196S, *Headquarters and Headquarters Detachment, Medical Battalion, Engineer Amphibian Brigade,* October 1944.

8-197, *Medical Company, Battalion, Engineer Amphibian Brigade,* July 1942.

8-197S, *Medical Company, Battalion, Engineer Special Brigade,* April 1943.

8-197S, *Medical Company, Battalion, Engineer Special Brigade,* October 1944.

9-97, *Ordnance Platoon, Engineer Amphibian Brigade,* July 1942.

9-97S, *Ordnance Maintenance Company, Engineer Special Brigade,* April 1943.

9-97S, *Ordnance Maintenance Company, Engineer Special Brigade,* October 1943.

9-97S, *Ordnance Maintenance Company, Engineer Special Brigade,* October 1944.

9-97T, *Ordnance Maintenance Company, Engineer Special Brigade,* January 1946.

9-97, *Ordnance Maintenance Company, Amphibious Support Brigade,* July 1951.

9-97A, *Ordnance Maintenance Company, Amphibious Support Brigade,* June 1953.

9-97R, *Ordnance Maintenance Company, Amphibious Support Brigade,* April 1955.

10-275, *Quartermaster Battalion, Engineer Amphibious Brigade,* July 1942.

10-276, *Headquarters and Headquarters Company, Quartermaster Battalion, Engineer Amphibian Brigade,* July 1942.

10-276S, *Quartermaster Headquarters and Headquarters Company, Engineer, Special Brigade,* April 1943.

10-276S, *Quartermaster Headquarters and Headquarters Company, Engineer, Special Brigade,* September 1943.

10-276T, *Quartermaster Headquarters and Headquarters Company, Engineer, Special Brigade,* January 1946.

10-277, *Quartermaster Company, Amphibious Support Brigade,* February 1951.

10-277A, *Quartermaster Company, Amphibious Support Brigade,* October 1952.

10-277R, *Quartermaster Company, Amphibious Support Brigade,* March 1955.

17-115, *Amphibian Tank Battalion,* January 1944.

17-115, *Amphibious Tank Battalion,* June 1950.

17-115A, *Amphibious Tank Battalion,* September 1953.

17-115R, *Amphibious Tank Battalion,* April 1955.

17-115D, *Armored Amphibious Battalion,* May 1959.

17-116, *Headquarters and Headquarters and Service Company, Amphibious Tank Battalion*, January 1944.

17-116, *Headquarters and Headquarters and Service Company, Amphibious Tank Battalion*, June 1950.

17-116A, *Headquarters and Headquarters and Service Company, Amphibious Tank Battalion*, September 1953.

17-116R, *Headquarters and Headquarters and Service Company, Amphibious Tank Battalion*, April 1955.

17-116D, *Headquarters and Headquarters Company, Armored Amphibious Tank Battalion*, May 1959.

17-117, *Amphibian Tank Company*, January 1944.

17-117, *Amphibious Tank Company*, June 1950.

17-117A, *Amphibious Tank Company*, September 1953.

17-117R, *Amphibious Tank Company*, April 1955.

17-117D, *Armored Amphibious Company*, May 1959.

17-125, *Amphibian Tractor Battalion*, April 1944.

17-125, *Amphibious Tractor Battalion*, August 1950.

17-125A, *Amphibious Tractor Battalion*, August 1953.

17-125R, *Amphibious Tractor Battalion*, April 1955.

17-126, *Headquarters and Headquarters and Service Company, Amphibian, Tractor Battalion*, April 1944.

17-126, *Headquarters and Headquarters and Service Company, Amphibian, Tractor Battalion,* August 1950.

17-126A, *Headquarters and Headquarters and Service Company, Amphibian, Tractor Battalion*, August 1953.

17-126R, *Headquarters and Headquarters and Service Company, Amphibian, Tractor Battalion*, April 1955.

17-127, *Amphibian Tractor Company*, April 1944.

17-127, *Amphibious Tractor Company*, August 1950.

17-127A, *Amphibious Tractor Company*, August 1953.

17-127R, *Amphibious Tractor Company*, April 1955.

20-300, *Amphibious Support Brigade*, December 1951.

20-300A, *Amphibious Support Brigade*, October 1953.

20-300R, *Amphibious Support Brigade*, April 1955.

20-301, *Headquarters and Headquarters Company, Amphibious Support Brigade*, June 1951.

20-301A, *Headquarters and Headquarters Company, Amphibious Support Brigade*, June 1953.

20-301R, *Headquarters and Headquarters Company, Amphibious Support Brigade*, April 1955.

20-511, *Amphibious Support Regiment*, April 1953.

20-511R, *Amphibious Support Regiment*, April 1955.

20-512, *Headquarters, Headquarters and Service Company, Amphibious Support Regiment,* April 1953.

20-512R, *Headquarters, Headquarters and Service Company, Amphibious Support Regiment,* April 1955.

55-9, *Transportation Harbor Craft Company, Amphibious Support Brigade,* December 1951.

55-9A, *Transportation Harbor Craft Company, Amphibious Support Brigade,* May 1953.

55-9R, *Transportation Harbor Craft Company, Amphibious Support Brigade,* April 1955.

55-9C, *Transportation Harbor Craft Company, Amphibious Support Brigade,* January 1956.

55-37, *Amphibian Truck Company,* April 1943.

55-37, *Amphibian Truck Company,* May 1944.

55-37, *Transportation Amphibious Truck Company,* November 1948.

55-37A, *Transportation Amphibious Truck Company,* August 1952.

55-37B, *Transportation Amphibious Truck Company, Army or Communications Zone (Type B),* September 1953.

55-37, *Transportation Amphibious Truck Company, Army or Communications Zone,* May 1954.

55-37R, *Transportation Amphibious Truck Company, Army or Communications Zone,* April 1955. (Superseded by TOE 55-137C, January 1957.)

55-137C, *Transportation Amphibious Truck Company,* January 1957. (Supersedes TOE 55-37R, April 1955.)

55-137D, *Transportation Amphibious Truck Company,* April 1961.

55-137H, *Transportation Medium Lighter Company (ACV),* June 1980. (Supersedes TOE 55-139H, January 1976.)

55-138E, *Transportation Light Amphibian Company,* July 1962.

55-138G, *Transportation Light Amphibian Company,* July 1968.

55-138H, *Transportation Light Amphibian Company,* December 1975.

55-139E, *Transportation Medium Amphibian Company,* February 1963.

55-139G, *Transportation Medium Amphibian Company,* August 1967.

55-139H, *Transportation Medium Amphibian Company,* January 1976. (Superseded by TOE 55-137H, June 1980.)

55-140E, *Transportation Heavy Amphibian Company,* February 1963.

55-158T, *Transportation Amphibian General Support Company,* October 1962.

Books, Articles, and Reports

Adcock, Al. *WWII US Landing Craft in Action: Warships Number 17.* Carrollton, TX: Squadron/Signal Publications, 2003.

Agnew, James B. "From Where Did Our Amphibious Doctrine Come?" *Marine Corps Gazette,* Vol. 63, No. 7 (July 1979): 52–59.

Alexander, Barton S. "Reports of Lieutenant Colonel Barton S. Alexander, US Army, Engineer Officer of Operations from April 20 to July 12." Washington, DC, 28 January 1863. *Official Records of the Rebellion,* Vol. 11, Chapter 23, Part 1: "Peninsular Campaign, Reports."

Alexander, James H. "Roots of Deployment—Vera Cruz, 1914." In *Assault from the Sea: Essays on the History of Amphibious Warfare,* edited by Merrill L. Bartlett. Annapolis, MD: Naval Institute Press, 1983.

Alexander, Joseph H. *Utmost Savagery: The Three Days of Tarawa.* Annapolis, MD: Naval Institute Press, 1995.

———. *The U.S. Navy and the Korean War, Fleet Operations in a Mobile War: September 1950–June 1951.* Washington, DC: Department of the Navy, Navy Historical Center, 2001.

———. *Storm Landings: Epic Amphibious Battles in the Central Pacific.* Annapolis, MD: Naval Institute Press, 1997.

Almond, Edward M. *The Edward M. Almond Papers.* US Army Military History Institute.

———. "Personal Notes Covering Activities of Lt. Gen. E.M. Almond During Military Operations in Korea, 31 August 1950–15 July 1951" (Almond Diary). US Army Military History Institute.

Amory, Robert. *Surf and Sand, the Saga of the 533d Engineer Boat and Shore Regiment and 1461st Engineer Maintenance Company, 1942–45.* Andover, MA: Andover Press, 1947.

Anderson, Charles R. *The U.S. Army Campaigns of World War II: Algeria–French Morocco.* CMH Pub 72-11. Washington, DC: GPO, n.d.

———. *The U.S. Army Campaigns of World War II: Papua.* CMH Pub 72-7. Washington, DC: GPO, 1992.

———. *The U.S. Army Campaigns of World War II: Guadalcanal.* CMH Pub 72-8. Washington, DC: GPO, n.d.

———. *The U.S. Army Campaigns of World War II: Leyte.* CMH Pub 72-27. Washington, DC: GPO, n.d.

———. *The U.S. Army Campaigns of World War II: Western Pacific.* CMH Pub 72-29. Washington, DC: GPO, n.d.

Appleman, Roy E. *Disaster in Korea: The Chinese Confront MacArthur.* College Station, TX: Texas A&M University Press, 1989.

———. *Escaping the Trap, The US Army X Corps in Northeast Korea, 1950.* College Station, TX: Texas A&M University Press, 1990.

———. *Ridgway Duels for Korea.* College Station, TX: Texas A&M University Press, 1990.

———. *Roy Appleman Collection, 1945–1989.* US Army Military History Institute.

———. *United States Army in the Korean War: South to the Naktong, North to the Yalu.* Washington, DC: GPO, 1961.

Appleman, Roy E., James M. Burns, Russell A. Gugeler, and John Stevens. *United States Army in World War II, The War in the Pacific, Okinawa: The Last Battle.* Washington, DC: Historical Division, Department of the Army, 1948. Reprinted 1984, 1991.

Army Transportation Association Vietnam Home page. grambo.us/atav/default.html (accessed 10 February 2008).

Arnold, A.V. "Preparation for a Division Amphibious Operation." *Military Review,* Vol. XXV, No. 2 (May 1945): 3–11.

Association of the United States Army. "Force Projection Capability for a Transforming Army," May 2002. ausa.org/PDFdocs/tsv.pdf (accessed 31 March 2006).

Atkinson, Rick. *An Army at Dawn: The War in North Africa.* New York, NY: Henry Holt & Co., 2002.

———. *The Day of Battle: The War in Sicily and Italy, 1943–1944.* New York, NY: Henry Holt and Company, 2007.

Atwater, Charles B., Jr. *Soviet Amphibious Operations in the Black Sea, 1941–1943.* www.globalsecurity.org/military/library/report/1995/ACB. htm (accessed 12 February 2008).

Atwater, William F. "United States Army and Navy Development of Joint Landing Operations, 1898–1942." PhD diss, Duke University, 1986.

Baeggol Sadan Yeoksa, 1947 nyeon 12 weol 1 il buto, 1980 nyeon 10 weol 31 il ggaji [History of the Skeleton Division from 1 December 1947 to 31 October 1980]. Seoul: ROK 3d Division, 1980.

Bailey, Alfred D. *Alligators, Buffaloes and Bushmasters: The History of the Development of the LVT Through World War II.* Occasional Paper. Washington, DC: History and Museums Division, Headquarters, US Marine Corps, 1986.

Baldwin, Hanson. Series of articles on PORTREX in the *New York Times*: "Vieques 'Invasion' Slated for Today," 8 March 1950; "D-Day on Vieques Finds Going Tough," 9 March 1950; "Navy Withdrawing in Caribbean Area," 10 March 1950; "Last Action Today in Caribbean War," 11 March 1950; "Vieques 'Captured' As Exercise Ends," 12 March 1950; "Portrex May Bring Operating Changes," 14 March 1950.

Balkoski, Joseph. *Omaha Beach: D-Day, June 6, 1944.* Mechanicsburg, PA: Stackpole Books, 2004.

———. *Utah Beach: The Amphibious Landing and Airborne Operations on D-Day, June 6, 1944.* Mechanicsburg, PA: Stackpole Books, 2005.

Ballard, John R. *Upholding Democracy: The United States Military Campaign in Haiti, 1994–1997.* Westport, CT, and London: Praeger, 1998.

Ballendorf, Dirk Anthony, and Merrill Lewis Bartlett. *Pete Ellis: An Amphibious Warfare Prophet, 1880–1923.* Annapolis, MD: Naval Institute Press, 1997.

Barbey, Daniel E. *MacArthur's Amphibious Navy: Seventh Amphibious Force Operations, 1943–1945.* Annapolis, MD: Naval Institute Press, 1969.

Barlow, Jeffrey G. *Revolt of the Admirals: The Fight for Naval Aviation.* Washington, DC: Naval Historical Center, Department of the Navy, 1994.

Barr, David G. *Address by Major General David G. Barr, USA, Before the Army War College, Fort Leavenworth, Kansas, 21 February 1951.* US Army Military History Institute.

Barrett, Michael B. *Operation ALBION: The German Conquest of the Baltic Islands.* Bloomington, IN: Indiana University Press, 2008.

Barry, Gregory. *Amphibious Operations.* (Pictorial survey, World War II to Vietnam.) London: Blandford, 1988.

Bartlett, Merrill L., ed. *Assault from the Sea: Essays on the History of Amphibious Warfare.* Annapolis, MD: Naval Institute Press, 1983.

Bates, James C. "What Army Logisticians Should Know About the Marine Corps." *Army Logistician*, Vol. 35, No. 4, July–August 2003. almc. army.mil/alog/issues/JulAug03/know_about_marinecorps.htm (accessed 3 August 2007).

Bauer, K. Jack. *Surfboats and Horse Marines, US Naval Operations in the Mexican War, 1846–48.* Annapolis, MD: Naval Institute Press, 1969.

Bayne, J.K. "Operation Portrex: I.A. Medical Officer on 'Operation Portrex.'" *US Armed Forces Medical Journal*, Vol. 1, No. 10 (October 1950): 1227–1234.

Beasley, O.B. "Supporting a Major River Crossing." *Military Engineer*, Vol. XLIII, No. 291 (January–February 1951): 11–14.

Beaumont, Roger A. *Joint Military Operations: A Short History.* Westport, CT: Greenwood Press, 1993.

Bechtol, Bruce E., Jr. *Avenging the General Sherman: The 1871 Battle of Kang Hwa Do.* Quantico, VA: Marine Corps University Foundation, 2002.

Beck, Alfred M., Abe Bortz, Charles W. Lynch, Lida Mayo, and Ralph F. Weld. *United States Army in World War II, The Corps of Engineers: The War Against Germany.* Washington, DC: Historical Division, Department of the Army, 1985.

Becker, Marshall O. *The Amphibious Training Center.* Study No 22. Washington, DC: Historical Section, Army Ground Forces, 1946.

Bermudez, Joseph S., Jr. "Korean People's Army Guerrilla and Unconventional Warfare Units, June 1950–September 1950," Part 3, korean-war.com/ Archives/2000/03/msg00016.html (accessed 20 January 2007).

———. "Korean People's Army—766th Independent unit—revision," militaryphotos.net/forums/showthreat.php?t=41529 (accessed 28 February 2007).

———. *North Korean Special Forces.* Annapolis, MD: Naval Institute Press, 1998.

Bernstein, Lewis. *Learning and Transmitting Lessons in the Pacific War: From GALVANIC to FLINTLOCK, November 1943–February 1944.* Unpublished paper prepared for the Conference of Army Historians, 13–15 July 2004.

Birtle, Andrew J. *The Korean War: Years of Stalemate, July 1951–July 1953.* CMH Pub 19-10. Washington, DC: Center of Military History, 2000.

———. *The U.S. Army Campaigns of World War II: Sicily.* CMH Pub 72-16. Washington, DC: GPO, n.d.

Black, Robert W. *Rangers in Korea.* New York, NY: Ballantine Books, 1989.

———. *Robert W. Black Collection.* US Army Military History Institute.

Blackman, Raymond V.B., ed. *Jane's Fighting Ships, 1952–53.* New York, NY: McGraw-Hill, 1953.

Blair, Clay. *The Forgotten War: America in Korea 1950–1953.* New York, NY: Times Books, 1987. Reprinted, Doubleday Anchor, 1989.

———. *Clay and Joan Blair Collection.* US Army Military History Institute.

Blore, Trevor. *Commissioned Bargees: The Story of the Landing Craft.* London and New York, NY: Hutchinson, 1946.

Blumenson, Martin. *The Patton Papers, 1885–1940.* Vol. 1. Boston, MA: Houghton Mifflin, 1972.

———. *United States Army in World War II, The Mediterranean Theater of Operations, Salerno to Cassino.* Washington, DC: Historical Division, Department of the Army, 1969. Reprinted 2002.

———. "MacArthur's Divided Command." *Army*, Vol. 7, No. 4 (November 1956): 36–44.

Borch, Gunnar, and Massimo Annati. "Maritime Sealift—Organizations and Assets." *Naval Forces*, Vol. XXVI, No. VI: 12–24.

Bolte, Charles L. *Conversations Between General Charles L. Bolte, USA, Ret., and Mr. Arthur J. Zoebelein.* 3 vols. US Army Military History Research Collection, Senior Officers Debriefing Program. Carlisle Barracks, PA: Military History Institute, 1972. US Army Military History Institute.

———. Interviews by Dr. Maclyn Burg on 17 October 1973, 14 August 1974, and 29 January 1975 for the Eisenhower Library. US Army Military History Institute.

———. "History of First Days in England, 1941–1942," n.d. [but not earlier than August 1945]. US Army Military History Institute.

———. "Special Observers Prior to Activation of the European Theater of Operations," October 1944. US Army Military History Institute.

Boose, Donald W., Jr. "The Decision to Cross the 38th Parallel." In *The Encyclopedia of the Korean War,* edited by Spencer C. Tucker. New York, NY: ABC Clio, 2000.

———. "The Korean War Truce Talks: A Study in Conflict Termination." *Parameters*, Vol. XXX, No. 1 (Spring 2000): 107–108.

———. "The United Nations Command in the Korean War: A Largely Nominal Connection." Paper presented 8 June 2000 at the Conference of Army Historians.

———. *U.S. Army Forces in the Korean War 1950–1953.* Battle Orders No. 11. Oxford, UK: Osprey Publishing, 2005.

Bradford, James C. "The Missing Link: Expeditionary Logistics." *Naval History*, Vol. 20, Issue 1 (February 2006): 54–61.

Braitsch, Fred, Jr. "The Korean Marine Corps." *Leatherneck,* Vol. 36, No. 1 (1953).

Brittain, Thomas B. "Amphibious Operations." US Army War College Lecture, 52/2-3-M, 10 January 1952. US Army Military History Institute.

Brown, James B. "Joint Amphibious/Air Assault Operations." *Joint Force Quarterly* (Autumn/Winter 1998–99): 48–52.

Brown, John M., III. "USARPAC: The Army's Expeditionary Force in the Pacific." *Army*, Vol. 55, No. 10 (October 2005): 115–118.

———. "What Army Logisticians Should Know About the Navy." *Army Logistician*, Vol. 35, No. 6 (November–December 2003). almc.army.mil/

alog/issues/NovDec03/What_Army_ShouldKnow_Navy.htm (accessed 12 October 2007).

Buell, Thomas B. "Naval Leadership in Korea: The First Six Months." In *The U.S. Navy in the Korean War,* edited by Edward J. Marolda. Annapolis, MD: Naval Institute Press, 2007.

Buker, George E. *Blockaders, Refugees & Contrabands: Civil War on Florida's Gulf Coast, 1861–1865.* Tuscaloosa, AL: University of Alabama Press, 1993.

———. *Riverine Warfare: Naval Combat in the Second Seminole War, 1835–1842.* PhD diss, University of Florida, 1969.

———. *Swamp Sailors in the Second Seminole War.* Gainesville, FL: University of Florida Press, 2005.

———. *Swamp Sailors: Riverine Warfare in the Everglades, 1835–1842.* Gainesville FL: University Presses of Florida, 1975.

———. *The Penobscot Expedition: Commodore Saltonstall and the Massachusetts Conspiracy of 1779.* Annapolis, MD: Naval Institute Press, 2002.

Burdick, Charles B. *The Japanese Siege of Tsingtau.* Hamden, CT: Archon Books, 1976.

Burne, Alfred H. "Amphibious Operations—Lessons from the Past." *Fighting Forces* (October 1939): 324–343.

———. "Risk in War." *Fighting Forces* (April 1944): 13–18.

Bykofsky, Joseph, and Harold Larson. *United States Army in World War II, The Transportation Corps: Operations Overseas.* Washington, DC: Historical Division, Department of the Army, 1957. Reprinted 1972, 1990, 2003.

Cagle, Malcolm W., and Frank A. Manson. *Sea War in Korea.* Annapolis, MD: Naval Institute Press, 1957.

Callahan, Shawn M. *The Impact of Fastship and High Speed Sealift on Strategic Sealift.* Research Report. Maxwell Air Force Base, AL: Air Command and Staff College, Air University, 1998. fas.org/man/dod-101/sys/ship/docs/99-021.pdf (accessed 25 March 2005).

Cannon, M. Hamlin. *United States Army in World War II, The War in the Pacific, Leyte: The Return to the Philippines.* Washington, DC: Historical Division, Department of the Army, 1954. Reprinted 1987, 1996.

Caraley, Demetrios. *The Politics of Military Unification: A Study of Conflict and the Policy Process.* New York, NY: Columbia University Press, 1966.

Carr, Michael W. "Army Watercraft: Thoughts on Future Training and Use." *Transportation Corps* (Summer 2005): 11.

Cebrowski, Art. "Sea Basing: Poised for Takeoff." *Force Transformation* (15 February 2005): 1–8.

Chandler, Melbourne C. *Of GarryOwen in Glory: The History of the Seventh United States Cavalry Regiment.* Annandale, VA: The Turnpike Press, 1960.

Changjin Journal. libraryautomation.com/nymas/changjinjournalTOC.html (accessed 21 August 2008).

Chapin, John C. *Breaching the Marianas: The Battle for Saipan*. Marines in World War II Commemorative Series. Washington, DC: History and Museums Division, Headquarters, US Marine Corps, 1994.

Chen, Jian. *China's Road to the Korean War: The Making of the Sino-American Confrontation*. New York, NY: Columbia University Press, 1994.

Chisholm, Donald. "Escape by Sea: The Hungnam Redeployment." *Joint Force Quarterly* (Spring/Summer 2001): 54–62.

———. "Negotiated Joint Command Relationships." *Naval War College Review*, Vol. 53, No. 2 (Spring 2000): 65–124.

Clapham, Lathrop B. "The Gallipoli Expedition until May 6, 1915." In *Monographs of the World War,* 92–108. Fort Benning, GA: US Army Infantry School [1923?]. US Army Military History Institute.

Clark, Eugene Franklin. *The Secrets of Inchon: the Untold Story of the Most Daring Covert Mission of the Korean War.* Introduction and epilogue by Thomas Fleming. New York, NY: Putnam's, 2002.

Clarke, Jeffrey J. *The U.S. Army Campaigns of World War II: Southern France*. CMH Pub 72-31. Washington, DC: GPO, n.d.

———. "The Champagne Campaign." *Military History Quarterly*, Vol. 20, No. 2 (Winter 2008): 37–45.

Clarke, Jeffrey J., and Robert Ross Smith. *United States Army in World War II, The European Theater of Operations, Riviera to the Rhine*. Washington, DC: Historical Division, Department of the Army, 1993.

Cleaver, Frederick W., George Fitzpatrick, John Ponturo, William Rossiter, and C. Darwin Stolzenbach. *UN Partisan Warfare in Korea, 1951–1954*. Baltimore, MD: Johns Hopkins University Operations Research Office, June 1956.

Clifford, Kenneth J. *Amphibious Warfare Development in Britain and America from 1920–1940*. New York, NY: Edgewood, 1983.

———. *Progress and Purpose: A Developmental History of the United States Marine Corps, 1900–1970*. Washington, DC: History and Museums Division, US Marine Corps, 1973.

Cline, Ray S. *United States Army in World War II, The War Department, Washington Command Post: The Operations Division*. Washington, DC: Office of the Chief of Military History, Department of the Army, 1951.

Cline, Ray S., and Maurice Matloff. "Development of War Department Views on Unification." *Military Affairs*, Vol. XIII, No. 2 (Summer 1949): 65–74.

Coakley, Robert W., and Richard M. Leighton. *United States Army in World War II, The War Department, Global Logistics and Strategy: 1943–1945*. Washington, DC: Historical Division, Department of the Army, 1969. Reprinted 1989.

Cole, Alice C., Alfred Goldberg, Samuel A. Tucker, and Rudolph A. Winnacker, eds. *The Department of Defense: Documents on Establishment and Organization, 1944–1978*. Washington, DC: Office of the Secretary of Defense, Historical Office, 1978.

Cole, General Eli K., and Major [NFN] Watkins. *Joint Overseas Operations, Overseas Expedition: A Compilation of Joint Articles by General Cole, Major Watkins.* Fort Humphreys, VA: Engineer School, 1932.

Cole, Merle T. "Cape Cod Commando Training." *Military Collector & Historian,* Vol. 58, No. 2 (Summer 2006): 95–101.

Cole, Ronald H., Walter S. Poole, James F. Schnabel, Robert J. Watson, and Willard J. Webb. *The History of the Unified Command Plan 1946–1993.* Washington, DC: Joint History Office, Office of the Chairman of the Joint Chiefs of Staff, 1995.

Coll, Blanche D., Jean E. Keith, and Herbert H. Rosenthal. *United States Army in World War II, The Corps of Engineers: Troops and Equipment.* Washington, DC: Historical Division, Department of the Army, 1958. Reprinted 1974, 1988, 2002.

Collins, J. Lawton. *War in Peacetime: The History and Lessons of Korea.* Boston, MA: Houghton Mifflin, 1969.

Condit, Kenneth W. *The History of the Joint Chiefs of Staff: The Joint Chiefs of Staff and National Policy, Vol. II, 1947–1949.* Wilmington, DE: Michael Glazier, Inc., 1979. Reprinted: Washington, DC: Office of Joint History, Office of the Chairman of the Joint Chiefs of Staff, 1996.

Conn, Stetson, Rose C. Engelman, and Byron Fairchild. *United States Army in World War II, The Western Hemisphere, Guarding The United States and Its Outposts.* Washington, DC: Historical Division, Department of the Army, 1984. Reprinted 1995, 2000.

Cook, Henry B. "Sea Basing and Maritime Pre-positioning.*" Army Logistician,* Vol. 36, No. 3 (May–June 2004): 36–39.

Cook, Harry E. *The Harry E. Cook Papers.* US Army Military History Institute.

Cooper, Norman V. *A Fighting General: The Biography of Gen Holland M. "Howlin' Mad" Smith.* Quantico, VA: Marine Corps Association, 1987.

Cosmas, Graham T. *An Army for Empire: The United States Army in the Spanish–American War,* 2d Edition. Shippensburg, PA: White Mane Publishing Company, 1994.

———. "Joint Operations in the Spanish–American War." In *Crucible of Empire: The Spanish–American War & Its Aftermath,* edited by James C. Bradford. Annapolis, MD: Naval Institute Press, 1993.

Cosmas, Graham A., and Terrence P. Murray, *U.S. Marines in Vietnam: Vietnamization and Redeployment, 1970–1971.* Washington, DC: History and Museums Division, Headquarters, US Marine Corps, 1986.

Cowart, Glenn C. *Miracle in Korea: The Evacuation of X Corps from the Hungnam Beachhead.* Columbia, SC: University of South Carolina Press, 1992.

Cowings, John S., and Kim Nam Che. *Twelve Hungnam Evacuees.* Seoul, Korea: Headquarters, Eighth US Army, 1975.

Craig, Malin. "Report of Army Participation in *Grand Joint Exercise No. 4,* Hawaii, February 1932." Presidio of San Francisco, CA: Headquarters, Ninth Corps Area, 1932.

Creswell, John. *Generals and Admirals: The Story of Amphibious Command.* New York, NY: Longmans, Green, 1952.

Croizat, Victor J. *Across the Reef: The Amphibious Tracked Vehicle at War.* Quantico, VA: Marine Corps Association, 1989. Reprinted London: Blandford, 1989, 1992.

Crowl, Philip A. *United States Army in World War II, The War in the Pacific, Campaign in the Marianas.* Washington, DC: Historical Division, Department of the Army, 1960. Reprinted 1985, 1989, 1995.

———. Memorandum for the Chief of Military History. "Critique of Proposed Training Circular, 'Doctrines Governing Joint Amphibious Operations' submitted by the Office of the Adjutant General, Department of the Army, 21 December 1954," 21 April 1955. US Army Center of Military History.

Crowl, Philip A., and Edmund G. Love. *United States Army in World War II, The War in the Pacific, Seizure of the Gilberts and Marshalls.* Washington, DC: Historical Division, Department of the Army, 1955. Reprinted 1985, 1989, 1995.

Crowley, Joseph P. "Does the Army Need the Theater Support Vessel? If So, How Many?" USAWC Strategy Research Project Paper, 3 May 2004.

Cunliffe, James W. *James W. Cunliffe Papers.* US Army Military History Institute.

Curtis, Donald McB. "Inchon Insight." Letter to the editor, *Army*, Vol. 35, No. 7 (July 1985): 5.

Cutler, Thomas. *The Battle of Leyte Gulf: 23–26 October 1944.* Annapolis, MD: Naval Institute Press, 2001.

Daley, Robert W. "Burnside's Amphibious Division." In *Assault from the Sea: Essays on the History of Amphibious Warfare,* edited by Merrill L. Bartlett, 88–94. Annapolis, MD: Naval Institute Press, 1983.

Daugherty, Leo J., III. "Away All Boats: The Army–Navy Maneuvers of 1925." *Joint Force Quarterly* (Autumn/Winter 1998–99): 107–113.

Davis, Richard E. *Research and Development of Assault Ships.* Colorado: Naval Amphibious School, 1966.

Davis, W.J. "Japanese Operations at Tsing Tao, 1914." In *Monographs of the World War,* 684–695. Fort Benning, GA: US Army Infantry School [1923?].

Davis, Vernon E. *The History of the Joint Chiefs of Staff in World War II, Organizational Development, Vol. I, Origin of the Joint and Combined Chiefs of Staff.* Washington, DC: Historical Division, Joint Secretariat, Joint Chiefs of Staff, 1972.

———. *The History of the Joint Chiefs of Staff in World War II, Organizational Development, Vol. II, Development of the JCS Committee Structure.* Washington, DC: Historical Division, Joint Secretariat, Joint Chiefs of Staff, 1972.

de Kerchove, René. *International Maritime Dictionary.* Princeton, NJ: D. Van Nostrand Company, Inc., 1948. Second Edition, October 1961.

DeSpain, L.A. "The Development and Employment of the Landing Vehicle, Tracked." Student Paper. Fort Knox, KY: Instructor Training Division,

General Instruction Department, US Army Armored School, 1 May 1948.

D'Este, Carlo. *Bitter Victory: The Battle for Sicily.* New York, NY: E.P. Dutton, 1988.

Devers, Jacob. "OPERATION DRAGOON: The Invasion of Southern France." *Military Affairs*, Vol. X, No. 2 (Summer 1946): 2–41.

———. "Major Problems Confronting a Theater Commander in Combined Operations." Address at the Armed Forces Staff College, 8 October 1947.

Dictionary of American Naval Fighting Ships (DANFS). http://www.history.navy. mil/danfs/ (accessed 15 January 2007).

"Disembarking of Troops from Transports." *Journal of US Artillery* (January 1914).

Dod, Karl C. *United States Army in World War II, The Corps of Engineers: The War Against Japan.* Washington, DC: Historical Division, Department of the Army, 1966. Reprinted 1982, 1987.

Donahoe, Patrick, and Laurence McCabe. "Controlling the Rivers." *U.S. Naval Institute Proceedings,* Vol. 132, No.1 (January 2006): 26–30.

Donigan, Henry J. "Peleliu: The Forgotten Battle." *Marine Corps Gazette* (September 1994): 96–103.

Doyle, James Henry. "Amphibious Operations." Lecture, Army War College, 12 February 1953. US Army Military History Institute.

Doyle, James H., and Arthur J. Mayer. "December 1950 at Hungnam." *U.S. Naval Institute Proceedings*, Vol. 105, No. 4 (April 1979): 44–55.

Drea, Edward J. *The U.S. Army Campaigns of World War II: New Guinea.* CMH Pub 72-9. Washington, DC: GPO, n.d.

———. *MacArthur's ULTRA: Codebreaking and the War Against Japan, 1942–1945.* Lawrence, KS: University of Kansas Press, 1992.

Drum, Carroll H. *Vietnam Studies, Base Development in South Vietnam 1965–1970.* Washington, DC: Department of the Army, 1972.

Dudash, Paul A. *The Paul A. Dudash Papers.* US Army Military History Institute.

Dudley, William S. "The War of 1812 and Postwar Expansion." In *Encyclopedia of the American Military*, Vol. 1.

Dudley, William S., ed. *The Naval War of 1812; A Documentary History, Vol. II.* Washington, DC: Naval Historical Center, 1992.

Dunn, Brian J. "Rethinking Army–Marine Corps Roles." *Joint Force Quarterly* (Autumn 2000): 38–42.

Dunnavent, R. Blake. "Muddy Waters: A History of the United States Navy in Riverine Warfare and the Emergence of a Tactical Doctrine, 1775–1989." PhD diss, Texas Tech University, 1998.

———. *Brown Water Warfare: The U.S. Navy in Riverine Warfare and the Emergence of a Tactical Doctrine, 1775–1970.* Gainesville, FL: University of Florida Press, 2005.

Dwyer, John B. *Commandos from the Sea: The History of Amphibious Special Warfare in World War II and the Korean War.* Boulder, CO: Paladin Press, 2002.

Dyer, George C. *The Amphibians Came to Conquer: The Story of Admiral Richmond Kelly Turner.* 2 vols. Washington, DC: GPO, 1972.

Edwards, Paul M. *The Inchon Landing, Korea, 1950: An Annotated Bibliography.* Westport, CT: Greenwood Press, 1994.

————. *Small United States and United Nations Warships of the Korean War.* Jefferson, NC, and London: McFarland & Company, 2008.

Edwards, Spencer P., Jr. "Katusa—An Experiment in Korea." *U.S. Naval Institute Proceedings,* Vol. 84, No. 1 (January 1958): 31–37.

Eglin, Henry W.T. "General Scott's Landing at Vera Cruz, March 9, 1897." *Coast Artillery Journal,* Vol. 68, No. 3 (March 1928): 244–247.

Ellison, Marvin C. "Landing Craft in River Crossings." *Military Engineer,* Vol. XXXVII, No. 241 (November 1945): 447–449.

Ent, Uzal W. *Fighting on the Brink: Defense of the Pusan Perimeter.* Paducah, KY: Turner Publishing Co., 1996.

Estes, Kenneth W. *Marines Under Armor: The Marine Corps and the Armored Fighting Vehicle, 1916–2000.* Annapolis, MD: Naval Institute Press, 2000.

Evanhoe, Ed. *Dark Moon: Eighth Army Special Operations in the Korean War.* Annapolis, MD: Naval Institute Press, 1995.

Fahey, James C. *Ships and Aircraft of the United States Fleet, 1945.* New York, NY: Ships and Aircraft, 1945. Reprinted, Annapolis, MD: Naval Institute Press, 1976.

Falk, Stanley L. "Comments on Reynolds: 'MacArthur as Maritime Strategist.'" *Naval War College Review,* Vol. XXXIII, No. 2 (March/April 1980): 92–99.

Fergusson, Bernard. *The Watery Maze: Story of Combined Operations in World War II.* New York, NY: Collins, 1961.

Field, David D. *The David D. Field Papers.* US Army Military History Institute.

"Field Exercise in Massachusetts." *Army and Navy Journal* 52 (28 August 1909): 1474–1478.

Field, James A., Jr. *The Japanese at Leyte Gulf: The Sho Operation.* Princeton, NJ: Princeton University Press, 1947.

————. *History of United States Naval Operations, Korea.* Washington, DC: GPO, 1962.

Fisher, David Hackett. *Washington's Crossing.* New York, NY: Oxford University Press USA, 2004.

Fischer, Joseph, Richard Stewart, and Stanley Sandler. *Operation UPHOLD/RESTORE/MAINTAIN DEMOCRACY.* Fort Bragg, NC: US Army Special Operations Command, Directorate of History, Archive, Library and Museums, 1997.

Flemings, Amos W. *Observers' Handbook: Joint Exercise MIKI.* San Francisco, CA: Fort Winfield Scott, 1949.

Foster-Carter, Aiden. "Pyongyang Watch: The Dam Nuisance." *Asia Times* on line, 16 May 2003. atimes.com/koreas/DE16Dg03.html (accessed 23 March 2007).

Fowle, Barry W., and John C. Lonnquest, ed. *Remembering the "Forgotten War":*
U.S. Army Engineer Officers in Korea. Alexandria, VA: Office of History,
Headquarters, US Army Corps of Engineers, 2005.

Fowler, Delbert M. "Bridging the Han River." *Military Engineer,* Vol. XLIII, No.
296 (November–December 1951): 414–416.

———. "Operations at the Hwachon Dam, Korea." *Military Engineer,* Vol. XLIV,
No. 297 (January–February 1952): 7–8.

Fowler, William M., Jr. *Empires at War: The French and Indian War and the*
Struggle for North America, 1754–1763. New York, NY: Walker and
Company, 2005.

Frances, Anthony A. *History of the Marine Corps Schools.* Quantico, VA: Marine
Corps Schools, 1945.

Frank, Benis M., and Frank I. Shaw. *History of the United States Marine Corps*
Operations in World War II, Vol. V, Victory and Occupation. Washington,
DC: Historical Branch, G3 Division, Headquarters, US Marine Corps,
1968.

Frank, Richard B. *Guadalcanal.* New York, NY: Random House, 1990.

———. "The Amphibious Revolution." *Naval History,* Vol. 19, No. 4 (August
2005): 20–26.

Friedman, Norman, and A.D. Baker. *U.S. Amphibious Ships and Craft; An*
Illustrated Design History. Annapolis, MD: Naval Institute Press, 2002.

Fulton, William B. *Vietnam Studies: Riverine Operations 1966–1969.* Washington,
DC: Center of Military History, 1985.

———. *Mobile Riverine Force: America's Mobile Riverine Force Vietnam.*
Paducah, KY: Turner Publishing Co., 1998.

Fuson, Jack C. *Transportation and Logistics: One Man's Story.* Washington, DC:
Center of Military History, 1994.

———. *The Jack C. Fuson Papers,* 1986.

Futrell, Robert Frank. *The United States Air Force in Korea, 1950–1953.*
Washington, DC: Office of Air Force History, US Air Force, 1983.

Gailey, Harry A. *"Howlin' Mad" vs. The Army: Conflict in Command, Saipan*
1944. Novato, CA: Presidio Press, 1986.

———. *MacArthur Strikes Back: Decision at Buna New Guinea 1942–1943.*
Novato, CA: Presidio Press, 2000.

Gammons, Stephen L.Y. *The Korean War: The UN Offensive, 16 September–*
2 November 1950. CMH Pub 19-7. Washington, DC: Center of Military
History, 2000.

Garand, George W., and Truman R. Strobridge. *History of the United States Marine*
Corps Operations in World War II, Vol. IV, Western Pacific Operations.
Washington, DC: Historical Branch, G3 Division, Headquarters, US
Marine Corps, 1971.

Garber, Robert. *Robert Garber Papers.* US Army Military History Institute.

Garfield, Brian. *The Thousand-Mile War: World War II in Alaska and the*
Aleutians. Garden City, NY: Doubleday, 1969.

Garland, Albert N. *Amphibious Doctrine and Training.* AGC Study No. 6. Fort Monroe, VA: Historical Section, Army Ground Forces, 10 May 1949.

Garland, Albert N., and Howard McGaw Smyth. *United States Army in World War II, The Mediterranean Theater of Operations, Sicily and the Surrender of Italy.* Washington, DC: Historical Division, Department of the Army, 1965. Reprinted 1986, 1991, 2002.

Garthoff, Raymond L. "Soviet Operations in the War With Japan; August, 1945." *U.S. Naval Institute Proceedings,* Vol. 92, No. 5 (May 1966): 50–63.

GHQ UNC, Operations Order No. 2, 2 October 1950. National Archives and Records Administration.

Gibson, Charles Dana, and E. Kay Gibson. *Dictionary of Transports and Combatant Vessels, Steam and Sail, Employed by the Union Army, 1861–1866.* Camden, ME: Ensign, 1992.

———. *The Army's Navy Series, Vol. I, Marine Transportation in War: The U.S. Army Experience, 1775–1860.* Camden, ME: Ensign Press, 1992.

———. *The Army's Navy Series, Vol. II, Assault and Logistics: Union Army Coastal and River Operations, 1861–1866.* Camden ME: Ensign Press, 1995.

Gilfillan, Edward S. *The Raid as an Amphibious Technique.* Washington, DC: National Research Council, Committee on Amphibious Operations, 1951.

Glantz, David M. *August Storm: The Soviet 1945 Strategic Offensive in Manchuria.* Fort Leavenworth, KS: Combat Studies Institute Press, 1983.

Glover's Marblehead Regiment. gloversregiment.org/history.html (accessed 5 May 2007).

Godsey, James P. "Soyang River Bailey Bridge." *Military Engineer,* Vol. XLIII, No. 296 (November–December 1951): 396–397.

Godson, Susan H. *Viking of Assault: Admiral John Leslie Hall, Jr., and Amphibious Warfare.* Washington, DC: University Press of America, 1982.

Goldberg, Harold J. *D-Day in the Pacific: The Battle of Saipan.* Bloomington, IN: Indiana University Press, 2007.

Goldstein, Jonas L. "*Cuba Libre!* Army–Navy Cooperation in 1898." *Joint Force Quarterly* (Summer 2000): 16–121.

Gole, Henry G. "War Planning at the U.S. Army War College, 1934–40, The Road to Rainbow." *Army History* 25 (Winter 1993): 13–28.

———. *The Road to Rainbow: Army Planning for Global War, 1934–1940.* Annapolis, MD: Naval Institute Press, 2003.

Grant, Rebecca. "An Air War Like No Other." *Air Force Magazine,* Vol. 85, No. 11 (November 2002).

Greenfield, Kent Roberts, ed. *Command Decisions.* New York, NY: Harcourt, Brace, 1959.

———. *American Strategy in World War II: A Reconsideration.* Baltimore, MD: The Johns Hopkins Press, 1963. Reprinted, Westport, CT: Greenwood Press, 1979.

Greenfield, Kent Roberts, Robert R. Palmer, and Bell I. Wiley. *United States Army in World War II, The Army Ground Forces, The Organization of Ground Combat Troops.* Washington, DC: Historical Division, Department of the Army, 1947. Reprinted 1983, 1988, 2004.

Greenwood, John T. "The U.S. Army and Amphibious Warfare During WWII." *Army History* PB-20-93-4, No. 27 (Summer 1993): 1–10.

Gregory, Barry. *Amphibious Operations.* (Pictorial survey from World War II to Vietnam.) London: Blandford, 1988.

Grover, David H. *U.S Army Ships and Watercraft of World War II.* Annapolis, MD: Naval Institute Press, 1987.

Gugeler, Russell A. *Army Amphibian Tractor and Tank Battalions in the Battle of Saipan 15 June–9 July 1944.* US Army Center of Military History. www.army.mil/cmh-pg/documents/WWII/amsai.htm (accessed 10 November 2007).

Gunner, Matthew J. "The Second Phase of the Gallipoli Campaign: May 6th to include the Battle of Sari Bair." In *Monographs of the World War.* Fort Benning, GA: US Army Infantry School [1923?].

Haas, Michael E. *In the Devil's Shadow: U.N. Special Operations During the Korean War.* Annapolis, MD: Naval Institute Press, 2000.

Ham, Myong-su. *"Badaro! Syegyero!"* ["To the sea! To the world!"], *Kukbang Ilbo (Korea Defense Daily),* 22, 27, 28, 29 March, 3 April 2006.

Hammond, William M. *The U.S. Army Campaigns of World War II: Normandy.* CMH Pub 72-18. Washington, DC: GPO, n.d.

Hancock, Daniel A. "The Navy's Not Serious About Riverine Warfare." *U.S. Naval Institute Proceedings,* Vol. 134, No.1 (January 2008).

Harding, Richard. *Amphibious Warfare in the Eighteenth Century: The British Expedition to the West Indies, 1740–1742.* Suffolk, UK: Boydell Press, 1991.

Harding, Stephen. *Sail Army: A Pictorial Guide to Current U.S. Army Watercraft.* Missoula, MT: Pictorial Histories Publishing Co., 2005.

Harmon, Larry D. "The 'Short List' for Achieving a Logistics Revolution." *Army Logistician* (March–April 2004): 34–37.

Harrison, Gordon A. *United States Army in World War II, The European Theater of Operations, Cross-Channel Attack.* Washington, DC: Historical Division, Department of the Army, 1951. Reprinted 1989, 2002, 2004.

Hart, Francis Russell. *The Siege of Havana, 1762.* Boston and New York: Houghton Mifflin Company, 1931.

Hayes, Grace P. *The History of the Joint Chiefs of Staff in World War II: The War Against Japan.* 2 vols. Washington, DC: Historical Section, Joint Chiefs of Staff, 1953, 1954.

Hayhurst, Fred. *Green Berets in Korea: The Story of 41 Independent Commando Royal Marines.* Cambridge, MA: Vanguard, 2001.

Hearn, Chester G. *Ellet's Brigade: The Strangest Outfit of All*. Baton Rouge, LA: Louisiana State University Press, 2000.

Heavey, William F. "Amphibian Engineers in Action." *Military Engineer,* Vol. XXXVI, No. 223 (May 1944): 145–152.

———. "Amphibian Engineers in Action, Part II, On To Corregidor." *Military Engineer,* Vol. XXXVII, No. 237 (July 1945): 253–262.

———. *Down Ramp! The Story of the Army Amphibian Engineers*. Washington, DC: Infantry Journal Press, 1947. Reprinted 1988.

Heinl, Robert D. *The Robert D. Heinl Papers*. US Marine Corps University Archives.

Heinl, Robert Debs. *Soldiers of the Sea: The U.S. Marine Corps, 1775–1962*. Annapolis, MD: Naval Institute Press, 1962.

———. *Victory at High Tide: The Inchon–Seoul Campaign*. Annapolis, MD: Nautical & Aviation Pub. Co. of America, 1979.

Heinl, Robert D., and John A. Crown. *The Marshalls: Increasing the Tempo*. Washington, DC: Historical Division, Headquarters, US Marine Corps, 1954.

Hermes, Walter G. *United States Army in the Korean War: Truce Tent and Fighting Front*. Washington, DC: Office of the Chief of Military History, 1966.

Hickins, Kenneth E. "Transforming Strategic Mobility." *Army Logistician*, Vol. 35, No. 3 (May–June 2003): 2–6.

———. "Strategic Mobility: The U.S. Military's Weakest Link." *Army Logistician*, Vol. 34, No. 6 (November–December 2002): 34–37.

"High Speed Sealift." *Global Security.Org*. globalsecurity.org/military/systems/ship/hss.htm (accessed 10 December 2007).

Hirrel, Leo. *The U.S. Army Campaigns of World War II: Bismarck Archipelago*. CMH Pub 72-24. Washington, DC: GPO, n.d.

Hitt, Parker. "Amphibious Infantry Fleet on Lake Lanao." *U.S. Naval Institute Proceedings* (February 1938): 234–249.

Hittle, J.D. "Jomini and Amphibious Thought." *Marine Corps Gazette,* Vol. 30, No.12 (May 1946): 35–38.

Hoffman, Carl W. *Saipan: The Beginning of the End*. Washington, DC: Historical Division, Headquarters, US Marine Corps, 1950. Reprinted Nashville, TN: Battery Press, 1988.

———. *The Seizure of Tinian*. Washington, DC: Historical Division, Headquarters, US Marine Corps, 1951.

Hoffman, Frank G. "Forcible Entry is a Strategic Necessity." *U.S. Naval Institute Proceedings* (November 2004): 2.

Hoffman, Jon T. *From Makin to Bougainville: Marine Raiders in the Pacific War*. Washington, DC: Marine Corps Historical Center, 1993.

———. "Legacy and Lessons: The New Britain Campaign." *Marine Corps Gazette*, Vol. 82, No. 2 (February 1998): 56–67.

———. *Once a Legend: "Red Mike" Edson of the Marine Raiders*. Novato, CA: Presidio, 1994.

———. "Stepping Forward Smartly: 'Forward . . . from the sea,' the Emerging Expanded Naval Strategy." *Marine Corps Gazette*, Vol. 79, No. 3 (March 1995): 30.

———. "The Central and Northern Solomons." *Marine Corps Gazette* (February 1994): 60–65.

———. "The Legacy and Lessons of Iwo Jima." *Marine Corps Gazette*, Vol. 79, No. 2 (February 1995): 72–75.

———. "The Legacy and Lessons of Okinawa." *Marine Corps Gazette*, Vol. 79, No. 4 (April 1994): 64–71.

———. "The Legacy and Lessons of Operation DOWNFALL." *Marine Corps Gazette*, Vol. 79, No. 8 (August 1995): 59–64.

———. "The Legacy and Lessons of Operation OVERLORD." *Marine Corps Gazette* (June 1994): 68–72.

———. "The Legacy and Lessons of Operation TORCH." *Marine Corps Gazette* (December 1992) 60–63.

———. "The Legacy and Lessons of Operation WATCHTOWER." *Marine Corps Gazette* (August 1994): 68–73.

———. "The Legacy and Lessons of Peleliu." *Marine Corps Gazette* (September 1994): 90–94.

———. "The Legacy and Lessons of Tarawa." *Marine Corps Gazette* (November 1993): 63–67.

———. "The Legacy and Lessons of the Campaign in Italy." *Marine Corps Gazette* (January 1994): 65–69.

———. "The Legacy and Lessons of the Marianas Campaign." *Marine Corps Gazette* (July 1994): 76–81.

———. "The Legacy and Lessons of the New Guinea Campaign." *Marine Corps Gazette* (September 1993): 74–77.

———. "The Legacy and Lessons of WW II Raids." *Marine Corps Gazette* (September 1992): 62–65.

———. "The Roles and Missions Debate." *Marine Corps Gazette* (December 1994): 16–19.

Holt, Thaddeus. *The Deceivers: Allied Military Deception in the Second World War.* New York, NY: Scribner, 2004.

Holzimmer, Kevin. *A Soldier's Soldier; A Military Biography of General Walter Krueger.* PhD diss, Temple University, 1999.

———. "Joint Operations in the Southwest Pacific, 1943–1945." *Joint Force Quarterly*, No. 38 (3d Quarter, 2005): 100–108.

———. *General Walter Krueger: Unsung Hero of the Pacific War.* Lawrence, KS: University of Kansas Press, 2007.

Hough, Frank O., Ludwig E. Verle, and Henry I. Shaw. *History of the United States Marine Corps Operations in World War II, Vol. I, Pearl Harbor to Guadalcanal.* Washington, DC: Historical Branch, G3 Division, Headquarters, US Marine Corps, 1958.

Houghton, Russell T. *The Amphibian Tractor Battalion.* Military Monograph Advanced Officers Class #2. Fort Knox, KY: Instructor Training Division, General Instruction Department, US Army Armored School, 6 May 1948.

Howe, George F. *United States Army in World War II, The Mediterranean Theater of Operations, Northwest Africa: Seizing the Initiative in the West.* Washington, DC: Historical Division, Department of the Army, 1957. Reprinted 1985, 1991, 2002.

Hughes, Wayne P. *Naval Maneuver Warfare.* globalsecurity.org/military/library/report/1995/CG.htm (accessed 7 July 2007).

Hyzer, Peter C. "Third Engineers in Korea, July–October 1950." *Military Engineer,* Vol. XLIII, No. 292 (March–April 1951): 101–107.

Ickes, Robert J. *Landing Vehicles Tracked.* AFV 16. Windsor, UK: Profile Publications, n.d.

Incat Internet site. www.incat.com/au/domino/incat/incatweb.nsf/v-title/Incat%20Home?OpenDocument (accessed 21 June 2008).

Infantry Journal. Letters to the Editor of *The Infantry Journal* on the subject of the "Smith *versus* Smith" articles and editorials. *The Infantry Journal,* Vol. LXIV, No. 2 (February 1949): 51; Vol. LXIV, No. 3 (March 1949): 49, 51–53; Vol. LXIV, No. 5 (May 1949): 51; Vol. LXIV, No. 6 (June 1949): 54; Vol. LXIV, No. 8 (August 1949): 34; and *United States Army Combat Forces Journal* [successor publication to *The Infantry Journal*], Vol. 4, No. 6 (January 1954): 8.

Infantry Journal. "'Navy War—Volume VII,' Review of [Samuel Eliot Morison's] *New Guinea and the Marianas.*" *Infantry Journal,* Vol. 14, No. 3 (November 1953): 44.

Isely, Jeter A., and Philip Crowl. *U.S. Marines and Amphibious War: Its Theory and Practice in the Pacific.* Princeton, NJ: Princeton University Press, 1951.

Itschner, Emerson C. "The Naktong River Crossings in Korea." *Military Engineer,* Vol. XLIII, No. 292 (March–April 1951): 96–98.

Jablonsky, David. *War by Land, Sea and Air: Dwight D. Eisenhower and the Concept of Unified Command.* Unpublished manuscript.

Jacobs, James Ripley. *The Beginning of the U.S. Army, 1783–1812.* Princeton, NJ: Princeton University Press, 1947.

James, D. Clayton. *The Years of MacArthur, Vol. II, 1941–1945.* Boston, MA: Houghton Mifflin Company, 1975.

———. *The Years of MacArthur, Vol. III, Triumph and Disaster 1945–1964.* Boston, MA: Houghton Mifflin, 1985.

James, D. Clayton, and Anne Sharp Wells. *Refighting the Last War: Command and Crisis in Korea 1950–1953.* New York, NY: The Free Press, 1993.

Jamison, J.W. *Development of Amphibious Doctrine.* Lecture presented at the Army and Navy Staff College. Washington, DC: Army and Navy Staff College, 1 May 1945.

Jessup, John E., and Louise B. Ketz, eds. *Encyclopedia of the American Military.* New York, NY: Charles Scribner's Sons, 1994.

Johnson, Robert Erwin. *Coast Guard-Manned Naval Vessels in World War II*. US Coast Guard Historian's Office. www.uscg.mil/hq/g-cp/history/h_cgnvy. html (accessed 9 February 2008).

Jones, Clifford. "Japanese Landing at Tsing-tao." *The Coast Artillery Journal,* Vol. 68, No. 6 (June 1928): 145–149.

Juskowiak, Terry E., and John R. Wharton. "Joint and Expeditionary Logistics for a Campaign-Quality Army." *Army Logistician*, Vol. 36, Issue 5 (September–October 2004): 2–8.

Kane, Douglas T., and Henry I. Shaw. *History of the United States Marine Corps Operations in World War II, Vol. II, Isolation of Rabaul.* Washington, DC: Historical Branch, G3 Division, Headquarters, US Marine Corps, 1958.

Karig, Walter, Malcolm W. Cagle, and Frank A. Manson. *Battle Report: The War in Korea.* New York, NY: Rinehart and Company, 1952.

Keiser, Gordon W. *The U.S. Marine Corps and Defense Unification, 1944–47.* Baltimore, MD: Nautical and Aviation, 1966.

Kelly, P.X. "The Amphibious Warfare Strategy." *The Maritime Strategy.* Annapolis, MD: Naval Institute Press, January 1986.

Kennedy, J.C. *Planning Amphibious Operations.* Fort Knox, KY: Instructor Training Division, General Instruction Department, US Army Armored School, 27 April 1948.

Keyes, Roger J.B. *Amphibious Warfare and Combined Operations.* Cambridge, UK: The University Press, 1943.

Killblane, Richard E. "Army Riverine Operations in Vietnam and Panama (What the Navy Won't Tell You)." Unpublished manuscript, n.d.

———. "Operation Iraqi Freedom/Enduring Freedom Trip Report 2008." Unpublished manuscript, April 2008.

———. "The History of Logistics-over-the-Shore (LOTS) Operations." Unpublished manuscript, n.d.

Kim, Myung Oak. "His Christmas Miracle, Savior of the People: Amid Korean War pullout, doctor found refuge for thousands being forgotten." *Philadelphia Daily News*, 24 December 2004, 7.

Kim, Captain Sang Mo. "The Implications of the Sea War in Korea from the Standpoint of the Korean Navy." *Naval War College Review*, Vol. XX, No. 1 (Summer 1967): 105–139.

King, Joseph E. "The Fort Fisher Campaigns, 1864–65." In *Assault from the Sea: Essays on the History of Amphibious Warfare,* edited by Merrill L. Bartlett, 95–104. Annapolis, MD: Naval Institute Press, 1983.

King, Toniya L. "Landing Craft Mechanized 8 Modification 2." *Transportation Corps* (Winter 2005–06): 20–21.

Kirkwood, R.G. "Artillery Loads for Navy Lighter for Landing Heavy Artillery." Fort Leavenworth, KS: The General Service Schools, 20 June 1928.

Klamper, Amy. "River War." *Seapower*, Volume 49, No. 2 (February 2006): 10–12.

Kretchik, Walter E., Robert F. Baumann, and John T. Fischel. *Invasion, Intervention, "Intervasion": A Concise History of the U.S. Army in Operation Uphold Democracy.* Fort Leavenworth, KS: US Army Command and General Staff College Press, 1998.

Krueger, Walter. *From Down Under to Nippon: The Story of Sixth Army in World War II.* Washington, DC: Combat Forces Press, 1953.

Krulak, Victor H. *First To Fight: An Inside View of the U.S. Marine Corps.* Annapolis, MD: Naval Institute Press, 1984.

———. "You Can't Get There From Here: The Inchon Story." In *First To Fight: An Inside View of the U.S. Marine Corps,* edited by Victor H. Krulak. Annapolis, MD: Naval Institute Press, 1984.

Kutta, Timothy J., Don Geer, and Perry Manley. "DUKW in Action." *Armor* 36. Carrollton, TX: Squadron/Signal Publications, 1996.

Ladd, James. *Assault from the Sea 1939–1945.* Newton Abbot, UK: David and Charles, 1976.

Lake, Deborah. *The Zeebrugge and Ostend Raids 1918.* Barnsley, South Yorkshire, UK: Leo Cooper, 2002.

Lambeth, Benjamin S. *Airpower Against Terror: America's Conduct of Operation Enduring Freedom.* Santa Monica, CA: RAND Corporation, 2005.

"Landing of Troops." *Journal of the United States Artillery,* Vol. 41, No. 1 (January–February 1914): 21–124.

Lane, Frederic L. *Ships for Victory, A History of Shipbuilding Under the U.S. Maritime Commission in World War II.* Baltimore, MD: The Johns Hopkins University Press, 1951.

Langley, Michael. *Inchon Landing: MacArthur's Last Triumph.* New York, NY: Times Books, 1979.

Larson, Eric V., Derek Eaton, Paul Elrick, Theodore Karasik, Robert Klein, Sherrill Lingel, Brian Nichiporuk, Robert Uy, and John Zavadil. *Assuring Access in Key Strategic Regions: Toward a Long-Term Strategy.* Santa Monica, CA: RAND Arroyo Center, 2004.

Larson, Harold. *The Army's Cargo Fleet in World War II.* Washington, DC: GPO, 1945.

Laurie, Clayton D. *The U.S. Army Campaigns of World War II: Anzio.* CMH Pub 72-19. Washington, DC: GPO, n.d.

Lawton, William S. *William S. Lawton Papers.* US Army Military History Institute.

Lay, Kenneth E. "Roads-Transport-Firepower in Korea." *Military Engineer,* Vol. XLIII, No. 296 (November–December 1951): 389–394.

Legere, Lawrence J. "Unification of the Armed Forces." PhD diss., Harvard University, 1950.

Leighton, Richard M., and Robert W. Coakley. *United States Army in World War II, The War Department, Global Logistics and Strategy: 1940–1943.* Washington, DC: Historical Division, Department of the Army, 1955. Reprinted 1984, 1995.

Lewis, Adrian. *Omaha Beach: A Flawed Victory.* Chapel Hill & London: The University of North Carolina Press, 2001.

Linn, Brian McAllister. "America's Expeditionary War Transformation." *Naval History*, Vol. 19, Issue 5 (October 2006): 56–61.

———. *Guardians of Empire: The U.S. Army and the Pacific, 1902–1940.* Chapel Hill & London: The University of North Carolina Press, 1997.

———. *The U.S. Army and Counterinsurgency in the Philippine War, 1898–1902.* Chapel Hill, NC: University of North Carolina Press, 1989.

Linn, Thomas C. "Joint Operations: The Marine Perspective." *Joint Force Quarterly* (Winter 1995–96): 16–18.

Linn, Thomas C., and C.P. Neimeyer. "Once and Future Marines." *Joint Force Quarterly* (Autumn/Winter 1994–95): 47–51.

Lofgren, Stephen J. *The U.S. Army Campaigns of World War II: Northern Solomons.* CMH Pub 72-10. Washington, DC: GPO, n.d.

Logistics in the Korean Operation 6/50 to 7/53. S-AZ. Chapter IV, "Operation Chromite"; Chapter VI, "Water Transportation"; Chapter VII, "Corps of Engineers." Microfilm. *Armed Forces Oral Histories: Korean War Studies and After-Action Reports.* Bethesda, MD: University Publications of America, 1989.

Lorelli, John A. *To Foreign Shores: U.S. Amphibious Operations in World War II.* Annapolis, MD: Naval Institute Press, 1995.

Lott, Arnold S. *Most Dangerous Sea: A History of Mine Warfare and an Account of U.S. Navy Mine Warfare Operations in World War II and Korea.* Annapolis, MD: Naval Institute Press, 1959.

Love, Edmund G. "Smith versus Smith." *Infantry Journal,* Vol. LXIII, No. 5 (November 1948): 3–13.

———. *The 27th Infantry Division in World War II.* Nashville, TN: Battery Press, 1982, reprint. Originally published, Washington, DC: Infantry Journal Press, 1949.

Lovering, Tristan, ed. *Amphibious Assault: Manoeuvre from the Sea.* Rendlesham, Woodbridge, Suffolk, UK: Seafarer Books, 2007.

Lowe, Christian. "Beyond the Beach." *Armed Forces Journal* (January 2005): 20–25.

Lundquist, Edward H. "Fleet Experimentation Lays Groundwork for New Concepts at Sea." *Naval Forces,* Vol. XXIX, No. 11 (2008): 20–25.

MacArthur, Douglas. *Reminiscences.* New York, NY: McGraw-Hill Book Company, 1964, Second Printing.

MacGarrigle, George L. *The U.S. Army Campaigns of World War II: Aleutian Islands.* CMH Pub 72-6. Washington, DC: GPO, 1991.

———. *United States Army in Vietnam: Combat Operations: Taking the Offensive, October 1966 to October 1967.* Washington, DC: Center of Military History, US Army, 1998.

Magee, Douglas R., Jr. *The Striking History of the 1097th Transportation Company.* Panama: USARSO Printing Plant, 1997.

Malcom, Ben S., with Ron Martz. *White Tigers: My Secret War in North Korea.* Washington, DC: Brassey's, 1996.

Malkasian, Carter A. "Charting the Pathway to OMFTS: A Historical Assessment of Amphibious Operations from 1941 to the Present." Center for Naval Analyses, July 2002.

Mann, Frank L. "Operation Versatile: Korean Saga of the 2d Engineer Special Brigade." *Military Engineer,* Vol. XLIV, No. 299 (May–June 52): 168–173.

Marolda, Edward J. "Wars and Conflicts of the U.S. Navy, Korean War, Naval Battles." Naval Historical Center. history.navy.mil/wars/korea/navalbattles.htm (accessed 10 March 2007).

Marolda, Edward J., ed. *The U.S. Navy in the Korean War.* Annapolis, MD: Naval Institute Press, 2007.

Mason, Colonel A.T., USMC. JCS Special Monograph on Amphibious Warfare (unpublished draft), Chapter 2, "Domestic Affairs—1942; ARCADIA, Organization and Training, Ships, and Craft," File HRC 451.94 "Amphibious Warfare Before WW II." Historical Resources Branch, Center of Military History, Washington, DC.

Matloff, Maurice. *United States Army in World War II, The War Department, Strategic Planning for Coalition Warfare: 1943–1944.* Washington, DC: Historical Division, Department of the Army, 1959. Reprinted 1970, 1994, 2003.

———. *World War II: A Concise Military History of America's All-Out, Two-Front War.* New York, NY: Galahad Books, 1982.

Matloff, Maurice, ed. *American Military History.* Washington, DC: GPO, 1988.

Matloff, Maurice, and Edwin M. Snell. *United States Army in World War II, The War Department, Strategic Planning for Coalition Warfare: 1941–1942.* Washington, DC: Historical Division, Department of the Army, 1953. Reprinted 1986, 1990, 2000.

Matray, James I. "Truman's Plan for Victory." *Journal of American History* (September 1979): 314–333.

Maund, L.E.H. *Assault from the Sea.* London: Methuen, 1949.

———. "The Development of Landing Craft." *The Journal of the Royal United Service Institution,* Vol. XC, No. 558 (May 1945): 212–217.

McCaffrey, William J. *William J. McCaffrey Papers, 1967–1997.*

McCaskey, D.L. *The Role of Army Ground Forces in the Development of Equipment.* Study No. 34. Washington, DC: Historical Section, Army Ground Forces, 1946.

McCollam, William, Jr. "Raising the Tidal Basin Lock Gates at Inchon, Korea." *Military Engineer,* Vol. XLIV, No. 298 (March–April 1952).

McDaniel, LTC Alva T., MAJ Francis A. Cooch III, MAJ George V. Labadie, CPT Edwin W. Piburn Jr., and CPT James R. Porta. *The Armored Division as an Assault Landing Force.* Research Report. Fort Knox, KY: US Army Armored School, 1951–52.

McGee, John Hugh. *John Hugh McGee Papers, 1950–51.* US Army Military History Institute.

McGee, William L. *Amphibious Operations in the South Pacific in WWII, Vol. I, The Amphibians are Coming! Emergence of the 'Gator Navy and its Revolutionary Landing Craft.* Santa Barbara, CA: BMC Publications, 2000.

McGourty, Wayne E. Photograph Collection, 1943–53.

McGrath, John J. *The Korean War: Restoring the Balance, 25 January–8 July 1951.* CMH Pub 19-9. Washington, DC: Center of Military History, 2001.

McMichael, Scott. "Force Projection." *Army Concepts Summaries.* Fort Monroe, VA: Headquarters, US Army Training and Doctrine Command, 2004.

McNerney, Charles D. *The Charles D. McNerney Papers.* US Army Military History Institute.

Medina, Joseph F. "Official Biography: Joseph V. Medina." usmc.mil/genbios2. nsf/biographies/DA9C6F9E36A7015885256D730013425D?opendocu ment (accessed 31 May 2007).

Mercogliano, Salvatore R. "Korea: The First Shot (Military Sea Transportation Service in Korean War)." usmm.org/msts/korea.html (accessed 24 June 2007).

———. "Merchant Ships Used in the Korean War." usmm.org/koreaships.html (accessed 24 June 2007).

———. "Military Sea Transportation Service (MSTS) Ships in the Korean War." usmm.org/koreashipmsts.html (accessed 24 June 2007).

———. "Military Sea Transportation Service and Merchant Ships Participating in Inchon, Korea Invasion." usmm.org/inchonships.htm.l (accessed 24 June 2007).

———. "Military Sea Transportation Service and Merchant Ships Participating in Hungnam, Korea Redeployment." usmm.org/hungnamships.html (accessed 24 June 2007).

Mesko, Jim. *Riverine: A Pictorial History of the Brown Water Navy in Vietnam.* Carrollton, TX: Squadron/Signal Publications, 1985.

Milkowski, Stanlis D. "To the Yalu and Back." *Joint Force Quarterly* (Spring/ Summer 2001): 38–46.

Miller, Edward S. *War Plan Orange: The U.S. Strategy to Defeat Japan 1897– 1945.* Annapolis, MD: Naval Institute Press, 1991.

Miller, John, Jr. *United States Army in World War II, The War in the Pacific, Guadalcanal: The First Offensive.* Washington, DC: Historical Division, Department of the Army, 1949. Reprinted 1989, 1995.

———. *United States Army in World War II, The War in the Pacific, Cartwheel: The Reduction of Rabaul.* Washington, DC: Historical Division, Department of the Army, 1959. Reprinted 1984, 1990, 1995.

———. "MacArthur and the Admiralties." In *Command Decisions,* edited by Kent Roberts Greenfield. New York, NY: Harcourt, Brace, 1959.

Millett, Allan R. "Assault from the Sea: The Development of Amphibious Warfare Between the Wars: The American, British, and Japanese Experiences." In *Military Innovation in the Interwar Period*, edited by Williamson Murray and Allan R. Millett. Cambridge, UK: Cambridge University Press, 1996.

———. *Semper Fidelis: The History of the United States Marine Corps.* New York, NY: The Free Press, 2003.

Milner, Samuel. *United States Army in World War II, The War in the Pacific, Victory in Papua.* Washington, DC: Historical Division, Department of the Army, 1957. Reprinted 1989, 2003.

Moenk, Jean R. *A History of Large-Scale Army Maneuvers in the United States, 1935–1964.* Fort Monroe, VA: Historical Branch, Office of the Deputy Chief of Staff for Military Operations and Reserve Force, US Continental Army Command, December 1969.

Montross, Lynn. Series editor. *U.S. Marine Operations in Korea, 1950–1953.* 5 vols. Washington, DC: Historical Branch, G3, US Marine Corps, 1955–72.

Montross, Lynn, and Nicholas A. Canzona. "Large Sedentary Targets on Red Beach." *Marine Corps Gazette*, Vol. 44, No. 9 (September 1960): 44–50.

———. *U.S. Marine Operations in Korea, 1950–1953, Vol.1, The Pusan Perimeter.* Washington, DC: Historical Branch, G3, 1954.

———. *U.S. Marine Operations in Korea, 1950–1953, Vol. II, The Inchon-Seoul Operation.* Washington, DC: Historical Branch, G3, 1955.

———. *U.S. Marine Operations in Korea, 1950–1953, Vol. III, The Chosin Reservoir Campaign.* Washington, DC: Historical Branch, G3, 1957.

Montross, Lynn, Hubard D. Kuokka, and Norman W. Hicks. *U.S. Marine Operations in Korea, 1950–1953, Vol. IV, The East-Central Front.* Washington, DC: Historical Branch, G3, 1962.

Montross, Lynn, Pat Meid, and James M. Yingling. *U.S. Marine Operations in Korea, 1950–1953, Vol. IV, Operations in West Korea.* Washington, DC: Historical Branch, G3, 1972.

Morison, Samuel Eliot. *History of United States Naval Operations in World War II.* Boston, MA: Little, Brown and Company, 1947–1962:

    Vol II. *Operations in North African Waters, October 1942–June 1943.* 1946.

    Vol V. *The Struggle for Guadalcanal, August 1942–February 1943.* 1949.

    Vol VI. *Breaking the Bismarcks Barrier, 22 July 1942–1 May 1944.* 1950.

    Vol VII. *Aleutians, Gilberts and Marshalls, June 1942–April 1944.* 1960.

    Vol VIII. *New Guinea and the Marianas, March 1944–August 1944.* 1953.

Vol IX. *Sicily—Salerno—Anzio, January 1943–June 1944*. 1954.

Vol XI. *Invasion of France and Germany, 1944–1945*. 1955.

Vol XII. *Leyte, June 1944–January 1945*. 1958.

Vol XIII. *The Liberation of the Philippines: Luzon, Mindanao, the Visayas, 1944–1945*. 1959.

Vol XIV. *Victory in the Pacific, 1945*. 1960.

Morrison, Robert K., and Phillip E. Pournelle. "Widen the Lens for JHSV." *U.S. Naval Institute Proceedings*, Vol. 134, No. 6 (June 2008): 54–58.

Morton, Louis. *United States Army in World War II, The War in the Pacific, Strategy and Command: The First Two Years*. Washington, DC: Historical Division, Department of the Army, 1962. Reprinted 1989.

Mossman, Billy C. *United States Army in the Korean War: Ebb and Flow, November 1950–July 1951*. Washington, DC: Office of the Chief of Military History, 1990.

Mountcastle, John W. "From Bayou to Beachhead: The Marines and Mr. Higgins." *Military Review* 60 (March 1980): 20–29.

Mowry, George E. *Landing Craft and the War Production Board, April 1942 to May 1944*. Washington, DC: Civilian Production Administration, Bureau of Demobilization, 1946.

Muir, Malcolm, Jr. "Sea Power on Call: Fleet Operations, June 1951–July 1953." In *The U.S. Navy in the Korean War*, edited by Edward J. Marolda. Annapolis, MD: Naval Institute Press, 2007.

Mullen, Mike. "What I Believe: Eight Tenets That Guide My Vision for the 21st Century Navy." *U.S. Naval Institute Proceedings*, Vol. 132, No. 1: 13–16.

Mundy, Carl E., Jr. "Reflections on the Corps; Some Thoughts on Expeditionary Warfare." *Marine Corps Gazette* (March 1995): 26–29.

Murray, Williamson, and Allan R. Millett. *A War to be Won; Fighting the Second World War, 1937–1945*. Cambridge, MA: Belknap Press of Harvard University Press, 2000.

Narr, David G. *The David G. Narr Papers*. US Army Military History Institute.

Nash, Gordon C. "Expeditionary Warfare: 'Taking the Fight to the Enemy.'" *Naval Forces*, Vol. XXVI, No. 5 (2005): 8–19.

National Research Council. Committee on Amphibious Operations. *Amphibious Operations: Synopsis*. Serial No. NRC:CAO: 002. Washington, DC: NRC, 1950.

Naval Staff History Office. *Invasion Europe*. London: HMSO, 1994.

Newell, Clayton R. *The U.S. Army Campaigns of World War II: Central Pacific*. CMH Pub 72-4. Washington, DC: GPO, 1992.

Nichols, Charles S., Jr., and Henry I. Shaw Jr. *Okinawa: Victory in the Pacific*. Washington, DC: Historical Branch, G3 Division, Headquarters, US Marine Corps, 1955. Reprinted Rutland, VT: C.E. Tuttle Co, 1966.

Nihart, Brook. "Amphibious Operations in Colonial North America." In *Assault from the Sea: Essays on the History of Amphibious Warfare*, edited by Merrill L. Bartlett, 46–50. Annapolis, MD: Naval Institute Press, 1983.

Noel, Captain John V. *Oral History*. Annapolis, MD: Naval Institute Press.

Norman, Albert. *Operation Overlord, Design and Reality*. Westport, CT: Greenwood Press, 1970.

O'Connor, Raymond G. "The U.S. Marines in the 20th Century: Amphibious Warfare and Doctrinal Debates." *Military Affairs,* Vol. 38, No. 3 (October 1974): 97–103.

O'Daniel, John W. *The John W. O'Daniel Papers*. US Army Military History Institute.

Ogden, D.A. "Our Business is Beachheads: The Third Engineer Special Brigade in the Southwest Pacific." *Military Engineer,* Vol. XXXVII, No. 236 (June 1945): 207–210.

Ogden, David A. *Amphibious Operations: Lecture before the Engineer School, Fort Belvoir, Virginia—March 15, 1949*. Fort Belvoir, VA: US Army Engineer School, The Engineer Center, 1949.

———. *Amphibious Operations of Especial Interest to the Army*. Fort Belvoir, VA: US Army Engineer School, The Engineer Center, 1951.

Ohls, Gary J. "Fort Fisher: Amphibious Victory in the American Civil War." *Naval War College Review*, Vol. 59, No. 4 (Autumn 2006): 81–99.

"Operation Load Up." *Quartermaster Review*, Vol. XXX, No. 3 (November–December 1950): 40–41, 109–110.

Ott, David Ewing. *Vietnam Studies: Field Artillery, 1954–1973*. Washington, DC: Department of the Army, 1975.

Paddock, Alfred H., Jr. *U.S. Army Special Warfare: Its Origins*. Lawrence, KS: University Press of Kansas, 2002.

Paik Sun Yup (Paek Son-yop). *From Pusan to Panmunjom*. Washington, DC: Brassey's (US), 1992.

Painter, Dean E. "The Army and Amphibious Warfare." *Military Review* 45 (August 1965): 36–40.

Palmer, Michael A. *Origins of the Maritime Strategy: American Naval Strategy in the First Postwar Decade*. Washington, DC: Naval Historical Center, 1988.

Partin, John W. *Special Operations in Operation EARNEST WILL/PRIME CHANCE I*. MacDill Air Force Base, FL: US Special Operations Command, History and Research Office, April 1998.

Paschall, Rod. "Special Operations in Korea." *Conflict,* Vol. 155, No. 2 (November 1987).

———. *A Study in Command and Control: Special Operations in Korea, 1951–1953*. Carlisle Barracks, PA: US Army Military History Institute, 1989.

Penrose, Jane, ed. *The D-Day Companion*. Oxford, UK: Osprey Publishing, 2004.

Phips, Sir William. *Dictionary of Canadian Biography Online*. biographica/EN/ShowBio.asp?BioId=345816 (accessed 15 June 2005).

Pick, Lewis A. "The Story of BLUE JAY." *Military Engineer*, Vol. XLV, No. 306 (July–August 1953): 278–286.

Pike, Shepard L. *Landing and Operations at Gallipoli, Apr 25, 1915: Study.* Washington, DC: Army War College, 1929.

Pitt, Barrie. *Zeebrugge.* New York, NY: Ballantine Books, 1958.

Plotts, Jared. "U.S. Marine Corps Brig. Gen. Joseph V. Medina: Marine General Leads Strike Group into History." *Defend America News,* 10 June 2004. defendamerica.mil/cgi-bin/prfriendly.cgi?http://www.defendamerica .mil/profiles/jun2004/pr0601004a.html (accessed 31 May 2007).

Pogue, Forrest C. *United States Army in World War II, The European Theater of Operations, The Supreme Command.* Washington, DC: Historical Division, Department of the Army, 1954. Reprinted 1989, 1996.

Polk, John Fleming. "Vera Cruz, 1847." In *Assault from the Sea: Essays on the History of Amphibious Warfare,* edited by Merrill L. Bartlett. Annapolis, MD: Naval Institute Press, 1983.

Polmar, Norman, and Peter B. Mersky. *Amphibious Warfare: An Illustrated History.* London: Blandford, 1988.

Possony, Stefany T. "Amphibious Strategy." *Marine Corps Gazette* (June 1945): 3–6.

Potter, E.B. *Admiral Arleigh Burke: A Biography.* New York, NY: Random House, 1990.

Powell, Herbert B. *Conversations between General Herbert B. Powell and Lieutenant Colonel Philip J. Stevens and Others, Vol. I, Senior Officer Debriefing Program.* Carlisle Barracks, PA: US Army Military History Institute Research Collection, 1972.

Prados, John. *Presidents' Secret Wars: CIA and Pentagon Covert Operations from World War II through the Persian Gulf.* Chicago, IL: I.R. Dee (Elephant Paperbacks), 1996.

"Public Misstatement by Lieutenant General Holland M. Smith." *Infantry Journal,* Vol. LXIII, No. 6 (December 1948): 45.

Pye, W.S. "Joint Army and Navy Operations." *U.S. Naval Institute Proceedings,* Part 1, Vol. 50, No. 12 (December 1924): 1963–1975; Part II, Vol. 51, No. 1 (January 1925): 1–14; Part III, Vol. 51, No. 2 (February 1925): 233–245; Part IV, Vol. 51, No. 3 (March 1925): 386–399; Part V, Vol. 51, No. 4 (April 1925): 589–599; Part VI, Vol. 51, No. 6 (June 1925): 975–1000.

Quinn, William W. Photograph Collection, 1933–75.

Quirk, Robert E. *An Affair of Honor: Woodrow Wilson and the Occupation of Veracruz.* Lexington, KY: University of Kentucky Press, 1962.

Raad, Robert H. "Amphibious Operations." Lecture, US Army War College, 10 October 1955. US Army Military History Institute.

Radford, Arthur William. *From Pearl Harbor to Vietnam: The Memoirs of Admiral Arthur W. Radford.* Edited by Stephen Jurika Jr. Stanford, CA: Hoover Institution Press, 1980.

Reed, Rowena. *Combined Operations in the Civil War.* Annapolis MD: Naval Institute Press, 1978.

Rehkopf, Ned B. "The Landing at Gallipoli." *The Coast Artillery Journal*, Vol. 68, No. 6 (June 1928): 475–491 and Vol. 69, No. 1 (July 1928): 19–35.

Republic of Korea Ministry of National Defense. *6.25 Jeonjaengsa, 2, Bukhan ui Jeonmyeonnamchim gwa Bangeojeontu (The Korean War, Vol. 2, The North Korean All-out Southern Invasion and the Early Defensive Battles)*. Seoul: Ministry of National Defense Military History Compilation Research Institute, 2005.

———. *Hanguk Jeonjang Sa* [History of the Korean War], *Vol. 3*. Seoul: Ministry of National Defense, 1970.

———. *The History of United Nations Forces in the Korean War*. 6 vols. Seoul: War History Compilation Committee, 1971–77.

———. Korean Institute of Military History. *The Korean War*. 3 vols. Lincoln and London: University of Nebraska Press, 2000.

Reynolds, Clark G. "MacArthur as Maritime Strategist." *Naval War College Review*, Vol. XXXIII, No. 2 (March/April 1980): 79–102.

Richmond, Herbert. *Amphibious Warfare in British History*. Exeter, UK: A. Wheaton & Company, 1941.

Ridgway, Matthew B. *Matthew B. Ridgway Papers, 1907–1993*. US Army Military History Institute.

Risch, Erna. *Quartermaster Support of the Army: A History of the Corps, 1775–1939*. Washington, DC: GPO, 1962.

Roberts, Claude L., Jr. "2d Engineer Special Brigade." In *Remembering the "Forgotten War": U.S. Army Engineer Officers in Korea*, edited by Barry W. Fowle and John C. Lonnquest. Alexandria, VA: Office of History, Headquarters, US Army Corps of Engineers, 2005.

Robinson, Matthew T. "Integrated Amphibious Operations Update Study (DoN Lift 2+)—A Short History of the Amphibious Lift Requirement." Center for Naval Analysis, July 2002.

Ross, Steven T. *American War Plans 1890–1939*. London: Frank Cass, 2002.

———. *American War Plans 1941–1945*. London & Portland, OR: Frank Cass, 1997.

———. *American War Plans 1945–1950*. New York & London: Garland Publishing, Inc., 1988.

Rottman, Gordon L. *Landing Ship, Tank (LST) 1942–2002*. New Vanguard 115. Oxford, UK: Osprey Publications, 2005.

———. *Inch'on 1950: The Last Great Amphibious Assault*. Oxford, UK: Osprey Publications, 2006.

———. *Saipan & Tinian 1944: Piercing the Japanese Empire*. Oxford, UK: Osprey Publications, 2004.

———. *US Special Warfare Units in the Pacific Theater 1941–45: Scouts, Raiders, Rangers and Reconnaissance Units*. Battle Orders No. 12. Oxford, UK: Osprey Publications, 2005.

———. *US World War II Amphibious Tactics: Army & Marine Corps, Pacific Theater*. Elite No. 117. Botley, UK: Osprey Publishing, 2004.

————. *US World War II Amphibious Tactics: Mediterranean & European Theaters.* Elite 144. Oxford, UK: Osprey Publications, 2006.

Rowny, E.L. "Engineers in the Hungnam Evacuation." *Military Engineer,* Vol. XLIII, No. 295 (September–October 1951): 315–319 plus photo.

Rubel, Robert C. "Principles of Jointness." *Joint Force Quarterly* (Winter 2000–01): 45–49.

Ruppenthal, Roland G. *United States Army in World War II, The European Theater of Operations, Logistical Support of the Armies, Volume I: May 1941–September 1944.* Washington, DC: Historical Division, Department of the Army, 1953. Reprinted 1985, 1989.

Russell, John H. "The Birth of the Fleet Marine Force." *U.S. Naval Institute Proceedings,* Vol. 72, No. 1 (January 1946).

————. "The Genesis of Fleet Marine Force Doctrine: 1879–1899." *Marine Corps Gazette,* Vol. 35, Nos. 4–7, 11 (April–July 1955, November 1955).

Sargent, Herbert H. *The Campaign of Santiago de Cuba.* 3 vols. Chicago, IL: McClurg, 1907.

Saryukjeonsa [History of Amphibious Operations]. Daejeon, ROK: *Heguntaehak* [Navy War College], 25 October 2004.

Schnabel, James F. *The History of the Joint Chiefs of Staff: The Joint Chiefs of Staff and National Policy, Vol. I, 1945–1947.* Wilmington, DE: Michael Glazier, Inc., 1979. Reprinted: Washington, DC: Office of Joint History, Office of the Chairman of the Joint Chiefs of Staff, 1996.

————. *United States Army in the Korean War, Policy and Direction: The First Year.* Washington, DC: GPO, 1972. Reprinted 1992.

Schnabel, James F., and Robert J. Watson. *The History of the Joint Chiefs of Staff: The Joint Chiefs of Staff and National Policy, Vol. 3, The Korean War, Part One.* Washington, DC: Office of the Chairman of the Joint Chiefs of Staff, 1998.

————. *History of the Joint Chiefs of Staff: The Joint Chiefs of Staff and National Policy 1951–1953, The Korean War, Part Two.* Washington, DC: Office of the Chairman of the Joint Chiefs of Staff, 1998.

Sebastian, J. "So What Makes It Amphibious Airspace?" *Air Land Sea Bulletin,* Issue No. 2006 (1 January 2006): 5–6.

Selkirk, Wyatt I. "The Co-Operation of Land and Sea Forces." *Journal of the Military Service Institution of the United States,* Vol. XLVI, No. 164 [CLXIV] (March–April 1910): 313–324.

Shaw, Henry I., Bernard C. Nalty, and Edwin C. Turnbladh. *History of the United States Marine Corps Operations in World War II, Vol. III, Central Pacific Drive.* Washington, DC: Historical Branch, G3 Division, Headquarters, US Marine Corps, 1966.

Shepherd, Lemuel C. *Korean War Diary covering period 2 July to 7 December 1950.* Lemuel C. Shepherd Papers. Marine Corps University Archives.

Sheldon, Walter J. *Hell or High Water; MacArthur's Landing at Inchon.* New York, NY: Macmillan, 1968.

Sherrod, Robert Lee. "An Answer and Rebuttal to 'Smith *versus* Smith,' The

Saipan Controversy," with additional commentary by *Infantry Journal* editors and a copy of a letter by Lieutenant General (Retired) Robert C. Richardson Jr., in rebuttal to a series of articles by Lieutenant General H.M. Smith that appeared in the *Saturday Evening Post* on 11 December 1948. *Infantry Journal,* Vol. LXIV, No. 1 (January 1949): 14–28.

―――. *On to Westward: The Battles of Saipan and Iwo Jima.* Baltimore, MD: Nautical & Aviation Publishing Company of America, 1990.

Ships of the Republic of Korea Navy: Pak Tu San PC-701. Naval Historical Center. history.navy.mil/photos/sh-fornv/rok/roksh-mr/paktusn.htm (accessed 20 June 2006).

Shulimson, Jack. "Daniel Pratt Mannix and the Establishment of the Marine Corps School of Application, 1889–1894." *Journal of Military History* 55 (October 1991): 469–485.

―――. "First to Fight: Marine Corps Expansion, 1914–1919." *Prologue* 8 (Spring 1976): 15–16.

―――. "Marines in the Spanish–American War." In *Crucible of Empire: The Spanish–American War & Its Aftermath,* edited by James C. Bradford. Annapolis, MD: Naval Institute Press, 1993.

―――. *The Marine Corps Search for a Mission: 1880–1898.* Lawrence, KS: University Press of Kansas, 1993.

―――. *U.S. Marines in Vietnam: An Expanding War, 1966.* Washington, DC: History and Museums Division, Headquarters, US Marine Corps, 1982.

Shulimson, Jack, and Charles M. Johnson. *U.S. Marines in Vietnam: The Landing and the Buildup, 1965.* Washington, DC: History and Museums Division, Headquarters, US Marine Corps, 1978.

Sigley, Woodrow B. "Command Relationship in Major Amphibious Warfare." Norfolk, VA: Armed Forces Staff College, 1954.

Simmons, Edward Howard. *Over the Seawall: U.S. Marines at Inchon.* Washington, DC: History and Museums Division, Headquarters, US Marine Corps, 2000.

Skaggs, David C. "The KATUSA Experiment: The Integration of Korean Nationals into the U.S. Army, 1950–1965." *Military Affairs,* Vol. 38, No. 2 (April 1974): 53–58.

Smith, Charles R. *U.S. Marines in Vietnam: High Mobility and Standdown, 1969.* Washington, DC: History and Museums Division, Headquarters, US Marine Corps, 1988.

Smith, Cornelius C., Jr. "Our First Amphibious Assault." *Military Review,* Vol. XXXVIII, No. 11 (January 1959): 18–28.

Smith, General Holland M., and Percy Finch. "'Practically Always Right,' Review of *Coral and Brass*." *Infantry Journal,* Vol. LXIV, No. 2 (February 1949): 55.

Smith, Holland M. *Coral and Brass.* New York, NY: Scribner's, 1949.

Smith, Kenneth V. *The U.S. Army Campaigns of World War II: Naples–Foggia.* CMH Pub 72-17. Washington, DC: GPO, n.d.

Smith, Lynn D. "A Nickel After a Dollar." *Army* (September 1970): 25–34.

Smith, Robert Ross. *United States Army in World War II, The War in the Pacific, The Approach to the Philippines.* Washington, DC: Historical Division, Department of the Army, 1953. Reprinted 1984, 1996, 2002.

———. *United States Army in World War II, The War in the Pacific, Triumph in the Philippines.* Washington, DC: Historical Division, Department of the Army, 1963. Reprinted 1968, 1984, 1991.

———. "Luzon Versus Formosa." In *Command Decisions,* edited by Kent Roberts Greenfield. New York, NY: Harcourt, Brace, 1959.

Special Problems in the Korean Conflict. S-AN Chapter II, "X Corps." Microfilm. *Armed Forces Oral Histories: Korean War Studies and After-Action Reports.* Bethesda, MD: University Publications of America, 1989.

Speer, Charles E. "From Battle of Sari Bair, August 10, 1915, to include Third Phase of the Gallipoli Campaign Evacuation, January 9, 1916." In *Monographs of the World War,* 114–124. Fort Benning, GA: US Army Infantry School [1923?].

Spivey, Owen. "High-Speed Sealift: Deployment Support for the Future." *Army Logistician,* Vol. 31, No. 1 (January–February 1999): 124–126.

Stanton, Shelby L. *America's Tenth Legion, X Corps in Korea, 1950.* Novato, CA: Presidio Press, 1989.

———. *Vietnam Order of Battle.* Washington, DC: U.S. News Books, 1981.

Stewart Obituary. Biography of Major General George Craig Stewart; Obituary of General Stewart in *Assembly,* Vol. LIV, No. 1, September/October 1995.

Stewart, George Craig. "Korea: August, 1950–December 15, 1950." Unpublished manuscript. US Army Military History Institute.

Stewart, Richard W. *The Korean War: The Chinese Intervention, 3 November 1950–24 January 1951.* CMH Pub 19-8. Washington, DC: Center of Military History, 2000.

Stokesbury, James L. *British Concepts and Practices of Amphibious Warfare, 1867–1916.* PhD diss, Duke University, 1968.

Strahan, Jerry E. *Andrew Jackson Higgins and The Boats That Won World War II.* Baton Rouge, LA: Louisiana State University Press, 1994.

Strong, Paschal N. "Engineers in Korea—Operation 'Shoestring.'" *Military Engineer,* Vol. XLIII, No. 291 (January–February 1951): 11–14.

Stubbs, Mary Lee, and Stanley Russell Connor. *Army Lineage Series, Armor–Cavalry, Part I: Regular Army and Army Reserve.* Washington, DC: Office of the Chief of Military History, US Army, 1969.

Stueck, William. *The Korean War: An International History.* Princeton, NJ: Princeton University Press, 1995.

Swan, W.N., foreword by Sir John Collins. *Spearheads of invasion: an account of the seven major invasions carried out by the Allies in the Southwest Pacific area during the Second World War, as seen from a Royal Australian Naval Landing Ship Infantry.* Sydney: Angus and Robertson, 1954.

Sweetman, Jack. *The Landing at Veracruz, 1914.* Annapolis, MD: Naval Institute Press, 1968.

Taaffe, Stephen R. *MacArthur's Jungle War: The 1944 New Guinea Campaign.* Lawrence, KS: University Press of Kansas, 1998.

Tata, Anthony J. "A Fight for Lodgment: Future Joint Contingency Operations." *Joint Force Quarterly* (Spring 1996): 82–89.

Telfer, Gary L., and Lane Rogers. *U.S. Marines in Vietnam: Fighting the North Vietnamese, 1967.* Washington, DC: History and Museums Division, Headquarters, US Marine Corps, 1984.

"The Army Magazine Hooah Guide to Army Transformation." ausa.org/PDFDocs/Hooah_Guide_web.pdf (accessed 6 April 2006).

The History of Army Transportation Units in Vietnam. grambo.us/atav/history.htm (accessed 13 February 2008).

Thomas, Evan. *Sea of Thunder: Four Commanders and the Last Great Naval Campaign 1941–1945.* New York, NY: Simon & Schuster, 2006.

Thornton, Gary J.E. *The U.S. Coast Guard and Army Amphibious Development.* Student paper. US Army War College Military Studies Program Paper. Carlisle Barracks, PA, 1987. handle.dtic.mil/100.2/ADA180972 (accessed 11 February 2008).

Tolley, RADM Kemp. Oral History: "Amphibious Group Two Participation in Korean War." US Naval Institute, Annapolis, MD.

Tomblin, Barbara Brooks. *With Utmost Spirit: Allied Naval Operations in the Mediterranean, 1942–1945.* Lexington, KY: University Press of Kentucky, 2004.

Trask, David F. *The War With Spain in 1898.* New York, NY: Macmillan, 1981.

Trauth, Stephen R., James C. Barbara, Patrick A. Papa, Christine Maluchnik, Donald R. Paskulovich, Kerry B. Riese, Ralph P. Pallotta. "Army Transformation at Sea: The New Theater Support Vessel." *Military Review* (November–December 2005).

Triplet, William S. *The William S. Triplet Papers.* US Army Military History Institute.

———. *A Colonel in the Armored Divisions: A Memoir, 1941–1945.* Edited by Robert H. Ferrell. Columbia, MO: University of Missouri Press, 2001.

Trudeau, Arthur G. *Doctrine and Techniques in Amphibious Operations.* Washington, DC: Army Services Forces, 1946.

———. *Engineer Memoirs.* Oral History of Lieutenant General Arthur G. Trudeau. EP 870-1-26. Fort Belvoir, VA: US Army Corps of Engineers, Office of the Chief of Engineers, 1986.

———. *Oral History Transcripts & Papers of LTG (Ret) Arthur G. Trudeau.* US Army Military History Institute.

———. "The Engineer Amphibian Command." *Military Review,* Vol. XXIII (September 1943): 13–24.

Truscott, Lucian K. *Command Missions: A Personal Story.* New York, NY: E.P. Dutton and Company, 1954.

Truver, Scott C. "The Sea Base: Cornerstone of the U.S. Tri-Service Maritime Strategy." *Naval Forces*, Vol. XXIX, No. II (2008): 9–19.

Tuttle, William G.T., Jr. "The Importance of Transportation to the Army's Future Force Capstone Concepts 2015–2020." *Transportation Corps* (Winter 2005/2006): 7–9.

Urbahns, Paul W. "Ft. Knox's Ark: The LST Building." www.aths.com/history-ftknox.html (accessed 28 February 2008).

US Army and Navy Staff College. *Joint Overseas Operations: Final Draft, 15 August 1946.* 2 vols. Part 2: Washington, DC: Army and Navy Staff College, 1946; Part 1: Norfolk, VA: Armed Forces Staff College, 1950.

US Coast Guard. *Coast Guard Manned LSTs.* US Coast Guard Historian's Office. www.uscg.mil/history/WEBCUTTERS/USCG_LST_Index.html (accessed 9 February 2008).

———. *U.S. Coast Guard-Manned LCI(L)s, Landing Craft Infantry (Large).* US Coast Guard Historian's Office. www.uscg.mil/history/WEBCUTTERS/USCG_LCI_Index.html (accessed 9 February 2008).

US Congress. House. Select Committee on Post-War Military Policy. *Hearing Pursuant to H.R. 465.* 78th Congress, 2d Session, 1944.

———. Committee on Military Affairs. *Hearings on H.R. 515 (Universal Military Training).* 79th Congress, 1st Session, 1946.

———. Committee on Expenditures in the Executive Departments. *Hearings on H.R. 2319 (National Security Act of 1947).* 80th Congress, 1st Session, 1947.

———. Committee on the Armed Services. *Hearing on H.R. 234 and Unification and Strategy.* 81st Congress, 1st Session, 1947.

———. Committee on the Armed Services. *The National Defense Program—Unification and Strategy: Hearings.* 81st Congress, 1st Session, 1949.

———. Committee on the Armed Services. *Unification and Strategy: A Report of Investigation.* House Document 600. 81st Congress, 2d Session, 1950.

US Congress. Senate. Committee on Military Affairs. *Hearings on S. 84 (a bill to provide for a Department of Armed Forces and other purposes) and S. 1482 (a bill to establish a Department of Military Security and other purposes).* 79th Congress, 1st Session, 1945.

———. Committee on Naval Affairs. *Hearings on S. 2044 (a bill to unify departments and agencies relating to Common Defense).* 79th Congress, 2d Session, 1946.

———. Committee on Armed Services. *Hearings on S. 758 (National Security Act of 1947).* 80th Congress, 1st Session, 1947.

———. Committee on Armed Services. *National Security Act Amendments on 1949: Hearings on S. 1269 and S. 1843.* 81st Congress, 1st Session, 1949.

US Department of Defense. *Directive 5100.1,* "Functions of the Department of Defense and Its Major Components." Washington, DC: Department of Defense, 1 August 2001. dtic.mil/whs/directives/corres/pdf/d51001_080102/d51001p.pdf (accessed 10 February 2007).

————. *Joint Chiefs of Staff Special Historical Study: Roles and Functions of the JCS, a Chronology*. Washington, DC: GPO, 1987.

US Department of Defense News Release. "Department of Army Unveils Active Component Brigade Combat Team Stationing," 27 July 2005. army.mil/modularforces/index.htm (accessed 21 February 2006).

US Departments of the Army and the Air Force. "Functions of the Armed Forces and the Joint Chiefs of Staff" (Key West Agreement). *Joint Army and Air Force Bulletin No. 18*. Washington, DC: Departments of the Army and the Air Force, 13 May 1948.

US War Department. *United States Army Transport Service Regulations, 1908*. Washington, DC: GPO, 1908.

————. The Adjutant General's Office. "Notes on Fleet Landing Exercise No. 2, Culebra, P.R.," AG 354.23 (3-24-36), 30 March 1936.

Utz, Curtis A. *Assault from the Sea: The Amphibious Landing at Inchon*. Washington, DC: Naval Historical Center, Department of the Navy, 1994. (US Navy in the Modern World Series, No. 2.)

————. "Assault from the Sea: The Amphibious Landing at Inchon." In *The U.S. Navy in the Korean War*, edited by Edward J. Marolda. Annapolis, MD: Naval Institute Press, 2007.

Vagts, Alfred. *Landing Operations: Strategy, Psychology, Tactics, Politics, From Antiquity to 1945*. Harrisburg, PA: Military Service Publishing Company.

Van Fleet, James A. *The James A. Van Fleet Papers, 1892–1973*. US Army Military History Institute.

Vego, Milan. "Warfare Concepts: Riverine Warfare." *Naval Forces*, Vol. XXIX, No. 11 (2008): 26–33.

Venzon, Anne Cipriano. *From Whaleboats to Amphibious Warfare: Lt. Gen. "Howling Mad" Smith and the U.S. Marine Corps*. London and Westport, CT: Praeger, 2003.

Villa, Brian Loring. *Unauthorized Action: Mountbatten and the Dieppe Raid*. Oxford, UK: Oxford University Press, 1989.

Villahermosa, Gilberto. "The 65th Infantry Regiment: Prelude to Inchon: The Puerto Rican Exercises of 1950." valerosos.com/PreludetoInchon.html (accessed 30 June 2006).

Walker, Stanley. "Logistics of the Inchon Landing." *Army Logistician* (July–August 1981): 34–38.

Wardlow, Chester. *United States Army in World War II, The Transportation Corps: Responsibilities, Organization, and Operations*. Washington, DC: Historical Division, Department of the Army, 1951. Reprinted 1980.

————. *United States Army in World War II, The Transportation Corps: Movements, Training, and Supply*. Washington, DC: Historical Division, Department of the Army, 1956. Reprinted 1978, 1990, 2003.

Wass de Czege, Huba, and Zbigniew M. Majchrzak. "Enabling Operational Maneuver From Strategic Distances." *Military Review* (May–June 2002). leavenworth.army.mil/milrev/English/MayJun02/wass.htm (accessed 25 September 2007).

———. "Executive Summary." Army Transformation Roadmap 2003.

Watson, Mark Skinner. *United States Army in World War II, The War Department, Chief of Staff; Prewar Plans and Preparations*. Washington, DC: Department of the Army Historical Division, 1950.

Webb, William J. *The Korean War: The Outbreak, 27 June–15 September 1950*. CMH Pub 19-6. Washington, DC: Center of Military History, 2000.

Weddell, Kevin J. *Lincoln's Tragic Admiral: The Life of Samuel Francis DuPont*. Charlottesville and London: University of Virginia Press, 2005.

"Who Won the War?" *Infantry Journal*, Vol. LXIV, No. 1 (January 1949): 2.

Williams, R.C. "Amphibious Scouts and Raiders." *Military Affairs*, Vol. XIII, No. 3 (Fall 1949): 150–157.

Willmott, H.P. *Empires in the Balance: Japanese and Allied Pacific Strategies to April 1942*. Annapolis, MD: Naval Institute Press, 1982.

———. *The Battle of Leyte Gulf: The Last Fleet Action*. Bloomington, IN: Indiana University Press, 2005.

Willoughby, Charles Adam. *MacArthur: 1941–1951*. New York, NY: McGraw-Hill Book Company, 1954.

Willoughby, Charles Andrew. Photograph Collection, 1942–1962. US Army Military History Institute.

Willoughby, Malcolm F. *The U.S. Coast Guard in World War II*. Annapolis, MD: Naval Institute Press, 1957.

Winters, Harold A. *Battling the Elements: Weather and Terrain in the Conduct of War*. Baltimore, MD: Johns Hopkins University Press, 1998.

Wise, Harold Lee. *Inside the Danger Zone: The U.S. Military in the Persian Gulf, 1987–1988*. Annapolis, MD: Naval Institute Press, 2007.

Wiser, Edward. "One Size Does NOT Fit All: A dialogue between industry and government is producing new mount for the riverine cavalry." *U.S. Naval Institute Proceedings,* Vol. 134, No. 6 (June 2008): 26–31.

Witt, Linda, Judith Bellafaire, Britta Granrud, and Mary Jo Binker. *"A Defense Weapon Known to Be of Value": Servicewomen of the Korean War Era*. Hanover and London: University Press of New England.

Woodward, C. Vann. *The Battle for Leyte Gulf*. New York, NY: The Macmillan Co., 1947. Reprinted with an introduction by Evan Thomas. New York, NY: Skyhorse Publishing, 2007.

Young, Peter. *Storm from the Sea*. Annapolis, MD: Naval Institute Press, 1989.

Weigley, Russell F. *History of the United States Army*. Bloomington, IN: Indiana University Press, 1984.

Wright, Burton, III. *The U.S. Army Campaigns of World War II: Eastern Mandates*. CMH Pub 72-23. Washington, DC: GPO, 1993.

Zaloga, Stephen J., Terry Hadler, and Mike Badrocke. *Amtracs: US Amphibious Assault Vehicles*. Osprey New Vanguard 30. Oxford, UK: Osprey Publishing, 1999.

Zhang, Shu Guang. *Mao's Military Romanticism: China and the Korea War, 1950–1953*. Lawrence, KS: University of Kansas Press, 1995.

Appendix A

Korean Geographical Names

(In National Institute of the Korean Language style and, in parentheses, Modified McCune-Reischauer [*Times-Herald*] style.)

Baengnyeongdo (Paengyong-do)
Busan (Pusan)
Cheongcheon (Ch'ongch'on) River
Cheongjin (Ch'ongjin)
Cheongpyeong (Chungp'yong)
Cheonsu (Ch'onsu) Bay
Cheorwon (Ch'orwon)
Chodo (Ch'o-do)
Chongcheon (Ch'ongch'on) River
Chuncheon (Ch'unch'on)
Daecheon (Taech'on)
Daecheongdo (Taech'ong-do)
Daedong (Taedong) River
Daegu (Taegu)
Daejeon (Taejon)
Daepo-ri (Taep'o-ri)
Daebudo (Taebu-do)
Dancheon (Tanch'on)
Deokjeok (Tokchok) Islands
Deungsangot (Tungsan-got)
Dokseok-dong (Toksokdong or Toksong-ni)
Dongcheon-ri (Tongch'on-ni)
Donghae (Tonghae)
Eocheongdo (Och'ong-do)
Gaeseong (Kaesong)
Ganghwa (Kanghwa)
Gangneung (Kangnung)
Ganggu-dong (Kanggu-dong)
Ganseong (Kansong)
Gapyeong (Kap'yong)
Geojedo (Koje-do)
Geum (Kum) River (Geumgang)
Geumcheon (Kumch'on)
Gimhwa (Kumhwa)
Gimpo (Kimp'o)

Gojeo (Kojo)
Goseong (Kosong)
Gunsan (Kunsan)
Gunu-ri (Kunu-ri)
Guryeongpo-ri (Kuryongp'o-ri)
Gyeonnaeryang (Kyonnaeryang) Channel
Gyodongdo (Kyodong-do)
Hamheung (Hamhung)
Heunghae (Hunghae)
Heungnam (Hungnam)
Hwacheon (Hwach'on)
Incheon (Inch'on)
Jangjeon (Changjon)
Jangsa-dong (Changsa-dong)
Jangsangot (Changsan-got)
Jangyeon (Changyon)
Jejudo (Cheju-do)
Jeongdongjin (Chongdongjin)
Jeongju (Chongju)
Jindong-ri (Chindong-ni)
Jinhae (Chinhae)
Jinnampo (Chinnamp'o)
Jukbyeon (Chukpyon or Jukpyon)
Jumunjin (Chumunjin)
Majeon-ri (Majon-ni)
Nakdong (Naktong) River
Nakdong-ri (Naktong-ni)
Nakpung-ri (Nakp'ung-ni)
Namdo (Nan Do, Nam Do)
Poseungmyeon (Posung Myon)
Pyeonggang (P'yonggang)
Pyeongtaek (P'yongt'aek)
Pyeongyang (P'yongyang)
Samcheok (Samch'ok)
Seogang (Sogang)
Seokdo (Sok-do)
Seoncheon (Sonch'on)
Seongjin (Songjin)
Sinchang (Sinch'ang)
Socheongdo (Soch'ong-do)
Solseum (Sol-sum)

Sukcheon (Sukch'on)
Suncheon (Sunch'on)
Suyeong (Suyong)
Tongyeong (T'ongyong)
Uijeongbu (Uijongbu)
Uljin (Ulchin)
Weonju (Wonju)
Wonpo-ri (Wonp'o-ri)
Yeongdeok (Yongdok)
Yeongdeungpo (Yongdungp'o)
Yeongheung (Yonghung)
Yeongheungdo (Yonghong-do)
Yeongheung (Yonghung) Bay
Yeongil (Yongil) Airfield and Bay
Yeongju (Yongju)
Yeongsan (Yongsan)
Yeongwon (Yongwon)
Yeonpyeongdo (Yonpyong-do)
Yeosu (Yosu)
Yeseong (Yesong) River
Yucheon-ri (Yuch'on-ni)

Appendix B

Landing Ships, Craft, and Vehicles in Use during the Korean War

Amphibious Force Flagship (AGH)

A converted Maritime Commission C2-S-AJ1 type freighter, the *Mount McKinley,* AGC-7, was built in 1943. It served as the flagship of Amphibious Force, Far East in 1950–51 and in 1953. The figure shows the *Mount McKinley* off Heungnam during the December 1950 evacuation with LSU-637 alongside. During the war, the *Mount McKinley* participated in the Incheon, Wonsan, and Heungnam amphibious operations.

Length Overall: 459' 3"
Beam: 63' 0"
Maximum Draft: 28' 2"
Top Speed: 15 knots
Light Tonnage: 7,650
Crew: 622
Armament: two 5-inch guns; four twin 40-mm guns, ten twin 20-mm guns

Attack Transport (APA)

The *Bayfield* (APA-33), a Maritime Commission C3-S-A2 type, was built in 1943. Shown above is the *Bayfield* en route to the 1950 PORTREX Amphibious Exercise near Puerto Rico prior to the Korean War. During the war, the *Bayfield* participated in the Incheon, Wonsan, and Heungnam amphibious operations.

Length Overall: 492' 0"
Beam: 69' 6"
Maximum Draft: 28' 6"
Top Speed: 16.5 knots
Light Tonnage: 7,650
Crew: 575
Capacity: 1,226 troops (an APA normally carried one battalion landing team of approximately 1,000 troops)
Armament: two 5-inch guns, eight 40-mm guns

Attack Cargo Ship (AKA)

US Navy Photo, NHC

The *Union,* AKA-106, a Maritime Commission C2-S-AJ3 type built in 1944, is a typical AKA. The *Union* participated in amphibious exercise *Miki* in 1949, was part of Rear Admiral James C. Doyle's Amphibious Group One at the start of the Korean War, and participated in the Pohang and Incheon amphibious operations. The figure shows the *Union* in April 1945. Its Korean War appearance was almost identical.

Length Overall: 459' 2"
Beam: 63' 0"
Maximum Draft: 24' 6"
Top Speed: 15.5 knots
Light Tonnage: 6,433
Crew: 387
Capacity: normally carried the vehicles and heavy equipment of a regimental combat team
Armament: one 5-inch gun, eight 40-mm guns, sixteen 20-mm guns

Transport (AP)

US Navy Photo, NHC

Various types of ships served as personnel transports. The *General J.C. Breckinridge,* T-AP-176, a Maritime Commission P-2-S2-R2 transport was built in 1945. The "T" indicates that it was a Military Sea Transportation Service (MSTS) ship. The *General J.C. Breckinridge* participated in the Incheon, Wonsan, and Heungnam amphibious operations.

Length Overall: 622' 7"
Beam: 75' 6"
Maximum Draft: 25'
Top Speed: 21 knots
Light Tonnage: 11,450
Crew: 466
Capacity: 5,289 troops
Armament: four 5-inch guns, four 40-mm guns, twenty 20-mm guns

APD (High Speed Transport)

US Navy Photo, NHC

The *Begor,* APD-127, was built in 1944. During the Korean War, the *Begor* participated in the Heungnam amphibious operation and in special missions. The photograph shows the *Begor* off Heungnam as the port facilities were being destroyed on the last day of the evacuation, 24 December 1950.

Length Overall: 306' 0"
Beam: 37' 0"
Maximum Draft: 12' 7"
Top Speed: 23.6 knots
Light Tonnage: 2,130
Crew: 204
Capacity: 162 troops
Armament: one 5-inch gun, six 40-mm guns

Landing Ship, Dock (LSD)

US Navy Photo, NHC

The *Gunston Hall,* LSD-5, was built in 1943. During the Korean War, the *Gunston Hall* participated in the Incheon and Wonsan amphibious operations. Shown here is the *Gunston Hall* in the late 1940s, but its appearance would have been identical during the Korean War.

Length Overall: 457' 9"
Beam: 72' 2"
Maximum Draft: 18'
Top Speed: 15 knots
Light Tonnage: 4,490
Crew: 326
Capacity: 3 LSUs or 14 LCMs or 64 LVTs or 74 DUKWs (92 LVTs or 108 DUKWs if temporary decks and ramps were installed)
Armament: one 5-inch gun, twelve 40-mm guns

Landing Ship, Tank (LST)

Korean War Signal Corps Collection, MHI

Units of the 1st Cavalry Division prepare to disembark from an LST at Pohang, Korea, 18 July 1950. This LST is typical of those that participated in Korean War amphibious operations.

Length Overall: 327' 9"

Beam: 50' 0"

Maximum Draft: 7' 1" forward, 13' 6" aft (fully loaded), 3' 1" forward, 9' 6" after (fully loaded, beaching)

Top Speed: 10+ knots

Light Tonnage: 1,653

Crew: 108–125

Capacity: 70 trucks (average) or 20 M4 tanks or 17 LVTs or 22 DUKWs

Armament: varied, usually one or two 40-mm guns and six 20-mm guns

Landing Ship, Medium (LSM)

Office of Naval Intelligence

The LSM-258 is similar in appearance to those used in the Korean War.

Length Overall: 203' 6"
Beam: 34' 6"
Maximum Draft: 6' 4" forward, 8' 3.5" aft
Top Speed: 13.2 knots
Light Tonnage: 520 tons
Crew: 58
Capacity: 3 tanks or 6 LVTs or 9 DUKWs or 50 troops
Armament: one 40-mm gun, four 20-mm guns

Landing Ship, Medium, Rocket (LSM[R])

LSM(R)-536, later renamed USS *White River*, conducted operations off Chodo on the northwest coast of Korea in support of Partisan operations in 1952 and 1953.

Length Overall: 203' 6"
Beam: 34' 6"
Maximum Draft: 6' 6"
Top Speed: 13.2 knots
Light Tonnage: 605 tons
Crew: 81
Armament: one 5-inch gun, two 40-mm guns, three 20-mm guns, 75 rocket launchers (1,000 5-inch rockets per salvo).

Landing Ship, Utility (LSU)/Landing Craft, Utility (LCU)

LSU-1160 is a typical Korean War era LSU. Originally called a landing craft, tank (LCT) in World War II and redesignated landing ship, tank (small) (LST[S]) after the war, the type was redesignated LSU in late 1949 and this was the designation carried during the first 2 years of the Korean War. The type was redesignated landing craft, utility (LCU) on 15 April 1952.

Length Overall: 114' 2"
Beam: 32' 0"
Maximum Draft: 2' 10" forward, 4' 2" aft
Top Speed: 8 knots
Light Tonnage: 133 tons
Crew: 11
Capacity: three tanks, fifteen 2½-ton trucks
Armament: two 20-mm guns

Landing Craft, Mechanized (LCM)

US Navy Photo, NHC

The LCM was originally designed to carry tanks and other heavy vehicles. By the time of the Korean War, tanks had become too heavy for the LCMs and were transported in LSUs, LSMs, and LSTs. Like the LCVP, the LCM could be carried aboard amphibious ships. It was the workhorse of the Engineer Special Brigade and the 8206th Army Unit, Amphibious Training Center, during the Korean War.

The LCM(6) shown above was an enlarged 56-foot version of the World War II 50-foot LCM(3). The version currently in service with the Transportation Corps medium boat companies is the 74-foot LCM(8).

Length Overall: 56' 1.5"
Beam: 14' 0.25"
Maximum Draft: 3' forward, 4' aft
Top Speed: 9 knots
Light Tonnage: 22 tons
Crew: 5
Capacity: 1 medium tank or 120 troops
Armament: two .50-caliber machineguns or two 20-mm guns

Landing Craft, Vehicle, Personnel (LCVP)

US Navy Photo, NHC

The LCVP, carried in the davits of APAs, AKAs, APDs, and LSTs, was the ubiquitous personnel landing craft of World War II and Korea and could carry trucks up to one ton. In the background of this photograph, taken during the Incheon landing, is the SCAJAP LST-Q0-12.

Length Overall: 35' 10"
Beam: 10' 6"
Maximum Draft: 2' 2" forward, 3' aft
Top Speed: 8 knots
Light Tonnage: 8 tons
Crew: 3
Capacity: 36 troops
Armament: two .30-caliber machineguns

Landing Craft, Personnel, Ramped (LCP[R])

The LCP(R) was a ramped version of the original Higgins Boat, the spoon-bowed 36-foot LCP(L). The narrow ramp precluded the transport of vehicles, and in 1942 the LCP(R) was replaced by the LCVP. However, the LCP(R) was faster and had better sea-keeping qualities than the LCVP and thus was continued in use as a utility boat and for special operations by underwater demolition teams, reconnaissance teams, and raiders.

Length Overall: 35' 11.75"
Beam: 10' 9.5"
Maximum Draft: 2' 2" forward, 3' aft
Top Speed: 10 knots
Light Tonnage: 6.5 tons
Crew: 3
Capacity: 36 troops
Armament: two .30-caliber machineguns

Amphibious 2½-ton Truck (DUKW)

A restored DUKW amphibious 2½-ton truck identical to that of the Korean War era DUKW.

The DUKW was an amphibious version of the GMC CCKW 353 2½-ton truck (C = designed in 1942, C = standard cab, K = front wheel drive, W = rear wheel drive). The standard version was the DUKW 353 (D = designed in 1942, U = amphibious, K = all wheel drive, W = dual rear wheels).

Length: 31'
Width: 8' 2.5"
Top Speed: 45 mph on land, 6.3 mph in water
Weight: 19,570 pounds
Crew: 2
Capacity: one 105-mm howitzer or one ¼-ton truck or 5,350 pounds of cargo or 25 troops or 6 casualties on litters

Landing Vehicle, Tracked and Armored Landing Vehicle, Tracked (LVT4 and LVT[A]5)

The LVT was a troop and cargo carrier originally designed to cross coral reefs. Because it provided some protection to the troops on board, it was used to carry troops in an initial assault. The armored LVT (LVT[A]) had a turret-mounted artillery piece. The LVT(A)5 mounted a gyro-stabilized 75-mm howitzer that could be used as a direct-fire weapon during the amphibious assault and as an indirect fire artillery piece on land. The figure shows an LVT(A)5 (top) and two LVT4s at Camp Casey, Washington, in early 1950 preparing for amphibious exercise PORTREX.

LVT4:   *Length*: 26' 1"
           Width: 10' 8"
           Top Speed: 20 mph on land, 7.5 mph in water
           Weight: 27,400 pounds
           Crew: 2
           Capacity: one 105-mm howitzer or one ¼-ton truck or 5,350 pounds of cargo or 25 troops or 6 casualties on litters
           Armament: two .30-caliber machineguns

LVT(A)5:   *Length*: 26' 2"
           Width: 10' 8"
           Top Speed: 16 mph on land, 7 mph in water
           Weight: 39,460 pounds
           Crew: 6
           Armament: one 75-mm howitzer, three .30-caliber machineguns

Appendix C

Amphibious Terms, Abbreviations, and Acronyms: Army Doctrine in Effect from 1950 to 1953

Terms

Advance force—In a joint overseas expedition, a force preceding the main part of a joint task force to the objective. The advance force normally dissolves on D-Day and is redistributed to other parts of the joint task force. (The advance force prepares the objective by reconnaissance, minesweeping, preliminary naval and air bombardment, and underwater demolition operations.) (FM 17-34)

Amphibious forces—1. The ground, sea, and air forces equipped and trained for amphibious operations. 2. Permanent naval organizations established for planning, training, preparing, and conducting landing operations. (FM 60-10)

Amphibious operations—Types of (FM 31-5):

a. *Demonstration*: An expedition intended only as an exhibition of force, implying attack.

b. *Raid*: An assault expedition involving relatively small forces designed to land, accomplish a mission, and retire within a limited time.

c. *Occupation*: An assault expedition to seize and hold a prescribed area without continuing a land operation.

d. *Invasion*: A major landing assault with extensive forces and resources, involving continued operations on land against an active enemy.

Amphibious troops—The troops of all Services assigned to a joint amphibious task force for operations ashore, including the landing force, garrison, and base troops. (FM 60-10)

Assault craft—A landing craft employed for landing troops and equipment in an assault on an enemy beach. (FM 17-34)

Attack force—A subdivision of an expeditionary force consisting of assault shipping with embarked troop and supporting naval and tactical units, operating to establish a landing force on shore and support its operation thereafter. (FM 17-34)

Battalion landing team—An infantry battalion specially reinforced by necessary combat and service elements; the basic unit for planning an assault landing. A battalion landing team (BLT) normally is embarked aboard one APA or an appropriate number of smaller ships. Also referred to as a landing team. (FM 17-34)

Beach—Shoreline of landing area assigned to one combat team. Each beach is given a color designation and subdivisions of the beach are numbered from left to right as you face the beach. (FM 17-34)

Beach, colored—Shoreline of a landing area assigned for the assault to one regimental combat team (RCT). Each RCT beach is color coded, and BLT subdivisions are numbered left to right from seaward. (FM 60-10)

Beach dump—Area adjacent to a beach, utilized by the shore group for temporary storage of supplies and equipment. (FM 17-34)

Beachhead—A designated area on a hostile shore that, when seized and held, ensures the continuous landing of troops and materiel and provides the requisite maneuver space for the projected operations ashore. It is the physical objective of the amphibious part of an operation, and it corresponds to a bridgehead in land operations. (Its depth should be sufficient to protect the beach from ground-observed artillery fire.) (FM 17-34)

Beachhead line—An objective which fixes the limits of a beachhead; a main line of resistance based, if practicable, on terrain features that can be defended against enemy counterattack before the advance out of the beachhead. (FM 60-10)

Beach marker—A sign or device used to identify a beach, or certain activities thereon, for incoming waterborne traffic. Markers may be panels, lights, buoys, or electronic devices. (FM 17-34)

Beach master—The officer in command of the beach party; responsible for the beaching and unloading of boats. (Under the command of the shore party commander except for purely naval functions.) (FM 17-34)

Beach party—A Navy unit responsible for effecting and coordinating movement of a landing force and its supplies and equipment through the surf zone and onto the hostile shore. (See naval beach group.)

Billet—An assignment of quarters and duties aboard a naval ship. (FM 60-10)

Boat—Any small craft capable of being stowed aboard a ship. As a verb, to load personnel into a boat. (FM 17-34)

Boat assembly area—The area astern, to the quarter, or abeam of a transport where empty landing craft circle, awaiting a call to the ship to take on personnel or cargo. (FM 17-34)

Boat assignment table—A table showing the organization of a boat group and the assignment of personnel and materiel to each boat (or landing vehicle). (FM 17-34)

Boat group—The landing craft organization for landing a battalion landing team. It also denotes the landing craft carried by an attack transport. (FM 17-34)

Boat pool—Additional boats available to transports to aid or replace boats that become inoperative before or during an amphibious operation. (FM 60-10)

Boat rendezvous area—The area where boats rendezvous after being loaded and prior to movement to line of departure. (FM 17-34)

Boat space—The space and weight factor used to determine the capacity of boats and landing craft. With respect to landing craft, it is based on the requirements of one man with his individual equipment. (One man is assumed to weigh 224 pounds and to occupy 13.5 cubic feet of space.) (FM 17-34)

Boat team—A subordinate unit of the landing team, constituted to function from the predebarkation phase of the landing until normal unit organization has been reestablished ashore. It is the personnel, with their equipment, loaded in one landing boat charged with the performance of a task after debarking from the landing boat. (The senior officer or enlisted man in the boat is the boat team commander.) (FM 17-34)

Boat wave—The landing craft or LVTs within a boat group that carry those troops scheduled to land simultaneously or at approximately the same time. (FM 17-34)

Broach—To tend to be thrown broadside on the surface or in a seaway. Often currents flowing parallel to a shoreline have this effect on landing craft causing them to land broadside to the beach. (FM 60-10)

Brodie launching device—An overhead landing wire, erected ashore or aboard ship, for launching and recovering aircraft specially equipped for use with this device. (FM 60-10)

Build-up—The process of attaining prescribed strengths of units and levels of supply. Also may be applied to the means of accomplishing this process. (Troops, equipment, and supplies of the build-up are landed over beaches or in ports already captured to further the operation and for protection, operation, and expansion of the base.) (FM 17-34)

Cargo and loading analysis—A form prepared from the consolidated unit personnel and tonnage table of a landing force element. The form lists all cargo by organization, number of containers, type of equipment or supplies, weight, cubic measure, and where stowed. Also called a cargo list. (FM 60-10)

Cargo ship, attack (AKA)—A naval cargo vessel capable of being combat loaded and fitted with special equipment to permit it to carry and launch landing craft and to facilitate the unloading of cargo into landing craft from off shore. (Expanded definition based on that of FM 60-10)

Close support fire—Fire to support units ashore. It is placed on enemy troops, weapons, or positions whose proximity presents the most immediate and serious threat to the supported units. Close support vessels may be the light cruisers, destroyers, gunboats, LSM(R)s, LVT(A)s, or other support landing craft. (FM 60-10)

Combat cargo officer—The member of the Navy staff corresponding to the unit loading officer (q.v.). Each APA and AKA of the amphibious forces has in its regular complement a Marine Corps officer assigned duty as the ship combat cargo officer. Officers assigned this duty are trained in ship-loading schools.

The duties of the ship combat cargo officer, as promulgated in United States Fleet Publication 66, *Tactical and Operational Instructions, Amphibious Forces*, 7 July 1947, are to advise and assist the commanding officer of the ship in the following: (1) All matters relating to loading and unloading troop cargo and to embarking, billeting, and messing troops. (2) The preparation, in conjunction with the ship's first lieutenant, of detailed plans for loading and stowing cargo, for unloading cargo, and for billeting and messing troops. (3) Acting as liaison officer with the commanding officer of troops during the planning and operational phases of an amphibious operation. (4) Advising the unit loading officer in the preparation of detailed loading, stowage, and unloading plans. (5) The preparation, correction, maintenance, and distribution of the transport characteristics pamphlet.

During the embarkation and rehearsal phase, the combat cargo officer performs the following duties: (1) Maintains continuous liaison with the commanding officer of troops through the unit loading officer. (2) Maintains a progress report on the assembly of cargo on shore in order that the loading of all hatches may progress efficiently and without delay. (3) Ensures that loading and stowage plans are being followed. (FM 60-30)

Combat loader—An attack cargo ship or attack transport. The term was widely used early in World War II but less so during the Korean War.

Combat loading—The loading of assault troops with their essential combat equipment and initial combat supplies in the same ship or craft, and in a manner permitting immediate and rapid debarkation in desired priority to conform to the anticipated tactical operation of the unit for the landing attack. (FM 17-34)

Combat team—See regimental combat team (RCT).

Commander, landing force—Commander of the task organization of ground troops equipped and trained to carry out an amphibious assault landing. (FM 60-10)

Condition 1A—That condition of battle readiness on vessels carrying troops or materiel for an amphibious landing when all stations are fully manned for debarkation. (FM 60-10)

Control group—A naval task organization consisting of personnel, vessels, craft, boats, and the necessary communication facilities to control the ship-to-shore movement. (FM 60-10)

Control officer—A naval officer, designated by the attack force commander, charged with overall supervision of the ship-to-shore movement. (FM 60-10)

Control vessels, boats, and craft—In an amphibious operation, a vessel to guide and act as a headquarters for the control of waterborne traffic to and from the beach. (FM 17-34)

    a. *Primary control vessels:* Vessels used by central control, transport squadron control, and transport division control officers. (FM 17-34)

    b. *Secondary control vessels:* Vessels used by boat group and boat wave commanders and wave guide officers. (FM 17-34)

    c. *Special control vessels:* Vessels used by corps and division (army) commanders, boat flotilla commanders, senior beach masters, and shore group commanders. (FM 17-34)

Convoy loading—The loading of troops together with their equipment and supplies on vessels in the same convoy, but not necessarily on the same ship. (FM 60-10)

Davit loading—See rail loading. (FM 60-10)

D-Day—The term used to designate the unnamed day that an assault landing is to be made, an attack is to be launched, or a movement is to begin. (FM 17-34)

Deadweight ton—See tonnage.

Debarkation—The unloading of troops, equipment, or supplies from a ship or an aircraft. (FM 17-34)

Debarkation schedule—A schedule showing the type of boat, the station and time it is to report alongside a transport for loading, and the boat team it is to embark. This schedule is prepared by the landing force. (FM 17-34)

Debarkation station—A location definitely established at the rail of a transport where troops and materiel load into boats for the ship-to-shore movement. There are usually four or more such stations located on each side of an APA. (FM 17-34)

Deck loading—Cargo loaded on the open deck or on the hatch covers of vessels. (FM 60-10)

Deep support—The naval gunfire on inland targets to support the operation as a whole, as distinguished from close support, which is for the immediate benefit of front line troops. Normally fired by battleships and heavy cruisers (16-inch and 8-inch guns). (FM 17-34)

Deep support fire—Naval gunfire on inland shore targets to support the operation as a whole. The gunfire is usually provided by battleships, heavy cruisers, and light cruisers. (FM 60-10)

Demonstration—(1) An attack or a show of force, on a front where a decision is not sought, made with the object of deceiving the enemy. (2) In an amphibious operation, an exhibition of force which may be a feint or a minor attack. (FM 17-34)

Demonstration group—The vessels assigned the task of transporting and supporting the troops that are to participate in an amphibious demonstration. (FM 17-34)

Distance—(1) The space between adjacent individual ships or boats measured in any direction between foremasts. (2) The space between adjacent men, animals, vehicles, or units in a formation measured from front to rear. (3) In air operations, the term has no specialized meaning. (FM 17-34)

Division shore party—A shore party organized to support an assault infantry division in an amphibious operation. (FM 60-10)

DUKW control point—A point located on or near beach exits to control the shuttle movement of amphibious trucks between ships and transfer points on shore. (For DUKW, see Abbreviations and Acronyms.) (FM 60-10)

DUKW-truck transfer point—A beach installation consisting of revolving cranes at which sling loads are transferred from amphibious trucks to trucks for further movement. (FM 60-10)

Dunnage—Any material, such as boards, mats, planks, blocks, bamboo, etc., used in transportation and storage to support and secure supplies, to protect supplies from damage, or for convenience in handling supplies. (FM 7-34)

Embarkation—The loading of troops, with their supplies and equipment, aboard vessels or aircraft. (FM 17-34)

Embarkation area—In an amphibious operation, an area, including a group of embarkation points, in which final preparations are completed and through which personnel and loads for craft and ships are called forward to embark. A marshalling area. (FM 17-34)

Embarkation group—The basic organization for embarking landing force troops, equipment, and supplies. The group is composed of the troops and cargo to be embarked in a single transport division or similar naval task organization. An infantry RCT typically forms the nucleus of an embarkation group, but other types of embarkation groups may be formed around division artillery units, special battalions, division service and supply units, or a combination of these units. (FM 60-30)

Embarkation officer—The troop officer designated to plan and supervise the loading and unloading of troops, equipment, and supplies. Each unit from division down to the BLT and each team to be embarked on a single ship has an assigned embarkation officer. (FM 60-10)

Embarkation team—Any element or combination of elements of the landing force assigned to one vessel. (FM 60-30)

Fire support area—The sea area assigned to the fire support group to permit it to maneuver so as to carry out the naval gunfire support. (FM 17-34)

Fire support coordination center—A single location in which all communications incident to the control of the artillery, air, and naval gunfire are centralized to provide for coordination of fire support. (The artillery commander of the appropriate echelon acts as the fire support coordinator.) (FM 17-34)

Fire support group—Basic naval unit for the delivery of naval gunfire support. (FM 60-10)

Flagship—Headquarters ship of the amphibious force commander, from which naval, landing force, and air commanders exercise control of a landing operation. See AGC. (FM 60-10)

Floating dump—A dump of critical supplies held on boats, barges, or landing vehicles established afloat in the vicinity of a control vessel for quick dispatch to assault troops ashore. Also called offshore dump. (FM 60-10)

Garrison force—All units assigned to a base for defense, development, operation, and maintenance of facilities. Units operating from the base normally are included for logistical purposes. (FM 17-34)

Gross ton—See tonnage. (FM 60-10)

H-hour—(1) The term used to designate the hour for an attack to be launched or for a movement to begin. (2) In an amphibious operation, the clock time designated for the first wave to land on the designated beach. Other letters of the alphabet may be used; e.g., F-hour, G-hour. (FM 17-34)

Hatch crew—A group of deckhands, soldiers, marines, or civilians, with a petty officer or noncommissioned officer in charge, responsible for loading and unloading the cargo for a specific hatch (opening into the cargo spaces of the hull) of a ship. The hatch crew manhandles the cargo and rigs it in slings or nets for hoisting by boom. The hatch crew may include boom operators. They are also responsible for placing dunnage and balancing the load as well as battening (securing) the hatch. (Traditional definition.)

Headquarters ship—A naval vessel from which naval, landing force, and air commanders exercise control in landing operations. See AGC. (FM 17-34)

Heavy lift cargo—All cargo packages, other than pallets, weighing more than 800 pounds or occupying more than 100 cubic feet (definition for amphibious operations only). (FM 60-10)

Hydrography—The description and analysis of the characteristics of the earth's surface waters. The mapping of bodies of water.

Joint communication center—A communication center established for joint use of the Armed Forces. (FM 60-10)

In the stream—A ship is "in the stream" when it is being unloaded while at anchor in a harbor, rather than tied up at a pier, dock, or quay.

Interval—(1) The space between adjacent groups of ships or boats measured in any direction between the corresponding ships or boats in each group. (2) The space between adjacent individuals, vehicles, or units in a formation that are placed side by side, measured abreast. (3) In air operations, the term has no specialized meaning. (FM 17-34)

Joint—Connotes activities, operations, organizations, etc., in which elements of more than one Service of the Department of Defense participate. (FM 17-34)

Joint expeditionary force—A joint force organized to undertake a joint overseas expedition. (FM 17-34)

Landing area—Includes the beach, the approaches to the beach, the transport area(s), the fire support area(s), the air occupied by close supporting aircraft, and the land included in the advance inland to the initial objective. (FM 17-34)

Landing craft—A craft which is especially designed for beaching, unloading, or loading on a beach, and retracting. (This term generally is applied to nonocean-going vessels, less than 160 feet long, designed for use in landing operations; the designation landing craft (LC) is used with appropriate modifications to designate particular types.) (FM 17-34)

Landing craft availability table—A tabulation of all landing craft available to embark and transport troops and materiel ashore. It is prepared by the transport group commander and submitted to the commander of troop units for planning purposes. (FM 17-34)

Landing diagram—A graphic diagram of the organization of the boat group into waves, showing the distance between waves, expressed in minutes, after H-hour, and the interval between boats and formations, shown in yards. (FM 17-34)

Landing force—A task organization of troops, especially trained and equipped, assigned to carry out amphibious operations against a position or group of positions so located as to permit their seizure by troops operating under a single tactical command. Some of its elements may be transported by air. (FM 17-34)

Landing schedule—A schedule showing the place, hour, and priorities of landing of all units embarked on a transport. It further shows necessary coordination for the ship-to-shore movement to execute the desired scheme of maneuver, and planned supporting naval and air bombardment missions. (FM 60-10)

Landing ship—A large type assault ship, generally over 200 feet long, designed for long sea voyages and for rapid unloading over or onto a beach. (LS is the naval prefix used to designate these ships.) (FM 17-34)

Landing vehicle—Amphibious vehicles used in landing operations that are capable of operating on land and water; they include LVTs (landing vehicle, tracked) and DUKWs (amphibious trucks). (FM 17-34)

Lighter, Lightering—A lighter is a watercraft used to transport cargo or personnel between a vessel and the shore. Lightering is the transfer of cargo or personnel between a vessel and the shore. (*International Maritime Dictionary*)

Line of departure—A line designated to coordinate the departure of attack elements—a jump-off line. In amphibious operations, a suitably marked off-shore coordinating line to assist assault craft to land on designated beaches at scheduled times. (FM 17-34)

Line of transfer (transfer area)—A line designated between the line of departure and the beach for the purpose of coordinating the transfer of troops or supplies between naval craft and LVTs and DUKWs; generally marked by vessels that control traffic to the beach. (FM 17-34)

Loading analysis—See cargo and loading analysis. (FM 60-10)

Loading officer—An Army officer of the embarked unit who is trained to plan and supervise the loading and unloading of his unit's personnel and equipment aboard the ships assigned. (FM 17-34)

Loading point—Any location where ships or landing vessels are loaded with personnel, supplies, and equipment. (FM 60-10)

Main landing—The landing on which the ultimate success of the operation depends. It envisages the securing of a beachhead where assault forces can assume the offensive and continue operations inland against an active enemy. (FM 60-10)

Marker vessel—A vessel that takes accurate station at a designated control point for the purpose of controlling vessels in the ship-to-shore movement. (FM 60-10)

Maru—Japanese merchant ship. The word *Maru* is a suffic traditionally applied to the names of Japanese civilian vessels. The term was used by American mariners to differentiate Japanese merchant ships from those of other nations.

Mine group or mine warfare group—Task unit of a joint attack force assigned the mission of laying (emplacing) and sweeping (locating and neutralizing) mines in the objective area. Mine warfare group elements may be attached to the advance force. (FM 60-10)

Naval beach group (NBG)—Established after World War II to provide naval elements to an amphibious task force. At the time of the Korean War, there were two NBGs: NBG-ONE in the Pacific and NBG-TWO in the Atlantic. An NBG consisted of a headquarters section; a construction battalion (CB); two underwater demolition teams (UDT); a boat unit, which maintained and operated assault landing craft for the ship-to-shore movement of troops and equipment; and a beach master unit, which maintained the special teams to control boat traffic and conduct boat salvage operations in the surf. ("History of Naval Beachmaster Unit TWO," bmu2.surfor.navy.mil/Site%20Documents/History.aspx [accessed 11 April 2007].)

Naval gunfire liaison officer (NGLO)—A naval officer attached to an RCT or BLT, to advise that organization on all matters pertaining to naval gunfire support. He assists the fire support coordination center in the planning and coordination of naval gunfire support with artillery and air. (FM 17-34)

Naval gunfire officer (NGFO)—An officer on the staff of a division or higher landing force unit whose duties are to plan naval gunfire support for amphibious operations. (FM 60-10)

Naval gunfire support (NGS)—Fire support of troops in an amphibious assault or engaged in other operations on shore by naval ordnance on supporting vessels. Types of support (FM 17-34):

a. *Close support fire*: Naval gunfire delivered in close support of friendly troops, either ashore or in landing craft. It is fired on enemy troops, weapons, or positions which, because of their proximity, present the most immediate and serious threat to the supported unit. Support landing craft, destroyers, and antiaircraft batteries of cruisers and battleships provide close support fire.

b. *Deep support fire*: Naval gunfire delivered on objectives not in the immediate vicinity of friendly forces, but farther inland on enemy reserves, supply dumps, fire direction centers, artillery concentrations, etc. Battleships and cruisers provide deep support fire.

Naval gunfire support area—An appropriate station and maneuver area assigned to fire support ships from which they deliver naval gunfire support for a landing operation. (FM 60-10)

Naval platoon—Naval unit, commanded by the beach master, assigned to a battalion shore party. The unit is often called the beach party. (FM 60-10)

Naval task force—A subdivision of the naval attack force composed of ships appropriate for one specific mission. (FM 17-34)

Neap tide—The lowest level of high tide, occurring twice each month during the first and third quarters of the moon.

Objective area—A definite geographical area within which is located the objective to be seized or reached by the expeditionary troops or landing force. (FM 17-34)

Officer in tactical command (OTC)—In naval usage, the officer charged with tactical control of a formation. He is designated by proper authority to assume tactical command or, in the absence of such designation, he is the senior line officer present. (FM 60-10)

Offshore dump—See floating dump. (FM 60-10)

Organizational unit loading—The loading of troop units with their equipment and supplies in the same vessel, but without regard for any planned priority of debarkation. (FM 17-34)

Pallet—A portable platform on which materials are placed for convenient handling and stowage. (A low platform constructed of wood or steel and mounted on runners or rounded baseboards on which are stacked and secured ammunition, rations, or other supplies to facilitate handling from ship holds to beach dumps. Usually approximately 4x6 feet and having attached towing slings, they haul approximately one ton bulk cargo.) (FM 17-34)

Patrol torpedo boat (PT Boat)—A high-speed motorboat mounting 2 or 4 torpedo tubes, antiaircraft, and machineguns; and equipped with depth charges and smoke making apparatus. Used for coastal patrol and convoy. (FM 60-10)

Ponton (or, pontoon), N.L.—Navy lightered ponton; cube shaped, sheet steel, airtight cell from which ponton barges and causeways are assembled when required. (FM 60-10)

Preparatory fires—Intensive naval fires delivered on landing beaches and adjacent areas immediately prior to and during the approach to the beach of the assault landing craft of the leading waves. (FM 17-34)

Primary control vessel—Vessel used by the senior naval officer in control of landing craft for a transport squadron or transport division. (FM 60-10)

Profile loading plan—A profile view of a loading vessel with the itemized list of materiel stowed in the holds indicated in the proper hold spaces. See stowage diagram. (FM 60-10)

Rail loading—Loading personnel and materiel into landing craft suspended from ship davits (Welin type) prior to launching the craft. (FM 17-34)

Reconnaissance group—A task organization of the attack force designated to reconnoiter landing areas before D-Day. They may also do such tasks as locating enemy naval forces, locating beaches, establishing aids to navigation, clearing minefields, selecting suitable targets for naval gunfire, and clearing beach approaches of underwater obstacles. (FM 60-10)

Regimental combat team (RCT)—Reinforced infantry regiment operating as a balanced fighting unit of essential arms. The normal ground force ratio is one regiment of infantry, one battalion of artillery, and one company of engineers, but may be changed to meet the demands of the tactical situation. (FM 17-34)

Regimental shore party—The element of a division shore party that supports an RCT. When the RCT lands separately or at a location where it is not practicable to provide support from the division beach support area, a regimental shore party may be formed from an engineer shore company with necessary attachments. (FM 60-10)

Reserve force—A task organization of a joint amphibious task force consisting of the ships carrying the reserve troops, usually formed into a landing force that can land according to the general scheme of maneuver or as the tactical situation dictates. (FM 60-10)

Reserve supplies—Supplies accumulated in excess of immediate needs to ensure continuity of an adequate supply. (FM 60-10) Selected types of reserve supplies:

a. *Beach reserves*: An accumulation of supplies of all classes established in dumps on the beach; normally 5 to 10 days of supply of all classes. (FM 60-10)

b. *Individual reserves*: The supplies carried on the soldier, animal, or vehicle for his (or its) individual use. This generally includes the combat load of ammunition for all weapons in the BLT; normally 1 or 2 days of supply of all classes. (FM 60-10)

c. *Initial reserves*: Those supplies normally unloaded immediately following the assault waves; usually enough to begin and sustain combat until higher supply installations are established; normally 3 to 5 days of supply of all classes. (FM 60-10)

Rhino barge—Barge assembled from cube shaped, sheet steel, airtight pontons. (FM 60-10)

S-day—Sailing date for a scheduled operation. (FM 60-10)

Salvage group—A naval task organization designed and equipped to rescue personnel and to salvage equipment and materiel. (FM 60-10)

Screening group—A defensive unit of naval vessels employed to protect the attack force. It includes antisubmarine vessels and picket boats located seaward from the transport and fire support areas. (FM 60-10)

Secondary control vessel—Vessels used by naval boat group and wave commanders and wave guide officers. (FM 60-10)

Selective loading—Loading of supplies and equipment in cargo vessels so that specific items can be unloaded on call. (FM 60-10)

Senior Officer Present Afloat (SOPA)—The highest ranking officer aboard ship in a harbor when more than one vessel is in the harbor. He commands all naval operations afloat in that harbor. (Naval Historical Center. ("Glossary of U.S. Naval Abbreviations," www.history.navy.mil/books/ OPNAV20-P1000/S.htm [accessed 26 August 2008].)

Ship's platoon—Personnel furnished by the Army to handle materiel and equipment being loaded on or unloaded from assault ships. Their function is essentially that of hatch crews. (FM 60-10)

Shore fire control party—A specially trained unit of naval gunnery, artillery, and communication personnel for control of naval gunfire in support of troops ashore. A shore fire control party consists of a naval gunfire spotter team including a naval gunfire spotter, assistant spotter, and radio and wire teams; and a naval gunfire liaison team including a naval gunfire liaison officer who is supported by a radio team and a wire team. (FM 17-34)

Shore group—The appropriate number of shore party units to provide the logistical support for an RCT. (FM 17-34)

Shore party—A task organization formed for the purpose of providing logistic support within the beach area to landing force units during the early phases of an amphibious operation. Its basic mission is to unload supplies and equipment; provide services and facilities ashore; receive, segregate, and safeguard this materiel; maintain security of the beach area; evacuate casualties and prisoners of war; and re-embark other personnel as directed. (FM 17-34)

Shore party team—The shore party organization basically organized to support a battalion landing team in an amphibious operation. The shore party team is the basic unit of a shore party. In Army usage, the organization performing this mission takes the name of the major T/O&E unit involved, normally a shore company. (FM 17-34)

Special control vessel—A vessel used by corps and division commanders, boat flotilla commanders, senior beach masters, and division shore party commanders. (FM 60-10)

Spring tide—An exceptionally high tide that occurs during a full or new moon, when the sun, moon, and earth are approximately aligned.

Stevedore—One who works at or is responsible for the loading or unloading of a vessel in port. (FM 17-34)

Stores—In naval usage, this term is sometimes used instead of the term "supplies" to denote any article or commodity used by a naval vessel or station; for example, equipage, consumable supplies, clothing, petroleum products, ammunition, and medical supplies. (FM 60-10)

Stowage diagram—A schematic drawing of each hatch level showing stowage space for cargo. It may include overall dimensions, and indicate boom capacity, stanchions, and minimum clearance. (FM 60-10)

Support group—A task group of naval vessels and craft assigned to furnish naval gunfire support in an amphibious operation. Usually there is one support group for each attack force. The support group may consist of two or more support units. (FM 60-10)

Supporting arms coordination center (SACC)—An organization having the same functions as the fire support coordination center, but located aboard a ship and remaining afloat. (FM 60-10)

Tactical air control party (TACP)—A subordinate operational component of the land-based tactical air control group designed for the control of aircraft from forward observation posts. The tactical air control party operates at division, regimental, or battalion level. (Typically consists of one air officer and three enlisted men attached to each landing team and combat team for the purpose of directing and controlling air support.) (FM 17-34)

Tactical air coordinator (airborne) (TACA)—An air officer who coordinates, from an airplane, the action of combat aircraft engaged in close support of ground or sea forces. (FM 60-10)

Ton—A unit of volume or weight. In volume: measurement ton = 40 cubic feet; gross ton = 100 cubic feet. In weight: short ton = 2,000 pounds; long ton (weight ton) = 2,240 pounds; metric ton = 2,205 pounds (1,000 kilograms). (FM 60-10)

Tonnage—An expression of cubic content or weight used to indicate the aggregate of tons shipped, carried, handled, or mined; also to indicate a ship's weight, size, and carrying capacity. (FM 60-10)

    a. *Deadweight cargo tonnage*: The cargo carrying capacity, expressed in long tons. It is the part of the deadweight tonnage of the vessel that remains after deducting the weight of fuel, water, stores, dunnage, and other voyage items. Also known as cargo capacity tonnage.

    b. *Deadweight tonnage*: The carrying capacity of a ship, expressed in long tons. It is the difference between displacement tonnage loaded and displacement tonnage light. Light deadweight tonnage: total weight of the ship to exclude the weight of cargo, passengers, fuel, water, stores, and dunnage. Loaded deadweight tonnage: total weight including all those items listed above.

    c. *Displacement tonnage*: The weight of the ship expressed in long tons, either light or loaded.

    d. *Gross tonnage*: Total internal cubic capacity of a ship expressed in tons of 100 cubic feet capacity.

Tractor group—A term sometimes used to designate a group of landing ships in an amphibious operation that carries the amphibious vehicles of the landing force. (FM 17-34)

Transfer line—A line on the water at which the transfer of troops and supplies from landing craft to amphibious vehicles is made. Its location may be arbitrary, or may be dictated by the existence of reefs beyond which landing craft cannot navigate. (FM 60-10)

Transport quartermaster (TQM)—Each APA and AKA of the amphibious forces normally has in its regular complement a Marine officer, usually a captain, assigned duty as transport quartermaster. He maintains ship's data as it affects loading, unloading, billeting, and messing; performs liaison between the commanding officer of the ship and the commanding officer of the troops prior to embarkation; assists the loading officer in the preparation of detailed loading plans; and supervises cargo stowage in accordance with approved loading plans. (FM 17-34)

Transport, attack (APA)—A naval transport capable of being combat loaded and fitted with special equipment to permit it to carry and launch landing craft and to facilitate the unloading of personnel into landing craft from off shore. (Expanded definition based on that of FM 60-10)

Transport division—The attack transports and attack cargo ships required to carry personnel, supplies, and equipment of one RCT. (During the first part of World War II, a transport division typically consisted of three APAs and one AKA. By the end of the war, a transport division typically consisted of five APAs and two AKAs.) (FM 17-34)

Transport group—A subdivision of an attack force consisting of assault shipping and, when attached, its protective and service units, organized for the purpose of embarking, transporting, and landing troops, equipment, and supplies of the landing force. (FM 17-34)

Transport area—The sea area designated as a station area for transports debarking troops during the assault phase of a landing operation. (FM 17-34)

Transport squadron—Two or more transport divisions organized to carry a reinforced infantry division. (FM 17-34)

Underwater demolition team (UDT)—A naval unit organized and equipped to perform beach reconnaissance and underwater demolition missions in an amphibious operation. (FM 17-34)

Unit loading officer—Normally an officer of the senior organization within the embarkation team. He must have been trained in a ship-loading school. His assignment as unit loading officer will be temporary but, upon appointment, he will be relieved of all other duties. His principal duties as unit loading officer includes: (1) Acts as direct representative of the commanding officer of troops of the embarkation team in all matters pertaining to loading. (2) Effects liaison between the commanding officer of the ship and the commanding officer of troops. (3) Prepares detailed loading plans for the ship to which the embarkation team is assigned (assisted by the ship's combat cargo officer). (4) Coordinates and supervises the execution of the loading plan. (5) Assists in the execution of the unloading plan. (FM 60-30)

Unit personnel and tonnage table—A table showing total personnel and cubic measurements and weights of each class of material and number, size, and weight of each type of vehicle to be embarked by a combat unit. (FM 17-34)

Vessel—Any type of watercraft larger than a rowboat. (FM 60-10)

Wave—A formation of landing ships, craft, or amphibious vehicles required to arrive at the beach at about the same time.

Welin davit—A type of davit with a three-boat capacity that became standard on US amphibious ships during World War II. (*International Maritime Dictionary*)

Abbreviations and Acronyms

(Attack cargo ships, attack transports, landing ships, and landing craft are described in appendix B.)

AAA AW	Antiaircraft artillery automatic weapon. (FM 60-10)
AAOC	Antiaircraft operations center. (FM 60-10)
AAS	Artillery-air-spot (net). (FM 60-10)
AGC	Naval symbol for an amphibious force flagship (headquarters ship). (FM 60-10)
AH	Naval symbol for a hospital ship. (FM 60-10)
AK	Naval symbol for a cargo ship. (FM 60-10)
AKA	Naval symbol for a cargo ship, attack. (FM 60-10)
AMTANK	An amphibious tank that can operate both on land and in water. Landing vehicle, tracked (armored) (LVT[A]) is current terminology. (FM 60-10)

AMTRAC	An amphibious tractor used for the movement of troops and cargo from ship to shore in the assault phase of an amphibious operation, or for limited movement of troops and cargo over land or water. Landing vehicle, tracked (LVT) is current terminology. (FM 60-10)
ANGLICO	Air and naval gunfire liaison company. A Navy/Marine Corps unit attached to ground units to control naval gunfire and close air support.
AP	Naval symbol for a troop transport. (FM 60-10)
APA	Naval symbol for attack transport; a vessel capable of combat unit loading and transporting the bulk of an assault battalion landing team. (FM 60-10)
APD	Naval symbol for a destroyer-type high-speed transport. Korean War era APDs were converted from destroyer escorts. They were 300-foot long ships mounting a 5-inch gun and smaller guns and carrying four 36-foot landing craft. (FM 60-10)
BB	Naval symbol for battleship. Battleships that participated in the Korean War were 900-foot long ships capable of speeds greater than 30 knots and armed with nine 16-inch guns, twenty 5-inch guns, and many 40-mm and 20-mm guns. (FM 60-10)
BHL	Beachhead line. An objective that fixes the limits of the beachhead; a tentative main line of resistance based, if practicable, on terrain features that can be defended against enemy counterattack prior to advance out of the beachhead; occupied and organized as demanded by the situation. (FM 17-34)
BMNT	Beginning morning nautical twilight. (FM 60-10)
CA	Naval symbol for heavy cruiser (a cruiser mounting 8-inch guns as the primary armament). (FM 60-10)
CAP	Combat air patrol. (FM 60-10)
CL	Naval symbol for light cruiser (a cruiser mounting 6-inch guns as its primary armament). (FM 60-10)

COMLANFOR/CLF	Commander, landing force. (FM 60-10)
COMNAVFOR	Commander, naval force; commander of the naval units of the joint force. This officer also may be the task force commander. (FM 17-34)
COMTRANSDIV	Commander, transport division. (FM 60-10)
COMTRANSGROUP	Commander, transport group. (FM 60-10)
COMTRANSRON	Commander, transport squadron. (FM 60-10)
COMTRACTORS	Commander, tractor group. (FM 17-34)
CV	Naval symbol for aircraft carrier. A CV was an 855-foot long ship carrying more than 80 aircraft and with a speed of more than 30 knots. (FM 60-10)
CVE	Naval symbol for escort aircraft carrier built on a merchant ship hull. About 500 feet long, carrying about 20 aircraft, and with a speed of 18 knots, they were used primarily to escort convoys and to deploy Marine or Navy aircraft supporting ground troops ashore. (FM 60-10)
CVL	Naval symbol for a light aircraft carrier built on a light cruiser hull. Less than 700 feet long, carrying about 35 aircraft, and with a speed of more than 30 knots. (FM 60-10)
DCP	DUKW control point. (FM 60-10)
DD	Naval symbol for destroyer. Korean War era destroyers were 380 to 390-foot long ships mounting six 5-inch guns and smaller weapons. (FM 60-10)
DE	Naval symbol for destroyer escort. Korean War era DEs were 300-foot long ships carrying two 5-inch guns. (FM 60-10)
DMS	Destroyer minesweeper. A destroyer modified to be capable of locating and neutralizing naval mines.
DUKW	A 2½ ton, 6x6 truck capable of operating on both land and water. DUKW was a General Motors Corporation designation based on their product codes: D = 1942 model, U = amphibious, K = all-wheel drive, and W = dual rear wheels. (FM 60-10)

FAC	Forward air controller. (FM 60-10)
FSCC	Fire support coordination center. (FM 60-10)
FSG	Fire support group. (FM 60-10)
HF	High frequency (radio). (FM 60-10)
LC	Landing craft. (FM 60-10)
LCI	Landing craft, infantry. (FM 60-10)
LCM	Landing craft, mechanized. (FM 60-10)
LCP(L)	Landing craft, personnel (large). (FM 60-10)
LCP(R)	Landing craft, personnel (ramped). (FM 60-10)
LCS	Landing craft, support. (FM 60-10)
LCVP	Landing craft, vehicle, personnel. (FM 60-10)
LEX	Naval term for a practice landing, a landing exercise. (FM 17-34)
LO	Loading officer. (FM 60-10)
LSD	Landing ship, dock. (FM 60-10)
LSM	Landing ship, medium. (FM 60-10)
LSMR, LSM(R)	Landing ship, medium, rocket. (FM 60-10)
LST	Landing ship, tank. (FM 60-10)
LSTH, LST(H)	Landing ship, tank (casualty evacuation). An LST configured to care for personnel casualties. (FM 60-10)
LSU	Landing ship, utility. (FM 60-10) (Designated landing craft, tank (LCT) until 10 April 1949, then redesignated landing ship, tank (small) (LST[S]). Redesignated LSU in late 1949. Redesignated landing craft, utility (LCU) on 15 April 1952.)
LSV	Landing ship, vehicle. (FM 60-10)
LVT	Landing vehicle, tracked. (FM 60-10)
LVT(A)	Landing vehicle, tracked (armored). (FM 60-10)
MSL	Mean sea level. (FM 60-10)
MSTS	Military Sea Transport Service. (FM 60-10)
MTB	Motor Torpedo Boat (see PT Boat).

MTT	Mobile Training Team. An element of a Marine Corps Troop Training Unit (TTU). (See TTU.)
NATU	Naval amphibious training unit. (FM 60-10)
NGF	Naval gunfire. (FM 60-10)
NGFO	Naval gunfire officer. (FM 60-10)
NGLO	Naval gunfire liaison officer. (FM 60-10)
N.L. Ponton	Navy lightered pontoon. (FM 60-10)
OTC	Officer in tactical command. (FM 60-10)
PC	Submarine chaser. A 173-foot long patrol craft armed with one or two 3-inch guns as well as 20-mm and/or 40-mm guns, .50-caliber machineguns, and depth charges. During the Korean War, they were widely used by the ROK Navy as patrol vessels.
PT Boat	Patrol torpedo boat. Also called a motor torpedo boat (MTB). An 80-foot long boat capable of speeds greater than 40 knots and armed with two or four torpedoes, 20-mm and .50-caliber guns, and, sometimes, depth charges. (FM 60-10)
RCT	Regimental combat team. (FM 17-34)
SACC	Supporting arms coordination center. (FM 60-10)
S/AS	Ship-air-spot (net). (FM 60-10)
SCAJAP	Shipping Control Administration, Japan. (FM 17-34)
SFCP	Shore fire control party. (FM 17-34)
SS	Naval symbol for submarine.
TAC	Tactical air command (net). (FM 60-10)
TACA	Tactical air coordinator (airborne). (FM 60-10)
TACC	Tactical air control center. (FM 60-10)
TACP	Tactical air control party. (FM 60-10)
TAD	Tactical air direction (net). (FM 60-10)
TADC	Tactical air direction center. (FM 60-10)
TAF	Tactical air force. (FM 60-10)
TAO	Tactical air observation (net). (FM 60-10)

TAR	Tactical air request (net). (FM 60-10)
TRANSDIV	Transport division. (FM 60-10)
TRANSGROUP	Transport group. (FM 60-10)
TRANSRON	Transport squadron. (FM 60-10)
TTU	Troop training unit. A Marine Corps organization designed to provide amphibious training to Marine Corps or Army units. (FM 60-10)
UDT	Underwater demolition team. A Navy unit primarily intended for beach reconnaissance, to destroy enemy beach obstacles, and to guide landing forces coming ashore. During the Korean War, Navy UDTs also conducted amphibious raids. (FM 17-34)
UP&T Table	Unit personnel and tonnage table. (FM 60-10)
VHF (Radio)	Very high frequency.

Index

Omaha Beach, Normandy, France, June 1944, 40, 59, 69, 101, 286
OPAL Beach (Incheon), 180–181, 188, 191–192, 200
RED Beach (Incheon), 165–166, 176–180, 188, 209, 211
Thon My Thuy, Vietnam, Utah Beach, Wunder Beach, 339
Utah Beach, Normandy, France, June 1944, 59, 151, 286, 289
Utah Beach, Vietnam, Thon My Thuy, Wunder Beach, 339
WANDA Beach (Incheon), 339
Wunder Beach, Vietnam, Thon My Thuy, Utah Beach, 339
YELLOW Beach (Incheon), 166, 178, 180–181
beaching, 7, 114, 122, 135, 235, 341, 425, 436, 443
Beauchamp, Colonel Charles E. (USA), 189, 212
Betio, Tarawa, Gilbert Islands, Landing, November 1943, 50–51
Bismarck Archipelago, 19, 31, 47
Black Sea Coast, Cold War Plans for Amphibious Operations on, 73
Blamey, General Sir Thomas (Australian Army), 54–55
Blockade Board of 1861 (Civil War), 14, 85
Bloody Ridge, Korea, Battle of, 296, 298
Borg-Warner Corporation, 30
Borneo, 65
Boscowen, Admiral Edward (Royal Navy), 11
Boston Whalers (boats), 341, 345
Bradley, Brigadier General Joseph S. (USA), 133, 250, 301, 310
Bradley, General Omar (USA), 69, 104
brigade combat team (BCT), 344, 347, 356
Brind, Admiral Sir Patrick (Royal Navy), 144
Briscoe, Vice Admiral Robert P. (US Navy), 322
British Army, 1, 8, 11–12, 19, 26–28, 30–33, 35–36, 39, 42–43, 49, 52, 60, 262
British Army Units
    17th Port & Maritime Regiment, 346
    27th Brigade, 224
British Chief of Combined Operations, 32
British Combined Operations Headquarters (COHQ), 30, 33, 39
British Commonwealth Forces (BCOF) (Japanese Occupation), 27, 80
British Navy. *See* Royal Navy
British Royal Marines, 19, 144, 232, 240, 270, 288
British Royal Marines, 41st Independent Commando (*see also* Drysdale, Lieutenant Colonel Douglas B.), 144, 154, 190, 209, 212, 231, 248, 270, 292, 295, 304
Brock, Captain Jeffrey V. (Royal Canadian Navy), 237–238
Brown, Major General Albert (USA), 48
Brown, Major General Jacob (USA), 12, 85
Buckner, Lieutenant General Simon Bolivar, Jr. (USA), 1, 64–65
Bukhan (Pukhan) River, Korea, 146, 237, 252, 261, 271–279, 284, 287, 308
Burnside, Major General Ambrose E. (USA), 14, 16, 85
Burnside's Coast Division (Civil War), 14, 16

Busan (Pusan), Korea, 111, 113, 115, 123, 126–130, 133–134, 136, 140, 155, 157–158, 160, 168–172, 175, 182, 185, 205, 210–211, 218–223, 226, 229, 233, 235, 240, 249, 252–253, 255–256, 259, 263–264, 266, 268, 270, 289, 295, 415

Butaritari Island, Makin Atoll, Gilbert Islands
    Landing by 165th RCT, USA, November 1943, 50, 99
    Landing by 2d Raider Battalion, USMC, August 1942, 42

Butler, Major General Benjamin F. (USA), 14

Caen, France, 57–58
Calabrian Coast, Italy, Landing, September 1943, 49
Caldera, Secretary of the Army Louis, 346
Callaway, Lieutenant Colonel John B. (USA), 275–278, 283
Cam Ranh Bay, Vietnam, 359
Cambodia, 337–338, 340
Camp Drake, Japan, 121, 123
Camp Edwards, Massachusetts, US Army Amphibious Training Center and Engineer Amphibious Command, 37–38, 348
Camp Gordon Johnson, Florida, Amphibious Training Site, 38, 65
Camp Haugen, Japan, 293
Camp Lejeune, North Carolina, 338
Camp McGill, Japan, Far East Command Amphibious Training Site, 82–83, 108–109, 119–120, 122–123, 143–144, 292, 295, 314, 316–317, 320
Camp Younghans, Japan, 293
Camp Zama, Japan, 123, 245
Canada, 32, 117, 331
Canadian Navy (Royal Canadian Navy) Ships (HMCS)
    Athabaskan (destroyer), 172–173, 238
    Cayuga (destroyer), 238
    Sioux (destroyer), 238
Cape Breton Island, Canada, Fortress of Louisburg, Captured 1745 and 1758, 11
Cape Cod, Massachusetts, Amphibious Training Site, 37, 94
Cape Fear River, North Carolina, Amphibious Training Site, 16
Cape Gloucester, New Britain, Landing, December 1943, 46
cargo ship (AK), 2, 5, 8, 26, 29, 38, 81–83, 111, 113, 122, 163, 168, 189, 220–221, 226, 229, 235, 239, 242, 249, 251, 262, 421, 438, 450–451
Caroline Islands, 53
Carrabelle, Florida, Amphibious Training Site, 37–38, 65
Casablanca, Morocco, Landing, November 1942, 43–44
Castine Peninsula, Maine, Raid on (1779), 12
Central Intelligence Agency (CIA), 145, 154, 226, 259, 269
Central Pacific Area, 56, 61
Central Pacific Force, 50
Central Pacific Offensive, 33, 52, 55
Central Pacific Operations, World War II, 49, 56
Chaney, Major General James E. (USA), 27, 91

Chang Chae Hwa (ROK Partisan Leader), 267

Chauncey, Commodore Isaac (US Navy), 12, 85

Cheongcheon (Ch'ongch'on) River, Korea, 228, 234, 236, 415

Cherbourg, France, 57, 72, 101

Chesapeake Bay, 35

Chief of Logistics (G4), US Army Staff, 80, 94, 118, 149, 224, 246, 266, 307

Chief of Naval Operations (CNO), US Navy, 20, 25–26, 33, 79, 94, 155, 204, 331

Chief of Operations (G3), US Army Staff, 79–80, 96, 98, 100, 103, 107–109, 118, 120, 149, 151, 171, 189, 205, 246, 258, 294, 302, 304–309, 326

Chigasaki Beach, Japan, Amphibious Training Site, 82–83, 109, 115, 292–293, 316, 319, 321

Chinese Military Forces, 118, 228, 231–232, 234–235, 241–242, 246–249, 251–254, 256–257, 259–260, 262, 266, 271, 276–280, 282–284, 286–288, 291–292, 294, 296, 301, 318, 321

Chinese People's Volunteer (CPV). *See* Chinese Military Forces

Chinese Spring Offensive, April 1951, 284, 287

Chodo (Ch'o-do), Korea, 140, 175, 219, 233, 257–258, 263, 267–270, 288–289, 295, 415, 427

Choi Nam Yong (Commander, ROK Navy), 113

Civil War, American, 14, 16, 24, 85–86, 143, 146

Clance, First Lieutenant James W. (USA), 176, 209

Clark, General Mark W. (USA), 43, 49, 73, 322

Clark, Lieutenant Eugene F. (US Navy), 174, 201, 208–209

Clark, Vice Admiral J.J. (US Navy), 323–324

Coast Guard, 12, 26, 36–37, 91–92, 94

Collins, General J. Lawton (USA), 76, 79, 104, 156, 160, 169, 172, 204–205, 208, 217, 235, 239–240, 245

combat loaders. *See* amphibious ships, combat loaders

Combined Operations Headquarters (COHQ) (British), 30, 33, 39

combined task force (CTF), 292, 234, 303

Commander, Task Force 90 (*see also* Doyle, Rear Admiral James H.), 233

Command and General Staff School, 24

Commander in Chief of the US Fleet, 33

Commander in Chief of the US Pacific Fleet, 33, 79

Commander in Chief, Far East (CINCFE), 79, 147–149, 155, 160, 169, 193, 204–205, 207–208, 223, 245, 248–250, 285, 292–293, 302–303, 308–310, 315, 317–318, 322, 325

Commander in Chief, United Nations Command (CINCUNC), 117, 209, 247, 260, 285, 322, 324, 326

Commander, Task Force (CTF) (US Navy term), 233

Commander, Task Force 90 (CTF 90). *See* US Navy Units, NAVFE Task Force 90 (NAVFE Amphibious Force)

Commander, United States Naval Forces, Far East (COMNAVFE), 116–117, 124, 247–249, 262, 303, 309, 315, 318, 322–323

Conduct of War and Analytical Studies Courses, 24

Far East Command (FEC), 7, 79, 82, 107–109, 149, 156, 205–206, 245, 251, 301, 303, 315, 325

    area of responsibility (AOR), 79, 81, 116, 222

    G2, 119, 121, 144, 149, 174, 189, 209, 236

    G3, 79–80, 108, 118, 120, 148–149, 171, 189, 308

    General Headquarters (GHQ), FEC, 2, 79, 81–82, 100, 108–109, 114, 118–120, 123, 143–144, 148–149, 154, 168, 171, 174, 207, 209, 212, 215, 224, 284, 293, 301, 306, 308–309, 325

    GHQ FEC Provisional Raider Company, later renamed 8245th Army Unit, X Corps Raider Company, 144–145, 174–175, 186, 190, 209, 211–212

    Headquarters and Service Command, FEC, 143

    Japan Logistical Command (JLC), 222

    Joint Special Operations Staff, 174

    Joint Strategic Plans and Operations Group (JSPOG), 55, 79, 118–119, 148, 155, 157, 159, 193, 218, 309

    Special Activities Group (SAG), 144–145

Farragut, Navy Flag Officer David G. (US Navy), 14

Farrell, Brigadier General Francis (USA), 132

fast transports (APD). *See* amphibious ships, high-speed transports (APD)

Fellers, Brigadier General William S. (USMC), 109, 120

field artillery battalion (FAB). *See* US Army Units, battalions, field artillery battalions (FAB)

Flaherty, Captain Michael J. (US Navy), 239

Fleet Landing Exercises (FLEXs). *See* exercises

Fleet Marine Force (FMF), 23, 57, 70, 155, 167, 188, 209–210, 290

fleet volunteers. *See* Royal Navy Units, fleet volunteers

Flying Fish Channel (Seo-sudo), Korea, 172

Foley, Boatswain's Mate Warren (US Navy), 142

Food Machinery Corporation (FMC), 30

force beachhead line (BHL), 178, 182–183

forcible entry operations, 8, 327

Ford General Purpose Amphibian (GPA). *See* amphibious vehicles, ¼-ton, general purpose amphibian (GPA)

foreign humanitarian assistance (FHA), 4

Formosa (Taiwan), 32–33, 36, 54–55, 60–62, 101, 116, 159

Forney, Colonel Edward H. (USMC), 83, 119–120, 149, 160, 206, 211, 236, 240–242

Forrestal, Secretary of Defense James V., 71

Fort Eustis, Virginia, 188, 330, 348, 355–356

Fort Fisher, Landings, 1864, 1865, 16, 24, 86

Fort Knox, Kentucky, 73, 95, 106

Fort Lewis, Washington, 25, 37, 68, 80, 120, 331, 347

Fort Story, Virginia, 338

Fort Worden, Washington, 66, 120, 313–314

Fox, Major General Alonzo P. (USA), 119, 149, 193

Franklin, Brigadier General William B. (USA), 15–16
Franklin's division (Civil War), 16
Fremont, Major John C. (USA), 13
French and Indian War (1754–63), American Part of the Seven Years' War (1756–63), 11, 84
French Army units
519th Logistics Regiment, 346
French fortress of Louisburg, Canada, Captured 1745 and 1758, 11
French Indochina, 31
French Morocco, 43, 96
French North African Colonies of Morocco, Algeria, and Tunisia, Landings, November 1942, 31
Fukuoka, Japan, 115–116
Fulton, Colonel William B. (USA), 341–342, 353
Funston, Brigadier General Frederick (USA), 18
Fuson, Lieutenant General Jack C. (USA), 348–349, 356

G3 Miscellaneous Division (Eighth Army), 258, 294
Gaeseong (Kaesong), Korea, 112, 140, 175, 219–220, 224–225, 233, 237, 251–252, 258, 263, 268, 270, 272, 289, 295, 297, 300, 321, 324, 415
Gallipoli Peninsula, Landing 1915, 19, 24, 87, 89–90
Ganggu-don (Kanggu-dong), Korea, 131–132, 415
Gangneung (Kangnung), Korea, 112–113, 116, 140, 175, 191, 219, 233, 237, 260–261, 263, 268, 270, 287, 289, 295, 297, 300, 320, 323, 415
Ganseong (Kansong), Korea, 140, 164, 175, 179, 219, 233, 237, 262–263, 268, 270, 272, 288–290, 295, 297, 300, 415
Gavutu-Tanambogo Islands, Solomon Islands, Landing, August 1942, 41
Gay, Major General Hobart R. (USA), 120–121, 123, 125, 150
General Headquarters (GHQ), 2, 26, 28–29, 36, 55, 79, 81–82, 100, 108–109, 114, 118–120, 123, 143–145, 148–149, 154, 157–159, 161-162, 168, 170–171, 174–175, 186, 190, 207–209, 211–212, 215, 218, 220, 224, 228, 245, 284–285, 293, 301, 306, 308–309, 317, 322, 325
Geojedo (Koje-do), Korea, 135–138, 140, 175, 219, 233, 255, 263, 268, 270, 289, 295, 415
German forces, 49
German Samoa, Occupied by Japanese Forces, 1914, 19
Ghormley, Rear Admiral Robert (US Navy), 26–27, 33, 41
GHQ FEC Amphibious Training Program, 2, 81–82, 109, 114
Gibbons, Lieutenant Colonel John B. (USA), 120–121, 126–127, 129
Gibraltar, 43–44
Gilbert Islands, 42–50
Gilberts, Marshalls, and Marianas Operations, 332
Gimpo (Kimpo) Airfield, 112, 164, 168, 173, 177, 179, 186–187, 190–191, 194–195, 197–198, 252, 260–261, 287
Gimpo (Kimpo) Peninsula, Korea, 224, 322
Gimpo (Kimp'o), Korea, 220, 252, 415

468

470

Jumunjin (Chumunjin), Korea, 112–113, 140, 157, 175, 219, 233, 263, 268–270, 289, 295, 416
Junker, Navy Captain Alexander F. (US Navy), 81, 117
Jutland Peninsula, Denmark, 72

Kanto Plain, Japan, 255, 292–293, 316
Ke In-Ju (ROK Army Counterintelligence Colonel), 174
Kean, Major General William B. (USA), 129
keel boats, 12
Kelly, Captain Samuel G. (US Navy), 236–238, 262
Kennedy, Captain Thomas J. (USA), 281–282, 307
Key West Agreement, 1948, 71–72, 76–77, 105, 327, 345
Key West, Florida, Marine Port of Embarkation, 1898, 16, 71
Kiland, Vice Admiral Ingolf N. (US Navy), 255, 288
Kim Ok Gyeong (Lieutenant, ROK Navy), 114
Kim Paik-il (Brigadier General, ROK Army), 222–223, 235
Kim Suk Won (Brigadier General, ROK Army), 132, 134
Kim Sung Eun (Lieutenant Colonel, ROK Marine Corps), 170
Kim Yong Bae (Lieutenant Colonel, ROK Army), 113
King William's War (War of the League of Augsburg 1689–97), 11
King, Admiral Ernest J. (US Navy), 33, 38
Kinkaid, Vice Admiral Thomas C. (US Navy), 53
Kiska Island, Alaska, Landing, August 1943, 32, 42, 48–49
Ko Kung Hong (Lieutenant Colonel, ROK Army), 113
Kobe, Japan, 115, 168, 172, 176
Kojo Feint (Operation DOMINO), October 1952, 322–323, 326
Korean Augmentation to the US Army (KATUSA) Program, 171, 230
Korean Military Advisory Group (KMAG), 80, 132–135, 152, 185, 288
Korean National Police, 132, 135, 189
Krueger, Lieutenant General Walter (USA), 46, 52, 55, 61, 76, 97, 100, 143
Kwajalein Atoll, Marshall Islands, Landing, January 1944, 52–53

Lake Erie, Battle of, 1813 (War of 1812), 12
landing craft
    landing craft, assault (LCA) (Royal Navy), 30
    landing craft, infantry (gunboat) (LCI[G]), 39
    landing craft, infantry (large) (LCI[L]), 39, 49
    landing craft, mechanized (LCM), 8, 30, 39, 46, 48, 52, 63, 65, 82, 119, 122, 125–126, 129, 150, 163, 177, 182, 201, 221, 224, 230–231, 256, 266, 316, 319–320, 330, 339, 341–342, 346, 353, 424, 429, 454
    landing craft, personnel (large) (LCP[L]), 29, 431, 454
    landing craft, personnel (ramped) (LCP[R]), 29–30, 141–142, 431, 454
    landing craft, support (large) (LCS[L]), 39
    landing craft, tank (LCT), 8, 30, 37, 39–40, 46, 64, 150, 330, 428, 454
    landing craft, utility (LCU), 8, 150, 330, 339, 341, 346, 353, 428, 454

LINE WYOMING, 271–272, 274, 284

PYEONGYANG–WONSAN Line, 293, 299

Lingayen Gulf, Philippines, Landing, January 1945, 24, 62–64

Linn, Brian McAllister, 16, 86, 88, 91

Litzenberg, Colonel Homer L. (USMC), 197

lodgment areas (beachhead), 7, 14, 23, 28, 30, 36–37, 46, 49, 51–52, 56–57, 59, 68–70, 72, 74–78, 92, 99, 111, 135, 137, 157–158, 162, 166, 177–179, 182–183, 220, 232, 240, 270, 296, 298, 332, 337, 348–349, 436, 444, 452

logistic support vessel (LSV), 346, 454

logistics-over-the-shore (LOTS) operations, 5, 329–331, 338–341, 346, 351, 353

Louisburg, Canada, Capture of (1745, 1758), 11, 84

Lovell, General Solomon (Continental Army), 12

Lucas, Major General John P. (USA), 52, 93

Luzon, Philippines, 24, 54–55, 60–63, 101–102

M-24 light tanks, 123

MacArthur, General Douglas (USA), 1, 2, 5, 11, 27, 33, 38, 40–41, 45–46, 50, 53–55, 60–61, 63, 65, 67, 69, 74, 79–84, 95–97, 99–100, 104, 114, 116–121, 123, 126, 143–144, 149, 155–162, 167–171, 176, 186, 192–193, 195, 203–205, 207–209, 211, 217–219, 222–224, 226–228, 231, 234–235, 240–241, 243, 245–247, 254–255, 260, 262, 271, 284–285, 291–292, 301

Maines, Corporal John W. (USA), 176, 209

Makin Atoll, Gilbert Islands. *See* Butaritari

Malay Barrier, 31

Manchuria, 19, 72, 118, 146, 227, 234

Manila Bay, Philippines, Battle of, 1898, 17, 20, 62, 64

Marblehead Mariners. *See* Glover, John, Continental Army, 14th Massachusetts Continental Regiment

Marianas Islands, 18, 50, 54, 61, 80, 100, 108, 332

Marine Air Group (MAG), 126, 151, 168, 190

Marine Corps developments, 88

Marshall Islands, 18, 51–52

Marshall, General George C. (USA), 32, 69, 218

Martinique Island, French West Indies, Planning for Occupation of, 1940, 26

Marus (Japanese Merchant Ships), 17, 124–125

Masan, Korea, 127–130, 135–136, 140, 175, 219, 233, 254, 261, 263, 268, 270, 287, 289, 295

McCaffrey, Lieutenant Colonel William J. (USA), 206, 223, 249

McClellan, Major General George B. (USA), 14–15

McGee, Colonel John (USA), 257–258, 269

McNair, Major General Lesley J. (USA), 28, 91

Medina, Brigadier General Joseph V. (USMC), 345, 354

Mediterranean Sea, 44

Mediterranean Theater of Operations (MTO), World War II, 1, 5, 39, 43, 49, 52, 56, 60, 69, 93, 95–96, 98, 101, 157, 188, 286, 308, 337

Medium Boat Company, 341–342, 344, 346
Merchant Ship *Luxembourg Victory,* 230
Merritt, Major General Wesley (USA), 17, 105
Mexican War, 1846–47, 13
Mexico City, Mexico, Capture of, 1847, 13, 88
Mid-Pacific doctrine, 68–69, 75, 162, 332
Midway, Battle of, June 1942, 32
Miles, Major General Nelson A. (USA), 17, 86
Military Demarcation Line (MDL), Korea, 299, 313
Military District of Puerto Rico (MDPR), 331, 351
Military Sea Transportation Service (MSTS) (*see also* MSTS ships), 2, 17, 81, 87,
    117, 120, 122, 124–126, 163, 170, 190, 194, 221, 229, 238, 241, 243, 251,
    317, 422, 454
Miller, Warrant Officer W.R. (USA), 162
Mindanao, Philippines, Landings, March–July 1945, 50, 54, 60–61, 64, 102
Miryang Battalion. *See* ROK Guerrilla Forces, Independent Mobile Unit, Miryang
    Guerrilla Battalion
    Jangsa-dong Operation, 183–184
Miryang, Korea, 127–128, 140, 175, 183, 185, 210, 219, 233, 263, 267–270, 289,
    295
Mississippi Marine Brigade, US Army (Civil War), 15
Mississippi River, 14
Mobile Riverine Force (Vietnam), 341–343, 353
Moji, Japan, 115, 117
Morobe Bay, Papua New Guinea, 46
Morocco, 31, 43–44, 93, 96
Moros (Philippine Ethnic Group), 20
Moscow, Russia, 31
Moseby's Raiders (Civil War), 143
Mosquito Fleet, Seminole Wars, 13
Mountbatten, Vice Admiral Lord Louis (Royal Navy), 32–33, 96
MSTS Ships
    David C. Shanks (T-AP-180), 124
    Fred C. Ainsworth (T-AP-181), 124
    General David I. Sultan (T-AP-150), 243
    General Edwin D. Patrick (T-AP-180), 124
    General John Pope (T-AP-110), 170
    General Leroy Eltinge (T-AP-154), 221
    General W.M. Black (T-AP-113), 170
    General Weigle (T-AP-119), 229
    Oglethorp (T-AKA-100), 122–124
    Titania (T-AKA-13), 122–124
Munich, Germany, 25
Munsan, Korea, 112, 219, 225, 237, 252, 261, 287
Murray, Lieutenant Colonel Raymond L. (USMC), 151, 177

Pyeonggang (P'yonggang), Korea, 112, 140, 175, 219, 233, 237, 261, 263, 268, 270–272, 287, 289, 291, 295, 297, 300, 323, 416

Pyeongtaek (P'yongt'aek), Korea, 112, 237, 252, 254, 261, 287, 291, 416

Pyeongyang (Pyongyang), Korea, 112, 117, 140, 157, 173, 175, 218–220, 223–225, 227–228, 233–234, 236–237, 252, 257, 263, 265, 268, 270, 289, 292–293, 295, 297, 299–300, 416

Pyo Yang-moon (ROK official), 189

Pyrenees Mountains, France and Spain, 72, 106

Qingdao (Tsingtao), China, Japanese Landings, World War I, 1914, 18

Qua Viet River, Vietnam, 339

QUADRANT, World War II Conference of Allies, August 1943, 49

Quang Ngai province, Vietnam, 340, 343

Quantico, Virginia, 23, 86, 89, 92, 149, 248

Quebec, Canada, Capture of (1759), 11, 49, 84, 160

Quinn, Lieutenant Colonel William (USA), 236

Rabaul, New Britain, 31, 33–34, 40, 45, 47, 50, 53, 97–98

Radford, Admiral Arthur W. (US Navy), 79, 116, 155, 160

Radio Hill, Wolmido, Korea (Incheon), 176

Radio, SCR-300 (walkie-talkie), 184

Raider Company, GHQ FEC Provisional Raider Company, later 8245th Army Unit, X Corps Raider Company, 143–145, 174–175, 186, 190, 209, 211–212

Rangers, US Army, 3, 11, 40, 42, 153, 274–280, 282–284, 305–307

regimental landing team (RLT), 29

Reinholt, Norwegian Cargo Ship, 114

Republic of Korea (ROK). *See* ROK

Republic of Korea Army. *See* ROK Army

Republic of Vietnam Army (ARVN), 341, 353

retracting, 7, 122, 443

Reuland, Sergeant First Class Nicholas (USAF), 133

Revision of *Doctrine for Amphibious Operations*, 1967, 334

Revolutionary War, 1775–83, 11–12

Rhee, President Syngman (ROK), 117, 203, 217–218

Rhone Valley, France, Operations, August 1944, 60, 72

Richardson, Lieutenant General Robert C., Jr. (USA), 56

Richmond, Virginia, Operations Against, 1862, 14

Ridgway, Lieutenant General Matthew B. (USA), 159, 205, 249, 251, 254–255, 259–260, 262, 271, 273–274, 276, 284–286, 291–293, 296, 298–299, 301, 303–305, 307–310, 314–316, 321–322

Rio Grande River, Landings, 1846, 13

riverine operations, 3, 6, 9, 11, 14, 345, 353–354

Roanoke Island, North Carolina, 1862, 14

Roberts, First Lieutenant Claude L., Jr. (USA), 178, 200, 209

Robertson, Lieutenant General H.C.H. (British Army), 80

Rodgers, First Lieutenant Russell L. (USAF), 133

ROK Army units
  Battalions
    2d Yeongdeungpo Separate Battalion, 132
  Corps
    I Corps, 222–223, 231, 234–235, 237, 239, 241, 252, 260, 288, 290, 294,
      296, 298–299
    II Corps, 183, 234, 237, 252
  Divisions
    3d Division (*Baegol* [Skeleton] Division), 123, 130–131, 135, 152, 183–
      184, 194, 201, 219, 239
    5th Division, 288
    8th Division, 112–113, 288
    9th Division, 288, 290
  Regiments
    10th Regiment, 113
    17th Regiment, 112, 167–168, 170, 196, 198–200, 213
    21st Regiment, 8th ROK Division, 113
    22d Regiment, 3d ROK Division, 131–132
    Min Force, 129
ROK forces, Partisans (*see* also ROK Partisan units), 116, 125, 139, 148, 217–
  218, 228–229, 254, 257–258, 288, 302–304, 310, 313, 321, 427
ROK Guerrilla Forces, Independent Mobile Unit, Miryang Guerrilla Battalion,
  183–185, 201, 211, 254, 257–258, 269, 294, 302, 318–319, 324
ROK Marine Corps Units,
  Battalions
    2d Korean Marine Corps Battalion, 189, 194
    Kim Sung-eun Unit, 135–137, 139
  Companies
    41st KMC Company, 264, 268
    42d KMC Company, 264, 294
  Regiments
    1st Korean Marine Corps (KMC) Regiment, 166, 170, 179
ROK Merchant Marine Vessels
  Chochiwon-ho (LST-665), 185
  Munsan-ho (LST-667), 184–185
ROK National Police (KNP) Units
  KNP Kangwon Battalion, 132
ROK Navy Units
  Task Group (TG) 95.7, 257
ROK Navy vessels
  landing ships, tank, LST-801, 114, 153, 172, 201, 264, 268
  minesweeper, AMS-501, 264
  motor minesweepers
    YMS-504, 137
    YMS-512, 113, 136

481

Ship-to-Objective Maneuver (landing operations), 6, 345
Expeditionary Warfare, Family of Concepts, 5, 9, 345, 354
US Marine Corps Units
  1st Combat Service Group (Fleet Marine Force Pacific), 167, 188–189, 210, 212
  Air Units
    1st Marine Air Wing (MAW), 80, 168, 228
    Marine Air Group 33 (MAG 33), 126, 151, 168, 190
  Battalions
    1st Amphibian Tractor Battalion, 1st Marine Division, 190, 197, 199
    1st Battalion, 5th Marine Regiment, 190, 196
    1st Engineer Battalion, 1st Marine Division, 201, 214
    1st Marine Raider Battalion, 141
    1st Shore Party Battalion, 1st Marine Division, 167, 179, 188, 190, 201–202, 240
        Headquarters and Service Company, 179, 197
        Group A, Team #3, 179
    2d Battalion, 5th Marine Regiment, 177, 190, 194, 196
    3d Battalion, 5th Marine Regiment, 176–177, 190, 194, 196
    3d Battalion, 11th Marines (Artillery), 196
    7th Motor Transport Battalion (Fleet Marine Force Pacific), 167, 210
  Brigades
    1st Marine Brigade, 25–26, 168
    1st Marine Provisional Brigade, 126
    9th Marine Expeditionary Brigade, 343
  Companies
    1st Marine Division Reconnaissance Company, 142
    Weapons Company, 3d Battalion, 1st Marines, 1st Marine Division, 178, 280
  Divisions
    1st Marine Division, 2, 28, 35, 41, 46, 73, 80, 142, 145, 155–156, 158–160, 163, 166, 168–170, 172, 179, 188–191, 193–194, 196–200, 209–210, 219–223, 228–229, 231–232, 234–236, 239–240, 243, 253, 256, 278–279, 288–290, 298, 302, 321–322
    2d Marine Division, 28, 41, 45, 50, 159
    3d Marine Division, 57
    4th Marine Division, 52–53, 56
  Marine Mobile Training Team (MTT), 121, 144, 160, 314
  Regiments
    1st Marines, also 1st Marine RCT, 178, 284
    5th Marines, also 5th Marine RCT, 126, 129–130, 142, 151, 157, 172, 178
    7th Marines, also 7th Marine RCT, 157, 172, 196–198, 213–214, 231, 271
    11th Marines (Artillery), 179, 188, 196, 279

About the Author

Donald W. Boose Jr., a retired Army colonel, teaches at the US Army War College. Much of his 30-year military career involved Northeast Asia political-military matters and included service as the Korean Politico-Military planner for the Joint Chiefs of Staff, 6 years with the UN Command Component of the Military Armistice Commission in Korea, and 3 years as the Assistant Chief of Staff for Strategic Plans and Policy (J5) for US forces in Japan. He is the author of *U.S. Army Forces in the Korean War,* coauthor of *Great Battles of Antiquity*, a major contributor to the *Encyclopedia of the Korean War*, coeditor of *Recalibrating the U.S.-Republic of Korea Alliance,* a major contributor to the *Encyclopedia of the Korean War,* and the author of many articles on the Korean War and Northeast Asia security issues. Professor Boose has a degree in Anthropology from Cornell University, a master's degree in Asian Studies from the University of Hawaii, and is a graduate of the US Army War College.